A Portrait of the Artist, 1525–1825

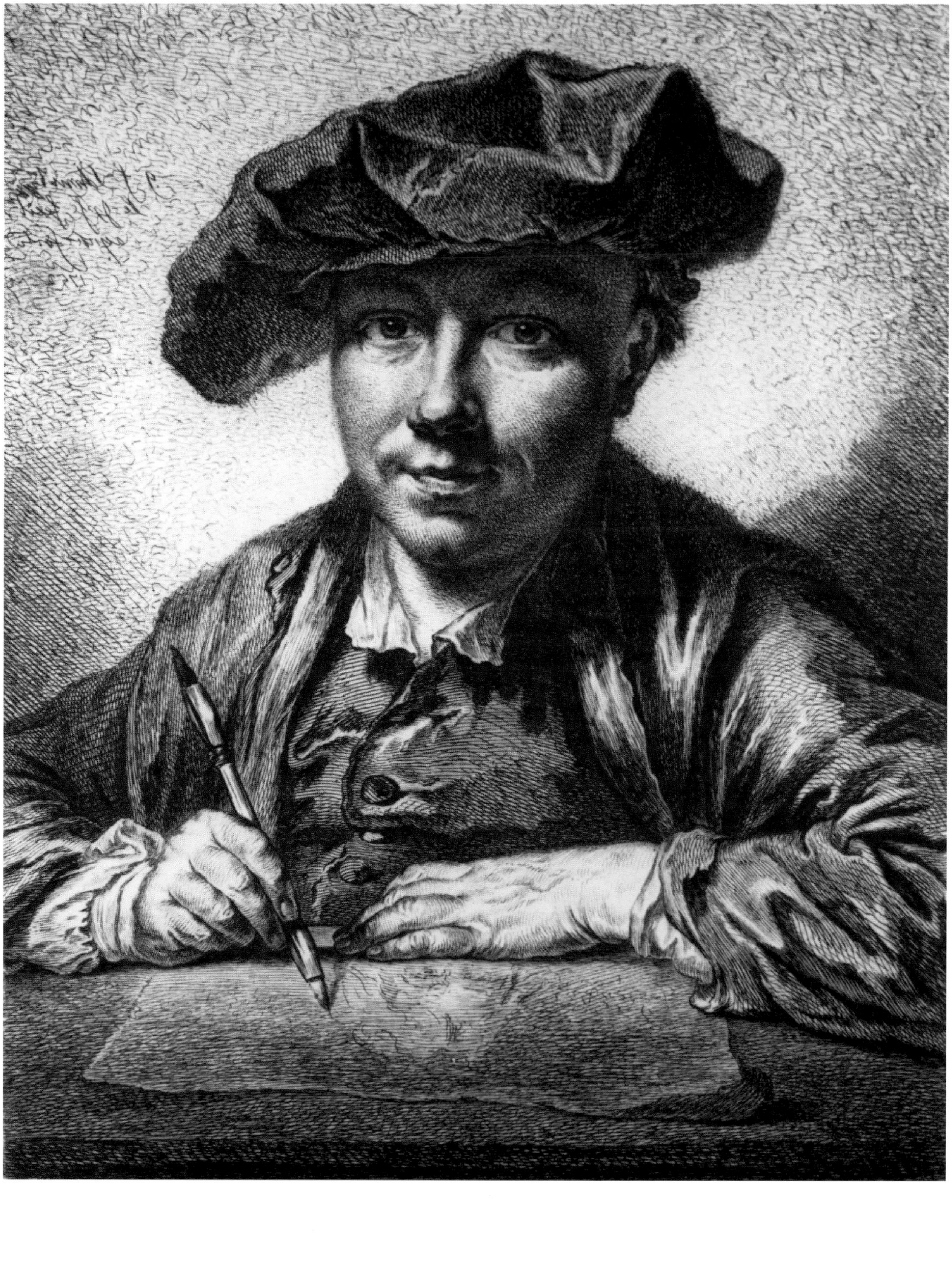

A Portrait of the Artist
1525–1825

Prints from the Collection of the Sarah Campbell Blaffer Foundation

James Clifton

with contributions by Leslie Scattone and Andrew C. Weislogel

The Museum of Fine Arts, Houston

A Portrait of the Artist, 1525–1825: Prints from the Collection of the Sarah Campbell Blaffer Foundation was published in conjunction with the exhibition organized by the Museum of Fine Arts, Houston, and the Sarah Campbell Blaffer Foundation.

EXHIBITION ITINERARY:

The Museum of Fine Arts, Houston
February 27–May 22, 2005

Herbert F. Johnson Museum of Art, Cornell University, Ithaca, New York
September 3, 2005–January 1, 2006

Design: Bruce Campbell
Typography: Mary Gladue, Aardvark Type
Printing: Chas. P. Young Co.

Jacket/cover illustrations: *(front)* Adriaen van Ostade, *The Painter* (cat. no. 39); *(back)* Francisco Goya, *Francisco Goya y Lucientes, Pintor (Self-Portrait)* (cat. no. 18).
Frontispiece: Georg Frederic Schmidt, *Self-Portrait* (cat. no. 14).

Library of Congress Cataloging-in-Publication Data
Clifton, James, 1958-
A portrait of the artist, 1525-1825 : prints from the collection of the Sarah Campbell Blaffer Foundation / James Clifton ; with contributions by Leslie Scattone and Andrew C. Weislogel.
p. cm.
Catalog of an exhibition at the Museum of Fine Arts, Houston, Feb. 27-May 22, 2005; and at the Herbert F. Johnson Museum of Art, Cornell University, Ithaca, N.Y.
Includes bibliographical references and index.
ISBN 0-89090-134-1 (hardcover : alk. paper) --
ISBN 0-89090-135-X (pbk. : alk. paper) 1. Artists and models in art--Exhibitions. 2. Prints, European--Exhibitions. 3. Prints--Private collections--Texas--Houston--Exhibitions. 4. Sarah Campbell Blaffer Foundation--Art collections--Exhibitions. I. Scattone, Leslie. II. Weislogel, Andrew. III. Museum of Fine Arts, Houston. IV. Herbert F. Johnson Museum of Art. V. Title.
NE962.A78C55 2005
769'.42'074764235--dc22

2004031022

Contents

Foreword

Born in Waxahachie and raised in Lampasas, both small towns in Texas, Sarah Campbell Blaffer (1885–1975) wanted to bring works of fine art, which she had come to know in Boston and Paris, to the people of her home state. In 1947, she established the Robert Lee Blaffer Memorial Collection at the Museum of Fine Arts, Houston, in honor of her late husband, who had been one of the major donors for the museum's first building, which had opened in 1924. Over the course of more than fifteen years, she purchased some thirty works for the museum, including significant paintings by Frans Hals, Canaletto, Auguste Renoir, and Paul Cézanne that remain highlights of the museum's collection. Sarah and Lee Blaffer's children also made generous contributions to the museum: their daughter, Jane Blaffer Owen, and her husband, Kenneth Dale Owen, gave an important painting by Edouard Vuillard; and their son, John H. Blaffer, and his wife, Camilla Davis Blaffer, provided funding for the construction of an addition to the museum. Designed by Kenneth Franzheim, the Robert Lee Blaffer Memorial Wing opened in 1953 with new quarters for the museum school and a gallery for the Blaffer Memorial Collection.

In 1964, Mrs. Blaffer established the Sarah Campbell Blaffer Foundation for religious, charitable, and educational purposes. A few years before Mrs. Blaffer's death in 1975, the foundation began applying its resources to the development of a collection of art that could travel throughout the state, providing viewers with a rare experience of fine art. Much of the Blaffer Foundation's collection of Old Master paintings is now exhibited in the Audrey Jones Beck Building of the Museum of Fine Arts, Houston, complementing and enhancing the museum's own collection. However, the foundation continues to circulate its collection of paintings and prints to other institutions. Mrs. Blaffer had a deeply felt love of art and a strong sense of its transformative potential for viewers. She once said that "in the creation of art we are fellow workers of God," and the attention to the self-reflection and creative powers of artists in *A Portrait of the Artist, 1525–1825: Prints from the Collection of the Sarah Campbell Blaffer Foundation* would surely have appealed to her. I am pleased that the Museum of Fine Arts, Houston, will be the first venue for the exhibition that will help fulfill Mrs. Blaffer's noble desire to share her love of art with others.

I would like to thank the trustees of the Sarah Campbell Blaffer Foundation for their initiation and support of this exhibition, including allowing the foundation's director, James Clifton, to serve as organizing curator. *A Portrait of the Artist, 1525–1825: Prints from the Collection of the Sarah Campbell Blaffer Foundation* and this accompanying catalogue exemplify the close and productive relationship between the museum and the foundation—a relationship that promises further exciting collaborations in the future.

Peter C. Marzio
Director
The Museum of Fine Arts, Houston

Preface and Acknowledgments

For the past thirty years, the Sarah Campbell Blaffer Foundation has collected and exhibited works of fine art, pursuing Mrs. Blaffer's vision of a "museum without walls" for the benefit of the people of Texas. Dozens of museums and galleries throughout Texas and in other states have hosted traveling exhibitions of Renaissance and Baroque paintings, as well as of prints by William Hogarth and Francisco Goya, from the Blaffer Foundation's collection. Although the foundation has had its own exhibition space at the Museum of Fine Arts, Houston, since 2001, works from its collection continue to circulate. In 1996, the foundation began collecting works of art for *A Portrait of the Artist, 1525–1825: Prints from the Collection of the Sarah Campbell Blaffer Foundation,* which, following its presentation at the Museum of Fine Arts, Houston, and the Herbert F. Johnson Museum of Art at Cornell University in Ithaca, New York, will be available for travel in Texas and elsewhere for years to come.

Although the Blaffer Foundation collection is limited chronologically to art produced up to the early nineteenth century, the issues addressed in *A Portrait of the Artist* resonate in modern and contemporary art as well, and the enduring interest of the topic guided the organization of the exhibition. This is not to suggest, however, that there are not significant differences in this regard between our own culture(s) and European culture(s) of several centuries ago. The image and the status of artists have not been static but have a reconstructable history, and notions of artists' roles in any society are not natural or absolute but can be historically situated. I hope that this exhibition and book will contribute to an understanding of the complex, varied, and shifting position of artists in European society, and may at least implicitly confirm Mrs. Blaffer's belief in the positive transformative power of artists and their work.

The organization of the exhibition and the production of the book accompanying it required the assistance and participation of many colleagues, to whom I am deeply grateful. Former curatorial assistants for the Blaffer Foundation, Britt Chemla and Celia Martin, and the foundation's administrator, Marilyn Steinberger, were indispensable in managing the collection from which the works in this exhibition are drawn. The dealers from whom these works were acquired, including Carolyn Bullard, Lesley Hill, Susan Lewis Kay, Armin Kunz, Christopher Mendez, Helmut Rumbler, Susan Schulmann, and Alan Stone, showed great interest in the project and provided insight into the objects. I received much needed scholarly guidance and assistance from current and former members of the curatorial staff of the MFAH, especially E. Peters Bowron, Leo Costello, Tina Llorente, Mary Morton, and Cindi Strauss, as well as from other colleagues and friends: Jonathan Bober, Allison Kelly Clifton, Peter Erickson, James Ganz, Nicole Hegener, Michael Ann Holly, Eik Kahng, Susan Kuretsky, Riccardo Lattuada, Amber Ludwig, Walter S. Melion, Otto Naumann, Andrew Robison, Kim Sloan, Philip Sohm, John T. Spike, Peter C. Sutton, Wendy Thompson, Mariët Westermann, and Thomas Willette. Thanks to the generosity of the Sterling and Francine Clark Art Institute, a summer sojourn in Williamstown, Massachusetts, in 2000 as a Clark Fellow allowed me to concentrate on some of the issues raised by the exhibition; for that opportunity I am grateful to Michael Conforti, director, and Michael Ann Holly, assistant director, research and academic programs. For considering the material with me I am grateful to my former Rice University students, especially Sarah Williams, who performed important research for the exhibition while an intern at the MFAH. Most of my research was conducted at the Hirsch Library of the MFAH, where I benefited greatly from the support of the staff, especially Jon Evans and Margaret Ford. Librarians at other institutions provided much needed information: John Hagood, formerly at the Hirsch Library and now at the Art Research Library, National Gallery of Art, Washington; Laura Schwartz, Fine Arts Library, University of Texas, Austin; and Ann Blecksmith and Tracey Schuster of the Getty Research Institute, Los Angeles. I am grateful to Diane Lovejoy, publications director at the MFAH, and Bruce Campbell, the designer of the exhibition catalogue. Christine Manca shepherded the catalogue into production and improved the text with her sensitive editing; I greatly appreciate both her efforts and her considerable patience. Kamila Bergen and Megan Wilson, interns in the publications department, assisted with the editorial process.

I extend thanks to Mary Gladue, who handled typesetting and prepared the index, and to Cynthia Bowman and her colleagues at Chas. P. Young Co., who printed this catalogue. Thanks also go to Thomas R. DuBrock, who photographed the works in the exhibition. Kem Schultz assisted in procuring the photographs for the comparative illustrations.

The mounting of the exhibition itself was made possible by the work of several departments at the MFAH, especially the registrar's, preparations, and design. I am especially grateful to Brooke Barclay and Robert Deeds for matting and framing the works.

A project that consists of collection building as well as exhibition requires the long-term commitment of an institution's trustees, a commitment that has been well demonstrated by the trustees, former and current, of the Sarah Campbell Blaffer Foundation: Gilbert M. Denman, Jr., Cecil Blaffer Furstenberg, Charles W. Hall, Edward Joseph Hudson, Jr., Robert Lee Hudson, Anne Dale Owen, and Jane Blaffer Owen. In its art programs, including this exhibition and book, the foundation continues to enjoy the support of the MFAH's trustees and director, Peter C. Marzio, for which we are grateful.

I appreciate especially the contributions of my coauthors, Andrew C. Weislogel, assistant curator and master teacher at the Herbert F. Johnson Museum of Art at Cornell University, Ithaca, New York; and Leslie Scattone, curatorial assistant of the Sarah Campbell Blaffer Foundation. Moreover, Leslie's work at every stage and every level of this project, pursued with great industriousness and good humor, has been invaluable.

Brief biographies of the artists—both designers and printmakers—are provided following the entries. The dimensions of the prints are described in millimeters and inches, with height before width, and the term "trimmed" indicates that a sheet has been cut within the plate-mark. Where possible, references to standard catalogues have been provided; those catalogues are listed in the References section. Short citations consisting of author and date refer to entries in the Bibliography. All translations are the authors', unless otherwise noted. The author of each entry is indicated by the following initials:

JC	James Clifton
LS	Leslie Scattone
AW	Andrew C. Weislogel

This catalogue is dedicated to the memory of Gilbert M. Denman, Jr., whose service as trustee to the Blaffer Foundation over many years was marked by aesthetic sensitivity, critical acumen, and refreshing wit.

James Clifton
Director, Sarah Campbell Blaffer Foundation

A Portrait of the Artist

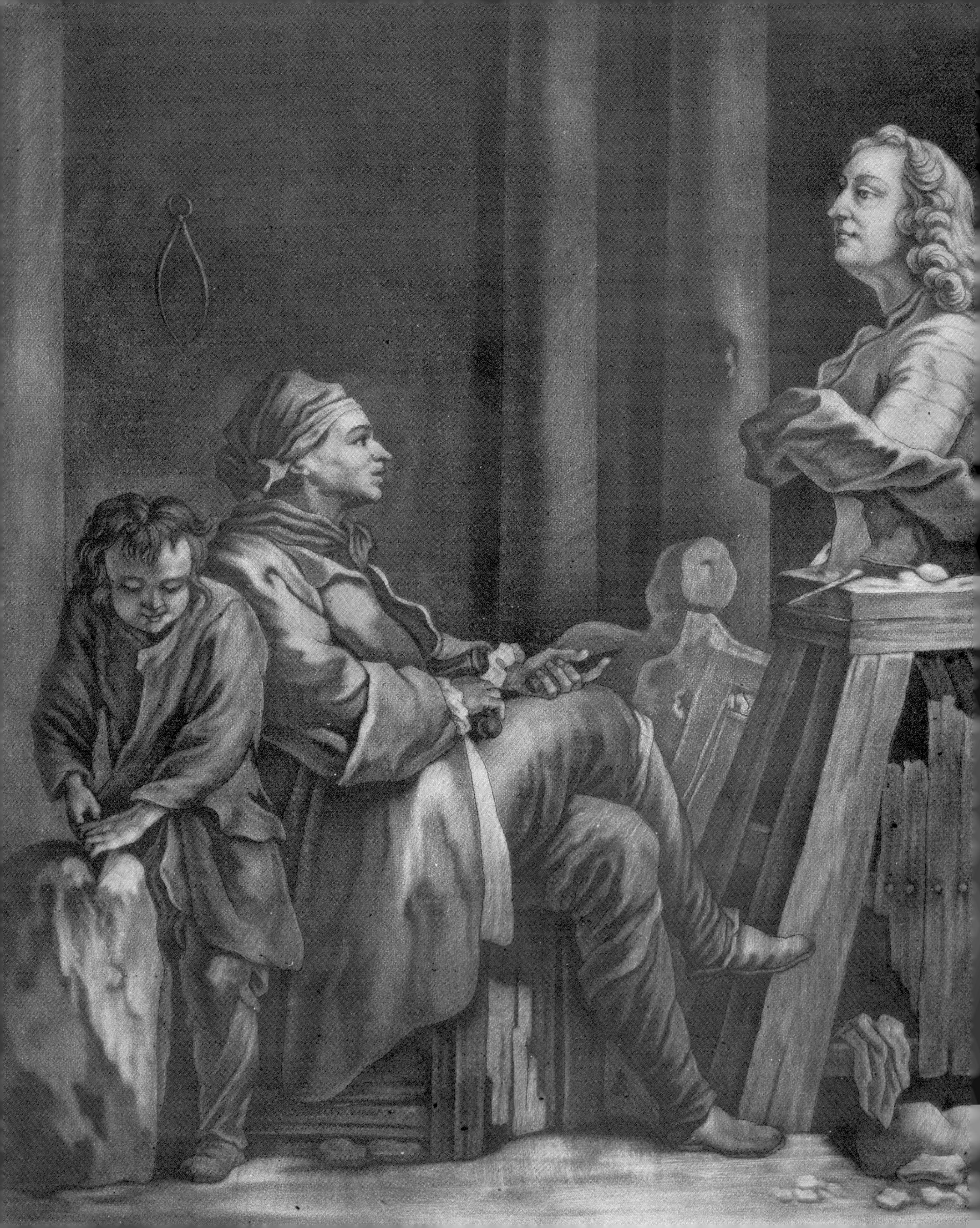

A Portrait of the Artist

Nothing is really so poor and melancholy than art that is interested in itself and not in its subject.
—George Santayana, *Reason in Art,* volume I of *The Life of Reason, or the Phases of Human Progress,* 1934

A substantial portion of the oeuvre of Bill Haley and the Comets from the mid-1950s consists of songs about rock and roll ("Rock around the Clock," "R-O-C-K," "Rock-a-Beatin' Boogie," "Don't Knock the Rock," and so on). Bill Haley may be the most salient example of the self-reflexive rock-and-roll musician, but he is not alone (one might think of Chuck Berry's "Roll Over Beethoven" and "Rock and Roll Music," for example). In the decades that have followed, scores, or even hundreds, of such songs have appeared, from the energetically industrious (Grand Funk Railroad, "We're an American Band") to the insipid (Jefferson Starship, "We Built This City") and the pseudoheroic (Deep Purple, "Smoke on the Water"). Similarly, although more diffused chronologically, following centuries and centuries of virtual absence, representations of artists began appearing in the late Middle Ages, at first sporadically, and then with increased frequency, so that by the seventeenth century they could be considered quite common and remain so to this day.[1] Along with self-portraits and portraits of other artists, came depictions of historical or generic artists, allegories of the arts, and depictions of artists' markets—that is, the kinds of images included in this book and exhibition.

Is it a poverty of imagination that allows artists to repeatedly address the narrow worlds in which they operate? Self-indulgence? Narcissism? Self-consciousness may operate as self-definition or self-validation, the result of the novelty of a form or status, or perhaps in reaction to the perception of a threat to that form or status. In the case of images relating to the visual arts, artists were redefining their relationship with broader society, which led to a new social status, and also to a defense against threats to that new status. The development of such imagery is not at all smooth or linear; in some periods and countries it is more important than in others; some artists have no proclivity for it, while others seem to revel in it. A lack of unity may also be the result of "creative frictions" between sets of social and psychological dichotomies: artist/artisan; corporate/individual identity; inner self/outward persona.[2] Nonetheless, there emerges a broadly consistent imagery in much of Europe from the sixteenth century until it shifts noticeably, or at least intensifies, in the nineteenth century. This exhibition examines a relatively small but representative group of the thousands of prints on the theme that were produced during that period.

Individualism and the Status of the Artist

Representations of artists—whether generic or specific, ostensibly at work or posed for the viewer—were infrequent until the fifteenth century but were quite common by the seventeenth. Their proliferation corresponds to a significant change in the professional and social status of the makers of images, from anonymous, replaceable, modestly remunerated craftsmen to (potentially) unique, irreplaceable, highly valued artists.[3] The characterization of their activity shifted from manual to intellectual, and the perception of their products changed from craft to liberal art. Needless to say, such gross generalizations are subject to numerous variations and exceptions, especially given the extensive chronological and geographical parameters of the Middle Ages and Renaissance; for example, Italian sculptors and architects of the twelfth century seemed to enjoy greater renown than their predecessors in Italy or contemporaries elsewhere, but they still did not achieve the status of artists of later periods. The status of artists in the Middle Ages had presumably declined from that of classical antiquity, from which we know the names and major works of many artists, although even in antiquity artistic activity was not universally esteemed. Although

Opposite: Johann Jakob Haid. *The Sculptor* (detail, cat. no. 45).

Renaissance apologists for the nobility of the visual arts frequently recalled the exaltation of individual artists in antiquity, also inherited from antiquity was the prejudice against manual labor which bore on the attitude toward artists in the Middle Ages and through the Renaissance.

The change in artists' status was roughly contemporaneous with what many have seen as an increased individualism in European society. Jacob Burckhardt's *The Civilization of the Renaissance in Italy* (1860) has exercised an enormous influence on modern historians' conceptions of the nature of the Renaissance. According to Burckhardt, one of the constitutive elements of the Renaissance was the development of the individual.[4] His famous passage on the subject is worth quoting in full:

> In the Middle Ages both sides of human consciousness—that which was turned within as that which was turned without—lay dreaming or half awake beneath a common veil. The veil was woven of faith, illusion, and childish prepossession, through which the world and history were seen clad in strange hues. Man was conscious of himself only as member of a race, people, party, family, or corporation—only through some general category. In Italy this veil first melted into air; an *objective* treatment and consideration of the State and of all the things of this world became possible. The *subjective* side at the same time asserted itself with corresponding emphasis; man became a spiritual individual, and recognized himself as such.[5]

Thus corporate identity was replaced with individual identity. Burckhardt recognized precedents for the new attitude already within the Middle Ages, but they were isolated and without echoes, and "at the close of the thirteenth century Italy began to swarm with individuality."[6] This new individuality manifested itself in both the "impulse to the highest individual development," that is, the formation of "complete men,"[7] and "a new sort of outward distinction—the modern form of glory."[8]

Burckhardt's thesis has, not surprisingly, been associated by art historians with the rise of portraiture in the early modern period—hence its particular significance in the present context—this in spite of Burckhardt's reticence on the connection both within *The Civilization of the Renaissance in Italy* and his later lengthy essay on portraiture, as well as his outright rejection of it in a later lecture.[9] Burckhardt's 1885 lecture on "The Beginning of Modern Portrait Painting" considers more Northern European art than Italian, and he explicitly points out that "in the second half of the fifteenth century, the painted single portrait [*Einzelporträt*] [is] in Italy still nowhere near as frequent as the cult of political power, of fame, and of beauty would lead one to expect."[10] Nonetheless, Gottfried Boehm has claimed that, "seen in broad historical measure, the independent portrait could first arise when man had learned to understand himself and establish himself as individuality."[11] While Boehm does not cite Burckhardt, suggesting perhaps the extent to which Burckhardt's thesis has become fundamental, Creighton Gilbert is more explicit in creating a pseudo-Burckhardtian thesis about individualism and portraiture: "The portrait is indeed the best illustration of the Burckhardtian definition of the Renaissance as the rediscovery of the world and of man. It emphasizes both rediscoveries: of the human individual and the world of physical matter."[12] In this view, as a sub-genre of portraiture, self-portraiture would be thought to bear a similar—although perhaps more complex—relationship to the "development of the individual."

Within the fairly narrow world of artists, there seems to be much evidence to substantiate Burckhardt's thesis that individualism was a hallmark of the Renaissance. Michael Baxandall concludes from his analysis of fifteenth-century contracts for paintings that the patrons' concern with the value of the materials to be used—that is, gold and ultramarine—was gradually displaced by a concern with the painters' skill, so that a contract might specify that the entire work was to be done by the hand of the master (that is, without workshop assistance). Furthermore, patrons began to distinguish not just levels of skill but also pictorial styles among painters.[13] Artists were thus no longer seen simply as interchangeable workmen equally capable of completing a task with essentially equal results. John Shearman has pointed out another symptom of a new conception of art: from around 1520, patrons wanted a work from the hand of a particular master, irrespective of its subject matter or even medium, "an example of his unique virtù, or his art."[14]

There also seems to be much evidence within the smaller world of artists to substantiate Gilbert's pseudo-Burckhardtian thesis that the proliferation of portraiture is the result of increased individualism. Undoubtedly there are more self-portraits, both independent and in the context of other pictures, produced in the Renaissance than in the Middle Ages, even though this increase in production seems to lag behind the moment of emerging self-awareness identified by Burckhardt by a century or more (which is in accord, more broadly, with the dating most scholars give to the Italian Renaissance in terms of the development of literature and other forms of writing, as opposed to the development in the visual arts). Artists also participated in the general increase in the production of biographies, with their emphasis putatively on the individual, as well as so-called "ego-documents"—that is, autobiographies, diaries, journals, memoirs, and letters.[15]

Burckhardt's thesis has been criticized on several fronts:[16] for example, that his terminology surrounding "the individual" is vague; that the shift toward greater individualism occurred earlier or was not so dramatic as Burckhardt suggested; or that the shift is not unique to the Italian Renaissance and is therefore not constitutive of it, nor is it distinguished from other cultures. Yet most writers accept, either implicitly or explicitly, the notion that there was, in fact, a shift toward greater individualism, which has even been described as "rampant."[17] But there is an important distinction between this formulation and Burckhardt's, which may also explain his reluctance to associate the development of the Renaissance individual with the development of the Renaissance portrait: Burckhardt is concerned not with "ordinary people," who remain ordinary even if they can afford to have themselves portrayed, but with a few extraordinary individuals—"complete men"—who, in Burckhardt's conception, define their culture by rising above it. Some artists in the early modern period were thought to be extraordinary, and would thus fulfill Burckhardt's criteria—for example, Giotto was already noted as such by Dante around 1300 and was included by Giovanni Villani in his biographies of famous Florentines in the 1380s[18]—but only much later were artists as a group thought to be extraordinary.

Individual and Corporate Identity

Individuality is mitigated when a corporate identity is of greater importance, which Burckhardt saw as prevalent in the Middle Ages. But it is also mitigated when one seeks to conform to the behavior and character of others. The value placed on exemplarity remained as strong in the early modern period as it had been in classical antiquity and the Middle Ages.[19] In the context of the development of autobiography, Karl Joachim Weintraub discussed the balance between the pursuit of an exemplary model and a concern with uniqueness. For Weintraub, the pursuit of the model left little room for individuality: "Despite all variation, the men who sought to follow such models saw virtue in approaching and fulfilling an exemplary way of being human while placing very little value on idiosyncratic differences—if at all."[20] At the other end of the spectrum, "the ideal of individuality is marked by the conviction that ultimately no general model can contain the specificity of the true self. The ineffable cannot be defined by the general—*individuum ineffabile est.* When the belief in individuality reaches its full force, this individual difference is seen to be a matter of great value in itself."[21] Like hagiographic literature, early modern biographies provided *exempla* (occasionally negative ones) with a didactic value. The subject was praised, but generally not for characteristics or achievement that were inimitable or unique.

The biographical projects of Giorgio Vasari, whose *Lives of the Eminent Painters, Sculptors, and Architects* of 1550 and 1568 was enormously influential, and later writers emphasize individuals in their very structure: discrete *vite* of artists, whose life and work are made distinct from those of others by the format of the biographies. But they also provided *exempla* for imitation, and the repetition of form from one biography to the other tends to dilute any sense of uniqueness, especially when the events described often conform to topoi, such as the discovery of the precocious artist's talent, and therefore have less to do with an individual than with an ideal.[22] Furthermore, the aggregate of the biographies has a corporate significance. Vasari, for example, treats the artists within the context of a tradition that takes the strong form of a biological narrative: the birth, growth, maturity, and potential decline of the arts. His biographies are filled with comments indicating that his overarching concern was with the progress of art—he dismissed the career of a certain Boccaccino, for example, by reporting that "without having ever made any improvement in art, he passed from this life at the age of fifty-eight"—and he manipulated information in favor of rhetorical purposes that superseded the careers of the artists he treated. The fundamental concern with art's progress as a collective and nearly autonomous endeavor has led to the reasonable, but paradoxical, conclusion that his work, though composed of more than one hundred sixty lives of individual artists, is essentially anti-individualistic.[23]

There are several ways in which corporate intrusion into the ego-documents of even the most egocentric—or at least self-conscious—of artists might occur, for example, through reference either to groups to which the artist belongs or to other artists to be imitated. Artists occasionally signed paintings with reference to their membership in a group, especially as an academician, or their nationality. Albrecht Dürer signed several monumental paintings between 1506 and 1511 indicating either his hometown of Nuremberg or, as in the *Feast of the Rose Garlands (Rosenkranz Madonna),* his name as "Albertus Dürer Germanus" (fig. 1). Painted in Venice as a means "to silence those

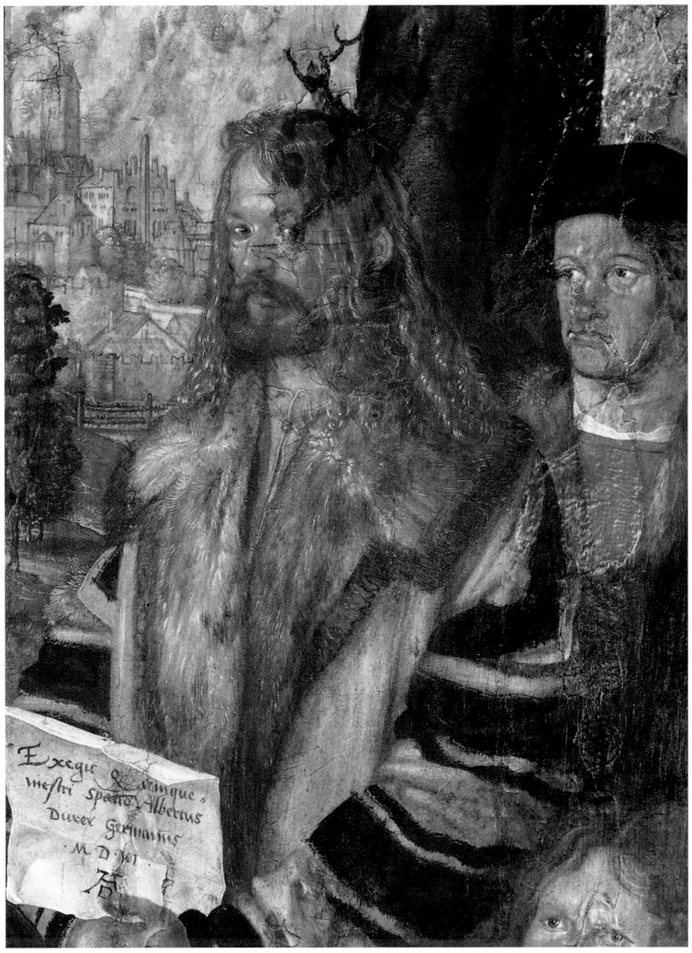

Fig. 1. Albrecht Dürer. *Self-Portrait* (detail of *Feast of the Rose Garlands*). 1506. Oil on panel, 162 x 194.5 cm (63¾ x 76⅝ in.). National Gallery, Prague.

who said that I was good as an engraver but did not know how to handle the colors in painting," the *Feast of the Rose Garlands* and his nationalistic signature proclaim that not just Dürer himself but the school of painting he represents can vie with the Venetian artists in painting.[24] In these paintings, Dürer included his own likeness next to the signatory inscription; such bystander self-portraits, besides "registering authorship," as Joseph Leo Koerner has pointed out, "can articulate an artist's corporate identity (his allegiance to family, church, confraternity, guild, or patron)."[25]

The autobiography of the Italian goldsmith and sculptor Benvenuto Cellini is one of the most remarkable ego-documents of the sixteenth century, "surely that of a freely standing, independent personality," as Burckhardt described it.[26] Yet after a brief introduction in which he avers that anyone who has achieved great things should write an autobiography, Cellini begins the story of his life with a genealogy in which he finds himself descended from a high-ranking officer to Julius Caesar and founder of Florence. Cellini does not hesitate to recount (and exaggerate) his own accomplishments, but he also finds his significance within a corporate structure as the proud scion of a great family. The autobiographical *Memoriale* of Baccio Bandinelli, another artist of considerable self-attention (see cat. nos. 1, 21), gives even greater shrift to his (false) ancestry: around one-fifth of the *Memoriale* passes before Bandinelli begins to talk of himself. He places particular emphasis on the family's relations with the Medici, suggesting that his status is defined not just by himself or even by his family, but by his family's relationship with a great family.[27] Even if he had not been inclined to think in such corporate terms, Bandinelli was in a sense forced to by the concern with family identity inherent in the order of the Knights of Santiago, to which Bandinelli sought entry.[28]

A pseudo-Burckhardtian approach to self-reflexive iconography tends to treat self-portraits as expressions of Renaissance individuality, focusing on individual identity at the expense of corporate identity. But artists' self-representations were often both. Diego Velázquez's *Las Meninas* is a case where a single picture advances both corporate and individual aims (fig. 2). Velázquez sought admission into the order of the Knights of Santiago, but his petition was rejected because he was, in the order's view, a manual laborer, still a common view in Spain in

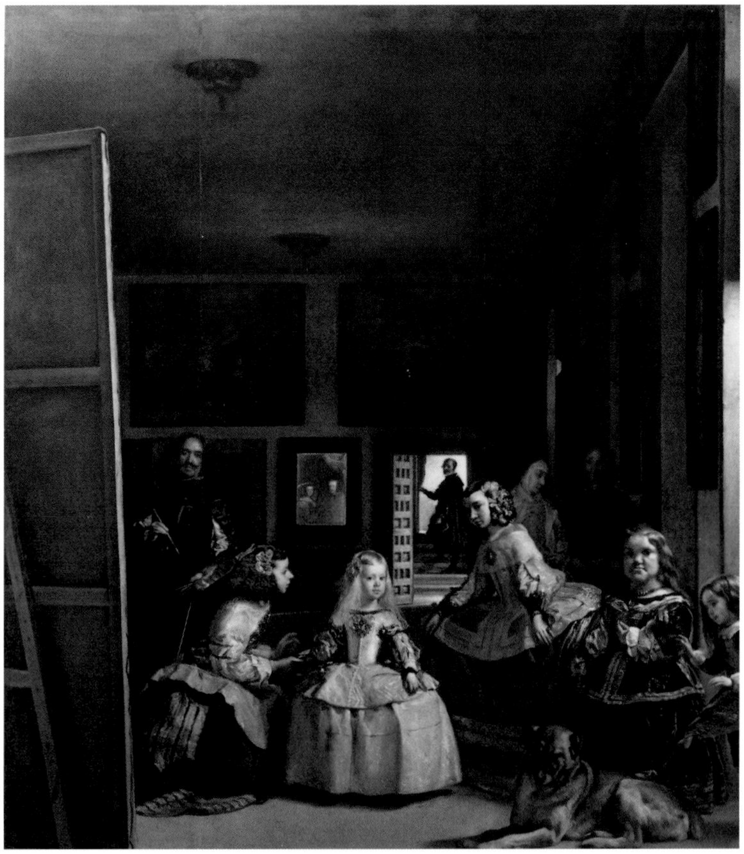

Fig. 2. Diego Rodriguez Velázquez. *Las Meninas*. 1656. Oil on canvas, 318 x 276 cm (125¼ x 108⅝ in.). Museo Nacional del Prado, Madrid.

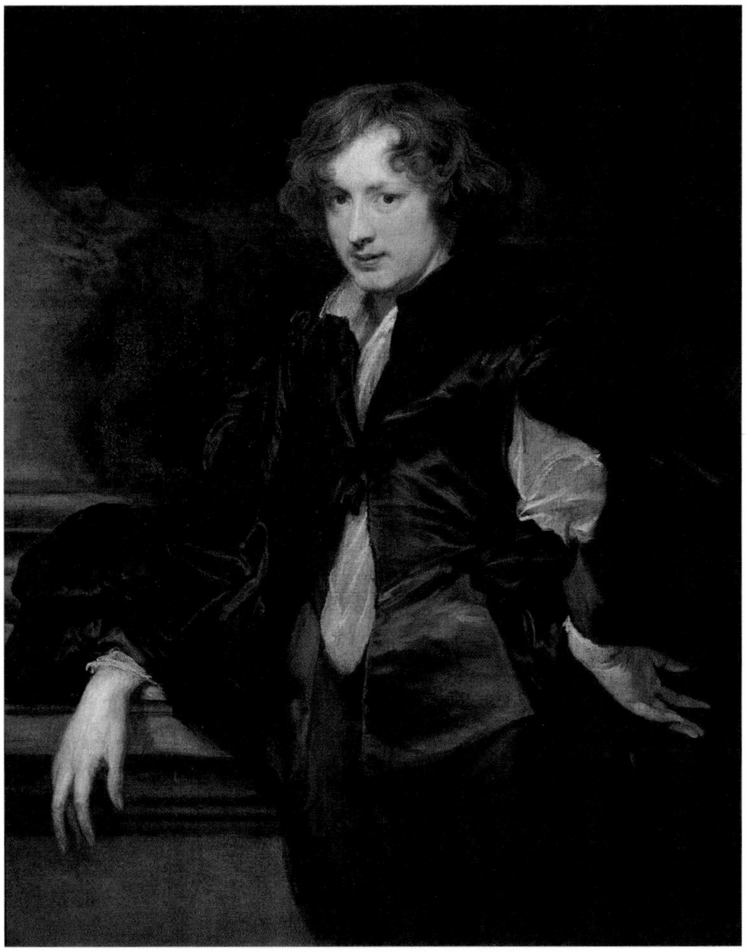

Fig. 3. Anthony van Dyck. *Self-Portrait.* 1622–23. Oil on canvas, 116.5 x 93.5 cm (45⅞ x 36¾ in.). The State Hermitage Museum, St. Petersburg.

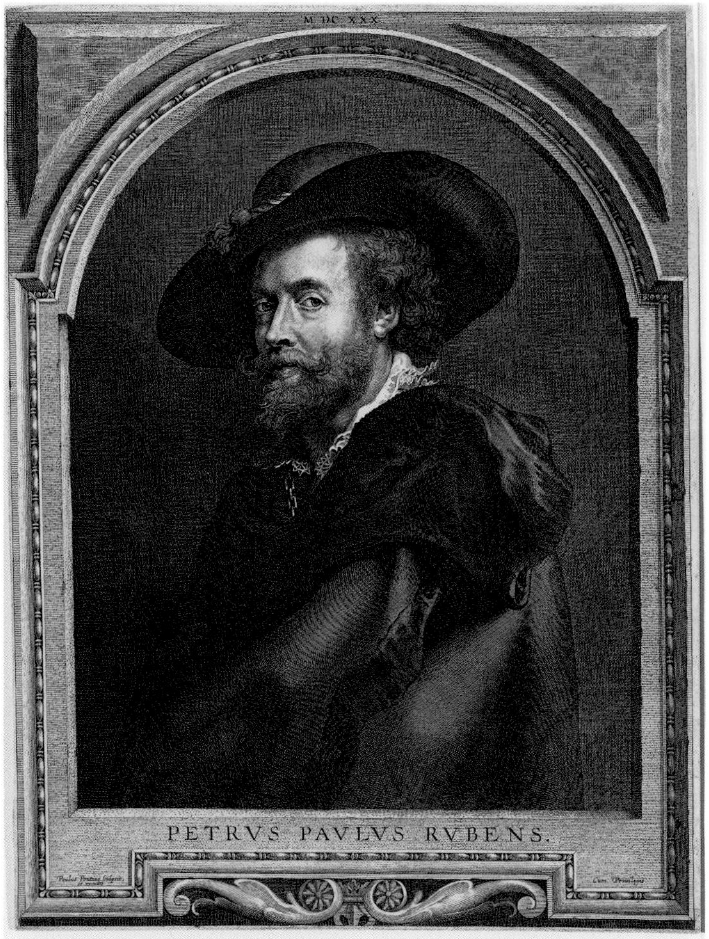

Fig. 4. Paulus Pontius. *Portrait of Peter Paul Rubens.* 1630. Engraving on laid paper, 368 x 273 mm (14½ x 10¾ in.). The Museum of Fine Arts, Houston; gift of Marjorie G. and Evan C. Horning.

the middle of the seventeenth century, but with legal ramifications, unlike in the rest of Europe. By showing (albeit indirectly, via a mirror) the king and queen visiting him during his work, he recalled the ancient story of Alexander visiting Apelles in his studio and, by extension, other indications culled from ancient texts that painting was a liberal rather than mechanical art. Velázquez thereby made simultaneous claims for the honors due himself and his profession. Where the corporate identity required defense or definition (especially caused by acknowledging, anticipating, or seeking to effect change), such could form the basis of self-representation. As individualized as artists became in the early modern period, they were still involved in a struggle for the improvement of their corporate status.[29]

Burckhardt's generalization that there was a shift from the corporate to the individual in the passage from the Middle Ages to the Renaissance has been rightly questioned; nonetheless, there remains an emphasis on individuality in the treatment of Renaissance portraiture and self-portraiture.[30] Self-portraiture and portraiture are commonly separated from each other as generic categories (as are autobiography and biography), thereby implying that the "ipseity"[31] of the self-portrait (or autobiography) is of paramount importance. To distinguish between self-portraits and portraits of other artists in the early modern period is to identify (or attempt to identify) a significant individuality, or more precisely that revelation of interiority, that individual self-consciousness that is of such interest to the modern mind. But to focus on that aspect of such works leaves aside aspects of the art that were probably of much greater import to the artists, their subjects, and their audience. The self-portrait may reveal what the artist thought of himself or establish how he wished others to think of him, but it is not necessarily significantly different from what another artist thought of him or wished others to think of him. Throughout the early modern period, artists continued to emphasize their corporate status, and it should not be surprising that, for example, Anthony van Dyck depicted himself as he did other artists (fig. 3; cf. cat. no. 5). That self-portraits conform to a type militates against the artist's sense that he or she is remarkably different from his or her colleagues.

Not all artists were eager self-portraitists. Peter Paul Rubens was reluctant to paint himself, although he did respond to a royal request from Charles I, overcoming, as he said, his modesty. The resultant image engraved by Paulus Pontius casts him as a gentleman, rather like the figures in van Dyck's etchings, and is not remarkably personal (fig. 4).[32] Nicolas Poussin produced two self-portraits in response to a request for a portrait from his friend and patron Paul Fréart de Chantelou, but only after he had concluded that an adequate likeness could not be produced by any other painter available locally, making Chantelou wait several years (see cat. no. 7).[33] What ensued may not be self-portraits in the modern sense of the term. The two paintings have been seen by Louis Marin as essentially theoretical exercises: "The figure we call Poussin's self-portrait masks, or to put it better, perhaps, is a mask for, Poussin's theoretical propositions concerning manners of painting."[34]

Fig. 5. Peter Paul Rubens. *Self-Portrait*. c. 1639. Oil on canvas, 109.5 x 85 cm (43⅛ x 33½ in.). Kunsthistorisches Museum, Vienna.

Artist Types

Representations of artists conformed to several different types in early modern Europe, more or less in concert with their social roles and status, whether real or desired. The most persistent representation was perhaps as a courtier or gentleman, as one would expect from the social aspirations, both individually and collectively, of artists. The ideal was established by Vasari's literary portrayal of Raphael. Van Dyck's *Iconography,* which was enormously influential on portraiture in general, consistently gives an aristocratic mien to the artists.[35] Quintessentially, Peter Paul Rubens, who achieved great wealth, was ennobled by Charles I of England, and functioned as a diplomat for the Archduchess Isabella of the Netherlands—which, however, led to Philip IV's characterizing him as "so mean a person" because he was a painter[36]—presented himself with no trace of his profession (fig. 5).[37] In his self-portrait in Vienna, from the late 1630s, he appears with gloves and a sword, trappings of the gentleman. The numerous self-portraits of the sculptor Baccio Bandinelli seemed to deny his profession, which was considered the most manual of the visual arts (cat. nos. 1, 21). Bandinelli claimed that he only wanted to be a scholar and a gentleman but was driven to sculpture by poverty.[38] Even with their attributes—conventionally, a palette and brushes—artists might appear to be in a state portrait, aggrandized with billowing drapery and monumental wigs, as in the case of numerous French portraits of the early eighteenth century, many of which were engraved as reception pieces for the Royal Academy of Painting and Sculpture.[39] The painters' adoption of a form originally reserved for the nobility demonstrates their idea of the "nobility" of their profession and "the artist as aristocrat."[40] Images in which the artist is presented as a scholar, as is the case with Nicolas Poussin (cat. no. 7), also de-emphasize the manual aspects of painting, in this instance in favor of the intellectual aspects.[41]

As Rudolf and Margot Wittkower have pointed out, tales of artists' eccentricity are ancient and proliferate from the fourteenth century on, many of them conforming to recurring motifs.[42] They see this typing of artists as a mark of their individualism, in that they stand outside the social mainstream,[43] but it was a type suppressed by artists in favor of one that corresponded more with a social and intellectual elite. Nonetheless, not all artists were portrayed as gentlemen; some seem to have cultivated the image as a social outsider. The group of (mostly) Northern artists in seventeenth-century Rome known as the Bentvueghels (birds of a feather) were infamous for their rowdy behavior, as one of them, Roeland van Laer, depicted (fig. 6).[44] Seventeenth-century Dutch artists often portrayed themselves

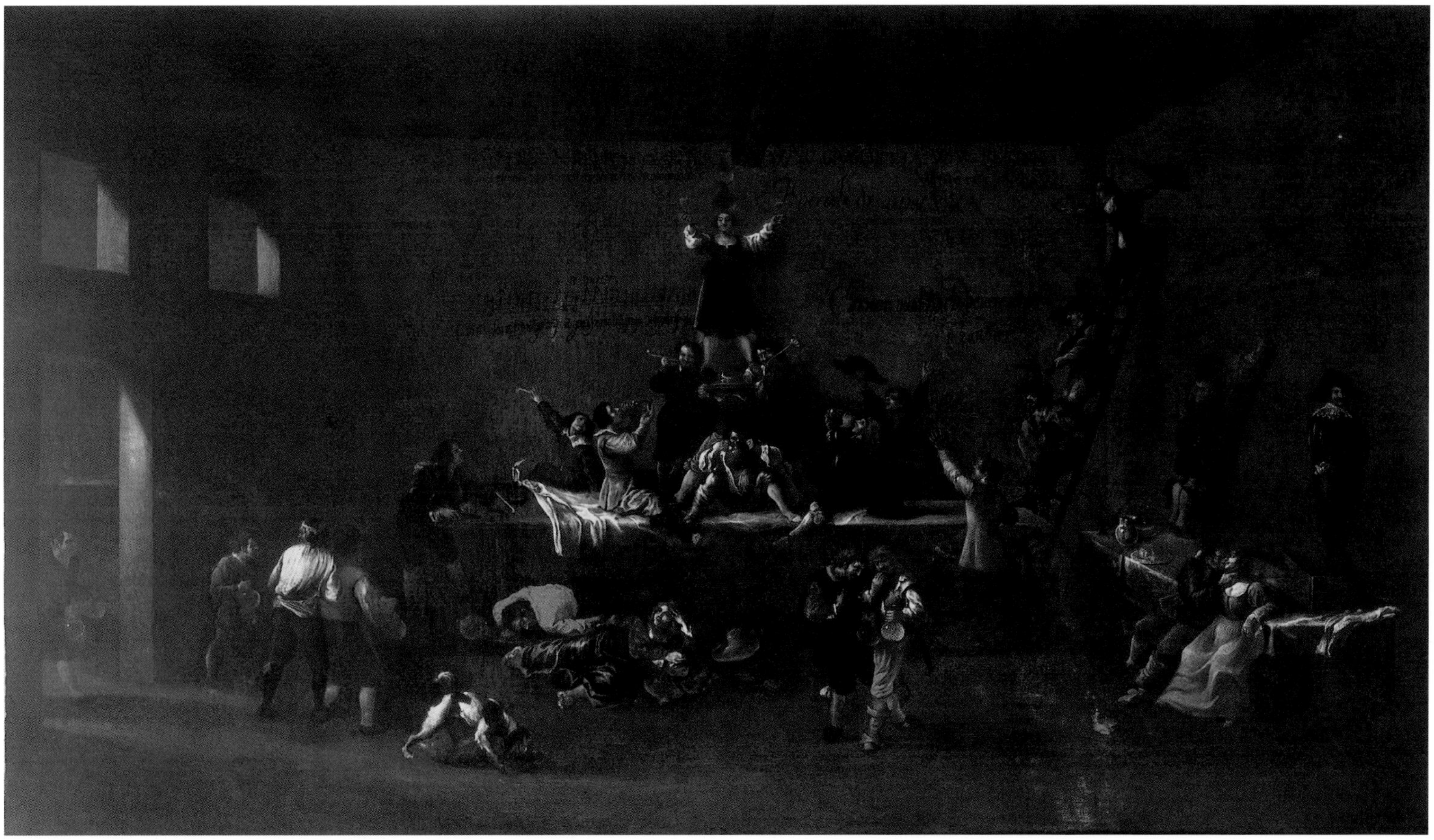

Fig. 6. Roeland van Laer. *Bentvueghels in a Roman Saloon.* c. 1626–28. Oil on canvas, 88.5 x 147.5 cm (34⅞ x 58⅛ in.). Museo di Roma.

as decidedly unsophisticated: smoking, drinking, guffawing, and carousing. These compositions may, however, be less self-portraits than embodiments of the five senses or enactments of roles like the prodigal son, which Rembrandt's painting of his wife, Saskia, and himself is understood to be (fig. 7).[45] Jan Steen portrayed himself many times, almost invariably playing comic roles, as a kind of inside joke.[46]

Although artists were considered craftsmen long before they were gentlemen, scholars, or outsiders, they were rarely represented as such until the seventeenth century, because the impulse to depict artists from the fifteenth century on generally went hand in hand with the desire to raise their status in society. Only after that more elevated status was largely secured could artists embrace their manual work in portraiture and depictions of their studios.[47] Anthonis Mor's famous self-portrait of 1558 in Florence (fig. 8) is an early example of an artist depicting himself at his easel, palette and brushes in hand.

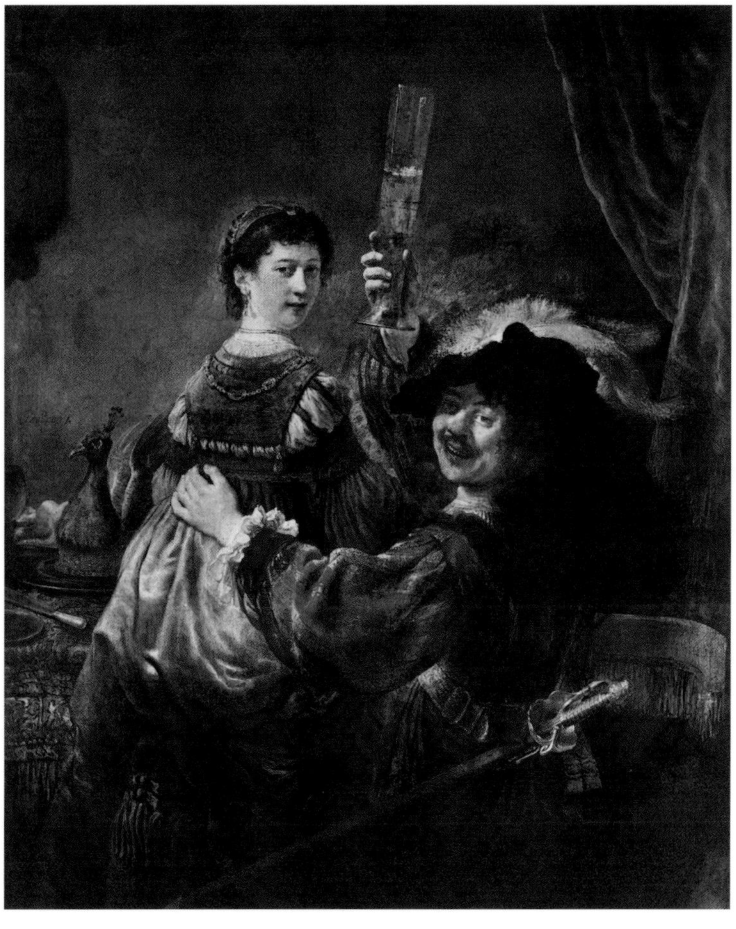

Fig. 7. Rembrandt van Rijn. *Rembrandt (Self-Portrait) and Saskia in the Parable of the Prodigal Son.* 1635–39. Oil on canvas, 131 x 161 cm (51⅝ x 63⅜ in.). Gemäldegalerie, Staatliche Kunstsammlungen, Dresden.

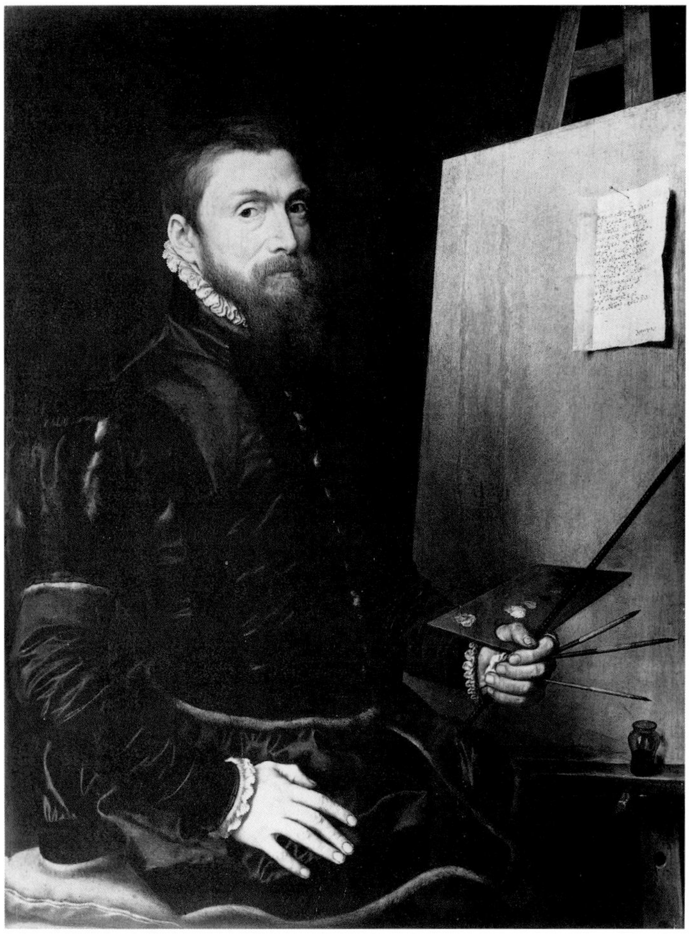

Fig. 8. Anthonis Mor. *Self-Portrait.* 1558. Oil on panel, 113 x 84 cm (44½ x 33⅛ in.). Galleria degli Uffizi, Florence.

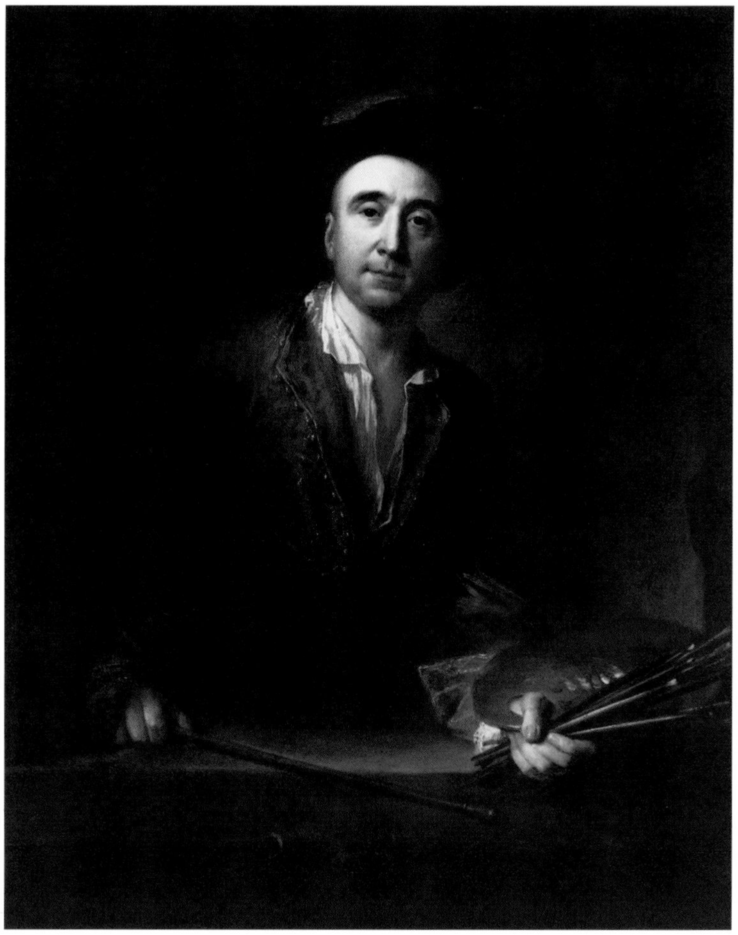

Fig. 9. François de Troy. *Self-Portrait.* 1704. Oil on canvas, 114.3 x 90.8 cm (46 x 35¾ in.). Sarah Campbell Blaffer Foundation, Houston.

Significantly, however, Mor subtly aborts this portrayal by not showing himself actually at work—the canvas is blank—and unites artisanal self-reflexivity with the humanist tradition by representing a piece of paper attached to the canvas inscribed with a Latin verse situating him in the classical tradition by averring his superiority to Apelles, the greatest of ancient painters. Mor further establishes his social dignity by signing as court painter to the Spanish king, Philip II.[48]

Seventeenth-century Dutch artists were much more likely than Italians to portray themselves as craftsmen, posing with their tools or at work in their studios. Celeste Brusati has discussed at length the proclivity of many Dutch artists "to associate and even to identify themselves with the representational craft of painting."[49] She identified two interrelated "cultural circumstances" that were determinative: the fact that Dutch artists in the sixteenth and seventeenth centuries strove to improve their social and professional status within the craft guilds, assimilating humanist principles of the liberality of art rather than adopting them in replacement of artisanal virtuosity;[50] and the value collectors placed on the artists' mimetic abilities evident in richly detailed still-life paintings. Even writers well acquainted with the humanist tradition within the visual arts that had emerged from Italy in the sixteenth century, such as Karel van Mander, whose *Schilderboeck* (1604) is enormously important as the first history of Netherlandish art, praised painters "for the patience, diligence and precision of their labors"; and in his well-known address to the painters of Leiden in 1641, Philips Angel emphasized the power of finely painted, mimetic pictures to captivate the viewer.[51] The emphasis on the artist's technical prowess is particularly evident in the many seventeenth-century Dutch still-life paintings in which the artist's image at the easel appears in one or more mirrors or other reflective surfaces, which are often convex, heightening the impression of the artist's skill in rendering complex perspectival views. A seminal work in this genre is Clara Peeters's *Still Life* of 1612, in which her specular image appears eight times in a gilt goblet.[52] Artists at work came to be a common motif in Dutch genre scenes, as in Adriaen van Ostade's etching (cat. no. 39). In the eighteenth

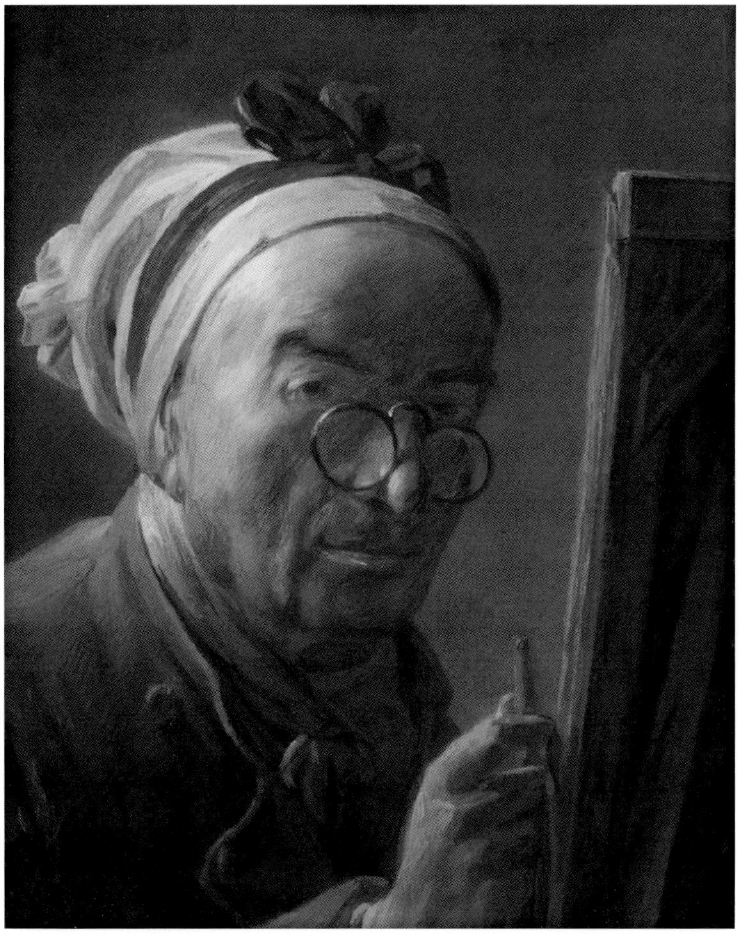

Fig. 10. Jean-Baptiste Siméon Chardin. *Self-Portrait at His Easel*. c. 1776. Pastel, 407 x 325 mm (16 x 12¾ in.). Musée du Louvre, Paris.

century, the image of the artist as craftsman passed readily into French art as well (cat. nos. 42–45), offering an alternative to the pseudo-state portrait, such as François de Troy's self-portrait exhibited at the Salon of 1704 (fig. 9) or Jean-Baptiste-Siméon Chardin's remarkable series of intimate pastel self-portraits from the 1770s (fig. 10).

All these types of portrayal appear in the drawn, etched, and painted work of Rembrandt. In works with his recognizable likeness—unparalleled for its time in its extent (more than seventy-five works) and variety—he appears as the prodigal son, a beggar, a saint, a gentleman, an artist, wearing elegant clothes, oriental clothes, work clothes, and so on.[53] There has been considerable debate about whether or not these works can be considered self-portraits in a meaningful way—the problem exacerbated by an uncertainty whether Rembrandt's features are even present in some works—and they have become part of the larger topic of the notion of the "self" in early modern times. Perry Chapman speaks most saliently of Rembrandt's "discovery of the self" and, borrowing a term from Stephen Greenblatt, his "self-fashioning." She sees the self-portraits as "generated by internal pressures," regardless of whether or not they were acquired by others, but the artist was also influenced by his social context, "deeply affected by the rising individualism of the age in which he lived."[54] An aspect of this individualism that became more prominent in the sixteenth and seventeenth centuries was religious self-examination, borne especially of the Protestant concept of the individual's unique and personal relationship to God.[55] Yet Rembrandt found individualism—at least as it developed in Italian humanism and was passed on to Dutch artistic culture—to be at odds with the realities of his bourgeois culture. He thus was forced "to invent a new concept of the artist," discovering "that he could gain selfhood more from his talent and professional identity than from his social status."[56] Rembrandt ultimately passes from "self-portraits based on Renaissance ideals"—that is, the gentleman-artist (fig. 11)—through the less "romanticized" images of himself at work (fig. 12), to "those expressing an independence of thought and feeling that is fundamentally modern (fig. 13)."[57] On the other hand, Ernst van de Wetering rejects this view as post-Romantic. Like Hans-Joachim Raupp before him, he is "convinced that the prevailing view of the self-portrait as a means for 'self-examination' is an anachronism when applied to the period before 1800," and that Rembrandt's self-portraits (a term that came into use only in the nineteenth century) are more properly thought of simply as "portraits of Rembrandt by Rembrandt."[58]

Self-Fashioning and Myth-Making

Stephen Greenblatt introduced the now widely used term "self-fashioning" into Renaissance studies to describe an individual's construction of his or her public persona, but the reverse of that medal—self-examination, interiority, "ipseity," and such—is notoriously vague and difficult to determine historically. Stephen Lukes discusses privacy as an aspect of individualism, finding relevance in "the whole tradition of Christian mysticism represent[ing] a cultivation of the private or inner sphere," from Augustine's engagement with the "complex and mysterious recesses of his inmost self" to a high point in the fourteenth century.[59] Burckhardt, on the other hand, saw the discovery or exploration of the "inward man" or "inward life" as a hallmark of the Italian Renaissance.[60] An alternative model for the development of the individual and his or her interior life places the historic shift in the time of Shakespeare, and often relates it

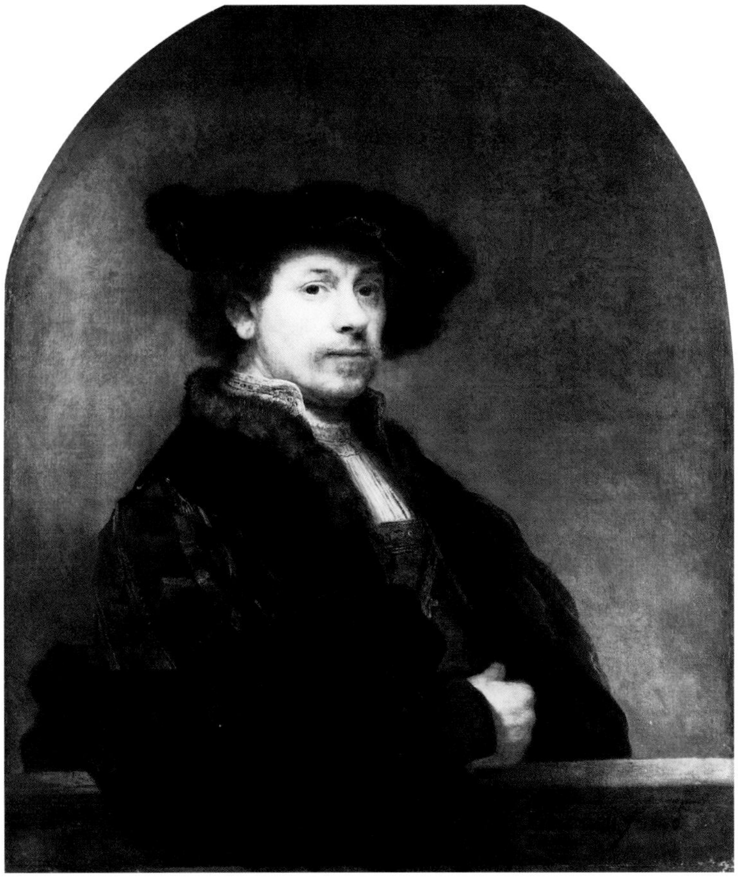

Fig. 11. Rembrandt van Rijn. *Self-Portrait as a Young Man.* 1640. Oil on canvas, 102 x 80 cm (40⅛ x 31½ in.). National Gallery, London.

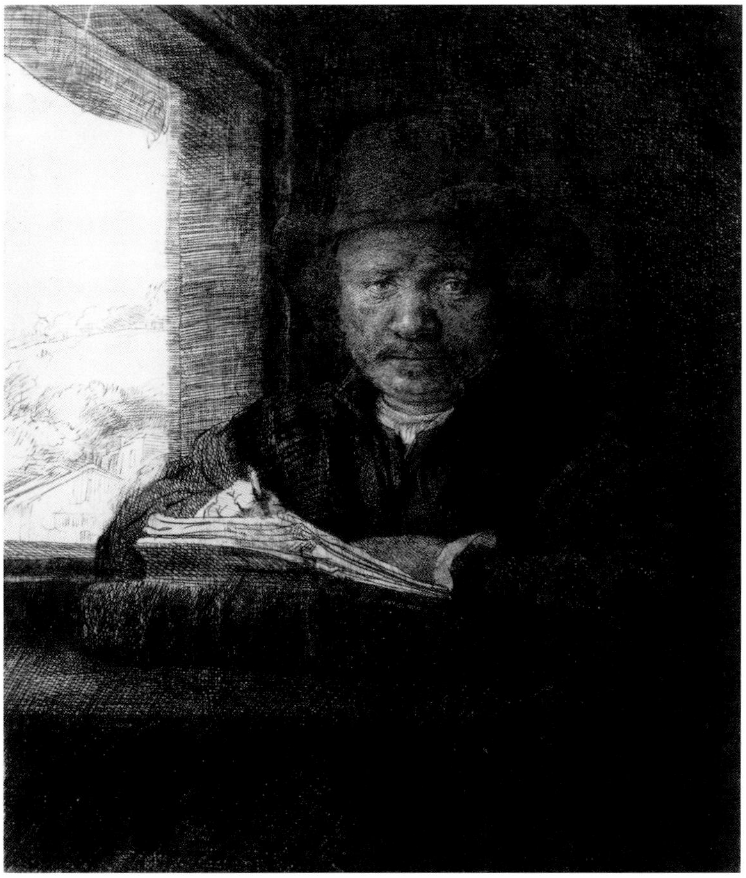

Fig. 12. Rembrandt van Rijn. *Self-Portrait Drawing at a Window.* 1648. Etching, drypoint needle and burin, 160 x 130 mm (6¼ x 5⅛ in.). The British Museum, London.

directly to Protestant poetics, first in England and subsequently in Holland.[61] Yet another view holds that an understanding of character as "essentially social, and not psychological, in nature," attending to the exterior rather than the interior of a person, is still predominant in the eighteenth century.[62] No single model will be able to account for all the forms of self-consciousness, and Peter Burke has usefully drawn attention to the "variety of 'Renaissance selves'" and the subtle differences between "self-consciousness, self-expression, self-presentation, and self-fashioning."[63] On balance, however, it should be borne in mind that most (or all) of the works in this exhibition—in fact, most prints of the period in general—were made for dissemination, and they are more likely to participate in the construction of a public persona than to reveal a private self.

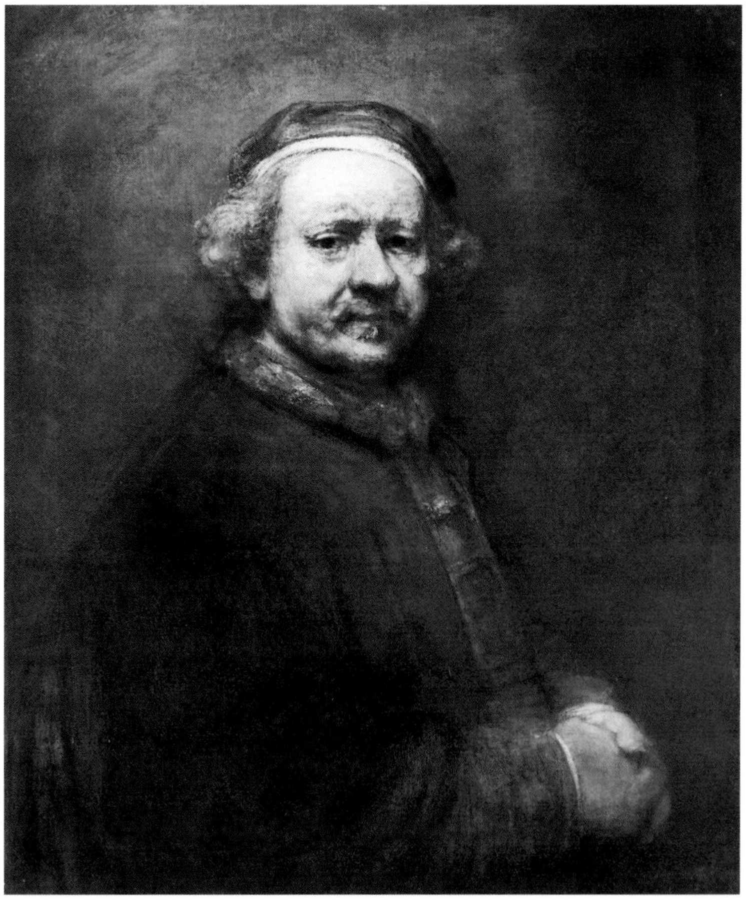

Fig. 13. Rembrandt van Rijn. *Self-Portrait at the Age of Sixty-Three.* 1669. Oil on canvas, 86 x 70.5 cm (33⅞ x 27¾ in.). National Gallery, London.

Self-fashioning is easily elided into myth-making. The "myths" of individual artists and of the "Artist" in general are inextricably entwined. Artists fashioned their own personas—through their works, their behavior, their writings, even their autobiographies (sometimes surrogate, in the case of Michelangelo's *Life,* written by Ascanio Condivi). This self-fashioning then became the seed of often extensive elaborations of the persona, which in turn re-read the works, letters, and so on, in light of the created myth, so that an artist's entire oeuvre could be seen as a visual manifestation of his biography, both external (his actions, whether real or imagined by later writers) or internal (his spiritual, mental, or emotional self).[64] The production of biographical and artistic meanings is simultaneous and interdependent; a *fortuna critica* of an artist's work and what we might call a *fortuna biographica* of the artist's life are therefore not simply parallel but mutually informing and even merging phenomena, so that life, persona, and work become a unified whole derived from, but not the same as, either a historical person or his artistic oeuvre.

There are tendencies toward this life/persona/work merger in the early modern period, as in, for example, Giovan Pietro Bellori's famous equation of Caravaggio's dark visage and manner of painting. An even more explicit connection, however, is William Hogarth's use of self-portraits as frontispieces to the bound folios of his collected prints (see cat. nos. 12, 41). Soon after Hogarth's death, John Nichols drew the connection even more tightly, as well as dramatically, recounting an anecdote of the origin of William Hogarth's *Tail Piece: The Bathos* (cat. no. 78). It was in the company of friends, "while the convivial glass was circulating round his own table," that Hogarth first proposed to produce as his "next undertaking . . . *The End of All Things.*" One of his friends replied that in that case, "'your business will be finished; for there will be an end of the painter.'" Hogarth sighed heavily, agreeing, and determined to begin his work the next day, approaching it "with a diligence which seemed to indicate an apprehension (as the report goes) that he should not live till he had completed it." He had nearly finished, when he cried, "'So far, so good, . . . nothing remains but this,'—taking his pencil in a sort of prophetic fury, and dashing off the similitude of a painter's pallet broken—'Finis,' exclaimed Hogarth, 'the deed is done—all is over.'—It is remarkable, that he died in about a month after this tail piece. It is also well known he never again took the pencil in hand."[65]

In the nineteenth century, Romantic notions of artists as outsiders and rebels, mad geniuses,[66] and so on, fueled the creation or extension of such myths, both of specific artists (especially the Old Masters) and of fictional ones.[67] A pronounced example of the conflation of an artist's life and work to create a Romantic ideal is Lady Morgan's much-maligned *The Life and Times of Salvator Rosa,* of 1824. Morgan's is an extreme formulation in which the "real" Salvator Rosa disappears and what we might call the "artistic persona" of "Salvator Rosa" becomes the biography's protagonist. Morgan's construction of "Salvator Rosa" is heavily dependent on the artist's work, both poetic and visual.[68] She provides accounts of Rosa's activities (such as supposed life among the bandits) based on the imagery of his work and discovers meaningful self-portraits (whether allegorical or actual likenesses) in his depictions of various historical figures.

By the eighteenth century, tradition had it that Rosa had lived for a time among the bandits of the wildest regions of the Abruzzi in southern Italy, based presumably on the inclusion of armed figures in Rosa's dramatic landscape paintings and in his prints known as the *Figurine.* The first published reference to the tradition is in William Gilpin's *Essay Upon Prints* of 1768;[69] a decade later John Hamilton Mortimer (called "the English Salvator" and "This Salvator of Sussex") produced a portrait of Salvator Rosa—part of a suite of fifteen etchings dedicated to Joshua Reynolds—in the dress of a soldier or bandit perusing a hefty volume of prints, his helmet and sword on a rock by his side (fig. 14).[70] Morgan's account of the sojourn with the banditti runs to some nine pages, replete (as usual) with background information on banditry in southern Italy. She introduced the idea that Rosa was at first captured by the banditti, then remained with them of his own accord, and she found relevance in one of the *figurine* (fig. 15); a passage gives some sense not only of Morgan's Romantic, novelistic approach, but also of the intimate association she regularly finds between art and life:

> There is one engraving which, though evidently done *a colpo di pennello,* seems so plainly to tell the story of the wandering artist's captivity, that it may, as an historic fact, if not as a *chef-d'oeuvre* of the art, merit a particular description. In the midst of rocky scenery appears a group of banditti, armed at all points, and with all sorts of arms. They are lying, in careless attitudes but with fierce watchfulness, round a youthful prisoner, who forms the foreground figure, and is seated on a rock, with languid limbs hanging over the precipice, which may be supposed to yawn beneath. It is impossible to describe the despair depicted in this figure: it is marked in his position, in the

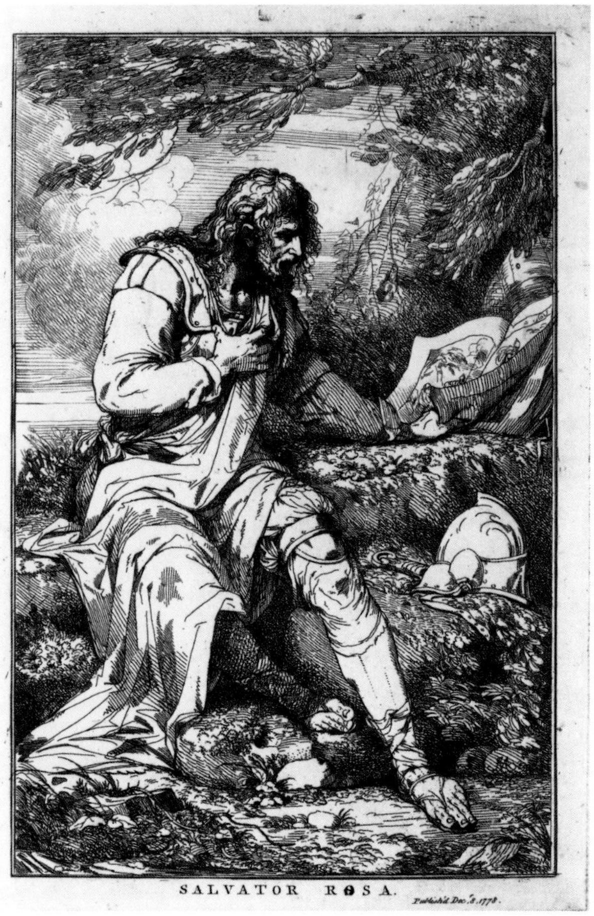

Fig. 14. John Hamilton Mortimer. *Salvator Rosa.* 1778. Etching. 300 x 201 mm (11¾ x 7⅞ in.). National Gallery of Art, Washington; Andrew W. Mellon Fund.

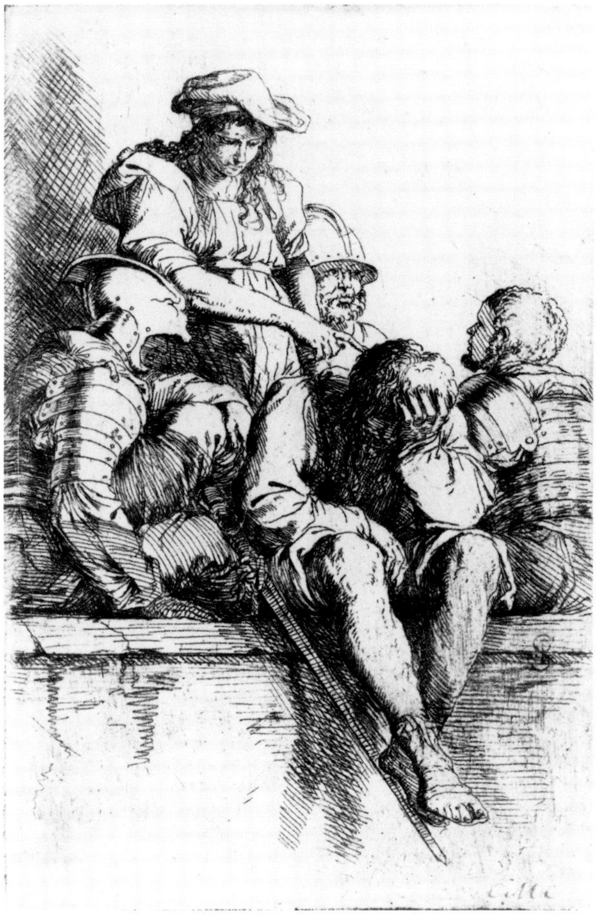

Fig. 15. Salvator Rosa. *Four Warriors and a Standing Youth.* c. 1656–57. Etching, 147 x 94 mm (5¾ x 3¾ in.). The British Museum, London.

> droop of his head, which his nerveless arms seem with difficulty to support, and in the little that may be seen of his face, over which, from its recumbent attitude, his hair falls in luxuriant profusion (and the singular head and tresses of Salvator are never to be mistaken). All is alike destitute of energy and of hope, which the fierce beings grouped around the captive seem, in some sentence recently pronounced, to have banished for ever. Yet one there is who watches over the fate of the young victim: a woman stands immediately behind him. Her hand stretched out, its forefinger resting on his head, marks him the subject of a discourse which she addresses to the listening bandits. Her figure, which is erect, is composed of those bold straight lines, which in art and nature constitute the grand. Even the fantastic cap or turban, from which her long dishevelled hair has escaped, has no curve of grace; and her drapery partakes of the same rigid forms. Her countenance is full of stern melancholy—the natural character of one whose feelings and habits are at variance, whose strong passions may have flung her out of the pale of society, but whose feminine sympathies still remain unchanged. She is artfully pleading for the life of the youth, by contemptuously noting his insignificance. But she commands while she soothes. She is evidently the mistress, or the wife of the Chief, in whose absence an act of vulgar violence may be meditated. The youth's life is saved: for that cause rarely fails to which a woman brings the omnipotence of her feelings.[71]

When the subject is taken up by a later artist, Thomas Jones Barker, in a painting of 1865, Rosa is embedded in a landscape of his own style (fig. 16).[72] Rosa's paintings come to life—with himself as protagonist—then are returned to paint by a later artist.

Morgan confidently finds Rosa's likeness in several works, including the great *Democritus in Meditation* in Copenhagen, all of which are then interpreted as spiritually revelatory self-portraits. It was shortly after his return to Rome, Morgan tells us, that his history paintings were criticized and buyers wanted only his small landscapes, much to the artist's irritation. "It was at this period that Salvator painted his fine picture of 'Job' [now in the Uffizi, Florence], for he, like the great subject of his selection, was one '*bitter in soul*.' In this noble picture, the sufferer

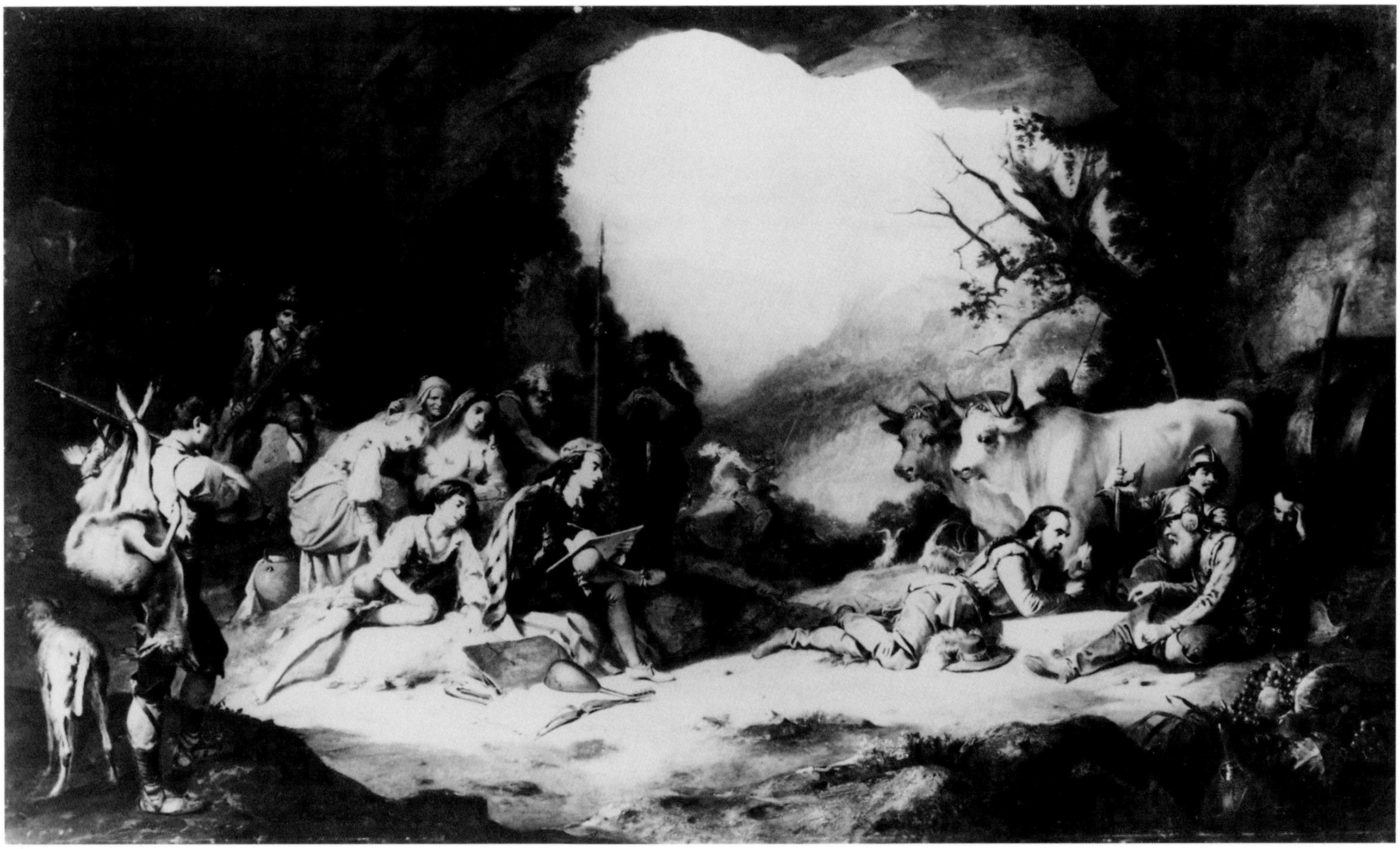

Fig. 16. Thomas Jones Barker. *The Studio of Salvator Rosa in the Mountains of the Abruzzi.* 1865. Oil on canvas, 111.8 x 180.7 cm (44 x 71⅛ in.). Joslyn Art Museum, Omaha.

appears equally tormented by the remonstrances of friends, and the inflictions of his destiny. One in the garb of philosophy is evidently reasoning with him in vain, while a rude soldier gives him all the uncalculated sympathy of deep-felt commiseration, so much more soothing to misery than the counsel of the prudent or the precepts of the wise. This is one of Salvator's finest works. It is a reproduction of himself."[73]

Art about Art

Morgan seems to be exalting Salvator Rosa the individual, but in fact her construction of his persona, in which his biography and works are inextricably intertwined, displaces both the artist and his work, and is thus in keeping with much of the critical theory of the last several decades, which has tended to undermine the putatively self-evident importance of both subject and object—that is, of the creator of a work and its ostensible subject matter. It tends to de-emphasize, or even negate, the authority of the author or artist over his or her own work, to remove the author/artist from a consideration of its meaning or significance.[74] The author might be retained as a concept, but he or she becomes, in Michel Foucault's phrase, an "author function,"[75] without regard for his or her existence as an individual responsible for the creation of the work, for investing it with meaning—the kind of individual we assume is portrayed in self-portraits.[76] The "death of the author" proclaimed by Roland Barthes and cheered by a host of others challenged the presumptions of individual autonomy and agency valued not just by liberal humanists but by others, especially Marxists and other contextualist historians, as well. The interest that self-portraiture has had is part of a broader concern with the individual, but this emphasis on the individual has as much to do with modern writers' situations within the context of Romanticism and liberalism (especially American) as it does with conditions within the early modern culture they study. Louis Montrose has referred, in another context, to "traditionalists who cherish liberal humanist ideals of individual self-determination,"[77] and it is precisely that liberal humanism, emphasizing the creative agency of individual artists, that would concern itself with apparently explicit representations of that individuality in self-portraits.

Both the ability of individuals to operate freely and the very concept of individualism have been challenged.

At the same time, and concomitantly, that the author/artist has been disembodied or eviscerated as creative agent, his or her creation—the artwork—has also suffered a loss or confusion of identity. A corollary of some structuralist and post-structuralist literary criticism is that texts (and anything that one might consider "texts," well beyond literary writing, including visual artworks) are ultimately about themselves, that is, about their own process of signification, thus supplanting the ostensible subject matter. In the visual arts, artworks could thus be understood as about the making, ontic status, or perception of artworks. Jan Mukařovský, for example, while recognizing that a picture can communicate through providing information (such as a portrait or a cityscape), argued that "the significance of a work of art as a work of art per se does not lie in communication. The work of art . . . is not oriented toward anything that is outside itself, toward any external aim"; thus "thematic meanings" carried by the representation of particular subject matter are extrinsic to its significance.[78] James Simpson has recently pointed to the varying "ground of meaning" for different critical schools as well as to the personified hypostases that have replaced the author for interpretative purposes; he identifies the ground of meaning and authorial hypostasis of the prevalent critical approach known as deconstruction as Textuality, suggesting the *reductio ad absurdum* that all art is about art.[79]

There is no doubt that the art in this exhibition is about art, and thus might even be considered hyper-self-reflexive, but its self-reflexivity has a validating iconographic component. George Santayana's complaint against art that is interested only in itself, quoted at the beginning of this essay, might be taken as a condemnation of the works in this exhibition and innumerable works like them. But the works are not so involuted as one might assume. They are self-conscious, self-reflexive, and probably occasionally self-indulgent, but they are not concerned *exclusively* with themselves. Rather, as suggested above, they participate in a process of self-definition that unfolds in an interplay with a broader context of social and historical factors. The artists operated simultaneously as unique persons but within historical and social constraints. They operated with regard to themselves as individuals, but also with regard to the various groups to which they belonged, resulting in a persistent creative tension. In many of the works in this exhibition and others like them, the individual is easily recognized, but so too are the representational conventions that have an anti-individualizing effect. There is a remarkable consistency in the accoutrements in images of artists, whether specific (self-) portraits or genre scenes, throughout the geographic and chronological limits of this exhibition and beyond. The same tools, like the chalk holder, appear over and again, regardless of whether the artist was noted for his or her especial use of them. Activities in workshop scenes are also repeated. They may or may not take place regularly in a particular workshop, but their prominent representation is used to define the subject. The precarious balance between individual and group manifests itself in the broad categories in which the exhibition is divided.

Icon

A measure of the rising status of artists is their inclusion in series of portraits of famous and illustrious men and women, both historical or contemporary. One of the most famous and extensive of these belonged to Paolo Giovio, papal historian and physician and Bishop of Nocera, who gathered about four hundred paintings and installed them in his villa—what he called a *musaeum*—in Como in the 1540s.[80] They represented figures from all over the known world, from antiquity to his own time. Artists were included with popes, kings, generals, poets, philosophers, and so on. Each was accompanied by an inscription indicating the nature of his achievement. He published many of the portraits in volumes that were later reissued, illustrated with woodcuts by Tobias Stimmer, ensuring their substantial influence. Giovio referred to the collection as a "temple of virtue" (*templum virtutis*), and it was exemplary, especially as it could be disseminated in published form: reading about the accomplishments of the great and seeing their images would induce the audience to strive to imitate them, not unlike conventional thinking on the function of hagiographic writing and images.[81]

In the early seventeenth century, the Roman artist Ottavio Leoni produced hundreds of portrait drawings, as well as around forty prints, many of them of artists.[82] Eighteen of the prints are of a common format—a bust-length portrait in a frame (dodecagonal for artists, simple oval or oval cartouche for others), inscribed with the sitter's name—and probably constitute the beginning of a series of famous men whose production was cut short by Leoni's untimely death. The artists are shown without attributes of their profession, and in the case of ennobled artists, such as Giovanni Baglione (fig. 17), Leoni shows the sitter wearing his insignia and describes him as a knight (*Eques*),

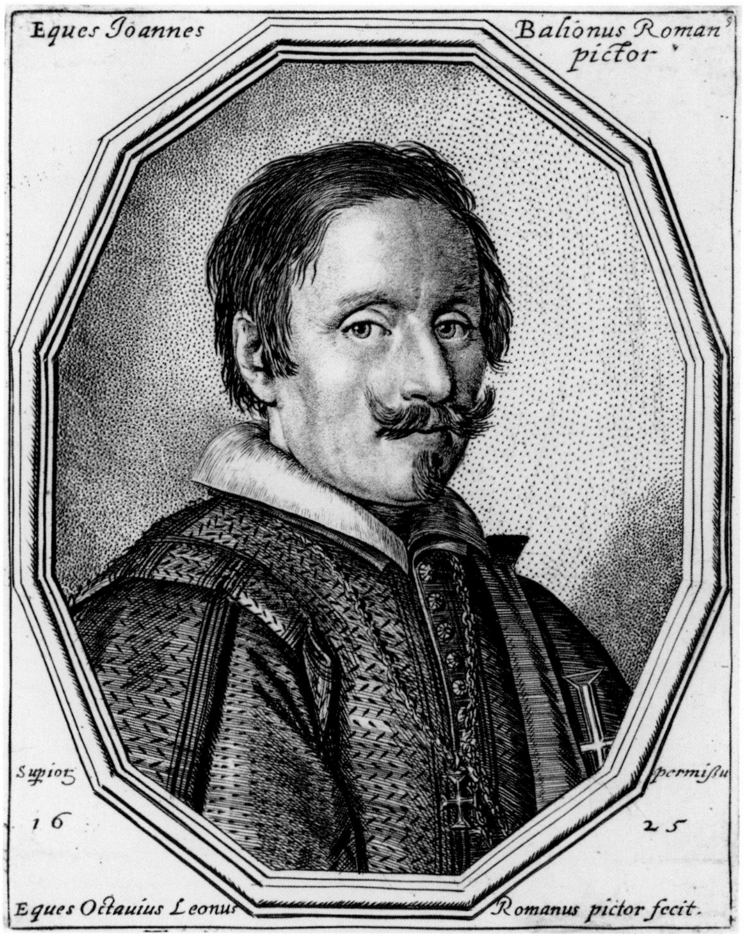

Fig. 17. Ottavio Leoni. *Portrait of Giovanni Baglione.* 1625. Engraving, 143 x 112 mm (5⅝ x 4⅜ in.). Private collection.

as he also describes himself in the signature. Baglione, who was also Leoni's earliest biographer, wrote that Leoni wanted to make "many portraits of various princes and virtuous persons of every profession."[83] Slightly later, a similar group of drawings and prints was made by Anthony van Dyck, again with a heavy concentration of artists' portraits. Van Dyck executed only a few of the prints himself, which were then reworked with others added and packaged as a series after his death (see cat. nos. 4–5). The sitters were shown with minimal attributes, and the artists are scarcely distinguishable visually from more socially elevated sitters. At the turn of the next century, artists (painters, sculptors, architects, printmakers, and a goldsmith) comprised fourteen of the one hundred subjects in Charles Perrault's two-volume *Les hommes illustres qui ont paru en France pendant ce siècle* (*The Illustrious Men Who Have Appeared in France during This Century,* 1696–1700). Nicolas Poussin (see cat. no. 7) and Pierre Mignard (cat. no. 10) appeared alongside such famous statesmen, prelates, nobles, and literati as Richelieu, Colbert, Descartes, Pascal, Corneille, Molière, and Racine. Perrault indicated explicitly that "the intention of this collection is to do honor to our century." Therefore, "one believed that one should not forget those who have excelled in the fine arts, and whose works have elevated France above the other states no less than the marvels of valor of our great captains, than the wisdom achieved by our great politicians, and than the admirable discoveries that our men of letters have made in all the sciences."[84] Although Perrault maintains some of the traditional hierarchy of social standing by grouping artists at the end of each volume, no further distinction is made between the artists and other subjects in the portrait or two pages of text allotted to each. Perrault's first volume apparently ruffled the feathers of some conservatives, whose objections were "advanced with a certain *air de hauteur,*" and in the preface to the second volume he both defended his book and acknowledged appropriate social distinctions:

> I have been reproached for having mixed artisans with princes and cardinals; it is true that in the same book there are encomiums on princes, cardinals, and artisans, but it is not at all true that I have mixed them together, and they are completely separated from each other in classes. As my principal intention was to give honor to our century, I believed that the genius and the extraordinary capacity of the workmen that it has produced is an advantage that I should not at all neglect, and that these excellent men contributed scarcely less to the glory of the century in which they lived than the great men of state and the great captains.[85]

Series comprised exclusively of artists' portraits closely resembled such groups of images of famous men. In 1572, Hieronymus Cock published in Antwerp twenty-three engraved portraits of artists with brief Latin poems extolling their achievements, with a combination of image and text comparable to the works in Giovio's *templum virtutis.* The texts were written by Domenicus Lampsonius, who in 1565 had published a biography of the artist Lambert Lombard with a portrait engraving.[86] Giorgio Vasari, who was in correspondence with Lampsonius, included woodcut portraits in his 1568 edition of his *Lives of the Eminent Painters, Sculptors, and Architects,* which was greatly enlarged and reworked from the first edition of 1550.[87] The combination of portrait (usually iconic, denuded of any appurtenances that its source image may have had) and text was imitated in later collections of biographies, both in Italy (by Giovan Pietro Bellori in 1672, Carlo Ridolfi in 1648, and Carlo Cesare Malvasia in 1678) and elsewhere (for example, Joachim von Sandrart in 1675, and Arnold Houbraken in

1718–21 [see cat. nos. 9, 11]). But a portrait need not be included in such a series to advocate the sitter's illustriousness: the mere fact of its existence establishes—or at least pretends to respond to—the sitter's importance, whether or not it includes a laudatory inscription.

The bust- or half-length figure, isolated from any narrative or even physical context, when coupled with a laudatory text, can function as the focal point of admiring attention, a secular version of non-narrative devotional images of Christ, the Virgin Mary, and saints—hence my use of the term "icon." Like so many images of saints who are sometimes indistinguishable from each other, portraits of artists share so many common characteristics, following general trends in portraiture, that the type often predominates over the individual. One of the definitions or hallmarks of "individualism" is autonomy.[88] With some notable exceptions, self-portraits are created of the artist's will, not coerced, or even commissioned, by someone else, and thus indicate his or her creative autonomy. So it may be surprising that self-portraits are often scarcely different from portraits by other artists (compare cat. nos. 5 and 16, for example), suggesting that portraitists provide for other artists the same self-presentation that they would provide for themselves. The format of the iconic portrait, its isolation from other figures as well as a context, proclaims the importance of individual identity, but the repetition of the format (including its occasional inclusion in series) suggests a corporate identity that extends not only to other artists but to other classes of sitters as well, classes of the wealthy and influential to which artists long aspired.

Work

Portraits of artists often show them at work, or, rather, pausing in work. In the images most closely approximating a common portrait format (especially half-length), the active aspects of the portrayal may appear essentially as attributes of the artist's profession, more elaborate perhaps but effectively the same, as if he were holding only a palette and brushes with no indication of setting. Thus an image such as Georg Frederic Schmidt's self-portrait, in which the artist's chalk-holder is poised above the paper on which he is working as he looks up to offer a full view of his face, differs in degree rather than in kind from Nicolas Poussin's self-portrait, in which the artist holds the chalk-holder to no immediate purpose (cat. nos. 14, 7). In at least one instance, such attributes were deemed by a patron to be essential to the representation, even though the broader context of a series of artists' self-portraits would make the sitter's profession clear: the agent in Amsterdam of Grand Duke Cosimo III de' Medici was instructed in 1676 to commission self-portraits from Frans van Mieris and Gerard ter Borch that would each show the artist either in the act of painting or holding some small work as an indication of his profession (fig. 18).[89] Work could also function as an attribute for groups as well as individuals, as in Johann Zoffany's group portrait of the London Royal Academicians, engraved by Richard Earlom, in which the pretense of a life drawing class in progress is scarcely pursued in the actions and postures of the members of the academy (cat. no. 28). The members of the Viennese Academy are more effectively portrayed at the task at hand, but the work remains a group portrait with a conventional indication of the group's raison d'être (cat. no. 29).

Representations of artists—whether specific or generic—should never be taken as unmediated "snapshots" of actual appearance or practice.[90] They aim at various kinds of effect, which may require a lack of, or selective, realism in portrayal. For example, they might be intended to demonstrate an artist's exalted status (or obscure a less exalted status). Baccio Bandinelli

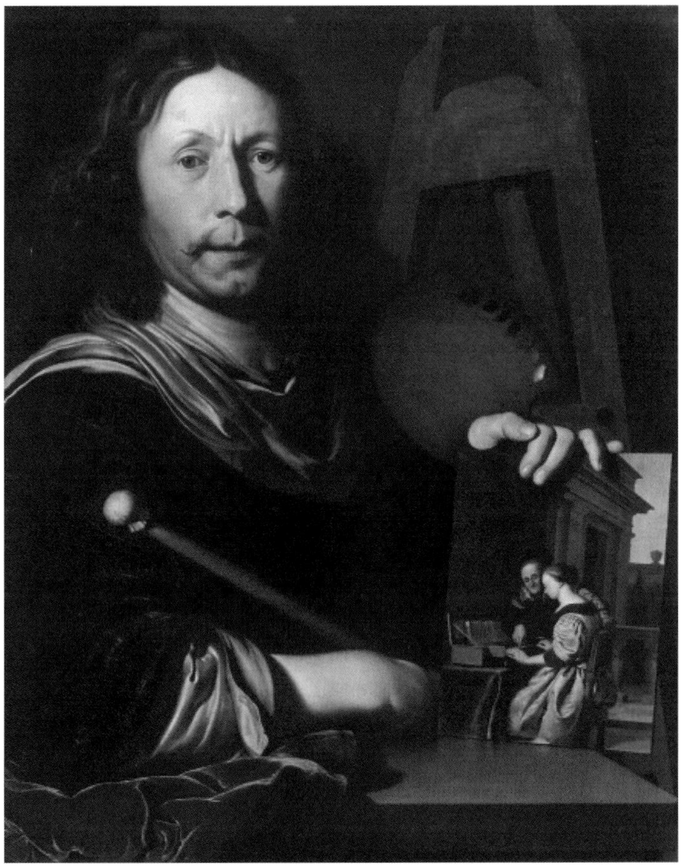

Fig. 18. Frans van Mieris. *Self-Portrait*. 1676–77. Oil on canvas, 72 x 57 cm (28⅜ x 22½ in.). Galleria degli Uffizi, Florence.

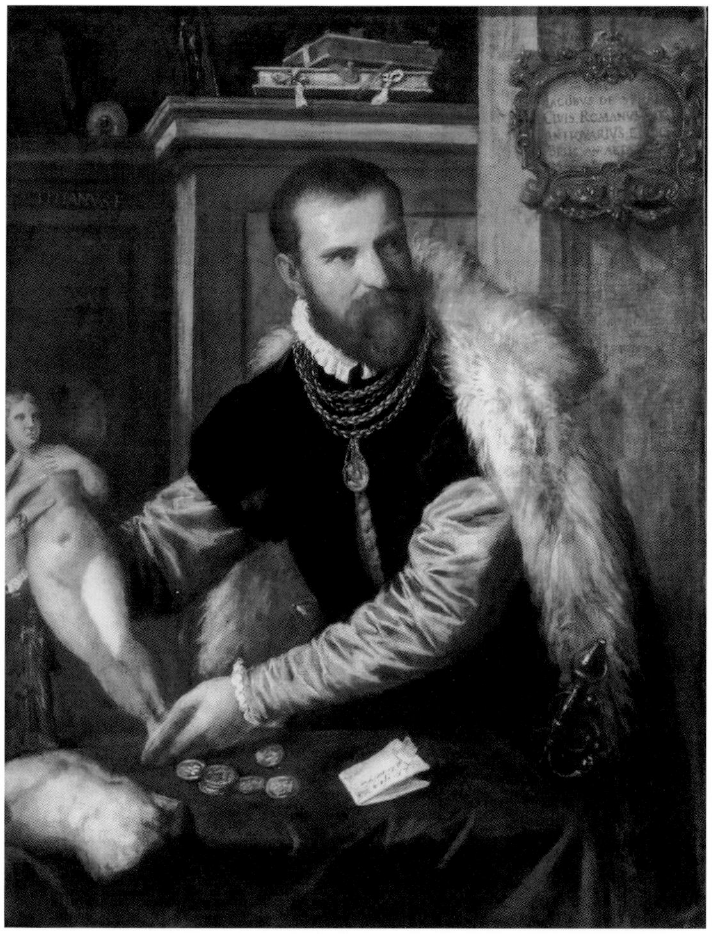

Fig. 19. Titian (Tiziano Vecelli). *Portrait of Jacopo Strada.* 1567–68. Oil on canvas, 125 x 95 cm (49¼ x 37⅜ in.). Kunsthistorisches Museum, Vienna.

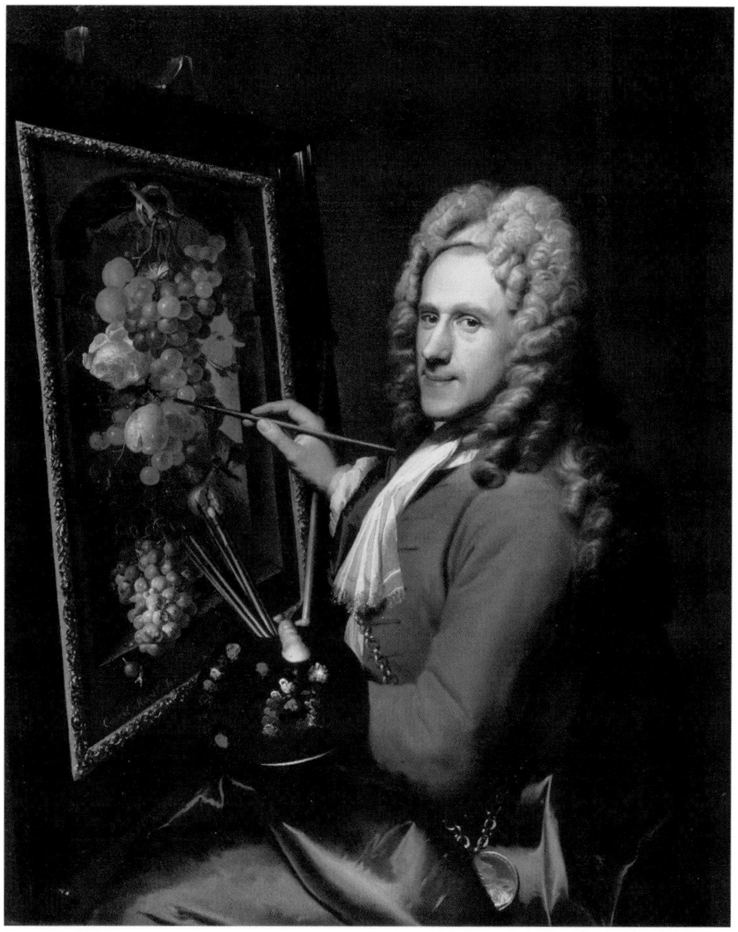

Fig. 20. Richard van Bleek. *Portrait of the Painter Coenraet Roepel.* Oil on canvas, 112.4 x 88.9 cm (44½ x 35 in.).

thus showed himself not as a sculptor whose sweaty labor might, in Leonardo's piquant expression, make him look like a baker covered with flour, but rather as a gentleman whose powers of invention are expressed through drawing and who holds small sculptures as might a collector (see cat. no. 1), like Titian's portrait of the architect and collector Jacopo Strada (fig. 19). In a painting recently on the London art market, Richard van Bleek showed the flower painter Coenraet Roepel at work on a painting—the palette, brushes, maulstick, and canvas on an easel all generic attributes, the flower painting a specific one—with no other indication of his work environment (fig. 20). Roepel's rather unlikely choice of attire for his work includes an honorary gold chain and medallion given to him by Johann Wilhelm, the Elector Palatine, in Düsseldorf in 1716, on which a portrait of the prince appears,[91] like that worn by numerous other artists in portraits (see cat. no. 2), and a grand peruke, which reveals just enough of his shaved pate to assure the viewer that it is a sign of his social status and not his real hair.

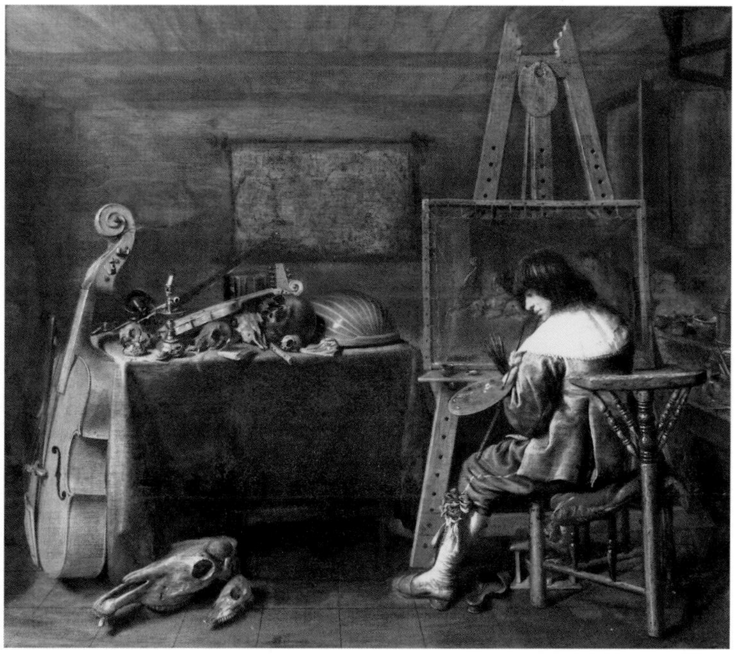

Fig. 21. Attributed to Jan Miense Molenaer. *A Painter in His Studio.* c. 1632. Oil on panel, 42.2 x 48.8 cm (16⅝ x 19¼ in.). Museum Bredius, The Hague.

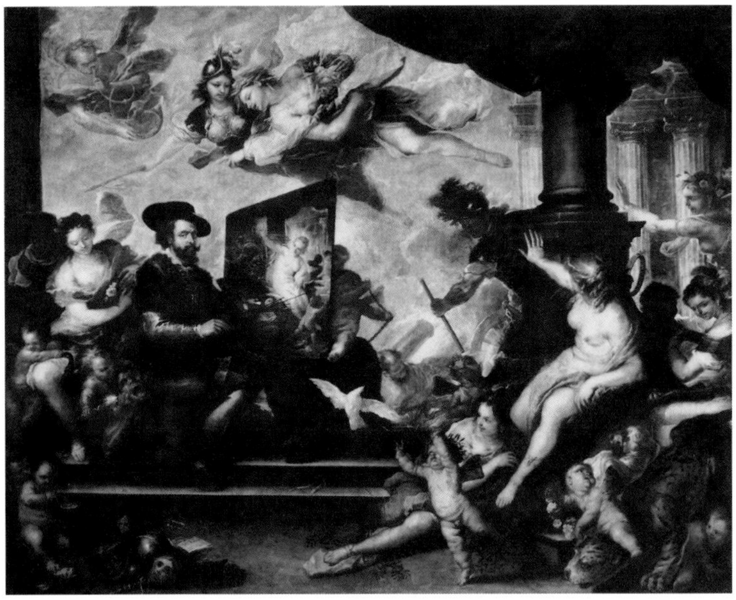

Fig. 22. Luca Giordano. *Rubens Painting the Allegory of Peace.* c. 1660. Oil on canvas, 337 x 414 cm (132⅝ x 163 in.). Museo Nacional del Prado, Madrid.

Representations of artists at work might also serve to emphasize the realism of the artist's work, possibly maintaining a fiction of how that realism came about. Images of artists with their models are common, whether of a sitter for a portrait or models for a history painting or genre scene, and the work in progress is often available for comparison against the model in the studio, as in a painting attributed to Jan Miense Molenaer, in which the model is a still life (fig. 21). Even in Luca Giordano's turbulent image of Peter Paul Rubens painting an allegory of peace, in which figures are flying all about, the female nude figure in distress on Rubens's canvas matches his putative model (fig. 22). In Martin Ferdinand Quadal's depiction of the Viennese Academy life class, Quadal shows himself in the center, at work on the very composition presented to the viewer—including himself—a *mise-en-abyme* that Johann Jacobe produced with engraved lines unlike the rest of the mezzotint (cat. no. 29). In outdoor scenes, the depicted artist may act as staffage, no different from shepherds or farmers or longshoremen going about their business, but he might also be a stand-in for the artist executing the painting, a signal that the landscape is true to life. An early and well-known example is a woodcut panoramic view of Florence, for which claims of veracity would be particularly important.[92] Often in these instances, when the artist's specific identity was not at issue, a three-quarter view from behind was conventional, allowing for a vicarious presence, a close identification of the depicted artist with both the depicting artist and the viewer (fig. 23; cat. no. 49).[93] Plein-air painting, as opposed to drawing, was highly unusual before the nineteenth century, but N. H. Tardieu's double portrait of Watteau and Jullienne (fig. 79.2) shows the artist at an easel out of doors, an unlikely scenario that was often repeated in nineteenth-century depictions of earlier artists, even Raphael.[94] The mimetic pretense of artists' work becomes the subject of parody in lithographs from the 1830s by Paul Gavarni of painters interacting with their models for religious subjects, Saints Peter and Mary Magdalen (figs. 24–25). Parody and comedy, as well as trivialization, are the signs of maturity in a genre, and Philibert-Louis Debucourt's *The Two Kisses* of 1786, in which the artist interacts with his model in a different way, would be unthinkable two centuries earlier (fig. 26).

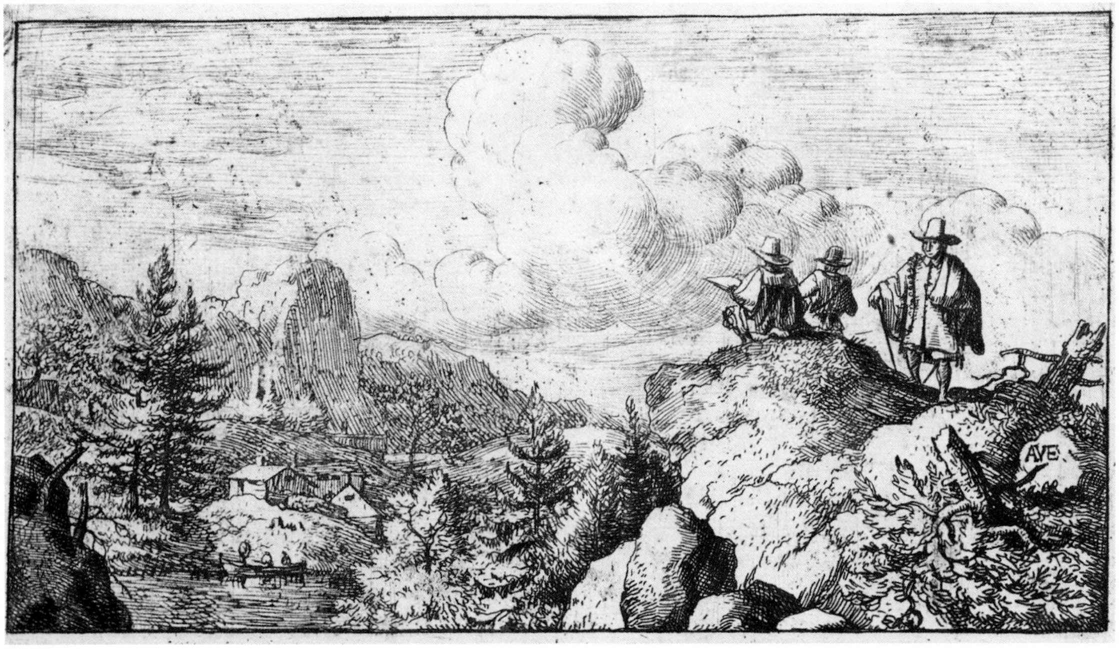

Fig. 23. Allaert van Everdingen. *The Draughtsmen.* n.d. Etching, 97 x 157 mm (3¹³⁄₁₆ x 6³⁄₁₆ in.). The Museum of Fine Arts, Houston; gift of William J. Hill.

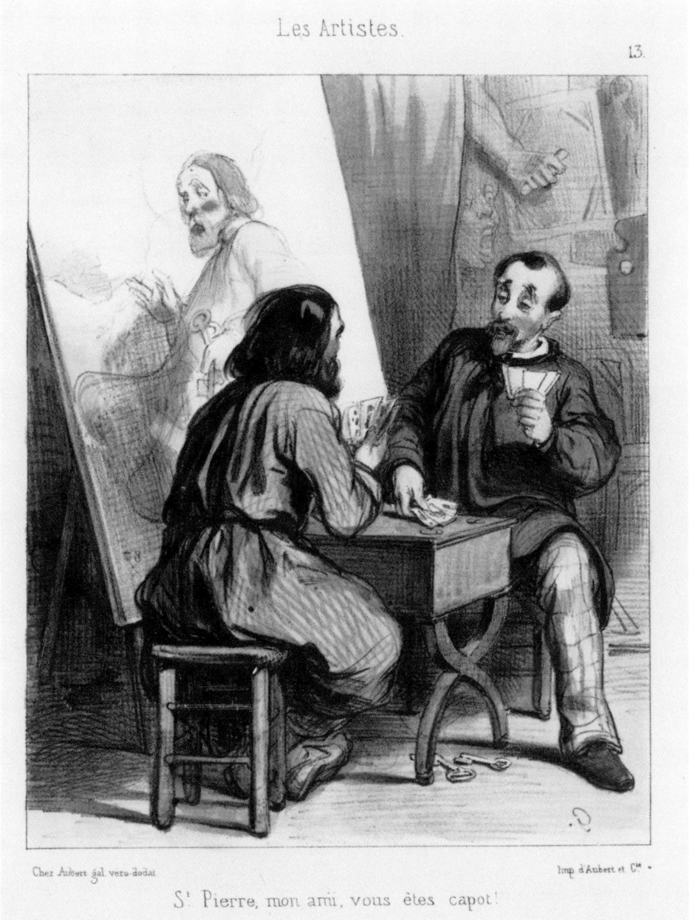

Fig. 24. Paul Gavarni. *Saint Pierre,* from the series *Les Artistes.* 1838. Lithograph in colors, image: 198 x 158 mm (7¾ x 6¼ in.). Sarah Campbell Blaffer Foundation, Houston.

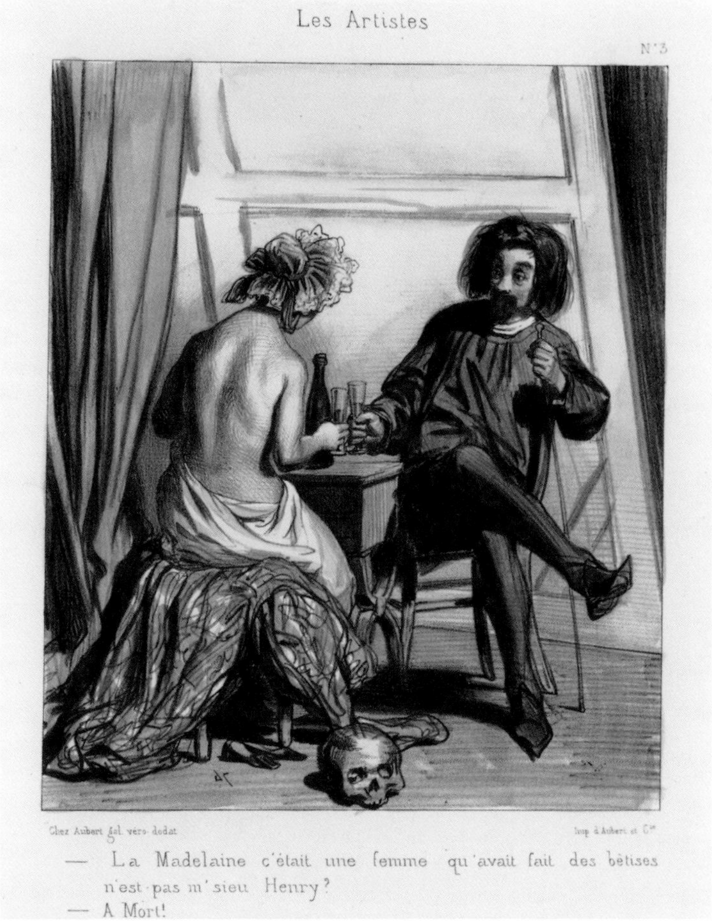

Fig. 25. Paul Gavarni. *La Madelaine,* from the series *Les Artistes.* 1838. Lithograph in colors, image: 197 x 162 mm (7¾ x 6⅜ in.). Sarah Campbell Blaffer Foundation, Houston.

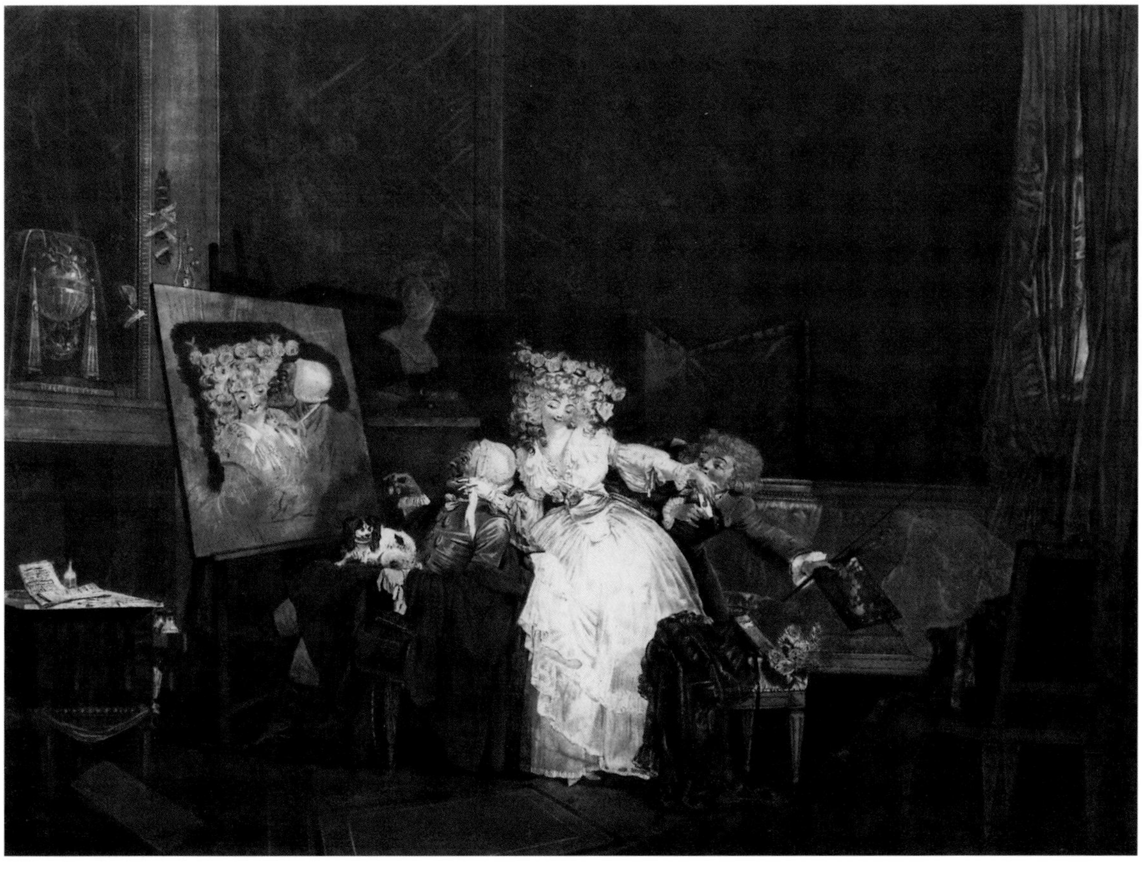

Fig. 26. Philibert-Louis Debucourt. *The Two Kisses (Les Deux Baisers).* 1786. Colored aquatint on laid paper, 272 x 365 mm (10$^{11}/_{16}$ x 14⅜ in.). Sterling and Francine Clark Art Institute, Williamstown, Massachusetts, 1955.1871.

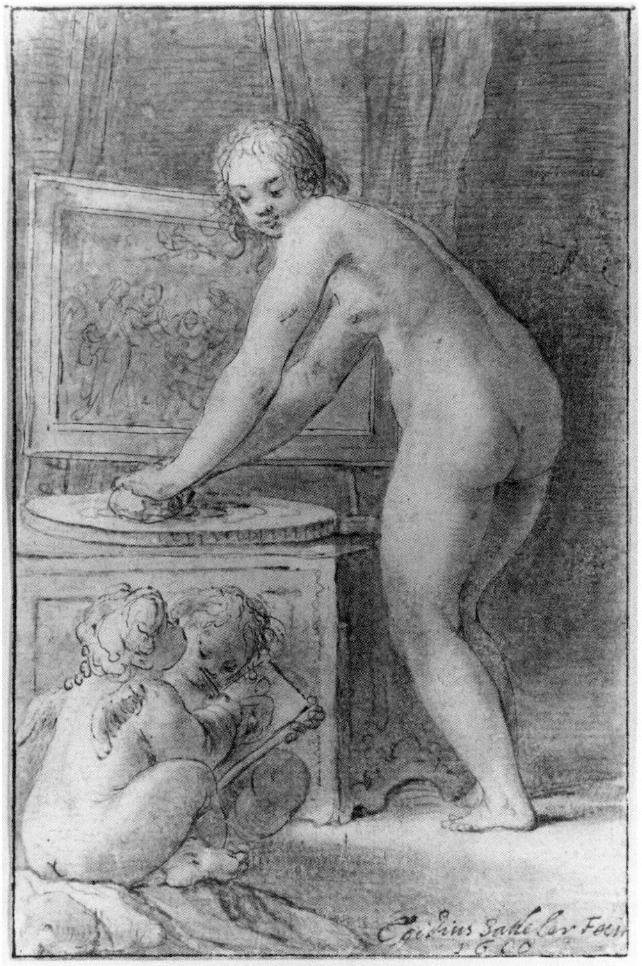

Fig. 27. Aegidius Sadeler. *Allegory of Painting.* 1610. Red and black chalk, pen and brown ink, grey wash. 131 x 86 mm (5⅛ x 3⅜ in.). Prentenkabinet der Universiteit Leiden.

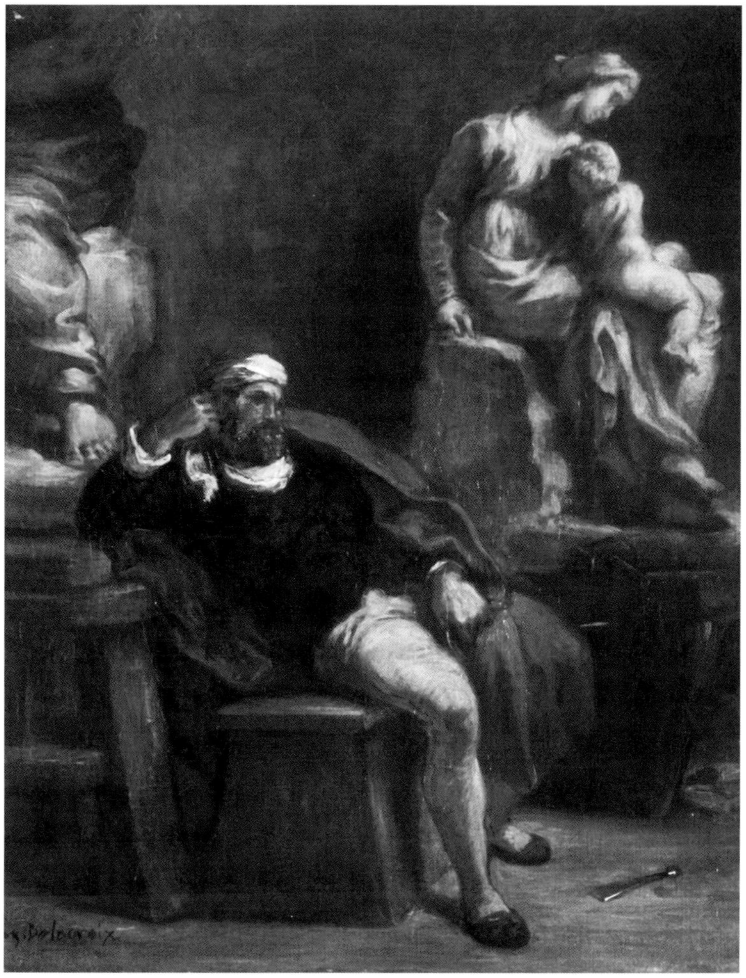

Fig. 28. Eugène Delacroix. *Michelangelo in His Studio.* c. 1850. Oil on canvas, 41 x 33 cm (16⅛ x 13 in.). Musée Fabre, Montpellier.

Representations of identifiable artists at work did differ from those of generic artists in one significant respect. While generic artists were often shown alone, as well as with studio assistance, identifiable artists were almost always shown without assistance, usually alone but sometimes in the company of sitters, visitors, family (for example, cat. no. 46), peers (for example, cat. no. 29), or, less frequently, students, although they are not assisting the master in his work (for example, cat. no. 21). That is, the specific portrait maintains a fiction of individual, unique, and unassisted production—the artist's *ingenium* visualized. By contrast, an invention like Joannes Stradanus's *Oil Paint,* while still exalting the artist, presents him as the head of a thriving, successful workshop (cat. no. 22). In this image, as in countless others, conventions are used to alert the viewer to both the profession depicted and the extent of the labor involved. Apprentices or assistants grinding pigments are almost *de rigueur* as a subsidiary activity in workshop scenes, regardless of whether or not the grinding of pigments would have taken place at the same time as, or in the presented spatial relationship with, the primary activity (usually the master executing a painting). The subject of the grinding of pigments could become so quintessentially representative of the artistic endeavor that it could appear in a scene of Saint Luke painting the Virgin and Child (cat. no. 32), and it was even allegorized, as in a drawing of 1610 by Aegidius Sadeler in which a nude personification of Painting (embodying Grace or Beauty) does the heavy labor (fig. 27).[95] As in other works, nude putti also take on studio roles, here in Sadeler's composition, drawing the female figure (see also cat. nos. 30, 55, 61). Several authors have argued persuasively for the corporate identity of the early modern artist's studio, determined by a recognizable style, without great regard to the involvement of the master in any particular phase of the operation.[96] But is this how artists depicted themselves, their peers, their generic representatives, and their studios? The artist as theorist and educator is certainly well represented,[97] as is the involvement of studio assistance at a low level (for example, the grinding of pigments), albeit limited to generic images. But what is not represented is an artist other than the master at the easel with brush in hand. Even in generic images in which assistants appear, such as Stradanus's composition or Adriaen van Ostade's several compositions of an artist's studio (cat. no. 39), the master's authority—and hence his unique artistic personality—is maintained.

Genius

In addressing the students of the Royal Academy in London, Joshua Reynolds tried in vain to stem the tide of what he saw as an irresponsible reliance on an innate, untrained genius, a term he uses for what we might call "talent." In his fifteenth and final "Discourse," of 1790, he acknowledged that he had laid himself open "to the sarcasms of those criticks who imagine our Art to be a matter of inspiration."[98] Michelangelo is the protagonist of this discourse, an artist who already in his lifetime was called "divine," whose style Reynolds himself called "the language of the Gods,"[99] who was taken up by the Romantics as an artist of unquestioned uniqueness and extraordinary sublimity,[100] whom Delacroix depicted around 1850 as a melancholic with as much *terribilità* as his works (fig. 28). In his first discourse, of 1769, celebrating the opening of the Academy, Reynolds had already taken aim at "that false and vulgar opinion, that rules are the fetters of genius."[101] More than twenty years later, he recognized Michelangelo's great genius but still not would accord it the preeminence or definition found in later writers:

> [H]e appears not to have had the least conception that his art was to be acquired by any other means than by great labour; and yet he, of all men that ever lived, might make the greatest pretensions to the efficacy of native genius and inspiration. I have no doubt that he would have thought it no disgrace, that it should be said of him . . . that he did not possess his art from nature, but by long study. He was conscious that the great excellence to which he arrived was gained by dint of labour, and was unwilling to have it thought that any transcendent skill, however natural its effects might seem, could be purchased at a cheaper price than he had paid for it.[102]

The term "genius" and its various cognates had been in use for centuries in relation to artists, with much the same meaning as Reynolds gave it.[103]

In the inscription to an etching of around 1662 (cat. no. 58), Salvator Rosa lists several qualities—sincerity, freedom, despising wealth and death, and so on—and proclaims: "This is my genius" (*hic meus est Genius*). In several ways Rosa set himself apart from society, which he critiqued through his art. His "genius" was precisely his conception of himself as an artist, rationally conceived and rationally pursued. Less that two centuries later, Lady Morgan uses the term "genius" many times in her "biographical Memoir" of Rosa. For Morgan, Rosa was a Romantic ideal: "a man, who, from the internal evidence of all he said, wrote, or painted, was evidently endowed with sensibilities approaching to malady, and who, gifted with the true temperament of genius, was framed to receive all impressions in their utmost force and intensity."[104] In Romantic thought, the artistic genius was endowed by God with a nearly preternatural power of imagination that ultimately set him against society and made him incapable of leading a normal life.[105]

During the course of the period represented by the works in this exhibition, there was considerable change not just to the term "genius," but also to how artists characterized the sources and aims of their work, whether God, poetry, love, nature, a muse, or an innate creativity. Notions of production, invention, fantasy, imagination, inspiration, and creativity were flexible but gradually shifted from the rational to the irrational, from the conventional to the eccentric, from the corporate to the highly individual; but the shift was not complete until the nineteenth century, and the earlier conceptions are still fundamental to most of the works presented here. Even Guérin's trilogy of lithographs, standing at the end of our period, addresses the artist's achievements in terms of industry and dedication, rather than transcendent genius as it has generally been construed since the nineteenth century (cat. no. 66)—not a surprising position for an active teacher like Guérin.

Market

Artists' representations of their market—whether patrons, clients, critics, or the vaguely interested public—manifest notions of their place and role in society. It has often been noted that stories of royal favors to artists, including visits to their studios, were used to advocate the elevated status of the visual arts, especially painting. The most important of them, told by Pliny the Elder in his *Natural History,* involved the painter Apelles and Alexander the Great, who was said to have visited the painter's studio often. Thus Francisco Pacheco wrote that Philip IV had a key to the studio in the royal palace that he had given to Diego Velázquez, and he "used to come and sit there for a while to watch Velázquez paint, much as Alexander the Great often visited Apelles in his workshop."[106] Artists most frequently represented Apelles's portraying Campaspe, the mistress of Alexander. Apelles falls in love with the beautiful woman, and Alexander gives her to the artist, "presenting not only his bedmate but his affection also to the artist" in an extraordinary show of generosity and appreciation for the artist's work (as well as an apparently utter disregard for Campaspe's wishes).[107] In Joos van Winghe's depiction of the story—a picture owned by Emperor Rudolf II—Alexander reaches to clap Apelles on the back while Cupid pokes the painter with his arrow of love (fig. 29).[108] More contemporary representations were also possible, as in Hans Burgkmair the Elder's portrayal of himself visited by the emperor Maximilian I (fig. 30).[109] An anecdote in Karel van Mander's biography of Dürer confirms the importance of imperial favor:

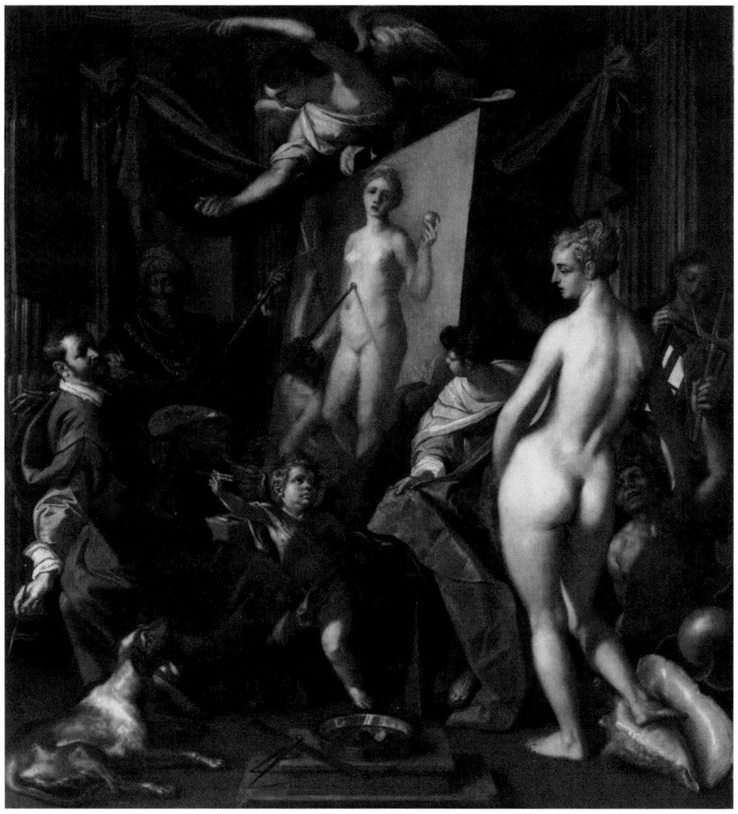

Fig. 29. Joos van Winghe. *Apelles Painting Campaspe.* c. 1600. Oil on canvas, 210 x 175 cm (82⅝ x 68⅞ in.). Kunsthistorisches Museum, Vienna.

> It is said . . . that Maximilian had him draw something so large on a wall that Albert could not reach high enough, whereupon the Emperor—in order to hurry things along—ordered one of the noblemen who happened to be present, to lie down so that Albert could stand on him and in that way finish his drawing. Upon which the nobleman courteously remonstrated with the Emperor that to be stepped upon thus by a painter would mean humiliation and contempt for the nobility. To which the Emperor replied that Albert was noble, yes more than a nobleman by virtue of his outstanding art, and that he could make a nobleman out of a peasant or an ordinary person but not such an artist from a nobleman.[110]

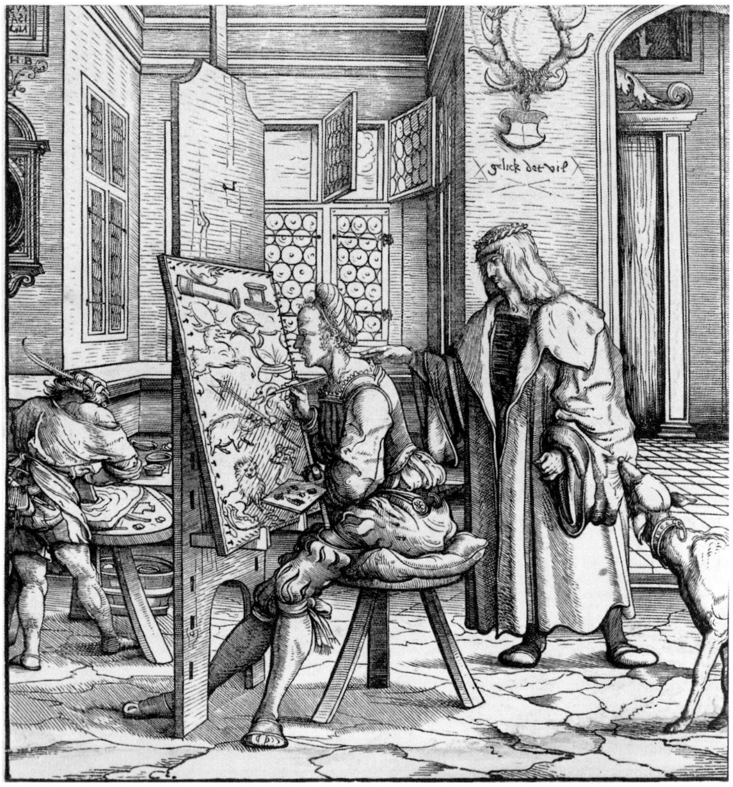

Fig. 30. Hans Burgkmair the Elder. *Emperor Maximilian I in the Artist's Studio.* 1512–16. Woodcut, approx. 220 x 195 mm (8⅝ x 7⅝ in.). Kupferstichkabinett, Staatliche Museen zu Berlin.

Some artists were fond of enumerating the times they had been visited by royalty and other august personages, a reversal of the roles in the court protocol that confirmed the exalted status of their profession—or at least their own practice of it. Benvenuto Cellini, for example, recounts four separate royal visits from Francis I, concluding the last with the observation: "Then he left saying: 'Good-bye, *mon ami*'—words rarely spoken by a king."[111] Self-portraits of artists with royal patrons are exceedingly rare (there was still the risk of violating decorum), and the most famous one, Diego Velázquez's monumental *Las Meninas,* in which the king and queen of Spain appear in the artist's studio (albeit only reflected in a mirror, a judiciously decorous conceit), was created during the artist's years-long struggle to gain admission into a noble order.[112] Royal munificence was acclaimed as fundamental for the flourishing of the arts in more abstract and general terms in celebratory allegories (see cat. nos. 73–75).

Patrons who were noble rather than royal, as in Abraham Bosse's depiction of a painter's studio (cat. no. 69), afforded the artist the opportunity not only to show the favor of acknowledgment accorded them by the patron but even to establish the social equivalence between patron and artist, whom Bosse explicitly calls "The Noble Painter."

In anecdotes of artists and their august patrons, mutual respect is exhibited. According to Filippo Baldinucci, when Maffeo Barberini became Pope Urban VIII, he had the sculptor Gianlorenzo Bernini brought to him and remarked, "It is a great fortune [for you], oh *cavaliere,* to see as pope the cardinal Maffeo Barberino, but ours is even greater that the cavalier Bernini lives during our pontificate."[113] In Cellini's recounting, during one of Francis I's many visits to the sculptor, the king remarked to him: "I don't know which is the greater, the pleasure of a prince at having found a man after his own heart, or the pleasure of an artist at having found a prince ready to provide him with all he needs to express his great creative ideas." Cellini, with false modesty, says that his own fortune was the greater, to which the king laughed and said that they were equal.[114] But complaints against august patrons are also to be found. As chummy as Cellini seemed to be with Francis, whom he continued to call a "remarkably fine man," he nonetheless left France under a cloud, claiming to be owed more than seven hundred crowns.[115] Cellini, at least by his own account, did not hesitate to put a patron like Duke Cosimo de' Medici in his place, thereby exercising authority over him. In a lengthy passage in his autobiography, Cellini recounts his rebuttal of Cosimo's charge that the model for his *Perseus* "'can't succeed in bronze, because the rules of art don't permit it.'" Cellini suggested that Cosimo may not understand the matter. When Cosimo insisted that he did, in fact, understand, Cellini answered, "'Yes, . . . like a patron, but not like an artist.'"[116] Salvator Rosa drew on a story from Pliny to make a similar point: he shows Apelles warning Alexander, however gently, that his ignorant discourse on a painting is amusing the apprentices (cat. no. 70). The subject is remarkable for the rarity of the depiction, but Rosa, not in royal service and also embittered against the broader patron class because he had not achieved the success he desired as a history painter, perhaps felt himself beyond the reach of potentially offended patrons. In fact, the print medium itself, with its multiple and relatively inexpensive impressions, signals the attempt to bypass the patron class.

Those non-artists who understood and appreciated art were greatly admired and respected (as well as financially relied upon) by artists. Aside from artists themselves, is there any more frequently met, or implicitly valued, figure in van Mander's *Schilderboek,* for example, than the "art lover"? The names given to para-artists over the centuries—*Liefhebber, virtuosi, amateurs, curieux, Liebhabern, connoisseurs*—suggest their love, interest, and knowledge,[117] and their importance for the marketing (and, indirectly, for the production) of art grew even as artists' dependence on patrons waned. Similarly, while much of the early art literature was written by artists—Giorgio Vasari is the most salient and important example, but one thinks also of Leonardo da Vinci, Karel van Mander, Giovanni Baglione, Charles-Alphonse Du Fresnoy, Joachim von Sandrart, Samuel van Hoogstraeten, and others—the contributions of non-artists (or non-professional artists), significant already in the sixteenth century, became more important and voluminous than that of the artists by the eighteenth century—like Anthony Ashley Cooper, the Earl of Shaftesbury, Horace Walpole, Comte de Caylus, Denis Diderot, Pierre-Jean Mariette, and Carl Heinrich von Heinecken. Sympathetic portraits of collectors abound; they were often friends of the artist, like Lucas van Uffel, painted by

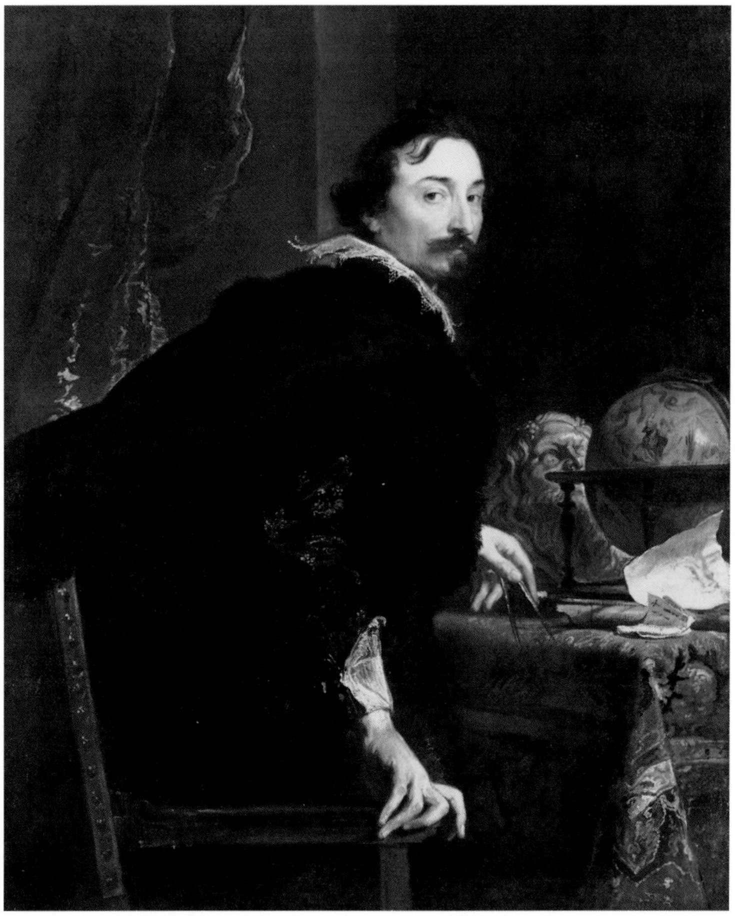

Fig. 31. Anthony van Dyck. *Portrait of Lucas van Uffel.* c. 1621–27. Oil on canvas. 124.5 x 100.6 cm (49 x 39⅝ in.). The Metropolitan Museum of Art; bequest of Benjamin Altman, 1913 (14.40.619).

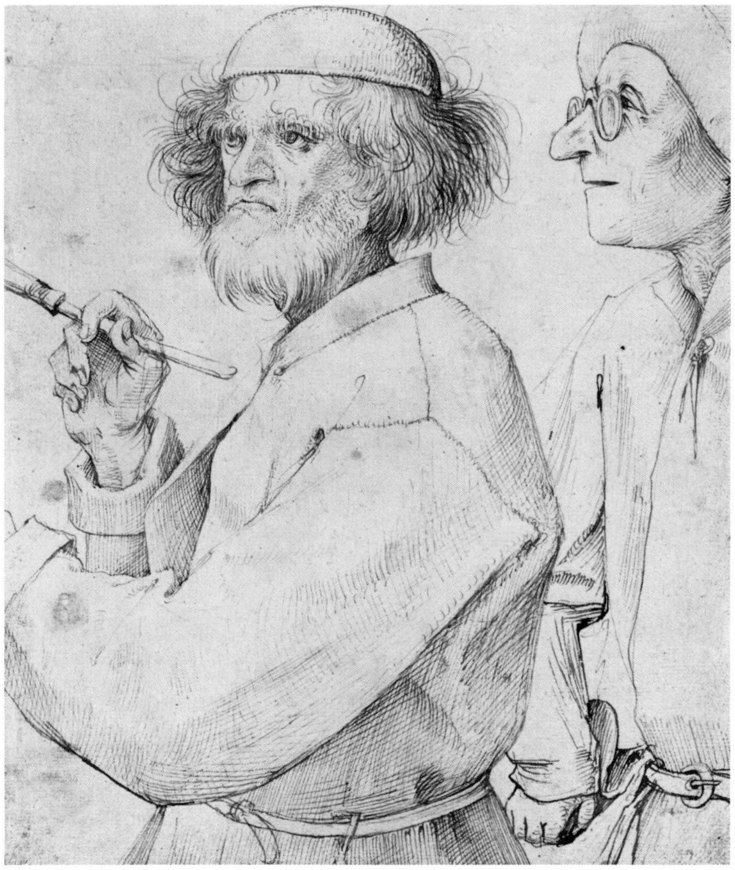

Fig. 32. Pieter Brueghel the Elder. *Artist and Connoisseur.* 1560s. Pen and ink, 255 x 215 mm (10 x 8½ in.). Albertina, Vienna.

Anthony van Dyck with attributes of his intellectual and aesthetic interests (fig. 31). An engraving ostensibly after a design by Antoine Watteau shows the artist with his friend, the *amateur* Jean de Jullienne, enjoying leisure together as equals (see cat. no. 79).

Not surprisingly, however, the pretensions of patrons and collectors readily became the object of scorn and derision. A famous drawing by Pieter Brueghel the Elder depicting a painter at work, observed by a bespectacled, long-nosed man clutching a money bag, has often been interpreted as a satire on artists' clients (fig. 32).[118] The client's eagerness and the artist's scowl do suggest an imperfect relationship, and the eyeglasses may also indicate a metaphorical blindness, although they were an ambiguous or inconsistent symbol in the period (see cat. no. 36). By the late eighteenth century, following the vitriol poured on them by Rosa, Hogarth, and others (cat. nos. 58, 76–77), such figures were frequently and openly mocked, as in a drawing by Thomas Rowlandson (fig. 33). Even in ostensibly neutral representations of public exhibitions, artists showed their awareness of the greater interest of some in fashionable self-display than in art (cat. nos. 81–82).

Not all of those interested in art were extremely wealthy, and prints afforded some a relatively economical way to indulge their passion, like the man holding an impression of Rembrandt's *Hundred Guilder Print*—an object much desired by collectors—painted by Rembrandt's pupil, Aert de Gelder (and sometimes called a self-portrait, fig. 34), or the generic "print lover" depicted by Daniel Chodowiecki (fig. 35). The print-seller's stall

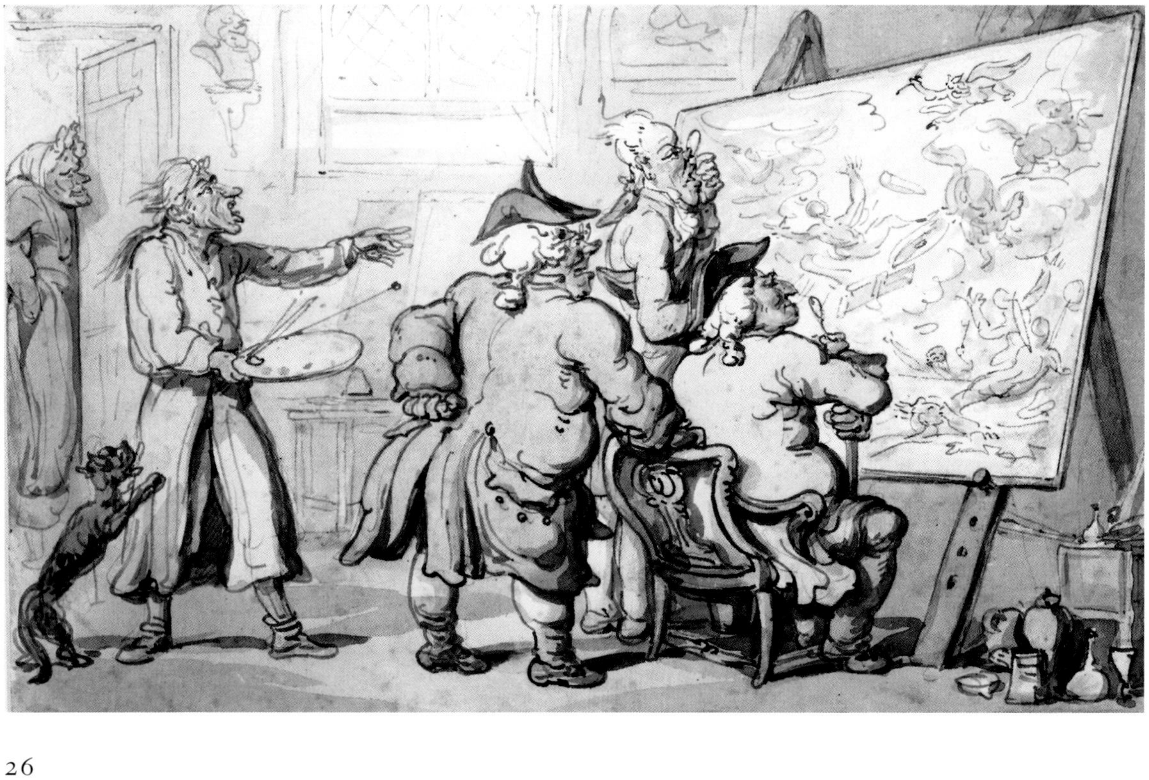

Fig. 33. Thomas Rowlandson. *Connoisseurs in the Studio.* n.d. Pen and watercolor, 146 x 235 mm (5¾ x 9¼ in.). Courtesy of the Huntington Library, Art Collections, and Botanical Gardens, San Marino, California; Gilbert Davis Collection.

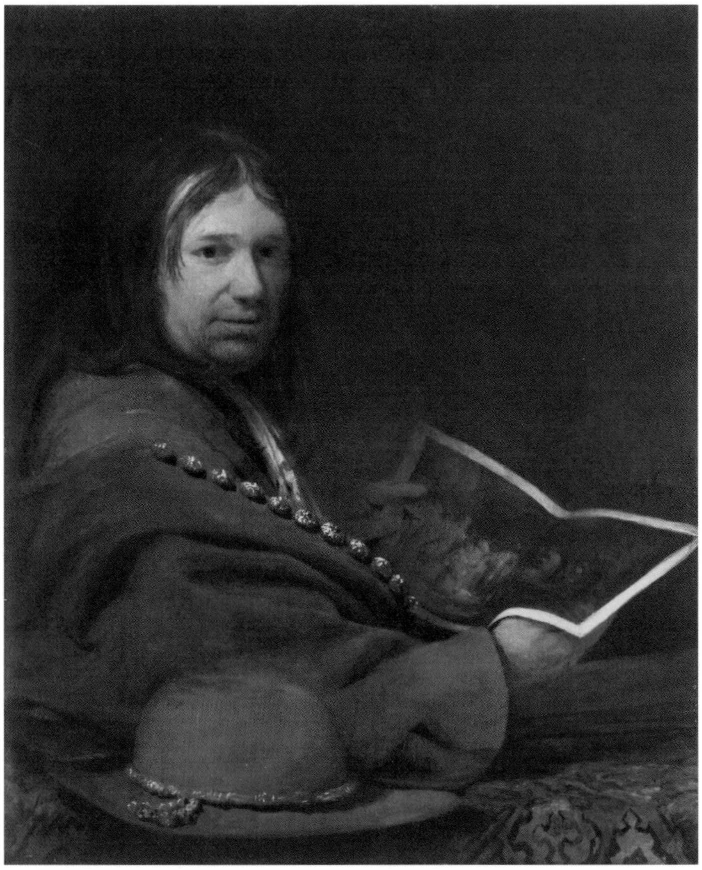

Fig. 34. Aert de Gelder. *Portrait of a Collector.* After 1685. Oil on canvas, 79 x 64 cm (31⅛ x 25¼ in.). The State Hermitage Museum, St. Petersburg.

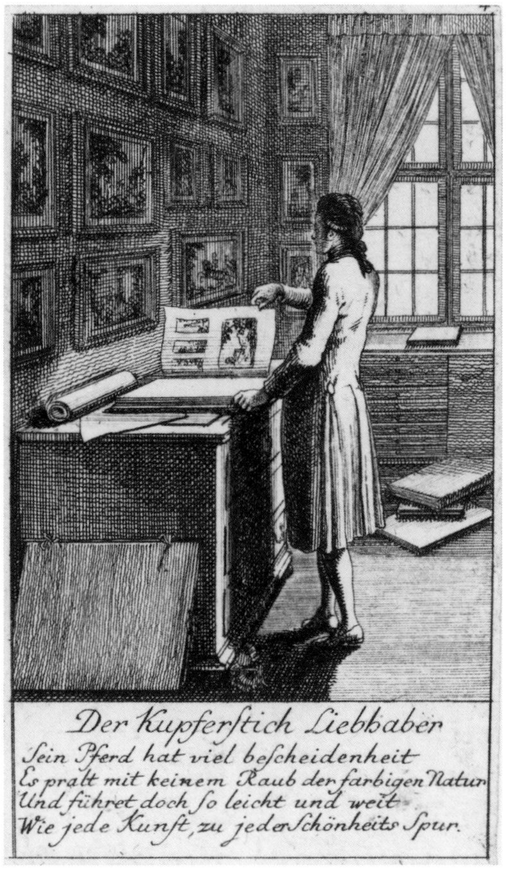

Fig. 35. Daniel Nikolaus Chodowiecki. *The Print Lover.* 1780. Etching, 240 x 115 mm (9½ x 4½ in.). C. G. Boerner Fine Art, New York.

on the street, depicted by Nicolas-Toussaint Charlet, was clearly accessible to those of modest income (cat. no. 84). At the same time, Chodowiecki's and Charlet's images exemplify two different markets for prints: those interested primarily in their artistic qualities and those interested primarily in their narrative or documentary qualities (although one could be interested in both). Already several centuries before, King Francis I's interest fell on the side of the former when he expressed a desire to have an object by the hand of Michelangelo, even small, irrespective of medium or subject.[119] The interest of the famous seventeenth-century English diarist, Samuel Pepys, lay with the latter: he owned a huge collection of prints, including around one thousand eight hundred portraits, which he gathered as part of an encyclopedic project to document the world.[120] The demand for prints was both deep socially and broad geographically: their relative affordability and multiplicity allowed them to be acquired and collected by people even of fairly modest means and to be disseminated all over Europe and beyond. The ways in which artists represented themselves, their peers, and their profession formed a consistent, enduring self-portrait.

James Clifton

1. For overviews of the origins and development of self-portraiture, see Holsten 1978; Asemissen and Schweikhart 1994, 49–90; Woods-Marsden 1998.
2. See Smith 2001, 356.
3. For an introduction to the topic, see Blunt 1940, 48–57; Kristeller 1951–52, 502–503, 513–15; Wittkower 1963, 1–16; Castelnuovo 1990; Posner 1993; Warnke 1993; Woods-Marsden 1998; Barker, Webb, and Woods 1999.
4. Summarized by Burke 1997, 17.
5. Burckhardt 1958, 143.
6. Ibid.
7. Ibid., 147.
8. Ibid., 151.
9. Pointed out by Warnke 1998.
10. Burckhardt 1959, 225; quoted by Warnke 1998, 81. Warburg's criticism of Burckhardt rested precisely on the example of the lack of consideration of connections between the rise of individualism and the visual arts: "So gab er in seiner 'Kultur der Renaissance' einerseits die Psychologie des socialen Individuums ohne Hinblick auf die bildende Kunst, wie er andrerseits in seinem 'Cicerone' nur 'eine Anleitung zum Genuss der Kunstwerke' bieten wollte" (Warburg 1902, 5).
11. Boehm 1985, 31; quoted by Warnke 1998, 81. According to Köstler 1998, 12, it has become a "Pavlovian reflex" to associate portraiture and the concept "individual."
12. Quoted by Warnke 1998, 213, n. 3. Warnke 1998, 83, argues against the proposition: Current research confirms "[d]oubts as to whether the history of portraiture presupposes a history of individuation . . . . It is clear that a person commissioning a portrait wanted, as a rule, to see his individuality linked to more general norms and claims. The individually fashioned face in a portrait is in the end also a system of preordained signs used to achieve an ideal image." For all his close attention to Burckhardt's thesis about the development of the individual, including its problems, Burke 1988, 1995, and 1997, does not acknowledge Burckhardt's clear disassociation of the development of the individual and portraiture, saying only that Burckhardt "himself never filled the gap between his famous discussion of individualism" and the late essay on portraiture (Burke 1988, 24). On the contrary, Burke uses portraiture to rework and revalidate Burckhardt's thesis (Burke 1997).
13. Baxandall 1988, 1–27. For Northern Europe, Barker, Webb, and Woods 1999, 120–21.
14. Shearman 1967, 44. On the question of individual style (as aspect of the rise of the artist as an individual), see Wittkower 1961, 300–301; Kemp 1987.
15. For "ego-documents" and their relevance to Burckhardt's thesis, see Burke 1997, 21. On early examples of artist biographies, see Barker, Webb, and Woods 1999, 36.
16. For a summary, see Burke 1995; Burke 1997; Elmer 2000, 8ff., 16–17. Hughes 1990, 36, takes issue with a corollary of the Burckhardtian thesis (without naming Burckhardt) in the context of artists' studio production: "If there is marked change in the nature of the renaissance and the modern studio, it is not necessarily best seen as a linear progress from a larger to a smaller unit, or, to put it in the more provocative form we keep glancing at, from the principle of collaboration towards the exercise of individual talent."
17. Macfarlane 1978, 196, quoted by Greenblatt 1980, 264, n. 44. Warnke 1998, while arguing against a tight connection between the development of the individual and the development of portraiture, seems to accept the existence of the former, which he refers to as "the objective historical development of the individual" (p. 82). Burke 1995 is an explicit attempt to "save" Burckhardt's famous thesis. There are also numerous writers who support Burckhardt's dating for the shift as well as its general outline. Writing of the High Middle Ages, for example, Ullmann 1967 (who also finds medieval precedents for developments in the Renaissance) describes an organological conception of society, with the "absorption of the individual by the community or by society": what mattered was "not the individual, . . . but . . . the office which the individual occupied," not "the individual, but society, the corpus of all individuals" (quoted by Lukes 1973, 46–47). See also Barker, Webb, and Woods 1999, 54: "One of the enduring fascinations of the art of the late medieval period is precisely that it belongs to a culture that did not on the whole adopt the later preoccupation with the cult of the individual."
18. Barker, Webb, and Woods 1999, 56.
19. See Lyons 1989.
20. Weintraub 1978, xv–xvi.
21. Ibid., xvi.
22. See Kris and Kurz 1979, who refer to these repetitious biographical motifs as "artist anecdotes" (p. 10) and "fixed biographical themes" (p. 11). Burke 1997, 23, notes that biographies and autobiographies of individuals follow patterns—recognizing the exemplarity of such patterns—but, unlike Weintraub, does not see a problematic contradiction therein, simply noting that people in the Renaissance were taught to model themselves on the exemplary figures of antiquity, and following the model (in biographical writing) also imposed order on apparent chaos. However, in my view, the dichotomy exemplarity/individuality remains closely allied with corporate/individual and poses similar reservations about the Burckhardtian thesis.
23. Alpers 1960, 212. For Vasari's comment on Boccaccino, see Clifton 1996, 29–30.
24. For the quotation, see Panofsky 1955, 109–10. Concerning the artist's social status, however, Dürer commented famously that he was a gentleman in Italy but only a parasite at home (Barker, Webb, and Woods 1999, 105).
25. Koerner 1993, 112.
26. On Cellini's autobiography, see Weintraub 1978, 115–41, who quotes Burckhardt ("*auf sich selbst gestellte Persönlichkeit*") (p. 121).
27. The high regard in which his father was held by Piero de' Medici and Lorenzo il Magnifico is described at Bandinelli 1905, 418–19 where he was said to be "fra i più cari amici." This is not to suggest that Bandinelli's ties to the Medici were not, in fact, substantial; see Pilliod 1998, 258 n. 35.
28. See Bandinelli 1905, 423–24.
29. Burke 1997, 25, notes that the development of the self-portrait was "related not only to self-awareness but also to the rise in the status of the artist." He goes on to describe the dual individual/corporate nature of portraiture in general.
30. E.g., Burke 1997, 17.
31. The term is from Sawday 1997, 30.
32. Magurn 1955, 101–102.
33. Colombier 1929, 226.
34. Marin 1999, 190.
35. See Manuth 1999, 45. Berger 2000, 354, comments that self-portraits that do not show the painter at work dissemble in that they pretend to be portraits rather than self-portraits.
36. In a letter to Isabella of June 6, 1628, quoted by Freedberg 1998, 42.
37. Brusati 1990–91, 168, cites Rubens's *Four Philosophers,* which also includes a self-portrait, as exemplifying the trend in self-portraiture in which artists "dissociat[e] themselves pictorially from the artisanal aspects of their art."
38. See Weil-Garris 1981, 235–36.
39. Johnson 1982.
40. Manuth 1999, 42.
41. On "the theoretical construct of the learned artist," see Levy 1984.
42. Wittkower 1961; Wittkower 1963, 67ff.
43. Burke 1987, 82–87, uses the term "social deviant." Wittkower 1961, 298, sees the emergence in the early sixteenth century in Italy of "an idiosyncratical professional caste with immensely strong leading individuals," as the birth of the "modern type of artist."
44. See Levine and Mai 1991, 209–11.

45. See Raupp 1984, 311–28.
46. Chapman 1996; see also cat. no. 9.
47. See Woods-Marsden 1998, 5.
48. See Brusati 1990–91, 173.
49. Ibid., 170.
50. Samuel van Hoogstraeten's hierarchy of subject-matter, set forth in his *Inleyding tot de hooge schoole der schilderkonst* (Rotterdam, 1678), 85–87, which places still-life at the bottom, is an adaptation of humanist principles. But Hoogstraeten is not here preaching to the choir; it is not a codification of existing thought in the Netherlands. Rather, the fact that he would need to argue the point indicates the priority given by collectors to artistic craftsmanship over subject matter. See Brusati 1990–91, 171 n.7.
51. Brusati 1990–91, 171.
52. Ibid., 172–75. These specular images were not without precedent in Netherlandish painting, as has often been pointed out. Jan van Eyck's *Van der Paele Madonna,* 1436 (Bruges, Groeningemuseum) includes a reflection of the artist at his easel in Saint George's armor. Though seventeenth-century artists may have been aware of, and alluding to, this motif in the altarpiece, it was not part of, or the initiation of, a continuous tradition in Netherlandish art.
53. On Rembrandt's self-portraiture, see especially Chapman 1990; White and Buvelot 1999. See also cat. nos. 6, 37–38. Alpers 1988, 59, also notes: "Among his works and those of his students and assistants there are probably more images which record the working operations of his studio . . . than there are of any other artist in Europe at the time."
54. Chapman 1990, 3, 4.
55. Ibid., 5, 105–27.
56. Ibid., 8.
57. Ibid., 9, 131.
58. Van de Wetering 1999, 19; he compares the concept to Poussin's portrait for Chantelou (on which, see above and cat. no. 7): for the artist and patron, "there was evidently no fundamental difference between a portrait of Poussin painted by another artist and one by Poussin himself" (p. 17). See also Raupp 1980, 7–8.
59. Lukes 1973, 59–66, esp. 61.
60. Burckhardt 1958, 303ff. Dante's early poetry is a watershed in this regard, by which the poet "marked . . . the boundary between medievalism and modern times. The human spirit had taken a mighty step toward the consciousness of its own secret life."
61. Aers 1992. Greenblatt 1980, who is concerned with the subject in sixteenth-century England, is not specific about the dating of the shift and recognizes its complexity , but—acknowledging the idea in both Burckhardt and Michelet—notes "the perception . . . that there is in the early modern period a change in the intellectual, social, psychological, and aesthetic structures that govern the generation of identities." On privacy and devotion in the English Renaissance, see Rambuss 1998.
62. Siegfried 1995, 107.
63. Burke 1997, 18–19.
64. For suggestive comments about this tendency—what she calls "the production of an artistic subject for works of art"—in modern art-historical writing, see Pollock 1980, 58–59 and *passim*. It has been seen as already operative in Vasari's *Vite* (Barker, Webb, and Woods 1999, 22). See also Kris and Kurz 1979, 119.
65. Nichols 1785, 403 (italics removed).
66. On the myth of the mad genius, see Pollock 1980, 64–65, who notes that "the notions of madness and art which produce the category 'mad genius' have little to do with clinical pathology or definitions of sanity, but circle around categories of difference, otherness, excess."
67. Although the Romantic image of the artist was a generalized one, the artists receiving the most extensive biographical treatment in the nineteenth century were precisely those artists whose previously created myths conformed to, and validated, the Romantic image (Michelangelo, Salvator Rosa, and Rembrandt, rather than Raphael, Rubens, and Bernini, for example). The same holds true for artists featured in motion pictures.
68. On Rosa, see also below and cat. nos. 58, 70.
69. Gilpin 1768, 83–84: "We are told, he spent the early part of his life in a troop of banditti; and that the rocky and desolate scenes, in which he was accustomed to take refuge, furnished him with those romantic ideas in landskip, of which he is so exceedingly fond; and in the description of which he so much excells. His *Robbers,* as his detached figures are commonly called, are supposed also to have been taken from the life." Quoted by Morgan 1824, 1:77n., as from the *Encyclopaedia Britannica,* s.v. *Rosa,* without reference to Gilpin; that Morgan herself cited a source for the story and that the source was Gilpin does not seem to have been noticed, since Morgan was accused until 1970 of having invented the story. Quoted by Sunderland 1970, 527; see also Sunderland 1973, 785.
70. See Sunderland 1970.
71. Morgan 1824, 1:81–83. Quoted in part by Wallace 1979, 13.
72. On the painting, see Barryte 1989.
73. Morgan 1824, 1:124.
74. See Wimsatt and Beardsley 1954; Barthes 1977; Moxey 1994, 51–61; Burke 1998; Moxey 2001, 124–42.
75. Foucault 1984.
76. For the tendency in narrative theory to replace "the author by the narrator, or the artist by an implied orchestrator of the image," see Bal 1998, 79.
77. Montrose 1992, 402.
78. Mukařovský 1976, 237; Mukařovský's essay was delivered as a lecture in 1944 but not published until 1966. For the supposedly paralyzing limitations of iconology, which is "concerned with thematic meanings alone," see Veltruský 1976, esp. 252.
79. Simpson 2003, 219, 228.
80. See Pavoni 1985; Klinger Aleci 1998; Barker, Webb, and Woods 1999, 70.
81. On such images as *exempla,* see Klinger Aleci 1998, 70–72.
82. See Spike 1984, 12–19, 106–21. The other engraved portraits include Galileo, the poet Giambattista Marino, prelates, and nobility.
83. Baglione 1642, 322; unfortunately, according to Baglione, the effort of producing the etchings gave Leoni a fatal stomach ailment.
84. Perrault 1696–1700, 1:n.p. (*Préface*).
85. Ibid., 2:n.p. (*Avertissement*).
86. See Lampsonius 1956; Melion 1991, 143–72, and *passim.*
87. See Prinz 1966.
88. See Lukes 1973, 52–58.
89. Naumann 1981, 1:27–28, 125–26; Langedijk 1992, 88.
90. For a theoretical discussion of images depicting artists at work, see Stoichita 1997. He refers to paintings that include a specular image of an artist at work (on the painting at which the viewer is looking) as the "scenario of enclosed production" (p. 227) and uses variations on the phrase "scenario of production" (e.g., "scenario of production in the third person") (pp. 242, 244, and *passim*). The painter portrayed in an image is the "endotopic painter" and the artist who executed this portrayal is the "exotopic painter" (p. 242).
91. Van Gool 1750, 1:428.
92. On the woodcut, attributed to Lucantonio degli Uberti after Francesco Rosselli, see Schulz 1978, 429–30, 433.
93. By contrast, and with considerably different effect, Rembrandt's etching, *The Three Trees* (1643), includes an artist seated at the far right, looking out of the picture rather than at the scene presented to the viewer.
94. Haskell 1987, 108.
95. For this drawing, see Geissler 1979, 1:74, and Kaufmann 1982, 134, with the suggestion that the subject on the painting on the easel depicts Mercury and the Muses, implying a union of painting with the liberal arts. Cornelis Galle's engraving after the composition (Hollstein 379), however, seems to show a Judgment of Paris, another subject with appropriate connotations for the profession. The accompanying inscription names the subject *PICTVRA,* and notes the four qualities

needed for success in the art: boldness, industriousness, youth, and patience.

96. E.g., Hughes 1990, Alpers 1988.
97. Confirming the analysis of Hughes 1990.
98. Reynolds 1975, 280.
99. Ibid., 278.
100. See Duffy 1995, who notes the importance of Reynolds's fifteenth discourse for a revived interest in Michelangelo's art.
101. Reynolds 1975, 17.
102. Ibid., 281.
103. See Kemp 1977; Kemp 1989; Barker, Webb, and Woods 1999, 57, 83; Brann 2002.
104. Morgan 1824, 1:87.
105. See Shroder 1961, 1-59.
106. Trans. Enggass and Brown 1970, 188.
107. Pliny 1984, 325 (25.86-87), who notes that Alexander "was not even influenced by regard for the feelings of his favourite in having been recently the mistress of a monarch and now belonged to a painter."
108. See Asemissen and Schweikhart 1994, 20-21.
109. Ibid., 204.
110. Van Mander 1994-99, 1:93. Cf. the justification of his "mélange" of illustrious men, "les premiers de leur espece," by Perrault 1696-1700, 1:n.p. (Préface): those who are "distinguez par la seule force de leur genie, sont plus visiblement l'ouvrage du Ciel que la pluspart des autres hommes, comme Charles Quint le témoigna aux Grands d'Espagne qui murmuroient, de luy avoir vû ramasser le pinceau du Titien. Je puis, leur dit-il, faire en un moment une vingtaine d'hommes tous plus grands que vous, mails il n'y a que Dieu seul qui pusse faire un homme tel que le Titien."
111. Cellini 1956, 260, 268-69, 294, 302-304.
112. Brown 1978, 109, and *passim,* associates the painting with Velázquez's quest for knighthood. He was finally admitted into the order of the Knights of Santiago with the king's support, implied by the artist in *Las Meninas,* but only through an exception to the rule that members not practice a craft or manual labor, granted by Pope Alexander VI.
113. Baldinucci 1974, 5:593.
114. Cellini 1956, 271-72; cited by Barker, Webb, and Woods 1999, 97.
115. Cellini 1956, 320-21.
116. Ibid., 341.
117. See cat. nos. 51, 79-80.
118. Barker, Webb, and Woods 1999, 169-72. The drawing was copied at least four times, indicating its popularity.
119. Shearman 1967, 44.
120. Manuth 1999, 52.

ICON

How many honors artists have acquired through their wonderful works would be difficult to describe, for besides [gaining] fame and laudable report that covers the whole world, so they have also been regarded with great favor and esteem, especially by emperors, kings, and princes, and reckoned as marvels of their time. For they [the rulers] know well that it stands in their power to make great men but that artists alone are as if sent from heaven.

Samuel van Hoogstraeten, 1678

I have observed . . . that an artist is never so mediocre that he would not find an admirer.

Carl Heinrich von Heinecken, 1778

Attributed to Nicolas Beatrizet (1507 or 1515–c. 1565)

after Nicolò della Casa (active 1543–48)
after Baccio Bandinelli (1488–1560)

1. *Self-Portrait of Baccio Bandinelli, Seated in His Studio*

1548

Engraving, 414 x 305 mm (16¼ x 12 in.) (trimmed)

References: Bartsch XV, 279; Le Blanc 1

Inscription: 1548 *A.S. Excudebat.*

Purchased from Lutz Riester, Freiburg and London

1998.22

The Italian sculptor Baccio Bandinelli made more self-portraits than any other artist of the Cinquecento, including engraved ones which could be disseminated.[1] This imposing engraving, remarkable for its scale and full-length composition, has until recently attracted little attention. It reproduces (in reverse) an unfinished engraving of Bandinelli, attributable to Nicolò della Casa, which presumably follows a drawing by the sculptor himself.[2] The copy was probably produced without Bandinelli's oversight, perhaps by Nicolas Beatrizet for the Roman publisher Antonio Salamanca.[3] Salamanca's engraver used a slightly smaller plate, which may have been the cause of some compositional changes (such as the placement of figurines). He also had to fill in some areas left unfinished in the prototype engraving, including the face of the sitter.[4] The copyist's apparent misunderstanding of aspects of the prototype, his need to condense the composition, and his general carelessness resulted in startling distortions of perspective and uncertain spatial relationships, especially evident at the right side of the engraving.[5] Nicolò della Casa also produced a smaller portrait of Bandinelli (fig. 1.1), signed but not dated, again after a drawing by the sculptor.[6]

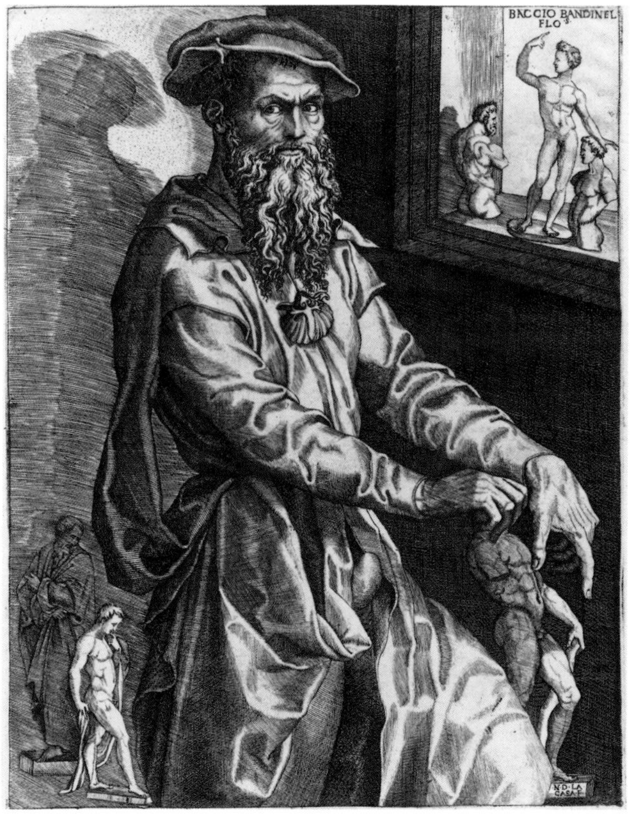

Fig. 1.1. Nicolò della Casa. *Portrait of Baccio Bandinelli.* Mid-16th century. Engraving, 292 x 218 mm (11½ x 8⅝ in.). Fine Arts Museums of San Francisco, Achenbach Foundation for Graphic Arts purchase, 1965.68.37.

Bandinelli was, by most accounts, ambitious and pretentious, and he became one of the leading artistic personalities of Florence in the sixteenth century.[7] Born Bartolomeo Brandin, the son of an impecunious—if also very successful—goldsmith and jeweler in Florence, Bandinelli took the name of a Sienese aristocratic family when he was attempting to gain admission to the order of the Knights of Santiago around 1530. He was admitted to the order by Charles V—the first artist to receive this honor—following his presentation to the emperor of a bronze relief of the *Deposition*.[8] In the smaller of the engravings (fig. 1.1), he wears the emblem of the Order of Santiago, a cross on a pilgrim's shell. In the larger composition, as in Enea Vico's engraving of Bandinelli's studio (where the sculptor appears, standing, at the far right) (cat. no. 21), he wears the cross on his breast.[9] In his portraits, Bandinelli is dressed as a gentleman rather than a craftsman; the codpiece on display in both engravings is an assertion of both upper-class fashion and potent masculinity.[10] In his autobiographical *Memoriale,* Bandinelli noted that members of the Order of Santiago opposed his nomination because his profession made him a manual laborer, but he said they opposed him "ignorantly, . . . not considering that

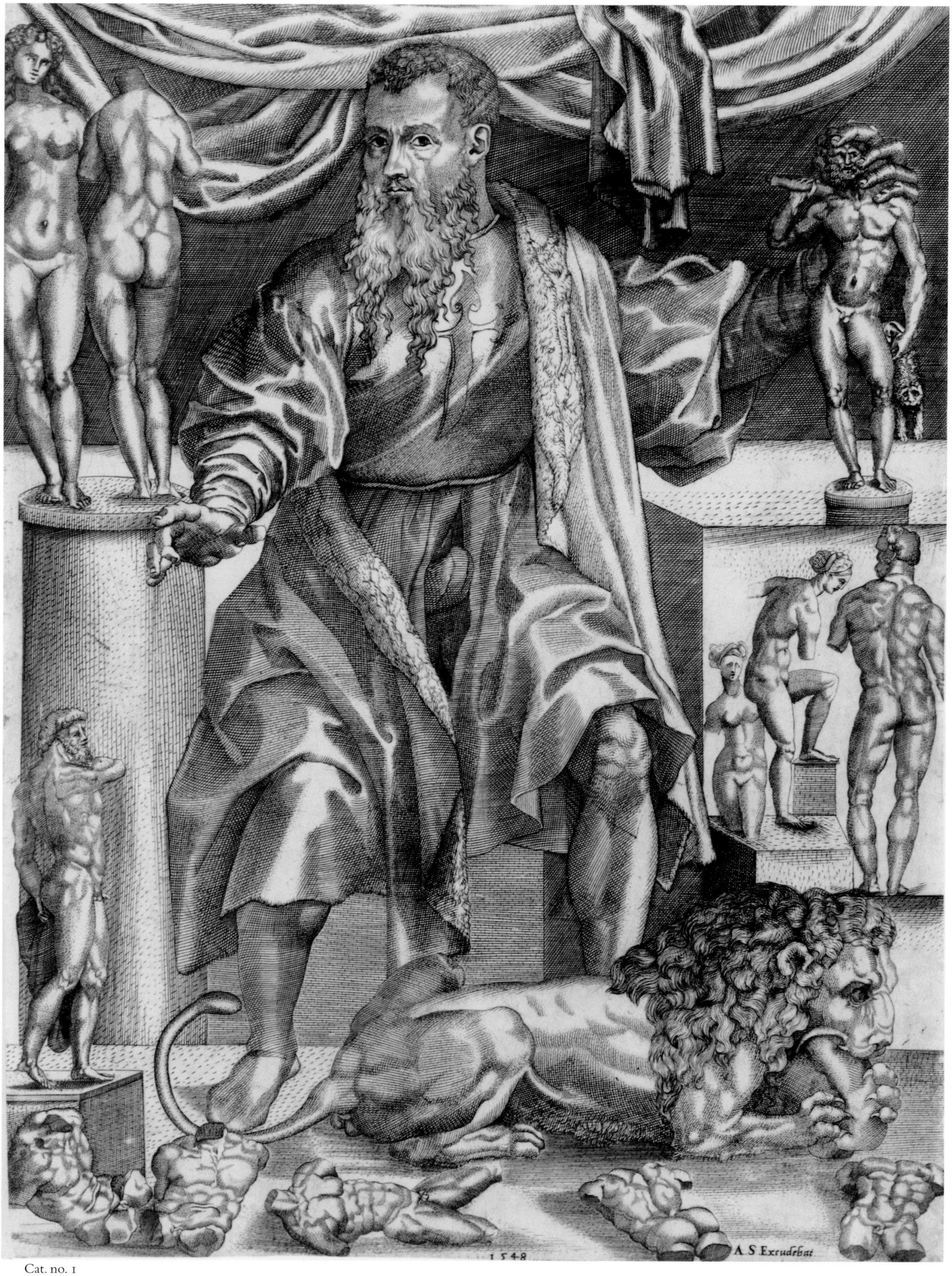

Cat. no. 1

in a nobleman every art is noble."[11] Even Leonardo da Vinci, in a famous passage comparing painting to sculpture, had stressed the manual aspects of the latter, which he characterized as "a highly mechanical exercise, often accompanied by great amounts of sweat composed of dust and converted into mud. With his face caked and all floured with marble dust, he looks like a baker, and covered with minute flakes that look as though it has snowed on his back."[12] Bandinelli naturally avoids such a rough self-presentation.

Bandinelli gained considerable power through his work for, and association with, the Medici family, and he was perhaps at the height of his power at the time of this portrait, in 1548. His most famous—if also much abused—work is the monumental *Hercules and Cacus* of 1534, which still stands before the Palazzo Vecchio in Florence, and Herculean imagery is met frequently in Bandinelli's work, including this portrait, in which the artist grasps a figurine of Hercules as part of his boldly expansive posture.[13] By the time of Bandinelli's activity, Hercules was explicitly associated with Medici rule, and the artist's emphasis on the figure would have confirmed his position as a faithful partisan.[14] The lion, which lies at Bandinelli's feet gnawing on an object that may be the lower thigh and knee of a sculpture (more readily apparent in Nicolò della Casa's unfinished engraving than in the present one), had been a frequent symbol of Florence since the Middle Ages. Erna Fiorentini interprets it here as the "skeptical and envious Florentine public," which had been so critical of Bandinelli's *Hercules and Cacus*.[15] It is worth noting, however, that the lion was not an unequivocal symbol of the Florentine public per se, especially when it gained associations with the Medici, Bandinelli's patrons, in the sixteenth century.[16]

Numerous small sculptures appear in portrayals of Bandinelli and his studio (cat no. 21 and figs. 21.1, 21.2), rarely repeated from one composition to another. Ancient sculptures, including the Belvedere Torso, provided a source and inspiration, but the figures are not exact copies. Kathleen Weil-Garris describes the artist in the smaller engraved *Self-Portrait* as "surrounded by models of his past works: they are his dictionary and treasury,"[17] even though there are far fewer works in that engraving than in this one. Her point, however, that Bandinelli tended to rework a limited vocabulary of forms, is even more evident in the present engraving, in that the multitude of figures are mostly closely related variations on the theme of a single figure in contrapposto. Bandinelli was an indefatigable draftsman, and this type of (most often male) single figure, whether derived from Michelangelo's colossal *David* or from antique models like the Apollo Belvedere,[18] is prevalent in his graphic work.[19] Such figurines were used by Bandinelli in teaching his students and emphasize the intellectual rather than manual aspects of his art (see cat. no. 21).

JC

1. On Bandinelli's self-portraits, see Weil-Garris 1981, 237; Galicka and Sygietyńska 1992; Woods-Marsden 1998, 139–47; Fiorentini 1999, 41–59, 137–57, who discusses Bandinelli's innovative use of printmaking in self-portraiture; and Fiorentini and Rosenberg 2002.
2. See Fiorentini 1999, 153–54, and Fiorentini and Rosenberg 2002.
3. For the attribution, see Fiorentini and Rosenberg 2002. Salamanca also published della Casa's portrait of the emperor Charles V and his set of prints after Michelangelo's *Last Judgment,* inscribed variously with the dates 1543, 1545, and 1548 (this last the date of the present portrait of Bandinelli).
4. Fiorentini and Rosenberg 2002, 44, have even suggested—implausibly, given the marked similarities to Bandinelli's other self-portraits—that Salamanca and his engraver were unaware that the sitter was Bandinelli.
5. The changes and infelicities are well catalogued by Fiorentini and Rosenberg 2002, 38–42.
6. Robert-Dumesnil 2. The engraving has been variously dated from c. 1540 to 1548 or later (Choux 1975, 177; Davis 1988, 77; Forlani Tempesti 1989, 23; Woods-Marsden 1998, 145). For Bandinelli's drawing, see Fiorentini 1999, 147–48, who dates it 1545–46.
7. On Bandinelli's life and character, see especially Weil-Garris 1981. He was accounted a notoriously difficult person, greedy and baldly ambitious, arrogant to his peers and servile to his superiors, but, to be sure, much of Bandinelli's posthumous reputation rests on the excoriating comments of his rival, Giorgio Vasari (see Pilliod 1998, 39).
8. On Bandinelli's knighthood (the exact date of which is debated), see Weil-Garris 1981, 247, n. 40; Weil-Garris Brandt 1989; Warnke 1993, 157, 160, 162, 169; Avery 1996, 3:157, 158; Fiorentini 1999, 41–42. Bandinelli may have been received first as a member of the lesser order of the Knights of Saint Peter in the mid 1520s, but the only evidence for this is his own *Memoriale* (Bandinelli 1905, 422 [see Weil-Garris Brandt 1989, 501 n. 28]).
9. See Olszewski 1981, 99, who also draws attention to the heraldic cross above the fireplace at left, and the entry on Vico's print (cat. no. 21).
10. Noted by Davis 1988, 77. On dress as a marker of the status of Italian Renaissance artists before Bandinelli, see Ames-Lewis 2000, 70–74. On codpieces, see Persels 1997.
11. Bandinelli 1905, 423; quoted by Fiorentini and Rosenberg 2002, 44.
12. Farago 1992, 256–57.
13. Weil-Garris 1981, 237, points out that all of Bandinelli's later self-portraits show him holding a statue of Hercules and interprets this identification with the subject as a defiant embracing—rather than embarrassed forgetting—of the *Hercules and Cacus*.
14. See Fiorentini 1999, 48–50; on Hercules and the Medici, see Wright 1994, esp. 336–37.
15. Fiorentini 1999, 51, who calls the object between the lion's claws "in der Realität Bandinellis Ruf."
16. On the gilded lion (Marzocco) that stood in the Piazza della Signoria from the late fourteenth to the early nineteenth century and its political associations, see Fader 1977, 24–60, esp. 34–35; Van Veen 1997, esp. 87ff; Johnson 2000, esp. 70.
17. Weil-Garris 1981, 235.
18. Forlani Tempesti 1989, 20, calls the *David* Bandinelli's "più o meno scomodo compagno di strada."
19. Ward 1988, 37, makes the point that Bandinelli's drawings are rarely direct copies from antique statues. For examples of drawings of standing nude male figures, see Forlani Tempesti 1989, and Ward 1988, cat. nos. 13, 23, 26, 29, 35, 40, 42, some of which represent Hercules. See also the drawing at Sotheby's, New York, January 26, 2000, lot 24.

    Davis 1988, 77, identifies the male nude at lower right with Bandinelli's *Adam and Eve* (Florence, Bargello), and the female figure on the column at the upper left—"possibly representing a variation on the antique Cnidian Venus"—as copied in a drawing by Bandinelli. On the drawing of the standing female nude after the antique, see Ward 1988, 37–38 (no. 16).

Aegidius Sadeler (c. 1570–1629)
possibly after Bartholomaeus Spranger (1546–1611)

2. *Portrait of Bartholomaeus Spranger and His Wife, Christina Müller*

1600

Engraving, 293 x 410 mm (11½ x 16⅛ in.) (trimmed)

Reference: Hollstein 332, ii/ii

Inscriptions: on banderole at upper left: *VIVIT NVMINE ET NOMINE*; on plaque above oval frame: *MORSINIQVA, QVID TANTVM / DECVS RAPIS. PIETAS AEQVA, / QVAE ET MORTVAM SERVAS*; in oval frame: *CHRISTINA MVLLERINA VXOR B. SPRANGER*; on plaque below oval frame: *ANIMVS MARITI / ANIMAM TVAM / SEQVITVR NONDV[M] / ASSEQVITVR. ET / LIGET SECVM SVA / ABIICIAT: TE NON / RECOLLIGIT*; on plinth at lower left: *QVIT ANTE DIEM VVLTIS. TE / TEMPVS VETAT OCCIDERE. TE / ARTES VOLV[N]T CLARAE CLARIOREM*; below image: *Priuatas lacrymas Bart. Sprangeri Egid. Sadeler miratus artem & amantem redamans, publicas fecit: et / eidem promutua beneuolentia dedicauit. Pragae Anno Seculari. Marco Sadeler excudit*; in manuscript at lower right: *181*

Purchased from Hill-Stone, New York

1999.22

This rich allegorical image is simultaneously a very personal portrait and an exaltation of the public function of the artist. It was generated in an intimate circle of artist friends at the court of the emperor Rudolf II in Prague, but was distributed widely, in keeping with Bartholomaeus Spranger's renown. At the left is a half-length figure of Spranger, one of the most influential European artists in the second half of the sixteenth century. As he turns toward the viewer, he points with a raised index finger to a bust of his recently deceased wife, Christina Müller, whom he had married in 1582. The inscription above her portrait contrasts unjust death, which has stolen such beauty, with just piety, which watches over the deceased. The portrait sits atop a sarcophagus, and before it is a figure of Thanatos (the genius of Death).[1] The skull he holds, as well as the inverted torch at his side and the overturned hour glass on which he treads, signify her death. Müller is flanked by figures of Faith and Virtue (in the guise of Minerva holding her Medusa shield) at left and right, respectively. The inscription below the portrait describes Spranger's unfulfilled yearning for his wife and the discarding of his things, namely the tools of painting and sculpture at the feet of Thanatos.[2]

Connecting the two halves of the composition are skeletal Death, who aims an arrow at Spranger, and winged Chronos (Time), who distracts Death with his hourglass, as if to say that Spranger's time has not yet come, as the inscription below the artist confirms. The inscription promises—as do the allegorical figures behind Spranger—that the arts will bring him even greater fame, offering further encouragement to overcome the paralyzing sadness induced by his wife's passing. Behind Spranger are three female figures representing the traditional branches of the arts of design—painting, architecture, and sculpture—each holding symbols of her art: maulstick, palette, and brushes; compass and square; and figurine, respectively. Above Spranger is Glory, who carries a laurel wreath and palm with which to reward the artist. At the upper left, with two trumpets, is Fame, whose banderole proclaims that the artist lives by both divine will and his own name. The traditional topos of the triumph of art and fame over death—to which this print itself would contribute—is thus recalled.

The print carries an inscribed dedication from the engraver, Aegidius Sadeler, without mention of the inventor of the composition: "Aegidius Sadeler has made public the personal tears of Bartholomaeus Spranger out of admiration for Spranger's art and out of love for those who love him; and he has dedicated [this print] to him on account of the feelings of good will between them."[3] The design is usually attributed to Spranger, although Jan Piet Filedt Kok has pointed out that the picture's subject (and, one might add, the dedication) would be more appropriate coming from a friend than from the artist himself. Filedt Kok is unwilling to attribute the design to Aegedius Sadeler, however, based on the style and quality of the image,[4] but such an attribution is not necessarily so far-fetched, since the crowded composition is, in many respects, a pastiche of conventional motifs known to Sadeler.[5] The work is certainly in Spranger's style, which would make sense in an homage to Spranger from an engraver whose works evince a mastery of several different figural styles, including Spranger's. The

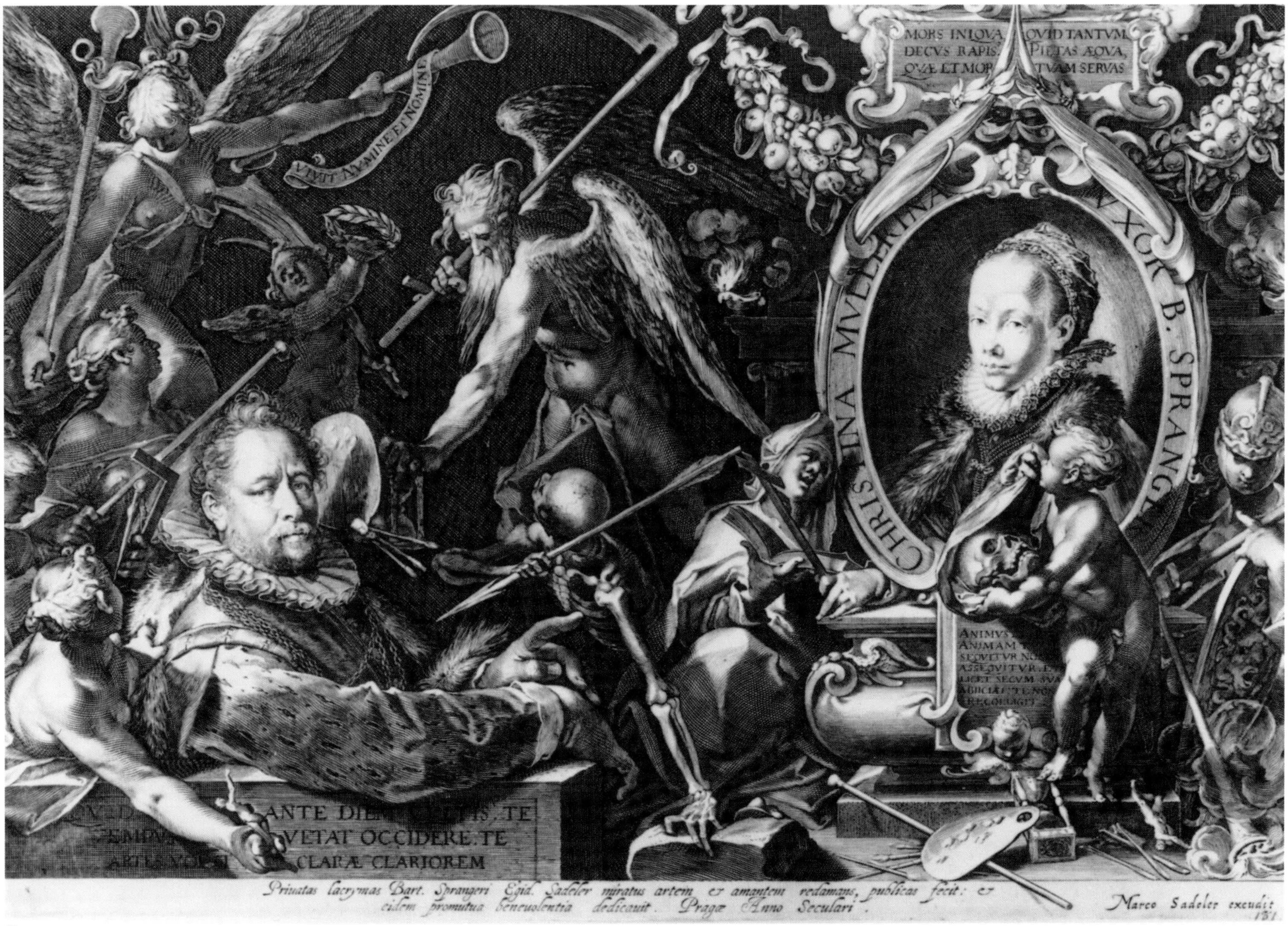

Cat. no. 2

figure of Spranger, in any case, is nearly identical to the bust in the engraved portrait by Jan Muller after Hans von Aachen of 1597 (fig. 2.1), another engraving made explicitly out of friendship with the sitter ("In perpetuam amici memoriam," according to the inscription). The Muller/von Aachen composition does not, however, include the fur draped around Spranger's shoulders, grasped by Sculpture, in Sadeler's engraving, nor the triple gold chain—a high honor—which had been granted to the artist, along with a coat-of-arms, by Rudolf II in 1588.[6]

JC

1. See Janson 1937, 446.
2. This interpretation of the inscription follows Mielke 1979, 43.
3. Translated by Filedt Kok 1996, 171.
4. Filedt Kok 1996, 171.
5. Limouze 1989, 9, has made the reasonable suggestion, based on the inscriptions, that this work and the portrait of Pieter Brueghel (see cat. no. 3) "were products of a collaboration between Sadeler and Spranger rather than being simple reproductions of finished designs."
6. On the wearing of honorary chains in portraits of the sixteenth and seventeenth centuries, see Held 1991a, 46–55, 184–86.

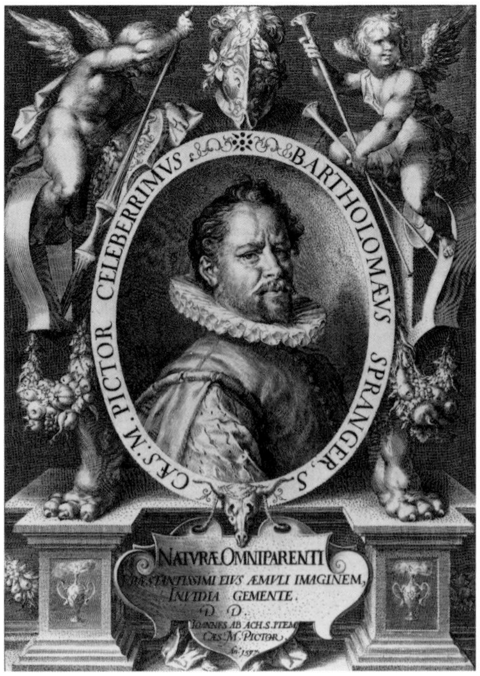

Fig. 2.1. Jan Muller after Hans von Aachen. *Portrait of Bartholomaeus Spranger.* 1597. Engraving, 261 x 185 mm (10¼ x 7¼ in.). Rijksmuseum, Amsterdam.

Aegidius Sadeler (c. 1570–1629)
after Bartholomaeus Spranger (1546–1611)

3. *Pieter Brueghel*

1606

Engraving, 305 x 211 mm (12 x 8¼ in.) (trimmed)

Reference: Hollstein 279, ii/ii

Inscriptions: in oval frame: *PETRVS BRVEGEL EX AMBIVARITIS BELGA PICTOR AEVI HVIVS INTER PRINCIPES*; at lower left: *Bar. Sprangers Inuentor.*; below image: *Ars Naturam vicerat, nisi et Ars per Naturam esset: Natura Artem aeternarat, nisi et Naturae nihil aeterni esset. Alumnus Altricem / aemulatus, quâ licuit adsecutus est: Altrix Aemulum alumnata, quâ datum prosecuta est. apagè liuor, Artem Naturae, Naturae foedus / sociat: apagè dolor, Naturam Arti, Artis foetus sufficit. Viuit in Arte Natura, quam Patris manus expressit: Viuit in Naturâ Ars, quam Fili / Genius adsequitur. illam, Naturâ ambiente Virgo Tritonis, Heroum choris inseruit: hunc, Arte prensante Majânatus Olifer, deses flumen / reduxit. redáccende facem Lucifuge, inique facis nisi Patrem in Filio noscis: adtolle tubam Terrigena, nihil agis nisi uterque tibi superstes est. / Patrem Filio, hunc in illo, sibi, utrumque seculis; Artis, Naturae / Posteritatis, cultor, admirator, amator Sac. Caes. Mai. sculptor / Egidius Sadeler, exhibet. M.DC.VI*

Purchased from Hill-Stone, New York

1999.17

Like Aegidius Sadeler's engraving of Bartholomaeus Spranger and his wife (cat. no. 2), this work is not only a portrait but also one of the many allegories of the arts that abounded at the imperial court of Rudolf II in Prague. In spite of the extensive inscription, including the name of the artist in the oval frame, there has been considerable uncertainty about the precise identity of the sitter; namely, is it Pieter Brueghel the Elder (c. 1525/30–1569), whose works were well represented in the emperor's collection, or his less famous son, Pieter Brueghel II (c. 1564–c. 1638), whose career consisted largely of the copying and imitating of his father's works? In an exhaustive analysis of the inscription, J. B. Bedaux and A. van Gool argued that the image portrays both father and son simultaneously, an argument that has found some acceptance.[1] The inscription makes several references to both father and son, most notably in asserting that "Nature lives in art, as expressed by the father's hand," and "Art lives in nature, as achieved by the son's genius."[2] Thanatos, the genius of Death, is reprimanded: "You are being unjust if you do not recognize the father in the son." Thus the art of the father, and therefore the father himself, lives on in the son. Nonetheless, the portrayal is very clearly commemorative and the sitter deceased. The portrayals of Pieter Brueghel and Christina Müller, Spranger's late wife, both are oval bust-length portraits on a sarcophagus, behind which is a fruit garland and before which is Thanatos (winged in the case of the Brueghel portrait) with a skull and upended torch of life, its flame dying and turning to smoke. The similarities were, surprisingly, only recently first noted.[3] The representation of Christina Müller is clearly funerary, and the same must be true of the representation of Brueghel. As Bedaux and van Gool pointed out, the epithet "painter among princes" (*pictor . . . inter principes*) in the frame could properly refer to Pieter Brueghel I but not Pieter II, but their further contention, that the phrase *aevi huius* could not refer to Pieter I, since he had been too long dead for "of our time" to make sense, is obviated if the phrase is translated as "of our age," which would make it perfectly applicable to Pieter I, no less than his son, as a "modern" artist. Spranger and Sadeler clearly flatter the son in this laudatory portrait of his father, but that son could just as, or even more, likely be Jan Brueghel, Pieter II's much more successful brother, who had visited Prague in 1604.[4]

Fame appears in both engravings, accompanying Spranger in the double portrait with his wife and blowing one of her trumpets in Brueghel's honor. In the latter instance, however, her foot rests on a globe, an attribute not of Fame but of Fortune.[5] The inscription calls for her to sound her trumpet, to make both father and son survivors. While fortune is unpredictable, even leading to a life cut short at an early age, as in the case of Pieter Brueghel I, fame ensures the perpetual survival of the artist's name.

Minerva (Athena), at the left of Brueghel's portrait, and Mercury (Hermes), above it, often appear together (or blended, as "Hermathena") in allegories of the arts produced by or known to Rudolfine artists.[6] Based on a reference by Cicero to a statue of Hermathena that he felt would be an appropriate ornament for his

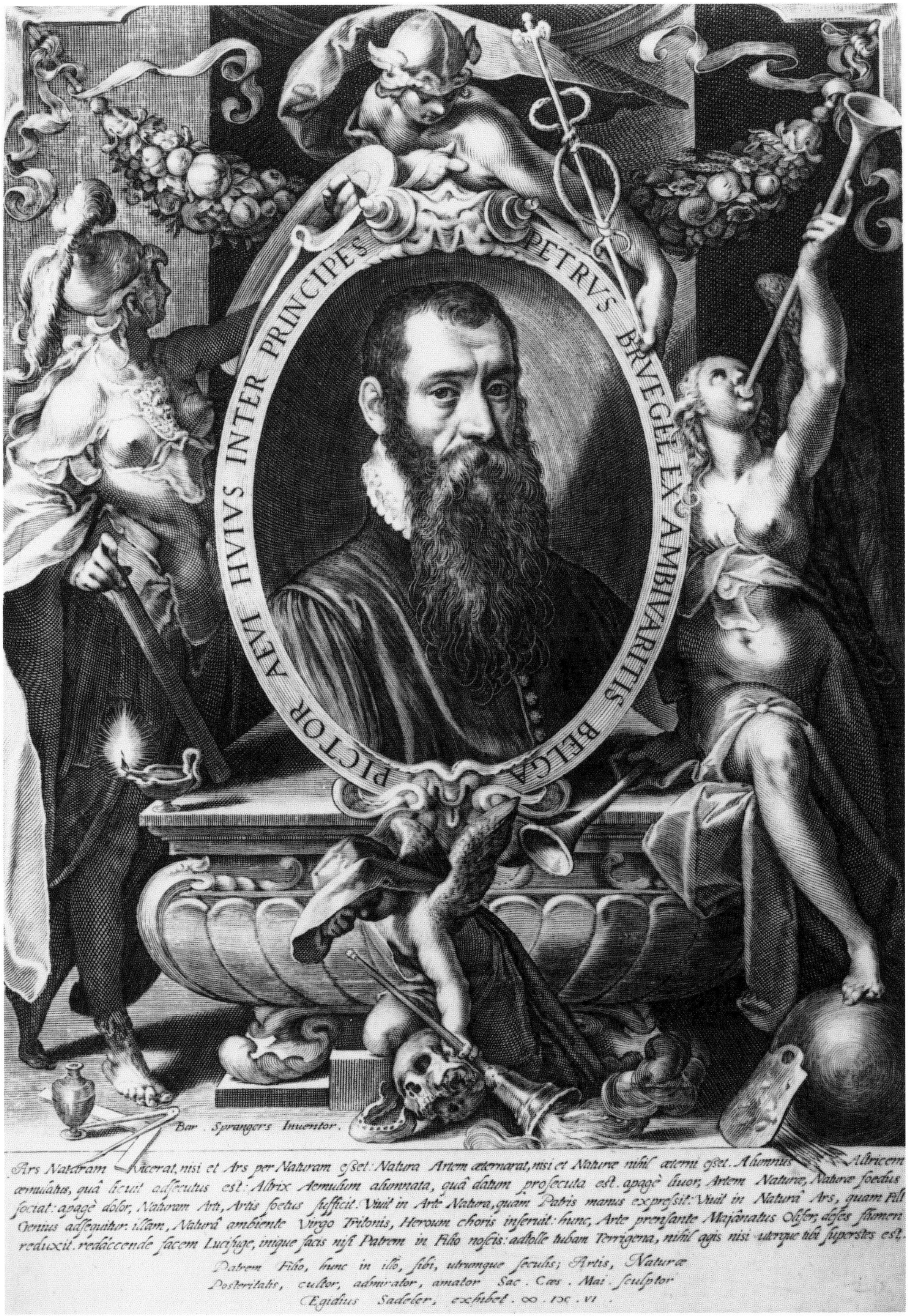
PICTOR AEVI HVIVS INTER PRINCIPES PETRVS BRVEGEL EX AMBIVARITIS BELGA
Bar. Sprangers Inuentor.
Ars Naturam uicerat, nisi et Ars per Naturam esset: Natura Artem æternarat, nisi et Naturæ nihil æterni esset. Alumnus Altricem
æmulatus, quâ licuit adsecutus est: Altrix Aemulum alumnata, quâ datum prosecuta est. apagè liuor, Artem Naturæ, Naturæ foedus
sociat: apagè dolor, Naturam Arti, Artis foetus sufficit. Viuit in Arte Natura, quam Patris manus expressit: Viuit in Naturâ Ars, quam Fili
Genius adsequitur: illam, Naturâ ambiente Virgo Tritonis, Heroum choris inseruit: hunc, Arte prensante Maianatus Olifer, deses flumen
reduxit. redaccende facem Lucifuge, inique facis nisi Patrem in Filio noscis: adtolle tubam Terrigena, nihil agis nisi uterque tibi superstes est.
Patrem Filio, hunc in illo, sibi, utrumque seculis; Artis, Naturæ
Posteritatis, cultor, admirator, amator Sac. Cæs. Mai. sculptor
Egidius Sadeler, exhibet. ∞. IϽC. VI.

Cat. no. 3

academy, the two gods were associated with academies—or, more abstractly, with an academic ideal—in the Renaissance and following. Not only are Mercury and Minerva protectors of the arts, but they also personify the educational goals of artists—eloquence and prudence or wisdom, respectively—goals borrowed from a humanist education in letters but gradually applied in the Renaissance as painting became accepted as a liberal art rather than manual craft to the ideal of a learned artist as well. They hold this significance in Spranger's 1595 design for the new coat-of-arms ordered for the painters' guild of Prague. The claim that artists worked under their aegis was a reminder that art-making was understood to be an intellectual activity, even for a painter with a reputation for close adherence to the coarser aspects of nature, like Pieter Brueghel. For example, in an engraving by Jan Muller after Spranger from 1592, Mercury presents a young artist, whose learning is indicated by the book at his feet, to be crowned by Minerva, while Painting, Sculpture, and Architecture, figured as in the double portrait of Spranger and his wife, look on (fig. 3.1). Fame is again present with her two trumpets.

JC

1. Bedaux and van Gool 1974; Depauw and Luijten 1999, 108; Limouze 1989, 9.
2. Translations from Bedaux and van Gool 1974, 137.
3. Filedt Kok 1996, 172.
4. Bedaux and van Gool 1974, 155–56, consider and dismiss this possibility, relying on a too narrow notion of imitation; that is, that the father lives on in the son through the son's strictest imitation of him (Pieter II copied his father's works innumerable times, Jan only a few). If Limouze 1988, 187–89, is correct that the relation between father and son in the inscription ultimately derives from Seneca, who advises writers to transform rather than blindly imitate their models (as the son is not an exact replica of the father), then the inscription would apply more aptly to Jan Brueghel than to Pieter II.
5. Limouze 1989, 9.
6. See especially Kaufmann 1982, 123–30; see also Levy-Van Halm 1991–92.

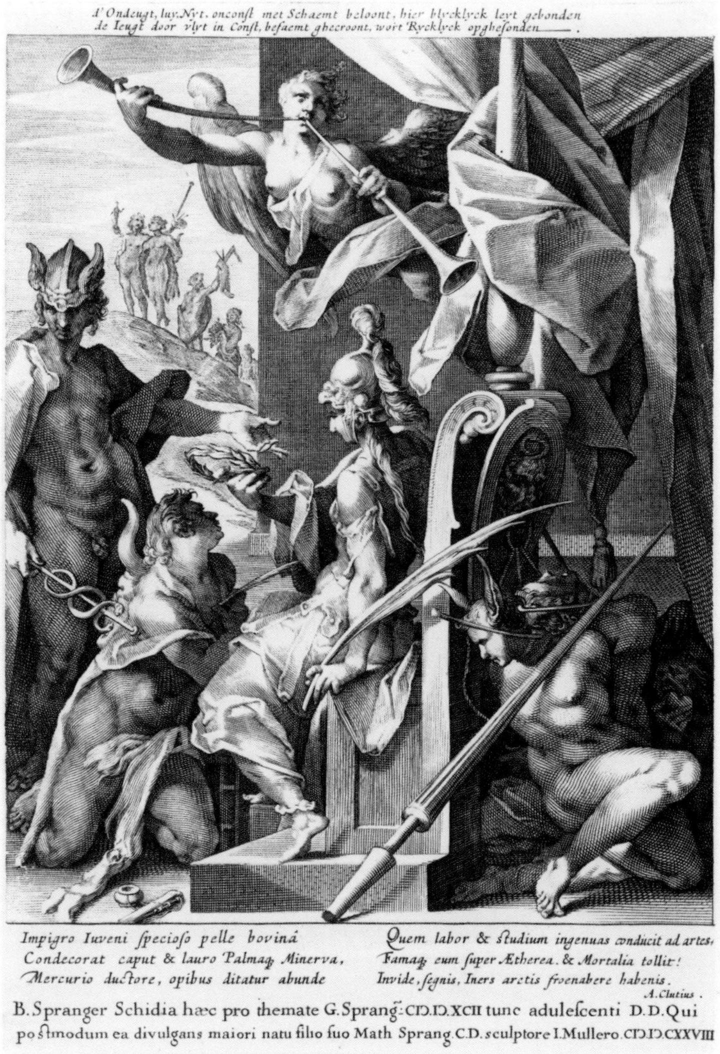

Fig. 3.1. Jan Muller after Bartholomaeus Spranger. *Mercury Leads Young Artists to Minerva.* 1592. Engraving, 283 x 176 mm (11⅛ x 6⅞ in.). The British Museum, London.

Anthony van Dyck (1599–1641) and Jacob Neeffs (1610–after 1660)

4. *Self-Portrait of Anthony van Dyck*

c. 1630/45

Etching and engraving, 243 x 157 mm (9⅝ x 6⅛ in.)

References: Hollstein 4, iii/iv; Mauquoy-Hendrickx 4, iv/vii; Turner and Depauw 1, iv/vii

Inscriptions: on the block below the bust: *ANT. VAN DYCK. Ant. van Dyck fecit aqua forti*; On the pedestal: *ICONES / PRINCIPVM / VIRORVM DOCTORVM, / PICTORVM CHALCOGRAPHORVM / STATVARIORVM NEC NON AMATORVM / PICTORIAE ARTIS NVMERO CENTVM. / AB / ANTONIO VAN DYCK / PICTORE AD VIVVM EXPRESSAE / EIVSQ[UE] . SVMPTIBVS AERI INCISAE. / ANTVERPIAE / Gillis Hendricx excudit*; at lower left: *Iac. Neeffs sculpsit*

Purchased from Kunsthandlung Helmut H. Rumbler, Frankfurt

2001.6

Anthony van Dyck's so-called *Iconography* consists of a hundred etched and engraved portraits of princes, generals, statesmen, intellectuals, artists, and collectors.[1] He began the series around 1630, and was still working on it at least in 1637, providing designs (either drawings or oil sketches) for engravers (ultimately nine participated, most prolifically Paulus Pontius and Lucas Vosterman), as well as producing some etchings by himself. The prints, excluding van Dyck's etchings, were distributed initially by Martinus van den Enden, but it was not until 1645, four years after van Dyck's death, that Gillis Hendricx produced the first full edition of the portraits, of which this print is the title page. Hendricx continued to reissue the prints over the next thirty years. The series acquired the name by which it is now commonly known only in 1759, when it was published with biographical texts and bore the title *Iconographie ou vies des hommes illustres du XVII. siècle.* Van Dyck's *Iconography* was by no means the first series of portraits of famous men and women, printed or otherwise. Particularly significant in the Netherlands was Domenicus Lampsonius's *Pictorum aliquot celebrium Germaniae inferioris effigies* of 1572, which consisted entirely of artists' portraits; it was reissued with addenda by Hendrick Hondius in 1610. Van Dyck probably also knew the extensive series of etched portraits produced in Italy during his sojourn there by Ottavio Leoni, whose self-portrait, in which he looks over his shoulder at the viewer, may have influenced van Dyck's choice of pose for his own self-portrait, ultimately used as the title page of the *Iconography*. The mixture of artists and non-artists in Leoni's series may also have influenced van Dyck's *Iconography*. Van Dyck's portrayals of his sitters were not unprecedented, but the series became enormously popular, helping to disseminate not only his portrait style—his poses became standard—but also the idea of the social and intellectual equality of artists with other persons of high standing.

The title page consists of a fictive sculptured bust of van Dyck set on a pedestal in an open landscape. Van Dyck's contribution to the composition is limited to the etched head: he never proceeded past a single-line indication of his collar and upper back.[2] By the time the head was used for the title page, the etching was not nearly as fresh and lively as in the first state, but it still contrasts sharply with Jacob Neeffs's heavy and rather lifeless engraving of the rest of the plate. Decorating the pedestal are, in addition to van Dyck's coat of arms, busts of Minerva and Mercury, as well as a trumpet of fame and a caduceus, which derive from a printer's mark designed by Rubens. The conjunction of the two gods had been used since the late sixteenth century to connote an academic ideal and, by extension, the intellectual stature of the arts, as in Sadeler's engraved portrait of Pieter Brueghel (cat. no. 3). Ironically, with the addition of the busts of Minerva and Mercury, Hendricx and Neeffs have allegorized the portrait, an approach in stark contrast to that of van Dyck in the *Iconography* (see cat. no. 5).

JC

1. On the *Iconography*, see Mauquoy-Hendrickx 1991; Depauw and Luijten 1999, 73ff.; Turner and Depauw 2002.
2. On the states of the print and the development of the design for the title page, see Mauquoy-Hendrickx 1991, 105; Depauw and Luijten 1999, 92–100; Turner and Depauw 2002, 2–12.

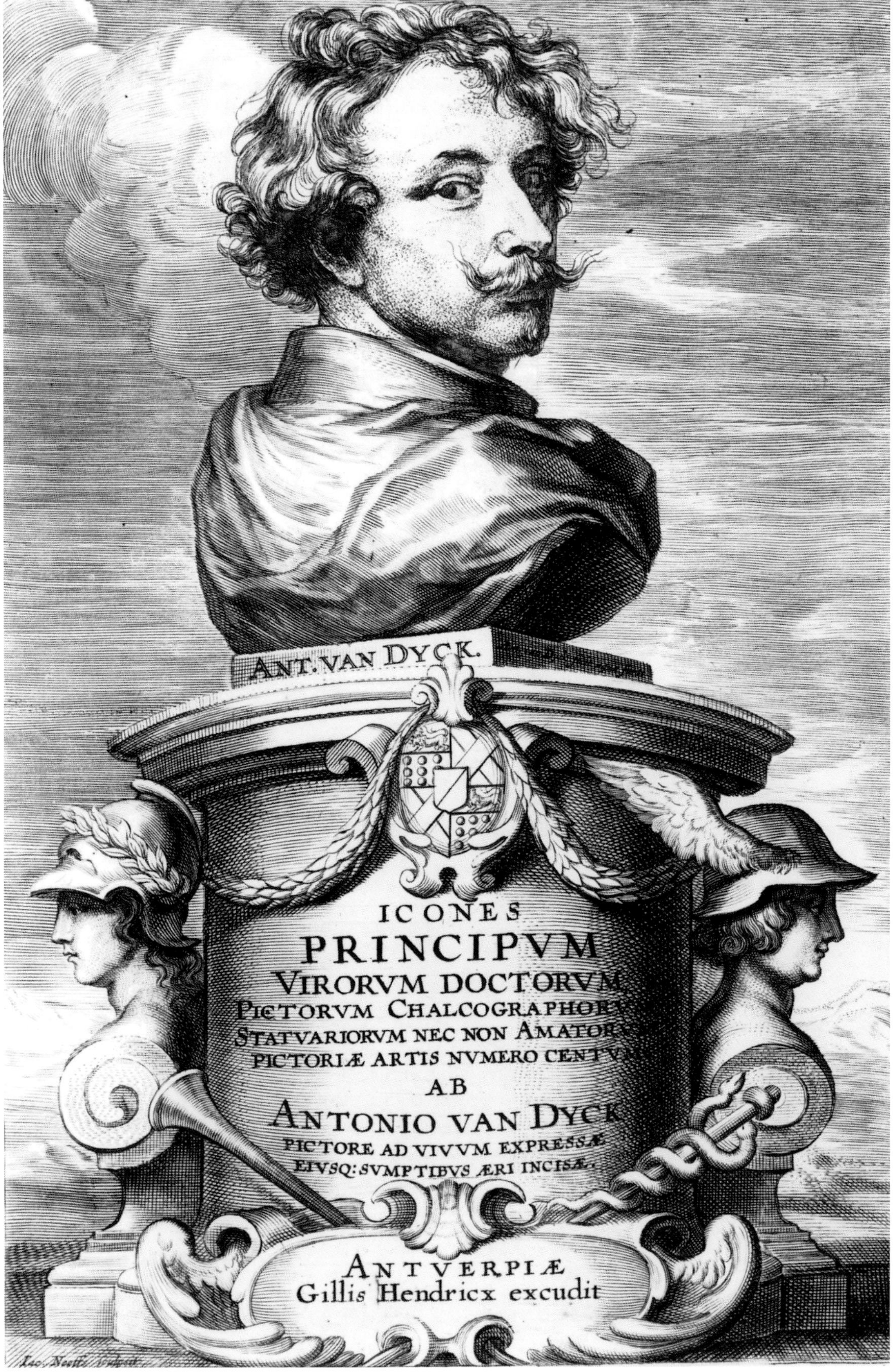
ANT. VAN DYCK.
ICONES
PRINCIPVM
VIRORVM DOCTORVM,
PICTORVM CHALCOGRAPHORV
STATVARIORVM NEC NON AMATORV
PICTORIÆ ARTIS NVMERO CENTV
AB
ANTONIO VAN DYCK
PICTORE AD VIVVM EXPRESSÆ
EIVSQ: SVMPTIBVS ÆRI INCISÆ.
ANTVERPIÆ
Gillis Hendricx excudit
Cat. no. 4

Anthony van Dyck (1599–1641)

5. *Pieter Brueghel the Younger*

c. 1630

Etching and engraving, 242 x 155 mm (9½ x 6⅛ in.)

References: Mauquoy-Hendrickx 2, iv/vi; Turner and Depauw 3, iv/vi

Inscription: *PETRVS BREVGEL / ANTVERPIAE PICTOR RVRALIVM ACTIONVM. / Ant. van Dyck fecit aqua forti. G. H.*

Watermark: Foolscap

Purchased from James Bergquist, Boston

1997.3

Anthony van Dyck's etched portrait of the artist Pieter Brueghel the Younger is one of more than a dozen etchings by him that comprised, along with engravings after his designs, the series of portraits of famous men and women known as the *Iconography,* published by Gillis Hendricx in 1645 (see cat. no. 4). Five of those etchings, including *Pieter Brueghel the Younger,* were not elaborated by an engraver, except for the addition of framing lines and inscriptions. The entire series of prints became enormously well known, but the etchings from van Dyck's hand were prized above the engravings made after his designs, as Giovan Pietro Bellori already noted in 1672.[1]

Van Dyck treated Brueghel as he treated his other sitters: in half-length, with little or no indication of profession (except princes, politicians, and soldiers, who are shown in armor, holding a baton).[2] Brueghel holds what seems to be a folded piece of paper. A brief inscription below each image identifies the sitter and his profession, in this instance as a painter of rural subjects from Antwerp.[3] Unlike some of his sixteenth- and early seventeenth-century predecessors, van Dyck eschewed fictive frames with allegorical figures and objects, and so his portrait of Pieter Brueghel the Younger contrasts markedly with the portrait of the sitter's father by Bartholomaeus Spranger and Aegidius Sadeler (cat. no. 3). Although the subject matter of Brueghel's paintings was rustic—coarse by some standards of the time—van Dyck presents him as elegant and dignified, in keeping with the other sitters in the *Iconography,* regardless of profession or social status, implicitly propagating the idea of painting as a liberal art and intellectual endeavor.

Two drawings of Brueghel by van Dyck, probably made from life at a single sitting, are known, in Chatsworth and in St. Petersburg, the latter of which supplied the model for the etching. Both the drawings include the motifs of the arm resting in the fold of a cloak, the hand holding a paper, and a column in the background. In the print, van Dyck typically elaborates the face in a strong chiaroscuro but barely indicates the remainder of the body, costume, and background.

JC

1. Depauw and Luijten 1999, 79.
2. On the development of the print and its various states, see Mauquoy-Hendrickx 1991, 103–104; Depauw and Luijten 1999, 104–108; Turner and Depauw 2002, 19–23.
3. In the fourth state (exhibited), the word "actionum" (actions) was substituted for "prospectuum" (views).

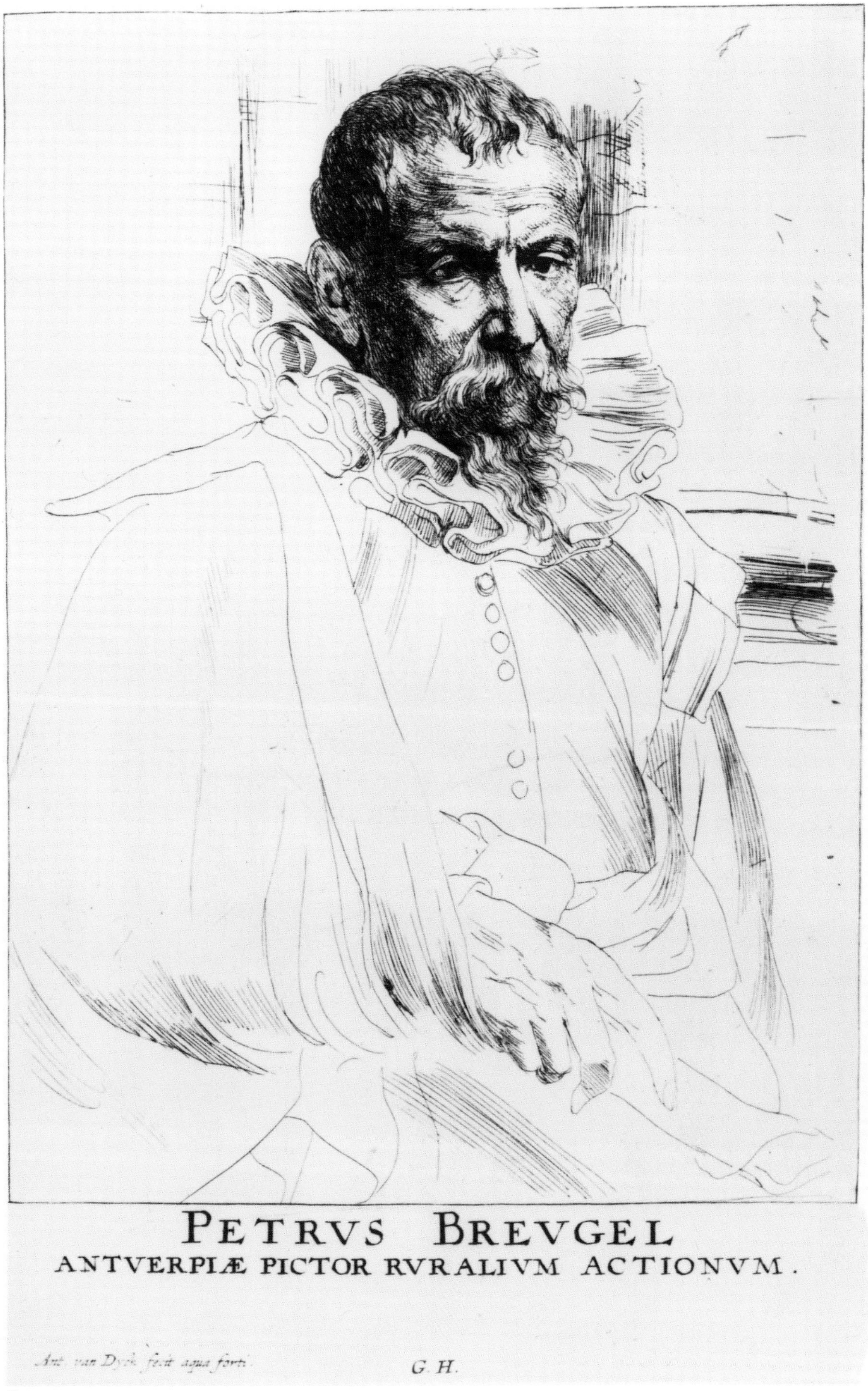
PETRVS BREVGEL
ANTVERPIÆ PICTOR RVRALIVM ACTIONVM.
Ant. van Dyck fecit aqua forti.
G. H.

Cat. no. 5

6. *Self-Portrait with Various Studies*

c. 1631–32
Etching, 99 x 105 mm (3⅞ x 4⅛ in.)
Bartsch, White and Boon 363, ii/ii
Purchased from C. G. Boerner, New York
1998.7

Like many artists, Rembrandt sometimes drew multiple, apparently unrelated figures on the same sheet. However, he also produced several etchings in this manner, three of which, over a lengthy period (around 1631–32, 1645, and 1651), include a self-portrait.[1] Figures and forms may be oriented differently in these works, so that the viewer must rotate the sheets to read them properly, as Rembrandt turned the plate to etch the different parts. In the earliest of these works, the young Rembrandt appears as a heavily shadowed head, with some indication of a collar and a blank space in lieu of a hat. Turning the sheet ninety degrees clockwise, we see a couple, stooped and supporting themselves with canes or "beggar's staffs," facing in opposite directions, and, above them, the head and shoulders of an elderly woman. Another ninety degrees shows the partial figure of a bearded and hatted man, apparently carrying a large sack behind him. One more turn reveals the head of a bearded man, his shoulders and cap barely indicated.

The print is typically catalogued not with the independent etched self-portraits, but with "sheets of studies" or "model sheets," as if the self-portrait is a motif equivalent to the other figures on the sheet, or at least as if the presence of the other forms indicates that Rembrandt was merely experimenting, practicing, or demonstrating something to students and that the work does not have the finish or clarity of the other self-portraits. Indeed, the incompleteness of the self-portrait, as well as the slightness and diverse orientation of the motifs, suggests that the plate had a function purely within the workshop. Yet there is evidence that the plate had a greater significance for Rembrandt. In the second state, the large areas of foul-biting (irregular etched areas), which were especially noticeable above the artist's head,[2] were either

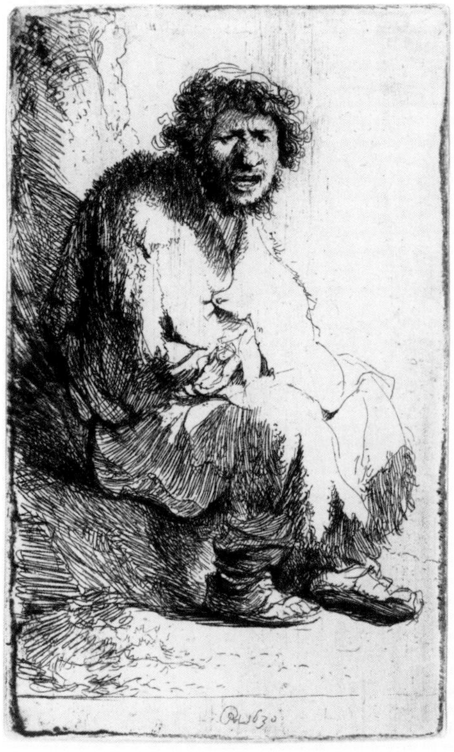

Fig. 6.1 (right). Rembrandt van Rijn. *Self-Portrait as a Beggar.* 1630. Etching, 116 x 70 mm (4⅝ x 2¾ in.). The British Museum, London.

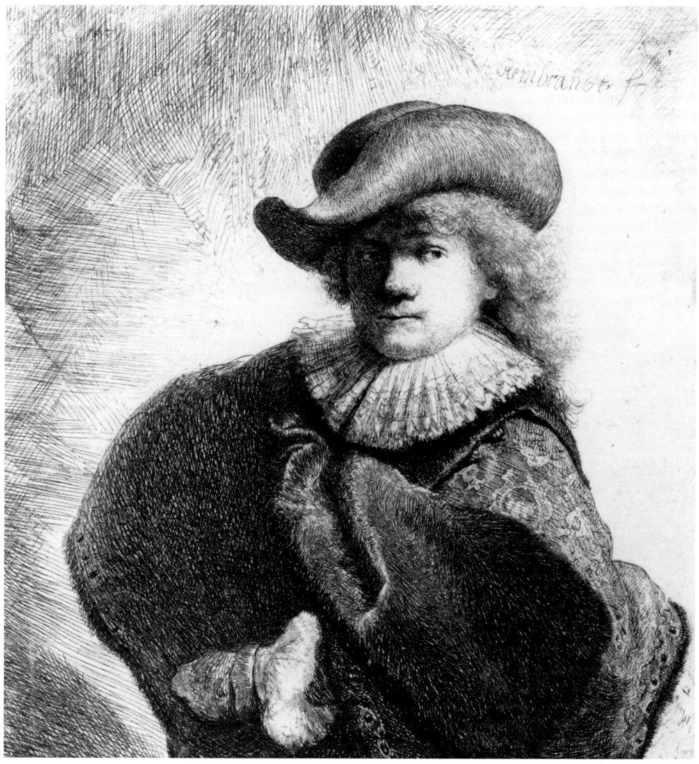

Fig. 6.2 (far right). Rembrandt van Rijn. *Self-Portrait with Hat, Hand on Hip.* 1631–33. Etching, 148 x 138 mm (5⅞ x 5⅜ in.). The British Museum, London.

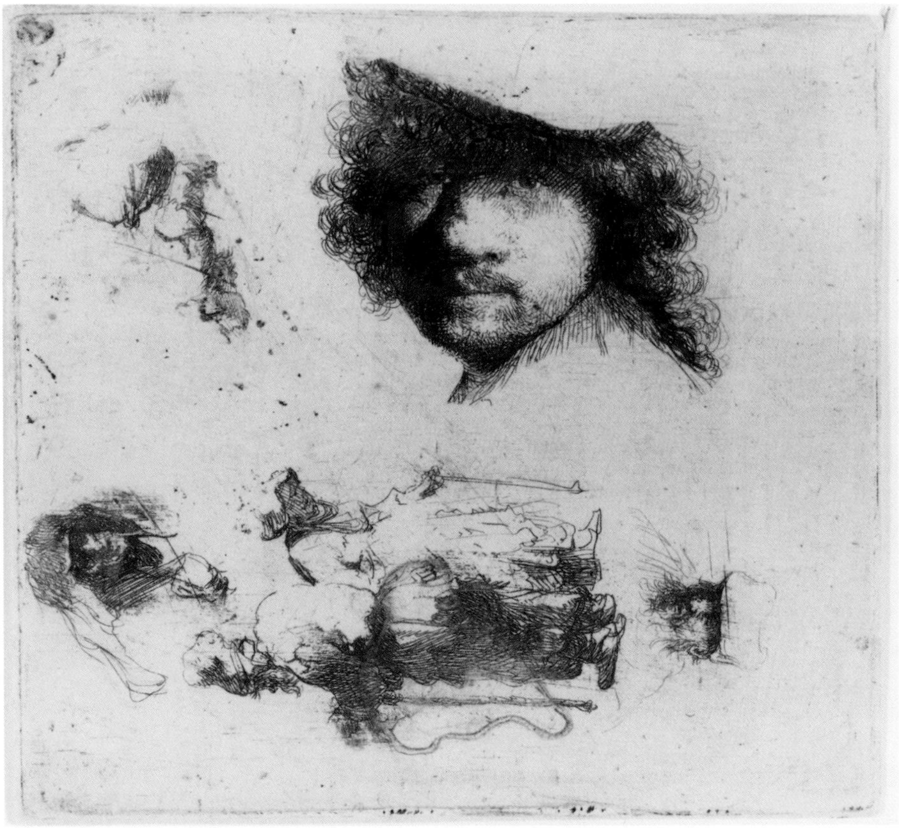

Cat. no. 6

removed or reduced. Furthermore, a substantial number of impressions, including two counterproofs (in London and Vienna), were pulled—more than would be useful for proofing purposes.

Several scholars suggest readings of the print that connect the self-portrait and the various studies. The couple on the sheet, as well as the man with the rucksack, may be plausibly identified as beggars or vagabonds, in keeping with the many images of such figures—both drawn and etched—produced by Rembrandt, especially early in his career.[3] Rembrandt was no doubt attracted to such figures, which he treated in an unusually sympathetic manner, perhaps in part because he shared, at least psychologically, their alienation from society.[4] Such would seem to be the significance of his etched self-portrait in the guise of a beggar (fig. 6.1). Rembrandt may also have cultivated the reputation of a marginal, or at least unprivileged, status as a means of projecting his personal genius.[5] It is worth noting, however, that there is nothing beggarly about Rembrandt's self-portrayal on the sheet with various studies. Although clothing is scarcely indicated, the collar and implicit hat may be likened to his sophisticated attire in his carefully etched *Self-Portrait with Hat, Hand on Hip* (fig. 6.2) and his painted self-portrait in Glasgow, both of the same period.[6] Rembrandt may have propagated a marginal or antisocial persona—albeit a fashionable one for artists—also by portraying himself as a melancholic, whether genuine or affected. His heavily shaded eyes, in the *Self-Portrait with Various Studies* as in numerous other self-portraits, suggest introspection, imagination, and creativity.[7]

JC

1. See also White and Buvelot 1999, 185, 189.
2. See White and Buvelot 1999, 141.
3. On Rembrandt and beggars, see Baldwin 1985; Held 1991b.
4. Held 1991b, 161.
5. Wheelock 2000, 18.
6. White and Buvelot 1999, 143–44, and 145–47, respectively. Wheelock 2000, 18–19, notes the "schizophrenic character of Rembrandt's self-images in the paintings and etchings" of this period, exemplified by the self-portrait as a beggar and the *Self-Portrait with Hat, Hand on Hip.*
7. On Rembrandt's melancholy, see Chapman 1990, 26–33. With regard to the *Self-Portrait with Various Studies,* Chapman 1990, 33, associates Rembrandt's melancholy with his self-portrayal among beggars, however incoherently organized, by asking "what better way to admit defeat and confess the fear of failure than to picture oneself among the end results of carelessness and idleness?"

Jean Pesne (1623–1700)
after Nicolas Poussin (1594–1665)

7. *Self-Portrait of Poussin (The Pointel-Cérisier Self-Portrait)*

c. 1661 (after the painting of 1649)

Engraving and etching, 357 x 246 mm (14 x 9⅝ in.) (trimmed)

References: Le Blanc 96, i/ii; Robert-Dumesnil 6, i/ii; Wildenstein 1, i/ii

Inscriptions: at upper center: *NICOLAVS POVSSINVS ANDELIENSIS ACADEMICVS ROMANVS PRIMVS / PICTOR ORDINARIVS LVDOVICI IVSTI REGIS GALLIAE ANNO DOMINI / 1649. ROMAE. AETATIS SUAE. 55.*; on spine of book: *DE LVMINE ET COLORE*; below image: *cum Priuil Regis / Viro egregio D. Cerisier amico suo et fautori beneuolentissimo / Apographum hoc Jconici, ex ejus museo, archetypi, quo se ipsum quondam expressit ad viuum N. Poussin, omniu[m] / quos nostra tulit aetas, pictorum, Jure merito, celebratissimus; in mutui amoris et grati animi monimentum / J Pesne D C Q*

Purchased from James Bergquist, Boston

1996.15

Jean Pesne's engraving is after a self-portrait by Nicolas Poussin usually identified as the painting now in the Nationalgalerie in Berlin. The painting is one of two self-portraits painted in successive years, 1649 and 1650; Poussin gave them to two of his most important patrons and friends: Charles Pointel and Paul Fréart de Chantelou. In 1647 and 1648, Poussin responded to Chantelou's request for a portrait of himself by claiming that there were no good portraitists in Rome. Then, in a letter of June 20, 1649, he revealed to Chantelou that he had executed a self-portrait, rather than having another artist paint it, but was not prepared to send it to Chantelou. Instead, he said he would paint another self-portrait and send the better of the two to Chantelou, who ultimately received the picture painted in 1650 (now in the Louvre in Paris).

The banker Pointel owned an important collection of paintings by Poussin, numbering at least ten.[1] Letters from Poussin to Chantelou, whose own collection of Poussin paintings was equally substantial, show that Chantelou was jealous of Pointel.[2] Poussin represented his self-portrait to Chantelou as an act of subservient friendship. We do not know if he adopted a similar stance for the self-portrait sent to Pointel, because their correspondence does not survive.

The popularity of the Pointel self-portrait is indicated by two engravings after it and over half a dozen painted copies,[3] as well as, extraordinarily, its use in a painting by Daniel Seghers as a fictive relief in a spot within a flower garland usually reserved for holy figures.[4] It was the basis for the portrait in Charles Perrault's first volume on famous men of the century, published in 1696 (fig. 7.1). Pesne's engraving of it served as the frontispiece of a folio

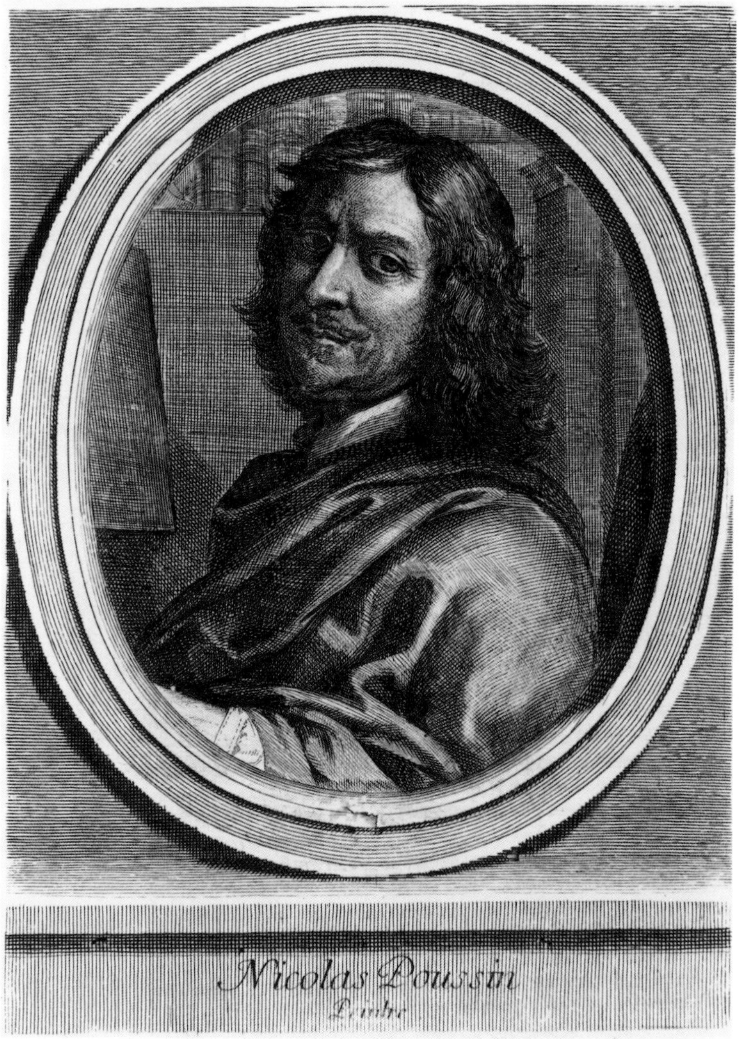

Fig. 7.1. *Self-Portrait of Poussin* from Charles Perrault, *Les hommes illustres*, vol. 1. 1696. Engraving, 252 x 178 mm (9⅞ x 7 in.). Sarah Campbell Blaffer Foundation, Houston.

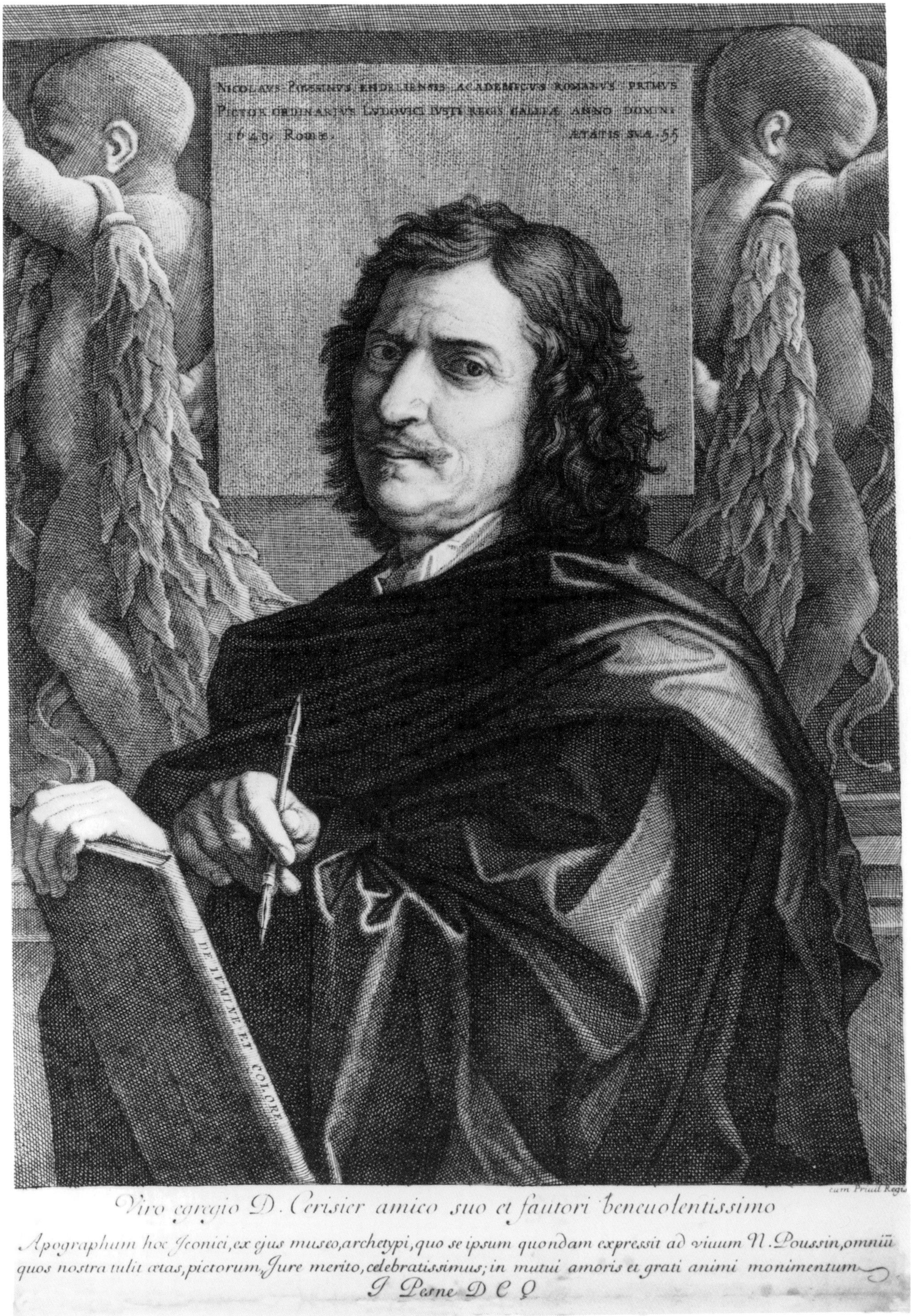
1649. Romæ.
ÆTATIS SVÆ. 55
cum Priuil Regis
Viro egregio D. Cerisier amico suo et fautori beneuolentissimo
Apographum hoc Jconici, ex ejus museo, archetypi, quo se ipsum quondam expressit ad viuum N. Poussin, omniũ quos nostra tulit ætas, pictorum, Jure merito, celebratissimus; in mutui amoris et grati animi monimentum
J. Pesne D C Q

Cat. no. 7

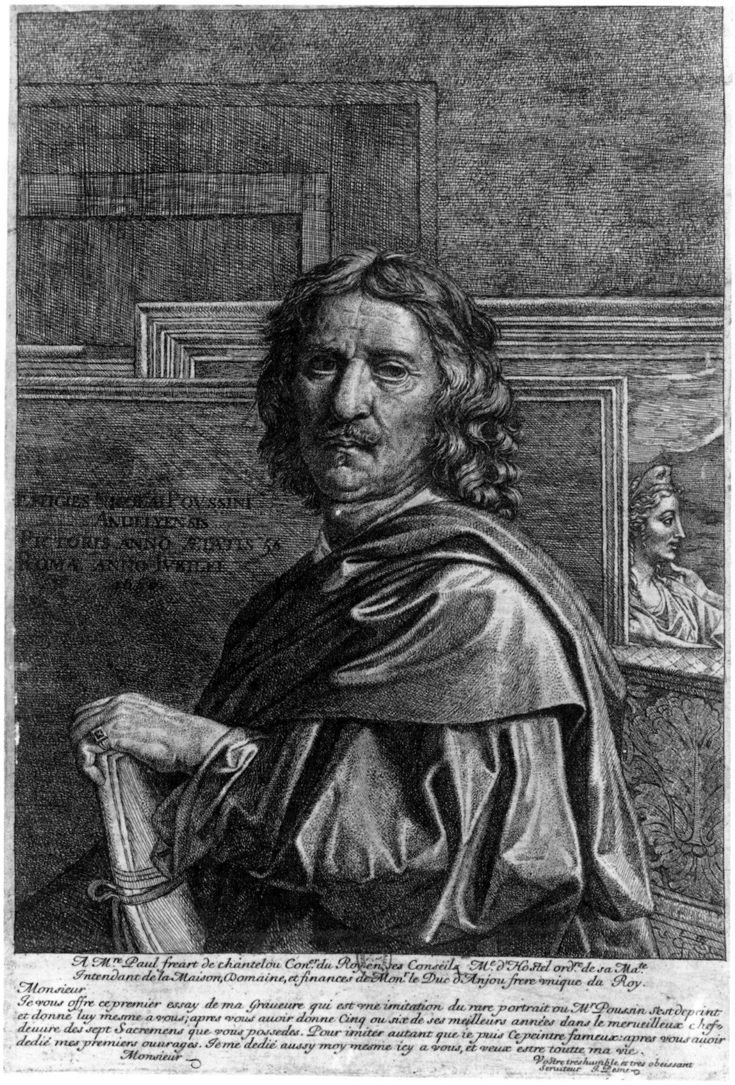

Fig. 7.2. Jean Pesne after Nicolas Poussin. *Self-Portrait of Nicolas Poussin.* 1650. Etching. Bibliothèque nationale de France, Paris.

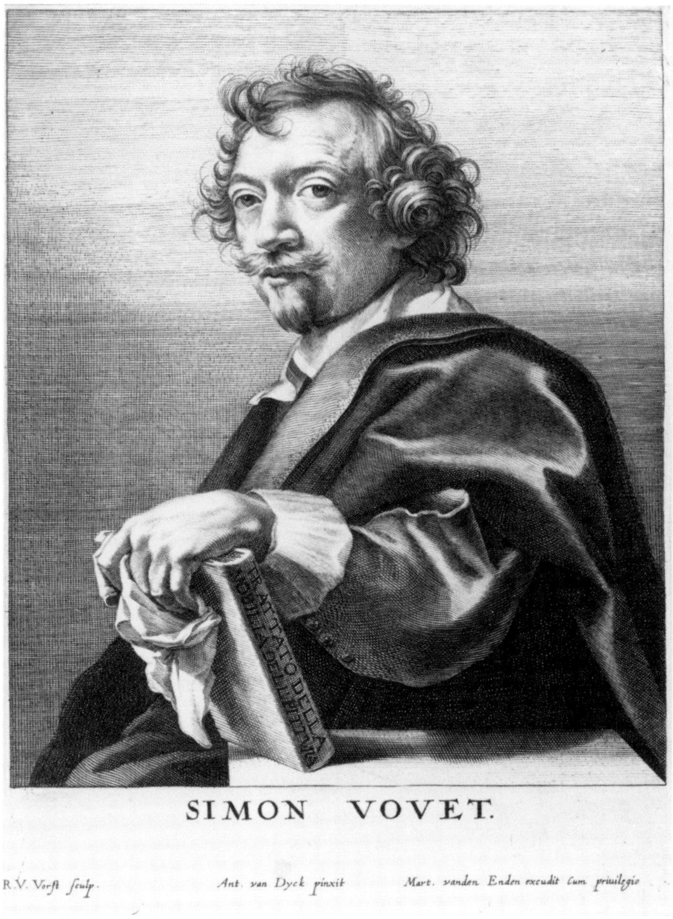

Fig. 7.3. Robert van Voerst after Anthony van Dyck. *Simon Vouet* (from *Iconography*). c. 1632–36. Engraving, 251 x 180 mm (9⅞ x 7⅛ in.). The British Museum, London.

of approximately fifty of his prints after Poussin's works.[5] The Chantelou picture proved even more popular, with some eight engravings based on it, including one by Jean Pesne (fig. 7.2) and a like number of painted copies.[6]

Pesne's engraving of the Pointel picture dates from the early 1660s.[7] The inscription below the image places the painting in the collection of the silk merchant Jacques Cérisier (or Serisier), where Gianlorenzo Bernini saw it in 1665 and pronounced it not as good a likeness as Poussin's self-portrait belonging to Chantelou (echoing Poussin's own opinion).[8]

The format of the two self-portraits is nearly identical, making all the more remarkable the differences between them, which Louis Marin has attributed to Poussin's theories of modal variation in painting. He characterizes the mood of the Pointel-Cérisier picture as one of "softness, gentleness, sadness," opposed to the "gravity, severity, modesty" of the Chantelou picture.[9] In both self-portraits Poussin represents himself as a scholar in academic dress, although there are also references to Poussin's profession. In the Chantelou painting, Poussin appears before a series of overlapping frames, one of which partially reveals allegorical figures said by Bellori to represent Painting embraced by the love of painting and friendship.[10] In the Pointel-Cérisier self-portrait, Poussin holds in one hand a chalk holder (*porte crayon* or *toccalapis*)[11] and in the other a volume, recalling the portrait of Poussin's compatriot Simon Vouet in Anthony van Dyck's series called the *Iconography,* in which the artist also wears an academic gown (fig. 7.3).[12] Unlike the portrayal of Vouet or the Chantelou self-portrait, which carry no direct sign of the artist's labor (Vouet's volume is tellingly entitled *Trattato dell Nobilità dell' Pittura,* that is, Treatise on the Nobility of Painting), the Pointel-Cérisier composition, with its chalk holder, acknowledges both the manual and the intellectual aspects of Poussin's work. As the artist had written to Chantelou in 1647, "To judge well is very difficult, if one does not possess both the theory and the practice [of painting]."[13]

The inscription on the spine of the book in the Pesne engraving—*De lumine et colore (On Light and Color)*—has engendered considerable confusion and comment.[14] It likewise appeared in the Berlin painting until technical examination indicated that it had been added later, possibly in imitation of Pesne's engraving, and it was removed. There was great interest in the prospect of Poussin writing a treatise on art, which he seems to have intended to do, and Cérisier had told Chantelou that he had seen such a book by Poussin "on lights and shadows, colors and measures" ("De lumine e umbre, colori e mesure"). Cérisier's interest may have led to the addition of the inscription to the book in the engraving, effectively an abbreviated form of this phrase, although Poussin had not, in fact, written such a treatise.[15] Anthony Blunt, thinking of Poussin as "a firm partisan of *disegno*" (that is, drawing and design), was baffled by the inscription on the book,[16] but recent scholarship has emphasized Poussin's debt to Leonardo da Vinci's theories of light and color. In the engraving—whether or not Poussin was directly responsible for the inscription on the book—the artist indicates with the chalk holder and the book the two conventionally accepted, fundamental parts of painting, drawing and color,[17] without prioritizing one over the other, as was often the case in the theoretical debates of the sixteenth and seventeenth centuries.

Several scholars have suggested that the composition is informed by the so-called *paragone,* the comparison of painting and sculpture that was of considerable interest in the sixteenth and seventeenth centuries. Thus, Oskar Bätschmann sees the book and the drawing instrument in the Pointel picture as indicating "the contrast between the transience of paintings and the permanence of sculptures" (as with the contrast between the "living" Poussin and the fictive stone background).[18] The painting has been likened to a funerary monument, comparable to those carved by Poussin's friend François Duquesnoy.[19] One author has described it flatly as "Poussin's tomb, both effigy and epitaph,"[20] although Poussin must have understood this connection metaphorically, since there is no indication that he felt himself close to death. One interpretation conceives it negatively—"Poussin insists . . . that painting, and here especially self-portraiture, is a kind of death in life in which the living voice is silenced"[21]—while another conceives it positively, as the triumph of art and fame over the transience of life.[22]

JC

1. For a list, see Blunt 1967, 214.
2. Marin 1999, 185; Cropper 1992, 495-96.
3. Blunt 1966, 7.
4. Warsaw, National Museum (Winters 2002, 92-93).
5. The folio, open to the title page (*Oeuvre de Nicolas Poussin par Pesne*) and frontispiece, is held by Dominique-Vivant Denon, the first director of the "Musée Napoléon" (i.e., the Louvre) in Paris, in a portrait of 1808 by Robert Lefèvre at Versailles (Paas and Mertens 2003, 205-206).
6. Blunt 1966, 8.
7. Pierre Mariette dated his impression 1660 (Wildenstein 1957, 99), but Cérisier, to whom the print is dedicated, did not acquire the painting from Pointel's estate until late 1660 at the earliest, and Cropper and Dempsey 1996, 146, suggest that the print may have been made to celebrate Cérisier's acquisition of the painting in early 1661.
8. Chantelou 1985, 110; on Cérisier, see p. 110, n. 54. For Poussin's opinion of the likeness, see Marin 1999, 184.
9. Marin 1999, 189.
10. Bellori's interpretation has generally been accepted only with reservations or not at all; see Bätschmann 1990, 47-48.
11. It is not a drawing pen or stylus, as it has sometimes been called; note the white tip on one end, black on the other (less evident in the engraving). The same instrument appears in self-portraits of Vanloo, Schmidt, Mengs, Boisseau, and Hayez (cat. nos. 13, 14, 16, 17, 20). For an elaborate interpretation of the significance of the instrument in this composition, see Winner 1987, 376-80.
12. Kauffmann 1960, 87; Winner 1987, 378, 396. On the *Iconography,* see cat. nos. 4, 5.
13. Marin 1999, 195.
14. See especially Cropper and Dempsey 1996, 145-74, with further bibliography.
15. In the illustration to Bellori's 1672 *vita* of Poussin by Albertus Clowet (Bellori 1976, 420), which is a combination of the two Poussin self-portraits (Carrier 1991, 132-33), the inscription becomes *DE LVM. ET VMB,* repeated in the frontispiece of Bellori's life of Poussin, where an allegorical female figure points to geometrical drawings and the inscription, "lumen et umbra" (light and shadow).
16. Blunt 1967, 265, n. 18.
17. Cropper 1984, 146.
18. Bätschmann 1990, 47; see also Winner 1987, 375-76.
19. Blunt 1966, 7; Blunt 1967, 266; Bätschmann 1990, 47.
20. Cropper 1984, 146; see also Cropper 1992, 497.
21. Cropper 1992, 497.
22. Winner 1987, 377-89. The laurel garland is comparable to the swags in the Sadeler portraits of Spranger and Brueghel (cat nos. 2, 3); such swags are often but not always funerary in significance (see Winner 1987, 386-87; Marin 1999, 191; Bätschmann 1990, 47).

Dirck de Braij (c. 1635–1694)

after Jan de Braij (c. 1627-1697)

8. *Salomon de Braij, Painter and Architect in Haarlem*

1664

Woodcut, 180 x 128 mm (7⅛ x 5 in.) (frame line)

With a counterproof of the first state, 183 x 130 mm (7¼ x 5⅛ in.) (frame line)

Reference: Hollstein 122 ii/ii and i/ii in reverse

Inscriptions: to the left of the sitter: *1664. / Oud 67.*; below image: *Salomon de Braij, Schilder en Bou-meester, tot Haerlem. / JDB*[ligature]*raij. f*[ecit]. *DB*[partially illegible ligature]

Purchased from Hill-Stone, New York

1996.4.1-2

Born in Amsterdam, Salomon de Braij (1597-1664) spent most of his life in Haarlem. As the inscription on this print proclaims, he was both a painter and an architect, but he was also a draftsman, printmaker, designer, urban planner, and writer, involved in many cultural projects in Haarlem, including the restructuring of the painter's organization, the Guild of Saint Luke. This print must have been made within months of his death on May 11, 1664, of the plague. The portrait was used in his *Bedenkingen over het uitleggen en vergroten der stad Haarlem (Considerations on the Extension and Enlarging of the City of Haarlem),* published posthumously in 1667. The portrait does not follow the pattern developed in the late sixteenth and seventeenth centuries by Lampsonius, van Dyck, and others in that it eschews the use of the sitter's hands for expressive purposes. Instead, the body, monumental though it appears, does not distract from the severe countenance. The small black cap is perhaps an attribute of de Braij's profession,[1] although it was quite commonly worn in mid-century.[2]

Three of Salomon de Braij's sons became artists: Joseph (died 1664), Jan, and Dirck. Jan and Dirck were both painters—Jan much more successfully so—but Dirck also produced etchings and woodcuts professionally, whereas Jan only dabbled in printmaking. Dirck made a few woodcuts after his father and brothers, inscribing them with both the designer's signature and his own monogram, as in this portrait of his father and a *Christ on the Cross* of 1663,[3] both after Jan and sharing the same form of inscription.[4] Jan noted that he drew his *Christ on the Cross* on the woodblock for his brother to cut, and he may well have done the same for the portrait of their father. Jan's drawing for Salomon's portrait (which the woodcut reverses), now in Berlin, is signed and dated 1657.[5] The woodcut medium was rarely used by later seventeenth-century Dutch printmakers—excepting often crudely cut broadsheets and other ephemera—and is unusual for portraiture in general. The

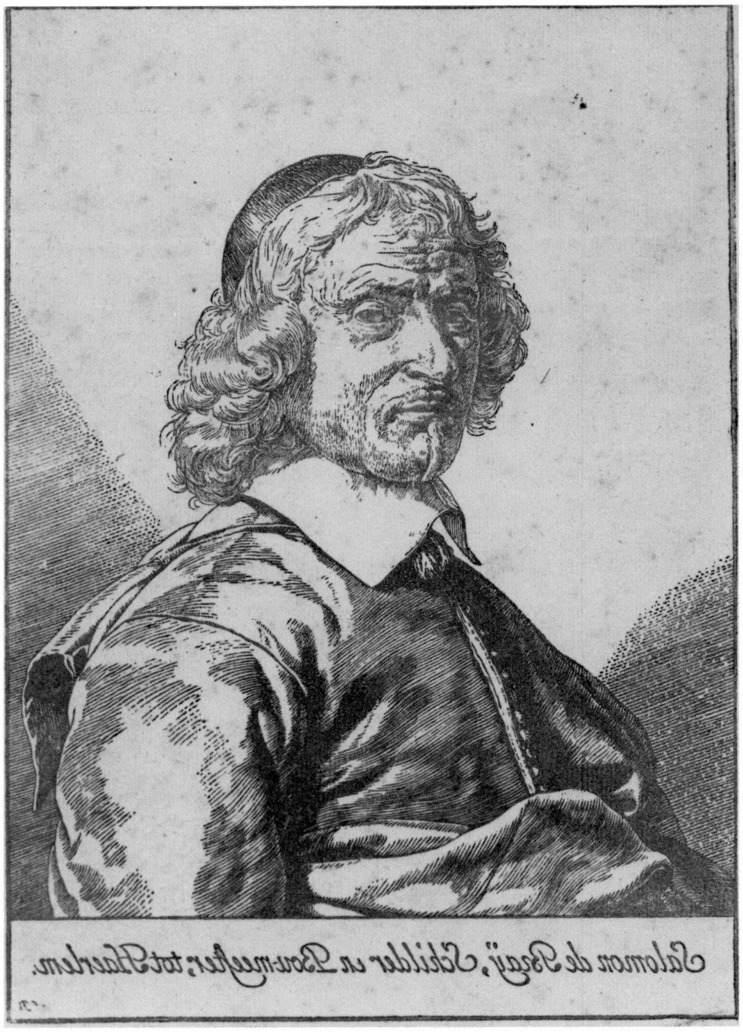

Cat. no. 8a. Counterproof in reverse of cat. no. 8.

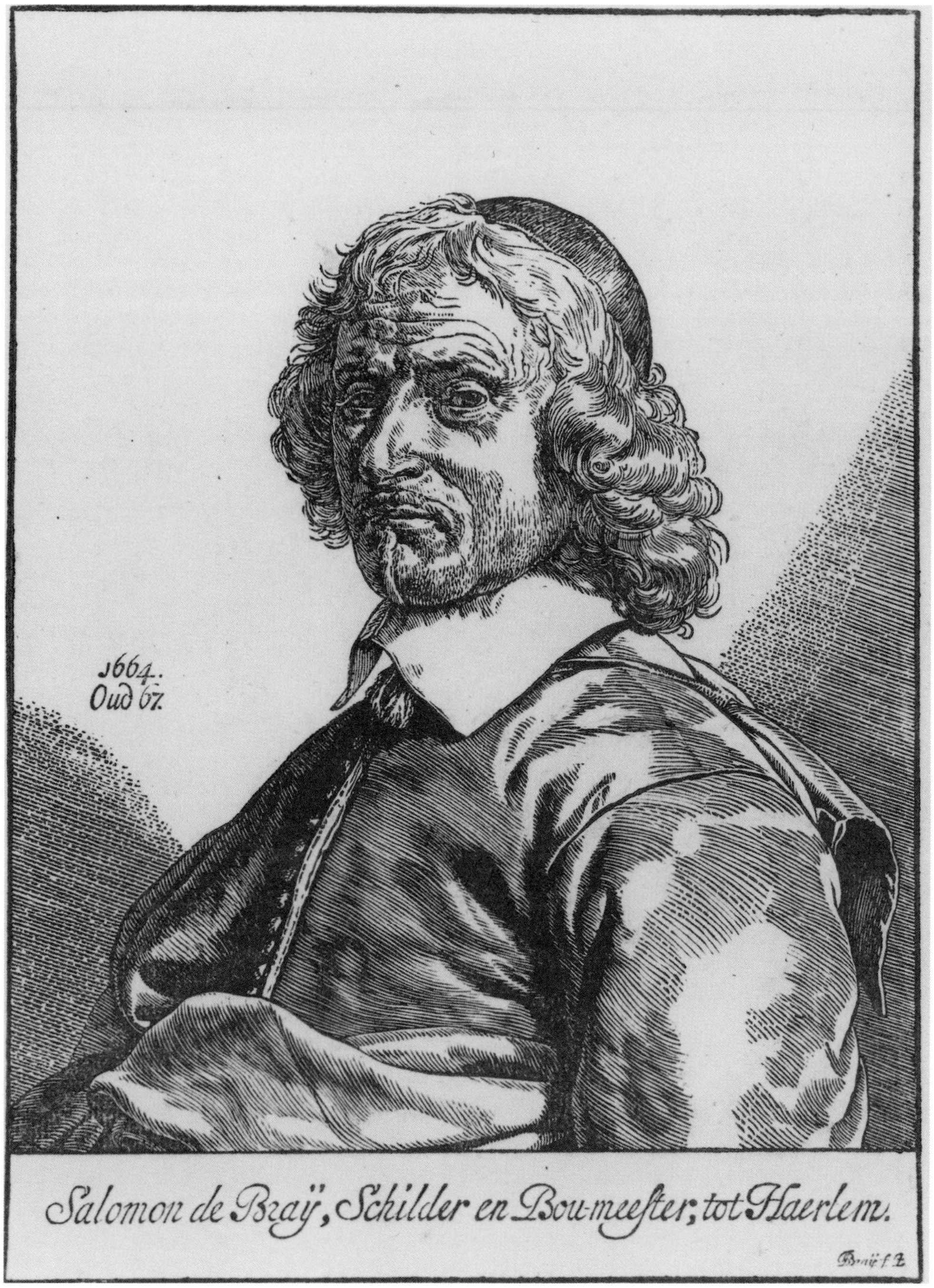

Cat. no. 8

sophistication of Dirck de Braij's woodcutting technique is evident in the *Salomon de Braij,* one of only a very few portraits he produced.

Exhibited also is a weaker impression in reverse (cat. no. 8A), which is probably a counterproof of the first state of the print, before the sitter's age and the date were added in the open field beside him, and with a less complete signature.

JC

1. Giltaij and Lammertse 2001, 387.
2. There are numerous examples in Jan de Braij's portrait oeuvre (see Von Moltke 1938–39, passim).
3. For the *Christ on the Cross* (Hollstein 25), see Giltaij and Lammertse 2001, 388–91.
4. The unusual practice of reproducing the designing artist's signature may derive from the practice of producing drawn copies, for archival purposes, of each other's paintings, including the signatures, in the de Braij family workshop (Giltaij and Lammertse 2001, esp. 368).
5. On the drawing, see Von Moltke 1938–39, 425–26, 501.

ABRAHAM BLOOTELING (1640–1690)
after Frans van Mieris the Elder (1635–1681)

9. *Self-Portrait of Frans van Mieris*

c. 1667

Mezzotint, 203 x 141 mm (8 x 5½ in.)

REFERENCE: Hollstein 185, ii/ii

INSCRIPTION: *Dus kon FRANS MIERIS hand, alleen met kool of kryt. / Op dood fransyn, syn zelfs Gedaente 't wesen geven: / Maer wie't Mirakel wil zien eelder Levend' leven; / Let hoe Penseel en verw met 't leven dingt om stryd. / Indien 't Pharhasius en Zeuxis mogten zien; / Sy staekten 't wedspel, streên wie d'eer kranshem zou bien. / Fr. Mieris delin. A. Blooteling. Fecit et exc. W.v.Heemskerk*

Purchased from Christopher Mendez, London

1996.12

Abraham Blooteling's mezzotint reproduces (and reverses) a self-portrait in black chalk on vellum now in London, which was executed in 1667, when the painter Frans van Mieris (1635-1682) was thirty-two years old (fig. 9.1). Although van Mieris painted many self-portraits (second only to Rembrandt in seventeenth-century Holland),[1] his drawn composition became the standard image for the artist.[2] Arnold Houbraken praised Blooteling's mezzotint, which became the basis of the portrait of van Mieris in Houbraken's important compendium of artists' lives, *De Groote Schouburgh der Nederlantsche Konstschilders en Schilderessen* of 1721 (fig. 9.2, here from the second edition of 1753):[3] "This drawn portrait was afterward engraved in mezzotint by Blooteling, and is preserved and treasured under the portraits of artists by those who love prints; and we have also not omitted to give the worthy portrait a place under so many dignified men . . . so that the remembrance may remain alive long."[4] Both the drawing—or a copy of it—and Houbraken's illustration appear in a three-generational portrait by Frans van Mieris the Younger from 1742 (fig. 9.3), which shows the last of the line of the artist's family with his father, Willem, and, through the images on the table, his grandfather, Frans the Elder.[5]

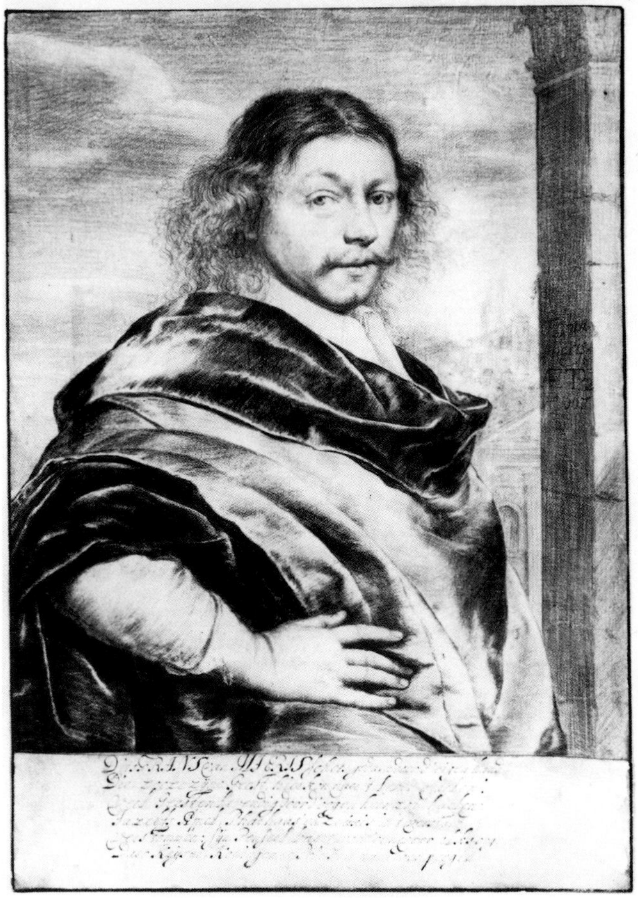

Fig. 9.1. Frans van Mieris the Elder. *Self-Portrait.* 1667. Black chalk on vellum, 197 x 137 mm (7¾ x 5⅜ in.). The British Museum, London.

The self-portrait drawing and Blooteling's mezzotint show the young but already accomplished artist posed assertively, his hand on his hip, next to a pillar. He is without the tools of his trade and wears an academic gown. Behind him is a hilly, Italianate landscape with a fragment of a Renaissance church (including a statue of Saint John the Baptist in a niche) in the middle ground, and another church in the background.[6] The non-Dutch setting recalls those he used in some of his paintings throughout his career, which must have appealed to the sophisticated tastes (or affectations) of his clientele, both local and international.

The inscription on the print was composed by Willem van Heemskerck (1613-1692), a family friend who, according to Houbraken, encouraged Frans van Mieris's father to allow his child to train as a glass painter rather than as a goldsmith.[7] Van Heemskerck

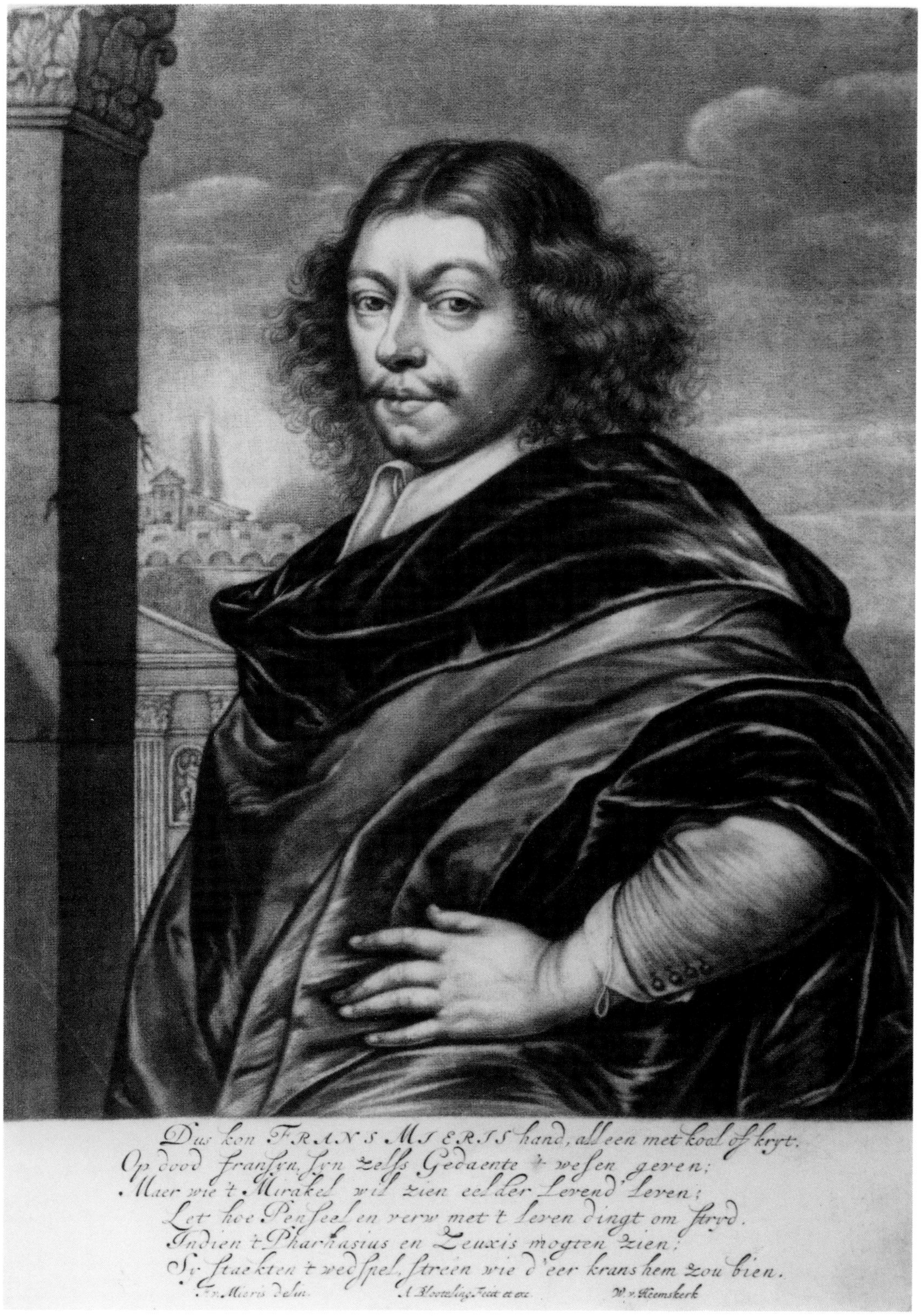

Cat. no. 9

owned two paintings by Frans van Mieris, and his portrait, painted by Frans's son Jan (1687), was also engraved by Blooteling. Van Heemskerck also wrote an epitaph for van Mieris's tomb in the St. Pieterskerk, Leiden.[8] Van Heemskerck's inscription on Blooteling's print refers to the celebrated contest between the ancient painters Zeuxis and Parrhasius, recounted by Pliny (35.65): "Thus could FRANS MIERIS's hand, with charcoal and chalk alone, / On parchment give life to his own shape: / But who wants to see the miracle living more nobly; / Note how brush and paint compete with life. / If Parhasius and Zeuxis could see it: / They would stop the contest, and would fight to give him the wreath of honour."[9] Zeuxis painted a picture of grapes so well that birds, fooled by the illusion, flew to them. But Parrhasius then painted a curtain so convincingly that Zeuxis asked that it be drawn back to reveal the picture beneath. Upon realizing his mistake, he acknowledged Parrhasius's victory, "saying that whereas he had deceived birds

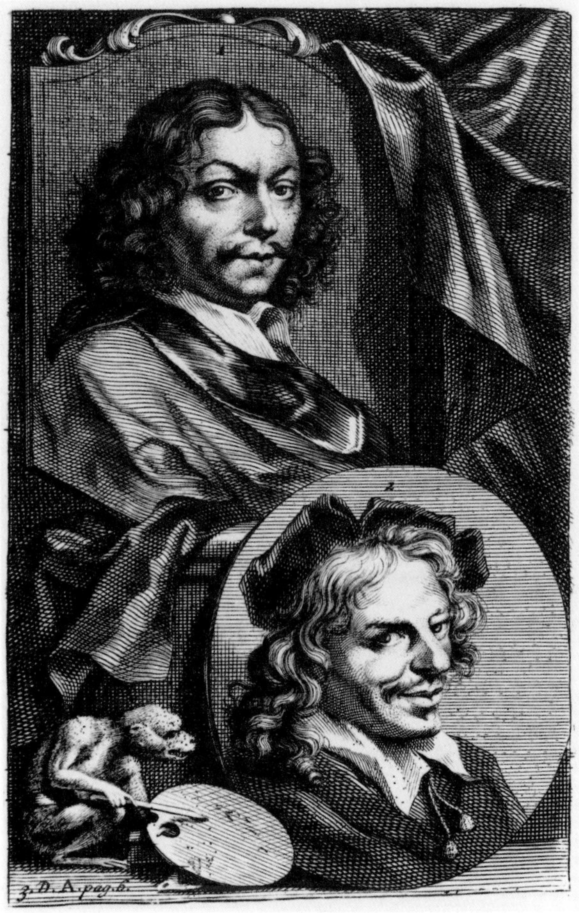

Fig. 9.2. *Portrait of Frans van Mieris and Jan Steen.* From Arnold Houbraken, *De Groote Schouburgh der Nederlantsche Konstschilders en Schilderessen* (volume 3). 1753. Engraving, 145 x 92 mm (5¾ x 3⅝ in.). Sarah Campbell Blaffer Foundation, Houston.

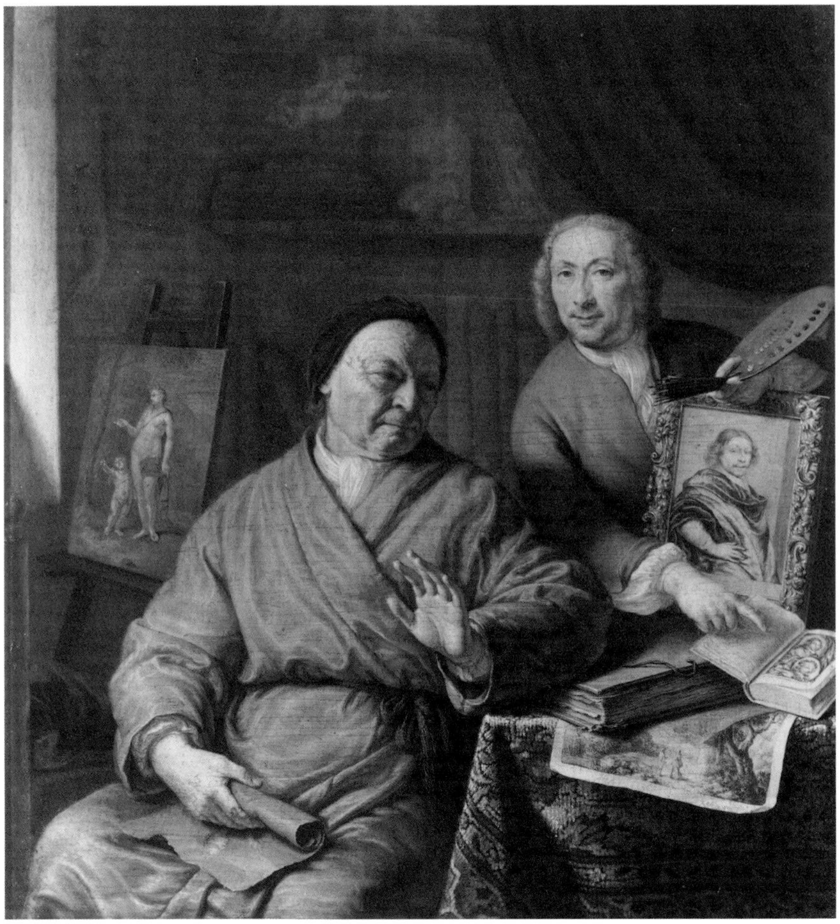

Fig. 9.3. Frans van Mieris the Younger. *De Drei Generaties (The Three Generations).* 1742. Oil on panel, 34 x 30.4 cm (13⅜ x 12 in.). Stedelijk Museum De Lakenhal, Leiden, Holland.

Parrhasius had deceived him, an artist." While the inscription is conventional in its references to ancient painters, its praise of the illusionistic qualities of van Mieris's work is particularly apt. He rivaled his master, Gerrit Dou (1613-1675), as the leading exponent of "fine painting" (*fijnschilderij*), whose richly detailed works were greatly admired and valued by collectors. Van Heemskerck's praise of van Mieris's use of chalk, quoted by Houbraken, is noteworthy because the "fine painters" were not particularly esteemed for their drawings, a naturally less mimetic medium than painting. Yet van Mieris's chalk drawing is perfectly matched by the mezzotint technique used by Blooteling—a technique which can effectively reproduce a variety of textures but not fine details—which also earned Houbraken's praise.

JC

1. See Naumann 1981, 1:125-34.
2. Two other prints after the drawing were made: one by van Mieris's pupil, Carel de Moor, and one by W. Baille in 1777, presumably after a copy of the drawing (Naumann 1978, 28).
3. The numerous portraits of artists in Houbraken's book appear as fictive paintings and prints, usually with two to four artists together. The contrast between the portraits of van Mieris and the more farcical portrait Jan Steen at the lower right was pointed out by Chapman 1996, 13.
4. Houbraken 1753, 3:5; trans. Naumann 1981, 1:200.
5. On this portrait, see Herzog Anton Ulrich-Museum 1993, 306-309. The copy of the drawing, in pen and ink, is in Amsterdam, Historical Museum, Fodor Collection (see Naumann 1978, 28, and fig. 24, p. 27).
6. Curiously, an oval painted copy of the drawing, probably by Willem van Mieris, sets the figure in a studio, with an easel in the background and palette and brushes in his hand (see Naumann 1981, 1:72, 1:127 and fig. 102).
7. Houbraken 1753, 3:2; Naumann 1981, 1:20.
8. The tomb no longer exists, but the epitaph is reported by Houbraken 1753, 3:12 (see also Naumann 1981, 1:203); another, unused epitaph was also written by van Heemskerck (Naumann 1981, 1:188; see also 1:20, 1:34).
9. Trans. Naumann 1981, 1:200, from Houbraken 1753, 3:5 (see also Naumann 1981, 1:196), who introduced several minor changes in spelling from the inscription on the print and substituted "Parkement" for "dood fransyn" (the latter more graphically conveys the animal origin of the parchment material). The inscription that accompanies the drawn self-portrait in London, on a separate piece of vellum, is of uncertain origin and differs from van Heemskerck's inscription on the print, referring, in addition to Parrhasius and Zeuxis, to another ancient painter, Apelles, to whom early modern artists were often compared (see, for example, cat. no. 39). A different set of verses, referring to Apelles and Zeuxis, accompanies a pen-and-ink copy of this drawn self-portrait (Naumann 1978, 28).

Gérard Edelinck (1640–1707)
after Pierre Mignard (1612-1695)

10. *Self-Portrait of Pierre Mignard*

1690-1700

Engraving, 251 x 185 mm (9⅞ x 7¼ in.)

Reference: Robert-Dumesnil 274, ii/ii

Inscriptions: lower left: *Se ipse Pinxit*; lower right: *Edelinck Sculp. C[um] P[rivilegio].R[egis]*; below ledge: *Pierre Mignard / Premier Peintre du Roy*

Purchased from Christopher Mendez, London

1996.13

Appointed as engraver to the king soon after his arrival in Paris in 1665, and later a member of the French Académie Royale de Peinture et de Sculpture, Gérard Edelinck ranks among the finest portrait engravers of the French seventeenth century. Edelinck's portrait of Pierre Mignard, Louis XIV's *premier peintre du roy,* aged seventy-eight, was engraved for Charles Perrault's influential two-volume book *Les Hommes illustres qui ont paru en France pendant ce siècle,* published in Paris in 1696 and 1700. Mignard's portrait appears near the end of the second volume. Edelinck furnished thirty-four of the fifty portraits in the second volume of Perrault's work, in addition to engraving the portrait of Perrault after François Tortebat that appears as the frontispiece to the first volume. Painters are relegated to the end of each volume, and Mignard is one of only six singled out for inclusion, the others being Poussin, Le Brun, Le Sueur, Vouet, and Blanchard.

This engraving of Mignard shows the painter in bust length in an illusionistic oval, his face turned toward us, and is taken in reverse from Mignard's full-length self-portrait of around 1690, now in the Louvre (fig. 10.1).[1] In the Louvre portrait, Mignard appears seated in a velvet armchair, surrounded by the attributes of painting (palette, brushes, and maulstick on the floor) and sketches prominently placed to remind us of his grandest commission, the frescoes in the cupola of the church of Val-de-Grace and the triumphal column for the Place Royale.[2] Looking directly at us, he sketches our portrait, holding a sketchbook propped in his lap.[3]

The Dutch engraver Cornelis Vermeulen produced the first engraving after the Louvre portrait, in 1690, a print that served as his reception piece to the Académie Royale and was listed as still hanging in its meeting chamber in Paris in 1715.[4] Vermeulen's engraving, and not Edelinck's, seems also to have provided the model for Robert Hecquet's frontispiece to the biography of Mignard that appeared in 1730.[5] Like Vermeulen, Hecquet retains the original orientation of the portrait, as well as the poised drawing hand and the damasked pattern of the gown.

That the Louvre portrait was also Edelinck's source for the engraving is further confirmed by Edelinck's exactness in copying the folds of Mignard's shirt collar and the lapels of his *robe de chambre*. However, in addition to cropping the composition of the painting down to a bust, Edelinck simplified the painter's pose, removing the drawing board and Mignard's right hand holding the chalk, and instead continuing the lapel and sleeves of his gown downward and out of the portrait oval. In addition, Edelinck changed the looping pattern of the painter's gown to more straightforward stripes. On the one hand, Edelinck no doubt intended all of these changes to differentiate his engraving from Vermeulen's earlier academy piece. But Edelinck's more sober depiction also seems to be deliberately in keeping with the more straightforward, factual writing style of Perrault's *Hommes illustres,* reflecting Perrault's desire to avoid unnecessary verbal or visual embellishment.[6] In his preface to the first volume, Perrault lays out the aesthetic tenor of the book: "For if it is true that one should take as goal to make well known the true character of whom one is speaking, it is no less true that nothing is more fitting to achieve this than a simple retelling of his actions, in which the man paints himself better than the finest orator using the most beautiful colors of eloquence would know how to do."[7]

Edelinck was accepted to the Académie Royale de Peinture et de Sculpture on March 6, 1677, a noteworthy achievement as only twelve other engravers had previously been accepted since the first, Abraham Bosse, in 1651.[8] The record of his *agrément,* or acceptance, shows that he was elected not only as "Académicien" but also "en la qualité de Conseiller,"[9] that is, with full privileges to participate alongside painters and sculptors in the governance of the Académie. Though invited in 1663, Pierre Mignard himself had refused to join the Académie, not wishing to play second fiddle to its undisputed guiding force—and Mignard's chief rival—Charles Le Brun. It is interesting to note that Edelinck's official reception piece, submitted to the Académie Royale on March 6, 1684, was a portrait of Le Brun.[10] After Le Brun's death in 1690, Mignard did accept the invitation, and was made director and first painter to the king.

AW

1. Nikolenko 1983, 94. Although it is unsigned and undated, the portrait's authenticity is supported not only on grounds of style and quality, but also because it was a gift to the French Academy from the painter's daughter, Catherine, comtesse de Feuquières, in 1696, in memory of her father (cf. cat. no. 60).
2. Nikolenko 1983, 93.
3. Other self-portraits by Mignard are documented, although not all are now accounted for. Perrault relates that the canvas on Mignard's easel when he died in 1695 was a *Saint Luke Painting the Virgin,* featuring a self-portrait of the artist. This work is now in the Musée des Beaux-Arts, Troyes. See Perrault 1696–1700, 2:92; Perrault 2003, 477.
4. Johnson 1982, 13.
5. Mazière de Monville 1730.
6. Perrault 2003, xxiii.
7. "Car s'il est vrai qu'on doit avoir pour but de faire bien connaître le veritable caractère de celui dont on parle, il n'est pas moins vrai que rien n'est plus propre pour y parvenir que le simple récit de ses actions, où l'homme se peint mieux lui-même que ne saurait faire le meilleur orateur avec les plus belles couleurs de l'éloquence." Perrault 1696–1700, n.p.; Perrault 2003, 8–9.
8. Johnson 1982, Appendix III, 191. The portrait engraver Robert Nanteuil (1623–1678) was instrumental in convincing Louis XIV that engraving required a level of skill comparable to that of painting; Louis XIV responded in 1659 with the Edict of Saint Jean de Luz, which elevated printmaking from the status of a craft to that of a liberal art like painting, and made engravers eligible for membership in the Académie Royale. See Campbell 1984–85, 28.
9. Johnson 1982, 68.
10. Ibid., 65.

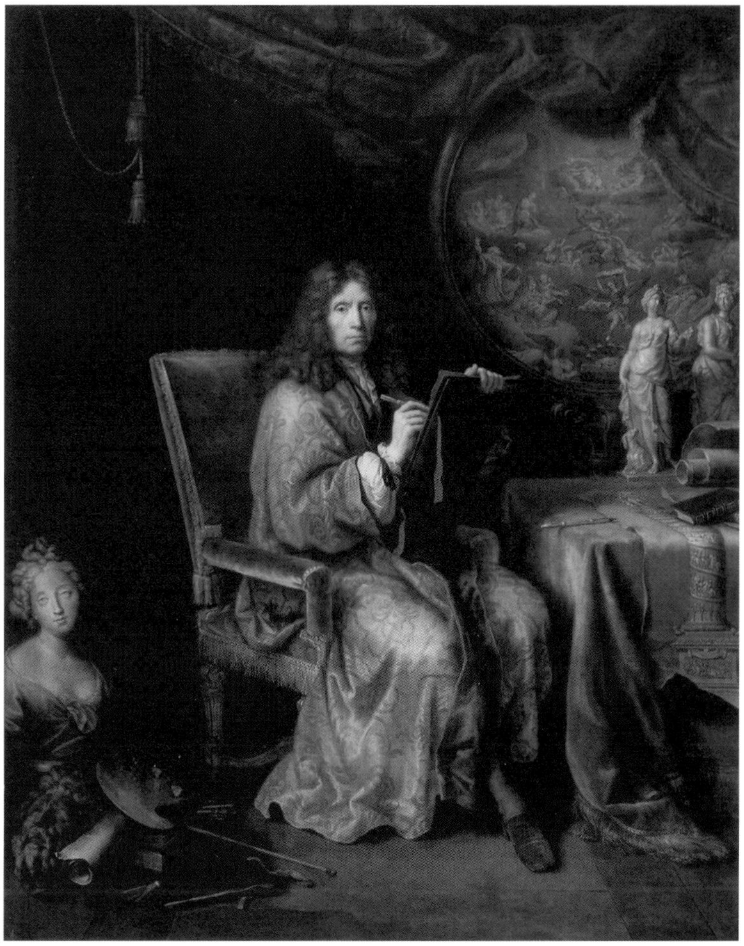

Fig. 10.1. Pierre Mignard. *Self-Portrait.* c. 1690. Oil on canvas, 235 x 188 cm (92½ x 74 in.). Musée du Louvre, Paris.

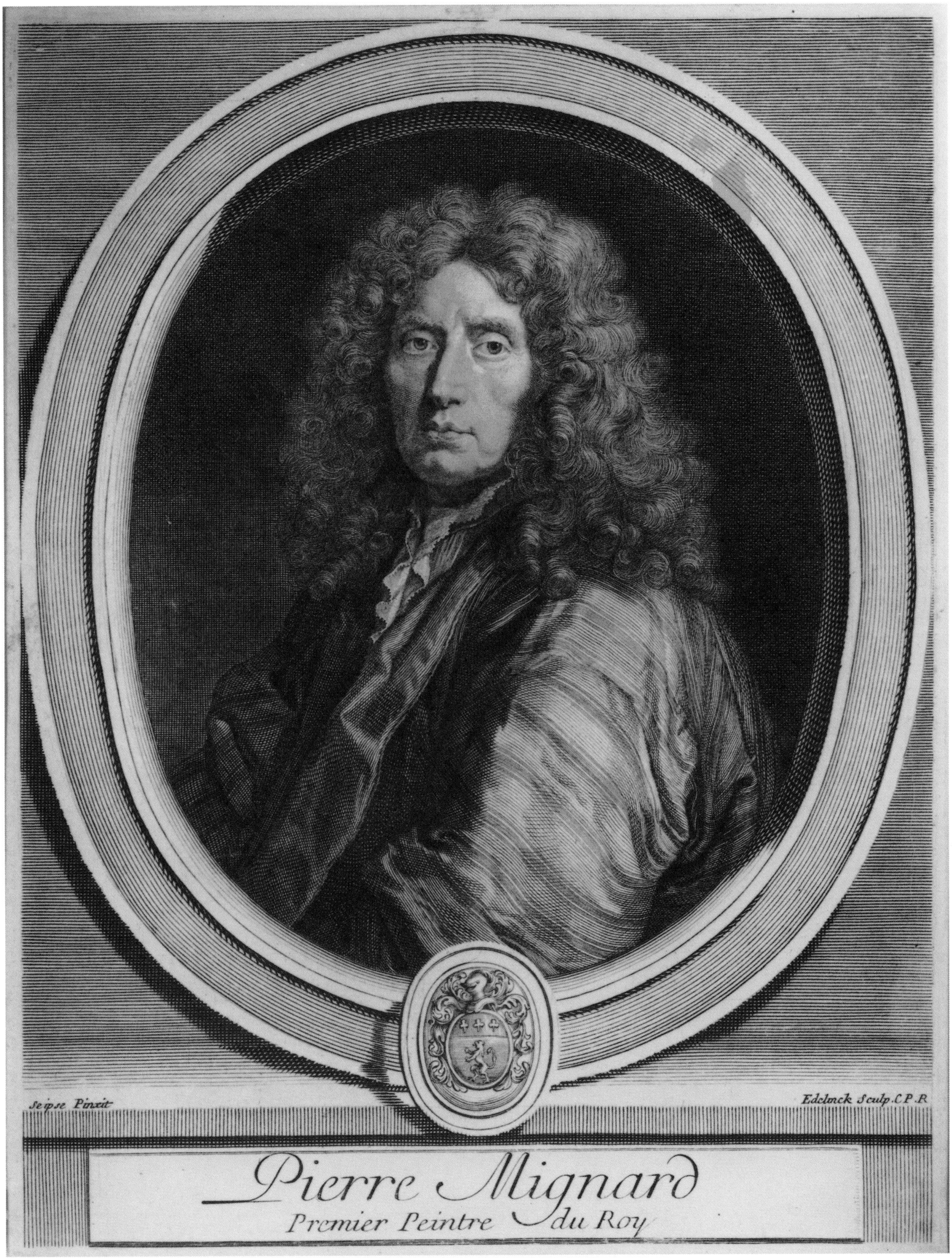
Se ipse Pinxit
Edelinck Sculp. C.P.R.
Pierre Mignard
Premier Peintre du Roy

Cat. no. 10

JACOB GOLE (1660–c. 1737)
after Ludolf Bakhuizen (1630–1708)

11. *Self-Portrait of Ludolf Bakhuizen*

1701

Mezzotint, 183 x 147 mm (7¼ x 5¾ in.) (image plate)

REFERENCE: Hollstein 41b

INSCRIPTIONS: above image (manuscript): *B3 Le portrait de L. Bakhuizen*; below image: *L. Bakhuizen out 71 jaar. / Aemula naturae Bakhusia dextra potentis / Vivi coloris artifex: / Picturae postquam implevit, genus omne, Tropaeum / in aere seponit sibi. / cum Privileg: ord: Holland: et West Frisiae. Janus Broekhusius.*

Purchased from August Laube, Zurich

1997.2.13

Although Ludolf Bakhuizen gained his considerable fame as a marine painter, he produced several self-portraits in the latter part of his career in which he is invariably dressed, as in Jacob Gole's mezzotint, as a successful burgher.[1] As Arnold Houbraken described him, he was "industrious, quiet, and bourgeois (*borgerlijk*) in his life."[2] Although Bakhuizen's self-portraits are all very similar in pose, Gole's mezzotint is based on a black chalk drawing by the painter.[3] That image makes its appearance in a series of self-referential representations of Bakhuizen and his family: as a fictive print (in larger scale than and reversed from Gole's mezzotint) lying on a table with the artist's hand atop it in a self-portrait from 1699, which the artist gave to the city of Amsterdam (fig. 11.1); as an oval miniature held by his son, Johannes Bakhuizen; and within this same portrait of his son shown hanging on the back wall is a portrait of his fourth wife, Anna de Hooghe.[4] It was also used, perhaps drawn directly from Gole's version, for the artist's portrait in Houbraken's *De Groote Schouburgh* (fig. 11.2).[5]

The Latin verses below the image in Gole's mezzotint (printed from a separate plate) were written by Bakhuizen's friend, Jan van Broekhuizen, a military functionary for the city of Amsterdam and an amateur poet. The verses are conventional, describing Bakhuizen's ability to rival mighty Nature with his vivid colors. They first make their appearance in a bust-length self-portrait drawing by Bakhuizen from 1698, which was designed as a frontispiece to

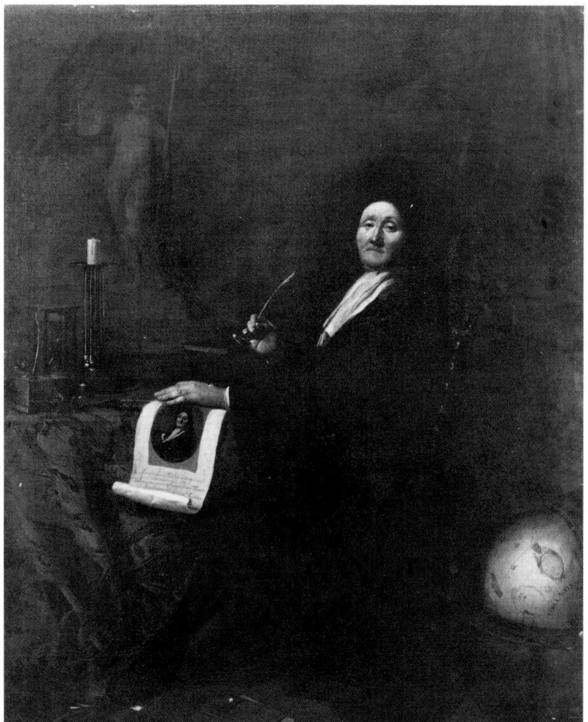

Fig. 11.1 (right). Ludolf Bakhuizen, *Self-Portrait.* 1699. Oil on canvas. Amsterdams Historisch Museum.

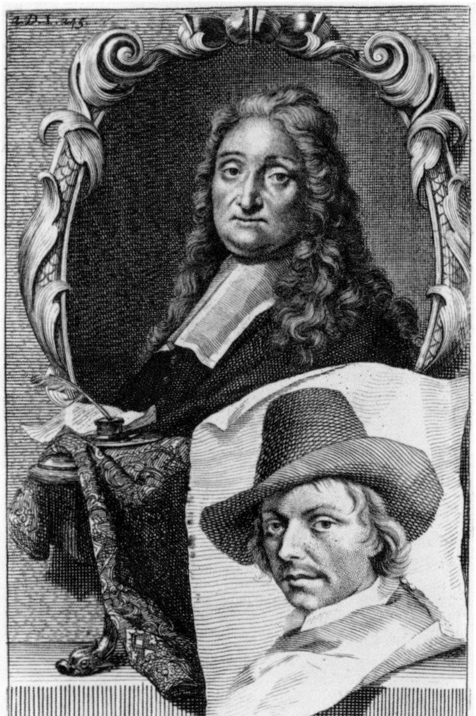

Fig. 11.2 (far right). *Portrait of Ludolf Bakhuizen and Vincent van der Vinne.* From Arnold Houbraken, *De Groote Schouburgh der Nederlantsche Konstschilders en Schilderessen* (volume 2). 1753. Engraving, 145 x 94 mm (5¾ x 3¾ in.). Sarah Campbell Blaffer Foundation, Houston.

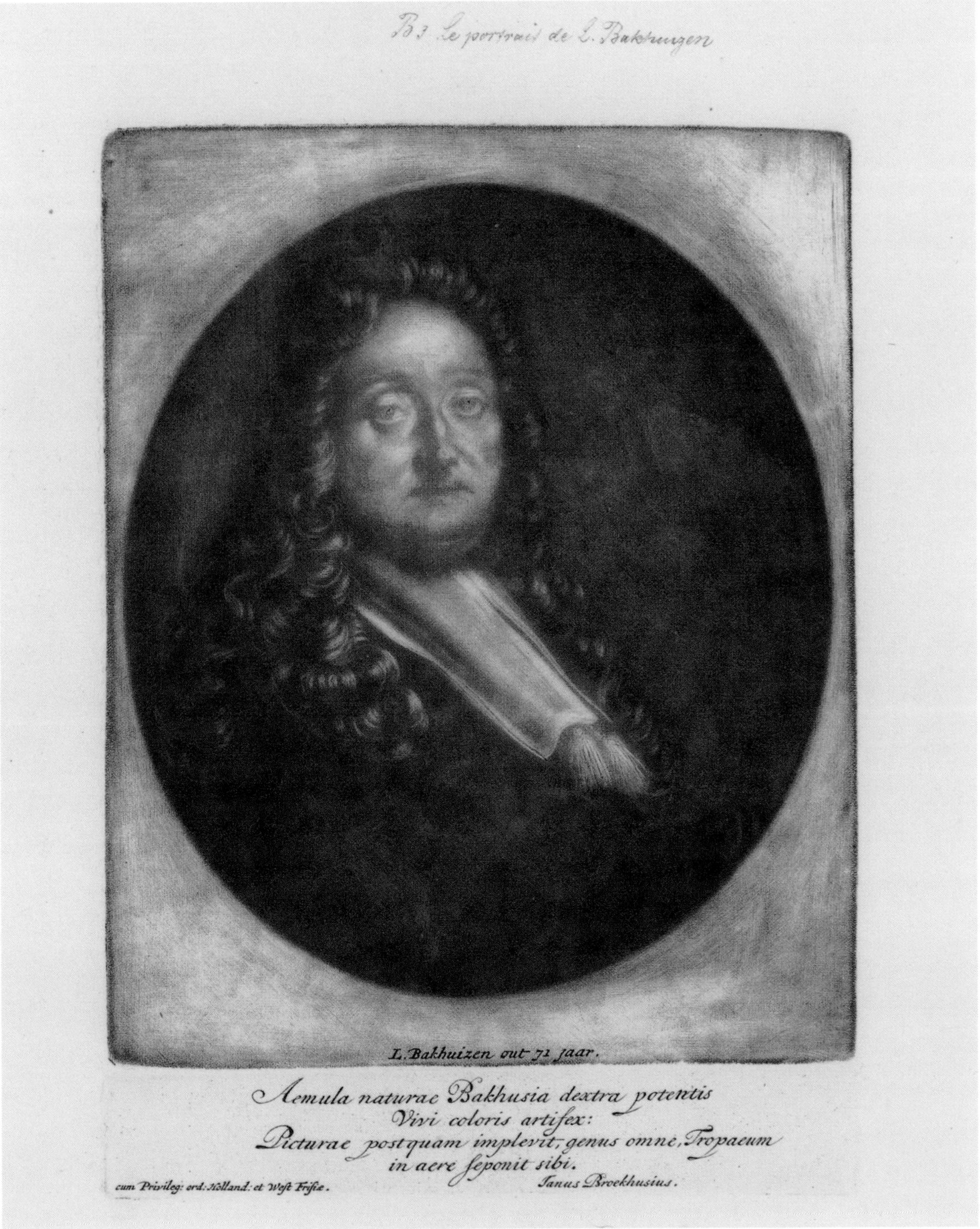
L. Bakhuizen out 71 jaar.
Aemula naturae Bakhusia dextra potentis
Vivi coloris artifex:
Picturae postquam implevit, genus omne, Tropaeum
in aere seponit sibi.
cum Privileg: ord: Holland: et West Frisiæ.
Janus Broekhusius.

Cat. no. 11

an instruction book on drawing that was never published,[6] and then appear again on the fictive print in his full-length portrait of the following year. Van Broekhuizen's comment that the portrait was a kind of trophy in copper (*Tropaeum in aere*) to the completed images made the inscription apt for Gole's print, which was published along with a series of ten etched marine scenes by Bakhuizen, called *D' Y Stroom en zeegezichten geteekent en geetst door Ludolf Bakhuizen Anno 1701 (The River Ij and Seascapes Drawn and Etched by Ludolf Bakhuizen in the Year 1701),* rather than in the unrealized instructional manual.

JC

1. Raupp 1984, 341–42, 497; Broos, Vorstman, and van de Watering 1985, 51, 64, 65, 107.
2. Houbraken 1753, 2:238.
3. Amsterdam, Rijksprentenkabinet, 40:548; see Broos, Vorstman, and van de Watering 1985, 107. Although Bartsch ascribed the mezzotint to Gole, it was thought by Wessely 1889, 111 (following Laborde) to be by Bakhuizen himself; Bakhuizen's printmaking is restricted to the late series of marine etchings (on which, see below), and the mezzotint is now accepted as Gole's work.
4. Rijksmuseum 1976, 96; Broos, Vorstman, and van de Watering 1985, 64, 65.
5. Houbraken 1753, facing 2:245.
6. Broos, Vorstman, and van de Watering 1985, 107–108.

William Hogarth (1697–1764)

12. *Gulielmus Hogarth (Self-Portrait)*

1748/49

Etching and engraving, 380 x 287 mm (15 x 11¼ in.)

Reference: Paulson 181, iv/iv

Inscriptions: on the palette: *The Line of Beauty*; below image: *Gulielmus Hogarth. / Se ipse Pinxit et Sculptsit 1749.*

Purchased from Andrew Edmunds, London

1983.5.89

Although Hogarth returns the viewer's gaze in this self-portrait, he looks out from a canvas within the print—a play on levels of reality rendered common by the eighteenth century in paintings, prints, and book illustrations. Other conventions apply: the swag of drapery, seemingly ubiquitous in Baroque portraiture, and the artist's tools in the foreground, in this instance a graver's burin in the center and a painter's palette at right. Unusual is the presence—prominence, even—of the dog, probably Trump, one of several pugs owned in succession by Hogarth, to which he sometimes compared himself.

Gulielmus Hogarth reproduces (and reverses, excepting the scar on his forehead) a painting now in the Tate Gallery, London, differing in a few, largely inconsequential details.[1] The painting is dated 1745 but seems to have evolved over a considerable period of time. The surface image of Hogarth in working clothes and a Montero cap covers an earlier self-portrait, replete with gold-buttoned waistcoat and wig. It has been suggested that Hogarth transformed the self-portrait after his trip to France in 1743 reminded him of French artists' tendency to portray themselves and their colleagues more casually, along with the tools of their trade, especially in the engraved reception pieces for the Royal Academy of Painting and Sculpture.[2] Hogarth's canvas recalls the oval surround of many of the French artists' portraits, although the latter generally consist of a fictive stone frame. A drape on occasion crosses an edge of the oval, as in Hogarth's composition,[3] which is, however, less provocative conceptually than the many French engravings in which a drape swathing the sitter crosses the bottom of the oval frame into the foreground of the image.[4]

The oval portrait rests on three books. In the painting, they are labeled with the names of William Shakespeare, Jonathan Swift, and John Milton, suggesting Hogarth's reliance on—and equality with—the great English representatives of drama, satire, and epic poetry.[5] But the names are omitted from the engraving, and the books become a more generic part of the composition's still life,

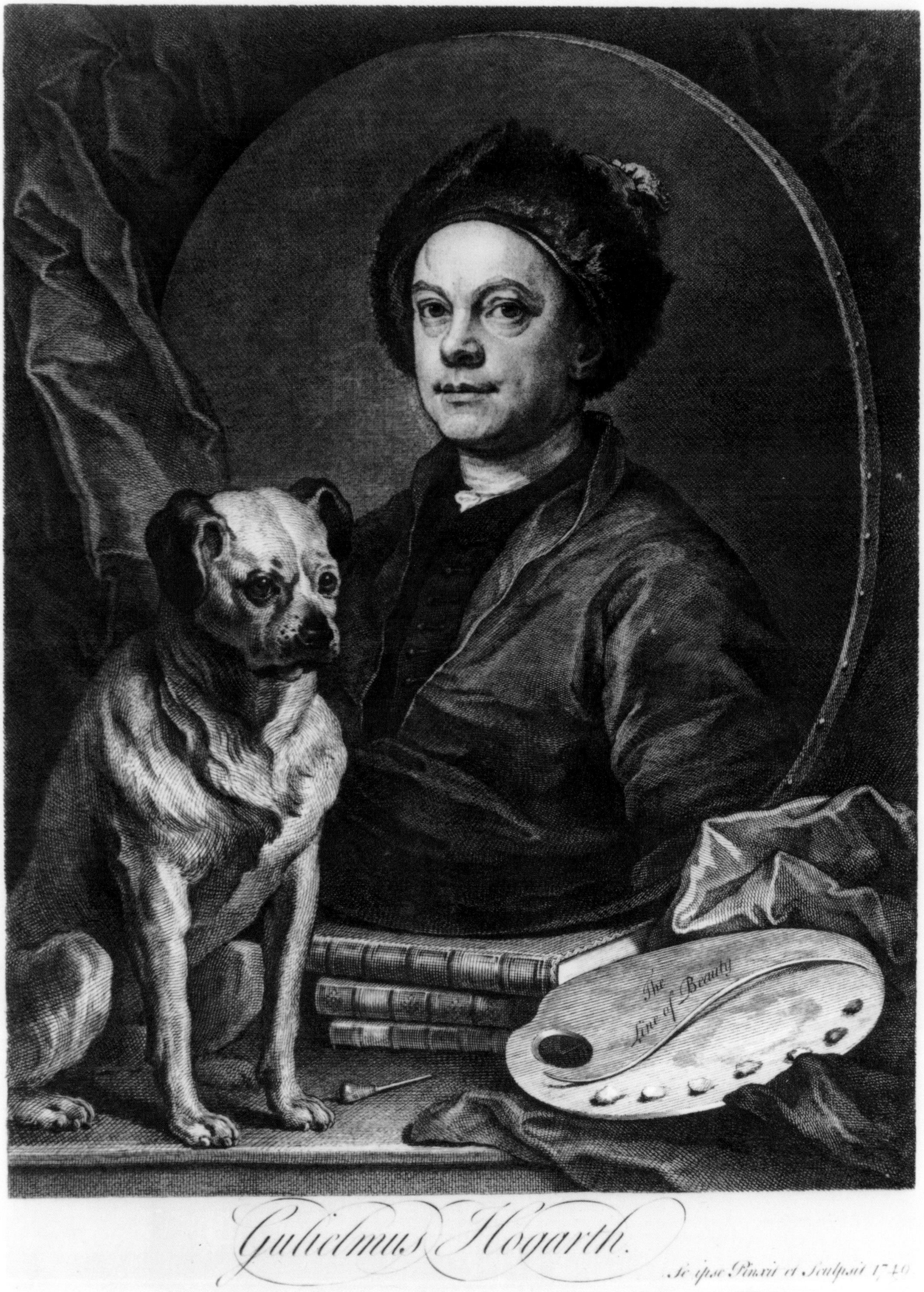
The Line of Beauty
Gulielmus Hogarth.
Se ipse Pinxit et Sculpsit 1749

Cat. no. 12

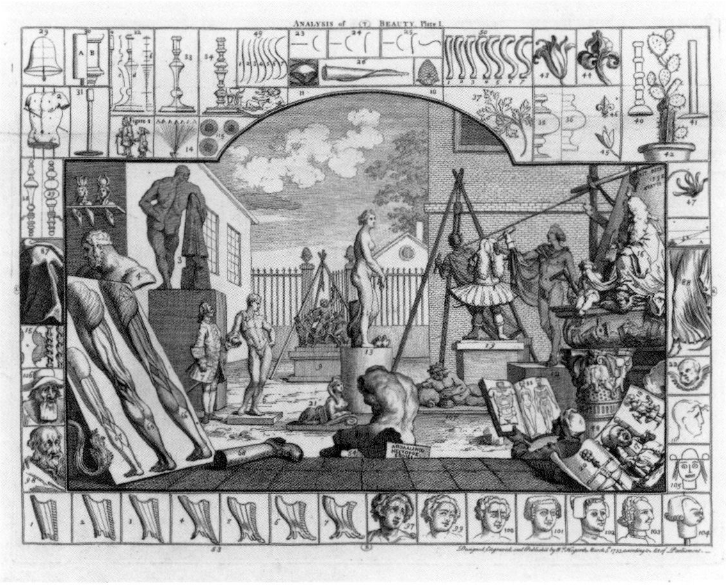

Fig. 12.1. William Hogarth. *The Analysis of Beauty, Plate 1.* March 1753. Etching and engraving, 391 x 505 mm ($15\frac{3}{8}$ x $19\frac{7}{8}$ in.). Sarah Campbell Blaffer Foundation, Houston.

not unlike the books which often appeared in seventeenth-century *vanitas* still lifes as emblems of transitory achievement, except that they literally prop up Hogarth, the painter of modern moral subjects.

On the palette in the foreground is a three-dimensional, serpentine line labeled "The Line of Beauty" (in the painting "and Grace" was appended to the inscription but later covered). It is the first appearance of a theoretical idea that was later elaborated in Hogarth's treatise and prints called *The Analysis of Beauty* (fig. 12.1). At the time of the print, it would seem that Hogarth had included it more for provocation and publicity than as a coherent theoretical statement. In the preface to *The Analysis of Beauty,* he recalls the introduction of the motif: "in the year 1745, [I] published a frontispiece to my engraved works, in which I drew a serpentine line lying on a painter's pallet, with these words under it, THE LINE OF BEAUTY. The bait soon took; and no Egyptian hierogliphic ever amused more than it did for a time, painters and sculptors came to me to know the meaning of it, being as much puzzled with it as other people, till it came to have some explanation; then indeed, but not till then, some found it out to be an old acquaintance of theirs. . . ."[6] Others would not admit acquaintance; as John Ireland noted, "Some called it the line of deformity, and others the line of drunkenness."[7]

As Hogarth indicates, *Gulielmus Hogarth* was used as the frontispiece to the bound folios of his engravings until it was replaced by *Hogarth Painting the Comic Muse* in 1759 (cat. no. 41).[8] Hogarth began making his engravings available in folios in 1737 and continued the practice until his death.

JC

1. On the painting, see Einberg and Egerton 1988, 110–14. Hogarth was careful to keep the scar, which he acquired in his youth and apparently deemed a distinguishing mark, accurately placed in the print; Ireland 1791, cxx, notes, "he frequently wore his hat so as to display it."
2. Einberg and Egerton 1988, 113–14. For examples, see Johnson 1982.
3. E.g., Johnson 1982, 77, 120.
4. Also comparable is Murillo's famous self-portrait in the National Gallery, which was in London already in Hogarth's time. The painting shows an oval portrait of the artist, situated on a tabletop on which also appear a palette and other implements; violating the illusion, the artist places his hand on the lower edge of the oval frame. Curiously, the print made after the painting in 1682 maintains the hand within the confines of the fictive oval canvas. See Royal Academy 1984, 148, 152, 188.
5. Einberg and Egerton 1988, 110. Early in his career, Hogarth had defended native English literature in response to the fashion for continental culture, in the print *Masquerades and Operas (The Bad Taste of the Town)* of 1723/24 (see Paulson 1989, 47–49).
6. Hogarth 1997, 6. The reference to the year 1745 is mistaken; it is the year of the painted self-portrait rather than the engraving.
7. Ireland 1791, 1:lxv.
8. On Hogarth's folios, see Paulson 1995, 39–40. In 1763, Hogarth reworked the plate of *Gulielmus Hogarth,* replacing the self-portrait with a figure of a bear representing his enemy Charles Churchill, thus rendering the original composition, according to Nichols 1785, 295, "very scarce." On the new composition, called *The Bruiser,* see Paulson 1989, 183–85.

GILLES DEMARTEAU (1722–1776)
after Carle Vanloo (1705-1765)

13. *Carle Vanloo, Peintre du Roy, Ecuier*

c. 1759-62

Crayon manner etching printed in brownish red ink, 489 x 364 mm (19¼ x 14⅜ in.)

REFERENCE: Leymarie 35

INSCRIPTIONS: lower right of image: *Carle Vanloo* and *Demarteau l^né*; below image: *CARLE VANLOO PEINTRE DU ROY, ECUIER CHEVALIER DE L'ORDRE DE S. MICHEL, / DIRECTEUR DES ELEVES PROTEGÉS PAR SA MAJESTÉ. / Dedié a Madame Vanloo son Epouse / Par son tres humble et tres Obeissant / Servieur Demarteau l'ainé. / Demarteau l^né Scul. Rue De la Pelterie*; in margin at upper left, handwritten: *N° 35*; below image at lower left, handwritten: *50* (?)

Purchased from Susan Schulman, New York

1999.14

Carle Vanloo came from a Flemish family of artists and, along with Watteau and Boucher, became one of the most celebrated painters in Europe during the reign of Louis XV. Demarteau's portrait reproduces a drawing *aux trois crayons* (in red, black, and white chalks) by Vanloo of 1757, which is now lost.[1] It shows the painter aged about fifty-two, wearing a comfortable *robe de chambre,* buttoned vest, and fur cap. Vanloo is visible from the waist up, standing or sitting behind a stone balustrade, his face animated as he addresses someone to his left, gesturing downward with his left index finger.

The conceit of the stone balustrade in front of Vanloo derives ultimately from Renaissance portraiture, in which there are many well-known examples of people posed behind similar stone sills or parapets. This device was used to set off the person portrayed, either literally by separating them from or elevating them above the viewer, or illusionistically by the contrast between dead stone and living flesh. Often, significant objects were draped over or set upon this ledge. Giorgione, for example, drew himself as the biblical David, resting Goliath's head on a stone sill. In French portrait engravings of the later seventeenth and early eighteenth century, this technique became formalized into a trompe-l'oeil socle or stone shelf situated below the oval framing the portrait bust; it often displayed attributes of the sitter's profession. Here, Vanloo acknowledges this long tradition, using the stone balustrade to set off his right hand, which clasps a chalk holder with dark and light chalks or crayons clamped at either end. That this drawing instrument is held in Vanloo's right hand seems to indicate that Demarteau did not reverse the original drawing in his print. Held in the same hand, or perhaps trailing out of his right sleeve, a white kerchief drapes over the balustrade, reinforcing the illusion of its three-dimensionality and stony hardness.

By including the chalk holder in this apparently informal portrait, Vanloo is telling us two things about himself. First, he is demonstrating membership in the academy of painters, whose art, in an academic sense, must always be based on drawing skill honed over long years of practice. On another level, like a painter who includes a paintbrush in his canvas, he is showing us the exact instrument he used to create the drawing Demarteau engraved, the instrument responsible for his signature sanguine drawings.

The printmaking process Demarteau used here further continues this connection to the original drawing. Crayon-manner etching, an invention that Demarteau claimed, was actually a process he developed with the talented but ultimately ill-starred printmaker Jean-Charles François (1717-1769). This process was based on the use of a wheel called a roulette, a metal-working tool modified and perfected for François by the instrument maker Alexis Magny,[2] which was covered with irregularly placed spikes. The roulette rolled across the ground on an etching plate in close approximation of the grain of a crayon or chalk line on paper. After years of experimentation, François began marketing fine simulations of chalk drawings in 1758. However, shortly after this success, François became absorbed in his invention of a procedure for soft-ground etching, and Demarteau soon outstripped his partner, now turned rival.

Demarteau made more than seven hundred crayon-manner etchings after drawings by the great draftsmen of the day, especially

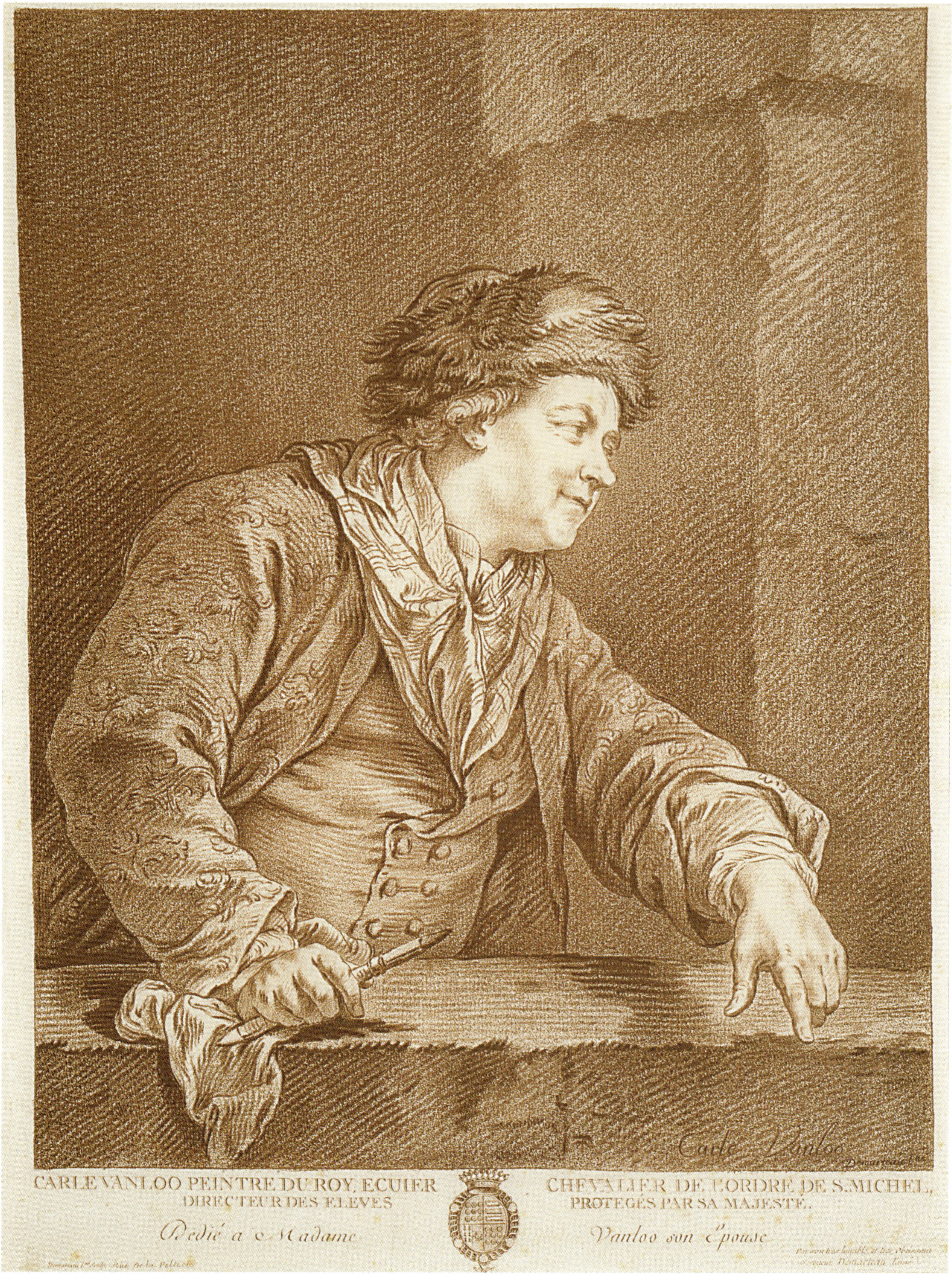
Carle Vanloo
CARLE VANLOO PEINTRE DU ROY, ECUIER CHEVALIER DE L'ORDRE DE S. MICHEL,
DIRECTEUR DES ELEVES PROTEGÉS PAR SA MAJESTÉ.
Dedié a Madame Vanloo son Epouse

Cat. no. 13

Boucher, Huet, and Vanloo. Of the more than thirty etchings Demarteau made after drawings by Vanloo, the vast majority are *académies,* studies of heads, or academic nudes meant for the instruction of drawing students. The crayon-manner technique made the dissemination of these drawings, with a high degree of fidelity, uniquely possible. The genial and informal self-portrait of Vanloo discussed here, with its dedication to Mme. Vanloo, clearly was meant for a different purpose, to trade on the celebrity of the artist. Because Demarteau did not begin consistently producing prints in the crayon-manner technique until around 1759, this portrait etching could not have been created before that date. Combined with the inscription which identifies Vanloo as "Peintre du Roy, Ecuier," making no reference to Vanloo's ultimate rank as *premier peintre du roy,* conferred upon him by Louis XV in 1762, the window for the creation of this print seems to be between 1759 and 1762. Like Vanloo's now-lost self-portrait, the drawings that he provided for the creation of two early crayon-manner etchings, François's *Corps de garde* and Demarteau's *Port de mer,* both date from 1757.[3]

Printmakers like François and Demarteau became assiduous experimenters in an effort to assert the continued relevance of printmaking in the realm of art. This hard work, coupled with the inventive spirit of the Enlightenment, resulted in greater technical advances in printmaking than had been made during any previous century.[4] This rapid progress caused a shift in the relationship between prints and the objects they reproduced. Scholars like George Levitine, who write about the almost total absence of the original artist's print in eighteenth-century France,[5] are indeed not far off the mark, both because of the new emphasis on collecting drawings and the vogue for displaying them, and because new technologies like crayon-manner etching made it possible for prints almost to stand in for drawings. No longer was a skilled engraver responsible for mediating a painting or drawing in black and white through the command of an entire vocabulary of engraved marks suited to different surface textures; instead, chalk drawings, and soon pastels and even paintings, could be faithfully and brilliantly reproduced in full color.

AW

1. Sahut 1977, 152, cat. no. 480.
2. Carlson and Ittmann 1984–85, 132.
3. Dandré-Bardon 1973, 66.
4. Levitine 1984–85, 18.
5. Ibid., 14–15.

Georg Frederic Schmidt (1712–1775)

14. *Self-Portrait*

1752

Etching with engraving, 210 x 172 mm (8¼ x 6¾ in.)

Reference: Wessely 102, ii/ii

Inscriptions: at upper left (in mirror image): *G. F. Schmidt / se ipse fecit / aqua forti / 1752*; below image: *G. F. Schmidt se ipse fec*

Purchased from Susan Schulman, New York, and Carolyn Bullard, Dallas

1999.10

Schmidt appears in bust-length, his arms resting on a table. He wears casual working clothes and seems to have paused in his work, holding the white chalk in a double-ended chalk holder to a sheet of paper. Here the instrument is not simply a professional attribute, as is often the case (see, for example, the nearly contemporaneous portrait of Anton Raphael Mengs, cat. no. 16), but is in use. The artist is working on a head, visible from the top to just below the eyes. It is probably male and possibly a self-portrait, although not as we see the artist here, since the sketched figure is hatless. However, the artist's penetrating gaze, as well as the sense of intimacy established by the nearness of the figure and the forward edge of the table to the picture plane, gives the viewer the impression that he or she is the sitter for the portrait. The disproportionately large head, accentuated by the wide, soft beret, adds to the sense of the artist's intensity.

Schmidt's early career had been spent as an engraver, often of reproductions of portraits. While official court engraver to Frederick the Great of Prussia in Berlin (from 1746), he began producing etchings, including this self-portrait whose medium he names specifically in the inscription at upper left (*aqua forti*), as he also did in his self-portrait of six years later (cat. no. 15). The reversal of the inscription suggests a level of spontaneity that is belied by the dense, though vigorous, working of the plate. The subtleties of direct light, reflected light, and shadow on the face are conveyed with fine cross-hatching, whereas the complicated folds of the garments are executed more broadly, but no less convincingly.

JC

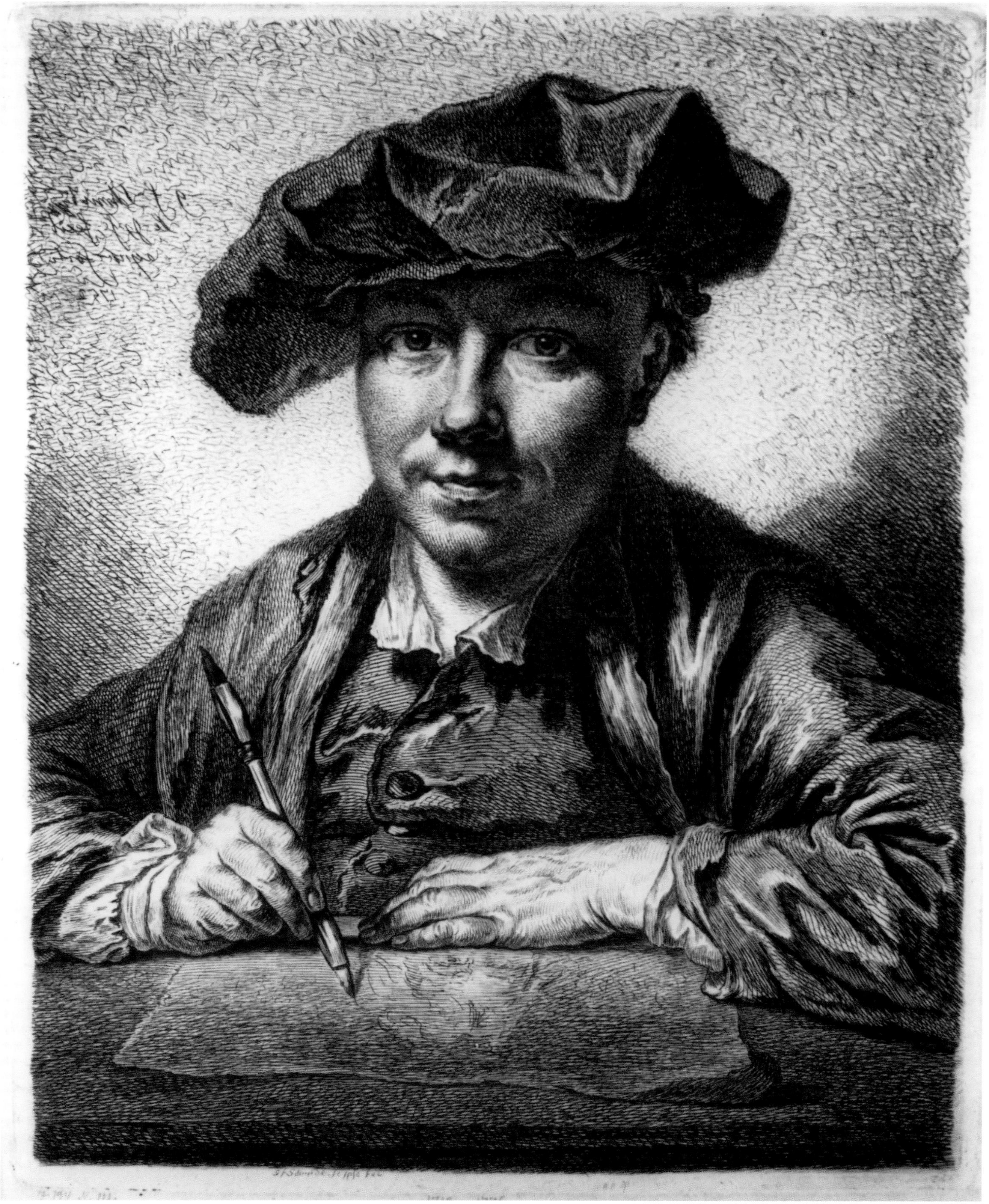
Cat. no. 14

reproduce the warm tonality of the Uffizi painting, and some colors are changed: the brown of the cloak has been replaced with green and the red of the scarf with dark gray. JC

1. On the painting, see Roettgen 1999–2003, 1:339–44.
2. Prinz 1971, 53.
3. Quoted from *La Real Galleria di Firenze,* in Prinz 1971, 230.
4. Quoted by Roettgen 1999–2003, 1:340.
5. Mengs appears with a volume of drawings in several of his self-portraits, from his early thirties to the last years of his life (Museo del Prado 1980, 16; Herzog Anton Ulrich-Museum 1980, 79–81; Rumbler 1993, no. 79; Roettgen 1999–2003, 1:345, 350).
6. Mengs 1787, VII; Fea goes on to call Mengs "un uomo straordinario, un pittor filosofo," with regard to "i suoi raziocinj metafisici sulla bellezza" (p. XI). He was also described as "painter philosopher" on a bronze portrait placed next to Raphael's in the Pantheon (Giuseppe Niccola d'Azara in Mengs 1787, XXIX).
7. In Mengs 1787, XXXVI.
8. Roettgen 1999–2003, 1:333–59.
9. Griffiths and Carey 1994, 15, 17.

Jean-Jacques de Boissieu (1736–1810)

17. *Self-Portrait*

1796

Etching, 380 x 297 mm (15 x 11¾ in.)

Reference: Perez 102, iv/viii

Inscriptions: upper left corner of plate held by artist: *J. J. DB*; lower right corner, below image: *J. J. DB. 1796.*

Purchased from James Bergquist, Boston

1999.1

Dressed in a comfortably bourgeois fashion and leaning on a table, the artist holds an image—a drawing or perhaps a copper plate[1]—of his wife, presenting the portrait to the viewer, whose eyes he meets. On the table are conventional references to his profession: a quill resting in an ink bottle, a chalk holder, a pen knife, a book, and a cast of an ancient sculpture, in this case the head of one of the sons of Laocoön. The classical head, uneasily balanced against the book behind it, seems intrusive, especially since Boissieu specialized in genre scenes and landscapes without direct reference to antiquity, but casts were common props in studios and representations of artists, irrespective of the nature of their own work (for example, see cat. no. 46).

Boissieu portrayed his wife, Anne-Roch Valous (born 1754, married 1773), in prints, drawings, and paintings. In a drawing of 1776, the young wife devotedly places a garland of flowers around a sculptured bust of her husband.[2] Her depicted devotion is requited in the present etching of twenty years later. From the sixteenth century onward, artists—most famously Rubens and Rembrandt—often portrayed themselves with their wives. Occasionally, the artist's wife (or other family member) is represented as a portrait within a self-portrait composition rather than as physically present.[3] The embedded portrait thus functions not only as a tribute to the artist's wife but also as a professional attribute and

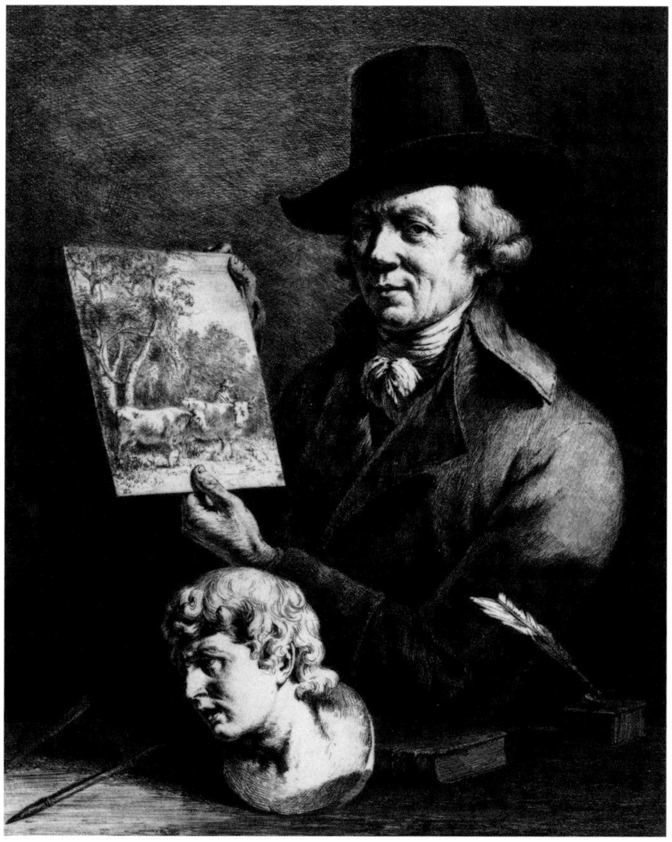

Fig. 17.1. Jean-Jacques de Boissieu. *Self-Portrait.* 1796. Etching, 285 x 228 mm (11¼ x 9 in.). Bibliothèque nationale de France, Paris.

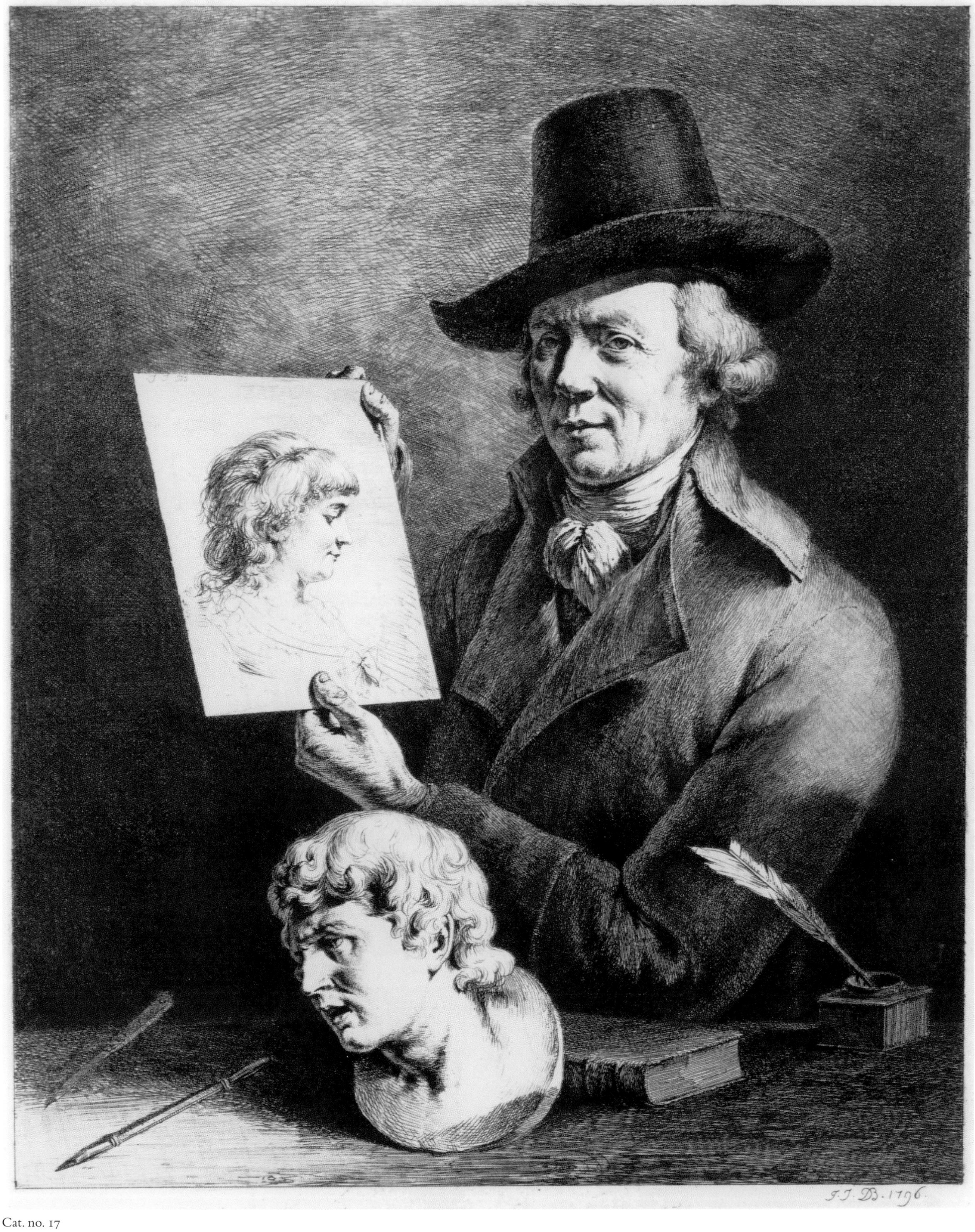

Cat. no. 17

reminder of the traditional notion of art's power to make the absent present.

After the fourth state of this print, Boissieu replaced the portrait of his wife with a landscape with two cows and a figure (fig. 17.1), a composition similar to the artist's etching known as *The Large Cows* (*Les Grandes Vaches*) and recalling Dutch landscapes of the seventeenth century.[4] It has been suggested that the self-portrait is a personal memorial to Boissieu's deceased wife (in this we might think of Sadeler's portrait of Spranger and his late wife, cat. no. 2); that the cast head, whose features, though twisted in anguish, recall Boissieu's own, signifies the widower's mourning; and that the appearance of the landscape in a later state marked the re-engagement of the artist with his art and market.[5] In a drawing for the composition, a more robust Madame de Boissieu appears in three-quarter view, her eyes also directed at the viewer;[6] the change to a profile with downcast eyes might have suggested a commemorative function. But the interpretation—at the very least problematic because of the artist's slight smile—was rejected by Marie-Félice Perez, who noted that Madame de Boissieu outlived her husband by nearly a quarter of a century.[7] It may be that the artist effaced his wife in favor of a bovine subject to refresh the market for the work, to which he was very attentive.[8]

JC

1. In his catalogue of his own works, published in 1801, Boissieu referred to the object as a drawing ("un dessin") (see Perez 1994, 365), in which he was followed by his grandson, Alphonse de Boissieu, in his catalogue raisonné of 1878. Roux 1934, 110, calls it a print, while Jay McKean Fisher in Carlson and Ittmann 1984–85, 310, and Perez 1994 (an edition of the 1878 catalogue), 227, call it a copper plate, reasonably responding to its rigidity and planarity.
2. Musée de l'Ain 1967, 19, and plate IV.
3. For a few examples, see Raupp 1984, 389, 393, 449.
4. Perez 1994, 196, no. 88.
5. Holsten 1978, 90; cf. Carlson and Ittmann 1984–85, 310.
6. Perez 1994, 226.
7. Ibid., 227, 386.
8. Carlson and Ittmann 1984–85, 308–10.

Francisco Goya (1746–1828)

18. *Francisco Goya y Lucientes, Pintor (Self-Portrait)*

1799

Etching, aquatint, drypoint, and burin, 215 x 151 mm (8½ x 6 in.)

Plate I from *Los Caprichos*

References: Delteil 38, iii/iv; Harris 36 III. 1

Inscriptions: upper right: *P. 1*; bottom: *Fran.co Goya y Lucientes Pintor.*

Purchased from R.W. Light & Co., Inc., Santa Barbara, California

1980.13

This self-portrait serves as the title page for Goya's *Caprichos,* the most ingenious and technically accomplished European print series of the eighteenth century. Combining poetic sensibility, devastating wit, a knowledge of Spanish folklore, and a mastery of the dramatic possibilities of the new medium of aquatint, Goya intended in the *Caprichos* to ridicule the follies of people of every social station and to provide an ongoing source for commentary and discussion. Goya depicts himself, dressed fashionably in coat and top hat, in bust length and approaching full left profile—an aloof, "third-person" depiction. This seemingly ordinary portrait serves as a frontispiece in much the same way as the portrait of a poet at the beginning of a book of verse. It also enables Goya to literally express contempt for the ills of society (including his own role in them, as we will see) as a member of the *ilustrados,* the intellectual cadre of the Spanish Enlightenment, who aimed to help cure them through pointing them out.

One of the most prominent aspects of the portrait is Goya's black beaver hat, which immediately draws the eye. It is a deliberate inclusion and a clue to seeing the portrait in the tradition of other artists' portraits that Goya knew. This is not a functional piece of headgear like the squat cylindrical hat with a metal armature to hold candles for night painting that Goya wears in his small 1798 self-portrait canvas (now in Madrid).[1] Rather, it is an element of style that connotes the gentlemanly status of the artistic profession. In this respect, Goya was also probably referring to the self-portrait etchings of Rembrandt. Goya once stated that he had had

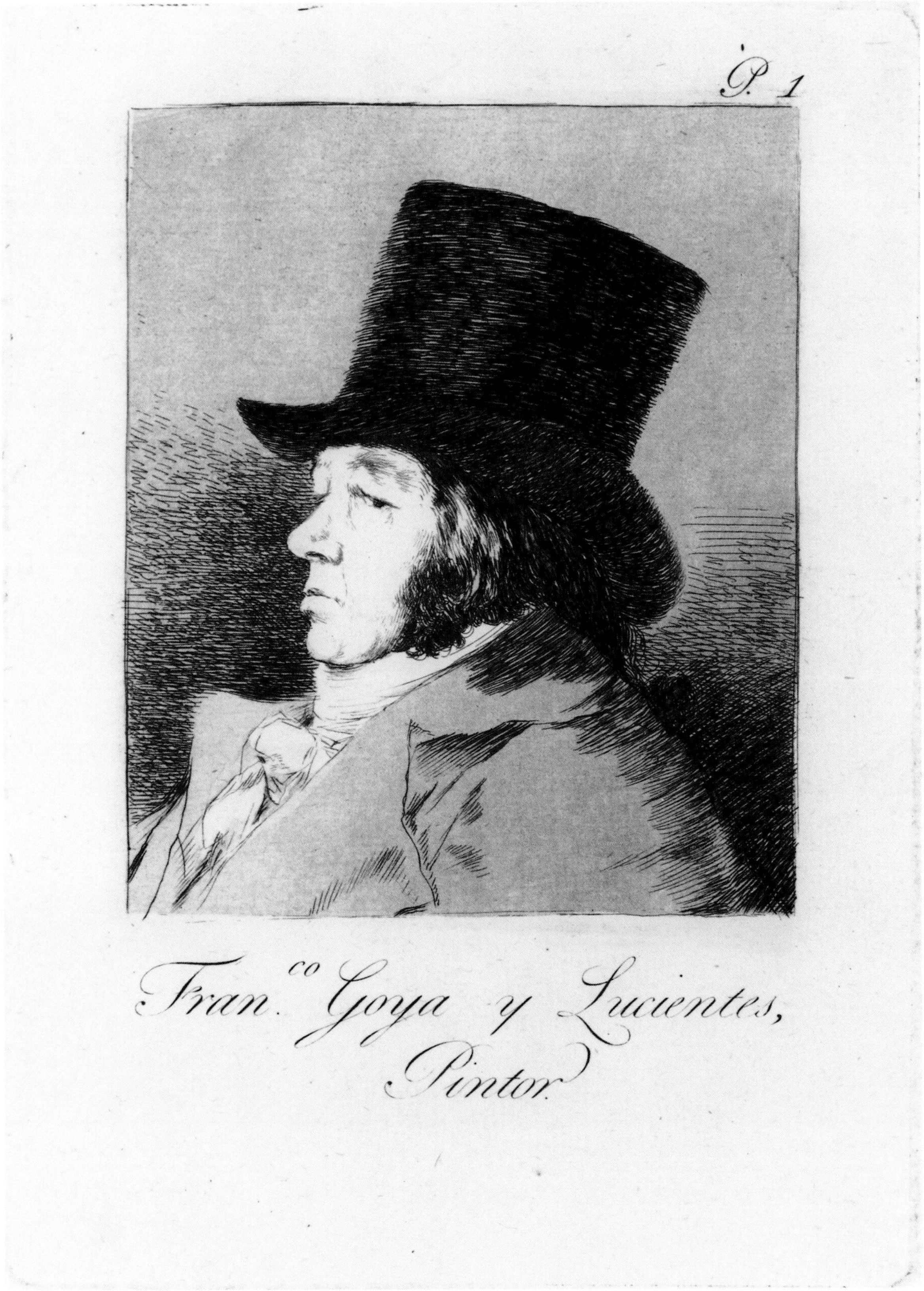

Cat. no. 18

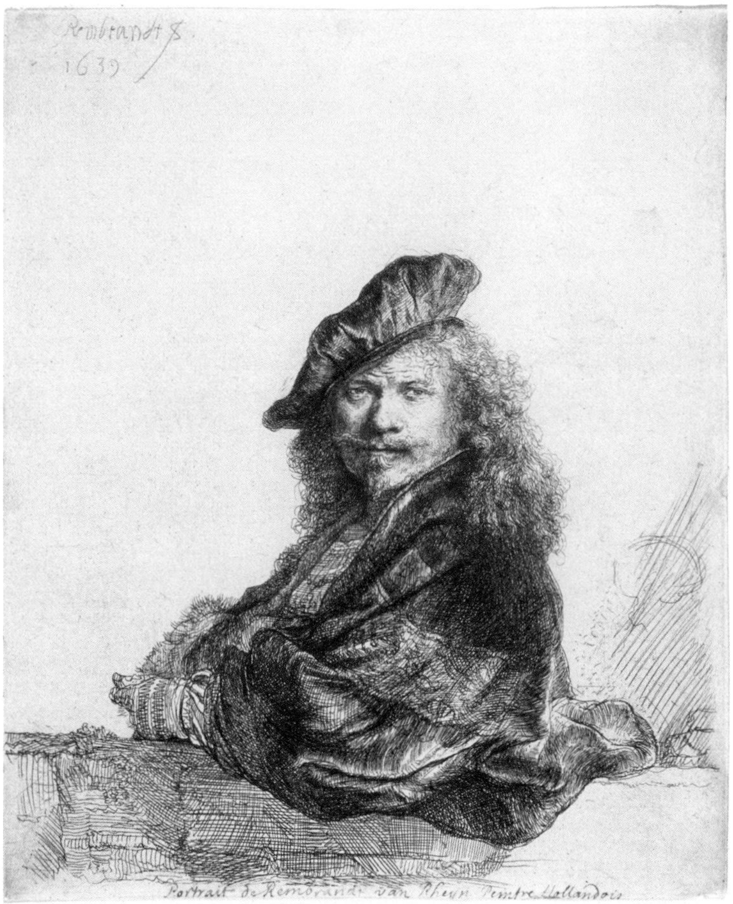

Fig. 18.1. Rembrandt van Rijn. *Self-Portrait Leaning on a Stone Sill.* 1639. Etching on laid, 200 x 162 mm (7⅞ x 6⅜ in.). Courtesy of the Herbert F. Johnson Museum of Art, Cornell University; bequest of William P. Chapman, Jr., class of 1895.

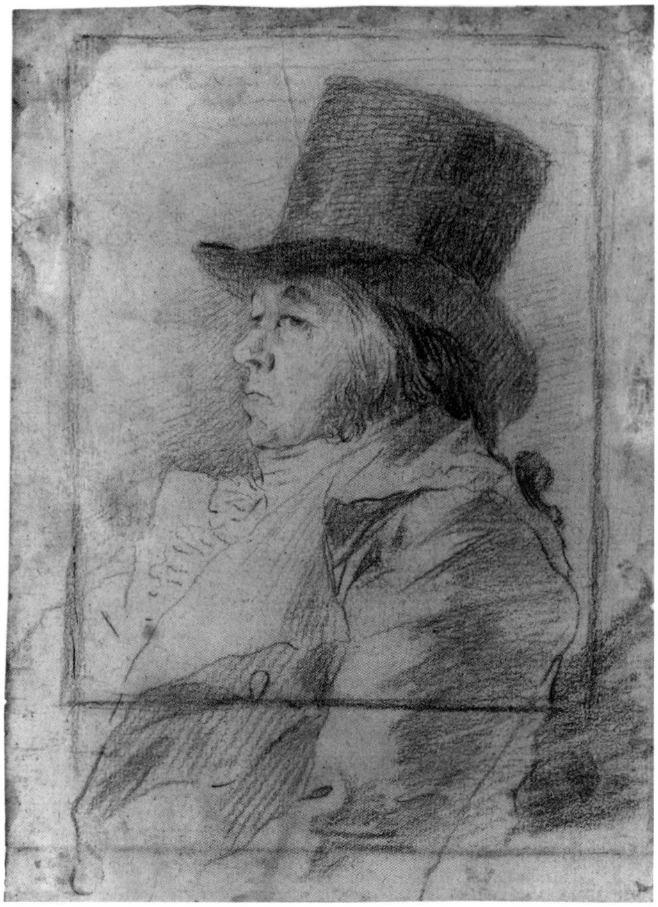

Fig. 18.2. Francisco Goya. *Portrait of the Artist.* Red chalk, 200 x 143 mm (7⅞ x 5⅝ in.). The Metropolitan Museum of Art; bequest of Walter C. Baker, 1971 (1972.118.295R).

"no other masters than Nature, Velázquez, and Rembrandt"[2]—an oft-quoted avowal, but one still valid for understanding the importance he assigned to Rembrandt's work. Goya had several opportunities to view Rembrandt prints, most notably in the collection of his good friend the poet Agustín Ceán Bermudez, whose love of collecting is underlined in Goya's portrait of him by a stack of prints displayed prominently on the table at his side.[3] Ceán recorded that he gave Goya a group of Rembrandt etchings when he was working on the *Caprichos*.[4] As a group, Goya's nearly forty known self-portraits, in their variety of media, dress, relationship to the viewer, and emotional affect, show a debt to Rembrandt, who himself returned constantly to his own likeness to express a range of ideas.

Perhaps most influential on Goya's self-portrait in plate I of *Caprichos* may have been etchings like Rembrandt's *Self-Portrait Leaning on a Stone Sill* of 1639 (fig. 18.1), which Goya could have known, for example, in the collection of Eugenio Izquierdo de Ribera y Lezuan, which though formed in Paris was brought to Madrid sometime before 1808.[5] In this portrait, Rembrandt presents himself as a Renaissance gentleman, modeling his sumptuous mantle and rakish beret on those in portraits by Raphael and Titian he sketched when he saw them at auction in Amsterdam. In so doing, Rembrandt was not only comparing himself to the great painters he admired, but making a statement about the exalted status of painting and his membership in an artistic elite. Perhaps Goya's gentlemanly appearance and stylish hat in the frontispiece of the *Caprichos* is a similar acknowledgment. Other Rembrandt self-portraits in Renaissance dress that Goya could have known include Bartsch numbers 26, 19, 20, and 17, all of which appear on the same page of Pierre-François Basan's bound edition of eighty-five restrikes of Rembrandt plates,[6] of which Ceán owned a copy.

The other major area of scholarly discussion of this portrait has been Goya's facial expression. Some art historians have seen, in the narrowed eyes, the jutting lower lip, and the slight upturn of the head, an expression of *mépris,* or contempt, according to the canon of facial expressions established by the French academic painter Charles Le Brun.[7] In addition, some contemporary reactions to the portrait read the facial expression as "satirical (*satirico*)" or malign (*maligno*)."[8] But what seems clear at the very least is that this is a sober depiction, meant to engender a serious reading of the works that follow it. Such an affect

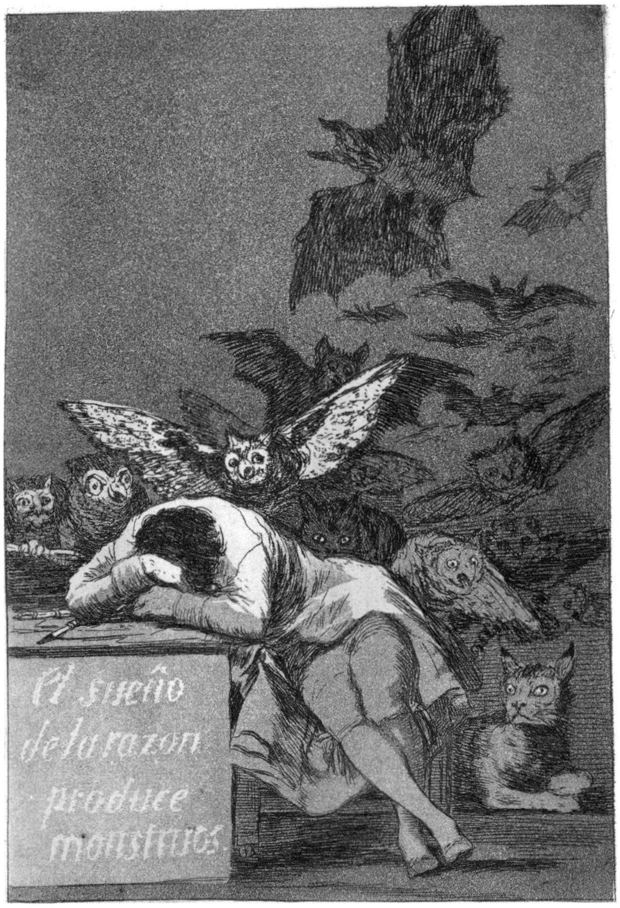

Fig. 18.3. Francisco Goya. *El sueño de la razón produce monstruos (The sleep of reason produces monsters)* Plate 43 of *Los Caprichos.* c. 1797. Etching and aquatint, 181 x 122 mm (7⅛ x 4¾ in.). Courtesy of the Herbert F. Johnson Museum of Art, Cornell University; Membership Purchase Fund.

would set an appropriate tone for a series of images whose expressed intent, as stated in the advertisement for *Los Caprichos* that appeared in the *Diario de Madrid* on February 6, 1799, was "the denunciation of human errors and vices (la censura de los errores y vicios humanos)." Goya's study in sanguine for the *Caprichos* plate I self-portrait, now in New York (fig. 18.2), includes the entire chest and the left arm down to the elbow. Goya, however, has sketched in a rectangle that crops the portrait down to its presentation in *Caprichos* plate I. The effect is to focus one's attention more on the profile and its expression, which Goya accentuates in the etching with an area of heavy, contrasting hatching adjacent to the face.

Even if Goya did intend to express a disdainful attitude, there is also a distance and haughtiness befitting a figure of importance. This self-portrait is not intended to elucidate the sitter's character, but rather to lend an air of mystery to the author of the *Caprichos.* By juxtaposing his respectable haberdashery and proud appearance with the moniker "Pintor," Goya seems to claim a legitimacy historically accorded to literary figures in Spain.[9] Indeed, the author of the *Diario de Madrid* announcement (most likely either Goya or his friend Ceán) brings up this very relationship:

> . . . Painting (like poetry) chooses from the universal that which it deems suited to its own ends: it reunites in a single fantastic personage circumstances and characteristics that nature has divided among many, and from this skillfully articulated combining comes the felicitous image by which a good craftsman attains the title of creator . . .[10]

Furthermore, the Spanish scientist Gregorio Gonzales Azaola, writing in the *Semanario patriòtico* of Cadiz in 1811, described the *Caprichos* as "80 engraved moral poems,"[11] a label that resonates with the advertisement in the *Diario de Madrid.* And Goya himself strengthened the literary connection of the *Caprichos* by captioning the second print of the series, directly after his self-portrait, with two lines from a satirical work by the poet Gaspar Melchor de Jovellanos.[12]

The poetic nature of the images and the positioning of Goya's self-portrait as a frontispiece further emphasize the associations with the printed book that Goya had already intended through the intimate size and sequential nature of the series, as well as through the interplay of images and captions. Goya was certainly aware of the publication of English satires in bound book format, as he offered the *Caprichos* for sale only as a complete set and not as individual sheets.[13]

One final point about this self-portrait pertains not directly to it, but to the fact that Goya initially intended the series to begin with a different image, which further demonstrates his grounding in a poetic sensibility. Through the mid-1790s, Goya's idea seems to have been to create a series called *Sueños,* or dreams, an idea he took from the *Sueños* of Francisco de Quevedo y Villegas, the seventeenth-century poet, a series of satirical visions of the various inhabitants of hell.[14] The title page for this series was to have been *El sueño de la razón produce monstruos (The sleep [or dream] of reason produces monsters)* (fig. 18.3). In the *Caprichos,* this composition, which shows the artist asleep at his desk assailed by bats and owls, became plate 43, the approximate midpoint of the series, immediately after which the subject matter turns from predominantly satirical to demonic and truly horrifying.

AW

1. Perez Sanchez and Sayre 1989, 41.
2. As quoted in Rose-de Viejo and Cohen 2000, 14.
3. Rose-de Viejo 2000, 18.
4. Ibid., 34.
5. Ibid., 78.
6. Basan c. 1789-97.
7. Perez Sanchez and Sayre 1989, cat. no. 38, p. 84.
8. Ibid., 86.
9. Ciofalo 2001, 65.
10. Translation in Montreal Museum of Fine Arts 2001, 27.
11. Wolf 1991, 18.
12. Ibid., 29.
13. Ibid., 30.
14. Perez Sanchez and Sayre 1989, xcviii.

Alexandre Clément
after Louis-Léopold Boilly (1761-1845)

19. *Réunion d'artistes*

1804

Stipple engraving, 504 x 384 mm (19⅞ x 15⅛ in.) (trimmed), with an engraved key, 442 x 373 mm (17⅜ x 14⅝ in.)

Inscriptions: *Peint par Boilly en 1800. Deposé à la Bibliotheque. Gravé par A. Clement. / RÉUNION D'ARTISTES / Dédiée aux Amateurs des Arts. / Tirée du Cabinet de Monsieur Bouillier. / À Paris chez l'Auteur, Cloitre des Bernardins Q [?].ion des Plantes N.o 136. & à l'Entrepôt de Thé, Rue des fossés Montmartre, N.o 6. / Imprimé par Bassand.* Engraved key: *Reunion d'Artistes. / Messieurs. / 1. . . . Corbet Sculpteur. / 2. . . . . Chenard Artiste du Théatre Italien. / 3. . . . Boilly Peintre de genre auteur du Tableau. / 4. . . . Percier Architecte de S. M. L'Empereur. / 5. . . . Bidault Peintre du Paysages. / 6. . . . Talma Artiste du Theatre Français / 7. . . . . Thiebaut Peintre et Architecte. / 8. . . . . Girodet Peintre d'Histoire. / 9. . . . Isabey Peintre des Relations Exterieures. / 10. . . . Drolling Peintre de genre. / 11 Baptiste ainé Artiste du Théatre Français. / 12. . . Swebach dit Fontaine Peintre de Batailles. / 13. . . Van-dael Peintre de Fleurs. / 14. . Mehul Compositeur de Musique. / 15. . . Le Thierre Peintre d'Histoire. / 16. . . Taunay Peintre de Paysages. / 17. . . Bourgeois Peintre en Miniatures. / 18 . . . Serangeli Peintre d'Histoire. / 19. . Le Mot Sculpteur / 20. . . Redouté Peintre de Fleurs / 21. . . Ménié Peintre d'Histoire. / 22. . . Chaudet Sculpteur. / 23. . . Fontaine Architecte de S. M. L'Empereur / 24. . De Marne Peintre de Paysages. / 25. . . Blot Graveur d'Histoire. / 26. . . C.les Vernet Peintre de Batailles. / 27. . . Bertault Graveur de Batailles / 28 . . . Hoffman Homme de Lettre. / 29. . . Gerard Peintre d'Histoire. / Deposée à la Bibliothèque en l'An 13.*

Purchased from Andrew Edmunds, London

2000.4.1-2

Compressed in an oval composition and set among clouds are the busts and heads of twenty-nine fashionable men in Paris at the turn of the nineteenth century: seventeen painters, three sculptors, three actors, two architects, two engravers, one composer, and one man of letters. Boilly himself appears at the top of the composition, between two figures wearing hats, looking out at the viewer. According to the inscription, Alexandre Clément's engraving is a copy of a painting by Louis-Léopold Boilly from 1800, although the painting is not now known.[1] The print is accompanied by an engraved key dated the thirteenth year of the French Revolution (1804-1805),[2] which names the figures and indicates their profession and, for the painters, their specialty: history, landscape, battle scenes, and so on.

The composition must be seen in conjunction with Boilly's most ambitious and famous group portrait, *A Reunion of Artists in Isabey's Studio* (fig. 19.1), exhibited in the Paris Salon of 1798. The painting includes thirty-one portraits, almost all of which are included in Clément's print,[3] which reproduces the busts and heads as they appear in the painting (reversed by the printing process), arranged so that they generally face toward the edges of the group. An important subset of Boilly's work consisted of representations of artists—both specific and generic—in their studios. With such works, and especially with *Isabey's Studio,* Boilly exalted the figure of the artist, in an elegant setting in which no manual labor is taking place, as sophisticated, cultured, and fashionable—"a new kind of cultural hero."[4] *Isabey's Studio* stirred considerable public interest upon its exhibition at the Salon, particularly in the identities and appearance of the figures.[5] Boilly's production of the oval painting shortly thereafter was presumably in response to the popularity of *Isabey's Studio* and may well have been intended from the beginning as a model for an engraving for wider distribution, although the latter was not produced until several years later. The success of *Isabey's Studio,* on which the oval composition relies, was instrumental in advancing Boilly's career as a portraitist.[6]

Susan Siegfried has argued that *Isabey's Studio* functioned to acquaint potential private patrons, on whom artists increasingly had to depend as public patronage diminished, with a new generation of artists, and has noted that Clément's print is pointedly dedicated to "Amateurs of the Arts"[7]—an attempt to cultivate new patrons as well as appeal to established ones. Boilly's oval composition does more than simply condense *Isabey's Studio* for quick

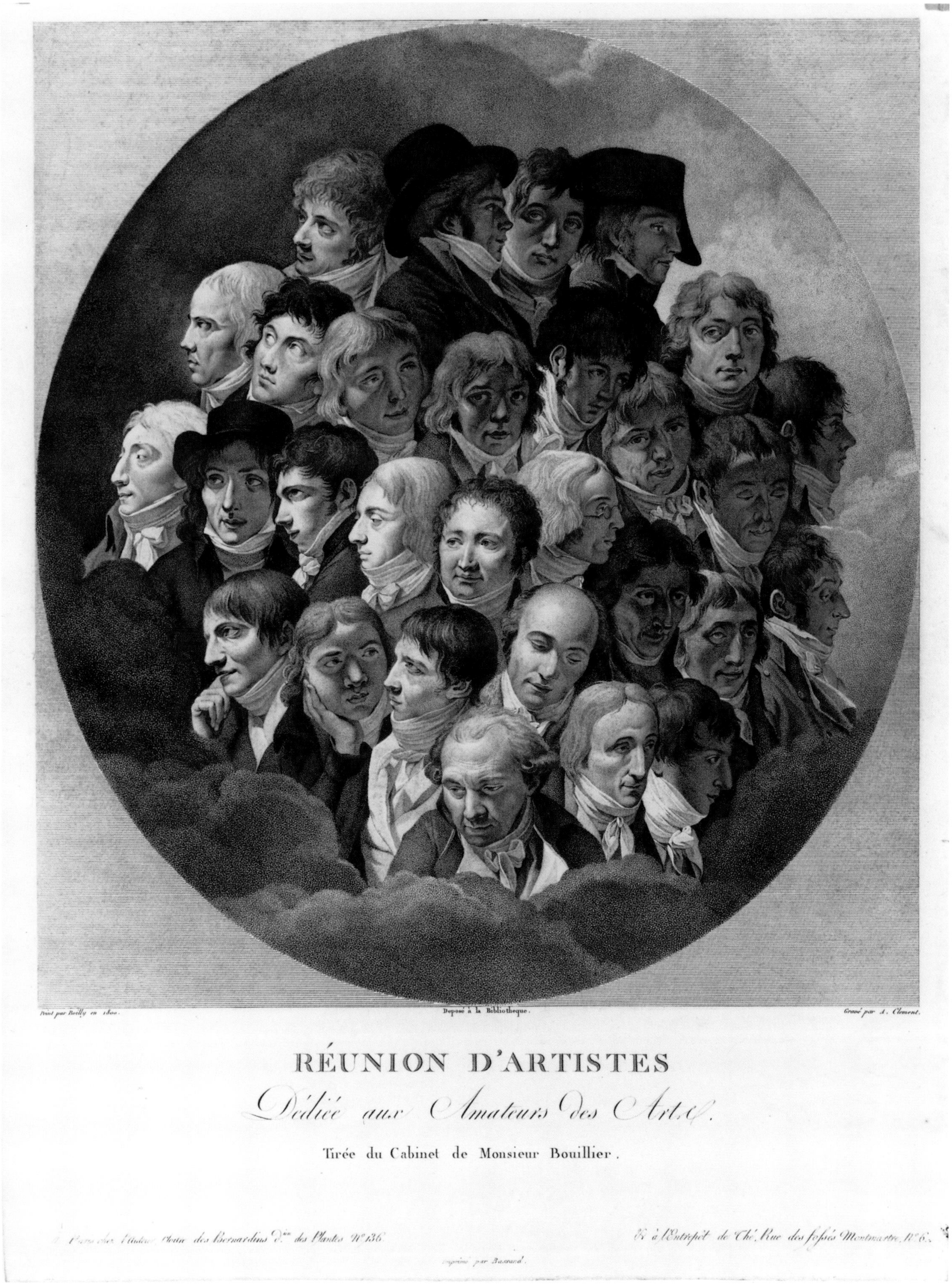
Peint par Boilly en 1800.
Deposé à la Bibliotheque.
Gravé par A. Clement.
RÉUNION D'ARTISTES
Dédiée aux Amateurs des Arts.
Tirée du Cabinet de Monsieur Bouillier.
imprimé par Bassand.

Cat. no. 19

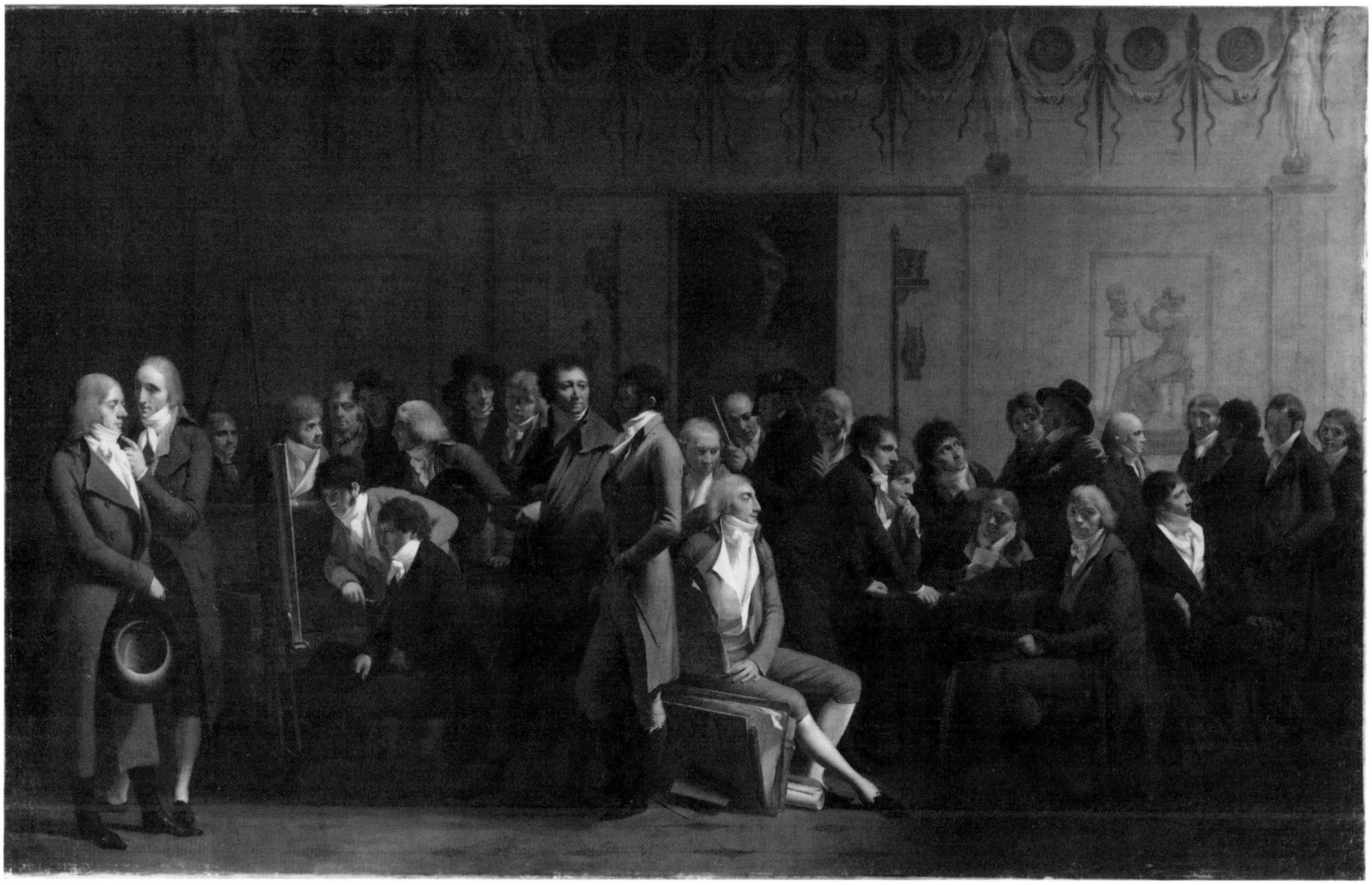

Fig. 19.1. Louis L. Boilly. *A Reunion of Artists in Isabey's Studio.* 1798. Oil on canvas, 71.5 x 111 cm (28⅛ x 43¾ in.). Musée du Louvre, Paris.

reference, however. By removing traces of genre or the pseudorealism of a conversation piece and replacing the isocephalic composition with one in which the figures are stacked in the clouds like angels and saints in a late medieval celestial hierarchy, Boilly, in a virtually unprecedented image, creates a pantheon of current creativity.

JC

1. The "Monsieur Bouillier" named as the owner of the painting in the engraving's inscription is otherwise not known. The painting may have later belonged to Boilly's friend and relative, the poet Antoine Vincent Arnault (1766–1834) (Laveissière 1988, 59–60).
2. According to Laveissière 1988, 60, 82, it was the appearance of the print which occasioned comments on *Isabey's Studio* in the *Le Moniteur universel* newspaper of November 15, 1804. As Laveissière 1988, 84, points out, the key may not have been engraved by Clément.
3. On the painting, the identification of the figures, and associated works, see Laveissière 1988, 52–84. For unknown reasons, Clément's print includes neither Pierre Paul Prud'hon nor Jean-Baptiste Jacques Augustin (Laveissière's nos. 3 and 31, respectively). Also, the identification of Pierre Gabriel Berthault in *Isabey's Studio,* based on his appearance in Clément's print (no. 27), is rejected by Laveissière 1988, 56 (no. 14), in favor of Jean Duplessi-Bertaux on the basis of a self-portrait of the latter. Both Berthault and Duplessi-Bertaux were engravers of battle scenes, as described in Clément's print. If Laveissière's identification is correct, Pierre Gabriel Berthault would be the only person represented in Clément's print but not in *Isabey's Studio.*
4. Siegfried 1995, 96; in this, as Siegfried points out, the painting recalls Zoffany's *The Academicians of the Royal Academy* (see cat. no. 28). The sitters are, for the most part, fairly young but not at the beginning of their careers, with an average age of thirty-five (Laveissière 1988, 61, citing a study by P. Bordes).
5. Siegfried 1995, 100.
6. Ibid., 101.
7. Ibid., 100–101.

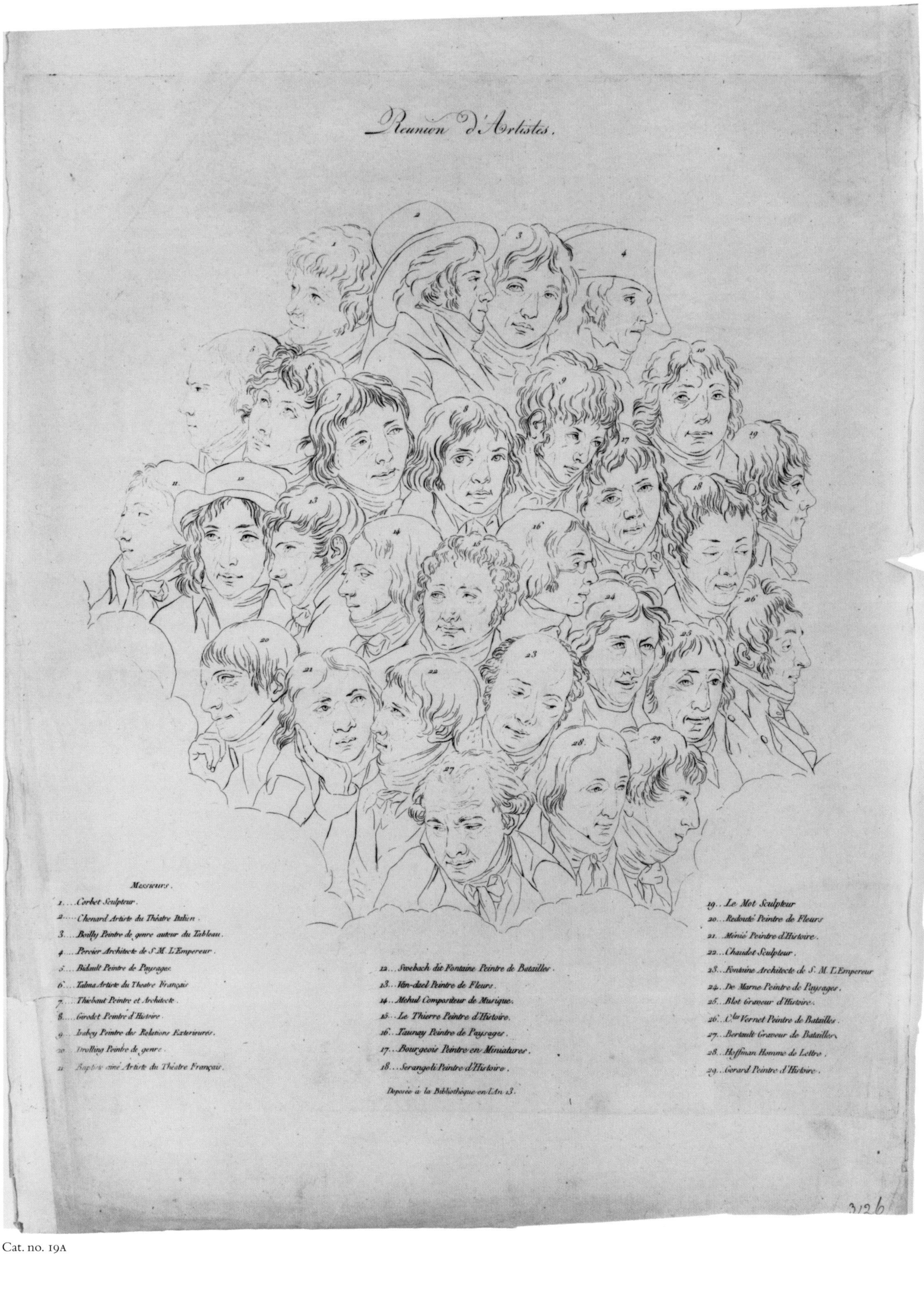
Reunion d'Artistes.
Messieurs.
1... Corbet Sculpteur.
2.... Chenard Artiste du Théatre Italien.
3... Boilly Peintre de genre auteur du Tableau.
4... Percier Architecte de S. M. L'Empereur.
5... Bidault Peintre de Paysages.
6... Talma Artiste du Theatre Français
7... Thiebaut Peintre et Architecte.
8.... Girodet Peintre d'Histoire.
9... Isabey Peintre des Relations Exterieures.
10. Drolling Peintre de genre.
11. Baptiste ainé Artiste du Théatre Français.
12... Swebach dit Fontaine Peintre de Batailles.
13.. Van-dael Peintre de Fleurs.
14.. Mehul Compositeur de Musique.
15... Le Thierre Peintre d'Histoire.
16.. Taunay Peintre de Paysages.
17.. Bourgeois Peintre en Miniatures.
18... Serangeli Peintre d'Histoire.
Deposée à la Bibliothéque en l'An 13.
19.. Le Mot Sculpteur
20... Redouté Peintre de Fleurs
21... Ménié Peintre d'Histoire.
22... Chaudet Sculpteur.
23... Fontaine Architecte de S. M. L'Empereur
24.. De Marne Peintre de Paysages.
25... Blot Graveur d'Histoire.
26.. C.les Vernet Peintre de Batailles.
27.. Bertault Graveur de Batailles.
28.. Hoffman Homme de Lettre.
29.. Gerard Peintre d'Histoire.
3126

Cat. no. 19A

Francesco Hayez (1791–1882)

20. *Self-Portrait*

c. 1828–30

Lithograph, 471 x 382 mm (18½ x 15 in.) (sheet size)

Inscription: lower center: *HAYEZ*; possibly traces of illegible inscription below the name in manuscript

Purchased from Hill-Stone, New York

2000.17

Francesco Hayez, the successful Italian history painter and portraitist, painted numerous self-portraits over the course of his very long career. Two of the relatively early ones are rather unusual, depicting himself with a group of friends in 1827, and with a tiger and a lion in 1831.[1] His personal appearance in the latter most resembles this undated lithographic self-portrait, which probably dates from around the same period. In both he sports long sideburns (he wore a full beard beginning at least in the late 1840s) and wears a large black velvet beret. Here he holds in his right hand a chalk holder pointing at his name inscribed on the desk.[2]

Hayez was not a prolific printmaker and, unlike his contemporaries, he worked directly on the lithographic stone himself rather than having his designs translated by someone else. His most fertile period of lithography was the late 1820s, when the Milanese Giuseppe Vassalli published a number of his works, especially an acclaimed series from 1828 consisting of sixteen scenes from *Ivanhoe,* half-length figures of four of the characters in the novel, a portrait of Sir Walter Scott, and a self-portrait.[3] The present self-portrait may also have been produced in conjunction with Vassalli, but it lacks Vassalli's address found on the other lithographs. In this impression, the design has been extended downward from the artist's name in lithographic crayon, presumably by Hayez himself, which suggests that it may be a proof and that the artist was considering altering the image, although he seems not to have made the change on the stone. The number of impressions may not have been numerous: one carries a manuscript note from the artist that it was his last one, which he gives with pleasure to a certain Signor Rivolta, presumably the Milanese Francesco Eugenio Rivolta, for whom Hayez painted in 1834 an episode from the war of Greek independence.[4]

JC

1. Mazzocca 1994, 186, 209.
2. Hayez's appearance is also very similar in another, undated lithograph self-portrait, in which he draws with the same instrument on sheets on a portfolio in his lap (Milan, Civica Raccolta Stampe A. Bertarelli).
3. Nicodemi 1962, vol. 2, plates 298–304; Gozzoli and Mazzocca 1983, 349–51; Mazzocca 1994, 190–91.
4. Nicodemi 1962, vol. 1, plate IV; Mazzocca 1994, 241.

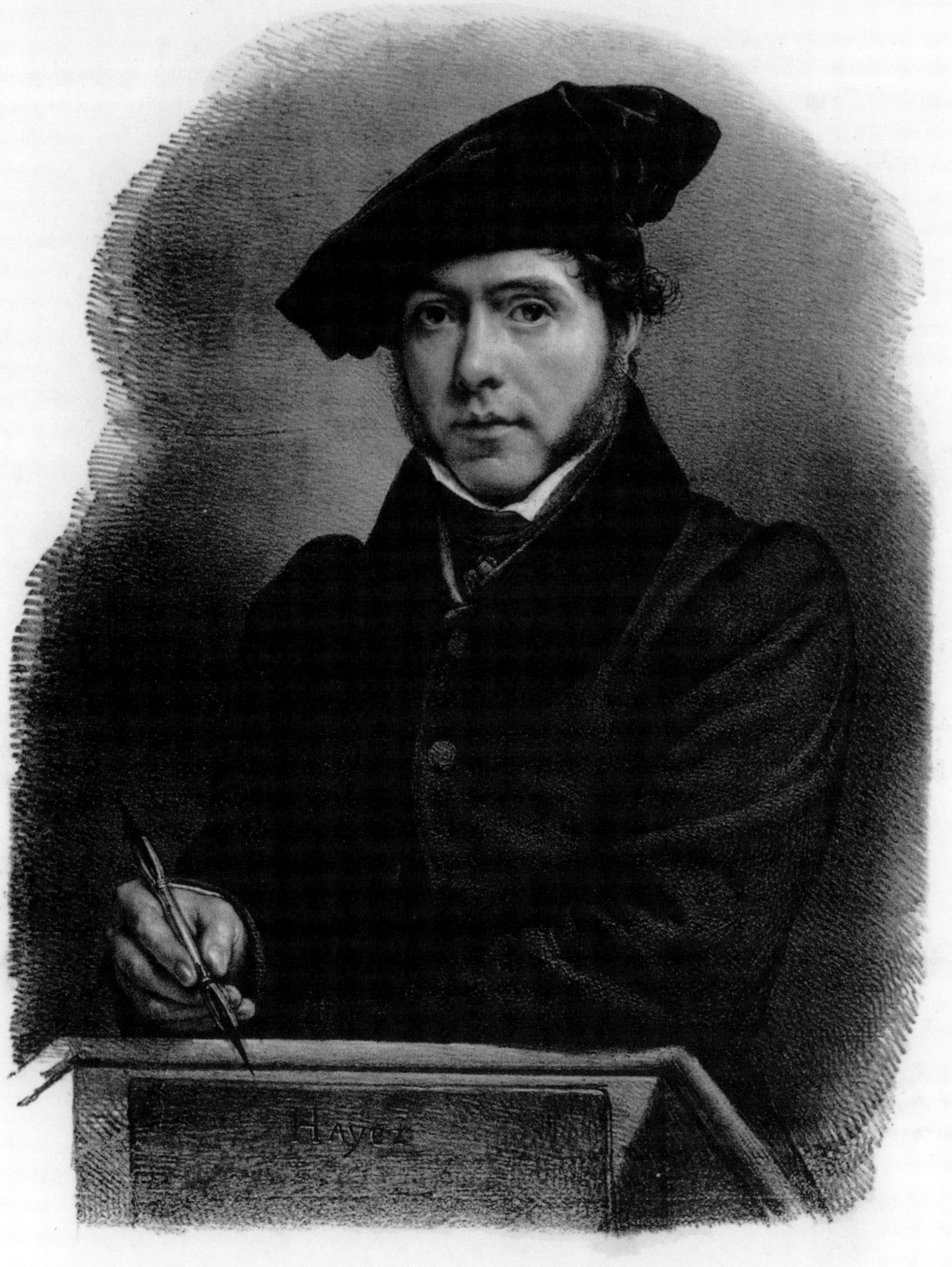

Cat. no. 20

WORK

Agostino [Carracci], beyond his excellence in the arts of drawing, painting, and engraving, also had a particular ability in speaking well on any subject, and especially on his profession. . . . A group of gentlemen found themselves in the rooms [of Agostino and his brother Annibale], and Agostino was discussing with great knowledge ancient statues, and he paused to celebrate especially the Laocoon, which they had recently seen. He would have liked Annibale to have said something about it, but the latter, who was very different from his brother in genius, in taste, and in how much discoursing pleased him, . . . seemed almost as if he held in very little regard this discourse of his brother. Whereby Agostino took offense and with resentment made fun of Annibale, as if to show that he didn't appreciate the study that they proposed to make of ancient statues . . ., since it seemed that Annibale, as if caring little, had forgotten or not seen it. . . . And while he saw his brother warming in the celebration of that ancient sculpture, and the others more than ever attentive in hearing him, he approached the wall of the room, and without anyone noticing him, he drew with charcoal the figure of Laocoon, and it was rendered as well as if he had had the original before his eyes. . . . When everyone became aware of it, they were extremely amazed, and Agostino admitted that . . . Annibale had imprinted it in his mind better than he and knew how to draw it in such a way that he [Agostino] certainly could not have achieved. . . . He praised the great prowess of his brother, which met the approval of everyone there. They waited to see if Annibale would say something. And finally, showing that he wanted them to leave, he said, laughing: "We other painters must speak with our hands."

Giovanni Battista Agucchi, c. 1607–15

Enea Vico (1523-1567)
after Baccio Bandinelli (1488-1560)

21. *The Academy of Baccio Bandinelli*

c. 1545-50

Engraving, 308 x 479 mm (12⅛ x 18⅞ in.) (trimmed)

References: Bartsch 49, undescribed state (ii/iii)[1]

Inscriptions: on the book at upper right: *Baccius / Bandi: / nellus / inueni / Enea ui: / go Par / megiano / sculpsit.*; at lower left: *Romae Petrus Paulus Palumbus forinis*

Purchased from Hill-Stone, New York

2000.28

Enea Vico's engraving of artists working in an interior lighted by candles and a fire seems to represent the Florentine "academy" of the sculptor Baccio Bandinelli. It has been associated with Bandinelli's comment in his autobiographical *Memoriale* referring to "the provisions conceded by his lordship the Duke [Cosimo I de' Medici] to the youths who studied under me in my private drawing academy [*a' giovani che nella mia Academia particolare del disegno sotto di me studiavano*], as is seen in the sheet designed by me and printed in Rome."[2] Bandinelli had established an academy at the Belvedere in the papal palace in Rome that was depicted in an engraving of 1531 by Agostino Veneziano (fig. 21.1). After returning from Rome to Florence in the spring of 1540, he established another academy. Although Vico's engraving is undated, it was probably produced around 1545-50, with Bandinelli's design perhaps preceding the execution of the print by a few years.[3]

Thirteen men and youths are gathered at a table and before an imposing fireplace, most of them occupied in drawing or watching others draw. On a shelf extending the length of the room are large books and figurines, mostly nude males fragmented as though they were copies of classical sculptures. Two more nude figures are on the floor in the foreground; all the sculptures resemble those in Veneziano's engraving of Bandinelli's Roman academy, as well as two engraved self-portraits of Bandinelli (cat. no. 1; fig. 1.1). Also on the floor are human skeletal remains, including two skulls.[4] Both the sculpted figures and the skeletons would become common appurtenances in representations of artists' workshops, studios, and academies (see, for example, cat. nos. 24, 28, 30, 31). Above the fireplace, two sculpted putti hold a wreath framing Bandinelli's coat of arms, which includes the cross of the order of the Knights of Santiago, to which the artist was admitted around 1530 (see

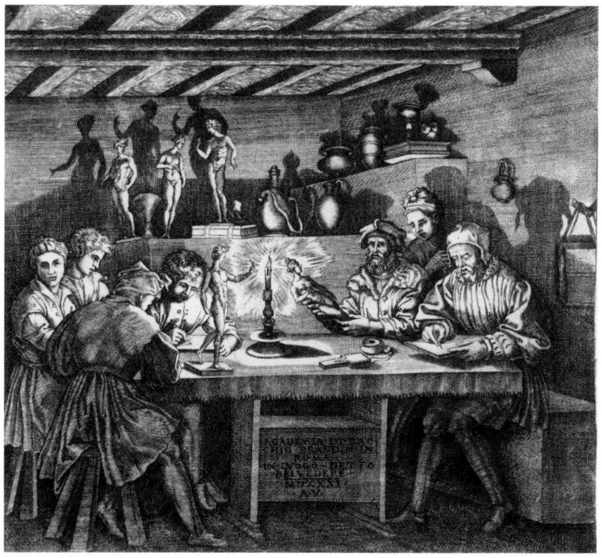

Fig. 21.1. Agostino Veneziano. *Baccio Bandinelli's Academy in Rome.* 1531. Engraving, 273 x 297 mm (10¾ x 11¾ in.). The British Museum, London.

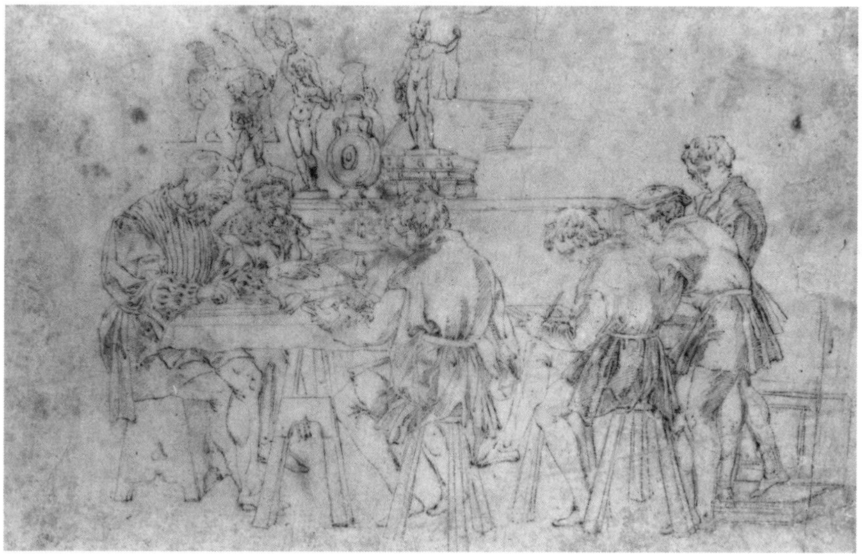

Fig. 21.2. Circle of Baccio Bandinelli. *An Artist's Studio.* Brown ink on paper. The British Museum, London.

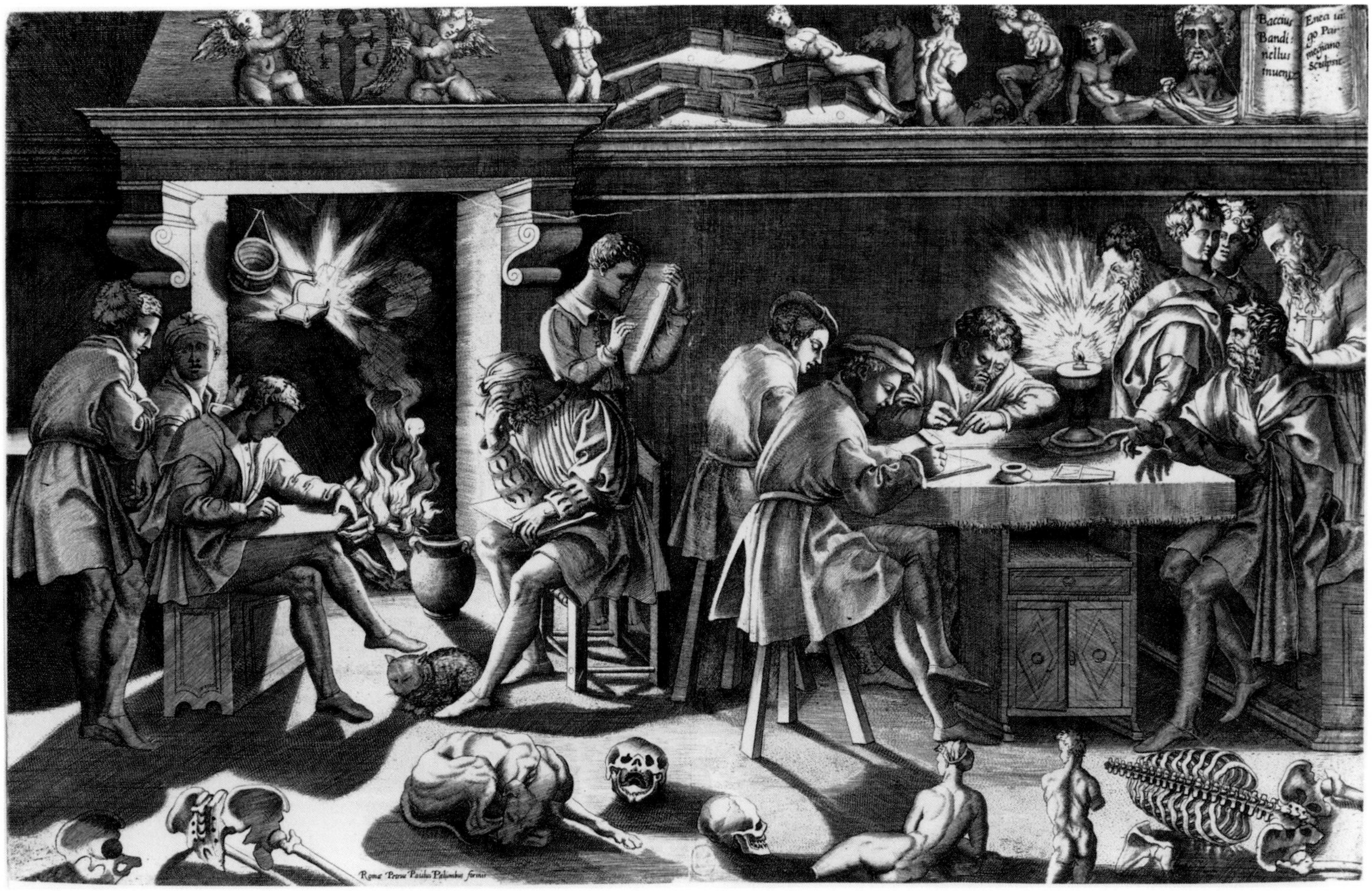

Cat. no. 21

cat. no. 1), as well as lilies, which the French king, Francis I, had allowed him to add.[5] The cross of Santiago also identifies the standing figure at the far right as Bandinelli.[6] The imposing figure seated at right and gesturing authoritatively recalls the *Moses* of Michelangelo; Bandinelli's rivalry with Michelangelo influenced his self-definition, and it is possible that Bandinelli intended the figure to represent the great sculptor himself.[7]

The right half of the engraving essentially reworks Agostino Veneziano's composition, with a very similar table and tablecloth, stools on the left and a bench for sitting on the right. A drawing from Bandinelli's circle (fig. 21.2) relates to a part of each engraving: the group around the table in Veneziano's composition and the three figures before the fireplace in Vico's. But it is not simply a pastiche after the engravings, as there are significant variations in the figures and the objects above and behind them. The reversal of direction suggests that it derives from preparatory drawings for the engravings.

The draftsmen in Veneziano's print may be drawing the sculpture on the table—a variation of the ancient Apollo Belvedere—and the strong shadows cast by the sculptures and vases in the background suggest that they are studying the effects of light on three-dimensional objects. In contrast, there are no sculptures at the table in Enea Vico's engraving, and none of the draftsmen seems to be drawing any object before him.[8] Only the work of the standing youth in the center of the composition is visible: a female nude unlike anything in the room. Their work is drawn from the imagination, representing a progression in both pedagogical and creative activity beyond the depiction of visible objects. The seated figure with his hand to his face has been said to be sleeping, but he might just as well be pondering, or his pose might also suggest the melancholic temperament of artists.[9] The strong artificial light within Vico's engraving has consequently been seen as "the visible sign of the higher illumination that guides the art of sculpture."[10]

Bandinelli was among the first to use the term "academy" in conjunction with artists. Associated with Plato and his followers in ancient Athens, the term was taken up in the fifteenth century to denote the places where Italian humanists gathered or the groups of "*academici*" themselves.[11] Bandinelli, who had ambitions as a poet and writer of art theory, was admitted to such a group, the Accademia Fiorentina, in 1545,[12] around the time of Vico's engraving; his use of the term to describe his own academy emphasizes the intellectual rather than the manual aspects of his art, an emphasis he was keen to maintain in all his self-representations. Of all the manual activities of the artist, drawing or *disegno*—a term that also meant design and suggested a thoughtful approach to the art—best emblematized the artist's claim to practice a liberal art, and Bandinelli's maintenance of an "Academia . . . del disegno," as well as his representation of it for public consumption, supported his claims to cultural and philosophical sophistication and even nobility.[13] The term "academy" does not imply an official organization, as it would later, from the founding of the Florentine Accademia del Disegno in 1563 and the subsequent proliferation of such organizations through the nineteenth century. As Francis Ames-Lewis has said in conjunction with Agostino Veneziano's engraving, at this time "the 'academia' was still a free, informal gathering of men of common interests for discussion and study."[14] Bandinelli's academy, however, was not simply a gathering of peers but also involved youths studying under the master, as he himself said, although they are depicted here very differently than the much younger boys in the later workshop images by Stradanus (cat. nos. 22, 23) and Fialetti (cat. no. 24).[15]

JC

1. The first state lacks the engraver's name; the third state has "Gaspar Albertus successor Palumbi" added at lower center. Bartsch, who listed only two states, seems to have been unaware of the state represented by the Blaffer impression, that is, with Enea Vico's name as engraver appearing on the book at upper right but without Alberti's below. For a description of the states, see Firenze e la Toscana dei Medici 1980, 264, no. 688. Two impressions (in Florence and New Haven) present alternative inscriptions on the book, but in both instances the inscriptions are manuscript. For a reproduction of the Yale University impression, see Gahtan and Jacks 1994, 43, no. 53 (illus. on p. 40).
2. Bandinelli 1905, 429; trans. Ward 1988, 67. Bandinelli goes on, however, to say that the print carried the inscription "Academia Bacci ex Senariis comitibus Bandinellis," which appears on neither the present engraving nor Agostino Veneziano's earlier depiction of Bandinelli's academy (fig. 21.1). Waźbiński 1987, 1:66 n. 63, suggests that the discrepancy results from the aged Bandinelli's "amplificazione tendenziosa del titolo della stampa" when he wrote his *Memoriale* late in life. Waźbiński 1987, 1:63ff., associates both the engraving and the comment in the *Memoriale* with Bandinelli's superintendency of the Opera del Duomo of Florence, assigned him by Cosimo I in 1540.
3. Weil-Garris 1981 (c. 1550); Olszewski 1981, 99 (1550); Waźbiński 1987, 1:66 (c. 1547); Ward 1988, 67 (not earlier than the mid-1540s, with the drawing slightly earlier). Fiorentini 1999, 45, 146–47, suggests that Bandinelli's original design dates to 1531–32 (therefore representing his Roman academy), that the self-portrait wearing the cross of Santiago was a late addition to commemorate this honor, and that the standing figure closest to the table is also a self-portrait already drawn before Bandinelli's knighthood. Eschenburg 2001, 86, wonders if this figure might be Duke Cosimo I.
4. On Bandinelli's interest in human anatomy, see Cazort, Kornell, and Roberts 1996, 142–43.
5. Bandinelli 1905, 420.
6. On self-portraits of Bandinelli in profile, see Ward 1988, 65–66; Galicka and Sygietyńska 1992.
7. On Bandinelli's rivalry with Michelangelo, see Weil-Garris 1981; she makes the highly tentative suggestion that the seated figure might be Michelangelo at 247 n. 41.
8. Noted by Goldstein 1996, 13; Fiorentini 1999, 46; cf. Weil-Garris 1981, 236. *Pace* Waźbiński 1987, 1:66, who says that "si vedono alcuni allievi che stanno disegnando figure umane, e altri che delineano figure geometriche."
9. Pevsner 1940, 40, described the figure as sleeping; Goldstein 1996, 13, as melancholic (cf. Weil-Garris 1981, 236); Fiorentini 1999, 46, "in 'Denkerpose'"; in Eschenburg 2001, 86, he is called "nachdenkend" and reminiscent of one of Michelangelo's *capitani* in the Medici Chapel of San Lorenzo, Florence. It is possible that the dog curled up in front of him is an allusion to the very similar (albeit reversed) dog in Albrecht Dürer's engraving *Melencolia I* (see Panofsky 1955, 156–71, esp. 162).
10. Weil-Garris 1981, 236, and 247 n. 39; see also Goldstein 1996, 13; Fiorentini 1999, 46.
11. See Pevsner 1940, 1–24, and, for Bandinelli, 39–42. See also Barzman 2000, 3–6.
12. Waźbiński 1987, 1:59, 68.
13. See Weil-Garris 1981, 235–36; Waźbiński 1987, 1:60ff.; Weil-Garris Brandt 1989, 2:497; Goldstein 1996, 14.
14. Ames-Lewis 2000, 59; cf. Pevsner 1940, 41.
15. Pevsner 1940, 41–42, recognizes that the younger figures in the two engravings might be Bandinelli's apprentices but asserts that "at this evening entertainment they are not present as trainees." Weil-Garris 1981, 235–36, asserts the pedagogical function of Bandinelli's academy.

Hans Collaert II (1566–1628)

after Joannes Stradanus (1523–1605)

22. *Oil Paint (Color olivi)*

c. 1590

Engraving, 203 x 270 mm (8 x 10⅝ in.)

Plate 14 from the *Nova Reperta*

Reference: From Hollstein 129–48 (Collaert), ii/ii

Inscriptions: at lower center: *Ioan. Stradanus inuent. Ioan. Galle excud.*; below image at left: *14.*; below image at center: *COLOR OLIVI.*; at bottom: *Colorem oliui commodum pictoribus, Inuenit insignis magister Eyckius.*

Purchased from Hill-Stone, New York

1998.9.14

Oil Paint (Color olivi) is the fourteenth of nineteen plates (plus a title page) in a series entitled *Nova Reperta (New Discoveries),* which illustrates mostly technological innovations since antiquity, from the production of sugar to the manufacture of eyeglasses, as well as the discovery of the New World. Designed by Joannes Stradanus in Florence around 1590, the plates were engraved by Theodor Galle and Hans Collaert and published in Antwerp by Philips Galle. The series was republished by Joannes Galle, Philips's grandson, and his name appears on this impression and the *Engraving in Copper (Sculptura in Aes)* (cat. no. 23). The title page is a visual synopsis of the first nine plates (fig. 22.1), to which the last ten were probably added shortly thereafter. It includes the name of Luigi (or Aloisio) Alamanni (1558–1603), probably not simply as a dedicatee (it lacks the customary encomiastic text of a dedication) but rather as the patron who commissioned the work. In 1587, Alamanni had commissioned a set of twenty-five drawings illustrating Dante's *Inferno* from Stradanus, presumably to be disseminated as prints, although only a title page was engraved (by Cornelis Galle in Antwerp), on which Alamanni's name appears. Alamanni, a frequent patron of Stradanus in the late 1580s, was a noble Florentine and member of the important scientific and literary groups, the Accademia degli Alterati and the Accademia Fiorentina.[1]

At the center of *Oil Paint (Color olivi),* a master painter stands on a platform, working on a Saint George and the Dragon on a large canvas. Behind him two older members of the workshop—perhaps journeymen—grind pigments and mix them with the oil medium. In the foreground, an apprentice places paints on a palette for the master's use. In the background at left, an advanced member of the workshop paints a portrait of a woman who is attended by a maid waiting patiently at her side. Behind the sitter are paintings in progress: a Madonna and Child and two bust-length portraits. Two apprentices in the foreground are performing exercises not directly connected to the workshop's production. The boy at right is repeatedly drawing the same form of an eye.[2] Model sheets for such anatomical parts were published shortly after the time of Stradanus's composition, and were probably known in some form already in the sixteenth century (see cat. no. 24); this student has no model in front of him, but it is possible that one of the older members of the workshop drew one, which he is then copying. At left, a more advanced student seems to be drawing a cast of a Roman female bust, with calipers handy on the table for exact measurement. A book on the table has a geometric form on its cover, suggesting the mathematical basis for painting and hence the validity of its claim to be a liberal art. Through the doorway at right, a figure carries a rectangle on his head; the means of carrying it suggests that it might have more weight than a canvas and is perhaps a stone like those used as a base for grinding and mixing pigments.

Stradanus drew artists at work on several occasions. Five sketches, perhaps roughly contemporaneous with the *Nova Reperta,* are varying compositional attempts on the theme of Zeuxis and the Maids of Croton, presumably for an unrealized or lost painting or engraving project.[3] Two of them include the conventional motif, also present in *Oil Paint (Color olivi),* of the color grinder.[4] One of Stradanus's best known compositions is an allegory of the practice of the arts, drawn in 1573, engraved by Cornelis Cort, and published in 1578, which is a montage of painting, sculpture, architecture, engraving, and the study of anatomy (fig. 22.2).[5] Although some of the activities reappear in *Oil Paint (Color olivi)* (namely, students drawing and a painter working on a large history painting), the later composition is cast much more as a functional workshop.

The inscription on *Oil Paint (Color olivi)* attributes the invention of oil as a medium—"convenient to painters," as it says in a gross understatement, since the innovation proved revolutionary—

Hans Collaert II (1566–1628)

after Joannes Stradanus (1523–1605)

23. *Engraving in Copper (Sculptura in Aes)*

c. 1590

Engraving, 203 x 272 mm (8 x 10¾ in.)

Plate 19 from the *Nova Reperta*

Reference: From Hollstein 129–48 (Collaert), ii/ii

Inscriptions: at lower left: *Ioan. Stradanus inuent.*; at lower right: *Ioan. Galle excud.*; below image at left: *19.*; below image at center: *SCVLPTVRA IN ÆS.*; at bottom: *Sculptor noua arte, bracteata in lamina Sculpit figuras, atque praelis imprimit.*

Purchased from Hill-Stone, New York

1998.9.19

This print, like cat. no. 22, belongs to a series of nineteen engravings called the *Nova Reperta (New Discoveries),* commissioned by Luigi Alamanni, executed by Hans Collaert and Theodor Galle after drawings by Joannes Stradanus, and published by Philips Galle. The publication of this series, commissioned by an Italian humanist from a Flemish expatriate in Italy and published by a firm in Antwerp, shows how the commerce of art across Europe had developed by this time. More importantly, it demonstrates the international reputation of Antwerp engravers, and of Galle in particular, as the acknowledged masters in the field of reproductive engraving.[1]

In this scene depicting a busy engraver's workshop, Stradanus presents an up to date accounting of the process of printmaking around 1600. The process begins near the right margin with the master engraver, wearing a pair of spectacles that perhaps indicate how his profession has affected his eyesight; he works with a burin on a copper plate from a model affixed to a vertical stand. Various burins, for achieving different line weights, and elongated objects, probably stones for polishing and burnishing areas of the plate and sharpening burins, lie on the workbench (along with a dish probably full of oil to whet the burnishing stones). Moving to the left, we see a table on which a shop assistant heats a copper plate engraved with a crucifixion scene over a charcoal brazier, in order to make the engraved lines more receptive to the thick printer's ink. Working with him at the table, another man inks and wipes a plate to prepare it for the press. To their left, we see the press itself, and an assistant who cranks the roller handle with both hands and one foot to apply enough pressure to force the paper into the lines of the plate; the physical exertion of the pressman and the bold diagonals of the crank give the act of printing a quasi-heroic aspect, as if the handle were the helm of a ship in stormy seas. The pressman has almost completed his pass, and we see the protective layers of blankets covering the plate as it emerges. Rows of finished prints dry on ropes on the left and rear walls of the shop.

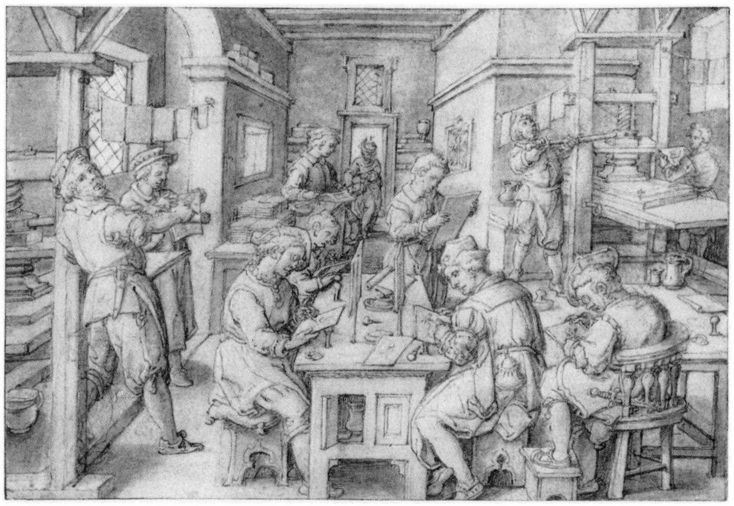

Fig. 23.1. Joannes Stradanus. *Engravers at Work.* Pen and brown ink with brown wash over black chalk, heightened with white, 187 x 274 mm (7⅜ x 10¾ in.). The Royal Collection, Her Majesty Queen Elizabeth II.

In a drawing now in Windsor Castle (fig. 23.1) that predates the finished drawing for plate 19 of the *Nova Reperta,* Stradanus rehearses the shop interior; he makes the act of engraving the central part of the composition. In the finished version, Stradanus has given greater emphasis to the presses; instead of marginalizing them at the left and right, he has devoted the entire left half of the composition to one press, while another is visible in the adjacent room at the rear. Stradanus has also updated the presses to the more modern roller variety.[2]

Perhaps the most significant change between this earlier conception and the finished version is that Stradanus decided to show

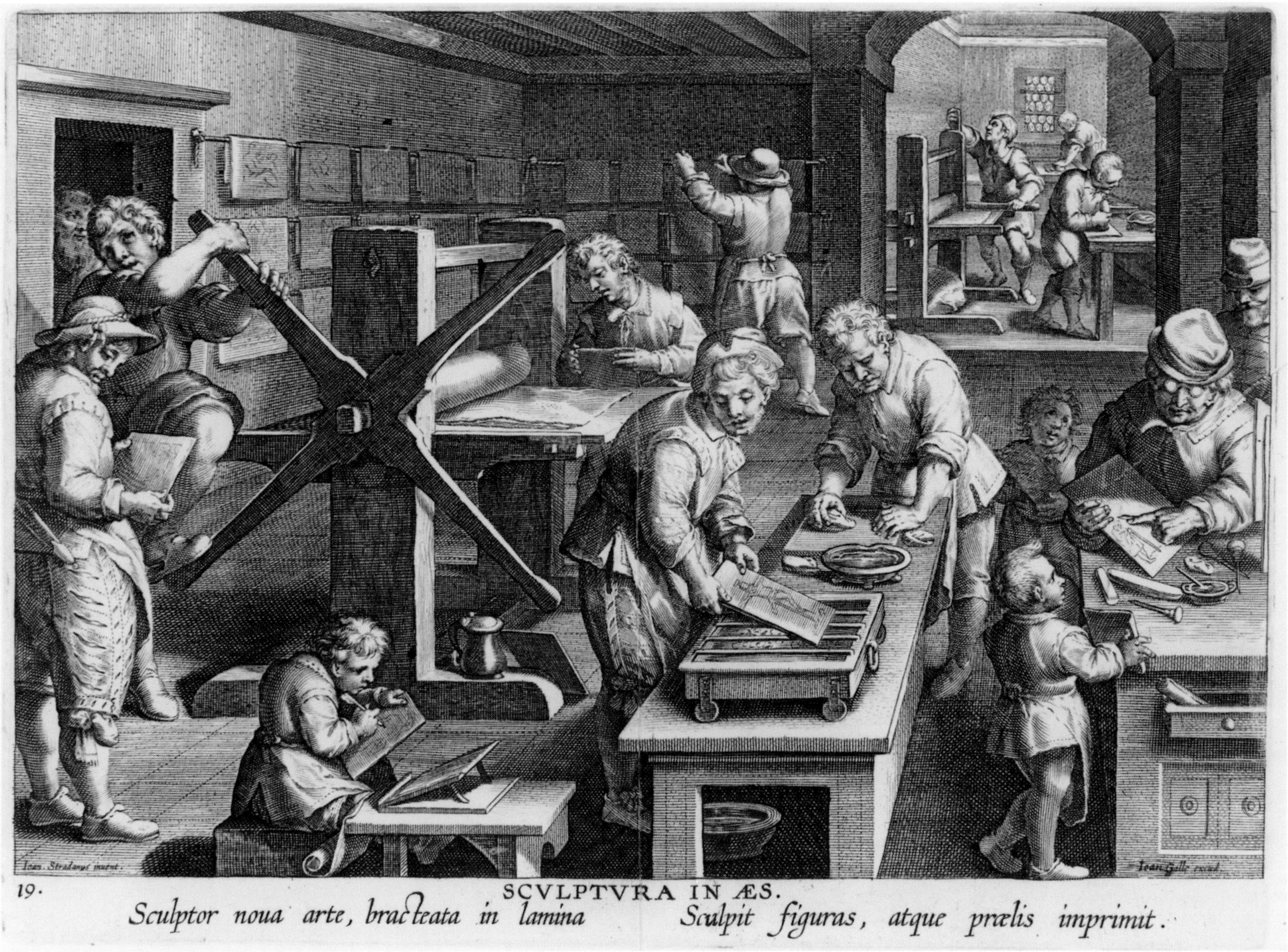

Cat. no. 23

us how apprentice engravers learn their art. The little apprentice at the lower left is busily at work copying a model print with a quill pen. Another shop worker, instead of examining the proof in his hand, looks over the shoulder of the boy in curiosity, as does the assistant warming the plate. Two other apprentices, having finished their copying assignments, rush to show their results to the master engraver. Thus, Stradanus communicates not only the technical and artisanal process of printmaking, but also the importance and the method of training a new generation of talent to keep the shop in business.

These sketching apprentices are interesting in light of the fact that both Stradanus and Philips Galle produced other works on the topic of training students through visual models.[3] Cornelis Cort's 1578 engraving of a drawing by Stradanus now referred to as *The Practitioners of the Visual Arts* (fig. 22.2) not only shows a group of young apprentices diligently sketching from a skeleton, a cadaver, and various sculptures, but also presents an engraver at work along with practitioners of painting, sculpture, and architecture. In 1589, Philips Galle had produced the first known Flemish drawing book for students, titled *Instruction et fondements de bien pourtraire (Instruction and rudiments of good drawing)*; this booklet of fourteen anatomical engravings was published, as the title page asserts, "for young apprentices, and all those who devote themselves to wishing to be Painters, Sculptors, Goldsmiths, and other craftsmen."[4] Engravers were certainly included in the last category.

The culture of Renaissance Europe dedicated itself above all to revering the arts and learning of the ancients in all forms of expression; great fame was to be gained by improving on their achievements. In art, this is best exemplified by the personal myth of the "divine Michelangelo" propagated by Vasari in his *Vite,* who believed that Michelangelo not only mastered the techniques of ancient sculptors, but was able to convincingly counterfeit them when he chose, and more importantly to surpass them. In a broader sense, the concept of novelty in many human pursuits in the sixteenth century was set against the backdrop of ancient wonders, and the *Nova Reperta* of Stradanus were conceived, perhaps by Alamanni, as a catalogue of modern achievements meant to stand comparison against those of the ancients. For example, Erasmus praised the invention of movable type as a novel invention undreamed of by the ancients,[5] a sentiment echoed in plate 4 of the *Nova Reperta,* which shows a print shop. We can extend Erasmus's point to engraving as well; as William Ivins observed, the significance of "being able to exactly repeat pictorial statements"[6] to all arenas of human endeavor has been vastly underestimated. Thus it is not only the beauty of an engraving and the skill of the engraver that should be celebrated, but also the ability of printmaking to record all of the other discoveries in the *Nova Reperta,* and to instruct others about them. In placing the depiction of engraving as the last in the series, Stradanus and Galle were certainly aware that in this particular instance, engraving had made all of the other discoveries possible. AW

1. For other examples of transalpine collaborations on engraving projects, see Riggs and Silver 1993, 53.
2. Baroni Vannucci 1997, 285.
3. Sellink 1992, 40–56.
4. "Pour la jeunesse aprentisue, & tous ceux qui s'adonnent à vouloir estre Peintres, Statuaires, Orfevres, & semblables Artisans."
5. Margolin 2001, 2.
6. Ivins 1953, 2.

Odoardo Fialetti (1573–1638)

24. *The Painter's Studio*

c. 1608

Etching, 112 x 155 mm (4⅜ x 6⅛ in.)

Reference: Bartsch 210

Inscription: lower left: *OF* (ligature) *F A2 N°208*

Purchased from C. G. Boerner, New York

2000.20

In the foreground of *The Painter's Studio,* five boys and young men are gathered before a table, on and under which are casts of sculptures, each a fragmentary part of a nude body (two with hooks for hanging on the wall). Two of the boys are actively drawing the male head on the table; another has set his drawing aside while he sharpens his pen; two others discuss a drawing of the head. At the lower edge of the image are an inkwell with quill pen, a pen case, calipers, and a square. In the background at left, before shelves of bowls, a figure bends to grind pigments. In the background at center, next to some palettes hanging on the wall, two painters work at easels, one standing and working on the sky in his picture, the other—bearded, apparently older, and probably the master of the workshop—seated.

Justus Sadeler, a member of the important Netherlandish family of engravers and publishers (see cat. nos. 2, 3) who settled in Venice, published more than forty etchings by Odoardo Fialetti for the instruction of students in art. The etchings were issued as one or more books, the plates appearing in different configurations in surviving bound volumes, for which two different title pages exist. One, dated 1608, is inscribed "Il uero modo et ordine, per dissegnar tvtte le parti, et membra del corpo hvmano" (The true means and method to draw all the parts and members of the human body) and carries a dedication to Cesare d'Este, Duke of Modena and Reggio (1562–1628) (Bartsch 198). The other, undated, is inscribed "Tutte le parti del corpo hvmano diuiso in piu pezzi" (All the parts of the human body divided into multiple pieces) (Bartsch 208) and is accompanied by a dedication on a separate plate to a Venetian nobleman, Giovanni Grimani (Bartsch 209). Bartsch called them *The Small Book of Drawing* and *The Large Book of Drawing,* respectively, based on the number of plates in volumes

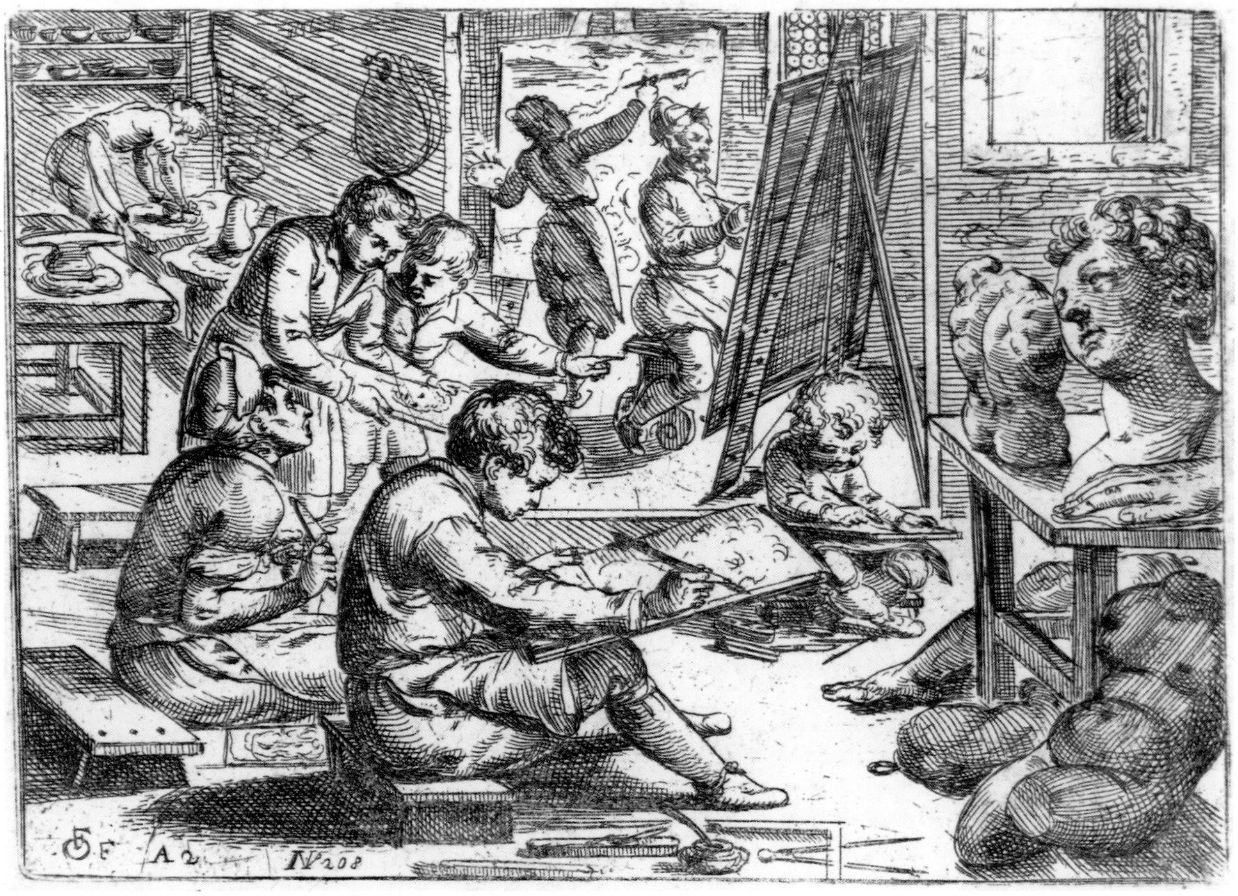

Cat. no. 24

he consulted rather than the plate size, which is very close in both instances. Some configurations include the title page for *Il uero modo,* with its dedication to Cesare d'Este, and the dedicatory page to Grimani as the only text.[1] The plate known as *The Painter's Studio* seems to have served as a sort of second frontispiece. *The Painter's Studio* is accompanied by another interior view, of artists measuring the proportions of both sculptures and a live figure with calipers (Bartsch 211). The rest of the etchings represent body parts—noses, ears, eyes, mouths, heads, hands, feet, arms, legs, torsos, knees—of sculptures and live figures, both in outline and shaded, as models for developing artists.

Precedents exist for the collection of motifs for use by artists, dating to the fifteenth century, but they were directed more toward professionals, providing them with models of objects for insertion in their own compositions.[2] Fialetti's, in contradistinction, is regarded as the first instructional manual for students (and perhaps also for amateurs).[3] Although the Bolognese Fialetti was working in Venice at the time of the publication of *Il uero modo,* the book, including the scene exhibited here, does not necessarily reflect traditional Venetian practice. It may derive from the educational ideals and methods of the famous Carracci academy in Bologna, whose products—both works of art and students—were to have an enormous effect on the development of European art in the seventeenth and eighteenth centuries. The Carracci, like Florentine and Roman artists, emphasized drawing, especially of the human figure, as the basis for painting—much more than sixteenth-century Venetian artists. Agostino Carracci's drawings of anatomical details (later engraved), which Fialetti may have known either from his early years in Bologna or through Agostino's visits to Venice, form an important precursor for Fialetti's etchings.[4] Classical sculpture was an important means toward an artistic understanding of the human form, and although collections of plaster casts of such sculpture, most famously Tintoretto's, existed in Venice, they were not used as rigorously for training as in Central Italy and as implied in Fialetti's etching of *The Painter's Studio.*[5] Fialetti's work also recalls Stradanus's view of a painter's studio, designed in Florence in the early 1590s (cat. no. 22): an apprentice in the foreground copies a classical bust and another repetitively draws eyes like those in two of the plates of Fialetti's drawing book (Bartsch 212, 213). JC

1. On the obscure publication history, see David P. Becker in Reed and Wallace 1989, 248-49; also, for different exemplars, Sopher 1978, 70, and Amornpichetkul 1984, 109. Rosand 1970, 45 n. 58, describes the page devoted to Grimani as "expressing gratitude . . . for his patronage" and therefore, implicitly, not in conflict with the dedication to Cesare d'Este. Also included in most bindings are two narrative compositions designed and etched by Palma Giovane (1548-1628), who participated to a greater extent in Giacomo Franco's more ambitious drawing manual, *De excellentia et nobilitate delineationis libri duo* (Venice, 1611) (see Rosand 1970, 5, 12-17). The reason for the dedication to Cesare d'Este is not known, although the duke was a knowledgeable collector and patron of art, and there were substantial connections between Venice and Modena during the time of Cesare's rule (1598-1628), especially including work by Palma Giovane (Mazza 1998, 51-52).
2. Gombrich 1961, 157ff.; Ames-Lewis 1981, 63-69; Amornpichetkul 1984, 109.
3. On the audience for the work, see Rosand 1970, 19.
4. For Fialetti and the Carracci academy, see Rosand 1970, 15; Maugeri 1982, 147-49. For the thesis of a "fundamental change in the artistic climate of Venice" represented by the publications of Fialetti et al., see Rosand 1970, passim, esp. 18-19. But see also Sohm 2001, 734, who argues that Fialetti's composition, with no reference to several fundamental aspects of *disegno,* suggests a more practical than theoretical approach, and thus "Fialetti e Franco consolidano e perpetuano la reputatzione dei veneziani maestri di *pratica,* deboli in sapere teorico, letterario, storico e archeologico."
5. In a pamphlet published in 1605, Federico Zuccaro, the reformer of the Roman Accademia di San Luca, suggested, in vain, that the Venetian Republic sponsor the instruction of artists in the rooms housing the extensive collection of ancient sculptures recently given to the state for public display by Giovanni Grimani (Rosand 1970, 33-34). On the collection, see Perry 1978. Giovanni Grimani, the Patriarch of Aquileia (d. 1594), was not the dedicatee of Fialetti's *Tutte le parti,* but Fialetti's extolling the "Ser[enissi]ma Casa Grimana" in the dedication and the appearance of (casts of) classical sculptures in several of his etchings, including *The Painter's Studio,* suggest a connection.

Sébastien Leclerc I (1637-1714)

25. *The Academy of Sciences and Fine Arts*

1698

Engraving and etching, 249 x 384 mm (9¾ x 15⅛ in.)

References: Le Blanc 310, viii/ix; *Inventaire du fonds français,* 859, ii/viii

Inscription: *L'ACADEMIE DES SCIENCES ET DES BEAUX ARTS / DEDIÉE AU ROY. / Par son tres humble tres obeïssant et tres fidèle Servieur et sujet Seb. le Clerc.*

Purchased from Kunsthandlung Helmut H. Rumbler, Frankfurt

1997.13

In a rich and complex work that has been called the artist's testament and an "allegorical self-portrait,"[1] a summation of Leclerc's wide-ranging interests, more than one hundred fifty male figures populate a large courtyard and loggia, participating in the activities of, as the title indicates, "the Academy of Sciences and Fine Arts." In both composition and subject, the image recalls two important Italian works: Raphael's monumental fresco in the Vatican Palace, *The School of Athens* (1510-1511), and Pietro Testa's engraving, *Il Liceo della Pittura* (The School of Painting, c. 1638); it is more ambitious than either in its abundance of figures and diversity of activities.

The personal nature of the image is manifested in the choice of activities in which the artist was interested and experienced. The basis for Leclerc's selection may be the Seven Liberal Arts, but he departs from them in significant ways. At the left are the *quadrivium*: Arithmetic, Geometry (although these two are not easily distinguished here), Astronomy, and Music. The *trivium* seems to be represented by the central group placed at the edge of the upper courtyard, although it might represent specifically Rhetoric, leaving out Grammar and Dialectics. Other figures exemplify arts sometimes associated with the Liberal Arts but not included among them. In the distant background are figures involved in sculpture and architecture. In the right middle ground, mechanical devices—gears, pulleys, levers, and so on—are featured. Painting is the focus of the figures in the background just to the right of center, under the colonnade, with students copying drawn heads under the tutelage of a master while a painter executes a large equestrian portrait. The plan of a military structure, spread out at the lower right, is a reminder that Leclerc worked as a military engineer as a young man. The inclusion of some activities is curious: at the lower edge of the image, just to the left of center, a bearded, turbaned, and ornately robed old man reads the palm of a young man while two

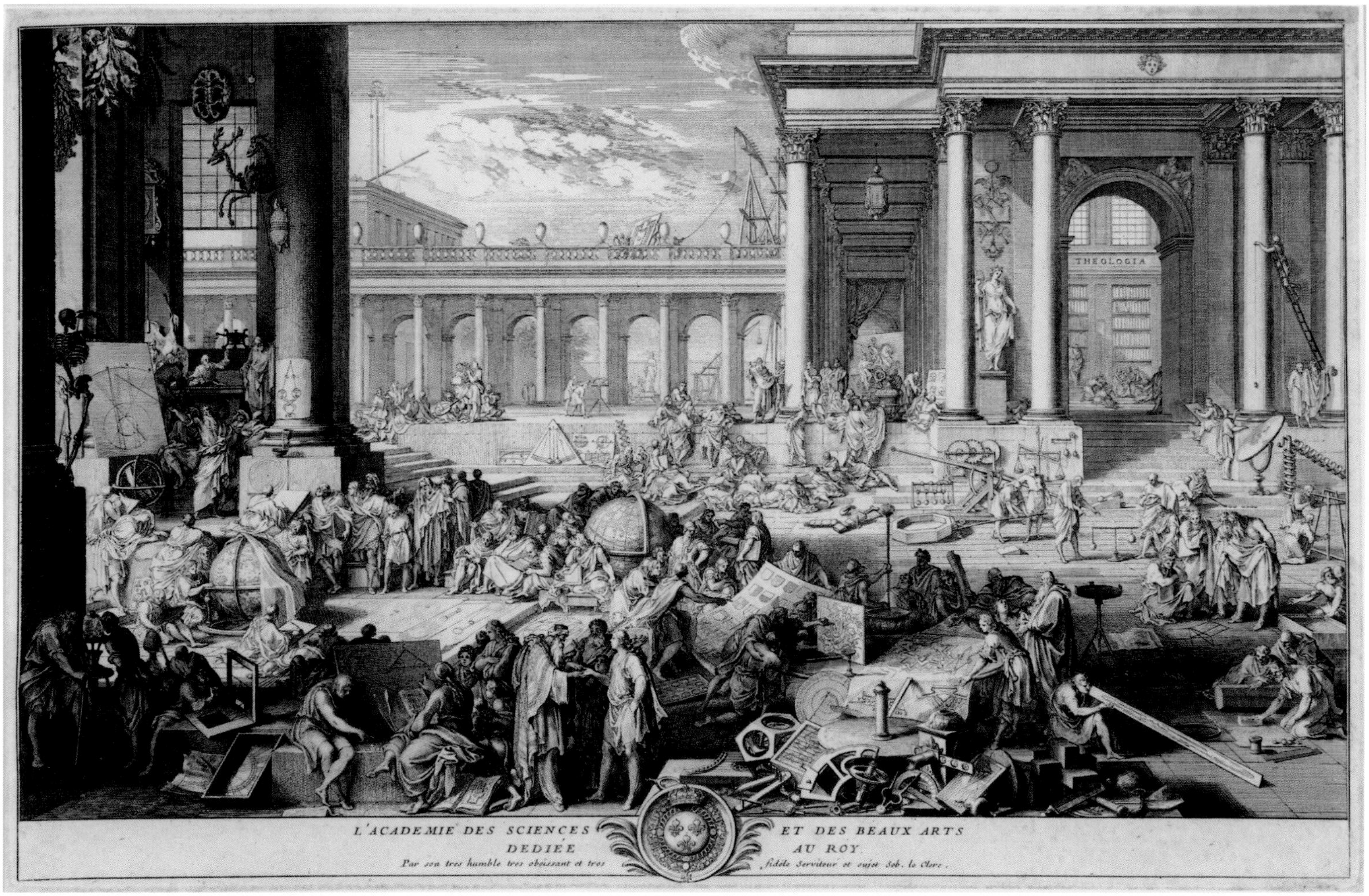

Cat. no. 25

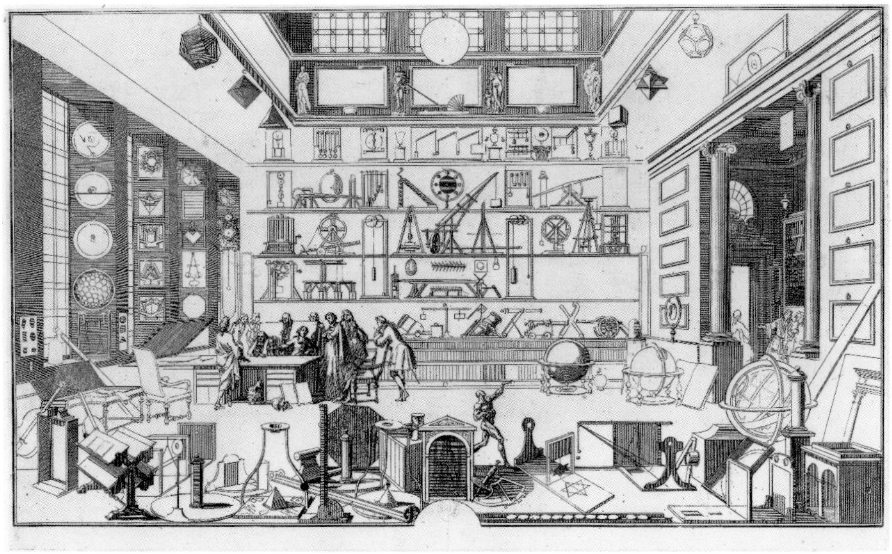

Fig. 25.1. Sébastien Leclerc. *Le Cabinet de Sébastien Leclerc.* 1712. Etching, 252 x 380 mm (9⅞ x 15 in.). Bibliothèque nationale de France, Paris.

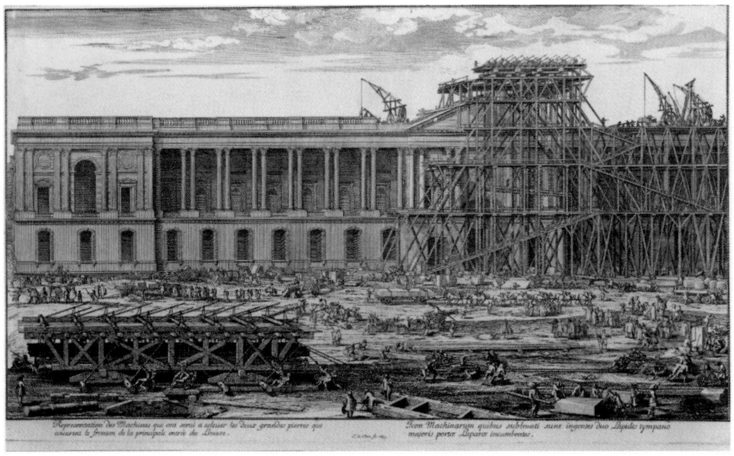

Fig. 25.2. Sébastien Leclerc. *Representation des Machines . . . (The Building of the Louvre, Paris).* 1677. Etching, 381 x 625 mm (15 x 24⅝ in.). Sarah Campbell Blaffer Foundation, Houston.

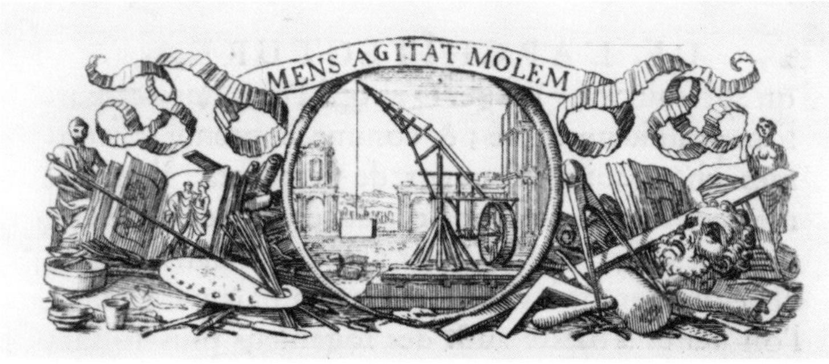

Fig. 25.3. Sébastien Leclerc. *Mens agitate molem* from André Félibien, *De principes de l'architecture, de la sculpture, de la peinture et des autres arts qui en dependent.* 1676. Etching, 44 x 110 mm (1¾ x 4⅜ in.). Bibliothèque nationale de France, Paris.

others look on in amazement;[2] and at the lower center of the image, occupying a prominent position, figures discuss a heraldic chart. The only art or science labeled is Theology, in a library in the background at right. The statue of Eternity between painting and theology, as well as the figure viewing an anamorphic image of a skull at the lower right, suggest an allegorical nature of the print that situates it within a tradition of *vanitas* imagery.[3]

An Academy of Sciences and Fine Arts, per se, did not exist, and the allegorical nature of the print is confirmed not only by the unrealistic nature of the setting and juxtaposition of diverse activities, but also by the pseudoclassical garb of the figures. Yet the print alludes to academies which flourished during the reign of Louis XIV, to whom it is dedicated. Leclerc was a student of Charles Le Brun, one of the founders of the Royal Academy of Painting and Sculpture, and he himself was admitted as a member in 1672, where he taught perspective and geometry. Leclerc was reputed to take great pleasure in intellectual and scientific conversation, which he represented in an unfinished etching of his ideal study (fig. 25.1).[4] Although he was not a member of the Académie des Sciences, many of his works are closely related to the activities of that institution and its members. Several motifs in *The Academy of Sciences and Fine Arts* relate to images in works that Leclerc himself had published or would publish later, illustrating his diverse yet overlapping interests: for example, the group of heads studied by young artists in the right background is close to a plate in Leclerc's *Principes de dessein* (1700); the geometric designs at the bases of the pilaster and column at the left are close to plates in his *Les Mouvements de Mercure et Vénus* (1706) and *Discours touchant le point de veuë* (1679). Leclerc's early work illustrating plants and animals, especially exotic ones, reappears in the motifs at the upper left corner of the print. More generally, the stone hoisting equipment in the far background recalls the machinery used in the construction of the façade of the Louvre, which Leclerc had depicted two decades earlier (fig. 25.2). Such a crane was also used as the central motif in a vignette which Leclerc etched for a book published by André Félibien, the historian of the Royal Academy of Painting and Sculpture, in 1676 (fig. 25.3), with a still-life recalling that at the lower right of *The Academy of Sciences and Fine Arts,* but less universal in its scope. The motto inscribed on the vignette, "The Mind Moves the Rock," claiming the priority of the intellect, might also serve for *The Academy of Sciences and Fine Arts,* the artist's later tour de force.

JC

1. Préaud 1983. Préaud's is the most exhaustive treatment of the image; see also Eschenburg 2001, 104.
2. Préaud 1983, 80, suggests that this figure represents medieval science, superseded by "la science opérative, appliquée, efficace."
3. See especially Préaud 1983, 81.
4. See Ibid.

WILLIAM PETHER (c. 1738–1821)
after Joseph Wright of Derby (1734–1797)

26. *An Academy*

1772

Mezzotint, 584 x 460 mm (23 x 18⅛ in.)

REFERENCE: Clayton P9, ii/ii

INSCRIPTIONS: on the portfolio at center: *An / Academy / Published by W. Pether / Feb^{y}, 25^{h}, 1772*; lower left: *Ios^{h} Wright, Pinx^{t}*; lower center: *Done from a Picture in / the Collection of the R^{t} Hon / Ld Melburne*; lower right: *W. Pether, Fecit.*

Purchased from C. G. Boerner, New York

1998.6

On a high square pedestal in a vaulted room sits a plaster cast or marble copy of the antique sculpture Nymph with a Shell. Six boys and young men sit or stand around it, two of them actively engaged in drawing the figure (another, at right, is looking at a drawing of the figure as seen from the other side). The youth standing at left is enrapt by the beauty of the female figure, whose drilled eyes give her a vitality lacking in the original. In the background at right is another cast or copy, this one of the Borghese Gladiator, offering a contrast between hard male musculature and supple female flesh.[1] Lighting in the room is limited to a single hanging lamp, which brilliantly illuminates the sculpture and creates dramatic contrasts of light and dark. William Pether's mezzotint, dated 1772, is an unreversed copy of a painting by Joseph Wright of Derby. The painting, now in the Yale Center for British Art, was exhibited at the Society of Artists in 1769 and purchased by the young Peniston Lamb, the first Lord Melbourne (1748–1829), who also acquired a *Blacksmith's Shop* from Wright.[2]

An Academy is one of around twenty strongly tenebristic paintings that Wright executed in the 1760s and early 1770s, inspiring the remark in 1772 that he was "the most famous painter now living for candlelight."[3] As Benedict Nicolson has pointed out, Wright might well have known the depictions of Baccio Bandinelli's academy, with their brilliant artificial light sources and deep shadows (cat. no. 21). His more immediate sources, however, were probably Dutch rather than Italian—not simply the Utrecht Caravaggists like Gerrit Honthorst with their candlelit genre scenes, but artists of later generations as well. Among the potential influences cited by Nicolson is Wallerant Vaillant's mezzotint of a boy reading in a studio (cat. no. 40).[4] In addition to the composition and the subject, Wright may well have responded to the rich tonal range of the medium of mezzotint itself, in which chiaroscuro effects could be so subtly rendered.[5] The technique became an important part of artistic production in England in the second half of the eighteenth century. Pether brilliantly translated Wright's compositions into mezzotint, and *An Academy* is a tour de force of the technique, apparent, for example, in the subtle effects of the lamplight partially obscured by the drape.

Ancient sculpture, whether original, copy, or cast, was widely collected in England in Wright's time. The Duke of Richmond's extensive collection of casts at Whitehall was made available to students from 1758 until around 1790 and would have been known to Wright.[6] Edward Edwards's description of this "admirable school for the study of painting and sculpture," to which boys of around twelve years of age were admitted, suggests the novelty that drawing antiquities for instructional purposes was in England:

> It consisted of a gallery or great room, fitted up with every conveniency requisite for the accommodation of students, and furnished with a number of gesses, or casts in plaster of Paris, moulded from the most select antique and modern figures at that time at Rome and Florence. To this elegant school, the young artists were invited by a public advertisement.
>
> In consequence of this invitation, several young artists of that time attended the room. . . . [A]nd it was in this school, that those young men acquired a purer taste in the knowledge of the human form, than had before been cultivated by the artists in England. . . .
>
> That this gallery was of the highest advantage to those who attended it, will easily be conceived, when it is known, that it was the first school opened in this country, where the beauties of the antique could be studied.[7]

But Wright's academy here is probably imaginary, and the composition focuses attention on the object of the draftsmen's work—centered in a lighted oval—rather than documents the activities of

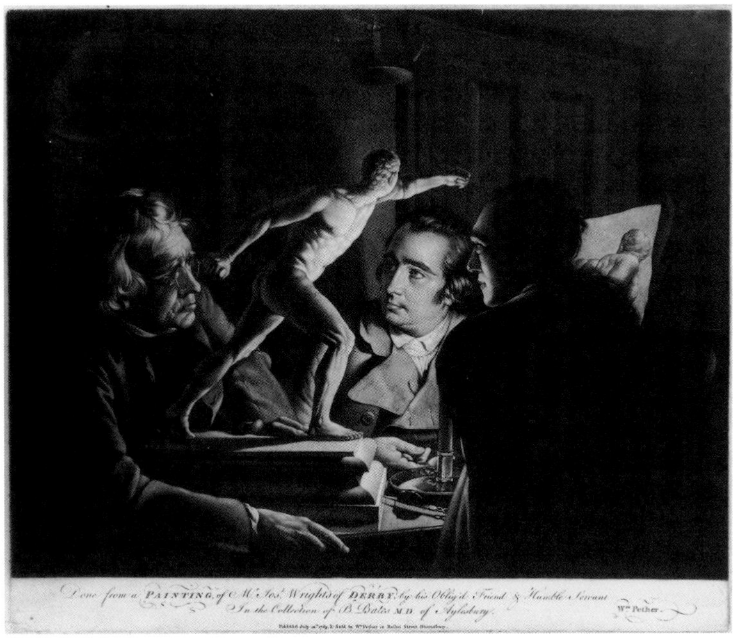

Fig. 26.1. William Pether after Joseph Wright of Derby. *Three Persons Viewing the Gladiator by Candlelight.* 1769. Mezzotint, 481 x 556 mm (18⅞ x 21⅞ in.). The Metropolitan Museum of Art, Harris Brisbane Dick Fund, 1953 (53.600.564).

an academy per se. Throughout his career, Wright drew ancient sculpture. Most of the extant drawings date from his visit to Italy in 1773–75, but several are earlier, including drawings of the Borghese Gladiator and the Nymph with a Shell.[8] Wright had also used the Gladiator to illustrate his contemporaries' fascination with antiquity in a painting of three men, one holding a drawing of the work, gathered around a small bronze copy of the sculpture. One of the figures, presumably the man on the right, was said by Edward Edwards to be a self-portrait.[9] This composition had also been reproduced in a mezzotint by Pether, published in 1769 (fig. 26.1).[10]

JC

1. Both the Gladiator and the Nymph with a Shell, now in the Louvre, were known from the seventeenth century and were at the Villa Borghese in Rome until around 1810, when they were sent to Paris. Full-size copies of both sculptures were in England, and those of the Gladiator abounded in the eighteenth century. See Haskell and Penny 1981, 221–24, 280–81. Bätschmann 1992, 252–53, noting the erotic element of the composition of *An Academy,* remarks that the shadows make the sculptural figure of the nymph interchangeable with the living and give it a "deceiving presence."
2. On *An Academy,* see Nicolson 1954, 72, 75; Nicolson 1968, 45–47, 106, 234; Egerton 1990, 63–64.
3. By James Northcote, quoted by Nicolson 1954, 72.
4. Nicolson 1968, 47; Egerton 1990, 64.
5. See Wax 1990, 84.
6. Nicolson 1954, 75 n. 12.
7. Edwards 1808, xvi, xviii. Edwards goes on to note that the foundation of the Royal Academy obviated the need for the Duke of Richmond's school, although it continued for some years and Edwards himself there "acquired the elements of all the little knowledge which he possesses in art" (xix). The subject of *An Academy* probably appealed to Wright for, among other things, the possibility to depict children, who appear in most of his early chiaroscuro paintings (see Nicolson 1954, 76).
8. See George Baker in Wallis 1997, 86–99, esp. 88–89.
9. Edwards 1808, 253; Egerton 1990, 61–62.
10. On the painting, see Nicolson 1968, 39–40, 234; Egerton 1990, 236.

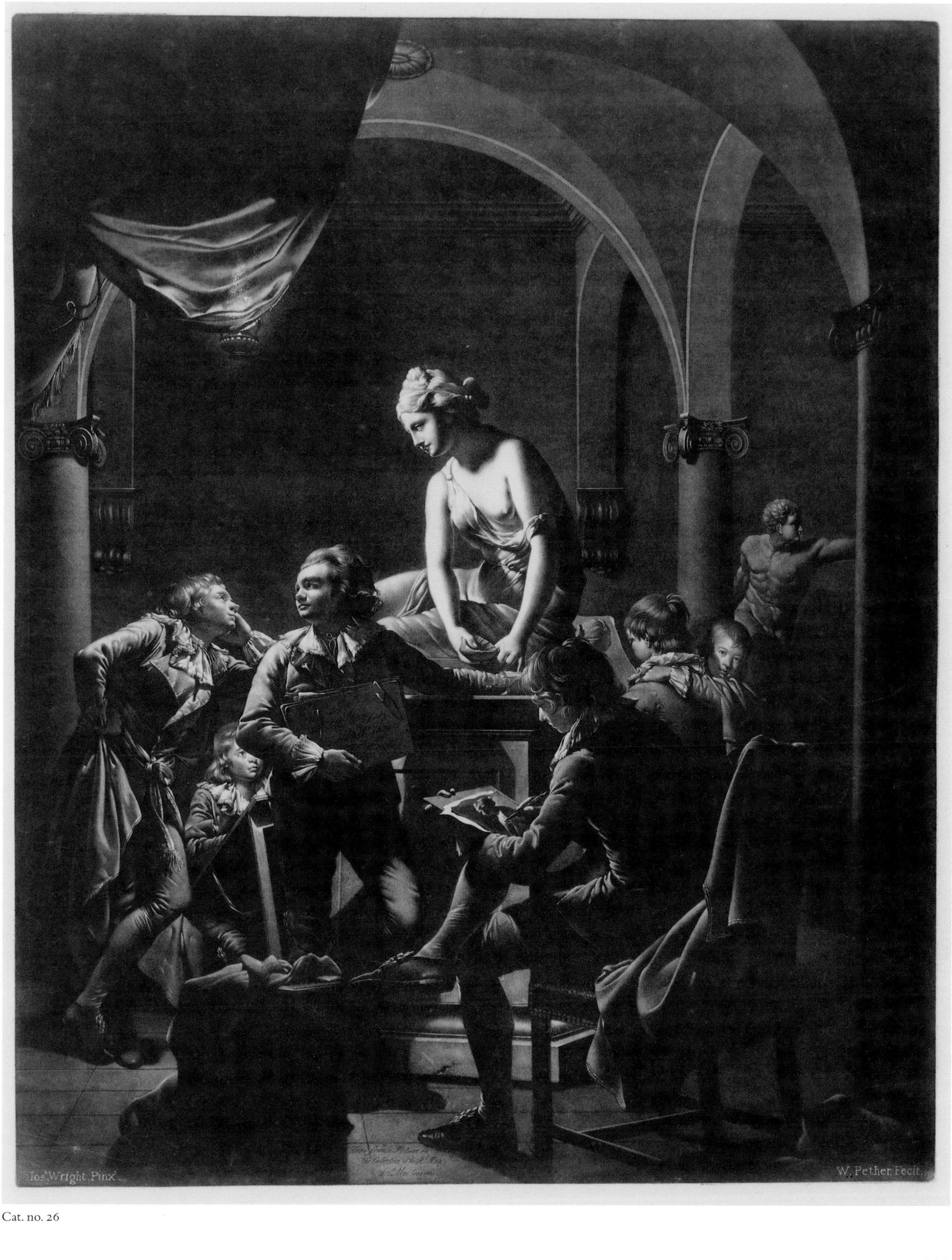

Cat. no. 26

Reinier Vinkeles (1741–1816)

27. *The Drawing Academy in Amsterdam*

1768

Engraving, 345 x 390 mm (13⅝ x 15⅜ in.)

References: Le Blanc 34, ii/ii; Nagler 28, ii/ii

Inscription: *R. Vinkeles ad vivum Delin 1764 et sculp 1768. / Afbeelding der TEEKEN ACADEMIE, zoo als Dezelve tot den Jaare 1767 Gehouden / werd boven het Corps de Garde van de Leydsche Poort te Amsterdam. / Opgedraagen aan den Wel Edelen Groot Achtbaaren Heer Mr WILLEM HUJGHENS, Heere van Honcoop, / Burgemeester en Raad der Stad Amsterdam, Mitsgaders Bewinthebber van de Oostindische Maatschappye / aldaar, en Hooft Directeur der Teeken Academie Door Zyn Wel EdlGr Achtb^r / Dienstw^e Dien^r R. Vinkeles.*

Purchased from James Bergquist, Boston

1999.2

The Amsterdam City Drawing Academy (De Amsterdamse Stadstekenacademie) began meeting in a room above the Leiden Gate (Leidsche Poort) in 1718.[1] In 1765, it was reorganized and in 1767 moved to larger quarters in the town hall, where it remained until it was dissolved in 1821, when the foundation of the Royal Academy of Fine Arts made it superfluous. From 1773 to 1792, a school for the training of the young to become professional artists was operated by the Drawing Academy, which itself was essentially a society of artists and dilettantes who met together to draw from the live model and plaster casts and to hear lectures, both practical and theoretical, presented by the academy's directors (six served simultaneously) and guests (most prominently and frequently the internationally renowned anatomist Petrus Camper).[2] In 1766, the academy began awarding annual prizes in life drawing.

Reinier Vinkeles's engraving depicts the Drawing Academy in its room above the Leiden Gate. Although it was produced in 1768, the engraving does not celebrate the opening of a new space, as did the later London and Vienna academy views (cat. nos. 28, 29), but rather documents the original space. The engraving is dedicated to Willem Huyghens, burgomaster of Amsterdam and *ex officio* director general of the Drawing Academy from 1767. Vinkeles was one of the directors of the academy as well as its secretary, but lectured on only one known occasion, speaking on contours in representations of the human figure, on March 25, 1767.[3] His view of the Drawing Academy proved influential on representations of groups of artists at work in other Dutch centers.[4]

In a room with a timbered ceiling, about twenty men, many arranged in two rows one above the other at right, are gathered around a nude male model (proposals for the use of a nude female model were rebuffed in the Drawing Academy).[5] Their instrument in every case is a chalk holder, and they hold drawing boards in their arms or on their laps, without the benefit of desks or of individual lamps evident in the views of life-study rooms in London and Vienna. The model, illuminated by a large, hanging, multiflame lamp as well as by a smaller spotlight, is seated on a podium next to a stove.[6] Drawing from plaster casts was practiced at the academy in the summer; in his description of the room, the city historian Jan Wagenaar mentioned that "along the walls, some plaster casts and other pictures [are] placed, for the practice of young and junior members"—yet only two-dimensional works are evident against the wall at right in the engraving.[7] Vinkeles proclaims in the inscription that, although the print was engraved in 1768, he drew it "from life" (*ad vivum*) in 1764. Attesting to his claim is a series of nearly twenty surviving study drawings for the composition, including one of the figure standing at the far right, identifiable as Cornelis Ploos van Amstel, an extremely influential dilettante draftsman, printmaker, collector, art theorist, one of the directors of the Drawing Academy (who had been instrumental in its reorganization in 1765), and a frequent lecturer at the academy.[8]

Vinkeles's engraving of the Drawing Academy appears in miniature in the lower ornamental border of a list of the subscribers of the print and the number of impressions they ordered.[9] The list was engraved by Vinkeles after a design by Jacob Otten Husly, another director of the Drawing Academy and frequent lecturer there who is seated in the foreground at the right of Vinkeles's view of the academy. Thirty men, nineteen of whom were named as members of the academy, were to receive a total of seventy impressions, three of which were explicitly accorded to Vinkeles as engraver of the work.

JC

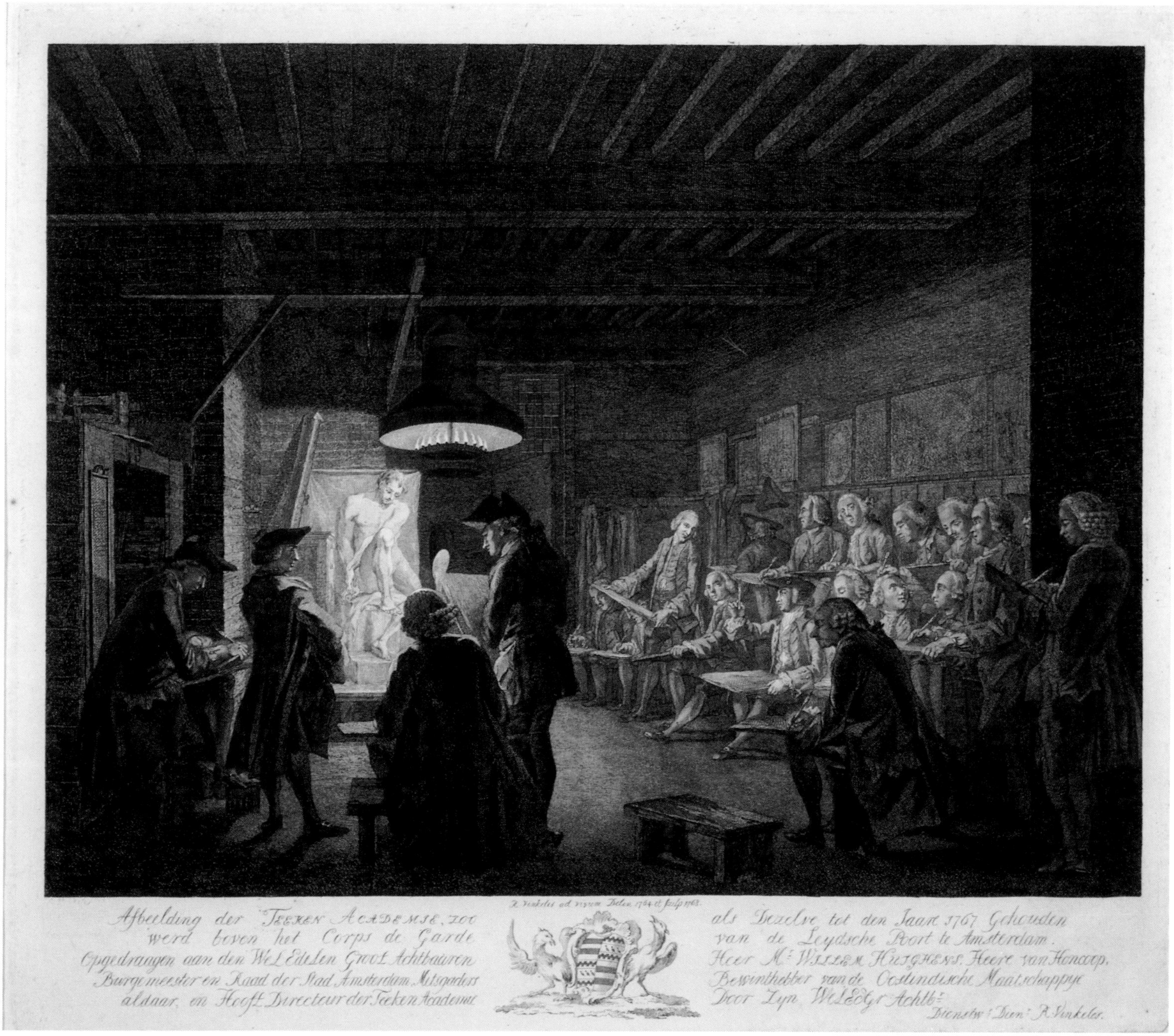

Cat. no. 27

1. On the Amsterdam City Drawing Academy, see Knolle 1979; Offerhaus 1979. For earlier academies in the Netherlands, see De Klerk 1986–1987; Akademie der Künste, Hochschule der Künste 1996, 51.
2. The lectures were disseminated in various ways: in summary in the *Nieuwe Nederlandsche Jaarboeken,* published individually (e.g., see Offerhaus 1979, 43–45), gathered and published together in 1785, and even, in the case of Camper's, translated into French, German, and English (see Knolle 1979, 11–13 and passim). For the role of dilettantes in the Drawing Academy, see also Knolle 1986–87.
3. Knolle 1979, 38.
4. Ibid., 30 n. 13.
5. Ibid., 21. A male model might, however, assume the pose of an ancient female sculpture (Offerhaus 1979, 62).
6. Another state of the engraving, very close in all other respects to the present state, shows the model as standing (Niemeijer 1962, 214, no. 35; Knolle 1979, 5). The academy models' poses alternated from week to week between those drawn from a classical repertoire—specifically those published by Jan de Bisschop (*Signorum Veterum Icones,* 1668–69) and François Perrier (*Icones et Segmenta,* 1638)—to "free" poses chosen by those responsible for arranging the model (*stellers*) (Offerhaus 1979, 61, according to a decision of 1766; see also Knolle 1979, 19–20). Renaissance and Baroque prototypes were also used (Offerhaus 1979, 62).
7. For Wagenaar's description, see Knolle 1979, 5. On the academy's collection of plaster casts, see Offerhaus 1979, 52–53.
8. For the drawings, see Niemeijer 1962, 212, no. 28; Knolle 1979, 10 and 30 n. 13, who also notes that the identities of other figures in the engraving are indicated on an impression in the Amsterdams Gemeentearchief.
9. Knolle 1979, 6, fig. 3.

Richard Earlom (1743–1822)
after Johann Zoffany (1733–1810)

28. *The Academicians of the Royal Academy*

1773

Mezzotint, 507 x 721 mm (20 x 28⅜ in.)

Reference: Chaloner-Smith 1, i–ii/ii

Inscription: below image: *J Zoffany pinxit Publish'd August 1st 1773 R. Sayer Excudit Rd Earlom sculpsit*

Purchased from Paul McCarron, New York

1996.7

The Royal Academy of Arts in London was founded late in 1768 under the aegis and with the financial support (until 1780) of King George III, who declared himself its "patron, protector and supporter."[1] In 1771, the king made available to the Royal Academy rooms in the Old Somerset House, a royal palace that included separate spaces for lectures, drawing from plaster casts, and drawing the live model. Probably to celebrate the opening of the new space and perhaps for the king himself, Johann Zoffany painted a group portrait of the members of the academy (fig. 28.1), ostensibly engaged in life study.[2] Most of those depicted were founding members, although Zoffany, who appears in the extreme left foreground, palette and brushes in hand, was nominated to the academy in 1769 by George III personally, an unusual distinction. Richard Earlom produced his mezzotint copy of Zoffany's composition (unreversed) in 1773. A later state of the impression carries a dedication to George III by the publisher, Robert Sayer.

In the life-study room two models were posed each night and drawn by the candlelight of the large lamp hanging from the ceiling. In Zoffany's composition, one model is being positioned by the keeper of the academy schools, George Michael Moser, who loops a rope around his right hand, and another is undressing. But also included in Zoffany's composition, arranged against the back walls, are casts of ancient and modern sculpture (although the academy had a separate space for full-length casts) and an *écorché* (flayed) figure, alluding to the Royal Academy's full academic program.[3] This *écorché* was used by Dr. William Hunter, Professor of Anatomy at the Royal Academy and pictured in the center of Zoffany's group portrait, his hand to his chin in apparently profound contemplation. The *écorché* also appears in a contemporaneous painting by Zoffany of Hunter lecturing at the Royal Academy (fig. 28.2).[4] In the life-study composition, the academicians are, for the most part, attentive to the posing of the model, but no one is prepared to

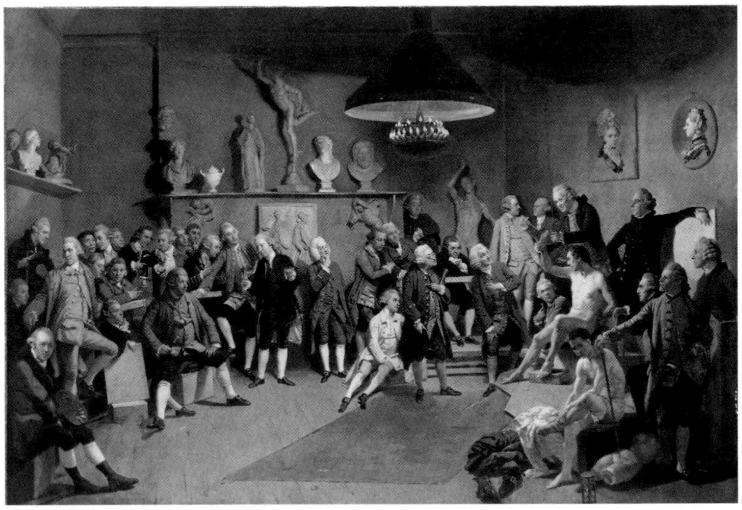

Fig. 28.1. Johann Zoffany. *The Academicians of the Royal Academy.* 1771–72. Oil on canvas, 100.7 x 147.3 cm (39¾ x 58 in.). The Royal Collection, Her Majesty Queen Elizabeth II.

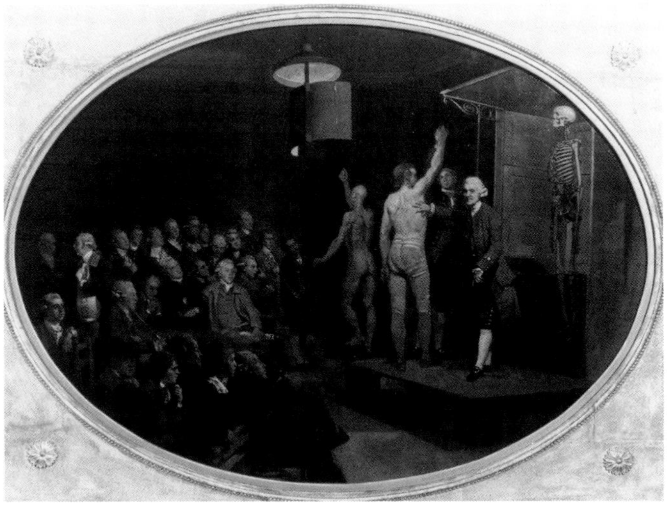

Fig. 28.2. Johann Zoffany. *Dr. William Hunter Lecturing at the Royal Academy.* c. 1775. Oil on canvas, 103.5 x 77.5 cm (40¾ x 30½ in.), oval. The Royal College of Physicians of London.

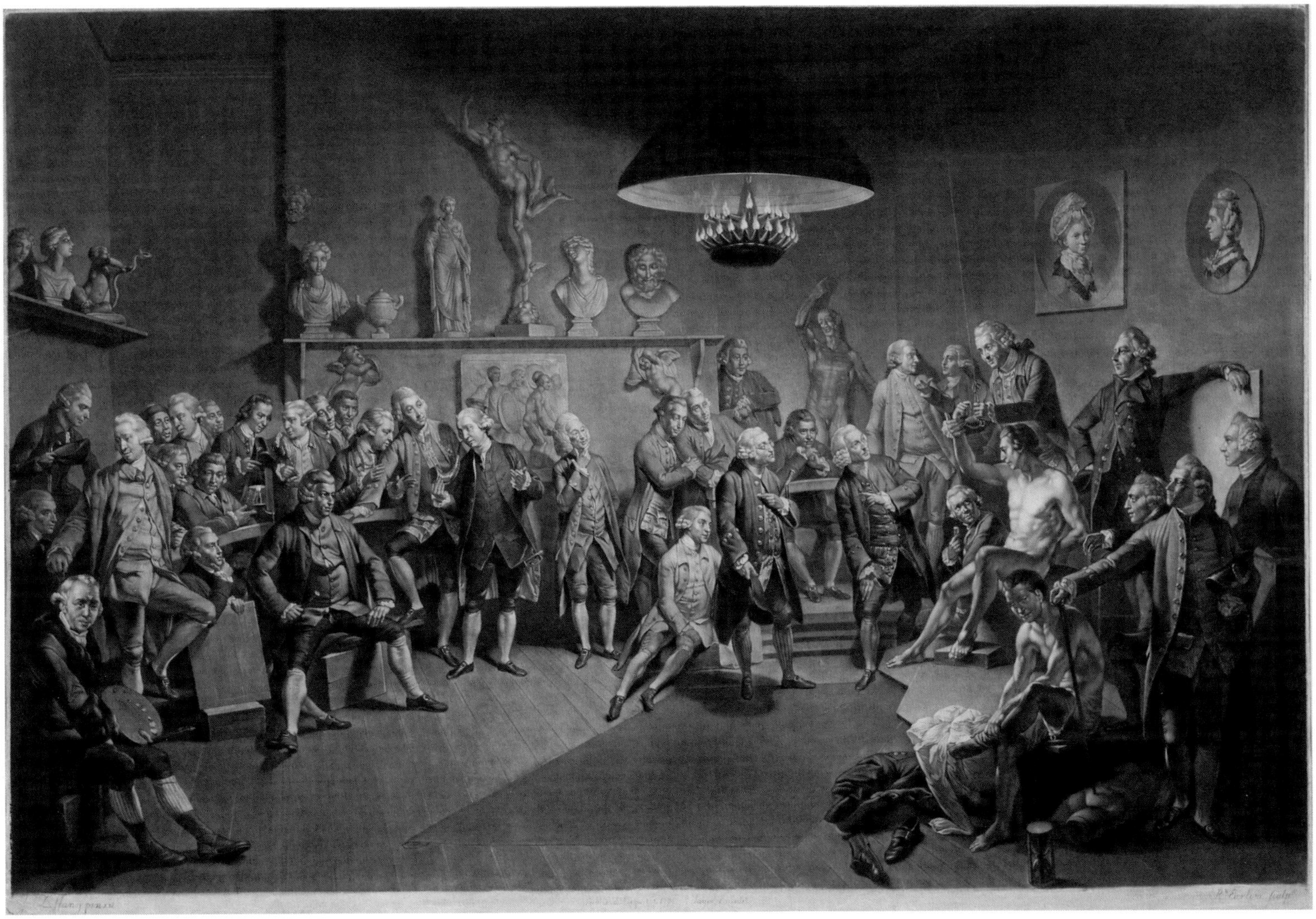

Cat. no. 28

draw him—indeed, the life study was for the instruction of students—although several are seated at the benches arranged in an arc for that purpose.[5] The poses of the figures are richly varied, from Francis Hayman boldly splayed at the left to Richard Cosway pompously resting his walking stick on a cast of a female torso while affecting the pose of the Apollo Belvedere.[6] Joshua Reynolds, the academy's president, stands just to the left of center, using his ear trumpet to listen to Francis Milner Newton, the academy's secretary. Giovanni Battista Cipriani appears, holding his hat and a cane, at the far left of the composition. In 1775, following a disagreement between Cipriani, who held the position of visitor at the time, and Moser, it was "resolved that the Visitor shall be considered as Master of the Living-Academy; and that neither the Keeper nor any other Academician shall presume to enter the Room whilst the Visitor is setting the Model, nor shall they give any instructions or Orders whatsoever whilst the Visitor is present. . . ."[7] The two women academicians (the history painter Angelica Kauffman, a founding member, and the flower painter Mary Moser) are represented only by portraits on the wall at right (on the square and oval canvas, respectively).[8] Women were not allowed to draw from the model in the Royal Academy until 1893,[9] and Zoffany was careful not to violate decorum.

The Royal Academy was not the first institution in England with life-study classes, nor was Zoffany's the first portrayal of English artists with a model. Paintings of life study, probably at both James Thornhill's academy and the Saint Martin's Lane Academy, exist, although the identification of the settings is uncertain.[10] One of the casts in the later painting, of around 1760 (fig. 28.3), reappears in Zoffany's painting of the life study at the Royal Academy.[11] According to "The Instrument of Foundation" of 1768, the Royal Academy was to maintain a "Winter Academy of Living Models, men and women of different characters . . . free to all Students who shall be qualified to receive advantage from such studies," and a "Summer Academy of Living Models, to paint after, also of Laymen with draperies, both Antient and Modern, Plaister Figures, Bas-reliefs, models and designs of Fruits, Flowers, Ornaments, &c., free to all artists qualified to receive advantage from such studies. . . ."[12] In his inaugural address on January 2, 1769,

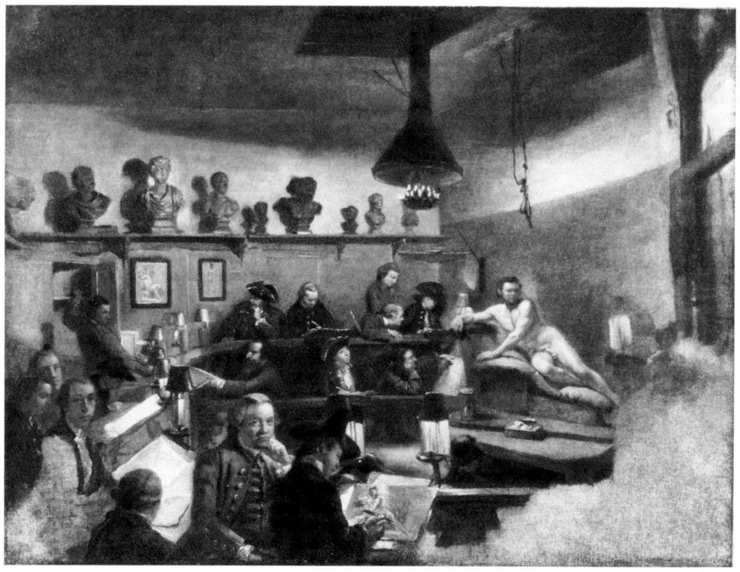

Fig. 28.3. British School. *A Life Class (St. Martin's Lane Academy?)*. c. 1760. Oil on canvas, unfinished, 48.2 x 64.7 cm (19 x 25½ in.). Royal Academy of Arts, London.

Reynolds urged a "scrupulous exactness" in the drawing of the model, the lack of which he saw as a failure in "all the Academies I have ever visited." Life study thus fit into Reynolds's larger scheme of art instruction, by which genius can only be realized through long labor and understanding of the rules of art,[13] a position underscored by Zoffany's setting his group portrait in the life-study room of the Royal Academy. JC

1. On the Royal Academy of Arts, see Hutchison 1968; and Hutchison 1986-87.
2. On the painting, which is in the Royal Collection, see Manners and Williamson 1920, 28-33 (a key identifying the figures is reproduced following p. 28); Webster 1976, 57-58.
3. Goldstein 1996, 54-55. The Academy's curriculum, with only an Antique School and a Life School, was much simpler than that of most other academies (Pevsner 1940, 177 n. 1). Avery 1998, 42, points out that one of the sculptures at the back is Giambologna's *Mercury in Flight*.
4. On the painting and the *écorché*, which Hunter had been instrumental in making for the Society of Artists, probably in the early 1760s, see Webster 1976, 58; Bignamini and Postle 1991, 87, 94-96.
5. The life-study room is presumably the setting for a student drawing by Thomas Rowlandson, inscribed as drawn at the Royal Academy and dated 1776, which depicts artists working on the bench (see Hayes 1972, 29-30).
6. For a feminist reading of his "pressing his stick dismissively into the damaged female torso," see Perry 1999, 148.
7. Quoted by Hutchison 1968, 61, from the General Assembly Minutes. On the role of the academy's nine visitors, see Hutchison 1968, 46.
8. According to Goldstein 1996, 55 (see also p. 62), the painting is "the first representation of a studio or academy including women in any form."
9. Pevsner 1940, 231; Nochlin 1971, 24.
10. See Bignamini and Postle 1991, 39-41. On Thornhill's and the Saint Martin's Lane academies, see Bignamini 1986-87, 442-43. See Bignamini 1986-87, 438, for Marshall Smith's remark in *Art of Painting* (1692) that one gains facility in drawing by "having studied Nuditys at the *Academy*."
11. The lamp in this painting makes a reappearance in a painting by Elias Martin, *Cast Room at the Royal Academy*; see Bignamini and Postle 1991, 41-43.
12. Hutchison 1968, 212.
13. Reynolds 1975, 18-21.

Johann Jacobe (1733-1797)

after Martin Ferdinand Quadal (1736-1808)

29. *Model Studio in the Imperial Academy of Art, Vienna*

1790

Mezzotint, 650 x 790 mm (25⅝ x 31⅛ in.)

References: Le Blanc 18, i/ii; Heller and Andresen 6, i/iii

Purchased from R. E. Lewis, Belvedere, California

1999.16

In 1692, the Viennese Academy of Painting, Sculpture, and Architecture (Akademie der Malerei, Bildhauerei und Baukunst) was founded. An academy of engraving (Kupferstecherakademie) was founded in 1766, and the Model-Stamping School (Erzverschneiderschule or Possier-, Verschneid- und Graveurakademie) in 1767. The three academies were combined in 1772 as the Imperial Academy of United Pictorial Arts (K. K. Akademie der Vereinigten Bildenden Künste), which consisted of five or six schools: painting (sometimes subdivided into history and landscape), sculpture, architecture, engraving, and model-stamping.[1] With the support of Emperor Joseph II and the ambitious leadership of the *Protektor*, Wenzel Anton, Prince Kaunitz-Rietberg (1711-1794), the Imperial

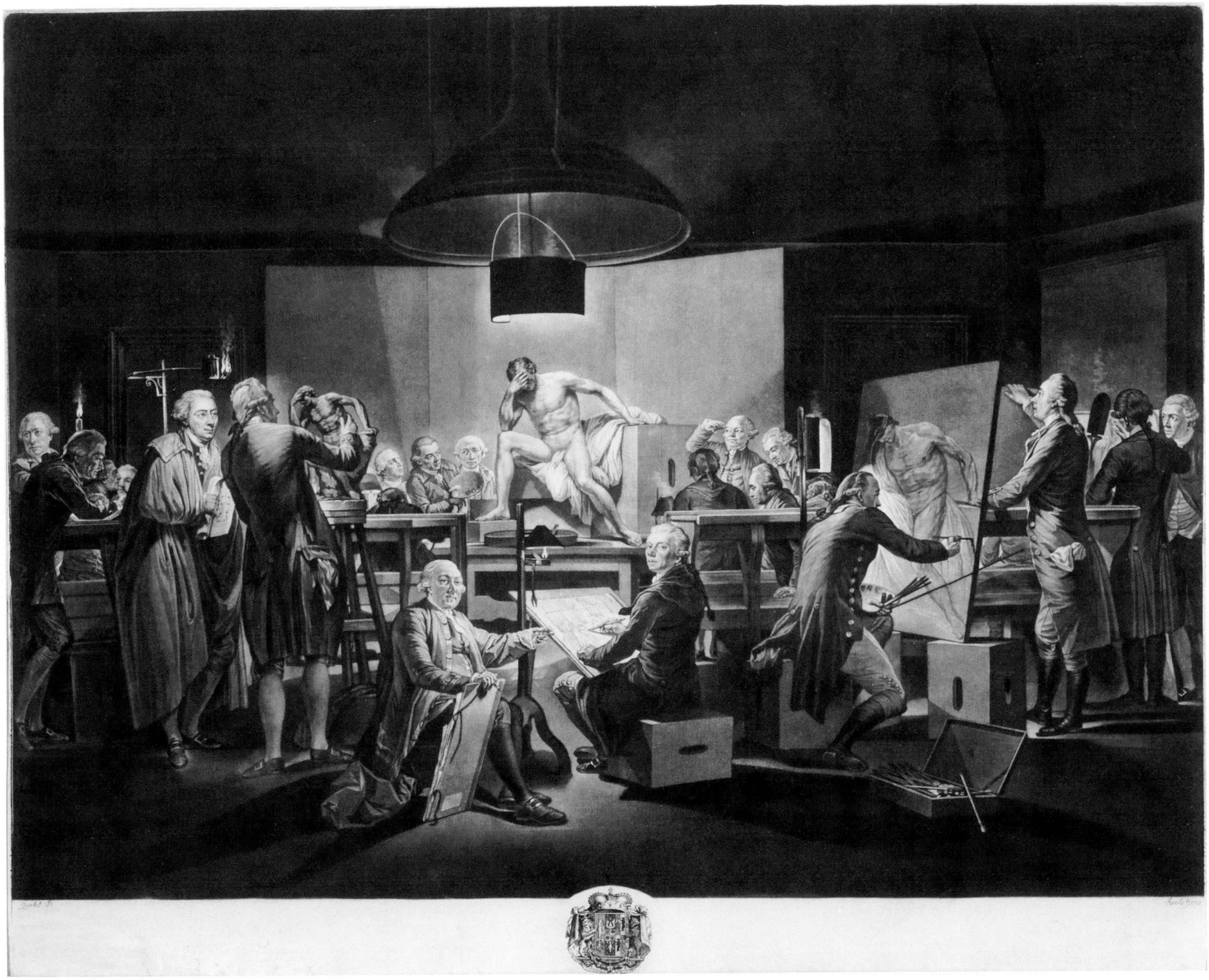

Cat. no. 29

Academy outgrew its quarters at the university and in 1786 became the most spacious academy in Europe when it took over the former Jesuit college of Saint Anna, which, with the suppression of the Jesuit order, had recently been secularized.[2] The next year, Martin Ferdinand Quadal painted the evening life-study class at the academy, which took place in a dedicated room on the fourth floor of the building.[3] In 1790, Johann Jacobe (or Jacobé) produced in mezzotint a close (unreversed) copy of Quadal's composition, and both works were exhibited together that year at the academy.

On a raised platform under lamps baffled to focus their light and vented to remove their smoke, a nude male poses as a "thinker," rather like one of the students in Enea Vico's engraving of Baccio Bandinelli's academy (cat. no. 21). Gathered around the model are about twenty men, many of whom are recognizable. At left, modeling the figure in clay, is Franz Anton Zauner (1746–1822), professor of sculpture at the academy. With him, holding a rolled-up building plan, is Johann Ferdinand von Hohenberg (1732–1816), professor of architecture. At the right side of the composition, working on a canvas, is the painter Heinrich Friedrich Füger (1751–1818), vice-director of the academy. In the center is the engraver Jacob Matthias Schmutzer (or Schmuzer, 1733–1811), director of the erstwhile Kupferstecherakademie and professor of the engraving school in the Imperial Academy, as well as Johann Jacobe's teacher. He directs the viewer's attention to Quadal himself, who turns away from his work, a chalk drawing of the present composition, toward the viewer. At the far left is Jacobe.[4] A later state of Jacobe's mezzotint carries a dedication (in French) to Kaunitz, who was not only the guiding force of the reformed academy, but also a personal supporter of many of the artists featured in Quadal's composition.

Quadal's painting of academicians gathered around a nude male model recalls Johann Zoffany's painting of the Royal Academy in London of 1771-72 (fig. 28.1) which Quadal probably saw while working in England in the 1770s. Richard Earlom's engraving after Zoffany's painting (cat. no. 28) would have been well known in Vienna. The mezzotint technique was most successfully practiced in England in the second half of the eighteenth century, and Jacobe, like the Viennese engraver Johann Gottfried Haid (see cat. nos. 44, 45) before him, had been sent to London to train in the technique.[5] Jacobe led a special school of mezzotint at the Imperial Academy, and Vienna became second only to London in importance in the practice of the art.[6] The comparison of Jacobe's mezzotint of academicians and a nude model with Earlom's was made explicit by the art writer, Johann Georg Meusel, who remarked on Quadal's painting in 1788: "Professor Jacobe . . . will also engrave this work of art on a sheet of royal-size paper in mezzotint, so that it will make a worthy counterpart to the famous London Academy after Zoffany, which one might call a representation from the theoretical point of view while this shows the practical side."[7] Indeed, Quadal's composition lacks the classical statuary of Zoffany's image, which might be construed as a reference to the theoretical aspects of the art, and much greater attention is given to actual working after the model than to discourse and contemplation.

The practice of working directly from the nude model had a centuries-old tradition in European art and was a fundamental part of academic training since the sixteenth century. The rendering of the nude figure was deemed a benchmark of an artist's abilities. In 1782, the president of the Viennese academy's advisory board, Baron von Kettler, suggested that contemporary, rather than classical, themes be used for competitions. Among the negative responses to the proposal was that of Joseph Freiherr von Sperges, a member (and, following von Kettler's death in 1783, president) of the advisory board who exercised considerable influence through his relationship with Kaunitz. Sperges remarked simply (and decisively) that there is "an opportunity such as this to choose from mythology or heroic ancient history, according to general custom, primarily because the artist can thereby prove himself in [the depiction of] the nude."[8] Unfortunately, the professors and advisors were perpetually disappointed with the results of the competitions, which revealed that the generally uneducated students were capable of little more than the depiction of the nude.[9]

JC

1. On the history of the Imperial Academy in the later eighteenth century, see Von Lützow 1877, esp. 51-90; Wagner 1967, 37-54; Kuijpers 1986-1987, esp. 379-82.
2. Pevsner 1940, 180.
3. The painting is in the academy's collection and is often assumed to have been the artist's reception piece for membership, but there is no documentation of his membership, and the painting was given to the academy by Anton Graf Lamberg-Sprinzenstein, whose portrait Quadal had painted in Naples in 1784. See Trnek 1997, 227, 250-251. For a floor plan, including the *Modellsaal,* see von Lützow 1877, 77.
4. For further identifications, see Trnek 1997, 251.
5. See Friesen 1980, 3-4, for Haid's and Jacobe's training in London.
6. Von Lützow 1877, 67.
7. Trans. Griffiths and Carey 1994, 86-87; see also Von Lützow 1877, 82 n. 3.
8. Quoted in Kuijpers 1986-87, 386.
9. Kuijpers 1986-87, 395.

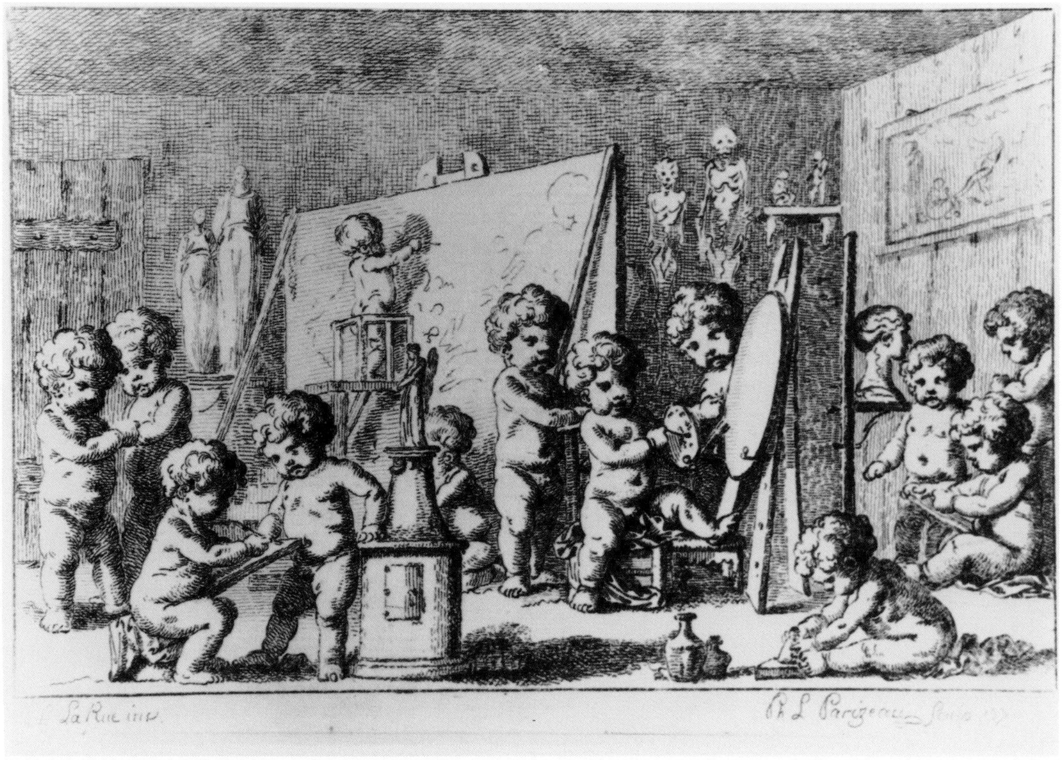

Cat. no. 30

Philippe-Louis Parizeau (1740–1801)
after Louis-Félix de La Rue (1730–1777)

30. *Artists' Studio with Children*

1771
Etching, 98 x 140 mm (3⅞ x 5½ in.)
Reference: Le Blanc 129
Inscriptions: below image: *L F La Rue inv.*; *Ph L Parizeau Sculp 1771*
Purchased from Kunsthandlung Helmut H. Rumbler, Frankfurt
1997.19

Following the success of Titian's paintings featuring numerous putti, compositions in which putti or toddlers frolic or pursue adult activities—often, but by no means exclusively, art production—became common in the seventeenth and especially the eighteenth centuries, probably as part of a general trend toward the increased attention to childhood in European culture.[1] At times, the children act in the service of allegory, as in Giovanni Andrea Podestà's *Allegory with Cupid and Putti* of 1640 (cat. no. 55) or William Hogarth's *Boys Peeping at Nature* a century later (cat. no. 61). At other times they simply substitute for adults and older children, as in this *Artists' Studio with Children*. French artists had a particular penchant for the type, although the phenomenon was spread internationally.[2] In 1669, for example, François Chauveau etched a composition by Pierre Mignard with children drawing a bust of Minerva, grinding colors, and so on, one of a pair of vignettes appearing in an edition of Molière's *La Gloire du Val-de-Grâce*.[3] François Boucher, one of the most successful and influential artists of the eighteenth century, was particularly fond of painting putti and small children in action. On several occasions he represented painting, sculpture, and architecture, along with other arts, such as music and poetry, as part of a decorative scheme, as in the eight panels painted for the marquise de Pompadour in

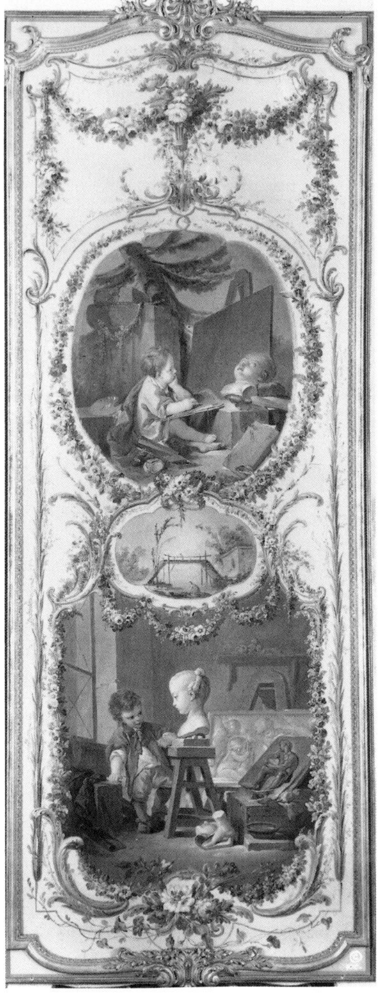

Fig. 30.1. François Boucher. *Painting and Sculpture* from *The Arts and Sciences*. c. 1750–52. Oil on canvas, 217.2 x 77.5 cm (85½ x 30½ in.). The Frick Collection, New York.

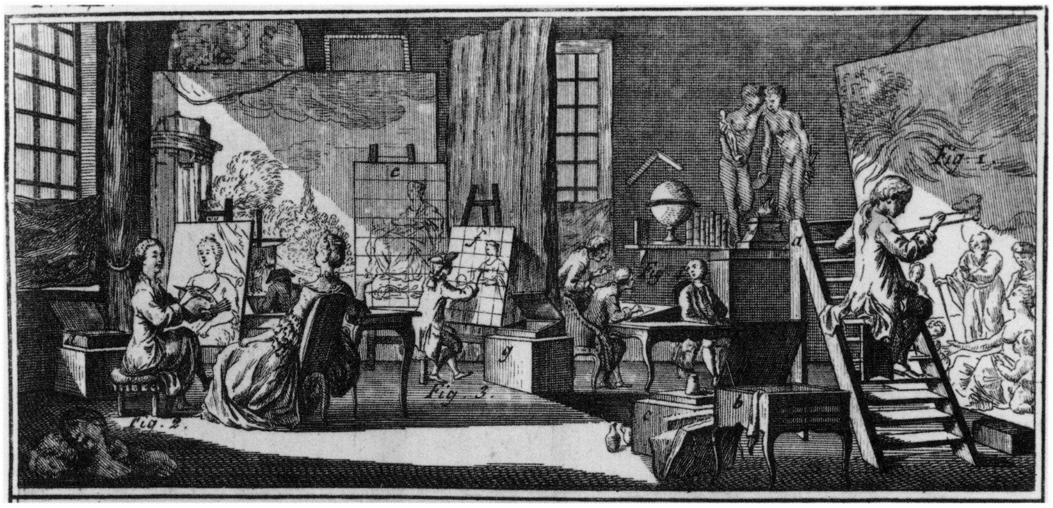

Fig. 30.2. *Painters' Workshop* from Denis Diderot and Jean le Rond d'Alembert, *Grande Encyclopédie*. c. 1767. Etching and engraving. 95 x 205 mm (3¾ x 8⅛ in.). Sarah Campbell Blaffer Foundation, Houston.

the early 1750s, now in the Frick Collection, New York (fig. 30.1), and the seven canvases for the Danish king Christian VII from 1756-57.[4] In Boucher's work, the more allegorical compositions tend to consist of nude putti, and the infantilized genre scenes, like the Pompadour panels, of clothed children.[5]

Louis-Félix de La Rue's composition, etched by Philippe-Louis Parizeau, combines these two approaches to the subject: small children (not winged putti) paint, draw, and sculpt in a large studio space.[6] At the far right, a child draws after a sculptured bust, which was commonly represented in other studio scenes as part of young artists' training (for example, cat. nos. 22-24), albeit by children of a more realistically capable age. The painters in the center of the image take on adult activities, painting an oval on an easel and a large canvas, to reach the upper portion of which the painter has to rely on a movable scaffold, comparable to one represented in the depiction of a painting studio in Diderot's and d'Alembert's *Grande Encyclopédie* (fig. 30.2). Other common motifs of the iconography of academies and studios appear, namely, casts of classical sculptures (although here remarkably elongated and without attention to specific prototypes) and skeletons (see, for example, fig. 28.1).[7]

JC

1. See, for example, Ariès 1962; Steward 1995.
2. See, for example, in addition to the Hogarth *Boys Peeping at Nature,* Joshua Reynolds's *The Infant Academy* of 1781-82, which was reproduced as a stipple engraving by Francis Haward in 1783, and copied several times (Martin Postle in Mannings 2000, 1:538-39); Joseph Wagner's *Children in a Studio,* c. 1750, after Jacopo Amigoni (Rumbler 1993, no. 51).
3. See Weigert 1951, 48, nos. 1049-1051; Rumbler 1993, no. 22. Cf. the print of c. 1729 by Frédéric Horthemels after Jean-Baptiste Vanloo, also a vignette, of children drawing, painting, and sculpting (Bruand and Hébert 1970, 379; Rumbler 1993, no. 42). See also Georgel and Lecoq 1987, 266.
4. See Ananoff 1976, 2:68-72, nos. 365-72, and 2:145-46, nos. 467-73, respectively; see also 1:200-201, no. 67; 2:60, no. 357; 2:127-29, nos. 444-48; 2:168-70, nos. 492-95; 2:210-11, no. 545.
5. Cf. Carle Vanloo's painting of a child portraitist (clothed) in San Francisco from 1753, also for the marquise de Pompadour (reproduced in Rosenblum 1986, 47).
6. Parizeau etched over a hundred compositions by La Rue in 1770-71, including many of children (Portalis and Béraldi 1880-1882, 3:271). The *Artists' Studio with Children* was paired with a similar work on sculpture (Le Blanc 130). La Rue's sculptural work also often involved representations of children.
7. See also Eschenburg 2001, 113, 117.

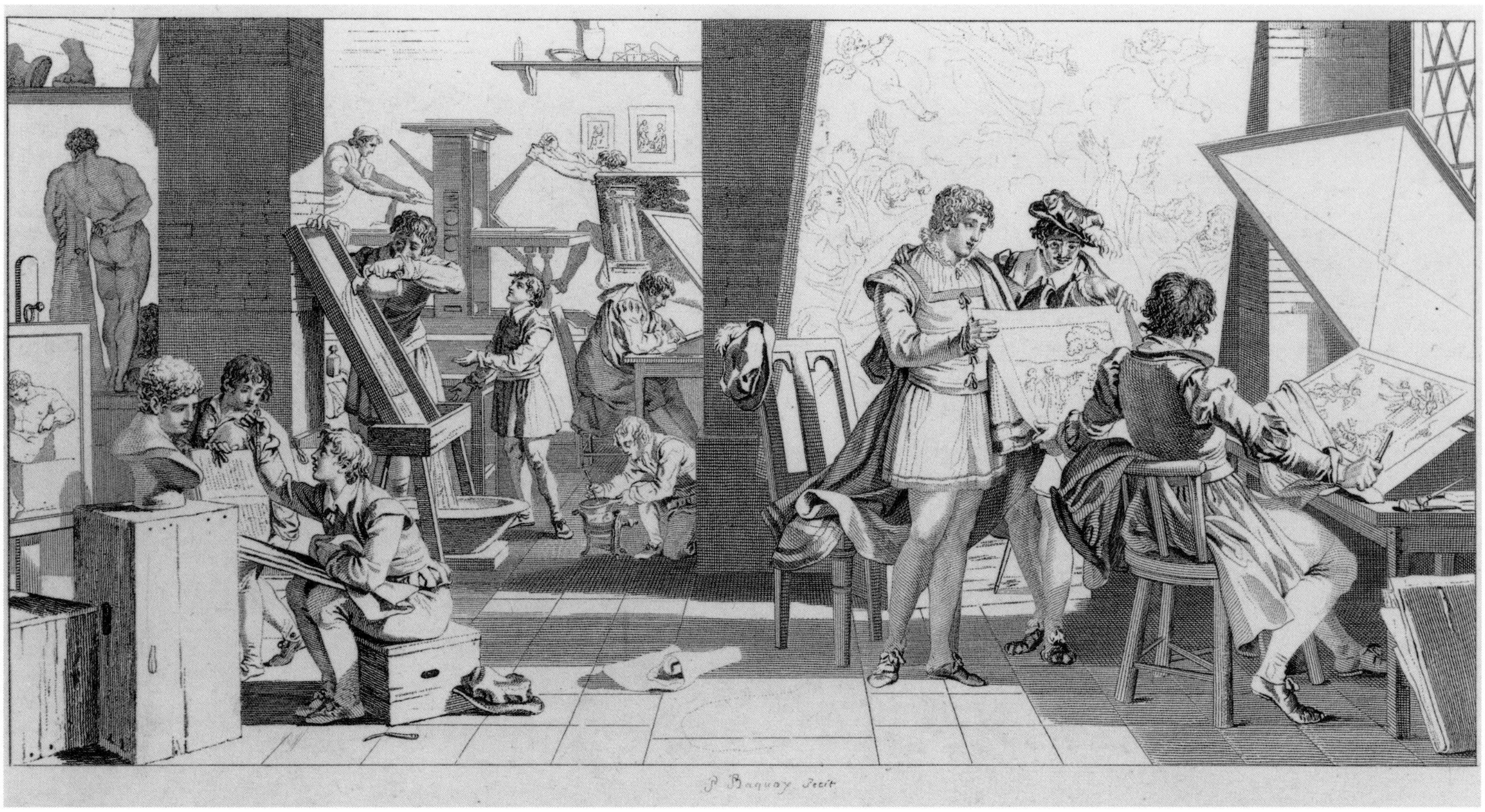

Cat. no. 31

Pierre-Charles Baquoy (1759–1829)
after Jean-Michel Moreau (called Le Jeune) (1741–1814)

31. *Studio of a Printmaker*

1806

Unfinished proof in etching, 110 x 216 mm (4⅜ x 8½ in.) (image size)

Inscription: below image: *P Baquoy fecit*

Anonymous gift, in memory of Spencer A. Samuels

2004.8

The depiction of an engraving workshop, which appears only in pure etching in the present impression, was fully engraved for publication in the multivolume *Le Musée français, recueil complèt des tableaux, statues et bas-reliefs, qui composent la collection nationale; avec l'explication des sujets, et des discours historiques sur la peinture, la sculpture et la gravure (The French Museum: Complete Collection of the Paintings, Statues, and Bas-reliefs that Constitute the National Collection, with an Explication of the Subjects and Some Historical Discourses on Painting, Sculpture, and Engraving),* published in Paris from 1803 to 1809 (fig. 31.1).[1] This large project involved other leading Parisian engravers of the period, including Charles-Clément Bervic, Robert Daudet, François Jacques Dequevauviller, and Jean Massard. Each of the four historical discourses (painting is separated into ancient and modern) includes a vignette of an artist's studio, as well as an allegorical tailpiece. All eight of these compositions were designed by Jean-Michel Moreau. Four were engraved by Jean-Baptiste Simonet and one by Emmanuel De Ghendt. Baquoy engraved three: the tailpiece to the discourse on modern painting, the vignette and the tailpiece to the discourse on engraving (fig. 31.2), in which Engraving gains the laurel crown already worn by Painting, and the two join hands.[2]

Moreau's composition recalls earlier representations of printmaking shops, such as the two images produced by Abraham Bosse

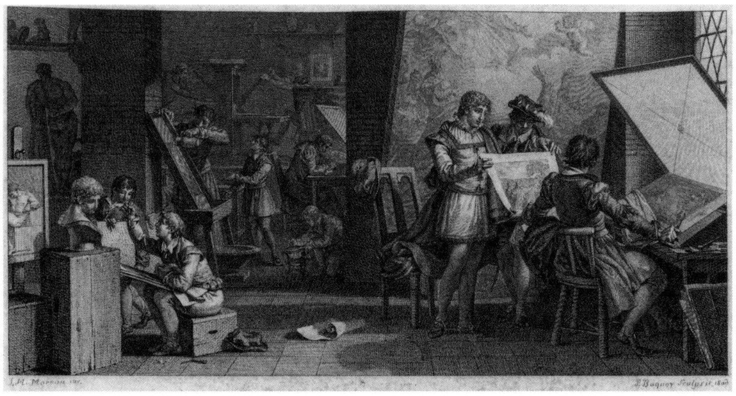

Fig. 31.1. Pierre-Charles Baquoy after Jean-Michel Moreau (called Le Jeune). *Studio of a Printmaker.* 1806. Etching and engraving. In *Le Musée français, recueil complèt des tableaux, statues et bas-reliefs, qui composent la collection nationale; avec l'explication des sujets, et des discours historiques sur la peinture, la sculpture et la gravure* (Paris, 1803–09). Fine Arts Library, The University of Texas Libraries, The University of Texas at Austin.

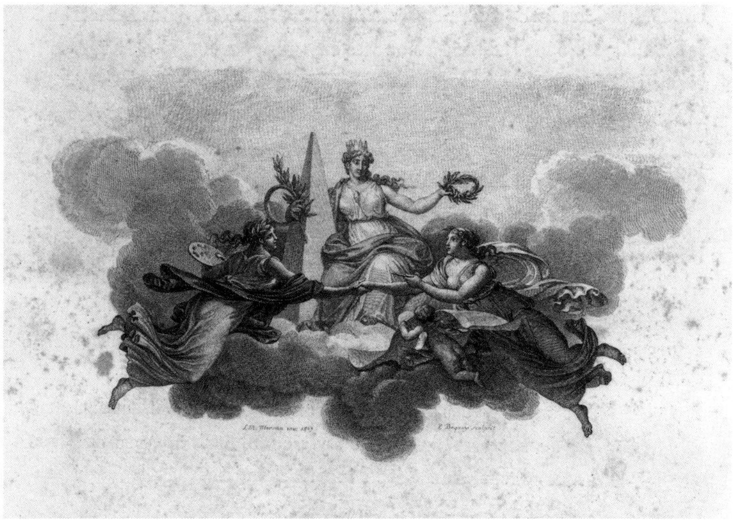

Fig. 31.2. Pierre-Charles Baquoy after Jean-Michel Moreau (called Le Jeune). *Engraving and Painting.* 1806. Etching and engraving. In *Le Musée français, recueil complèt des tableaux, statues et bas-reliefs, qui composent la collection nationale; avec l'explication des sujets, et des discours historiques sur la peinture, la sculpture et la gravure* (Paris, 1803–09). Fine Arts Library, The University of Texas Libraries, The University of Texas at Austin.

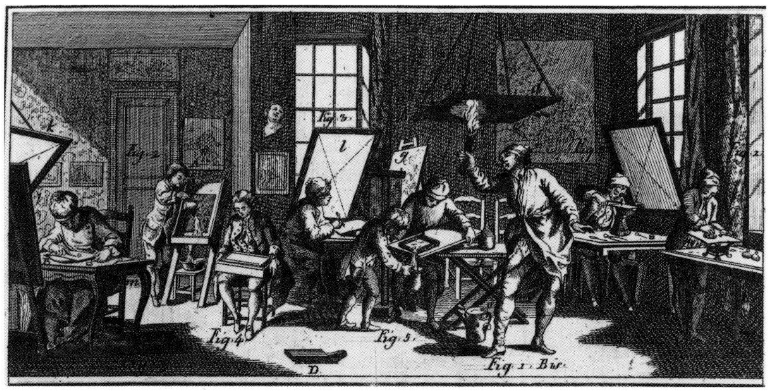

Fig. 31.3. A.-J. Defehrt after Benoit-Louis Prévost. *Engravers' Workshop* from Denis Diderot and Jean le Rond d'Alembert, *Grande Encyclopédie.* 1767. Etching and engraving, 96 x 199 mm (3¾ x 7⅞ in.). Sarah Campbell Blaffer Foundation, Houston.

in the 1640s (figs. 68.1, 68.2), and the engraving by A.-J. Defehrt after Benoit-Louis Prévost from 1767 in the fifth plate volume (*quatrième livraison*) of Diderot and d'Alembert's *Grande Encyclopédie* (fig. 31.3).[3] In both instances, text and illustration (with numerous depictions of individual tools and techniques supplementing the general view in the *Encyclopédie*) explain the activities undertaken in the production of etched and engraved plates and, in the case of Bosse, the pulling of impressions, represented more systematically and completely than in Baquoy's image. Unlike the figures in the Bosse and *Encyclopédie* compositions, Baquoy's figures wear historical dress, apparently of the sixteenth century, although the style of the large painting at the right suggests a seventeenth-century context. In any case, the dress is remarkably different from that of the artists in the contemporaneous group of portrait busts by Boilly (cat. no. 19), in keeping with the historical context of *Le Musée français*.

In Baquoy's print, not all the stages in the production of an engraving or etching are illustrated. In the center of the composition, a boy kneels over a burner, warming resin for the coating of a copper plate. Behind him, an artist bends over his work, his etching needle held like a pencil. Left of him, a man pours acid onto an etched plate held up at an angle above a basin collecting the run-off. After several pitchers of acid were poured, the plate would be turned and the process repeated. Some narrative interest is added at the far right to an otherwise illustrative depiction: the *explication* of the vignette relates that "the Artist is occupied in engraving with a burin a large history painting; an Amateur introduces to him a young Artist with his works, on which the Engraver gives his opinions." Between the engraver's work table and the window is a frame, covered with paper that is oiled or varnished for transparency, to diffuse the light. Behind this group is a large painting, an *Assumption of the Virgin,* presumably there to be copied as a print, although it is not the one on which the engraver is working, despite what is stated in the *explication*. He may be finishing a plate whose composition was first lightly inscribed through etching, a process that was common in this period, including for Moreau's composition itself. At the rear, a man, partially obscured by a landscape painting with an architectural element, pulls on one of the handles of the press and pushes on another with his foot, thereby moving the bed of the press, the engraved or etched plate, and the paper through the roller; the physical exertion required is evident in his posture and the bulging of his muscles. His companion at the press may be handling the cloths used to cover the plate.

The group in the foreground at left is not directly connected with the production of prints, but is familiar from earlier images of artists' studios in which apprentices learn to draw by copying sculptures (see cat. nos. 21–23). The text accompanying the illustrations on engraving in the *Encyclopédie,* probably written by Prévost, asserts that "engraving must be preceded by the study of drawing; this art is its foundation: it is the germ of taste that should enliven it [engraving]. No sentiment, no progress in engraving without an experience consummated in the practice of drawing."[4] Here a boy pauses as he walks past another boy raising a chalk holder to take an approximate measurement of the head of Antinous in front of him.[5] A knife for sharpening his chalk lies on the floor beside him. To the left is a framed depiction of a nude male figure, perhaps a life study, suggesting another stage in the young artist's instruction. At the rear is a large copy of the Farnese Hercules, often depicted from the back, above which are casts of two feet and a head on a shelf.[6]

JC

1. There were recent precedents for the publication of engravings after paintings in significant collections; e.g., Jacques Couché's *Galerie du Palais-Royal* (1786–1808); Jean-Baptiste Wicar's *Tableaux, statues, bas-reliefs et camées de la Galerie de Florence et du Palais Pitti* (Paris, 1789–1814).
2. In some exemplars of *Le Musée français,* one paginated discourse is bound at the beginning of each of four volumes of unpaginated plates (in these cases, the *Studio of a Printmaker* appears on page 1 of volume 3); in other exemplars, the four discourses are gathered together, though still paginated separately, into an unnumbered text volume. The "Discours historique sur la Gravure en taille-douce et sur la Gravure en bois" was written by Toussaint-Bernard Emeric-David; for a brief excerpt, see Gramaccini and Meier 2003, 349–50.
3. On "Gravure . . ." in the *Recueil de planches* of the *Encyclopédie,* see Walsh 2003, 25.
4. "La gravure doit être précédée par l'étude du dessein, cet art en est la base: c'est le germe du goût qui doit la vivifier. Nul sentiment, nul progrès en gravure sans une expérience consommée dans la pratique du dessein." Cf. the comments of Claude-Henri Watelet in the main entry on "Gravure" in the *Encyclopédie,* quoted in Gramaccini and Meier 2003, 358: "Il faut au moins indispendablement que le graveur sache bien dessiner, & qu'il s'entretienne toûjours dans l'habitude du dessein au crayon d'après la bosse & d'après la nature."
5. The famous Belvedere Antinous was in Paris from 1798 to 1815, displayed most of that time at the Musée Central des Arts (Haskell and Penny 1981, 141–43).
6. On the Farnese Hercules, see Haskell and Penny 1981, 229–32.

Dirk Jacobsz. Vellert (1480–85–after 1547)

32. *Saint Luke Painting the Virgin*

1526

Engraving, 170 x 121 mm (6¾ x 4¾ in.) (trimmed)

References: Bartsch, Hollstein 9

Inscriptions: on the stool at lower left: *D V*; on the parapet at lower center: *1526 IN IVLI 28*

Purchased from Susan Schulman, New York, and Carolyn Bullard, Dallas

1998.20

According to a medieval tradition, Saint Luke the Evangelist was a painter who portrayed the Virgin and Christ on several occasions. Images purporting to be by Saint Luke became potent objects of devotion. Luke was adopted as the patron saint of painters; their guilds and, eventually, their academies were dedicated to him. The subject of Saint Luke drawing or painting the Virgin and Child became common in the fifteenth century and following, often in association with the artist's professional life, and especially for altarpieces for the guilds.[1] Dirk Vellert was dean of the Antwerp Guild of Saint Luke in 1518 and again in 1526, the date of this engraving and of his woodcut depicting the arms of the guild. These prints, then, probably commemorate his position with the guild.[2]

Lorne Campbell's comment that "we can form some idea of the appearance of a painter's studio from representations of St Luke drawing or painting the Virgin" seems overly optimistic,[3] although some elements are clearly self-referential. Depictions of the subject might take place in elegant settings, often with an arcade or loggia open to the outside and with patterned marble or tile floors; this approach was taken in Vellert's engraving as well as in works by Rogier van der Weyden and by a follower of Dieric Bouts,[4] and has similarities with innumerable early Netherlandish representations of the Virgin and Child Enthroned. Vellert's architecture is covered with grotesques, which, along with the rounded arches and the exotic tower in the distance, assert the antiquity and exotic location of the narrative, or may be the artist's attempt to demonstrate himself conversant with relatively modern Italianate style.[5] The subsidiary space in the background at right includes a bed with drapes, as if it were the Virgin's bedchamber so often portrayed in early Netherlandish Annunciations. Jean Owens Schaefer

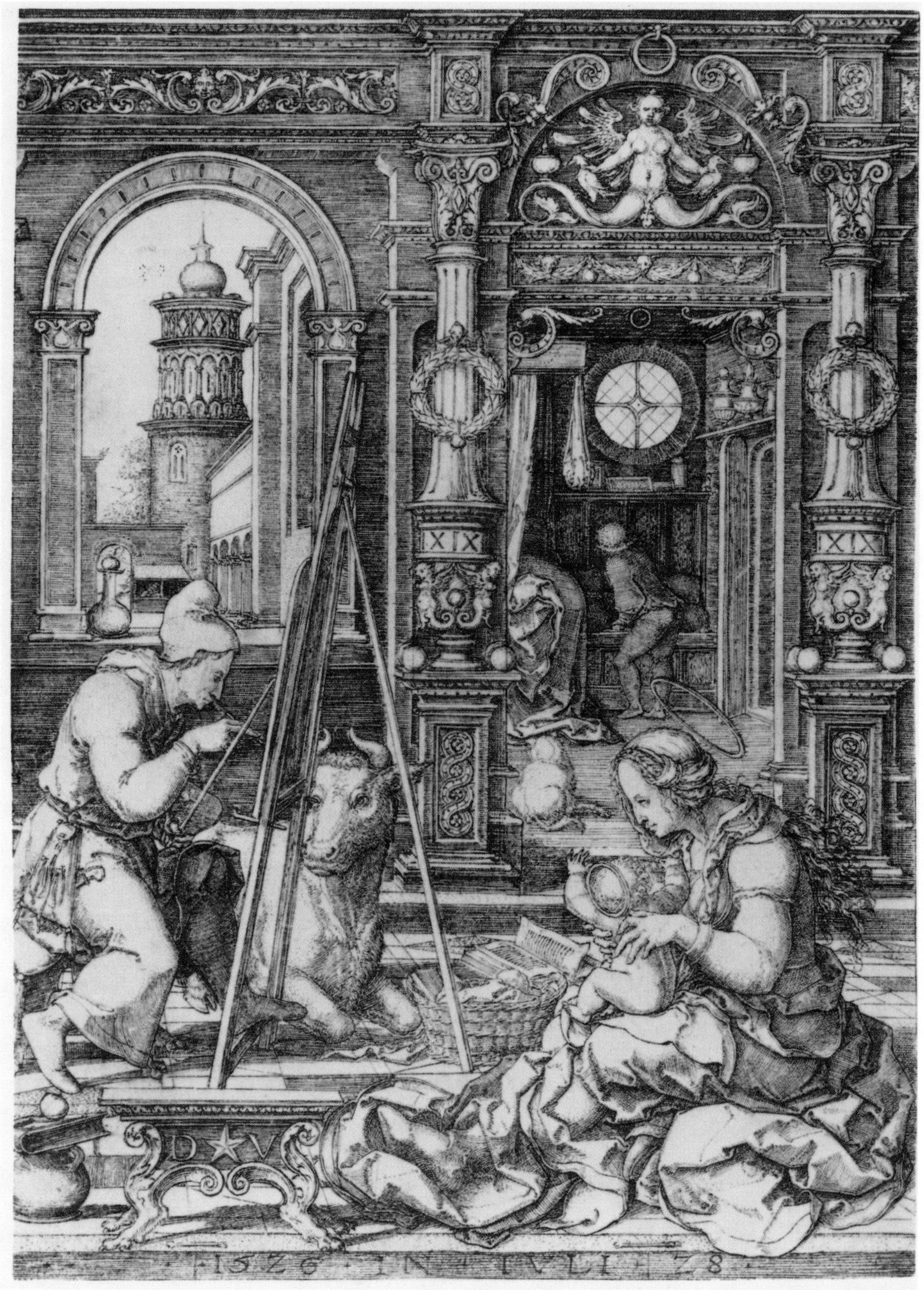

Cat. no. 32

has divided images of Saint Luke painting into two categories: those in which the painter appears with his live subjects in a domestic setting and those in which he is in his workshop and they appear to him as a vision.[6] Although she notes that by the third decade of the sixteenth century, the two types become less distinct, Vellert's image conforms to the former. Unlike the representations by van der Weyden and the follower of Bouts, Vellert's engraving shows the Virgin not enthroned but seated on the ground, a basket for domestic tasks and some scriptural reading at hand, more like a Virgin Annunciate. Most remarkably, Vellert depicts the Christ Child from the rear, his face averted from the viewer.

Saint Luke, in contemporary dress, is working intently on a panel. In a ubiquitous convention, his painting hand is supported by a maulstick held by the other hand, which also holds a palette. His left foot is on the base of the easel in a pose sometimes assumed in other representations of painters at work (for example, cat. nos. 34, 39, 69).[7] His attribute, a large ox, rests—rather incongruously, but placidly—at his side.[8] In the bedchamber, an apprentice or journeyman is grinding colors, a motif introduced by the late fifteenth century that Schaefer suggests "helps to identify Saint Luke as the master craftsman."[9] The figure of the ox became a common convention in the portrayal of artists' workshops in general, quite apart from representations of Saint Luke (see, for examples, cat. nos. 22, 24).[10] The flask for the examination of urine on the window ledge behind Luke alludes to his medical profession. References to Luke as a physician gained much greater emphasis in Maarten van Heemskerck's famous panel from around 1560, where they seem to suggest the scientific—especially anatomical—basis for the painter's art,[11] but the urinal could also come to refer to the sense of sight, as in Jan Saenredam's engraving after Goltzius (cat. no. 36).

JC

1. Veldman 1974, 98; Schaefer 1986, 415. For an overview of the subject, see Kraut 1986; Asemissen and Schweikhart 1994, 37-48; Költzsch 2000, 15-69.
2. Jacobowitz and Stepanek 1983, 318, 322.
3. Campbell 1981, 44.
4. Schaefer 1986, 423-24; the Boutsian painting is cited by Campbell 1981, 56 n. 12. The trappings of a workshop make sporadic appearances, perhaps beginning with the Boutsian painting, but the space is only occasionally fully realized as that of an obvious workshop (see Költzsch 2000, 35, 42, 64-69).
5. The grotesques recall the decoration in Jan Gossaert's painting of the same subject in Vienna from around 1522 (illus. in Schaefer 1992, 33); see also Jacobowitz and Stepanek 1983, 318. Költzsch 2000, 66, says that Vellert has placed his subject "in einen prachtvollen Palastraum."
6. Schaefer 1992, 31.
7. The pose of Vellert's Saint Luke—in profile, hunched over the panel, which is turned slightly away from the viewer—is very close to, and was possibly the model for, the Saint Luke in a painting of the same subject by the Master of the Holy Blood, a contemporary of Vellert's working in Bruges (illus. in Költzsch 2000, 36).
8. On the ox, see Georgel and Lecoq 1987, 106-109; the ox was naturalized as a small sculpture in later works like Guercino's *Saint Luke Displaying a Painting of the Virgin and Child* and Jan Steen's *The Drawing Lesson* (Walsh 1996, 68-69).
9. Schaefer 1986, 417.
10. On apprentices and journeymen (*compagnons*) in the workshop, see Campbell 1981.
11. Veldman 1974; Schaefer 1986, 419-20; Georgel and Lecoq 1987, 79.

Hendrick Goltzius (1558-1617)

33. *Pygmalion and Galatea*

1593

Engraving, 326 x 216 mm (12⅞ x 8½ in.)

References: Bartsch 138, iii/iv; Hirschmann 158; Strauss 315, iii/iv

Inscriptions: lower right of image: *R. Baudous excu. / Anno 1593 / HGoltzius Inve[n]t. et sculp.*; below image: *S[c]ulpsit ebur niueum quod virginis ora gerebat / Pygmalion, viuae dixisses virginis ora. / Ipse opus author amans in imagine flagrat eburna, / Munere Acidaliae cupido dein iuncta marita est. / F. Estius.*

Purchased from C. G. Boerner, New York

1998.17

Upon returning from his Roman journey undertaken in 1591-92, Goltzius engraved the subject of Pygmalion and Galatea, the story from Ovid's *Metamorphoses* about the sculptor who falls in love with his own creation. In this engraving, Goltzius blends his recent observations of ancient sculpture with a sensitivity to an Ovidian text that shows similarities—not lost on Goltzius—to his own status as an artist.

In formal terms, Goltzius adhered to the manner of his famous prints of Roman antiquities such as the Farnese Hercules and the Apollo Belvedere (the plates for which he had completed by 1592), by treating this subject as a play of white forms against a dark background.[1] Working, to use Karel van Mander's terminology, *uyt den gheest* ("from the memory of things seen"),[2] Goltzius was inspired by drawings he had made of other prominent ancient sculptures in Rome. The figure of Pygmalion is based on the Belvedere Torso;[3] the Galatea is a combination of the Venus Pudica or Venus of modesty, whose hands are posed to cover her breasts and pubis, and the Venus Felix, who draws her drapery around her hip with the right hand.[4]

Goltzius was well acquainted with Ovid's *Metamorphoses,* and in the late 1580s had published a series of fifty-two prints illustrating Ovidian narratives; these prints are notable for their originality in exploring more obscure transitional scenes and their sensitivity to Ovid's literary style.[5] Here, Goltzius largely adheres to the story of Pygmalion and observes many of its small details; for example, Ovid writes that after carving the statue, Pygmalion brings it many-colored flowers (*flores mille colorum*); we see two roses on the ground at the statue's feet, and what appears to be a flowery crown or chaplet leaning against its base. Pygmalion also offers the statue a pretty nosegay; the dissonance between this love token in his right hand and the chisel in his left, which reminds us of his creative act, expresses the profound confusion Pygmalion feels in Ovid's story.[6] The eyes of the statue appear blank, and at this moment, we imagine that Pygmalion's love cannot be reciprocated. However, Goltzius cleverly leaves the statue's eyes slightly shadowed, so that we are not entirely sure that life does not reside in them.[7] The suggestion of vitality in an inert statue, both visually in Goltzius's print and subtextually in his choice of the Pygmalion story, reflects contemporary ideas about what constituted a successful sculpture. Walter S. Melion has also posited that through Goltzius's combination and material transformation of famous marble sources (the Venus Pudica and the Venus Felix), first into the ivory statue in Ovid's tale, and thence by his skill as an engraver into the suggestion of living flesh, Goltzius makes an important statement about the ability of artifice and beauty not only to trick the viewer into thinking a statue is real, but to cause him to fall in love. This statement is in keeping with versions of the story of the artist seduced by his own creation in both ancient and contemporary literature.[8]

Goltzius was also surely aware of the connection he shared with Pygmalion as a fellow artist, and specifically between Pygmalion's chisel and his own burin. As Dorothy Limouze points out, the Latin word *sculptor* was used in Goltzius's day to describe both engravers and sculptors of three-dimensional works.[9] Also, in Jan Muller's 1597 engraving after Bartholomaeus Spranger, *Painting, Sculpture, and Architecture, Banned by the Turks, Withdraw to Olympus* (Bartsch 76), the allegorical figure of Sculpture holds both a statuette of Minerva and two burins, suggesting that engraving belonged to the same taxonomy as sculpture.[10] In the Pygmalion engraving, the point of Pygmalion's chisel even seems to be placed in one of the engraved lines shading the cushion on which he sits; this could be a visual witticism on Goltzius's part to underscore the parallel between chisel and burin.

In the masterful engravings of great antique sculptures Goltzius made after his return to Haarlem (e.g., the Apollo Belvedere and the Farnese Hercules), he had eminently proved his ability to render three-dimensional sculpture in a two-dimensional medium.[11] Goltzius also put his unique stamp on these famous works through *handelingh,* the distinctly individual matrix of engraved lines that mediates between the original sculpture and the viewer. In the case of the Pygmalion engraving, however, both the actual subject (though inspired by antique sculpture) and the *handelingh* are of Goltzius's own invention—a double act of creation. In this light, the inscription "H Goltzius invenit. et sculp." may take on new meaning; Goltzius, a new Pygmalion, has both "invented" and carved a new Galatea, and through the skill of his burin, brings her to life.

AW

1. Strauss 1977, 2:570.
2. Melion 1991, 63.
3. In the sixteenth century, the Belvedere torso was also known as the *torso di Michelangelo* because of Michelangelo's well-known esteem for it. Pygmalion's youthful and handsome frame highly resembles Michelangelo's seated *ignudi* on the Sistine ceiling, which indeed were Michelangelo's own experiments for "completing" the Belvedere torso. In addition to the compression of the abdomen, Goltzius takes the pose of Pygmalion's left arm and feet from the *ignudo* at the lower left of the Sistine fresco depicting the fall and the expulsion from the Garden of Eden. Although van Mander makes no specific mention of it, Goltzius would almost certainly have seen the Sistine ceiling during his visit to Rome; additionally, he could have known this particular *ignudo* from Adamo Ghisi's series of engravings after Michelangelo's *ignudi* (see Bartsch 42).
4. Limouze 1991–92, 444–45. Melion 2001, 157–58. Drawings of all three sculptures by Goltzius survive in the Teylers Museum, Haarlem.
5. Melion 2001b, 155.
6. Nesbitt 1992, 54.
7. Walter S. Melion also noted this intentional ambiguity. See Melion 2001b, 157.
8. Melion 2001b, 160.
9. Limouze 1991–92, 448.
10. Ibid.
11. Goddard and Ganz 2001, 41.

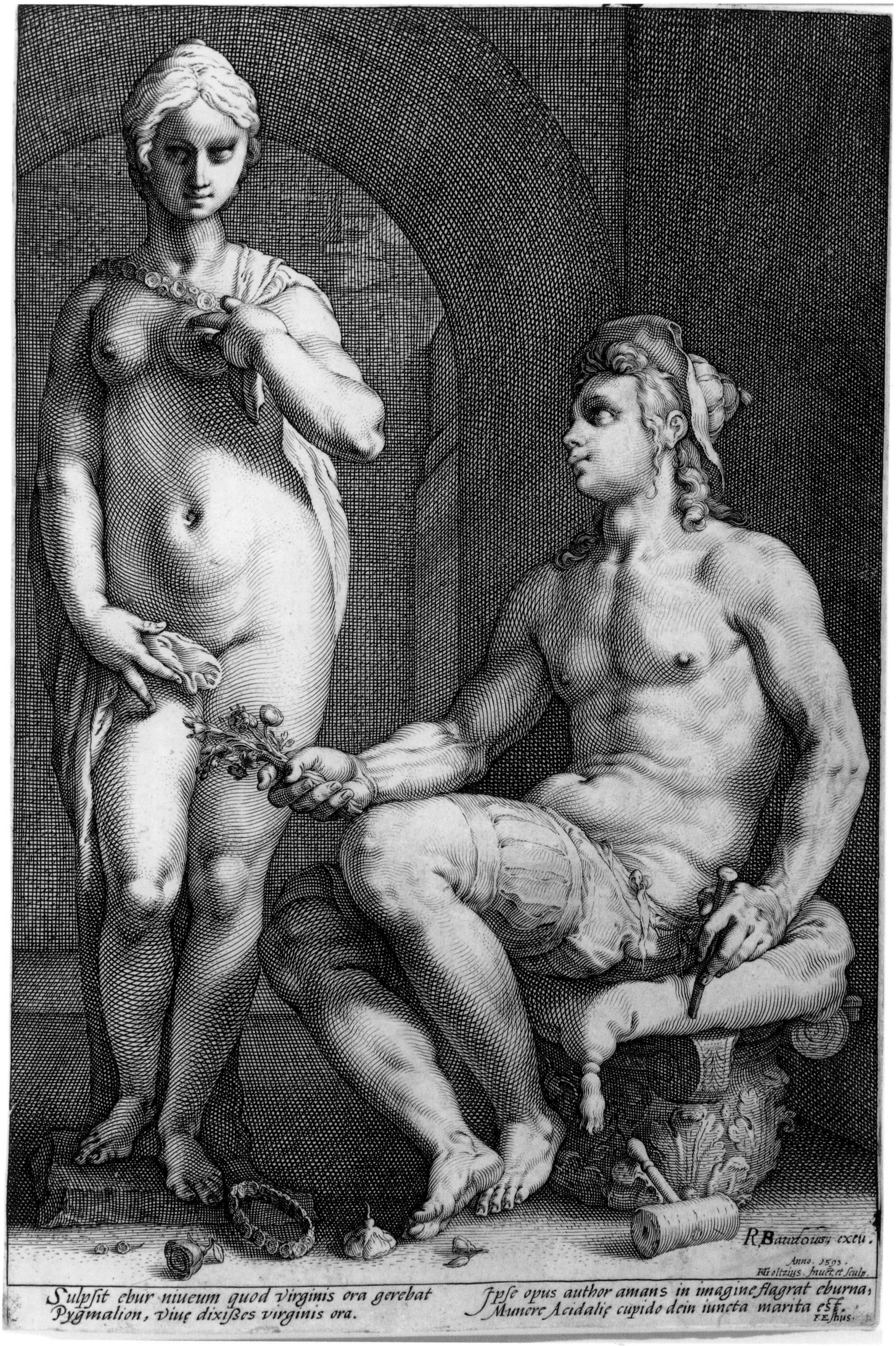

Anno. 1593.
Sulpsit ebur niueum quod virginis ora gerebat
Pygmalion, viuę dixißes virginis ora.
Ipse opus author amans in imagine flagrat eburna,
Munere Acidalię cupido dein iuncta marita est.

Cat. no. 33

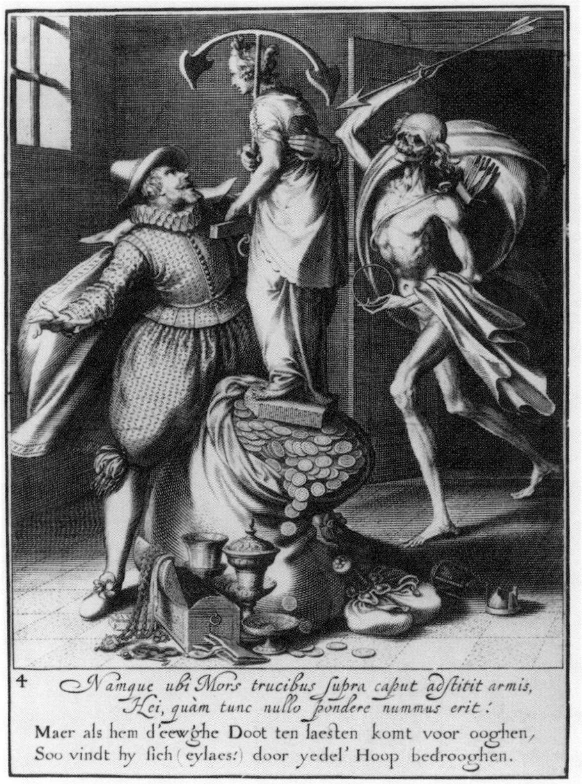

Fig. 34.3. Willem van Swanenburg. Plate 4 from *Allegory of the Misuse of Worldly Property.* 1609. Engraving, 216 x 159 mm (8½ x 6¼ in.). Sarah Campbell Blaffer Foundation, Houston.

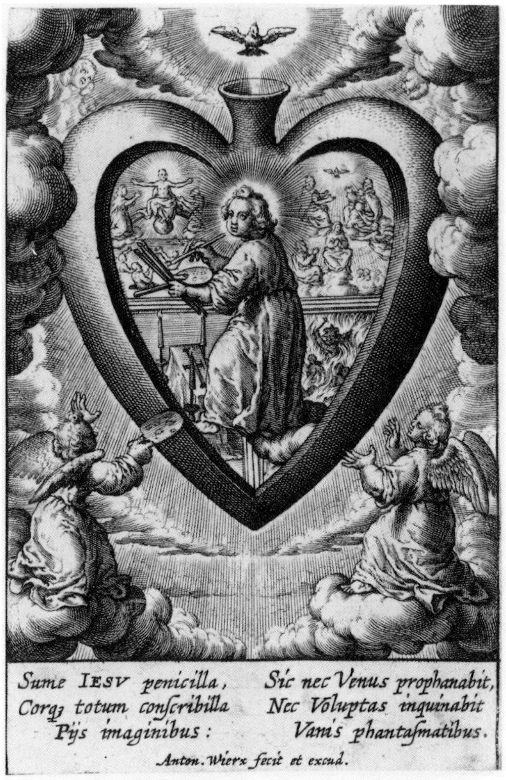

Fig. 34.4. Antonius II Wierix. *Jesus Painting the Four Last Things.* Engraving, 93 x 58 mm (3⅝ x 2¼ in.). Copyright Bibliothèque Royale de Belgique, Brussels.

bag of coins. Mirroring his action on the other side of the statue is a nude demon, characterized slightly differently than in the first print (now with bird feet rather than goat hooves),[3] who helps the man literally place his hope on worldly things. In the final print of the series (fig. 34.3), the man continues to embrace the statue of Hope, looking up to her with some desperation as Death enters the room, his arrow aimed at the uselessly wealthy man, who is "betrayed by vain hope."

The series follows works designed by Maarten van Heemskerck and etched by Dirk Volkertsz. Coornhert more than a half-century earlier, in 1550. Although they are not copies, with significant differences in settings, the clothing of the figures, and the inscriptions, the prints in the series retain the same fundamental meaning.

The motif of the artist at an easel had been employed for devotional purposes in representations of Saint Luke painting the Virgin and Child (see cat. nos. 32, 35), and in the middle of the sixteenth century it came to be used for religious allegories as well. The metaphor of the human heart, mind, or soul as a *tabula rasa* on which spiritual characteristics could be inscribed or depicted was a commonplace in Western literature since antiquity (the Dutch phrase *het hart verbeelden,* or "to paint the heart," was used in Coornhert's print).[4] Its use in devotional imagery of the later sixteenth and early seventeenth century—during which allegorical subjects flourished, especially in prints—is not surprising. Hans-Joachim Raupp has drawn attention to Heemskerck's composition as the first in which the metaphor is used negatively, with Satan painting evil on the human heart.[5] We meet Satan's artistic opposite in Antonius Wierix's engraving of the *Jesus Painting the Four Last Things* from his popular series *Cor Iesv amanti sacrvm* of around the turn of the seventeenth century (fig. 34.4). Here the divine artist is inside the heart, painting the Four Last Things, filling the heart with "pious images" (*pijs imaginibus*) instead of "empty phantasms" (*vanis phantasmatibus*).

For the clarity of the meaning of such works, the image of the painter—even a demonic painter—conforms to conventions of representation, regardless of their veracity. Thus, Satan is shown seated at an easel, using a maulstick to support his hand in the act of applying paint to the work, a palette and brushes held, along with the maulstick, in his left hand. On the ground are more tools of the artist, including a brush for removing excess charcoal from an underdrawing and a mortar for the grinding of pigments. Even Satan's eyeglasses, which Swanenburg added to the Heemskerck composition, had associations with painters, as in Jan Saenredam's engraving after Hendrick Goltzius of an *Allegory of Sight and the Art of Painting* (cat. no. 36).[6]

JC

1. The former title is Hollstein's, the latter from Veldman 1977, 82-85, discussing the Heemskerck/Coornhert series. See also Veldman 1971, where the series is referred to as *Allegorie van de Hoop op Geld.*
2. The shield shape is most evident in Heemskerck's preparatory drawing for the first print in the series (see Veldman 1977, 82 n. 112).
3. Veldman 1971, 75, argues that they are not the same creature.
4. See Veldman 1971, 73, who argues that the literal representation of such phrases indicates the conceptual priority of text over image in the series. She notes the change from a shield to a human heart as bringing the image more in line with the preexisting text, but it may rather suggest the simultaneous development of interdependent text and image.
5. Raupp 1984, 288-90, who also argues that in Swanenburg's version of the composition the emphasis has changed, in that the man's very act of viewing the sins painted by Satan leads to his entrapment by those sins; but neither the image nor the text, in my opinion, supports such an interpretation.
6. The eyeglasses in the Goltzius composition were interpreted negatively by Müller Hofstede 1984, 267, but Sluijter 2000, 109, pointed out their symbolic neutrality (or ambivalence), since they also appear prominently in Maarten van Heemskerck's famous self-portrait as Saint Luke in Haarlem.

Jacob Matham (1571-1631)

after Hendrick Goltzius (1558-1617)

35. *Saint Luke Painting the Virgin*

c. 1613

Engraving, 501 x 372 mm (19¾ x 14⅝ in.)

References: Bartsch 113, i/ii; Hollstein 143, i/ii; Widerkehr M. 29, i/ii

Inscriptions: on easel at right: *HG FECIT.*; on stool at bottom: *Cum privil. S. Caes. M.tis / Iac. Matham Sculptor.; in central cartouche below image: Spertatae p[er]bitatis viro D. Maximiliano Laignier Tw / jilotXcvh Opus hoc aeri incisum (cuius archetypum cala / mo ab H Goltzio notatum singulari beneficio imitandum dederat, et divulgandum) in grati animi signum D. D. Matham.*; flanking central cartouche lower left and right: *Nobilis ille Syrus, non vltimus arte medendi / Mystica taurina referens insignia frontis / Divinum formabat opus doctaq[ue] colorum / Temperit sacros audebat ponere vultus, / Et brevibus tantum tabulis includere numen. / In caelis sensere animae, cantusq[ue] cientes / Ad nova pennati coëunt spertacula fratres; / Atq[ue] iterum nato renovant praeconia Christo. / T Schrevelius.*

Purchased from Lutz Riester, Freiburg and London

1997.37

When Hendrick Goltzius married Jacob Matham's mother in 1579, the eight-year-old Matham became both Goltzius's stepson and his apprentice. Matham's first published engravings date from the late 1580s, and show the influence, as do those of his teacher, of Bartholomaeus Spranger's courtly Mannerist style. In all, Matham engraved over four hundred plates. In around 1600, Goltzius put aside engraving entirely, no doubt partly because of failing eyesight, but also because of his growing belief in the nobility of painting. After this point, Goltzius's drawings were distributed largely in the form of engravings by Matham.

The typology in Netherlandish art of depictions of Saint Luke, the patron saint of artists, is quite varied. Sometimes the Virgin is shown sitting for Saint Luke in his studio, as in the best known example, by Rogier van der Weyden. In other cases the Virgin appears to Saint Luke in a celestial vision. Matham's engraving belongs to still another type, in which the Virgin is not present in the room; we see her and the Christ Child only on the unfinished panel on Saint Luke's easel. Perhaps the evangelist's connection to the divine, symbolized by the hovering cherubim, with Saint Luke's attribute, the ox, at the top, inspires him to paint the Virgin and Child. Perhaps he is demonstrating his skill at working from memory. Whatever the case may be, because Saint Luke does not share the picture space with any other figures and because of his striking glance over his shoulder in our direction, this engraving is primarily a portrait and only secondarily a Saint Luke subject.

Twentieth-century scholarship seems to have answered the question of whose portrait Goltzius recorded here. The face in Matham's engraving has been possibly identified as that of the Haarlemite Jan Govertsz. van der Aar (born c.1645, died before 1612), based on similarities to a drawing in brown ink on parchment by Goltzius showing Jan Govertsz. as Saint Luke, dated 1614, now in the collection of the Veste Coburg in Germany.[1] Little is known about Govertsz. except that he was a friend (and possibly a patron) of Goltzius, and a collector of seashells; Goltzius painted Govertsz.'s portrait holding a seashell in 1603, a painting described by van Mander and properly reidentified by Emil Reznicek in 1959.[2] Further research has recently uncovered documentation indicating Govertsz. was a cloth merchant,[3] although little else about him is certain. Govertsz. was something of a favorite model for Goltzius, who made six other portraits of him, including one that shows up in a painting of *Susanna and the Elders* (1607) in which one of the two elders has his face.[4] In addition, a portrait drawing of Govertsz. by Jacob Matham has come to light, a freer interpretation of the subject wearing a turban, possibly copied from a drawing by Goltzius rather than taken from life.[5]

Apparent physiognomical discrepancies between the Saint Luke in Matham's engraving and the 1614 portrait of Govertsz. might be accounted for by Goltzius's original drawing having lost something in the transfer to Matham's engraving. However, this identification also ignores the name of another party to be found on the print itself. On the rectangular sheet tacked illusionistically to the margin at lower center we find the print is dedicated to a certain D[octor] Maximilien Laignier, about whom nothing has yet come to light. One possible explanation for this dedication would be that Saint Luke's face presents the likeness of Laignier, rather than that of Govertsz. In short, it seems likely that Matham's engraving does reproduce an eighth portrait by Goltzius of Jan Govertsz. van der Aar, as has been suggested. However, in the absence of Goltzius's original drawing, and because of the ostensible differences between the face in this engraving and other portraits of Govertsz., and, finally, compounded with the dedication of the print to the mysterious Maximilien Laignier, it would be premature to make this identification definitively.

The historical context of Goltzius's depiction of Saint Luke is also worth discussing here, as the many artists' guilds that bore Saint Luke's name were undergoing a considerable change during this time. Medieval guilds of Saint Luke were corporate urban entities, designed to regulate and promote local art production. Guilds devoted to painters and sculptors were structured along the same lines as those in other artisanal fields, like saddlery or rope making. In the mid-sixteenth century, writers like Giorgio Vasari promulgated the new concept of the individual artist, emphasizing artists' conceptual rather than manual abilities and advocating for an elevation in their professional and social status. Medieval guilds declined, while academies, with scholarly curricula that intellectualized painting and sculpture by offering training in perspective, mathematics, and anatomy, were on the rise. The first true example of such an academy was the Florentine Accademia del Disegno, founded in 1563 by Vasari; the Accademia di San Luca in Rome, founded in 1593, soon took most work away from Roman guilds through papal patronage. In Haarlem, although Hendrick Goltzius himself was never a member of a guild or academy, around 1600 he joined with Karel van Mander and Cornelis Cornelisz. van Haarlem to found a drawing school known as the Haarlem Academy. Jacob Matham was made dean of the Haarlem Guild of Saint Luke in 1605; in 1630, the year before his death, he aided in its restructuring into an official academy on the Italian model.

AW

1. Widerkehr 1991–92, 242. For a reproduction of this drawing, see Reznicek 1961, vol. 2, plate 442.
2. Reznicek 1960.
3. Nichols 1987, 246.
4. Ibid., 241.
5. Van Tatenhove 1983, 231.

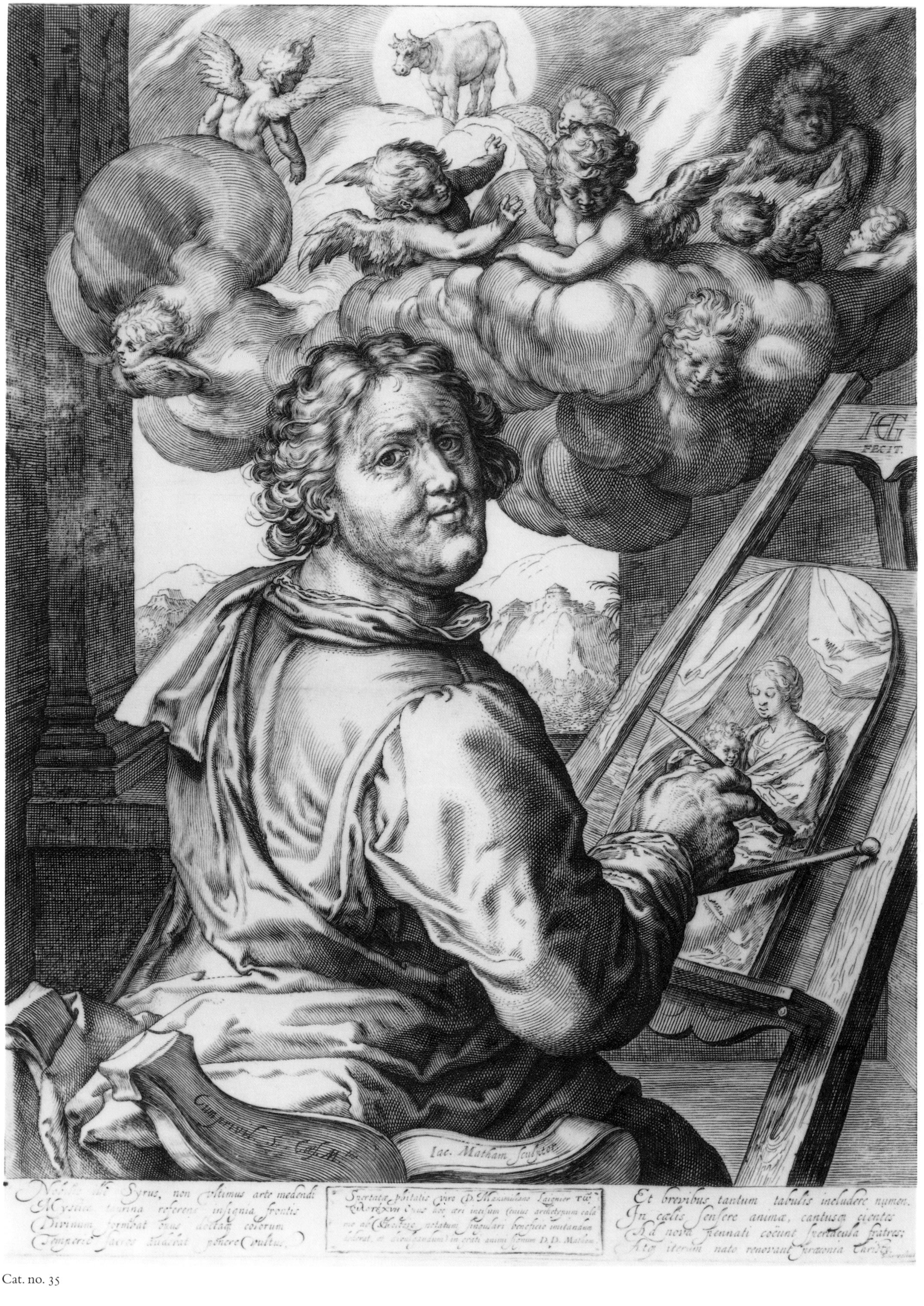
HG FECIT.
Iac. Matham Sculptor
Et brevibus tantum tabulis includere numen.
In cælis sensere animæ, cantusq cientes
Ad nova pennati coëunt spectacula fratres;

Cat. no. 35

JAN SAENREDAM (c. 1565-1607)

after Hendrick Goltzius (1558-1617)

36. *Allegory of Sight and the Art of Painting*

1616

Engraving, 244 x 184 mm (9⅝ x 7¼ in.)

REFERENCES: Bartsch 100; Hollstein 106, ii/iii

INSCRIPTIONS: lower left: *HG. Inuent. I. Saenr. scu. / R. de baudous excudit. 1616*; below image: *Haec memini nocuiße atque oblectaße videntes.*

Purchased from R. M. Light, Santa Barbara, California

1997.6

Hendrick Goltzius's complex allegorical invention probably dates from around 1600, at a time when he was beginning a dramatic career change from printmaker to painter. It was engraved by Jan Saenredam but first published nearly a decade after the engraver's death in 1607. A bespectacled artist paints Venus kneeling on the ground as she looks into a mirror held by Cupid. In the background are a scholar with an astrolabe, a doctor holding up a urinal for examination, and an astronomer with a compass and a large celestial globe. Further in the background are boats in a bay. An eagle flies toward a radiant sun. In the foreground lies a cat which, like Cupid, looks out at the viewer. A group of sundials and clocks are in the foreground at right, and an armillary sphere sits just behind Venus. What these diverse elements share in common is an association with the sense of sight.

The inscription, added at the time of the print's publication but in keeping with Goltzius's imagery, expresses ambivalence about the subject: "I know from experience that this harms and delights the viewers (or: those who see this)."[1] One interpretation of the image is essentially negative: the nude woman recalls personifications of worldliness and vanity (compare cat. no. 34), and as Venus she is the embodiment of corporeal lust. Thus the artist is not only an imitator of beauty and grace, but also of pleasure and luxury—a negative image accentuated by the visual similarity to images of Saint Luke painting the Virgin and Child (as in cat. no. 32), who are here displaced in favor of a nude woman. The doctors and scholars are satirized as foolish and blind, pursuing useless knowledge, and the cat symbolizes, among other undesirable traits, lasciviousness.[2]

In a magisterial study of the print's iconography, however, Eric Jan Sluijter properly interprets the work as a positive meditation on the visual arts—which Goltzius himself practiced, including the frequent depiction of sensuous nudes—with the painter appearing as "a worthy investigator of nature and a connoisseur of beauty *par excellence*."[3] As Sluijter has shown, in the many representations of the Five Senses in Netherlandish prints of the late sixteenth century (including several by Goltzius), Sight is often characterized by an attractive woman, sometimes nude, observing herself in a mirror, often accompanied by a cat, eagle, radiant sun, and boats or ships on water. The sun, which is emphatically represented in this image, not only provides the light that makes sight possible, but also symbolizes truth. The eagle appears elsewhere in Goltzius's oeuvre as both a symbol of Sight and attribute of Jupiter, patron of astronomers and other scholars. The bird's head on the easel seems to be that of a phoenix, which was associated with the sun, as well as with coloring and excellence in art and scholarship, by Goltzius's friend and biographer, Karel van Mander. The phoenix was also a personal emblem for Goltzius, as was the cherub's head worn on Venus's arm, indicating that the print is highly self-referential.[4]

The most significant novelties in this allegory of Sight are the three scholars and their instruments, the introduction of a painter whose work duplicates the mirrored image, and the characterization of Sight specifically as Venus. Goltzius had elsewhere depicted scholars in respectable contexts (including portraits) and here they "are dignified, learned investigators and experts on nature who demonstrate that Sight is the servant of their science."[5] The painter might indeed be likened to Saint Luke (his pose is quite similar to that of the saint in Jacob Matham's engraving after Goltzius [cat. no. 35]), but in a positive rather than negative sense. Luke and Apelles, whose portrayal of Alexander the Great's mistress Campaspe was a common subject, which Goltzius's combination of painter and nude woman here recalls, were "both portrayers of female beauty and grace *par excellence,* . . . so that the allusion to *the* exemplary painters" can validate the depiction of female beauty as an exemplary theme for the art of painting.[6] In Goltzius's time, the power of images of nude female figures to arouse sensual desire in the viewer (and in the painter) was both acknowledged and

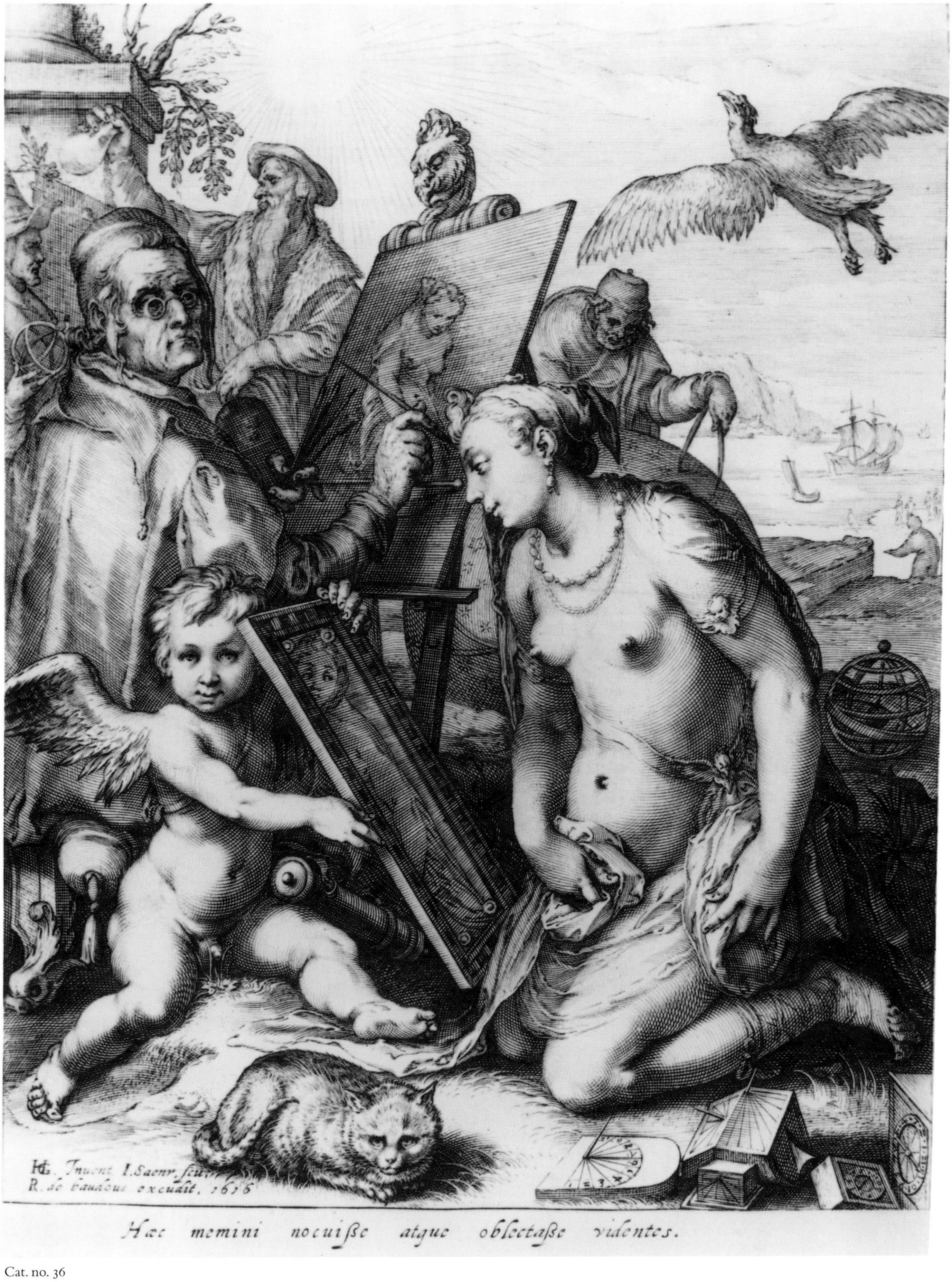
HG. Inuent. I.Saenr. scu
R. de Baudous excudit, 1616
Hæc memini nocuiße atque oblectaße videntes.

Cat. no. 36

feared, and Goltzius here seems to be alluding to that power in characterizing the artist's nude model as both Sight and Venus (the most seductive of goddesses), as well as directing the lascivious cat's and Cupid's gazes at the viewer. In defiance of the "art haters" who condemned sensual art, Goltzius embraced that aspect of the art in which he excelled, an aspect firmly rooted in artistic tradition in antiquity and again in the Italian Renaissance, providing delectation for his knowledgeable audience.

JC

1. Trans. Sluijter 2000, 90; he offers a slightly different translation at p. 146.
2. Raupp 1984, 293–301; and Müller Hofstede 1984, 266–69, who summarizes: "Auch das '*Gesicht*' ist ganz '*in malo*' zu lesen."
3. Sluijter 2000, 87–159 (the quotation from p. 144); originally published as Sluijter 1991–92. Most of what follows is derived from Sluijter's analysis.
4. In the *Allegory with Cupid and Putti* (cat. no. 55) by Giovanni Andrea Podestà, who may well have known Saenredam's print, the phoenix rising toward the sun is the hope of the highest good.
5. Sluijter 2000, 102.
6. Ibid., 109.

Rembrandt van Rijn (1606–1669)

37. *A Man Drawing from a Cast*

1641

Etching, 94 x 64 mm (3¾ x 2½ in.)

References: Bartsch, Hollstein 130; White and Boon 130, ii/iii

Purchased at sale, Sotheby's, New York

1998.10

By candlelight, in a study piled with books and papers, an artist draws from a bust of a child, an ink pot clasped in his left hand. In his etching *The Goldsmith* of 1655 (cat. no. 38), Rembrandt explores the relationship between the artist and his creation, whereas in this etching he considers one artist studying the creation of another long dead. In so doing, Rembrandt brings together elements of the *vanitas* still-life genre popular in Leiden early in his career—the bust, the books, and the candle in its holder. But instead of making a *vanitas* picture, Rembrandt uses these elements to communicate an intimate and meditative mood, and even inflect the work with wit and humor.[1]

Because Rembrandt, like other prominent artists of his time, took on pupils, he was undoubtedly familiar with the accepted procedure of teaching draftsmanship, in which students progressed from sketching after reproductive engravings of the human form, to drawing from casts and sculpture, and only then attempted to draw from a live model.[2] The practice of sketching from sculpture had greatly expanded in the early sixteenth century with the continual rediscovery of ancient works in Italy and the perfecting of casting procedures that permitted their multiplication. There is much evidence of the growing place of casts in Dutch art and artistic practice in the first half of the seventeenth century; for example, the frontispiece of Abraham Bloemaert's *Tekenboek,* published in Utrecht around 1650 (fig. 37.1), shows a young apprentice sketching from a plaster cast of an old man, while casts of heads, arms, legs, and torsos rest on the floor or hang on the wall. However, studying casts was not limited to students; fully trained artists of established reputation, Rembrandt included, continued to derive inspiration from them, and the frequent inclusion of casts in still lifes demonstrates that the masters who painted them were participants in this trend. For example, Pieter Claesz.'s *Vanitas Still Life with the Spinario,* painted in 1628, features a plaster cast of the famous work. The painter Cornelis van Haarlem owned over fifty casts upon his death in 1638,[3] and the 1656 inventory of Rembrandt's house, in addition to listing numerous works of antique sculpture, lists dozens of plaster casts located in various rooms, taken both from ancient models and living subjects.[4] Therefore, despite Rembrandt's awareness of the process of artistic education, the draftsman in the etching seems less likely to be a student than a full-fledged artist. The nighttime setting, the intimacy of the room, and the stacks of books speak of a private study rather than a studio. Also, this artist does not appear to be particularly young;

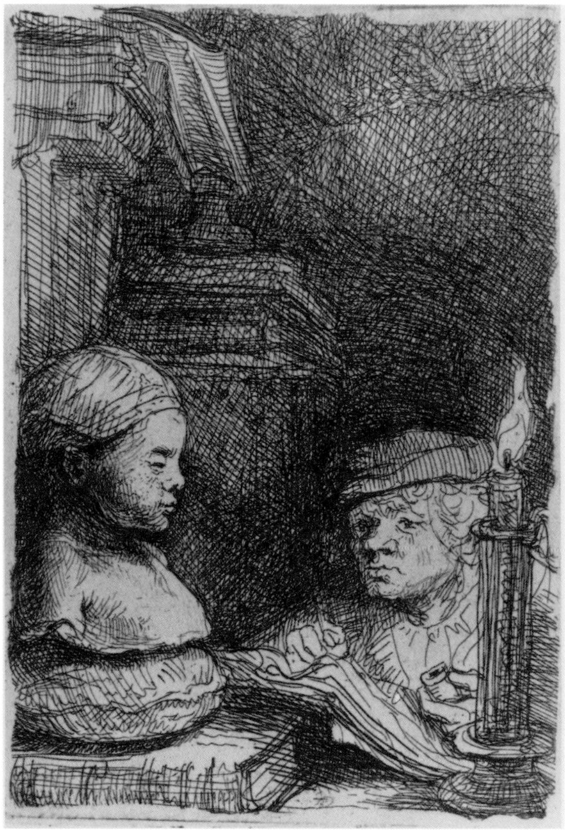

Cat. no. 37

the fleshiness of the face and the three sketchy wrinkles added to the left cheek suggest someone approaching middle age.

The plaster cast of the little boy in Rembrandt's etching appears to be the same cast on a shelf in the unattributed Leiden School *Still Life with Books,* c. 1628, in the Alte Pinakothek, Munich (fig. 37.2). This is a *vanitas* still life—a type popularized most importantly by David Bailly in Leiden, the hometown he and Rembrandt shared—an assortment of objects designed to present a moralizing message about the vanity of human pursuits. Rembrandt himself owned at least three *vanitas* pictures by other artists during his lifetime, which he apparently enjoyed retouching.[5] This oil on panel, by a painter probably associated with Jan Davidsz. de Heem during his Leiden period of 1625 to 1631, is a part of a Leiden subgenre of *vanitas* still lifes of books, which seems to have sprung up there because Leiden was a university town and learning was thus a fitting topic for this kind of moralizing.[6]

The Munich panel shows a variety of books, bound and unbound, among them a portfolio of engravings open to a print showing a horse and rider. Two other smaller casts, one perhaps a bronze, occupy the shelf with the bust of the little boy. This cast, which appears to be taken perhaps from an Antonine Roman portrait bust, shares the same overall shape and the clear delineation between upper arm and chest with the one in Rembrandt's etching, as well as the downward tilt of the chin, pursed lips, and heavy-lidded eyes. These similarities, along with the fact that Rembrandt and de Heem were both living in Leiden during the time when the painting was most likely created, increase the possibility that Rembrandt could have known this cast, and that he either obtained his own copy or was remembering it when he made this etching.[7]

In the Munich panel, what appears to be a portfolio of drawings—a sheaf of papers wrapped in soft leather—is visible in the lower right corner. The quill pen next to it speaks of writing, certainly, but quills were also used for drawing, and Rembrandt's artist uses one in the etching. Thus, with the presence of the casts, the Munich painting evokes the process of drawing from antique sculpture just as Rembrandt does. Furthermore, the books and papers piled everywhere in the etching reflect the basic compositional device of the Leiden book pictures. Whereas in the Leiden still lifes the books are presented as symbols of the vanity of learning, Rembrandt does not seem to be interested in that kind of message; in his etching, the books instead lend the artist a learned air

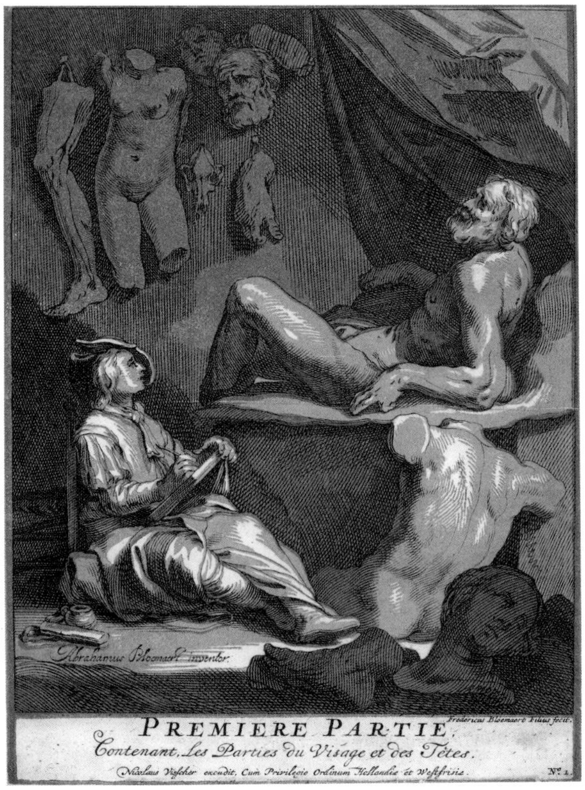

Fig. 37.1. Frederick Bloemaert. *Student Drawing from a Cast.* 1650. Etching and chiaroscuro woodcut on laid, 305 x 226 mm (12 x 8⅞ in.). Courtesy of the Herbert F. Johnson Museum of Art, Cornell University; Membership Purchase Fund.

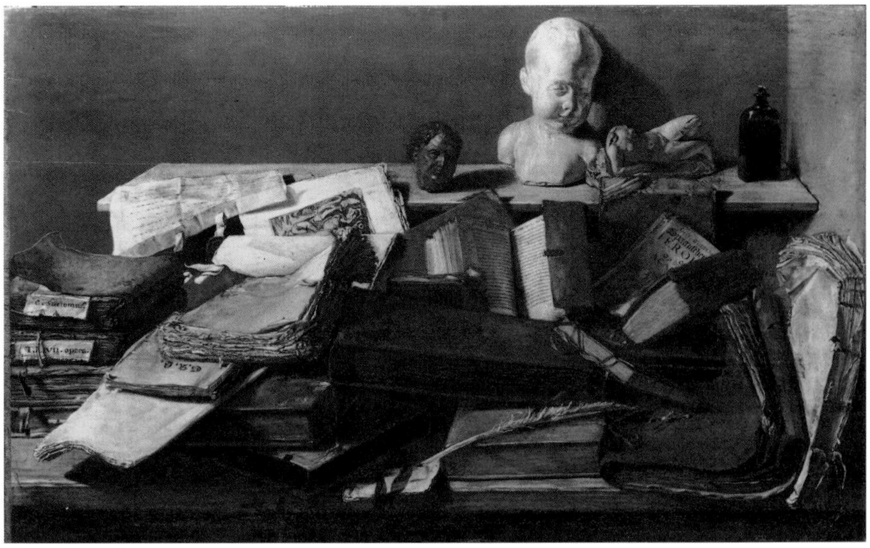

Fig. 37.2. Leiden School. *Still Life with Books.* c. 1628. Oil on panel, 61.3 x 97.4 cm (24⅛ x 38⅜ in.). Bayerische Staatsgemäldesammlungen, Alte Pinakothek, Munich.

and add to the meditative nature of the candlelit drawing session.

There is one significant difference between the two busts in these two works: the cap worn by the bust of the boy in Rembrandt's etching, complete with turned-up earflaps—an unlikely accoutrement for an ancient sculpture. Rembrandt was extremely fond of hats (for instance, thirty-two of the forty-odd figures in his famous *Hundred Guilder Print* wear headgear of some kind), and I believe this one serves an important function in the print. First of all, the cap connects the artist and his model by headgear, as in Rembrandt's etching *The Goldsmith,* humanizing the link between an inert statue and a living person. This connection is strengthened by the facial similarity of the bust's sculpted expression and the rapt attention of the artist, both with set jaw and pursed lips. With these similarities, Rembrandt sets up an interesting duality; the sculpture of the boy is ancient, but he is in the bloom of youth, whereas the artist is of the present but is showing his age. The bust, perhaps, represents the ideal world; the artist, with his lived-in face, represents the real one in which we live.[8]

The cap is also specifically of the type worn by Dutch children in the seventeenth century. Perhaps Rembrandt cannot resist jarring our expectations by placing this modern cap on what is probably an ancient sculpture, reminding us that although it is ancient and worthy of reverence, it is also a little child. Rembrandt thus makes an inanimate plaster cast into a living, breathing little boy. This is a gesture typical of Rembrandt—using a work of antique sculpture not to speak about antiquity so much as to convey a human presence that would be relevant to viewers in his own time. Finally, in this portrayal of an artist, arguably aged in the vicinity of Rembrandt's own thirty-five years, might we also see the man whose first three children, a son and two daughters, had all died in infancy, the last in the year before Rembrandt made this etching?[9] In this respect, the cast of the child might also take on a *memento mori* or memorializing role.

The final aspect of Rembrandt's composition meriting discussion here is the large candlestick with its lighted candle. Clifford Ackley has noted that this candle implies the artist is working late at night in dedication to his art.[10] But, whether burning brightly,[11] as here, sputtering, or completely extinguished, a candle commonly appears in *vanitas* still lifes as a *memento mori.* Thus it is possible that through the candle, more than half its life already gone,[12] Rembrandt is speaking about the passage of time and the omnipresence of death. In this sense, then, the two most prominent objects in the artist's study, the antique bust and the candlestick, pointedly bracket the artist, indicating his reverence for the past and the importance of returning to ancient sources, but also referring to Rembrandt's own personal experience of the uncertainty and brevity of life.

AW

1. On a technical note, this plate may be one that Rembrandt etched using the somewhat unorthodox method of building up a "dam" of wax around the edges of the plate and pouring the acid directly onto its surface, rather than submerging the entire plate in a trough of acid. The undulating border around the image seems to have been caused by the wax dam masking the edges of the plate. See Thomas E. Rassieur, "Looking Over Rembrandt's Shoulder: The Printmaker at Work," in Ackley 2003, 51.

2. Rembrandt's etching *A Nude Man Seated and Another Standing,* also called *The Walking Trainer* (Bartsch 194), which shows two apprentices posing in the studio, is an expression of this practice. J. A. Emmens explained the presence of the baby learning to walk in the background as an analogy of the importance of drawing to the young artist's training; just as the baby is aided in its efforts by a wheeled trainer, so the student's artistic development is aided by drawing from models; see Emmens 1968, 154–56.

3. Van Thiel 1965, 128.

4. Clark 1966, 193–209.

5. Clark 1966, 195 and 199.

6. Chong and Klock, 1999, 166. Jan Lievens also painted a still life in which books predominate, c. 1628, now in the Rijksmuseum; see p. 146–7.

7. That the cast in the Munich panel may have belonged to Jan Davidsz. de Heem is supported by the presence of what appears to be the same cast of a little boy in a *vanitas* still life by de Heem's grandson, David de Heem, now in the collection of the Graf von Schönborn, Pommersfelden. See Chong and Klock 1999, p. 15, fig. 6.

8. Many thanks to Frank Robinson for this observation.

9. The first, a boy named Rombertus, was baptized in December 1635 and lived only two months. The second, a daughter, Cornelia, was born in 1638, and lived only two weeks. A second daughter, also named Cornelia, was born in August 1640, and she died after two weeks as well.

10. Ackley 2003, cat. no. 86, 155.

11. For a brightly burning candle as a *memento mori,* see plate 21 of Joachim Camerarius, *Nucleus emblematum . . .,* vol. 1, Arnhem, 1611, as reproduced in de Jongh 1982, 206.

12. Clifford Ackley has described the candlestick in this print as adjustable. This is, I believe, still open to question; I believe this candlestick to be of the (nonadjustable) variety common in the Netherlands in the mid-seventeenth century, with a flaring base, a flange above the base, a tall stem made from grouped tubular columns, and another wide flange at the candle holder. If the candlestick is meant to be of this type, the candle in it would be at least half used up. For an example of this type, see Den Blaauwen 1979, 144. An example of a *vanitas* painting, albeit a later one, with just such a candlestick, is the one by Cornelis Norbertus Gijsbrechts, dated 1669, illustrated in De Jongh 1982, 204.

Rembrandt van Rijn (1606–1669)

38. *The Goldsmith*

1655

Etching, 78 x 57 mm (3⅛ x 2¼ in.)

References: Bartsch, Hollstein, White and Boon 123, i/ii

Purchased from Susan Schulman, New York, and Carolyn Bullard, Dallas

1998.19

In the mid-sixteenth century, makers of gold and silver *objets* began to reject the associations with manual labor and the medieval guild system that had traditionally been attached to their work, as painters and sculptors had done before them. Their quest is best exemplified by the autobiography and treatises on goldsmithing and sculpture written by Benvenuto Cellini. Silversmiths began to enter a new realm of appreciation and patronage as creative minds, and achieved an increasingly elevated social status. In the culturally aware climate of seventeenth-century Amsterdam, and in particular because of the advances of a few great practitioners of the art, silversmiths competed on the same level as painters and sculptors.[1] In the etching *The Goldsmith,* Rembrandt shows his awareness of this status.

Despite the traditional title of this print, during the Dutch golden age, this "goldsmith" would be more accurately termed a silversmith.[2] The tools on the workbench, the tongs, the glowing forge with its hood visible behind the smith, and especially the anvil and the hammer in his hand, indicate the profession of the silversmith, who shaped sheets of fine metals (including gold) into plates, basins, ewers, goblets, saltcellars, and the like.

Through his calm and reverent portrayal of the silversmith, Rembrandt emphasizes above all the intimate relationship between an artist and his work, like that between a parent and his child. The silversmith seems to be just putting the finishing touches on his creation, perhaps attaching it to its base,[3] and holds it to steady it. The result is a tender embrace, which is echoed in the statue, whose subject, Charity, holds one of her children in precisely the same way. Strengthening the kinship between artist and creation, Rembrandt bows the heads of the goldsmith and the figure of Charity toward one another, even wrapping their heads in similar cloths.[4] Finally, a horizontal band in the background (possibly the rung of a ladder leaned against the back wall) joins the brows of

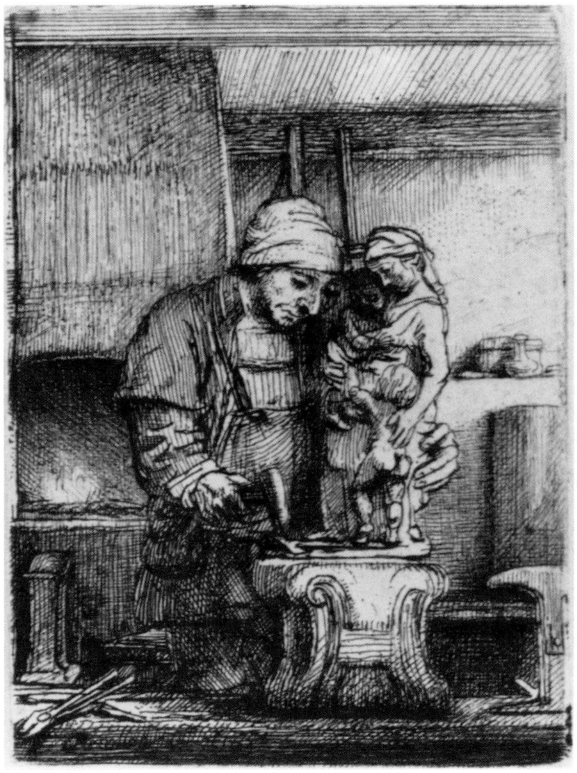

Cat. no. 38

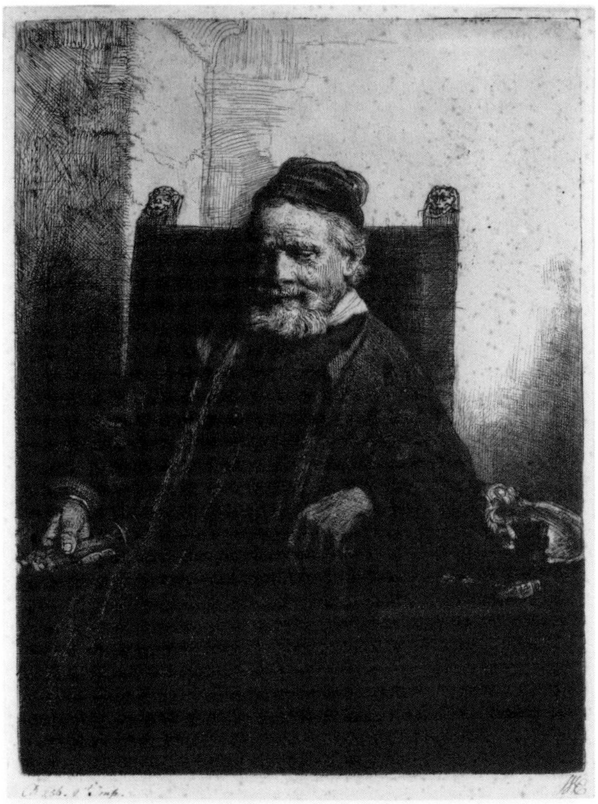

Fig. 38.1. Rembrandt van Rijn. *Jan Lutma.* 1656. Etching and dry point, first state, 199 x 150 mm (7 13/16 x 5 7/8 in.) (platemark); 208 x 155 mm (8 3/16 x 6 1/8 in.) (sheet). Catalogue raisonné: Bartsch 276 i; Hind 290 i. Museum of Fine Arts, Boston; Harvey D. Parker Collection, P 1067. Photograph copyright 2004 Museum of Fine Arts, Boston.

the two figures.[5] With all these bonds, the close-knit group of artist and sculpture in effect becomes a larger sculptural unit of its own. Given this intentional similarity, and Rembrandt's conspicuous choice of a figural work as the goldsmith's creation (instead of a dish or ewer), one cannot help but think Rembrandt may also be alluding to God's creation of man and woman in God's own image. The analogy between divine creativity and the artist's creative powers was a commonplace in the sixteenth century; Vasari advanced the legend of the "divine Michelangelo," a characterization still current in Rembrandt's day, and Dürer's treatise on human proportion—of which Rembrandt owned a copy[6]—also makes the analogy between God's creation and the artist's ability to continually produce new inventions.

This idea is perhaps supported by a compositional detail found in Rembrandt's superb etched portrait of his good friend, the silversmith Janus (or Jan) Lutma (fig. 38.1), made in 1656, one year after *The Goldsmith.* Lutma, an artist of immense skill and inventiveness, particularly in the creation of animal-inspired forms, produced works ranging from elegant serving pieces to the great choir screen of the Nieuwekerk in Amsterdam. In his portrait of Lutma seated in an armchair, Rembrandt places the master's hammer and a container of punches on the table next to him, along with a silver bowl in Lutma's baroque "lobate" style, of a type that still survives in the Rijksmuseum. However, in Lutma's right hand, the hand normally given significant gestures or objects in portraits,

Rembrandt places a work whose functional end (a candle-cup or the bowl of a goblet?) is cleverly cropped by the image's left margin. All that remains visible in Lutma's right hand is the human form that serves as the stem of the piece—a human form that Lutma's hand has created.

A work of the size and complexity of the figure of Charity in *The Goldsmith* would be a magnum opus for any silversmith, whose normal output would be smaller vessels and table furnishings on a functional scale, regardless of their flamboyance or costliness. In his etched portrait of Lutma, Rembrandt probably selected the pieces that would appear in the print in consultation with the sitter[7] as marks of artistic pride; these are both quite small, as we have seen. Furthermore, figural work, like the stem of the piece Lutma holds in his hand, was normally cast in solid silver (albeit alloyed with more copper, for strength);[8] the expense involved would again make a figure of this size extremely unusual. The other possibility that comes to mind with a sculpture of this size is that it might be cast in bronze, which would mean classifying the silversmith instead more as a sculptor. This is a difficult assertion to make, because of the presence of the proper tools for a silversmith (the hammer and anvil, and so forth). It seems on balance more likely that Rembrandt is both exaggerating the size of the normal work of a silversmith and humanizing the subject to emphasize the relationship between artist and creation, and to lend to this important but traditionally artisanal profession some of the aura of the sculptor. This modification seems to indicate Rembrandt's high degree of respect for the profession of silversmithing, and in particular for his good friend Janus Lutma. AW

1. Den Blaauwen 1979, xxvi.
2. I am grateful to Frank Robinson for pointing out the inaccuracy of this traditional title.
3. Ackley 2003, cat. no. 89, p. 159.
4. White 1969, 170–71.
5. Robinson 1980, 166.
6. Clark 1966, 205.
7. Hinterding, Luijten, and Royalton-Kisch 2000, 332.
8. Den Blaauwen 1979, xli.

Adriaen van Ostade (1610–1685)

39. *The Painter*

1647 (?)

Etching, 238 x 181 mm (9⅜ x 7⅛ in.)

References: Bartsch 32; Godefroy, Hollstein 32, vi/xii

Inscription: below image: *Pictor Apelliea pingas licet arte tabellam, / Quae modo pictores, et modo fallit aves, / Livor edax sed enim, nisi te fortuna bearit, / Auferret ingenio praemia digna tuo. / A. v. Ostade fecit.*

Purchased from C. G. Boerner, Inc., New York

1996.10

A modestly dressed painter sits in a tattered chair with one foot resting on the broken strut of his easel, at work on what appears to be a landscape or other outdoor scene. A maulstick steadies his hand as he paints not from a cast or model, but from a sketchbook propped open on a bench. Various accouterments of the trade occupy the rustic studio: two plaster casts are displayed on a shelf near a lute, which hangs on the wall; the painter's brushes and solvents set on a table by the window; an empty frame hangs on the wall at right; and additional canvases or panels lean against a cabinet behind the painter. Two apprentices prepare the artist's pigments in an alcove beneath the stairs. The artist is portrayed not as an academician, humanist, or status-seeking gentleman, but as a simple craftsman in a rustic studio reminiscent of van Ostade's peasant interiors.[1] The depiction of the artist in this etching has traditionally been identified as a self-portrait, but this position lacks support. In fact, the print hardly seems autobiographical at all, given that van Ostade was himself a successful and prosperous artist.

The etching is related to two paintings of the same subject by van Ostade, one in Dresden and the other in Amsterdam, though the print's composition does not directly replicate either panel.[2] The painting in Amsterdam is the earlier of the two and is more similar to the etching, although the artist here is apparently working from memory with no sketch present.[3] In the Dresden version, the space, which John Walsh describes as "picturesquely decrepit,"[4] is deepened to include a second room, the staircase is reconfigured, and only one assistant is present.[5] Here the artist works from a drawing attached to his easel. The painting in Dresden is signed and dated 1663 and may be associated with van Ostade's election to the position of Dean in Haarlem's Guild of Saint Luke in 1662. This raises the possibility that the painting in Amsterdam, and therefore the etching, may be connected to van Ostade's appointment as commissioner of the artists' guild in 1647.[6] A drawing reflecting the composition of the rare first state of the etching, which appeared at auction in 1984, may be a copy of van Ostade's lost preparatory drawing for the print.[7] The style of the sheet appears to be consistent with van Ostade's draftsmanship around 1647, and is comparable to another study of an artist's studio in Berlin,[8] which may be a rejected early sketch for the Amsterdam painting.[9]

Although the etching has long been dated to the 1660s by many scholars, including himself, Leonard Slatkes recently suggested a redating of the print to c. 1647.[10] Tom Rassieur has also suggested a dating of *The Painter,* to the first half of the 1650s or perhaps slightly earlier, based in part on its similarities with *The Dance in a Tavern* (Bartsch 49).[11] Theo Laurentius's technical study of watermarks found on van Ostade's prints seems to confirm the need for redating *The Painter,* given that impressions of the third and fourth states appear on paper in use in 1647–53.[12] He also asserts that all states after the sixth were printed posthumously on paper dating 1690–95,[13] although this would seem to contradict Trautscholdt's claim of having found the inscription *P. Mariette, 1670* (fifteen years before the artist's death) on an impression of the seventh state in the Dutuit collection in Paris.[14] Godefroy also records seeing this impression, although he describes it as the eighth state.[15] The dating of van Ostade's etchings remains an arduous task—one still very much open to debate—due in part to the fact that only ten of the fifty plates were dated.

The Latin inscription below the image refers to one of the great painters of classical antiquity: "Though you a painter, paint a painting with Apelles' art which now fools painters, and now the birds. Yet, gnawing envy, unless fortune bless you, will take away the prizes worthy of your talents."[16] The reference to an art that fools both birds and painters, however, should recall not Apelles but the celebrated contest between two other ancient artists, Zeuxis and Parrhasius, recounted by Pliny (see cat. no. 9). Pliny did relate, however, an anecdote in which neighing horses demonstrated the lifelikeness of a painting by Apelles of a horse (35.95). Trompe-l'oeil anecdotes pepper ancient and early modern accounts of artists' lives and are fundamental to notions of verism in both antiquity and the early modern period. It is to these notions that the inscription on van Ostade's print refers, in spite of its muddled reference, making a by then highly conventional claim regarding the artist's ability to rival nature.[17]

A collector's mark on the verso of the etching identifies the print as having belonged to the famed collection of Dutch and Flemish works on paper formed by John Sheepshanks (1787–1863, Lugt 2333), consisting of 7,666 prints and 812 drawings. Sheepshanks worked assiduously in the formation of his collection, his goal being to possess each print described in the first five volumes (i.e., those volumes detailing the Dutch and Flemish schools) of Bartsch's *Le Peintre-graveur* (Vienna, 1803–21). With very few exceptions, he accomplished this objective and even surpassed it by obtaining many prints unknown to Bartsch. The entire collection, with the exception of the prints by van Dyck and Rembrandt, was purchased by the British Museum in 1836 for 5,000 pounds.[18] The Blaffer etching was one of at least two impressions of van Ostade's *The Painter* accessioned by the British Museum in the Sheepshanks acquisition and was subsequently released as a duplicate.

Godefroy records the sixth state of *The Painter* as "très rare," and the Blaffer impression, at that time in the collection of M. Henry Oppenheimer, is one of only six listed by him.[19] In later states the plate size is reduced and the beginning of the fourth line of the inscription is corrected from *Auferret* to *Auferet.* The hat is later shortened, the collar reduced, and a prominent stripe is added to the back of the artist's jacket along with a ruffle of lace on his cuff. These altered details, which may very well change the intended meaning of the image and may have been made posthumously, are in keeping with the artist depicted in the related paintings.

LS

1. Stone-Ferrier 1983, 44, notes that the emphasis placed on the apprentices rather than the casts, as well as on their clothing and duties, is more in keeping with guild customs than academic training.
2. A painting in Philadelphia is nearly identical to the etching but is assumed to be a copy after a later state of the print (Philadelphia Museum of Art, John G. Johnson Collection, cat. 523). For a reproduction, see Philadelphia Museum of Art 1994, 86.
3. Panel, 37 x 36 cm. On the painting, see Rijksmuseum 1976, 430, no. A298; Hofstede de Groot 1976, 3:170–71, no. 97. The painting is signed with an atypical monogram (A.O.), which, according to Slatkes, renders it untrustworthy (Slatkes in Pelletier, Slatkes, and Stone-Ferrier 1994, 172; Slatkes in Van der Coelen 1998, 135).
4. Walsh 1996, 61.
5. *A Painter in His Studio,* 1663, oil on panel, 38 x 35.5 cm, Staatliche Kunstsammlungen, Gemäldegalerie Alte Meister, Dresden. Hofstede de Groot 1976, 3:171, no. 98. For a color reproduction, see Westermann 1996, 30.
6. Slatkes in Van der Coelen 1998, 135.
7. Christie's, Amsterdam, November 26, 1984, lot 39.
8. Schnackenburg 1981, 1:88, no. 40.
9. For a brief discussion of the two drawings in relation to the etching, see Slatkes in Van der Coelen 1998, 136.
10. Ibid., 136. Slatkes had previously maintained a more traditional dating of c. 1669, suggesting that at that time van Ostade returned to his earlier drawings. See Slatkes in Pelletier, Slatkes, and Stone-Ferrier 1994, 172.

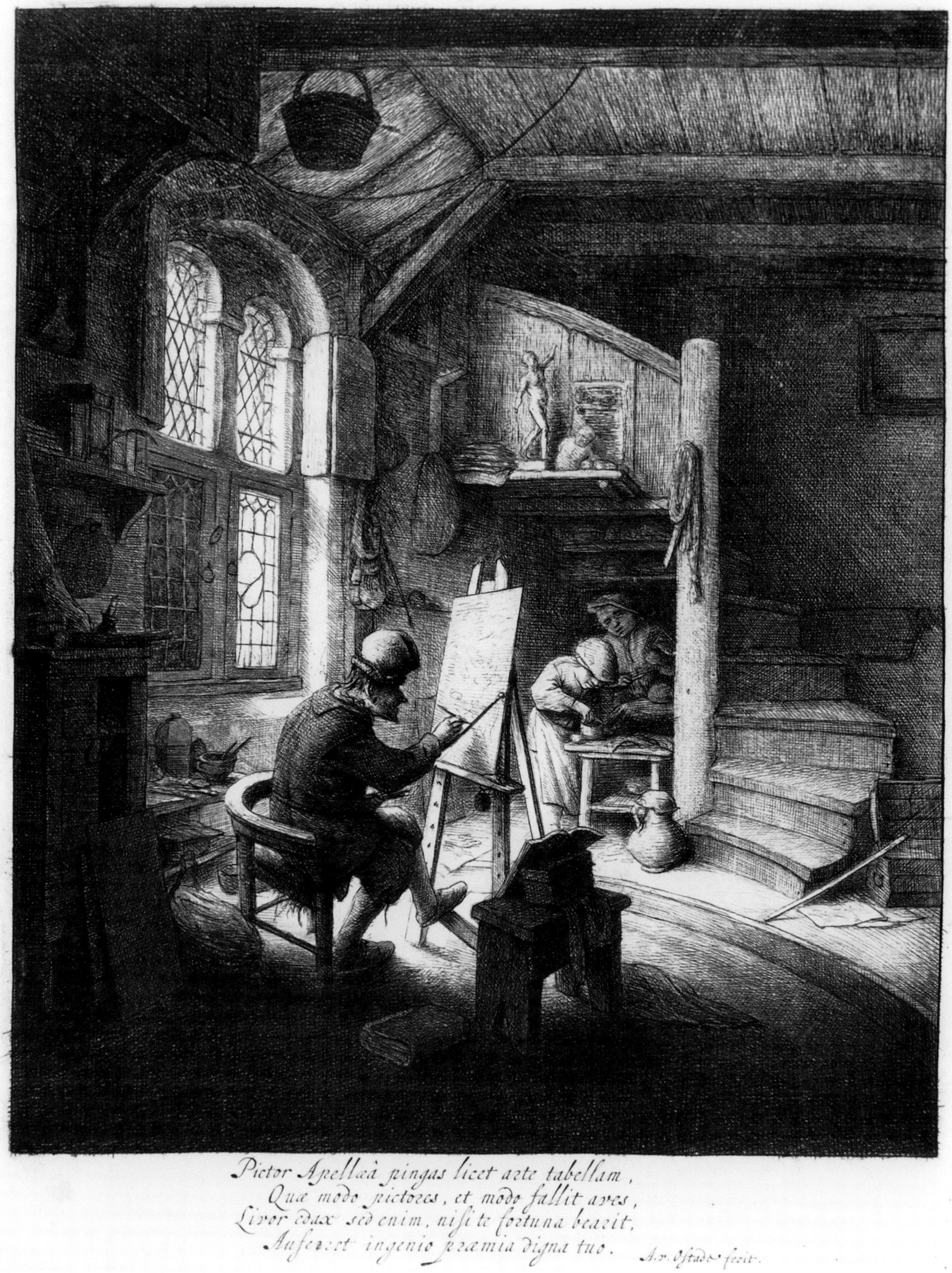
Pictor Apellæà pingas licet arte tabellam,
Quæ modo pictores, et modo fallit aves,
Livor edax sed enim, nisi te fortuna bearit,
Auferret ingenio præmia digna tuo.
A.v. Ostade fecit.

Cat. no. 39

depictions of artists' studios, it was famously the only sculpture by the revered artist outside of Italy, and Rembrandt owned a cast of the child from the group.[4] On the table behind the Christ Child are recognizable plaster casts of two Roman heads. On the left is the so-called Vitellius, the original of which, now in the Archaeological Museum in Venice, was known in the sixteenth century. A bronze copy of it was in the Amsterdam collection of the brothers Gerard and Jan Reynst in the first half of the seventeenth century, which Vaillant may have known, but plaster casts probably abounded throughout Europe.[5] It appears in the sculptor's studio represented by Abraham Bosse (cat. no. 68) and more prominently in another mezzotint of a young artist by Vaillant, after a painting in the Minneapolis Institute of Arts usually attributed to Michael Sweerts but probably by Vaillant himself (fig. 40.2).[6] The female head in profile in the *Boy Seated in a Studio* is similar to the cast shown in three-quarters view in Vaillant's painting *The Young Draftsman* in Lille.[7]

The mezzotint of the *Boy Seated in a Studio* reproduces (and reverses) Vaillant's own painting of c. 1666 in the Louvre.[8] The print closely follows the painting, except that it eliminates the cast of a foot hanging on the wall behind the Christ Child and the female face drawn in the open portfolio in front of the boy. Some elements are proportioned differently, especially noticeable in the reduced scale of the Christ Child's head (now less like the original sculpture) and the female head in profile behind him.

JC

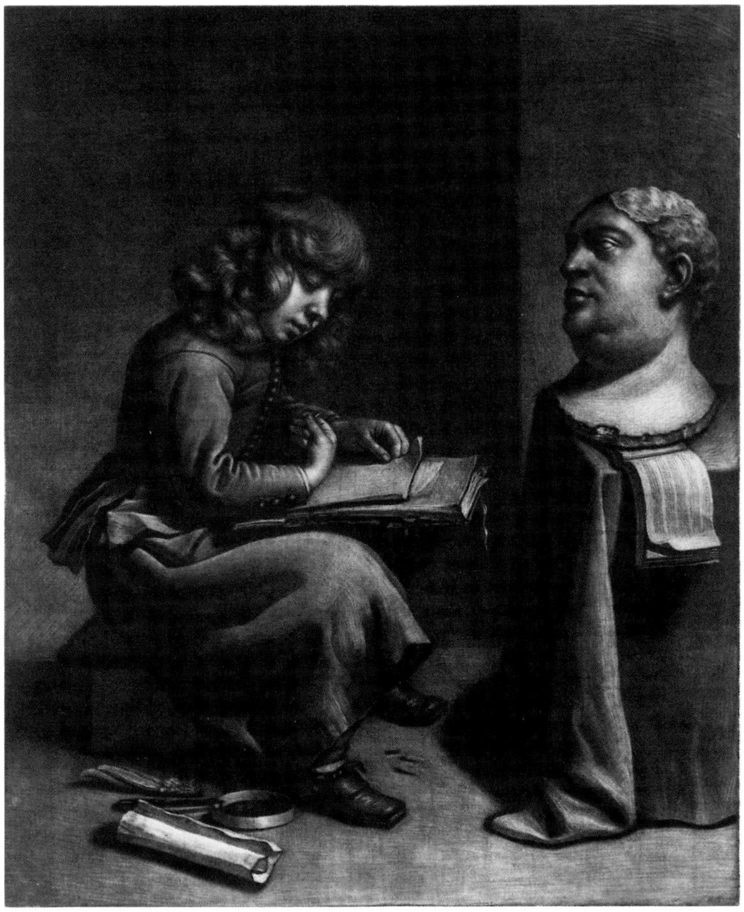

Fig. 40.2. Wallerant Vaillant. *Boy Drawing a Bust of the Roman Emperor Vitellius.* Mezzotint, 332 x 270 mm (13⅛ x 10⅝ in.). The British Museum, London.

1. See Grohn 1980.
2. See Sutton 1992, 212–15; De Jongh and Luijten 1997, 348–52.
3. On the implements, see De Jongh and Luijten 1997, 351–52.
4. Noted by Walter Liedtke in regard to Vaillant in Metropolitan Museum of Art 1992, 78.
5. On the sculpture, which is now presumed not to represent the Roman emperor Vitellius, and early modern copies, see Jitta 1972; Bailey 1977; Müller Hofstede 1985.
6. On the painting, which was attributed to Vaillant at its sale at Sotheby's, London, April 19, 1972, lot 86, see Waddingham 1976–77. The attribution to Sweerts, advanced by Waddingham and others, is rejected by Zafran 2002, 62, as well as by Peter C. Sutton, who views Vaillant as the probable artist (personal communication, for which I am grateful). It is often suggested that Sweerts's depictions of young artists at work influenced Vaillant, although most of Sweerts's compositions on the theme are multifigure works, and only the painting in Minneapolis is closely connected with Vaillant's images of a boy alone in a studio. On the print, see Ackley 1981, 272–73; Griffiths 1996, 148–49; De Jongh and Luijten 1997, 348–52.
7. Metropolitan Museum of Art 1992, 76.
8. On the painting, see Georgel and Lecoq 1982–83, 151–52. Another version, probably a copy after Vaillant, is at the National Gallery, London (see Levey 1981, 22, 24; MacLaren 1991, 1:439–40).

William Hogarth (1697–1764)

41. *William Hogarth Painting the Comic Muse*

1758

Etching and engraving, 403 x 351 mm (15⅞ x 13⅞ in.)

Reference: Paulson 204, v/vii

Inscriptions: on the book held by the painting on the canvas: *Comedy*; on the print in the volume at lower right: *ANALYSIS*; below the image: *Wm Hogarth SERJEANT PAINTER to His MAJESTY. / Publish'd as the Act directs, march 29 1758*

Purchased from Andrew Edmunds, London

1983.5.1

Hogarth, dressed in work clothes, sits before a canvas, raising a palette, brushes, and a palette knife as though he were in the process of painting, but rather stiffly and unconvincingly. On the canvas is the white-line drawing of a female figure holding a mask and a volume inscribed "Comedy." On a ledge behind the canvas is a bound book; another is propped against the foot of the easel. This latter is Hogarth's own *The Analysis of Beauty,* published in 1753, the first of its two large fold-out plates protruding from the volume (fig. 12.1). Behind the artist is a pot, across which an engraver's burin lies. The engraving reproduces (unreversed) a painting of c. 1757, which, however, lacks the two volumes and the pot and burin.[1] Like the self-portrait that gave rise to the *Gulielmus Hogarth* engraving (cat. no. 12), the painting of Hogarth seated at an easel evolved in stages on the canvas, with the artist painting over elements like a dog urinating on paintings, presumably Old Masters, which would have been in keeping with the more aggressive posture of *The Battle of the Pictures* (cat. no. 76) and *Time Smoking a Picture* (cat. no. 77).[2] The canvas on which the artist is working originally appeared behind him, in the center of the composition, and its current place was occupied by a large nude, presumably male, model of uncertain iconographic significance.

Hogarth made several minor changes in the plate, including to his face, although in the fifth state of the engraving, exhibited here, he is still smiling slightly.[3] He changed the print more radically in 1764, the last year of his life, darkening his face and transforming the mask held by Comedy into that of a satyr. In its multiple states the engraving was used (even by his wife after Hogarth's death) as a frontispiece to the bound volumes of his prints, replacing *Gulielmus Hogarth*. As much as the *Gulielmus Hogarth,* the iconography of the self-portrait suggests its use as a programmatic introduction to his graphic oeuvre. Here still is the reference to his (now fully mature and published) art theory, with *The Analysis of Beauty* replacing the "Line of Beauty" on the palette in the *Gulielmus Hogarth*.[4]

In his biographical anecdotes about Hogarth, John Nichols first called the figure in the painting-within-a-painting "the Muse of Comedy."[5] She has thus been referred to as Thalia, the muse associated with comedy, although a book is not generally one of her attributes.[6] She may just as easily be simply a personification of Comedy, whose attributes may—according to the influential *Iconologia* by Cesare Ripa—include a mask.[7]

The figure of Comedy on which Hogarth works in the composition is, paradoxically, unlike anything Hogarth painted in actuality. He uses the language of allegory, exalted in the traditional hierarchy of genres, to embody his low-genre subjects. The allegorical figure alerts the viewer to the serious purpose of the engravings in the folio, despite (or in addition to) their comic appeal.[8] Similarly, the presence of *The Analysis of Beauty,* a treatise which is almost entirely formal and technical, asserts the aesthetic quality of Hogarth's work, even as measured by traditional history painting and classical sculpture. Hogarth supports his pretensions to important work with an inscription emphatically naming his position as Serjeant Painter to the king, which he had assumed on July 6, 1757, following the resignation from the post of his brother-in-law, John Thornhill, who was in poor health.[9] The proud proclamation of the inscription is somewhat at odds with the reality of the position, which was comparable to, for example, that of the Serjeant Plumber, although it proved lucrative through the deputizing of all the painting and gilding of royal palaces and conveyances. It has been suggested that the emphasis placed on his title is cynical, drawing on the general knowledge that the position carried with it more income than honor, and that the pot with brushes at lower left alludes to the low degree of projects undertaken under his auspices (akin to, and even including, house painting).[10] It is certainly like Hogarth to poke fun at himself while satirizing the state of the arts in England—with increasing bitterness toward the end of his life. JC

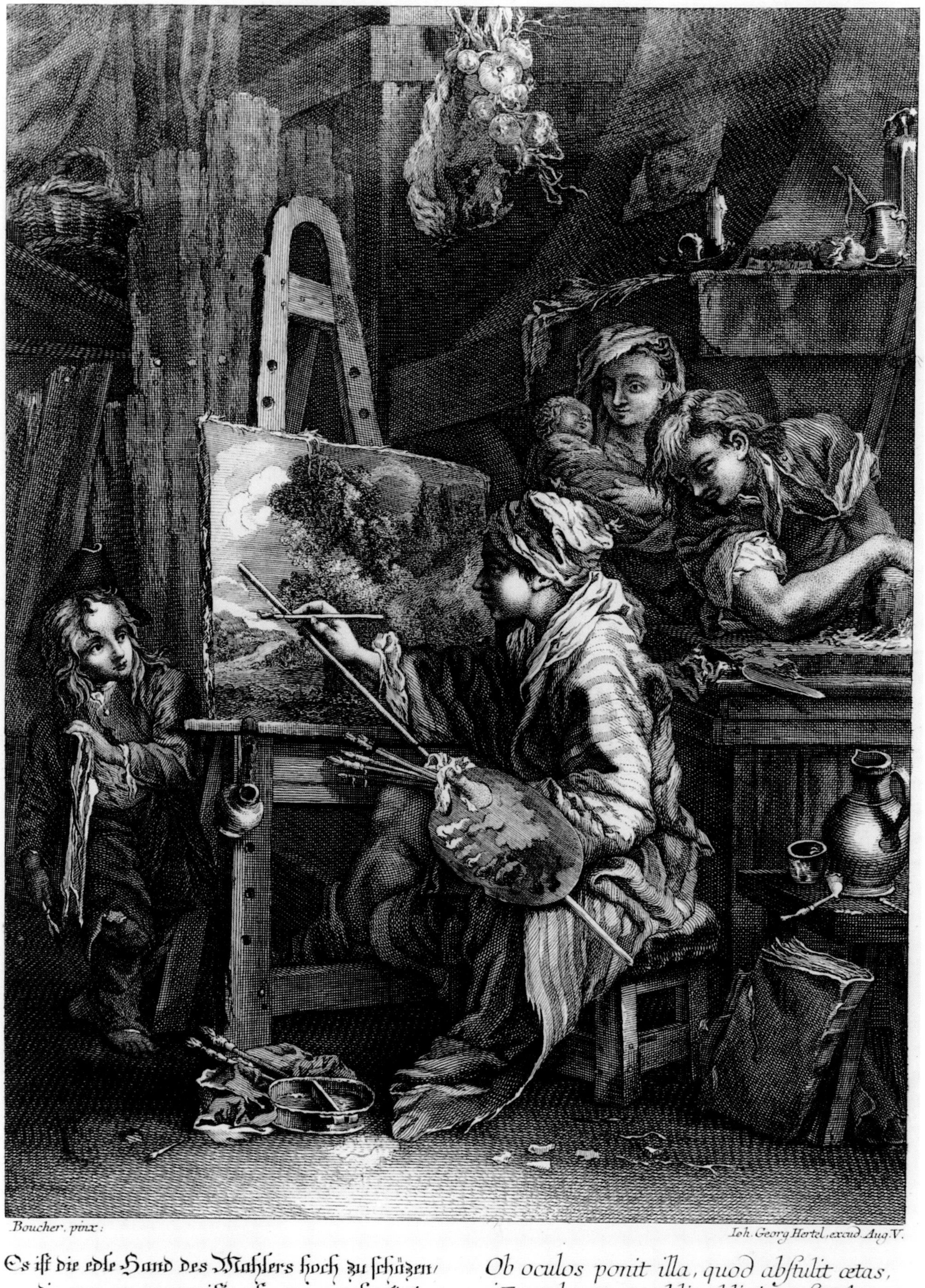

Boucher. pinx:

Ioh. Georg Hertel, excud. Aug. V.

Es ist die edle Hand des Mahlers hoch zu schäzen,
die, was vergangen ist, aufs neue præsentirt:
es kan des Keñers Aug sich ungemein ergözen,
wañ er beÿ dem Portrait den Pinsel weißlich führt.

Ob oculos ponit illa, quod abstulit ætas,
im̄ortalesque reddit oblivione sepultos:
præsentes facit et sæpe absentes amicos,
quare Laude numquam destituetur sua.

Nº. 12.

Cat. no. 42

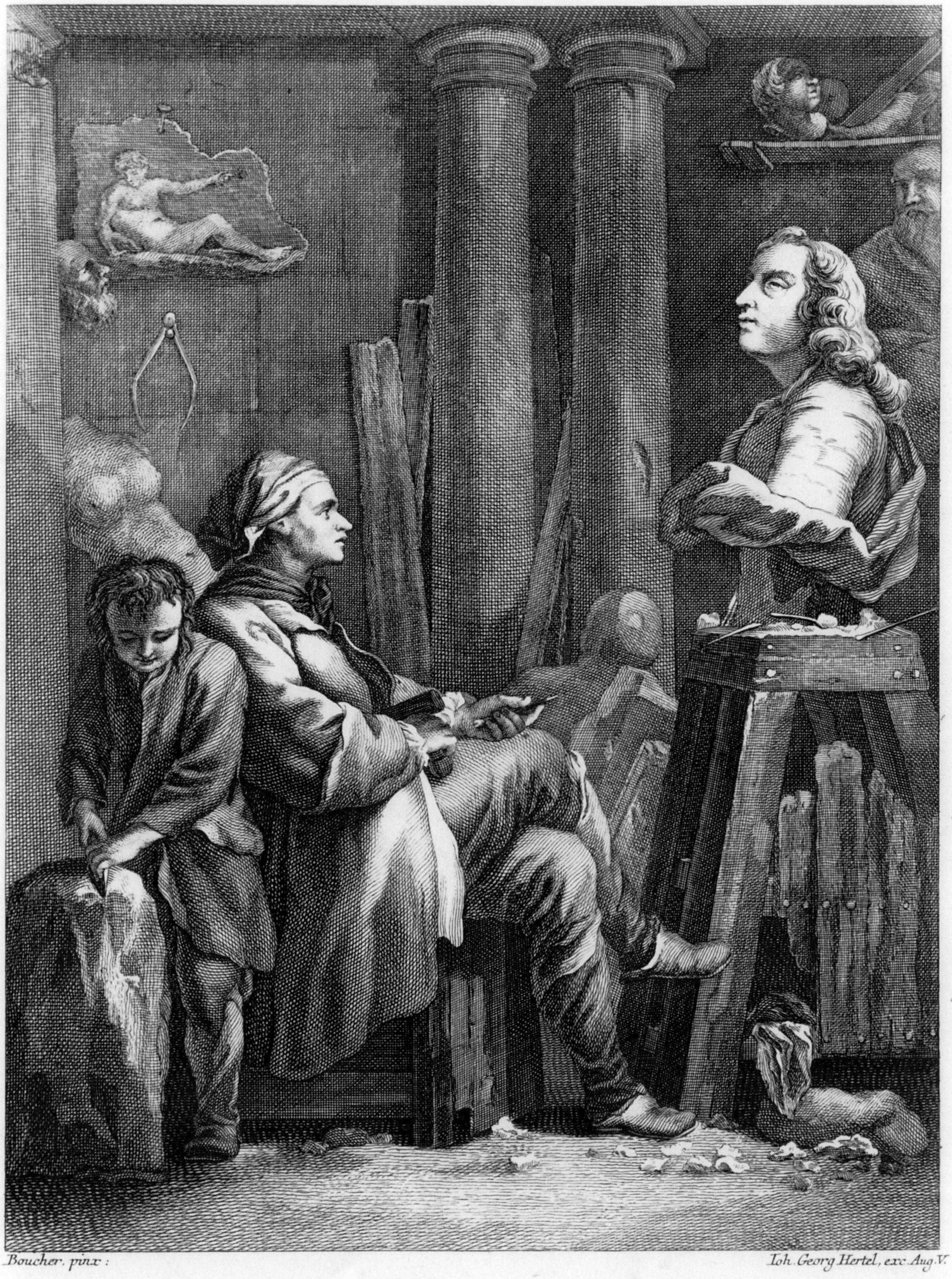
Boucher. pinx :
Ioh. Georg Hertel, exc. Aug. V.
Offt läst sich Holz u: Stein nicht gleich zu bolzen drehen,
ob gleich des Künstlers Hand den besten fleiß nicht spahrt:
doch läst zu weilen sich davon ein Bildnuß sehen,
so, als ein Angedenk, das Alterthum verwahrt.
Ex quovis Lapide non fit Mercurius
Licet perita Sculptoris sæpe manus:
oleum et operam impendat multo sudore,
donec Statua suavi aspectu oculos beat.
No. 12.

Cat. no. 43

The sale of the collection of the sculptor Jean-Baptiste Lemoyne on August 10, 1778, in Paris included a pair of paintings, described in the catalogue: "The one represents a sculptor in his studio, seated before a bust of the king Louis XV; next to him is a boy who sharpens his chisel. The other a painter working on a landscape; behind him is a color grinder; next to him is a woman holding her baby in swaddling-clothes. Behind the easel is visible a small boy who holds a portfolio. The two lovely pieces are full of gaity and delights. Paintings executed by M. Pierre and François Boucher."[1] The *Landscape Painter,* painted around 1732 and signed by Boucher, is in the Baron Edmond de Rothschild collection, Château de Prégny, and the *Sculptor* (or a version of it), painted years later by Jean-Baptiste-Marie Pierre, recently appeared at auction. Both paintings were engraved (in reverse) in 1752 by Marie-Madelaine Igonet, entitled *La Peinture* and *La Sculpture* and inscribed with Boucher's and Pierre's names, respectively,[2] as are the mezzotints after the paintings by Johann Jakob Haid (cat. nos. 44, 45). It is curious, then, that Johann Georg Hertel the Elder attributes both paintings to Boucher in the present engravings. It is not clear what models were used for the engravings published by Hertel that might have led to a misattribution. One would expect the engravings to have been based on Igonet's prints rather than the paintings themselves because they were more accessible to the Augsburg publisher, and the fact that Hertel's prints are in the same direction as the paintings suggests that they may have been taken after, and therefore reversed, from the prints. However, there are slight but notable differences between the two sets of prints, as well as the paintings—most obviously the introduction in the Hertel *Landscape Painter* of a female head on the drawing attached to the chimney, which is indecipherable in Boucher's painting and Igonet's engraving—that may indicate a different source. The identity of Hertel's engraver is also unclear; he may be one of the four artists working at this time on Hertel's luxuriously illustrated edition of Cesare Ripa's famous *Iconologia* (1758-1760).[3]

Both the artists depicted in Boucher's and Pierre's compositions are working in fairly shabby circumstances, much in contrast to the studios depicted by Abraham Bosse a century earlier (see cat. nos. 68, 69). The young painter wears an elegant housecoat, fashionable for portraits of artists like Pierre Mignard (fig. 10.1) but here rather tattered. We may presume the woman to be the artist's wife and the color grinder and the barefoot boy with the portfolio to be members of his shop. At the sale of the painting in 1828, the catalogue averred that the painter was Boucher himself and the boy his pupil, Jean-Baptiste Deshays (1729-1765), but the identification is unlikely: neither figure has the individualized features of a portrait, and Deshays, Boucher's eventual son-in-law, did not train with him as a youth.[4] At about the same period, Boucher painted a similar composition of a young landscape painter at work, this time alone

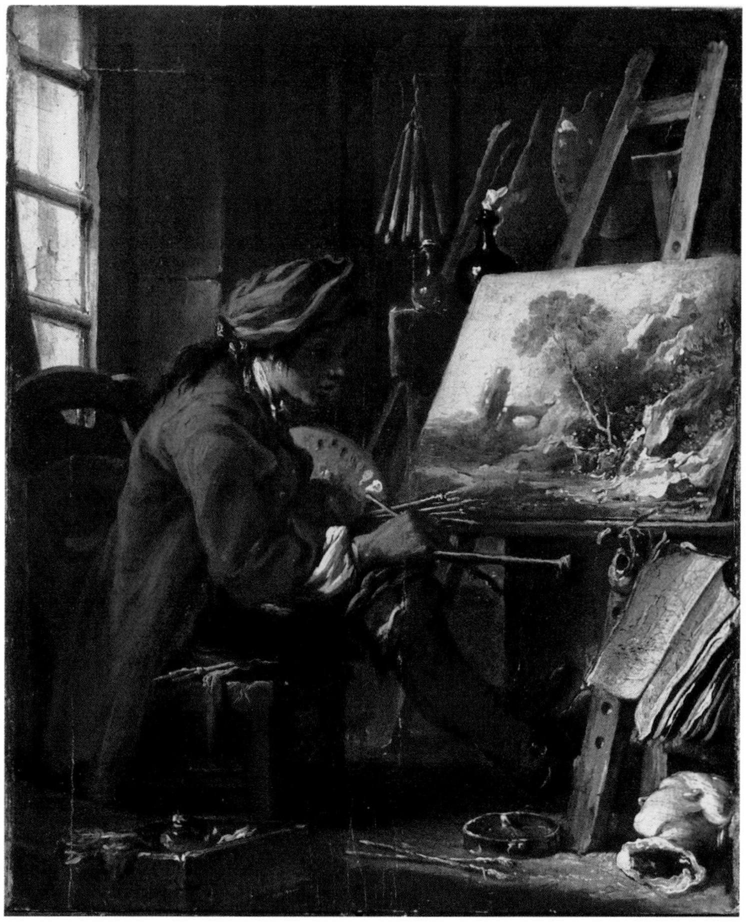

Fig. 43.1. François Boucher. *The Painter in His Studio.* c. 1732–35. Oil on canvas, 27 x 22 cm (10⅝ x 8⅝ in.). Musée du Louvre, Paris.

(fig. 43.1). In both instances, Boucher's painter is making a landscape "from memory," based on drawings made from life, attached to his easel in one painting and without direct benefit of drawings in the other.[5] Boucher's depictions of a landscape painter working both with and without drawings recall versions of a similar subject by Adriaen van Ostade in the previous century (see cat. no. 39).

Assuming that Boucher's *Landscape Painter* was in Lemoyne's collection long before his death in 1778, the sculptor may have commissioned a pendant from Pierre representing his own profession. Although the sculpture of Louis XV on the workbench matches no known portrait by Lemoyne, the sculptor had depicted the king on several occasions. At the 1828 sale of the painting along with its pendant, the sculptor was identified as Lemoyne himself and the assistant as his student Augustin Pajou,[6] which is probably as fanciful as the identification of Boucher and Deshays.

Hertel's inscriptions do not relate directly to the compositions; rather, they rehearse traditional and general notions of the painter's ability to make present the past and that which is absent, the sculptor's struggle against the material to produce a portrait which will preserve memory, and the pleasure that both painting and sculpture bring to the viewer's eye.

JC

1. Quoted by Ananoff 1976, 1:209.
2. On the painting by Pierre, see Sotheby's, New York, May 20, 1993, lot 40. The Sotheby's painting is described as being dated 1756, which would make it an impossible model for Igonet's 1752 engraving, although the sales catalogue notes that the Pierre *Sculptor* in the 1828 sale was described as dated 1748. On Igonet's engravings, see Bruand and Hébert 1970, 556, nos. 2–3. See also Ananoff 1976, 1:209; Metropolitan Museum of Art 1986, 150.
3. Namely, Jeremias Wachsmuth, Emmanuel Eichel, Jakob Wangner, and Christian Halbaur (see Maser 1971, xiv).
4. Ananoff 1976, 1:209–210; Ananoff and Wildenstein 1980, 91.
5. Metropolitan Museum of Art 1986, 150; Roland Michel 1990, 103.
6. See the Sotheby's sale catalogue, New York, May 20, 1993, lot 40. Bruand and Hébert 1970, 556, accept the identification of Lemoyne.

JOHANN JAKOB HAID (1704–1767), PUBLISHER
after François Boucher (1703–1770)

44. *The Landscape Painter*

c. 1760

Etching and mezzotint, printed in blue ink, 409 x 319 mm (16⅛ x 12½ in.)

INSCRIPTIONS: below image: *Peint par Bouch. I. Iac. Haid excud. A. V.; LA PEINTURE. / Die Mahler Kunst.*

Purchased from Kunsthandlung Helmut H. Rumbler, Frankfurt

1997.17

JOHANN JAKOB HAID (1704–1767), PUBLISHER
after Jean-Baptiste-Marie Pierre (1714–1789)

45. *The Sculptor*

c. 1760

Etching and mezzotint, printed in blue ink, 412 x 322 mm (16¼ x 12⅝ in.)

INSCRIPTIONS: below image: *Peint par Pierre. I. Iac. Haid excud. A. V.; LA SCULPTURE. / Die Bildhauer Kunst.*

Purchased from Kunsthandlung Helmut H. Rumbler, Frankfurt

1997.18

Johann Jakob Haid published copies of pendant compositions of a painter and sculptor in their studios by François Boucher and Jean-Baptiste-Marie Pierre, respectively, at about the same time that Johann Georg Hertel published his copies of the compositions (cat. nos. 42, 43). Both publishers worked in Augsburg, and they may have shared models for the prints, or Haid may have relied on the prints published by Hertel.[1] In Haid's versions, a great amount of detail has been eliminated, especially in the background, although the prints themselves are substantially larger than Hertel's. The mezzotint technique is capable of considerable detail and refinement (see, for example, cat. nos. 26, 28), but its primary attraction has been its ability to reproduce subtle tonal gradations. Details are not generally of paramount importance in the medium, and the naturally produced soft contours are welcomed (see, for example, cat. no. 40). Nonetheless, sometimes the composition is etched into the plate as a first step, before the overall use of the rocker or roulette that gives rise to mezzotint's characteristic tone, resulting in crisp contour lines.[2] Haid's engraver, even as he eliminated details, made extensive use of etching in both plates, with lines that are not always sure-handed. The lines were deeply etched and therefore appear prominently in the impressions. The most remarkable aspect of the prints' appearance, however, is their vivid

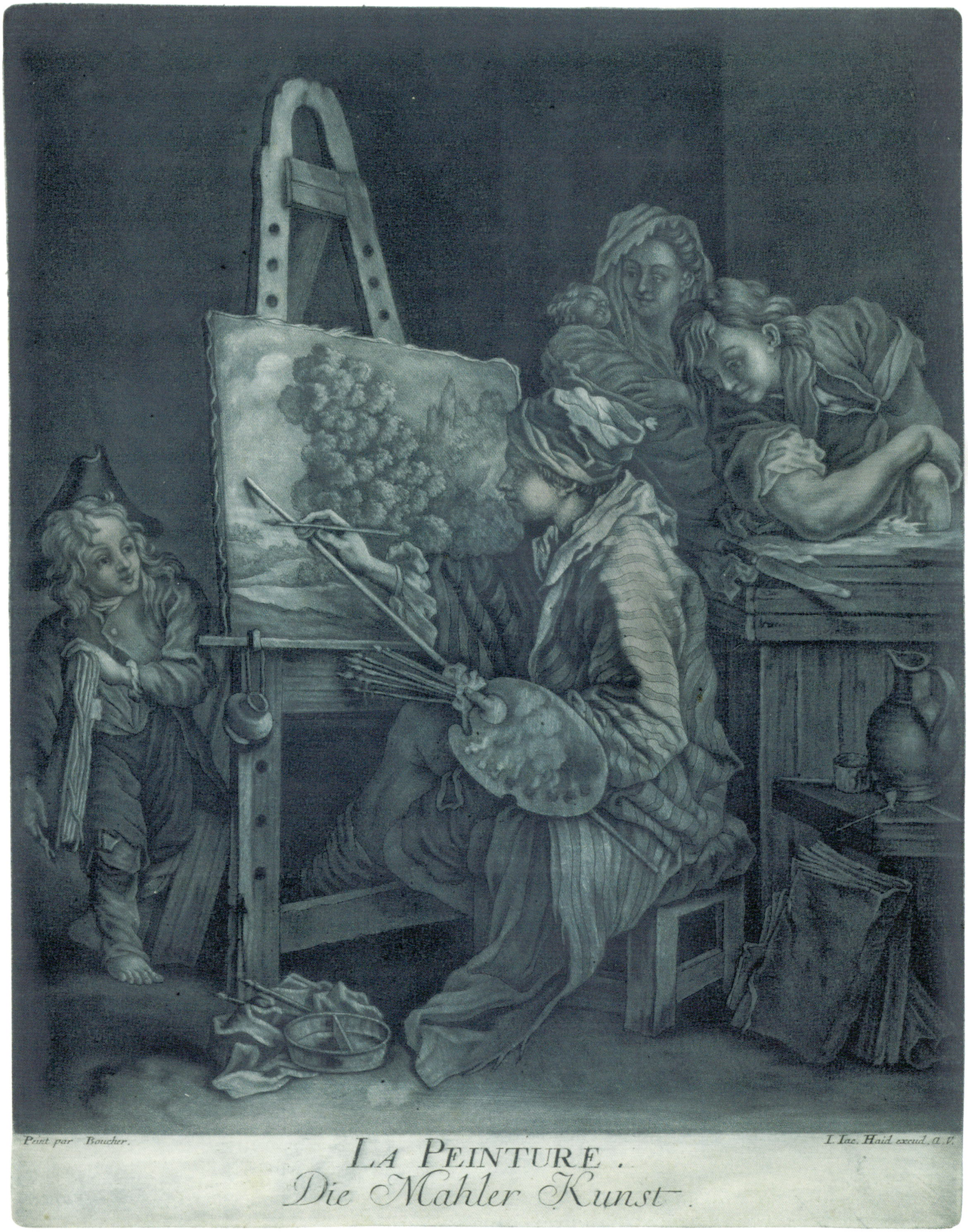
Peint par Boucher.
I. Iac. Haid excud. A.V.
LA PEINTURE.
Die Mahler Kunst.

Cat. no. 44

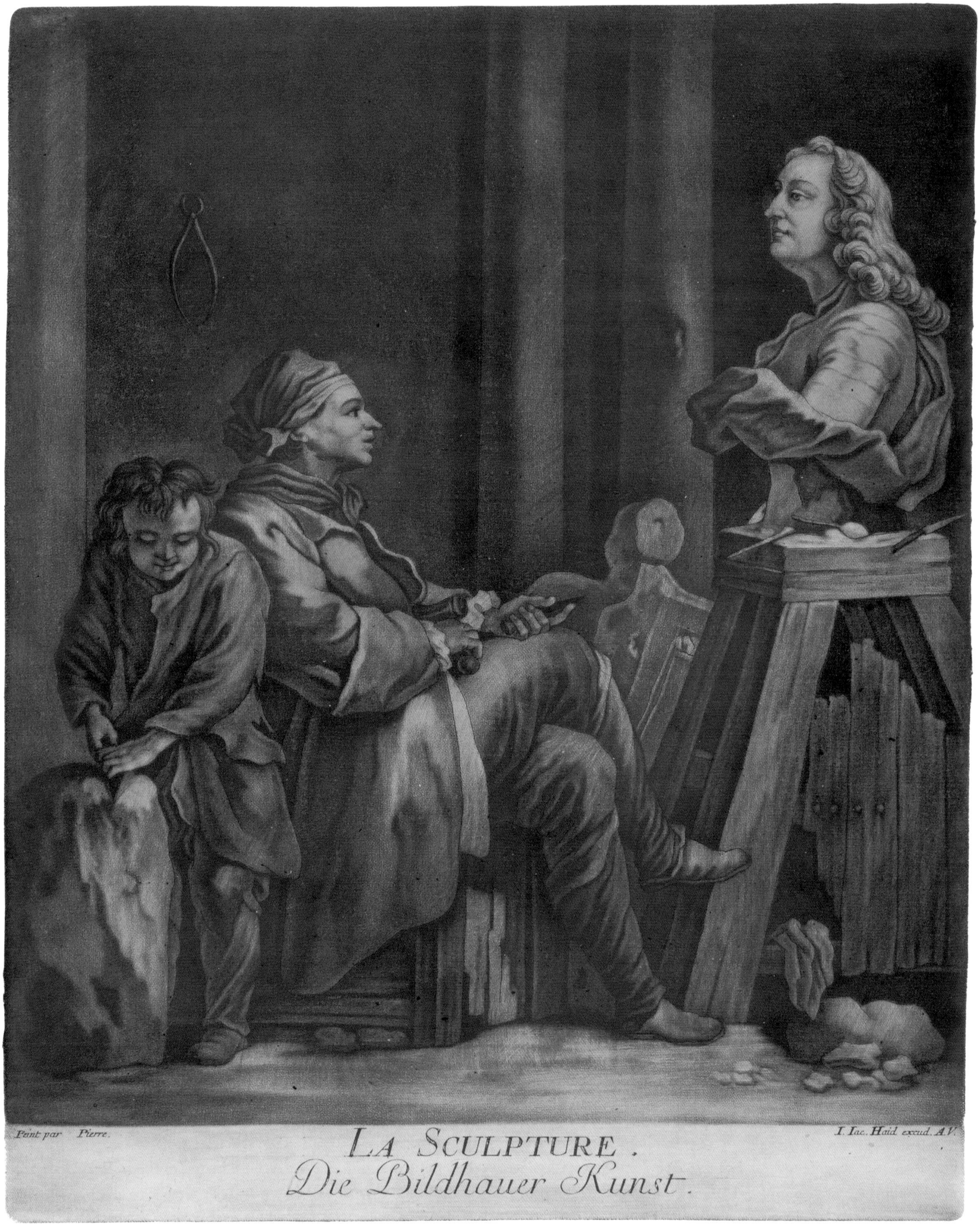
Peint par Pierre.
I. Iac. Haid excud. A.V.
LA SCULPTURE.
Die Bildhauer Kunst.

Cat. no. 45

man about to enter some kind of structure, possibly subterranean, on the other side of the river. Before the ruins—and remarkably close to them for his purpose, since they seem to have little fineness of detail—is a seated draftsman. Another figure, possibly a curious passerby, stands before him.

JC

1. On Mauperché, see Biard 1997.
2. For French artists, see Coquery 2000.
3. Robert-Dumesnil 28-51. Robert-Dumesnil divides the landscape into a suite of six small ones, two suites of medium-sized ones (to the second of which the present etching belongs), and miscellaneous large ones. A few of Mauperché's etchings were made after other artists, some after his own paintings, and some, as here, as an etching alone.

Unknown Northern Artist (?)

49. *Draftsman before Antique Ruins*

Second half of the seventeenth century (?)
Etching on blue paper, 312 x 231 mm (12¼ x 9⅛ in.) (trimmed)
Purchased from Kunsthandlung Helmut H. Rumbler, Frankfurt
1999.15

In front of a tall plastered brick wall are fragments of large ancient sculptures, vases, and architectural members, all in the disarray of neglect. Set into the wall is a cracked relief depicting a pagan sacrifice. Ivy grows from a sarcophagus whose broken lid has collapsed into its cavity. Weeds sprout along the top of the wall, the top of the relief, behind the stump of an Egyptian obelisk, and among the pieces on the ground. In the lower right corner of the composition, dwarfed by the jumble of ruins, an artist bends over the portfolio on his lap, drawing. The three-quarter view from behind the figure was a convention for the representation of an artist at work when his specific identity was not at issue. The etching apparently has not been published, and its attribution is highly uncertain.

The work is a capriccio; that is, it is an imaginary view of ancient ruins rather than a specific site. In this instance, unlike many other capricci, the ruins themselves are probably fictive rather than known works. Nonetheless, the image evokes the ruins in Rome, which were often depicted in the sixteenth century and following. Artists from Northern Europe frequently traveled to Italy as part of their artistic formation, drawn by the famous works of both antiquity and the Renaissance, and they spent much of their time making drawings after these works.[1] For example, the Haarlem artist, Maarten van Heemskerck, spent over four years in Rome in the 1530s, mostly drawing, especially works of ancient and contemporary art and architecture, including ruins. He proudly recalled his experience years later in his self-portrait of 1553, now in the Fitzwilliam Museum, Cambridge (fig. 49.1).[2] A painting by Anton Goubau from 1662 suggests the activities of these artists: at the right side of the composition a group draws (and, remarkably, sculpts) ancient ruins and sculptures—recognizable ones, including the Farnese Hercules, albeit placed in an imaginary setting (fig. 49.2).[3] Seventeenth-century Dutch artists visiting Italy produced mostly landscape drawings, often with ruins, and several of these artists, such as Willem van Nieulandt the Younger, Bartholomeus Breenbergh, and Herman van Swanevelt, used the drawings as the basis for etchings upon their return north.

Individual sculptures, particularly those of great fame, were naturally the object of visiting artists' particular interest, but the artists were also sensitive to the pictorial possibilities of views of architectural ruins and fragmented sculptures in situ, and depictions of antiquities early on became more than simply records of works to be admired and imitated. For example, the prints of Etienne Dupérac, a French artist resident in Rome for twenty years, published as *Vestigi dell'antichità di Roma* in 1575, showed views of ancient Rome (as well as more recent structures) with contemporary figures, including tourists, wandering among the ruins. They proved enormously popular, appearing in many editions through the next two centuries. Many of Heemskerck's evocative drawings show such sites, and private collections of ancient sculptures, whether real or imagined, were also represented in their abundant disarray, as in a print published by Hieronymus Cock in Antwerp

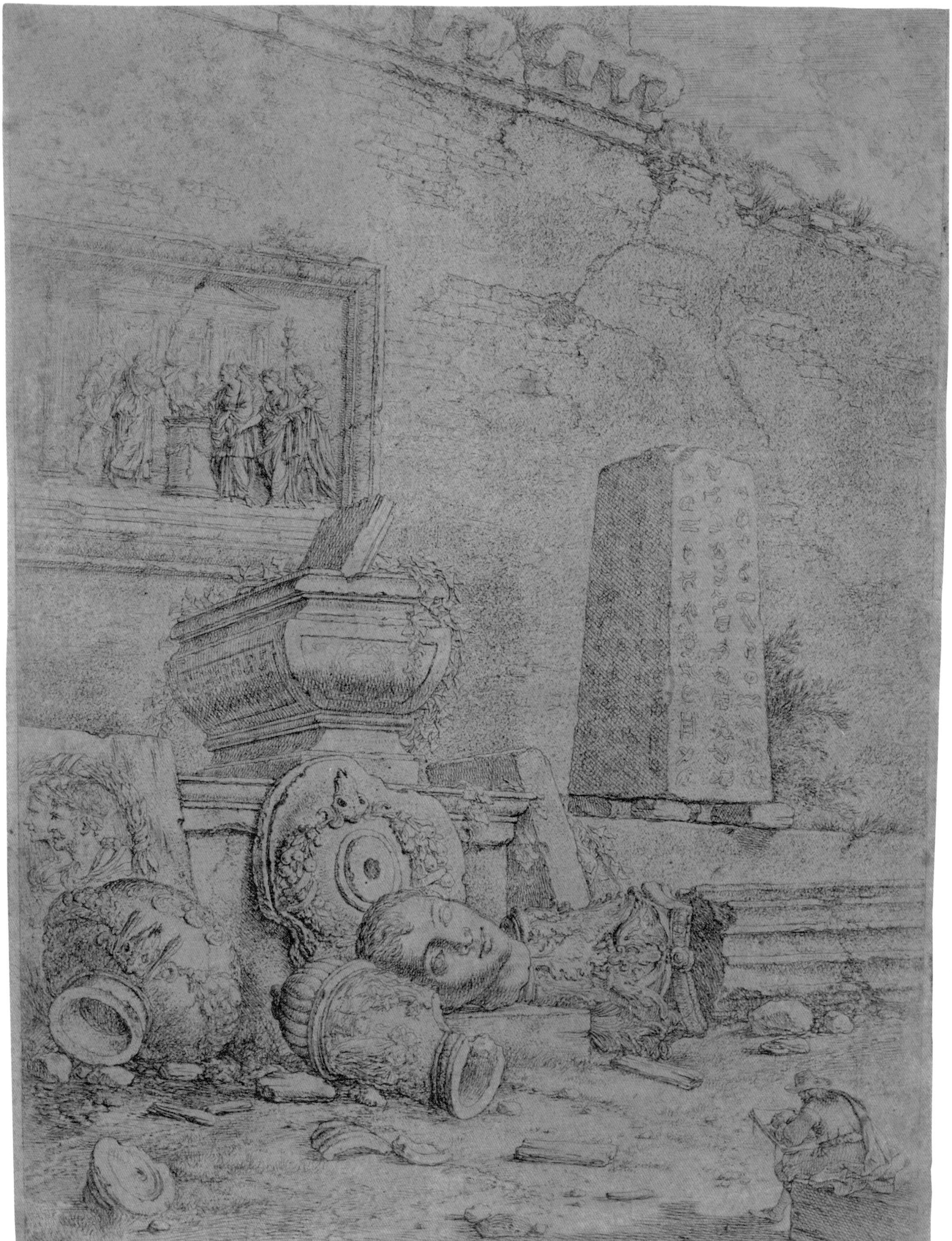

Cat. no. 49

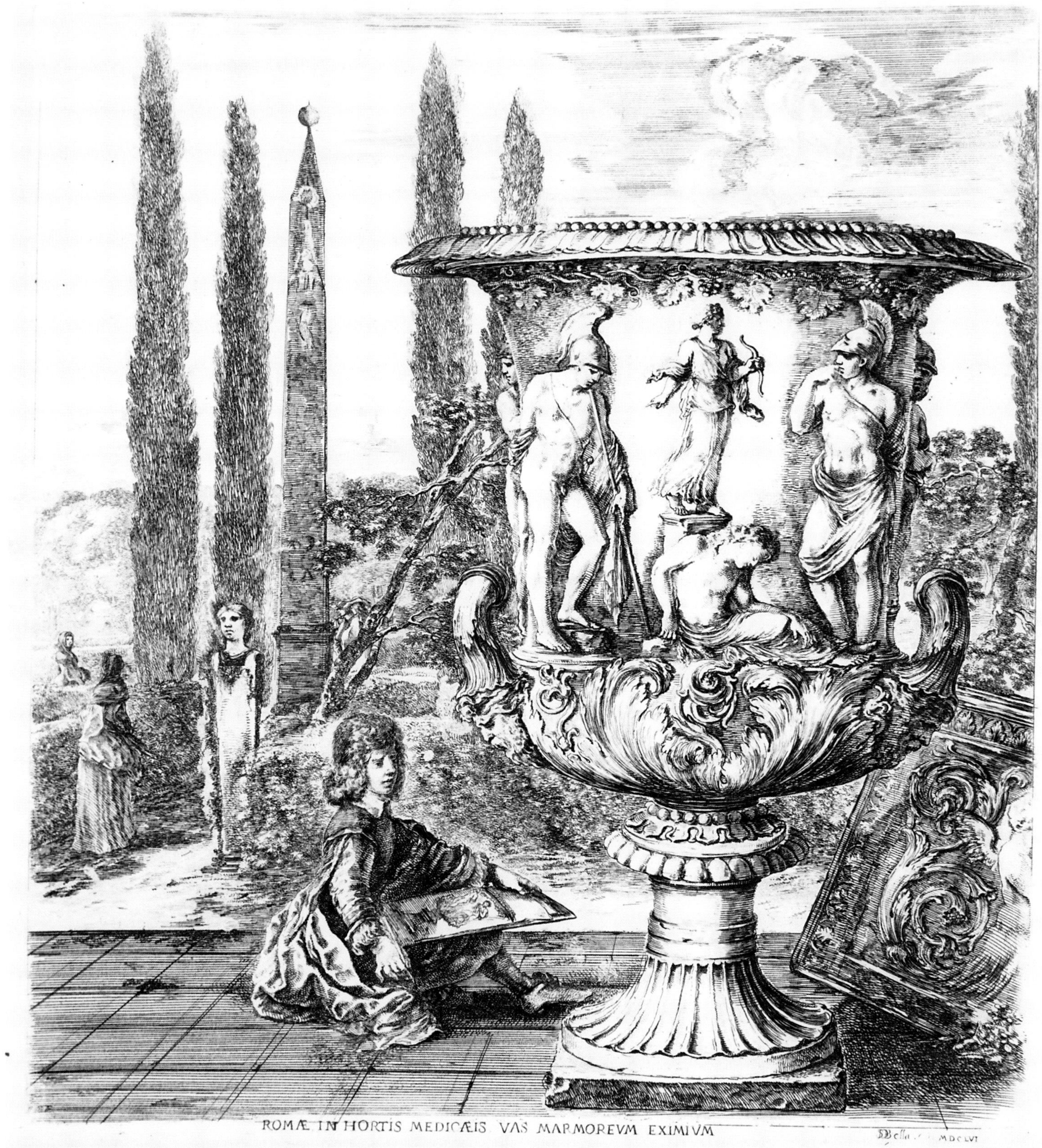

Cat. no. 50

Drawing occupied a unique place among the arts, especially in Florentine art theory which asserted that *disegno* was the origin of all other arts and that a knowledge of drawing was fundamental to the successful painter or sculptor.

By the seventeenth century, the arts had gained considerable social status, so that to see a print of Cosimo III sketching an antique vase is not surprising, as learning to draw was part of his princely education. By depicting the future grand duke engaged in leisurely drawing, della Bella—though himself a professional artist—reaffirms the noble status the arts had attained and seeks to validate his own elevated status as a draftsman and printmaker.

LS

1. De Vesme and Massar no. 832. The first state of this etching, known only through an impression at the Albertina, is inscribed with the date D.MDCL (which could be read as 1650), although De Vesme dismissed this as an imperfection in the biting of the plate, arguing that the artist probably intended the inscription to read A.D.MDCLVI (i.e., Anno Domini 1656). The Blaffer Foundation's impression of *The Medici Vase* probably dates to the late seventeenth century.
2. On the Medici vase, see Mansuelli 1958, no. 180; Haskell and Penny 1981, no. 82.
3. Haskell and Penny 1981, 316. See Boyer, 1929, 256–70.
4. Gaspari 1991, 447 n. 15.
5. Haskell and Penny 1981, 316. See Amelung 1897, 79–80. For the story of Iphigenia, see Ovid's *Metamorphoses,* 12.24–34. After considering Iphigenia and Cassandra as possible subjects, Mansuelli concludes that a more general mantic consultation is most likely the subject of the vase.
6. Evelyn 1955, 232.
7. Capecchi 1993, 107.
8. De Vesme and Massar 1971, 3.
9. Ibid., 42. For the engraved double portrait see De Vesme and Massar, no. 37. A preparatory drawing for the figure of Cosimo in *The Medici Vase* is housed in the Royal Collection at Windsor Castle. See Blunt 1954, no. 9.
10. Alberti 1966, 67. See also Summers 1987, 132.
11. "I recall reading that the ancients, especially throughout Greece, required boys of gentle birth to learn painting in school, as a decorous and necessary thing, and admitted it to first rank among the liberal arts; then by public edict they prohibited the teaching of it to slaves." Castiglione 1959, 77.

Isaac Beckett (c.1653–possibly 1715 or 1719)

after Simon Du Bois (1632–1708)

---

51. *Adriaan Beverland Drawing a Statue*

c. 1686

Mezzotint, 425 x 250 mm (16¾ x 9⅞ in.) (trimmed)

Inscription: below image: *Viro perillustri Hadriano Beverlando numismatim Insectorum Cochearam / Picturarum ac Librorum rariorum Vindici ac Statori Hanc Tab a Sim: du Bois delin L.M.Q.C. / I. Smith ex Is. Beckett*

Purchased from Andrew Edmunds, London

2000.3

Adriaan (or Hadrian) Beverland (1650–1716) was a notorious free-thinking writer.[1] During the 1670s, he was enrolled at several universities in the Netherlands and England, studying Latin literature and writing his first book, *De Prostibulis Veterum,* which, drawing on numerous quotations from classical antiquity, the Bible, and modern writers, discourses on the erotic nature of humankind. An advance section of that book, the *Peccatum Originale,* on the sexuality of Adam and Eve and original sin, was published anonymously in 1678 and then with the author's name in 1679. Beverland was arrested in Leyden and exiled. He moved to England where he remained controversial. During the 1680s, Beverland amassed a substantial personal library and collection of art. However, in the following decades, mentally unstable and impecunious, he was forced to sell his books (1693) and paintings (around 1711) to ease perpetual financial straits. Beverland was not a professional artist, and Isaac Beckett's mezzotint of him drawing among antiquities suggests a different characterization. The inscription describes him as a distinguished collector of coins, insects, shells, pictures, and books. As such, he is presented as a gentleman-scholar, what in the seventeenth century was called a *virtuoso* and in the eighteenth an *amateur.* Nonprofessional drawing was seen as an important element in the development and life of the *virtuoso.*[2]

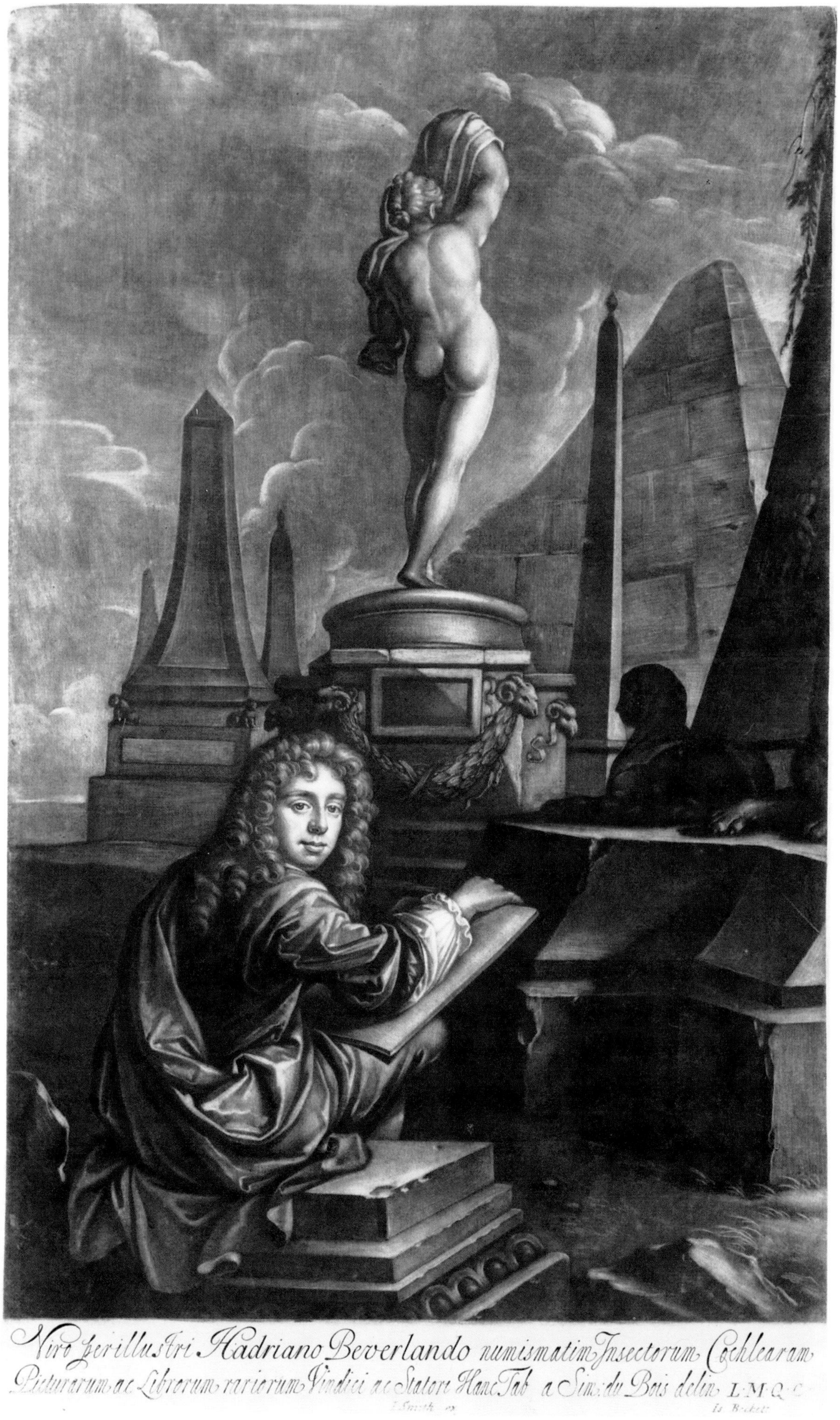
Viro perillustri Hadriano Beverlando numismatim Insectorum Cochlearam
Picturarum ac Librorum rariorum Vindici ac Statore Hanc Tab a Sim: du Bois delin L·M·Q·C
I. Smith ex
Is. Beckett

Cat. no. 51

Beckett's mezzotint is based on a composition by Simon Du Bois and was published by Beckett's student John Smith (1652–1742).[3] Du Bois was a friend of Beverland, who inherited Du Bois's art collection in 1708. The personal connection and perhaps the input of the sitter, as well as the fact that the image was probably never meant for a painting, may account for the unusual composition—a departure from Du Bois's more conventional portraiture—with its outdoor setting and Beverland's back to the viewer. Beverland sits on the square base of a column or pier and turns to the viewer. No drawing instrument is visible, and the tablet he holds is less specifically rendered than the portfolios often depicted with draftsmen, but he may be drawing the pseudoancient (Roman and Egyptian) sculptures and monuments, all in nearly pristine condition, rising before him.[4] Given Beverland's intellectual and, apparently, personal proclivities, the compositional centrality of the female nude is not surprising.

Beckett produced another mezzotint portrait of Beverland, in this instance after a painting in Amsterdam attributed to Arie de Vois, in which the writer appears in nearly full-length, seated and holding a pipe, with a woman who has a book open before her, presumably his *Peccatum Originale,* the title of which is inscribed below the image.[5] Horace Walpole called the mezzotint "Adrian Beverland and his wife," perhaps using the term loosely or ignoring the woman's deshabille.[6]

JC

1. On Beverland, see Dingwall 1962, 145–77; De Smet 1988.
2. See Sloan 2000, esp. 11–18.
3. O'Donoghue 1908–25, 1:183, lists three impressions of the mezzotint in the British Museum, of which one is a proof without letters, one without Smith's name, and one inscribed as in the present impression.
4. The statue of the nude woman recalls, but is not identical to, the famous Callipygian Venus (Haskell and Penny 1981, 316–18); similarly, the pyramid recalls that of Caius Cestius in Rome.
5. Bromley 1793, 232, cites the painter as "CDVoisLugd," but O'Donoghue 1908–25, 1:184, correctly reads the inscription as G. D. Vois. A reversed copy was produced as a mezzotint by Pieter Schenk (Hollstein 505). On portraits of Beverland, see Dingwall 1962, 176–77; De Smet, 149–50.
6. Walpole 1969, 3:240. Bromley 1793, 232, refers to the woman as Beverland's mistress.

William Hogarth (1697–1764)

52. *O the Roast Beef of Old England: The Gate of Calais*

1748/49

Etching and engraving, 380 x 454 mm (15 x 17⅞ in.)

Reference: Paulson 180, ii/ii

Inscriptions: on the tag, at center: *For Mad^m Grandsire at Calais.*; below image at left: *Painted by W. Hogarth*; below image at right: *Engraved by C. Mosley & W. Hogarth.*; below image at center: *O THE ROAST BEEF OF OLD ENGLAND, &c. / Publish'd according to Act of Parliament March 6th 1749.*

Purchased from Andrew Edmunds, London

1983.5.33

Hogarth had been to Paris in 1743 (in order to have his *Marriage A-la-mode* series engraved), before the outbreak of the War of Austrian Succession had made commerce with France difficult at best. He had apparently enjoyed himself, conducted business—his prints were increasingly popular in France—but remained Francophobic, consonant with his career-long antagonism toward continental culture (see cat. no. 76). In 1748, following the cessation of hostilities, he determined to go to France again, in the company of friends, for some rest and relaxation. Hogarth had an uneventful stay in Paris, although, according to one early account, he was rather an ugly tourist: "While Hogarth was in France, wherever he went, he was sure to be dissatisfied with all he saw. If an elegant circumstance, either in furniture, or the ornaments of a room, was pointed out as deserving approbation, his narrow and constant reply was, 'What then? but it is *French!* Their houses are all gilt and b—t.' In the streets he was often clamourously rude."[1] He may have accompanied his friends to Flanders and Holland; in preparing to return to England from Calais, he ran

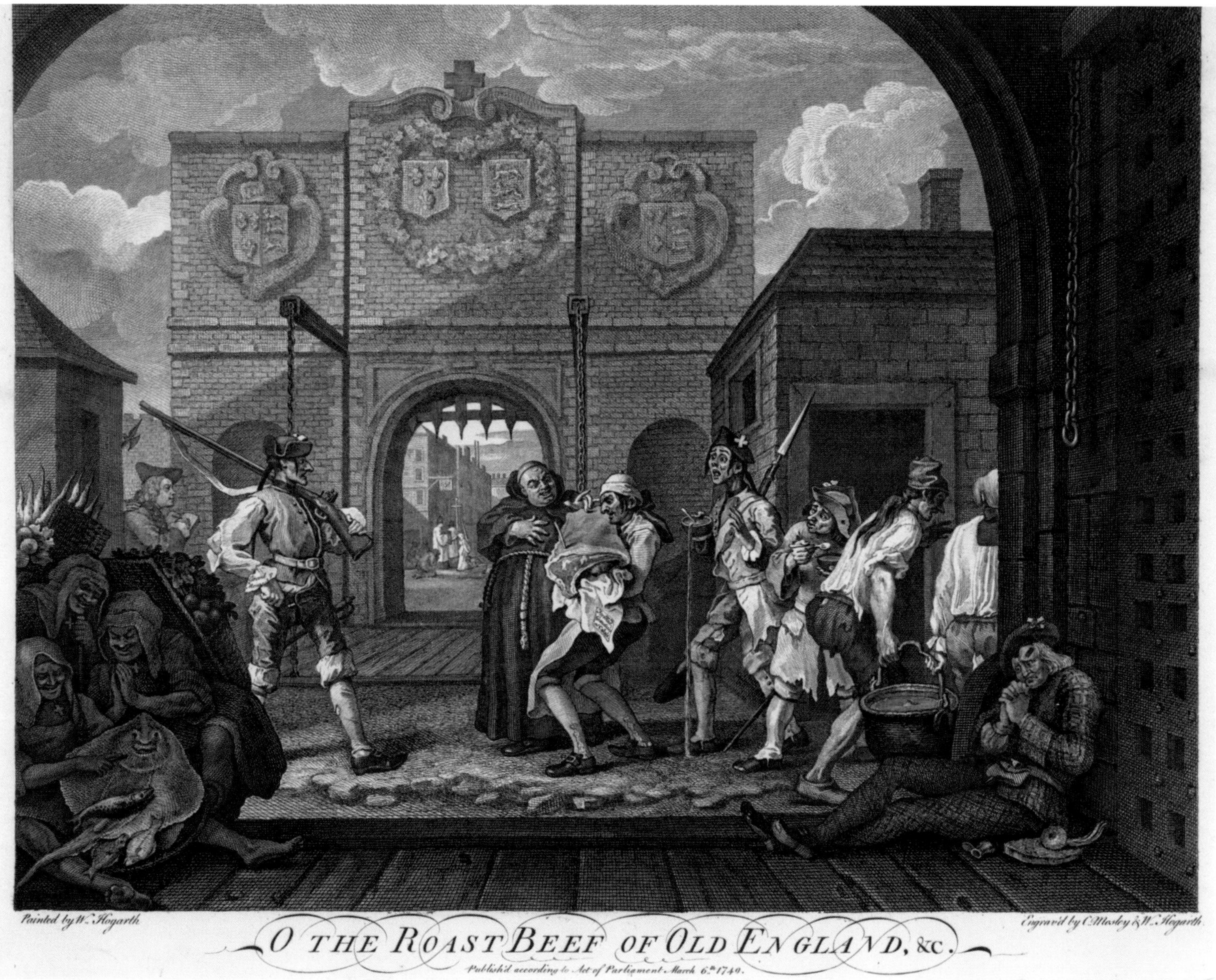
Painted by Wm. Hogarth
Engrav'd by C. Mosley & Wm. Hogarth
O THE ROAST BEEF OF OLD ENGLAND, &c.
Publish'd according to Act of Parliament March 6th 1749.

Cat. no. 52

into some trouble, which gave rise to a painting and a print upon his return to England.

Hogarth encountered trouble while sketching the Calais Gate (the old English tower fortifications, which had been built during the English occupation of Calais, 1346–1558), as he described in his "Autobiographical Notes": "I seiz by one of them [soldiers] and carrid to the governor (?) as a spy as I was santering about and obseving [the people] & the gate which it seem was built by the English when the place was in our possession. . . . [A]s I conceild none of the memorandum I had privately taken and they being found to be only those of a painter for own use it was Judged necessary only to confine me to my lodging till the wind changed for our coming away to England."[2]

In characterizing the French and his experience there, Hogarth was typically thinking in terms of contrasts: "The first time any one goes from hence to france by way of Calais he cannot avoid being struck with the Extreem different face things appear with at so little a distance as from Dover a farcical pomp of war, parade of riligion, and Bustle with little with very little bussiness in short poverty slavery and Insolence (with an affectation of politeness) give you even here the first specimen of the whole country nor are the figure less opposited to those of dover than the two shores. fish wemen have faces of [*word illegible*] leather and soldiers raged and lean."[3]

Hogarth used the incident as a springboard for a visual diatribe against France and the French, first as a painting (London, Tate Gallery), then as this unreversed engraving, which was executed in part by Charles Mosely.[4] England is represented metonymically by the solid gate decorated with English escutcheons and, at the center of the composition, a giant slab of beef, which, as its tag indicates, is destined for Madam Grandsire's, the English inn in Calais. Hogarth described the beef as "opposed the Kettle of soup meager,"[5] as Henry Fielding had contrasted the hearty English fare with less substantial French food in *Grub-street Opera* (1731), from which Hogarth took his title for this print.[6] A founding member (in 1735) of the nationalistic Sublime Society of Beefsteaks (their motto was "Beef and Liberty"), which met for a hearty meal weekly in season at Covent Garden Theatre, Hogarth uses the beef in *The Gate of Calais* as a symbol of English strength and substance.[7] The friar who admires the beef is the only well-fed Frenchman in the print, illustrating Hogarth's antipathy for the Roman Catholic Church.[8]

The artist himself appears in the background at left, his pencil raised to his sketch-pad, his arrest imminent: "my own figure in the corner with the soldier (?) hand upon my sholder is said to be tolerably like."[9]

JC

1. Nichols 1785, 49–50; quoted by Paulson, 1991–93, 2:354. As Ireland 1791, 1:286, succinctly puts it: "Extreme partiality for his native country, was the leading trait of his character; he seems to have begun his three hours voyage, with a firm determination to be displeased at everything he saw out of *Old England*."
2. Hogarth 1955, 228.
3. Hogarth 1955, 227–28. His most explicit contrast between England and France occurs in the pair of prints, *The Invasion* (Paulson 1989, 169–70).
4. On the print, see Paulson 1989, 139–40.
5. Hogarth 1955, 228.
6. Paulson 1989, 139.
7. On the Sublime Society of Beefsteaks, see Paulson 1991–93, 2:60–62; Rogers 2003, 80–86.
8. According to Nichols 1785, 290, Hogarth's friend, the engraver John Pine, was the model for the friar; he did not know to what purpose his features would be applied and subsequently, the object of some ridicule, tried to persuade Hogarth to change the friar's face (see also Ireland 1791, 1:292).
9. Hogarth 1955, 228.

GENIUS

The artist who has his mind thus filled with ideas, and his hand made expert by practice, works with ease and readiness; whilst he who would have you believe that he is waiting for the inspirations of Genius, is in reality at a loss how to begin; and is at last delivered of his monsters, with difficulty and pain.

Joshua Reynolds, 1769

The Fine Arts can be considered from two quite different points of view: practice, which one acquires with time and study, and genius, divine inspiration, which neither time nor study can give to him who does not naturally have it. . . . All that practice takes from industry, mechanics, and chemistry can thus be treated and taught with a rigorous exactitude; but genius, this noble fire that animates the artist and makes him give birth to sublime works, this feeling of truth, of beauty, this enthusiasm for that which is great and exalted, this exquisite sensibility that one can call the poetic part of art, finally this reunion of qualities that are indispensable to the superior talent, how to obtain them? Is it by the complete knowledge of rules and principles? No.

Aristide Michel Perrot, 1830

Hendrick Goltzius (1558-1617)

53. *The Circumcision, from the Life of the Virgin*

1594

Engraving, 480 x 355 mm (18⅞ x 14 in.)

References: Bartsch 18; Hirschmann 12, iii/v; Strauss 322; iii/v

Inscriptions: at lower left: *4*; on tablet at lower center: *1594 / HG* (monogram); in lower margin: *Cernis vt octaua sit circuncisus Jesus / Luce puer, tenero accipiens in corpore vulnus, / Ad normam veteris legis, ritumq[ue] receptum, / Isacidis multos obseruatumq[ue] per annos. / C. Schoneus.*

Purchased from Carolyn Bullard, Dallas, and Susan Schulmann, New York

2000.7

The circumcision of the Christ Child is described briefly in the Gospel according to Luke 2:21: eight days after his birth, the child was circumcised and given the name Jesus as ordained by the angel before his conception. Hendrick Goltzius situates the child in the center of a dense grouping of religious officials, family members, and onlookers. The setting is the church of Saint Bavo in Haarlem, where Goltzius lived. From behind a pier at the right edge of the crowd, Goltzius himself peers at the viewer. His presence signals a nexus of meanings, personal and professional.

The *Circumcision* belongs to a series of six large prints drawn from the early life of the Virgin Mary.[1] Karel van Mander, Goltzius's friend and biographer, gives them extensive attention in his biography of the artist, more attention than on any other prints, and they have come to be known as Goltzius's *Masterpieces (Meisterstücke),* in explicit reference to three famous engravings by Albrecht Dürer (1471-1528), the greatest of sixteenth-century printmakers, whose work was particularly revered late in the century. Goltzius certainly invited the comparison by rendering the *Circumcision*—the subject of a well-known Dürer woodcut—in Dürer's style, employing the German master's types of figures, clothing, and accessories, as well as his dense network of varied engraved lines and stippling.[2] The *Adoration of the Magi* was similarly rendered in the style of the other great Northern European printmaker, Lucas van Leyden, and the other four prints imitate the styles of Italian artists. Goltzius announces his stylistic flexibility and imitative skill in the dedication to Prince William of Bavaria, composed by Cornelius Schonaeus, which appears on the *Annunciation* and reads (in translation) in part as follows: "As Proteus changed amidst the waves out of burning love for the beautiful Pomona, so does Goltzius, the admirable engraver and inventor, with his varied art, for you, Oh Prince."[3]

Goltzius's emulation—in the double sense of rivalry and imitation—of the Old Masters was tested against the wit of artists and connoisseurs throughout Europe. According to van Mander:

> When these things [the *Masterpieces*] were ready and had hardly been seen by anyone he had very witty practical jokes played, in particular with the print of the *Circumcision,* engraved in the style of Albert Dürer, and in which Goltzius' self-portrait appears, this, along with his mark, he had burned out with a red-hot coal or iron and repaired again, after that he smoked and crumpled it as if it were very old and had been on this earth for many years. This print then, arriving thus disguised and masked in Rome, Venice, Amsterdam and also elsewhere, was eagerly seen with great admiration and pleasure by artists and art lovers who had knowledge of these things, and was also bought at a high price by some who were happy that they had been able to obtain such a piece by the art-full Nuremberger [Dürer], which had never been seen before. It was of course very funny that the master was praised everywhere way above himself; for when it was said or asked whether Goltzius could have made something like that, some people, who were not poor in art, replied that it was far beyond Golzius to be able to make anything that good in the whole of his life; and that it was easily the best by Albert Dürer that had been seen. . . . When then, after many rumours and much claptrap, the print was shown and came before the eyes of these people in its entirety and freshly printed, they stood (as the saying goes) with egg on their faces and were ashamed and bewildered for their being so cocky. Some became angry and blamed those who had played the joke. The same thing happened with the piece with the Three Kings in the manner of Lucas van Leyden. It was most remarkable that there were engravers, who believed themselves to have a good understanding of the working method and technique of the masters, who were deceived by it. The power of goodwill or envy amongst people, and of prejudice too, can be observed from this; for some

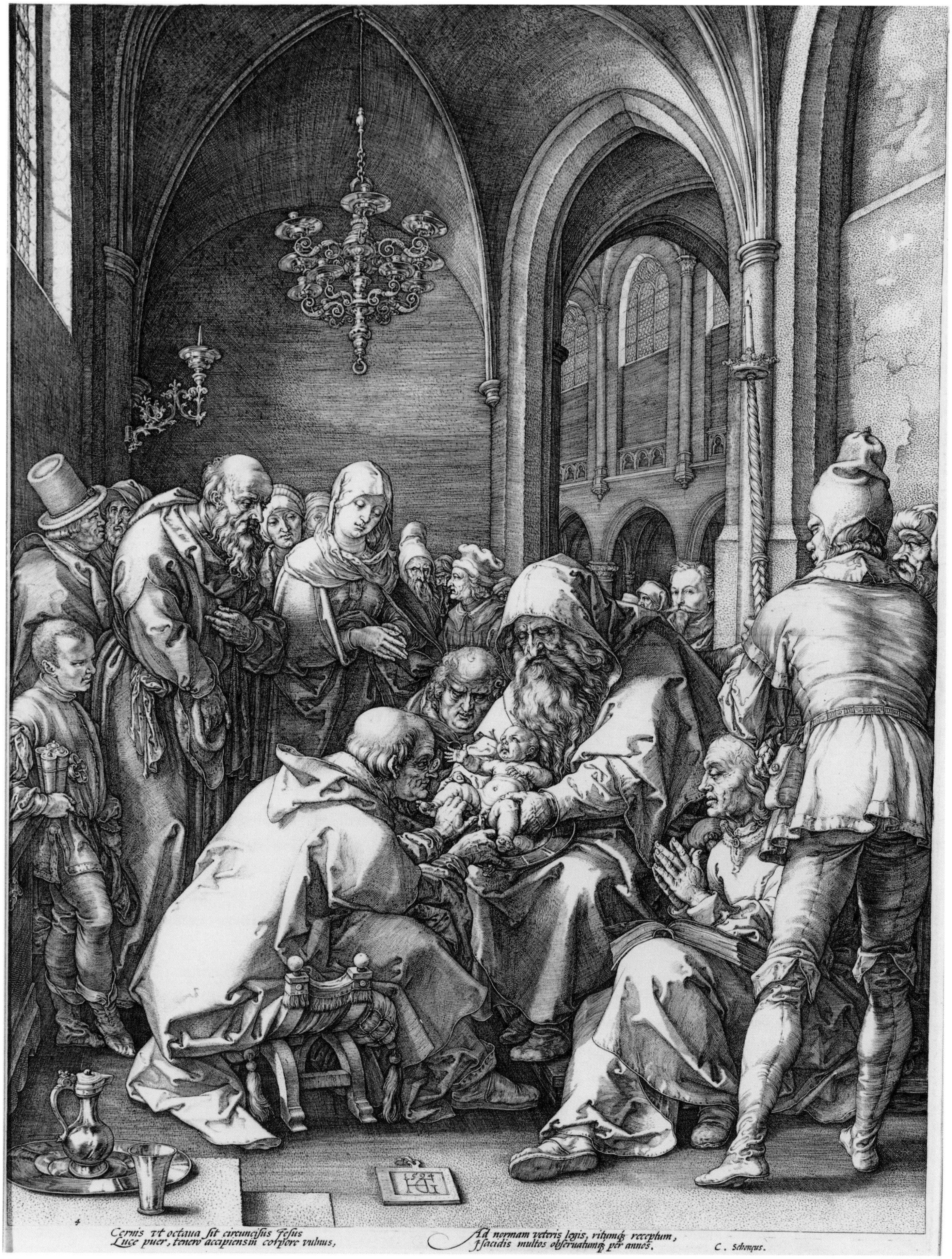
1504
HG
4
Cernis vt octaua sit circuncisus Iesus
Luce puer, tenero accipiens in corpore vulnus,
Ad normam veteris legis, ritumq; receptum,
Isacidis multos obseruatumq; per annos.
C. Schonęus.

Cat. no. 53

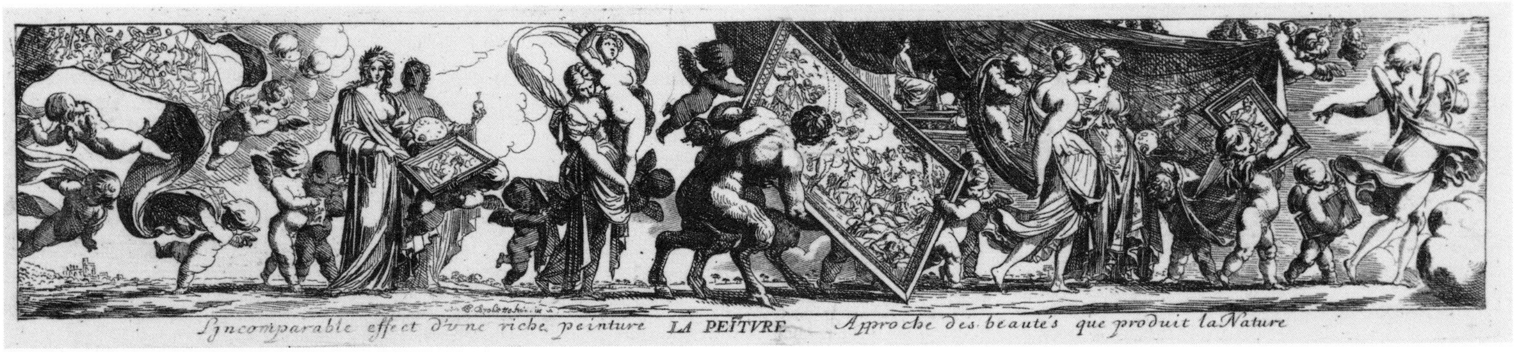

Cat. no. 54.1

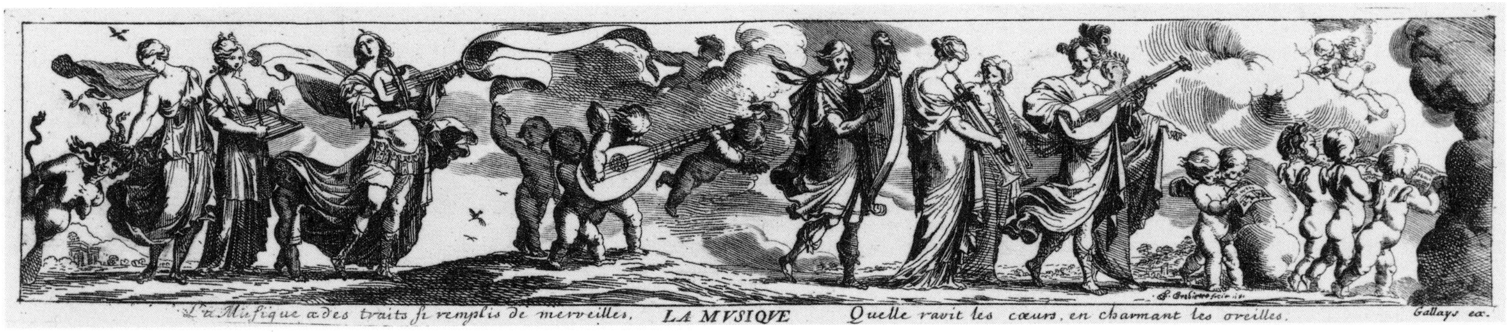

Cat. no. 54.2

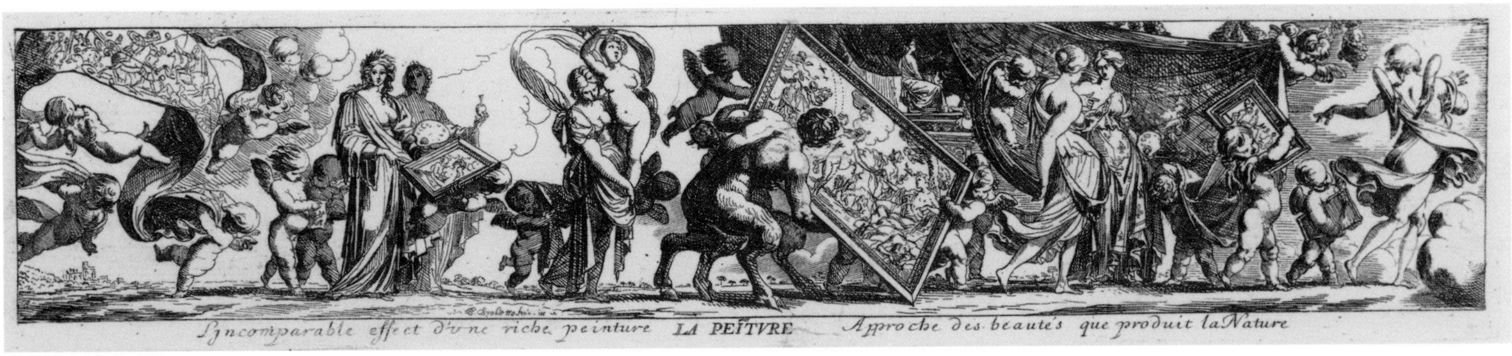

Cat. no. 54.1

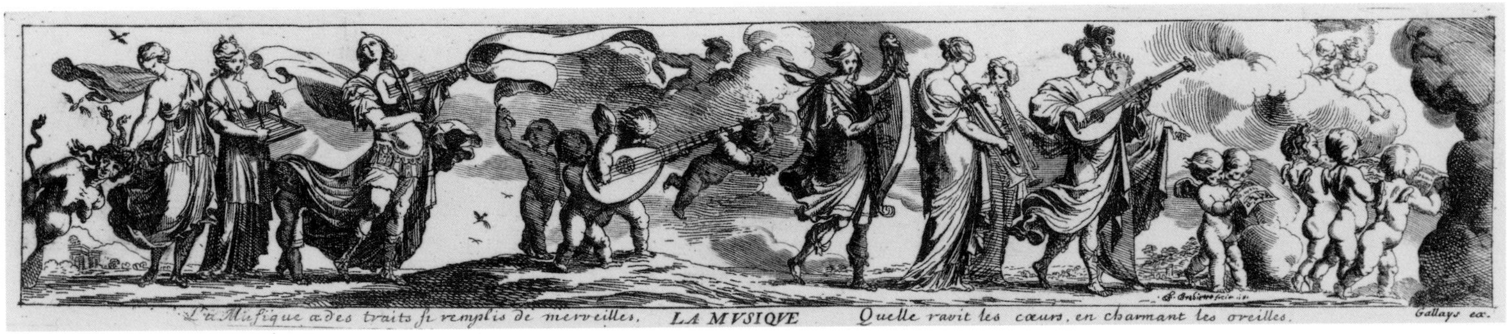

Cat. no. 54.2

Pierre Brebiette (c. 1598–c. 1650)

54. *The Triumph of Painting, Music, Grammar, and Arithmetic*

c. 1636

4 etchings, .1: 77 x 340 mm (3 x 13⅜ in.); .2: 75 x 340 mm (3 x 13⅜ in.); .3: 73 x 333 mm (2⅞ x 13⅛ in.); .4: 73 x 333 mm (2⅞ x 13⅛ in.)

Reference: *Inventaire du fonds français* 2, 166–70

Inscriptions: .1: at lower left: *P. Brebiette fecit in*; below image: *Lincomparable effect d'vne riche peinture LA PEI[N]TVRE Approche des beautés que produit la Nature*; in manuscript above image to right: *Brebiette*; in manuscript at upper right corner of paper: *27*; .2: at lower right: *P. Brebiette fecit in. [?]*; below image: *La Musique a des traits si remplis de merveilles, LA MVSIQVE Quelle ravit les coeurs, en charmant les oreilles. Gallays ex.*; in manuscript above image to right: *Brebiette*; in manuscript at upper right corner of paper: *28*; .3: at lower left: *P. Brebiette . in. f.*; below image: *Veux tu entre les arts ce qui est necessaire GRAMMAIRE. Suy les enseignements que prescrit la Grammaire*; in manuscript at upper right: *Brebiette Graveur / (N.° 37) . . .*; in manuscript at upper right corner of paper: *25*; .4: at lower right: *P. Brebiette fecit & in*; below image: *Les Atomes volants et les sablons lybiques ARITHMETIQVE. Peuuent estre nombrés dedans l'arithmetique.*; in manuscript above image to right: *Brebiette*; in manuscript at upper right corner of paper: *26*

Mounted on two sheets of paper, at the upper right corners of which are inscribed in manuscript: *33* (numbers 3 and 4); *34* (numbers 1 and 2)

Purchased from Hill-Stone, New York

2000.12.1–4

Brebiette's four prints celebrating the liberal arts[1] of painting, music, grammar, and arithmetic are unusual in that they convey serious information about how these disciplines were viewed in the form of delightful processions of mythological and allegorical personages. These prints are given the horizontal proportion of antique sculptural friezes, a format that Brebiette often used; there are over sixty in his corpus of roughly three hundred prints. Printmakers adapted this format ultimately from the sculptural friezes found on ancient Roman architecture and sarcophagi, and Brebiette undoubtedly participated in this trend during his seven years in Rome.[2]

Until the early seventeenth century, depictions of the liberal arts had largely been cast in the form of female personifications holding attributes. Brebiette's allegorical group makes reference to this tradition, but multiplies both figures and attributes. In the print inscribed *La Peinture,* a lighthearted procession of putti, fauns, and muses carries with them from left to right a selection of paintings and related objects. The two most important types of painting are represented: religious painting, by the Madonna and Child carried by the laurel-crowned muse at left, and history painting, by the large-scale canvas dragged by two fauns and a putto at center. The sketchbook tucked under the arm of the putto at the head of the procession communicates the importance of drawing as the foundation of painting, one of the tenets Renaissance art theory. Likewise, the muse who rather implausibly carries a statue of a female nude shows the importance of sketching from ancient sculpture to good painting practice.[3] Another pair of putti at left also examine a drawing (or perhaps a print) like urbane connoisseurs.

If Brebiette intended us to read the central painting as a *Judgment of Paris,*[4] as Sue Welsh Reed believes, then the woman in the center of the painting, and therefore the center of the print, would be Venus, whose beauty Paris chose over the military and political power offered by Minerva and Juno. Thus, Venus is the ultimate symbol of the divine beauty that painters strive to achieve in their art. This would support the print's caption that "The incomparable effect of a rich painting / proceeds from the beauties that Nature produces." Appropriately, the faun who carries the central picture seems spellbound by the counterfeit presentation of Venus.

Another interesting relationship to painting is suggested by the billowing fabric borne by putti at far left and at the right. Because of the vaguely historical subjects legible on them—we see soldiers and a mounted commander at left, and a horse and rider at the right—these are probably tapestries. Since the time of Raphael, tapestries had followed the designs of great painters, and it was during the third decade of the seventeenth century that painters, with Rubens leading the charge, began to exert a new influence on

who felt that Goltzius should be scorned and condemned with regard to his art, set him above both the best old masters and himself without realising it. And this was also done by those who habitually said that no better engravers than Albert and Lucas could be hoped for, and that Goltzius could not be compared to them. In short, these six pieces were enough to demonstrate what he was capable of in this art.[4]

No "disguised" impressions of the composition are known, but van Mander's point remains, that is, that Goltzius demonstrated his abilities in surpassing not only the two greatest masters of printmaking and overcame the perception that collectors apparently had of him. With the *Circumcision,* Goltzius may also have consciously entered into competition with a contemporary, Jan Sadeler, who was court engraver to Wilhelm V—Goltzius's dedicatee—and had executed a Düreresque *Circumcision* in 1581.[5] According to van Mander, Goltzius had visited Sadeler in Munich during his trip to Italy in 1591–92 without revealing his identity, as was his wont in order to hear what people thought of his art; Sadeler took him for a cheese merchant.[6] With the *Circumcision* of 1594, Goltzius accomplished the deception in his art that he had previously accomplished in person. His self-effacement in both instances, while it may have paid homage to his predecessors and allowed him to entertain unbiased criticism, was temporary and the ultimate outcome was the revelation of his artistic virtuosity.

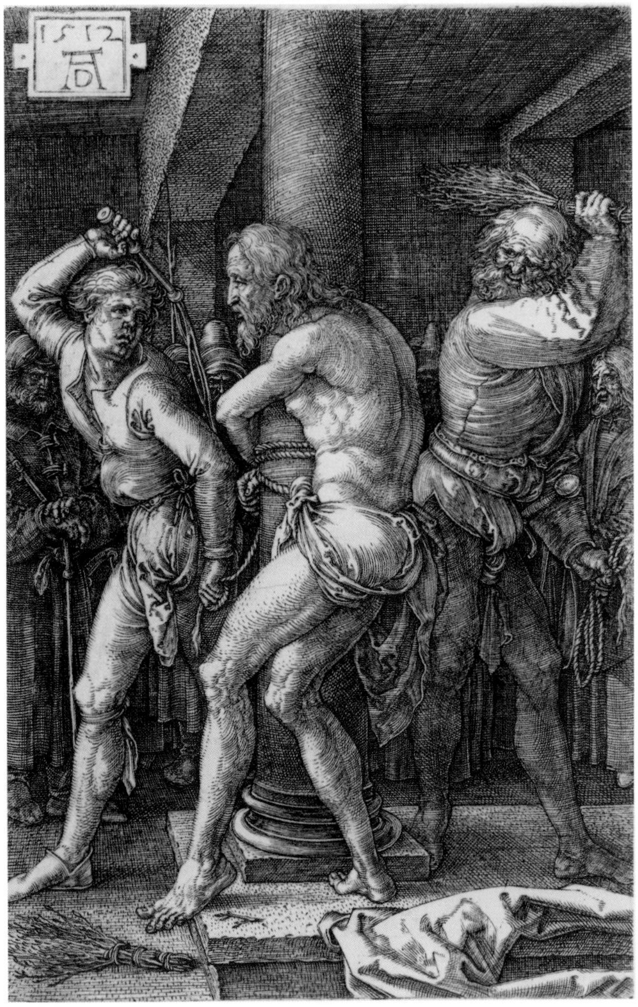

Fig. 53.1. Albrecht Dürer. *The Flagellation of Christ.* 1512. Engraving on laid paper, 117 x 75 mm (4⅝ x 3 in.). The Museum of Fine Arts, Houston, gift of Marjorie G. and Evan C. Horning.

Notwithstanding the professional concerns at work in Goltzius's emulation of Dürer, the *Circumcision* remains an illustration of a biblical narrative, whose devotional possibilities are not to be overlooked.[7] Although the dedication of the series appearing on the *Annunciation* is couched in professional terms, the series must also have been intended to appeal to the dedicatee's well-known Catholic piety. The inscriptions below the images all refer to the religious subjects, and the *Circumcision* was sometimes issued apart from the other prints in the series, without, therefore, explicit reference to Goltzius's protean skills. Situating a biblical narrative in a contemporary setting, which could heighten the devotional experience for the viewer, had been common for centuries. Also common was the inclusion of a self-portrait in such a narrative, in which the artist witnesses or even participates in the economy of salvation through Christ's incarnation and Passion, often for profoundly devotional purposes, as in Michelangelo's Florentine *Pietà.* Goltzius may have even had in mind a specific prototype from Dürer's engraved *Passion*—some have thought the figure in the right background of his *Flagellation of Christ* to be a self-portrait (fig. 53.1)—further deepening the connection between professional abilities and religious devotion.

JC

1. On the series, see the entry by Huigen Leeflang in Leeflang and Luijten 2003, 210–15.
2. See Melion 1992, 47.
3. Trans. Leeflang and Luijten 2003, 210.
4. Van Mander 1994–99, 1:397–98.
5. See Bloom 2001, 90–92.
6. Van Mander 1994–99, 1:390, 394.
7. See especially Melion 1992a, Melion 2001a; see also Bloom 2001.

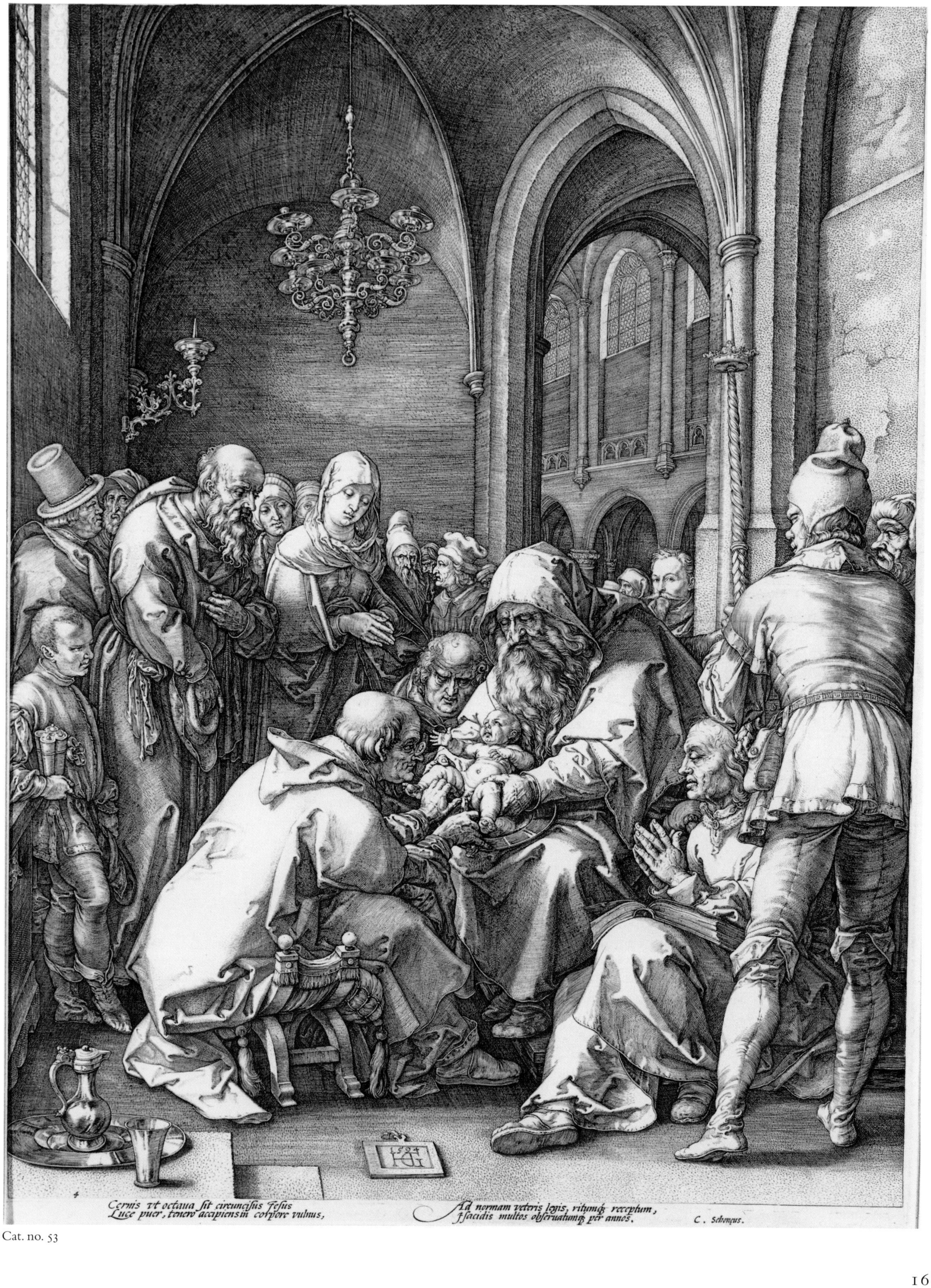
1594
4
Cernis vt octaua sit circuncisus Jesus
Luce puer, tenero accipiens in corpore vulnus,
Ad normam veteris legis, ritumqꝫ receptum,
Jsacidis multos obseruatumqꝫ per annos.
C. Schonęus.

Cat. no. 53

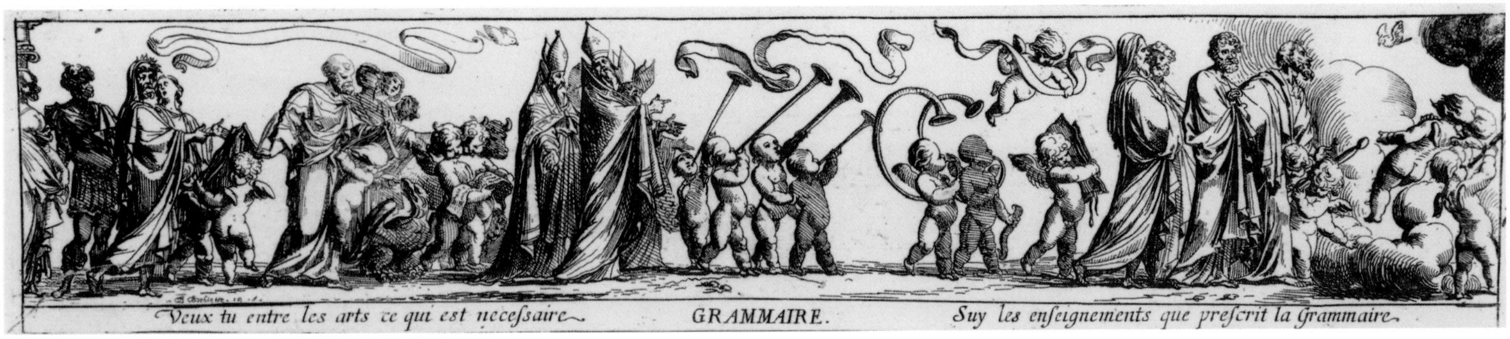

Cat. no. 54.3

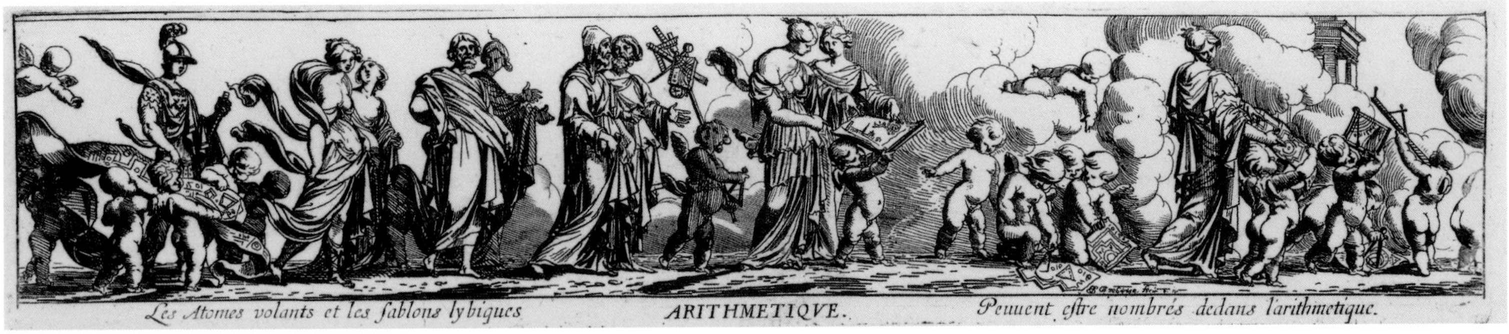

Cat. no. 54.4

Poesis for *Ptesis*), who leans on a closed volume, a quill pen in his hand and an inkpot by his side. On the other side of the painter is Music (*Musica*), playing a guitar, a sheet of music on the drapery in front of him. The right side of the composition comprises a *vanitas*: an allegory of the transience and vanity of earthly things. One putto balances an hourglass on his head, signifying fleeting time (*Tempus fluidum*).[1] Death is at hand (*Mors actat*) in the human skull indicated by the putto seated at the lower right, causing another to recoil in horror. Behind them, a putto raises aloft the ashes of heroes crowned with laurel (*Cineres Heroum*), which are then dispersed by the wind, a disembodied putto (*uentus discipat*). Yet another turns a lighted torch, the sign of life and death (*Vitaeq[ue] Necisq[ue] Est signum*), downward, thus indicating death (see also cat. no. 32). The shadow of death is not, however, impenetrable, since the phoenix rising from flames toward a human-featured sun is the hope of the highest good (*Spesq[ue] boni summi Phenix est*).[2]

Podestà's invention is forward-looking in that its grouping of painting, poetry, and music—what came to be called the Sister Arts in eighteenth-century England—was unusual in the seventeenth century, a period in which the conceptual system of the arts had shifted away from the medieval Seven Liberal Arts but had not yet arrived at a modern definition of the Fine Arts or *Beaux Arts*.[3] Comparisons among painting, poetry, and music were not uncommon in the Renaissance (mostly notably with Leonardo, who argues for the superiority of painting), initially because they were all seen as imitative arts, but ultimately also because they produced pleasure. But such comparisons and alliances were neither rigorous nor codified, and they were just as likely to involve other "arts," from grammar to astronomy to dance (cf. cat. nos. 54, 74). Although the two halves of Podestà's composition do not interpenetrate, the contiguity of the two themes of the Sister Arts and *vanitas* may suggest that the products of the arts are among the earthly things of no lasting import, which was a common motif in seventeenth-century art, including a related painting by Podestà (fig. 55.1).[4] The presence of the phoenix, however, may further suggest the ultimate triumph of the arts over mortality.

The popularity in the seventeenth and eighteenth centuries of pictures peopled by putti (see also cat. nos. 30, 61) may be traced to Titian's *Feast of Venus,* which was in the Villa Aldobrandini in Frascati from 1598 and the Villa Ludovisi in Rome from 1621 and was copied by Podestà.[5] Titian's painting had a direct impact in the 1620s and following in particular on the sculptor François Duquesnoy and the painter Nicolas Poussin; the latter was brother-in-law and teacher to Gaspard Dughet,[6] with whom Podestà was associated, and by the time Podestà arrived in Rome from Genoa around 1630, the taste for Titian's infants, supported by a more general taste for sixteenth-century Venetian painting, was in full bloom. Podestà also copied Titian's *Bacchanal of the Andrians,* which was at the Villa Ludovisi with the *Feast of Venus,* and produced a pair of bacchanal etchings of his own invention (which were, like the present *Allegory,* published by Francesco Salucio in 1640), but populated by putti, combining, as it were, elements of Titian's *Andrians* and *Feast of Venus*. His small known oeuvre, in painting and drawing as well as in etching, demonstrates a specialization in putti.

Podestà also owes a debt to artists other than Titian or Poussin and his circle. He had no known direct association with Guido Reni, to whom the *Allegory with Cupid and Putti* is dedicated and who was nearing the end of his life in Bologna at the time the print was produced, but he must have admired Reni's many images of the infant Christ, John the Baptist, and sundry putti, including his etching of *Angels in Glory* (which was based on a drawing by Podestà's famous compatriot, Luca Cambiaso).[7] While the pair of putti in the painting within Podestà's composition are reminiscent in their pose of figures in Reni's print,[8] they also recall the pairs of infants in the corners of Annibale Carracci's ceiling fresco in the Farnese Gallery in Rome. Annibale's putti are Eros and Anteros, who often battled and reconciled in the period and could represent either Profane and Sacred Love, or Love and Reciprocated Love, respectively.[9] In a pair of paintings by Podestà, Eros and Anteros fight and then embrace (in a pose derived from Titian's *Feast of Venus*), while doves kiss in the corner of the composition, as in the present etching.[10]

There was, to be sure, some doubt expressed that such infants, whose proportions suggested their extremely young age, could stand upright, much less plausibly perform all the activities in which they are shown to be engaged, but for centuries the Christ Child had moved as capably, and the quality of tenderness they evoked was a decisive attraction, even as a rhetorical device to convey the import of the subject matter.[11]

JC

1. Cf. the hourglass held by a putto in Duquesnoy's funerary monument for Ferdinand Van Den Eynde "as an indication that he bewails the transience of earthly life" (Colantuono 1989, 219).
2. The phoenix appears in conjunction with the sun in the *Allegory of Sight and the Art of Painting* by Jan Saenredam after Hendrick Goltzius (cat. no. 36; see Sluijter 2000, 104–108), which may have been known to Podestà.
3. See Kristeller 1951–52.
4. The painting was brought into connection with the present etching by Blunt 1958, 15.
5. On this painting and the representation of infants in seventeenth-century Rome, see Colantuono 1989.
6. For a Duquesnoyesque infant in a Poussin self-portrait, see cat. no. 7. Podestà may also be associated with Poussin through Poussin's intimate, Cassiano dal Pozzo, to whom Podestà's etching of the *Feast of Venus* is dedicated.
7. Bartsch 45.
8. Reed and Wallace 1989, 261.
9. See Martin 1965, 86–89; Dempsey 1968.
10. On the paintings, see Blunt 1960, 311 n. 12.
11. Colantuono 1989, 223.

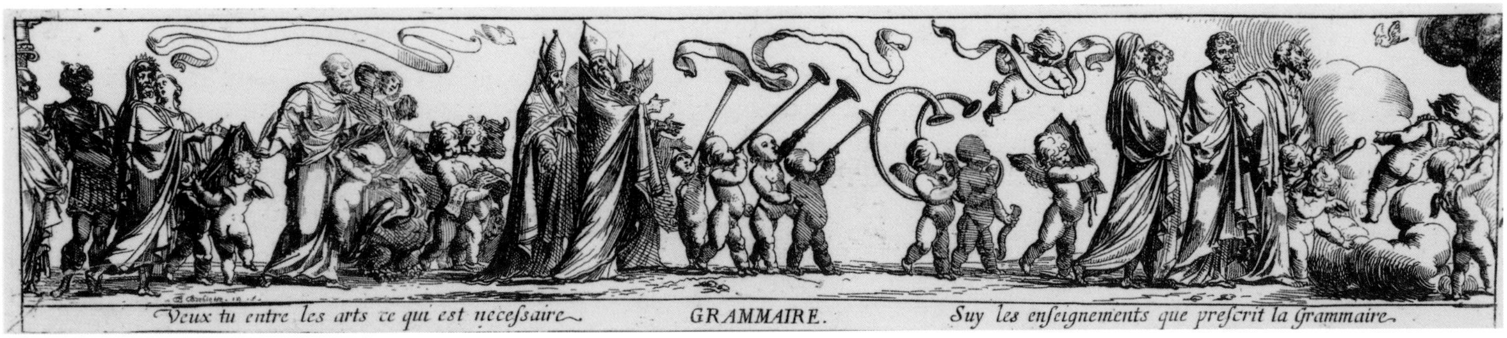

Cat. no. 54.3

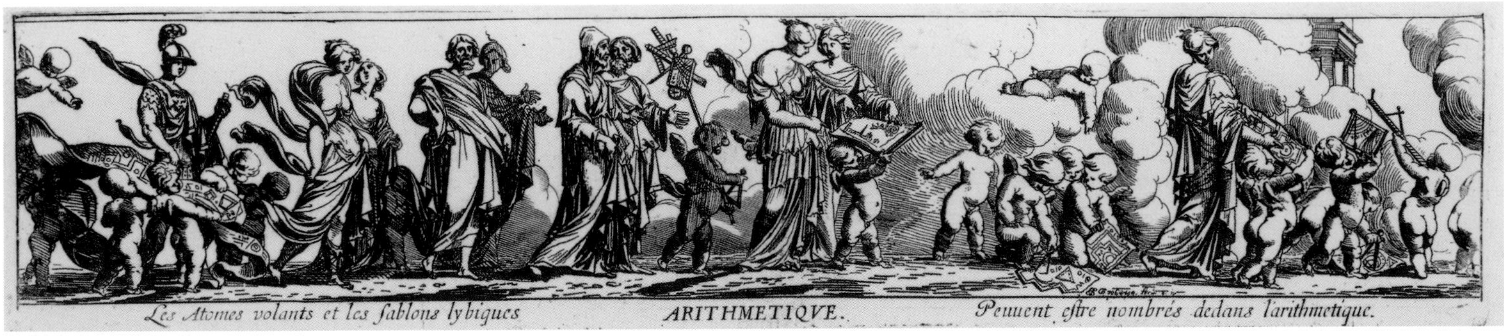

Cat. no. 54.4

tapestry makers; the success of the tapestry became more dependent on the reputation of the designing artist than ever before.[5]

La Musique is less complex, perhaps reflecting its being conceived by an artist and not a musician. Muses or female allegorical figures of some kind are again present, playing a variety of musical instruments, including lutes, sackbuts, and viols, while putti sing from sheet music. At the center, the man in classicizing dress playing the lyre is probably Apollo, ruler of the muses and god of music. At left, one of the muse figures grasps a gorgon by her snaky hair, forcing her to the ground; this presumably illustrates the subjugation of things evil and uncouth to the divine harmony of music.

Le Grammaire presents a quasi-Christian, quasi-pagan procession of authors, an equitable mix of classical writers, like the laurel-crowned poet at far left, with church fathers like Saints Peter and Paul at the head of the procession, identifiable by their attributes of keys and sword, respectively. Behind a group of mitered clerics, the gospel writers are also celebrated; the eagle of Saint John, the ox of Saint Luke, and the lion of Saint Mark surround an unidentified evangelist with quill poised to receive divine inspiration. The caption instructs us "if you desire the most necessary of the arts, follow the teachings prescribed by grammar."

In the fourth print, the caption boasts of arithmetic's encompassing powers, stating that "Every floating mote, and all the Libyan sands can be numbered by arithmetic." In fact, this image incorporates other members of the traditional *quadrivium* of the seven liberal arts. The two putti at far right, one with a quadrant and one with what appears to be a cross-staff, both navigational instruments, illustrate astronomy, while the various putti engaged in measuring shapes with dividers represent geometry. The pair of female figures at center who hold a drawing or print of a building with a tower (perhaps a church?) may be indicating the importance of these various quantifying arts to the lofty discipline of architecture; other drawings held by putti at the right and left of the composition also appear to be plans for buildings. AW

1. For a discussion of the liberal arts and the "sister arts" of painting, music, and poetry, see cat. no. 55.
2. Reed 1998, 243.
3. This statue, with her arm flung over her head, creating a bow of wind-filled drapery, is reminiscent of figures in rediscovered sculptural friezes Brebiette might have known in Rome, like the Aurae or winds on the Ara Pacis Augustae. See Simon 1968, 27.
4. Reed 1998, 208.
5. Joslyn 1996, 320.

Giovanni Andrea Podestà (1608–c. 1674)

55. *Allegory with Cupid and Putti*

1640

Etching and engraving

265 x 394 mm (10⅜ x 15½ in.)

Reference: Bartsch 5, i/iv

Inscriptions: upper left, on easel: *Al'Sig.r Guido Reni / And.P.D.D.D.*; lower left: *Romae apud Franciscum Saluucium 1640.* Verses, lower center and right: *Pulcher Amicitiam, et lasciuu[m] pingit Amore[m], / Dum Puer Idalius, spectat Phebea Ptesis, / Musica, quam sequitur, Princepsq[ue] huic surda sedenti / Mors astat, cuius timor est, qui horret Puer, alter / Fert Cineres Heroum, has uentus discipat; alter /Paruulus est Tempus fluidum, Vitaeq[ue] Necisq[ue] / Est signum in manibus collucet splendida, cui fax, / Spesq[ue] boni summi Phenix est, quae quatit alas.*

Purchased from Hill-Stone, New York

1997.28

At the edge of a wooded landscape, nude, winged infant boys enact an allegory, divided into two parts compositionally defined by the grove on the left and the open vista to the right. The left side of the image is dominated by a canvas set upon an easel. According to the inscription, the painter is Cupid (*Puer Idalius,* that is, Boy of Idalium, a city in Cyprus sacred to Venus), the only figure in the composition with the love god's quiver of arrows. He paints friendship and licentious love embracing (*Amicitiam, et lasciuu[m] . . . Amore[m]*)—a variation of the theme of Sacred and Profane Love—their torches united above their heads, their concord replicated by two doves in the lower left corner of the fictive canvas. The painter is watched by Apollonian Poetry (*Phebea Poesis,* reading

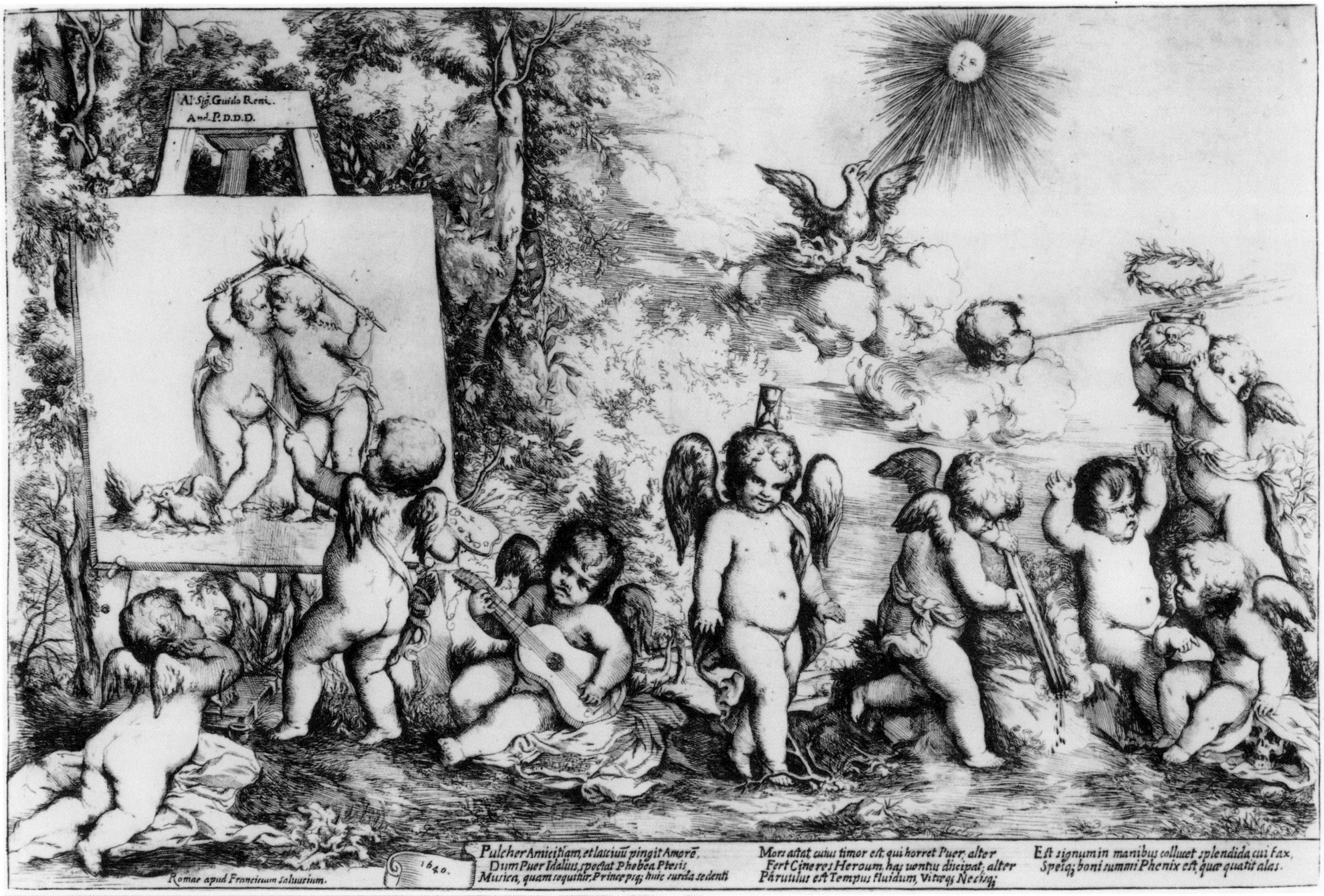

Cat. no. 55

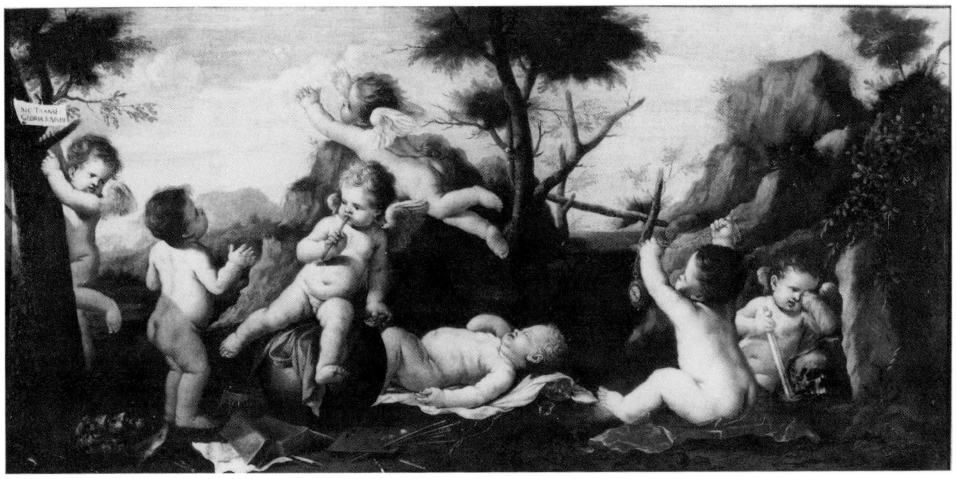

Fig. 55.1. Giovanni Andrea Podestà. *Vanitas (Allegory of Vanity).* Galleria Spada, Rome.

Poesis for *Ptesis*), who leans on a closed volume, a quill pen in his hand and an inkpot by his side. On the other side of the painter is Music (*Musica*), playing a guitar, a sheet of music on the drapery in front of him. The right side of the composition comprises a *vanitas*: an allegory of the transience and vanity of earthly things. One putto balances an hourglass on his head, signifying fleeting time (*Tempus fluidum*).[1] Death is at hand (*Mors actat*) in the human skull indicated by the putto seated at the lower right, causing another to recoil in horror. Behind them, a putto raises aloft the ashes of heroes crowned with laurel (*Cineres Heroum*), which are then dispersed by the wind, a disembodied putto (*uentus discipat*). Yet another turns a lighted torch, the sign of life and death (*Vitaeq[ue] Necisq[ue] Est signum*), downward, thus indicating death (see also cat. no. 32). The shadow of death is not, however, impenetrable, since the phoenix rising from flames toward a human-featured sun is the hope of the highest good (*Spesq[ue] boni summi Phenix est*).[2]

Podestà's invention is forward-looking in that its grouping of painting, poetry, and music—what came to be called the Sister Arts in eighteenth-century England—was unusual in the seventeenth century, a period in which the conceptual system of the arts had shifted away from the medieval Seven Liberal Arts but had not yet arrived at a modern definition of the Fine Arts or *Beaux Arts*.[3] Comparisons among painting, poetry, and music were not uncommon in the Renaissance (mostly notably with Leonardo, who argues for the superiority of painting), initially because they were all seen as imitative arts, but ultimately also because they produced pleasure. But such comparisons and alliances were neither rigorous nor codified, and they were just as likely to involve other "arts," from grammar to astronomy to dance (cf. cat. nos. 54, 74). Although the two halves of Podestà's composition do not interpenetrate, the contiguity of the two themes of the Sister Arts and *vanitas* may suggest that the products of the arts are among the earthly things of no lasting import, which was a common motif in seventeenth-century art, including a related painting by Podestà (fig. 55.1).[4] The presence of the phoenix, however, may further suggest the ultimate triumph of the arts over mortality.

The popularity in the seventeenth and eighteenth centuries of pictures peopled by putti (see also cat. nos. 30, 61) may be traced to Titian's *Feast of Venus,* which was in the Villa Aldobrandini in Frascati from 1598 and the Villa Ludovisi in Rome from 1621 and was copied by Podestà.[5] Titian's painting had a direct impact in the 1620s and following in particular on the sculptor François Duquesnoy and the painter Nicolas Poussin; the latter was brother-in-law and teacher to Gaspard Dughet,[6] with whom Podestà was associated, and by the time Podestà arrived in Rome from Genoa around 1630, the taste for Titian's infants, supported by a more general taste for sixteenth-century Venetian painting, was in full bloom. Podestà also copied Titian's *Bacchanal of the Andrians,* which was at the Villa Ludovisi with the *Feast of Venus,* and produced a pair of bacchanal etchings of his own invention (which were, like the present *Allegory,* published by Francesco Salucio in 1640), but populated by putti, combining, as it were, elements of Titian's *Andrians* and *Feast of Venus*. His small known oeuvre, in painting and drawing as well as in etching, demonstrates a specialization in putti.

Podestà also owes a debt to artists other than Titian or Poussin and his circle. He had no known direct association with Guido Reni, to whom the *Allegory with Cupid and Putti* is dedicated and who was nearing the end of his life in Bologna at the time the print was produced, but he must have admired Reni's many images of the infant Christ, John the Baptist, and sundry putti, including his etching of *Angels in Glory* (which was based on a drawing by Podestà's famous compatriot, Luca Cambiaso).[7] While the pair of putti in the painting within Podestà's composition are reminiscent in their pose of figures in Reni's print,[8] they also recall the pairs of infants in the corners of Annibale Carracci's ceiling fresco in the Farnese Gallery in Rome. Annibale's putti are Eros and Anteros, who often battled and reconciled in the period and could represent either Profane and Sacred Love, or Love and Reciprocated Love, respectively.[9] In a pair of paintings by Podestà, Eros and Anteros fight and then embrace (in a pose derived from Titian's *Feast of Venus*), while doves kiss in the corner of the composition, as in the present etching.[10]

There was, to be sure, some doubt expressed that such infants, whose proportions suggested their extremely young age, could stand upright, much less plausibly perform all the activities in which they are shown to be engaged, but for centuries the Christ Child had moved as capably, and the quality of tenderness they evoked was a decisive attraction, even as a rhetorical device to convey the import of the subject matter.[11] JC

1. Cf. the hourglass held by a putto in Duquesnoy's funerary monument for Ferdinand Van Den Eynde "as an indication that he bewails the transience of earthly life" (Colantuono 1989, 219).
2. The phoenix appears in conjunction with the sun in the *Allegory of Sight and the Art of Painting* by Jan Saenredam after Hendrick Goltzius (cat. no. 36; see Sluijter 2000, 104–108), which may have been known to Podestà.
3. See Kristeller 1951–52.
4. The painting was brought into connection with the present etching by Blunt 1958, 15.
5. On this painting and the representation of infants in seventeenth-century Rome, see Colantuono 1989.
6. For a Duquesnoyesque infant in a Poussin self-portrait, see cat. no. 7. Podestà may also be associated with Poussin through Poussin's intimate, Cassiano dal Pozzo, to whom Podestà's etching of the *Feast of Venus* is dedicated.
7. Bartsch 45.
8. Reed and Wallace 1989, 261.
9. See Martin 1965, 86–89; Dempsey 1968.
10. On the paintings, see Blunt 1960, 311 n. 12.
11. Colantuono 1989, 223.

Pietro Testa (1612–1650)

56. *The Triumph of the Virtuous Artist on Parnassus*

c. 1645

Etching, 415 x 569 mm (16⅜ x 22⅜ in.)

References: Bartsch 33, ii/iii; Bellini 33, ii/iii

Inscription: in margin at bottom: *All'Ill.mo Sig.r mio Sig.r et Pron Colendis.mo Il Sig.r Fra Gio: Tomaso Rondenino Caualier Gerosolimitano. / Chi camina per la uia della Virtu con la scorta del'lume della sapienza non può far á meno, che la fama non li appresti Corone, e trionfi, V.S. Ill.ma che calca anch'essa il medemo, sentiero miri in questo delineamento del Sig.r Testa espresso un ritratto delle sue uirtuose operationi, egli euenti del suo merito quale incantenera / il tempo eloserberá immortale, ad onta della morte, dall'espressione di questa uerita riconosca V.S. Ill.ma il mio ossequio et humiliss.te me li inchino Di V.S. Ill.ma Deuotissimo et obligatissimo Seruitore Gio: Domenico Rossi. D.D.D.*

Purchased from Hill-Stone, New York

1997.35

This richly allegorical etching celebrates the arrival of the virtuous artist on Parnassus, the sacred abode of Apollo and the Muses, symbolizing Testa's own triumph over vice. The artist is guided by Divine Wisdom, whose torch blinds Envy and Ignorance, illuminating the obstacles the virtuous artist must overcome along the path to Parnassus. At right, Hercules expels Avarice, who carries a basket of gold coins and chains on his back. A winged figure of Fame with trumpet in hand crowns the artist, whose ideal proportions are derived from the ancient Belvedere Antinous.[1] The artist gestures benevolently toward a figure, probably Venus, who reaches for a basket of flowers. Although the figure resembles Flora, the putto carrying her torch reinforces her identity as Venus. In this capacity the goddess of love functions much like the Venus Coelestis, who is symbolic of divine wisdom. Love is presented here as it is in Testa's *Altro diletto ch'imparar non trovo (I find delight only in learning),* whose title is derived from Petrarch's *Triumph of Love.*[2] The phrase articulates Testa's own concept of pleasure and can be applied to *The Virtuous Artist,* whose delight of learning (rather than of the flesh) and guidance by Divine Wisdom has led him to triumph on Parnassus.

Behind Venus are the Muses, including Clio, the Muse of history, who holds a trumpet, and Calliope, the Muse of epic poetry, with tomes in hand. The waters of the Castalian stream, the source of poetic inspiration, flow from the urn of a nymph, while Pegasus causes the Hippocrene stream to spring from a rock above. A winged figure of Time is shackled below at left and is kicked by Venus and the torch-wielding putto. This can be interpreted as a statement that true art and love of virtue halt the passage of time. To the right of Time is a monkey clinging to a rock to symbolize the ignorance and base ambition of contemporary artists who simply ape nature.[3] Many of these figures, undoubtedly informed by Ripa, appear in Testa's closely related print, *The Triumph of Painting on Parnassus* (fig. 56.1), in which a personification of Painting rides a chariot toward Parnassus, where the Muses await her.[4] Calliope is beckoned to greet Painting, and an inscription on a preparatory drawing in Frankfurt elucidates the significance of their meeting: "When Painting is united with Poetry she is worthy of Parnassus, that is, of immortality."[5]

The idea of Parnassus was prevalent in Testa's musings on art. In *The Virtuous Artist* and *The Triumph of Painting,* Testa promotes the notion that the artist (or, interchangeably, the profession itself), who has overcome many obstacles, is worthy to take his place on Parnassus along with poetry. In juxtaposing the fine arts with poetry,

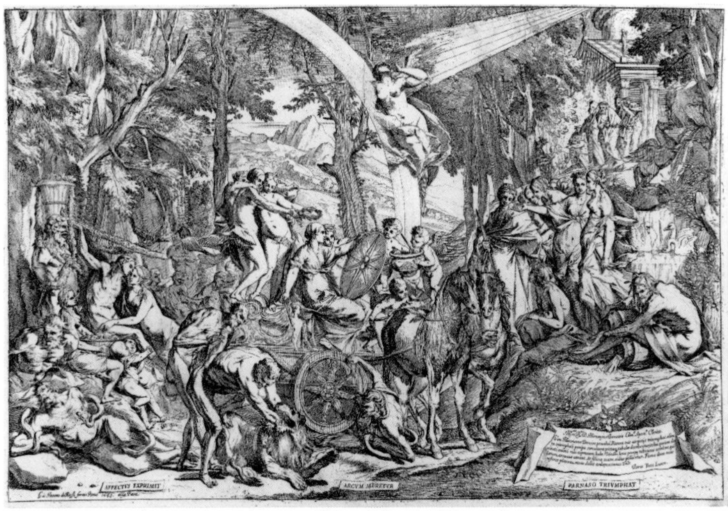

Fig. 56.1. Pietro Testa. *The Triumph of Painting on Parnassus.* c. 1648. Etching, 475 x 723 mm (18¾ x 28½ in.). Städelsches Kunstinstitut, Frankfurt.

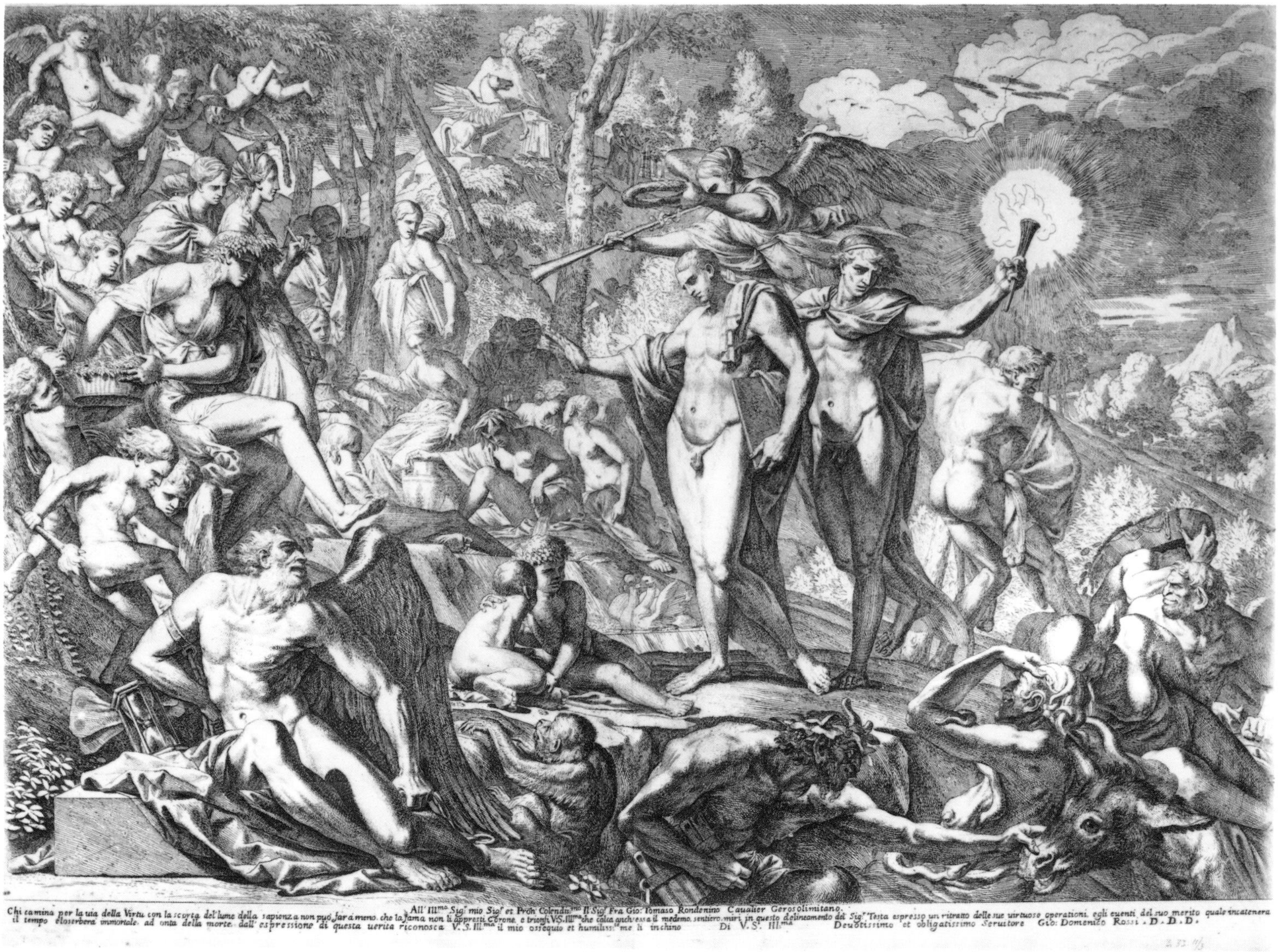

Cat. no. 56

Testa alludes to the *paragone,* or comparison, between painting and poetry. This debate had classical roots in Horace's phrase, *ut pictura poesis* (as is painting so is poetry), from his *Ars poetica,* which was often adopted by seventeenth-century artists and theorists who endeavored to raise the status of painting to equal that of poetry, considered a liberal art.

While other celebrated Renaissance and Baroque scenes of Parnassus—like those by Mantegna, Raphael, and Poussin—generally emphasize the tranquil sanctuary of the hilltop abode, Testa underscores the struggle of the artist in attaining this eminence, giving pictorial form to his preoccupation with the status of the artist and the profession of painting.[6]

Testa imagined his ideal Parnassus, which he described in the form of a letter to his patron, Girolamo Buonvisi.[7] In it he lauded the great geniuses of painting, whom he wished to join on the sacred mount. Testa offered special praise for the masters of classicism, including Raphael, the Carracci, Guido Reni, and his teacher, Domenichino. The literary form of a communication from Parnassus had been popularized earlier in the seventeenth century in Traino Boccalini's satire, *Ragguagli di Parnaso* (1611).[8]

The Triumph of the Virtuous Artist on Parnassus and several other prints from the same period show the new influence of Annibale Carracci on the style and content of Testa's works. The proliferation of clearly defined figures in *The Virtuous Artist* is reminiscent of the explosion of classicizing forms in the Palazzo Farnese.[9] In *The Virtuous Artist,* as well as in *Altro diletto ch'imparar non trovo,* the protagonist is forced to choose between the pleasures of learning and the indulgences of the flesh, a theme that recalls Annibale's *Choice of Hercules* from the Farnese Camerino (now in Naples, Capodimonte).[10]

Paolo Bellini has suggested, based on stylistic differences in the lower-right portion of the print, that it may have been completed by another artist, perhaps Giovanni Cesare Testa, Pietro's nephew.[11] Elizabeth Cropper refutes this notion, however, claiming that the stylistic differences—namely the lack of dense hatching around the eyes—differentiate the base, earthly passions from the virtuous mythological figures.[12] The second state of the print, shown here, bears a dedication by the publisher, Giovanni Domenico Rossi, to Giovanni Tomaso Rondenino, a Knight of Jerusalem and a member of a notable Roman family.

A painting now conserved at Schleissheim depicts the same subject and has long been attributed to Testa. The composition is in reverse from the print, which might indicate that the print was executed after the painting. However, the exact relationship between the two works remains unclear.[13] While several figure studies for *The Virtuous Artist* are extant, a highly finished drawing in Haarlem appears to be a *modello* for the print.[14] The sheet is squared for transfer and bears an inscription in the artist's hand, although it is smaller than the print. While there are differences between the drawing and the print, especially in the figure of the artist and the landscape behind him, the sheet certainly represents a late stage in the preparation of the etching.[15]

LS

1. On the Belvedere Antinous, see Haskell and Penny 1981, 141–43.
2. On Testa's *Altro diletto ch'imparar non trovo,* see Cropper 1988, 220–24.
3. The description of figures derives primarily from ibid., 224–26.
4. On *The Triumph of Painting on Parnassus,* see ibid., 151–55.
5. Ibid., 154. *Study for The Triumph of Painting on Parnassus,* c. 1642, pen and brown ink over black chalk on cream paper, 360 x 720 mm, Städelsches Kunstinstitut, Frankfurt, inv. 4405, reproduced in Cropper 1988, 153.
6. Harris and Lord 1970, 15.
7. For a transcription and commentary on Testa's notes regarding his ideal Parnassus, see Cropper 1984, 251–59.
8. Harris and Lord 1970, 20.
9. Cropper 1984, 56.
10. Ibid., 58–9.
11. Bellini 1976, 62.
12. Cropper 1988, 226.
13. Ibid., 226.
14. Pietro Testa, *Study for 'The Triumph of the Virtuous Artist on Parnassus,'* black chalk on pale buff paper, reinforced in pen and brown ink, squared in red chalk, 383 x 520 mm (15⅛ x 20½ in.), Teylers Museum, Haarlem.
15. Cropper 1988, 228.

Giovanni Benedetto Castiglione (1609–1664)

57. *The Genius of Castiglione*

1648

Etching, 371 x 249 mm (14⅝ x 9¾ in.)

References: Bartsch 23; Bellini 56, iii/iii

Inscriptions: on the folio held by the central figure: *Genium Io: / Benedeicti / Castilionis / Ianuen / Inu. Fe.*; on the music sheet: *HO VI PAR Potto* [or *Poldo*?] / *CHE SARA*; at lower right: *Ill.o atq. Oni.mo / D. / Ma. / Da Merusie Dño de / Clootuijcse bonar Artium / Maecenati dignissimo / Io: Iacobus De R ubcis. D.D.D.*; at lower center: *Si uendono in Roma da Gio: Iacomo de Rossi 1648*

Purchased from Kunsthandlung Helmut H. Rumbler, Frankfurt

1997.10

This allegorical self-portrait proclaims the genius of Giovanni Benedetto Castiglione, who is represented by the reclining youth. His posture recalls that of Michelangelo's Adam on the Sistine ceiling, calling to mind the process of (artistic) creation. The trumpet in the youth's hand, as well as the horn played by the putto and the drum, are traditional symbols of fame, and the laurel crown and billowing palm fronds are attributes of virtue. The palette, brushes, and sheet of music are all representative of artistic production, while the rabbit and birds symbolize fecundity. The female bust at center may represent *Invenzione*.[1] Both the youth and the bust appear in earlier works by the artist.[2]

While Castiglione makes use of traditional iconography codified in Cesare Ripa's *Iconologia* and other early modern emblem books seemingly to suggest an apotheosis of the artist, subtle but significant

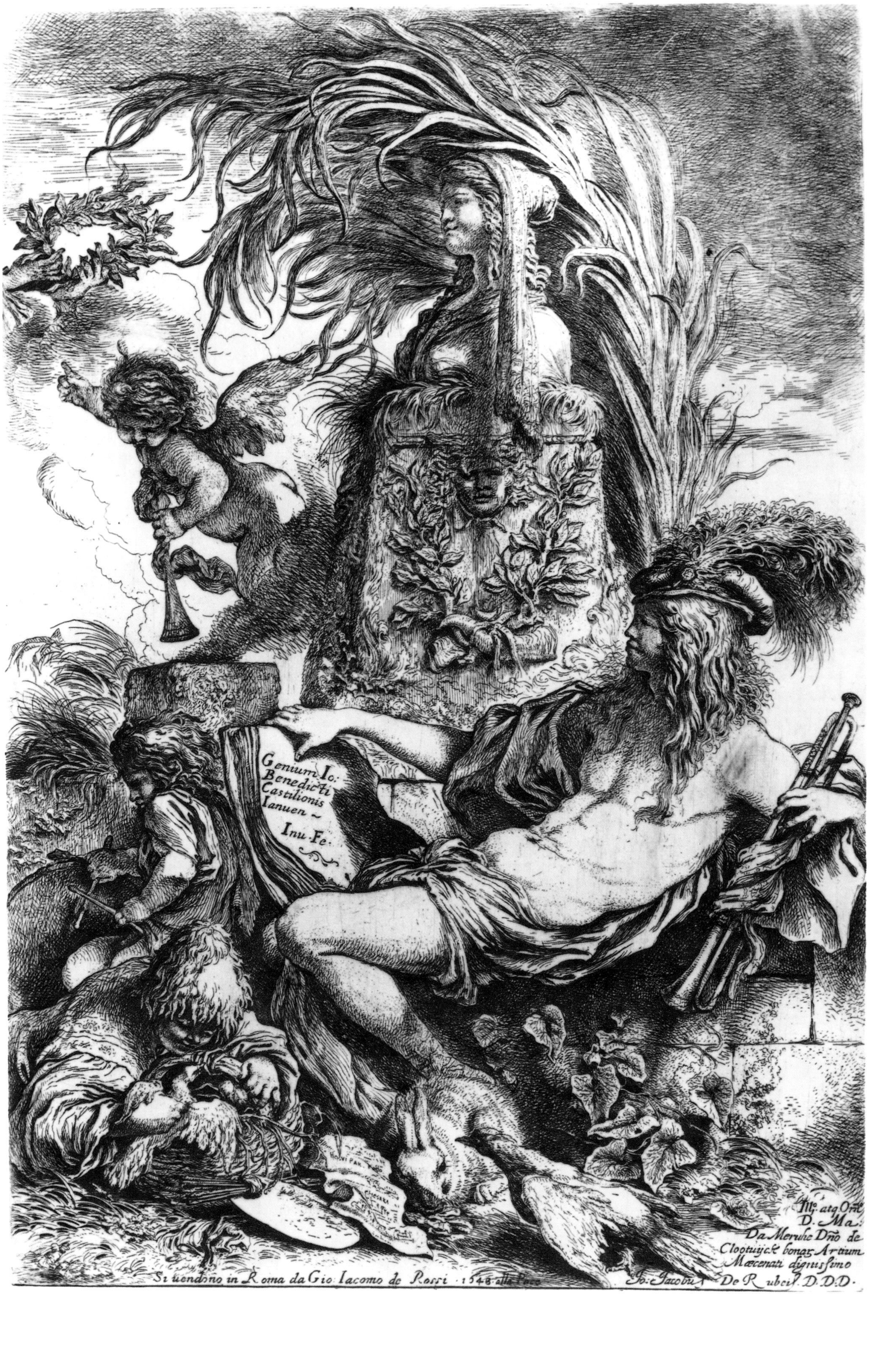
Genium Io:
Benedicti
Castilionis
Ianuen ~
Inu. Fe.
Illo atq Ornmo
D. Ma:
Da Meruhe Dño de
Clootuijck bonaq Artium
Mæcenati dignissimo
Si uendono in Roma da Gio: Iacomo de Rossi · 1648 alla Pace
Io: Iacobus De Rubeis. D.D.D.

Cat. no. 57

details reveal a reversal in the meaning of these conventional symbols. For example, the monument is overgrown with foliage, and the wrinkled music sheet and palette are carelessly discarded on the ground. Such details allude to the futility of human achievements, a theme which characterizes many of the artist's compositions, notably his *Melancholia* and *Temporalis aeternitas*.[3] Castiglione's interest in philosophical subjects was shared by contemporary artists like Pietro Testa, Nicolas Poussin, and Salvator Rosa, whose own self-proclamation of brilliance, *The Genius of Salvator Rosa,* of c. 1662 (cat. no. 58) certainly owes its concept to Castiglione's composition.

The Genius of Castiglione was published by Giovanni Giacomo de Rossi, one of the most important publishers in seventeenth-century Rome, in 1648, although it may have been executed while the artist was still in Genoa (1645-47).[4] It is dedicated to the Dutchman Matthys van de Merwede, Lord of Clootwyck, who was in Italy from 1647 to 1650. He was an art dealer and patron who circulated within the community of northern artists in Rome.[5]

LS

1. Accademia Ligustica di Belle Arti 1990, 208.
2. A drawing at Windsor Castle (inv. 3947) shows a boy in three-quarter view whose facial features are quite similar to those of the youth in *The Genius of Castiglione.* A second sheet at Windsor Castle, *Allegory of Abundance* (inv. 3893) includes a figure of the youth in the foreground at right. Another sketch, *Allegory in Honor of the Regent of Mantua* (inv. 4052), also at Windsor Castle, depicts a figure extremely similar in composition to the youth but in reverse, and a figure resembling the youth in reverse appears in a drawing at the Hamburger Kunsthalle (inv. 21152 B) as well. The monumental bust is found in reverse in a drawing at the Accademia in Venice.
3. Percy 1971, 143.
4. Percy 1971, argues that the plate was probably etched in Genoa, based on the inscription *Ianuen* on the book supported by the youth, which she believes was added by another hand at the time of publication in Rome. Bellini (1982, 1985) disagrees with this assessment, noting that this inscription appears even in the first state of the print, and no earlier impressions without it are known.
5. Bellini 1982, 150; Bellini 1985, 37. On van de Merwede, see Dalen 1900.

Salvator Rosa (1615-1673)

58. *The Genius of Salvator Rosa*

c. 1662

Etching and drypoint, 464 x 277 mm (18¼ x 10⅞ in.)

References: Bartsch 24; Wallace 113, iii/iii

Inscription: on the cartouche at lower right: *Ingenuus, Liber, Pictor Succensor, et Aequus, / Spretor Opum, Mortisque: hic meus est Genius. / Saluator Rosa*

Purchased from C. G. Boerner, New York

1997.7

Salvator Rosa's allegorical self-portrait derives, both compositionally and iconographically, from Giovanni Benedetto Castiglione's etching of 1648 (cat. no. 57), but it is both more ambitious and more personal.[1] It advances notions of the artist's work and life that are also met in his other works (prints, paintings, and satirical poetry), as well as in personal correspondence and early biographical anecdotes.

Six figures occupy the lower half of the composition. The nude Genius—that is, in seventeenth-century parlance, the artist's guiding or animating spirit—reclines at lower right, his left hand on a cornucopia spilling coins and jewels onto the ground. He is crowned with ivy, and his loins are draped, but he is otherwise nude. With his right hand he offers his heart to a seated female figure, Sincerity, who cradles a dove with her right hand and reaches out for the heart with her left. Behind him, another female figure, Liberty, holding a scepter in her right hand, leans over to place a hat on his head. At the lower left, a clothed female figure, Painting, kneels, her left hand steadying a canvas on which is drawn a nude male figure. On the ground at her knee are a square palette and brushes, which are placed through the hole of the palette in a conventional

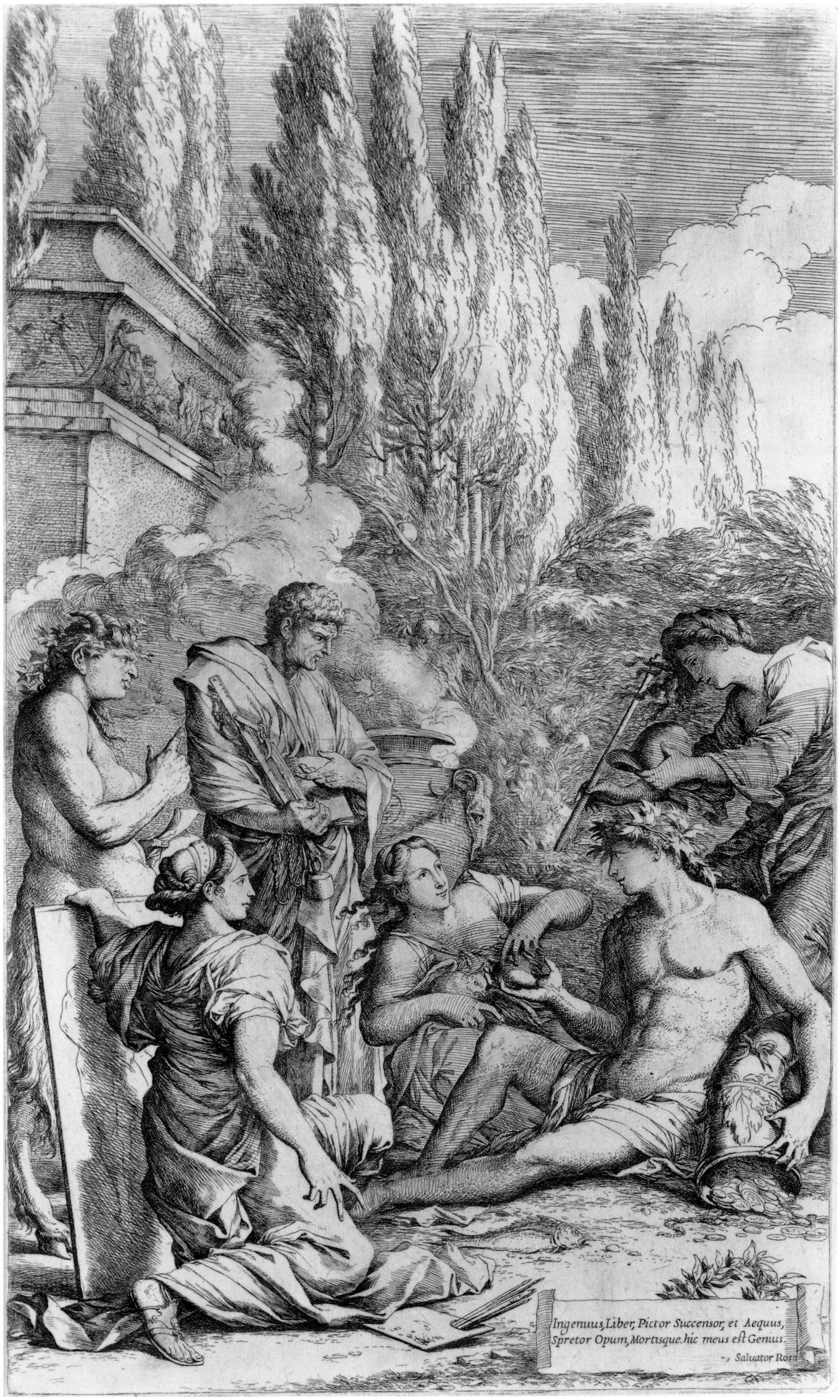
Ingenuus, Liber, Pictor Succensor, et Aequus,
Spretor Opum, Mortisque. hic meus est Genius.
Saluator Rosa

Cat. no. 58

arrangement. Standing above her, at the left edge of the image, is a nude female satyr (Satire), crowned, like Genius, with ivy; scowling, she holds a piece of paper in her left hand and gestures emphatically with her right. Standing beside her, toward the center of the composition, is a male, toga-clad figure, Stoic Thought, holding a set of scales as well as a book in his right hand and gesturing toward it with his left. Behind the figures are antique or pseudoantique objects: a smoldering urn decorated with a ram's skull and a garland; and a tomb, set on a high pedestal, decorated with reliefs. The figures conform for the most part to descriptions in Cesare Ripa's *Iconologia* and other handbooks of allegorical figures, but Rosa's combination of them is unprecedented and specific to himself. The inscription, most of whose terms effectively match the figures in the composition, summarizes the self-portrayal: "Sincere, free, fiery painter, and equitable, despiser of wealth and death, this is my genius."[2]

In Rosa's conception, the artist must be free from the demands of patrons. Rosa's chafing against the restrictions of the art patronage system of his time in Italy, in which painters with the highest ambitions—that is, history painters—usually worked on commission or even in the service of a princely patron and rarely on speculation, was not unprecedented, but his criticism of it and attempts to avoid it augured a dramatic shift in artist-client relations in the coming centuries. Rosa apparently resisted at every turn any kind of instruction from a prospective buyer, remarking that only coopers and brick makers work according to instructions given to them, not painters.[3] He wrote to his friend, Giovanni Battista Ricciardi, in 1664: "To painters of my condition and extravagant genius [*genio stravagante*], it is necessary to leave everything after the measurements free [*in libertà*], . . . and to content oneself with not wanting to tell fathers how to make sons."[4] According to Filippo Baldinucci, Rosa's contemporary and one of his earliest biographers, the artist did not want to accept an advance payment for a painting, not just "to preserve the freedom [*libertà*] to dispose of his paintings" as he wished, "but also in order not to enslave his will and virtue [*volontà e virtù*]" by having to finish one work instead of another in order to meet his obligations.[5] Rosa worked for the Medici court in Florence in the 1640s, but he left it, according to Baldinucci, not wanting ever again "the liberty of his spirit" to be subject to others, to be able to live for himself and his own studies without the annoyances suffered by those who carry the "golden chains of court."[6] Rosa made more use than most artists of the few public exhibitions in seventeenth-century Rome—annually at the Pantheon and at the church of San Giovanni Decollato—thereby establishing his fame with as wide a public as possible. Noting Rosa's use of public exhibition, Giovanni Battista Passeri, another contemporary biographer, added that "he preferred to make paintings according to his own genius [*di proprio genio*], it seeming to him to be more satisfying than obeying a restrictive command without his hands untied by the liberty of his fantasy; rather, he always expressed himself with his own genius [*si sfogava sempre col proprio genio*]."[7] His extensive production of prints—among the largest in seventeenth-century Italy—was itself an attempt to reach a broad, open market.

Freedom from the demands of patrons was to be achieved, in part, by a disinterest in wealth, suggested by Genius's neglect of the overturned cornucopia spilling its treasure and affirmed in Rosa's life by his biographers.[8] Death—represented by the tomb, the smoking urn, and the cypress trees—as well as wealth were to be scorned, as the inscription says. Rosa's independence allowed him to act as a satirist, suggested in the *Genius* by the presence of the female satyr with her admonishing gesture and the *Pictor Succensor* of the inscription: a "fiery painter" according to Richard Wallace's translation, but in Wendy Roworth's extended explication, a painter-satirist who is both inflamed by indignation and inflames his viewers to indignation through his work. The sincerity of his criticism is represented by the figure accepting Genius's heart, and its justness is indicated by the philosopher holding and pointing to a balance, the traditional symbol of justice.

The balance may also refer to a temperament untroubled by the vicissitudes of life which, along with the scorn of wealth and death, was a hallmark of the Stoic moral philosophy that was revived in the later sixteenth and seventeenth centuries, which Rosa embraced. Its themes are pervasive in his works, although the often-met charge that Rosa's stoicism was superficial and pretentious was already articulated by his contemporaries. After raising the issue of Rosa's vainglory and before describing his leaving the service of the Medici court, Baldinucci writes:

> From such an excessive love and appetite for glory was born in him . . . a fervent desire to appear in every deed and word almost a true philosopher. And it seems that walking among the spacious porticos of Athens in the company of the ancient Stoics continually occupied his thoughts, because one does not see among his infinite works, whether in verse or in painting, . . . anything that does not have in it invention, or composition that does not express some beautiful moral, or that does not represent in a lively way some of those so renowned men in their most memorable actions. Many and many more he showed in painting, and many in his etched prints. . . . Nor did his philosophical humor stop here, because he also used to give other outward signs.[9]

There is no reason, however, to think that Rosa did not take his own philosophical convictions (or pretensions) seriously. They were his guiding spirit, his genius.

JC

1. For the most extensive analyses of the print's iconography, see Wallace 1965; Roworth 1977, 69–110; see also Scott 1995, 159–62. Roworth 1978, 86, sees a closer source for Rosa's *Genius* in an engraving by Hendrick Goltzius entitled *Quies* (Hollstein 125).
2. Trans. Wallace 1965, 474. Roworth 1977, 94, offers an alternative translation: "Candid, Free, Painter who inflames through indignation, yet is Just and Equable, Scorner of Wealth and Death. This is my Genius."
3. Baldinucci 1974, 5:488; cf. Pascoli 1730–1736, 1:84 (cited by Haskell 1980, 11).
4. De Rinaldis 1939, 165 (trans. Wallace 1965, 473).
5. Baldinucci 1974, 5:483.
6. Ibid., 5:497.
7. Passeri 1772, 426.
8. See, for example, Baldinucci 1974, 5:497ff.
9. Ibid., 5:497.

Theodor Matham (1605/6–1676)

59. *Allegory of Painting*

c. 1655–58

Engraving and etching, 402 x 285 mm (15⅞ x 11¼ in.)

Reference: Hollstein 43, i/ii

Purchased from Kunsthandlung Helmut H. Rumbler, Frankfurt

1997.11

Matham's engraving shows an infant Cupid, his quiver of arrows behind him, crowning with laurel a female personification of Painting. She looks up into his face as she points with one hand toward the palette and brushes that she holds in the other. She seems to lean on a canvas or panel on which Cupid rather precariously sits. Her lower body is covered in extensive drapery, with just enough leg exposed to suggest that she is seated in a twisted posture. Yet her hair and clothing fly out behind her as if she is rushing toward Cupid or caught in a terrific wind. Cupid himself was sometimes shown as a painter (see cat. no. 55), and his crowning of Painting here suggests the mutual service of art and love (see also cat. no. 65).

The engraving reproduces in reverse and augments vertically a composition attributed in the seventeenth century to the Bolognese painter, Guido Reni (1575–1642). Versions of the composition abound, and the finest one, in the Cassa di Risparmio, Bologna, has been attributed to Francesco Gessi (1588–1649), one of Reni's followers.[1] A version of the composition, perhaps the one in Bologna, was part of the famous and vast collection of paintings and ancient sculptures belonging to the Reynst brothers, Gerard (1599–1658) and Jan (1601–1646), which were displayed both in Jan's house in Venice and in the brothers' house in Amsterdam.[2] The *Allegory of Painting* in the Reynst collection may have been one of the twenty-four paintings purchased from Gerard's estate in 1660 for the so-called "Dutch Gift" presented to King Charles II of England.[3]

The nearly two hundred paintings in the Reynst collection were almost exclusively Italian, especially Venetian, of the sixteenth and seventeenth centuries. Given the subject of the *Allegory of Painting,* it is not inconceivable that the picture was commissioned, either by Jan Reynst or as a gift to him, in honor of the collection itself. The Venetian Carlo Ridolfi dedicated his *Le Maraviglie dell'arte* (*The Marvels of Art,* Venice, 1648) to the Reynst brothers, praising them for their generous expenditures in erecting "two famous galleries" in Venice and Amsterdam, which were frequented by people of importance and talent ("da Personaggi, e da begli ingegni . . .").[4]

Matham's *Allegory of Painting* was one of thirty-four engravings of thirty-three paintings in the Reynst collection that appeared as a folio entitled *Variarum imaginum a celeberrimis artificibus pictarum caelaturae elegantissimis tabulis repraesentatae (Engravings of various subjects painted by most famous artists, presented in most elegant plates).*[5] The project to engrave some or all the paintings in the Reynst collection began around 1655 but apparently came to a halt upon Gerard's death in 1658. The completed plates by six engravers, including four by Theodor Matham, were issued probably in the late 1660s and possibly by the publisher Clement de Jonghe, who owned some of the plates, including that for Matham's *Allegory of Painting* (called *Ars pictoria* in the post-mortem inventory of de Jonghe's goods in 1679).[6] Matham's engraving, like all the prints in the *Caelaturae,* is unnumbered and without text, although the space at the bottom of the plate seems to have been reserved for a text that was never produced.

JC

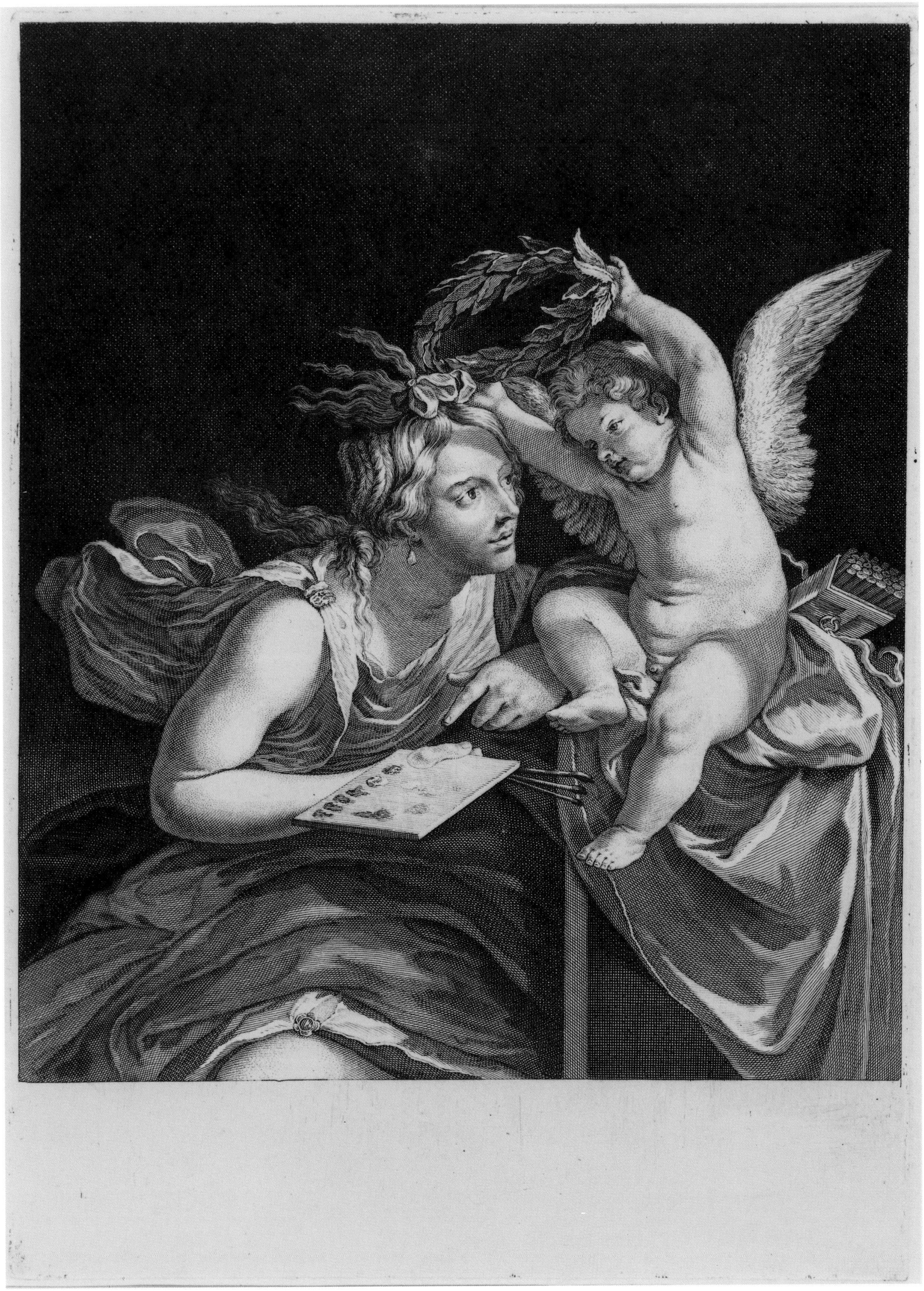

Cat. no. 59

1. See Spike 1982, 108.
2. On the Reynst brothers, see Logan 1979. In the brothers' extensive collection of antiquities was a so-called Vitellius, on which see cat. no. 40.
3. On the "Dutch Gift," see Mahon 1949–50; Logan 1979, 75–86. Two indifferent copies of the *Allegory of Painting* are in the English royal collection, but it is unlikely that either belonged to the Reynst brothers. The Reynst *Allegory* does not appear in the inventory of the collection of Charles II (some of the paintings of which are explicitly said to have been part of the "Dutch Gift"), but there may be a reference to the painting in an inventory of the collection of James II (Mahon 1949–50, 17; Logan 1979, 83, 143–44).
4. Quoted by Logan 1979, 11.
5. On the *Caelaturae,* see Logan 1979, 38–45, who provides the translation of the title (38, n. 1).
6. Logan 1979, 39, n. 3, who points out that de Jonghe may have purchased the plates from the sale of the Reynst estate in 1670.

JEAN DAULLÉ (1703–1763)
after Pierre Mignard (1612–1695)

60. *Catherine Mignard, comtesse de Feuquières (1652–1742)*

1735

Mezzotint, 469 x 320 mm (18½ x 12⅝ in.)

REFERENCE: Firmin-Didot 333, ii/ii

INSCRIPTION: below image: *Peint par P. Mignard. et Gravé par J. Daullé en 1735. / Catherine Mignard / Comtesse de Feuquiere. / Se vend chez l'Autheur Place de Cambray a Paris.*; on painting of Pierre Mignard: *P. Mignard p^r Peintre du Roy*

Purchased from Christopher Mendez, London

1998.13

In a biographical notice published at the beginning of the nineteenth century, this mezzotint was named as Daullé's first print, and it is generally acknowledged as his masterpiece, ranking with the best printmaking of the period.[1] It seems to have been on the strength of this print that the important portraitist Hyacinthe Rigaud came to prefer Daullé to make prints after his paintings.[2] At Daullé's death, most of his copper plates, including that of the *Catherine Mignard,* passed to his wife, Gabrielle-Anne Daullé, who used them to publish an edition of Daullé's collected works.[3]

Daullé's mezzotint reproduces, in reverse, a painting by Pierre Mignard (1612–1695), the subject's father, now in Versailles (fig. 60.1).[4] The exact date of the painting is unknown, although it is considerably earlier than the print, probably dating to 1690 or shortly later, when Mignard assumed the post of First Painter to the King, indicated in the inscription on his portrait held up by his daughter. The inscription may have been added to, or never appeared on, Mignard's portrait within the composition: that picture is now lost, but may be the one mentioned in Mignard's will of 1689 (that is, before he was named First Painter).[5]

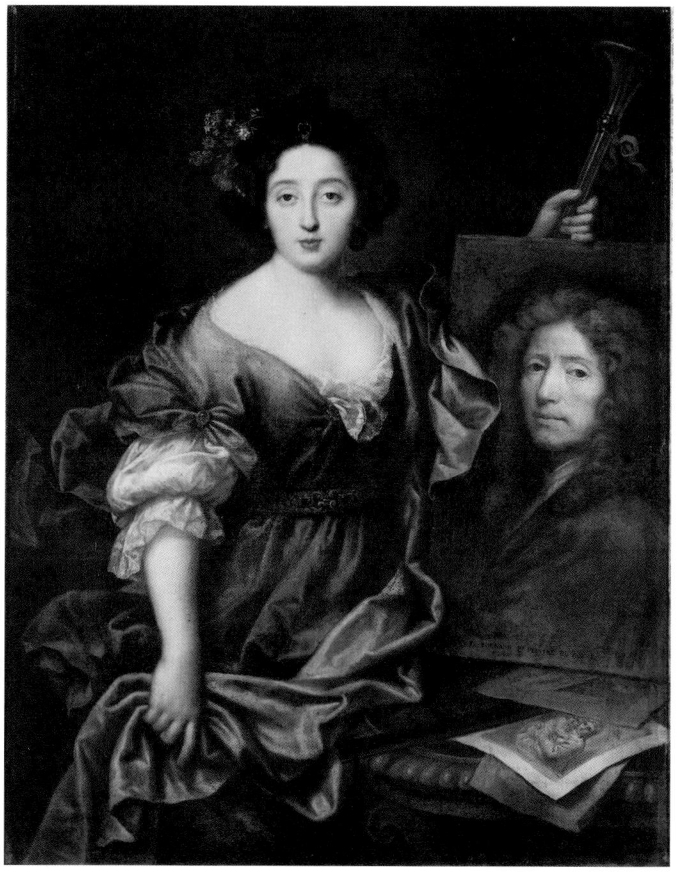

Fig. 60.1. Pierre Mignard. *Catherine-Marguerite Mignard.* Oil on canvas, 116 x 89 cm (45⅝ x 35 in.). Chateaux de Versailles et de Trianon.

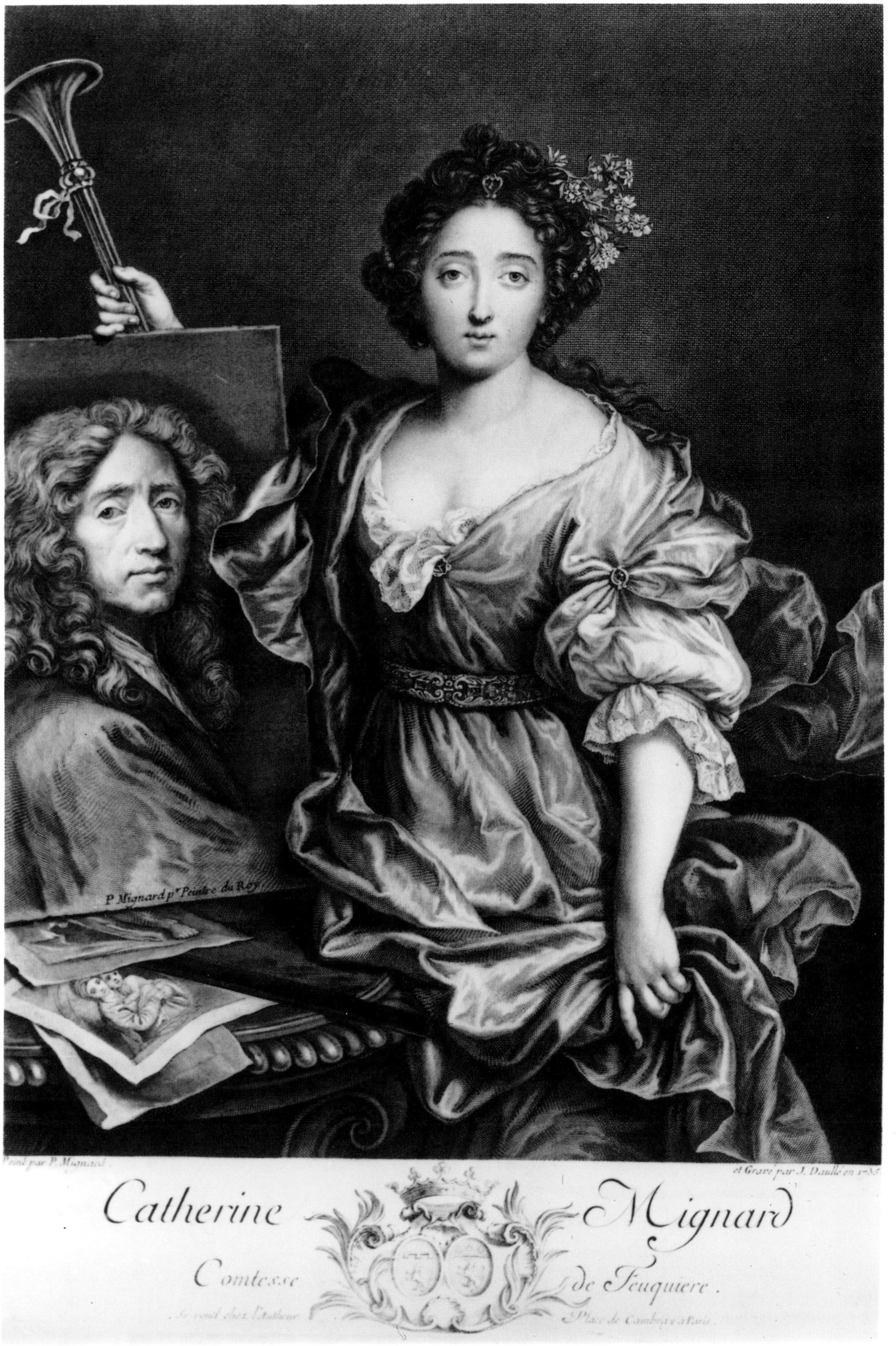
P. Mignard pr. Peintre du Roy
Catherine Mignard
Comtesse de Feuquiere.

Cat. no. 60

Within a few years of Mignard's death, Charles Perrault described the "tendresse singulière" between the painter and his daughter.[6] The portrayal of Catherine Mignard matches a bust in the lower left corner of Pierre Mignard's painted *Self-Portrait* in the Louvre (fig. 10.1), which was also painted late in the artist's life, around 1690, and was presented by Catherine to the Royal Academy of Painting and Sculpture in 1696, following her father's death.[7] With the exception of the sprig in her painted portrait, her hair is identically arranged, with pearls at either side and a jeweled piece above her brow. In both images, she wears a dress that bares her neck and much of her shoulders, with a lace chemise projecting from the breast. The shank of the square that lies on the table in the portrait of Catherine leans against her bust in the self-portrait of her father. Catherine Mignard plays a sort of allegorical role in each composition: in the Louvre self-portrait as something akin to a classical muse; in the Versailles painting as Fame, with whose trumpet, held in her hand above the canvas-within-the-canvas, she secures her father's renown.

On the table, in addition to the square, are several prints, presumably after Pierre Mignard. The *Madonna and Child* is typical of his work in Italy,[8] where he resided from 1635 to 1657; his paintings of the Madonna were so well known and distinctive that they were nicknamed Mignardes.

The large inscription at the bottom of the print identifies the sitter. Catherine Mignard (1652–1742) married the comte de Feuquières at around the age of forty, following her father's death,[9] and the heraldic device at the center combines the coats-of-arms of the Feuquières family with that of the Mignard, which also appears in Gérard Edelinck's portrait of Pierre Mignard (cat. no. 10).

JC

1. "Son premier ouvrage est d'après *Mignard,* et représente la Comtesse de Feuquieres, fille de ce peintre, dont elle tient le portrait" (Huber 1797–1808, 8:108; quoted by Johnson 1982, 125); see also Delignières 1873, IX, XXII, 34–35.
2. See Delignières 1873, IX–X, and Meyer 1992, 99, both citing Mariette.
3. Meyer 1992, 107–108; the plate for the *Catherine Mignard* appears as item no. 20 in the inventory taken after Daullé's death (Meyer 1992, 112).
4. On the painting, of which there are several versions, see Nikolenko 1983, 12, 83–84 (who dates the painting c. 1677); Bajou 1997, 197–98.
5. Nikolenko 1983, 84; Bajou 1997, 198. The portrayal of Mignard differs slightly from that of his larger Louvre *Self-Portrait,* mentioned below, as well as that of the model for Gerard Edelinck's print after a Mignard self-portrait (cat. no. 10).
6. Perrault 1696–1700, 2:92, who notes that Catherine Mignard married the comte de Feuquière.
7. Nikolenko 1983, 93–94.
8. See, for example, the painting in the Alte Pinakothek, Munich, reproduced in an engraving by François de Poilly (Nikolenko 1983, plates 31–32).
9. Nikolenko 1983, 12.

William Hogarth (1697–1764)

61. *Boys Peeping at Nature*

1731/51

Etching, 151 x 127 mm (6 x 5 in.)

Reference: Paulson 120, iv/iv

Inscription: *Receiv'd . . . of . . . / 5 Shillings being the first Payment for two large Prints / one representing Moses brought to Pharoah's [sic] Daughter. / The other S^t. Paul before Felix, wch I Promise to deliver / when finish'd, on Receiving 5 Shillings more. / N.B. They will be Seven and Six Pence / each Print, after the time of Subscribing.*

Purchased from Kunsthandlung Helmut H. Rumbler, Frankfurt

1997.24

Boys Peeping at Nature was Hogarth's first subscription ticket, which acknowledged the payment of half a guinea toward the full guinea price of his series of six prints, *A Harlot's Progress* of 1730/1, to be delivered on completion.[1] The print was used again in 1737, without alteration to the image, for *Strolling Actresses* and the series of the *Four Times of Day* (fig. 61.1). Hogarth again made use of it in 1751, for the two large prints of *Moses Brought to Pharaoh's Daughter* and *Paul before Felix,* this time with substantial

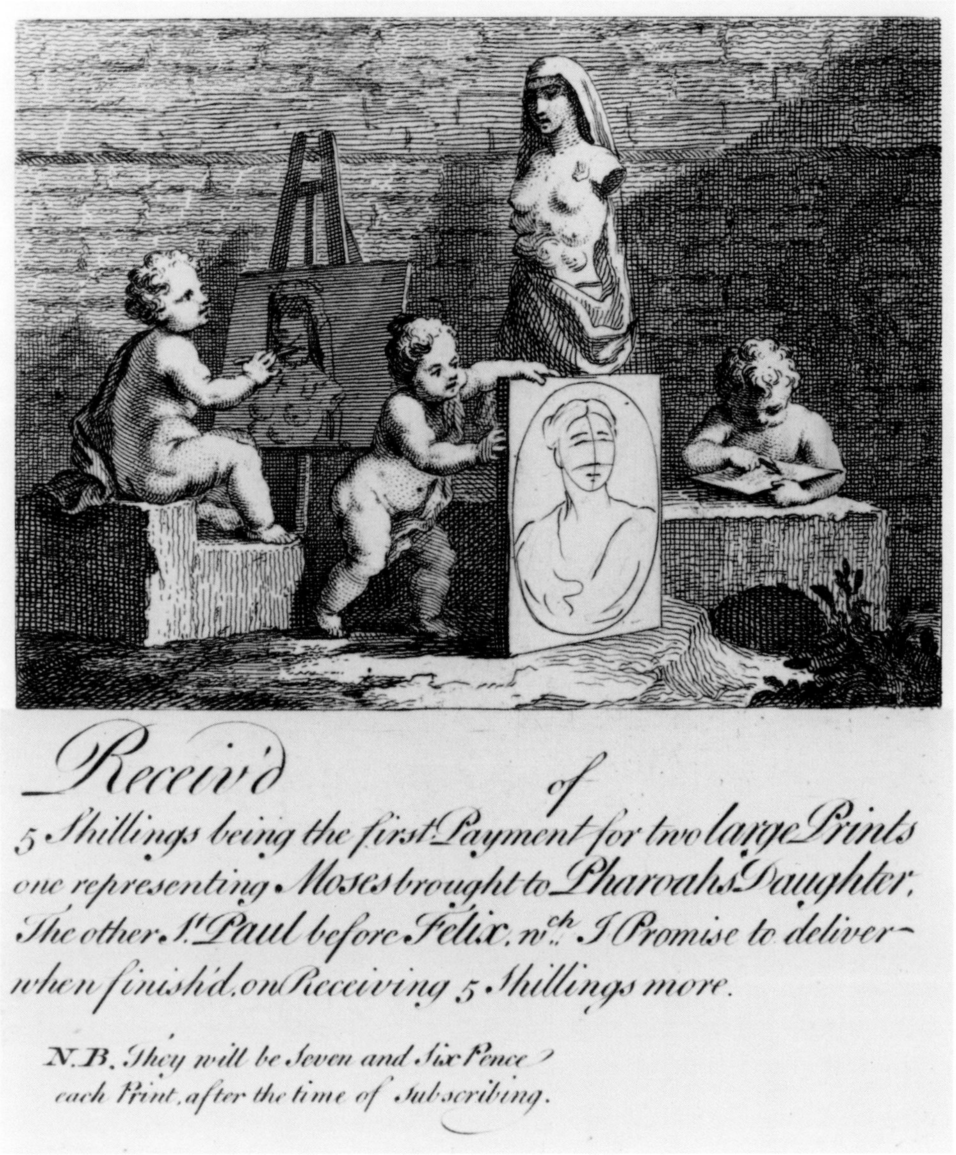

Cat. no. 61

alteration to the image. According to John Ireland, "Applications for the *gratis* etching were very frequent; and he found, to his great mortification, that the public were more eager to possess his little print, than either of the large ones. *To punish their want of taste,* he gave away no more, but fixed the price at two-thirds of the sum at which he published the large."[2]

In both versions of the print, a statue of the multibreasted Diana of Ephesus is surrounded by putti, one of whom is painting her on a canvas while another ignores her as he draws on a tablet. Such a use of putti in an allegorical composition was a commonplace by the eighteenth century (see cat. nos. 30, 55). The ancient multibreasted Diana had long represented Nature in the visual arts, including in the frontispiece to Gerard de Lairesse's *Groot Schilderboek,* a translation of which, with the same frontispiece, was published in London in 1707 as *Art of Painting.* There she appears on a canvas held by an allegorical figure of Painting (fig. 61.2, from the Dutch edition of 1712). Hogarth's most immediate source may have been a painting by Peter Paul Rubens and Jan Brueghel owned by his father-in-law, Sir James Thornhill.[3] Though the subject of the print may be, as Ronald Paulson has asserted, "the artist's imitation of nature,"[4] it is worth recalling that the object depicted by the putto at left is not unmediated nature but an ancient statue, and the casting of the image in allegorical terms places Hogarth within a classicist tradition against which he often chafed, a tradition which always paid at least lip-service to nature's fundamental importance for art, even as the imagination—represented here by the putto who draws without recourse to the statue—was also valued. He also mocks that tradition by having a young satyr lift the skirts of Diana for a fuller peep at nature. Hogarth's project with *A Harlot's Progress,* as with many of his later works, was to bring the

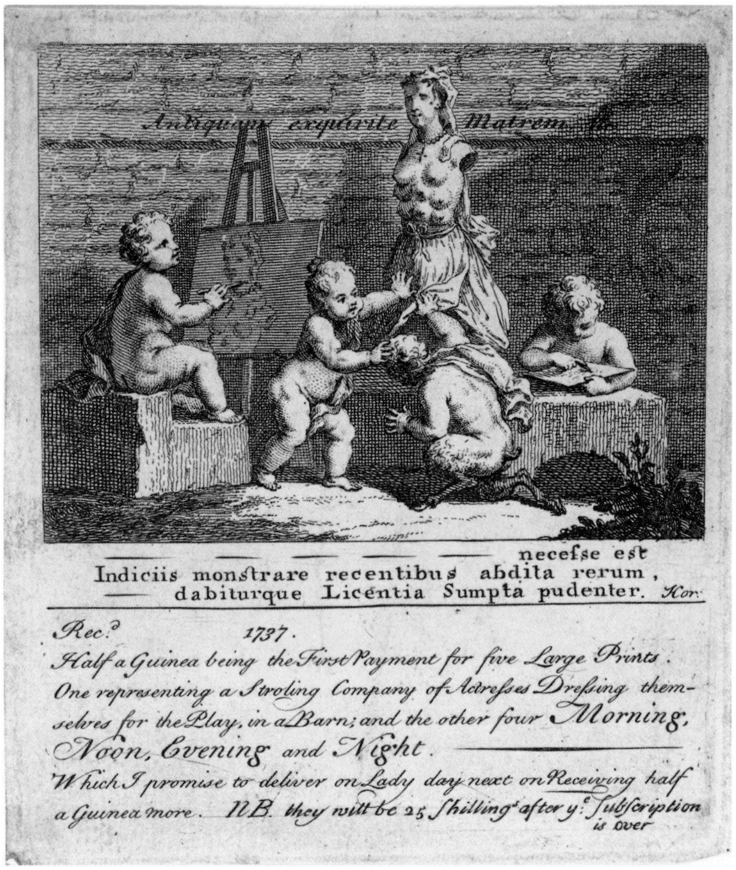

Fig. 61.1. William Hogarth. *Boys Peeping at Nature.* 1730–31. Etching, third state, 151 x 127 mm (6 x 5 in.). The British Museum, London.

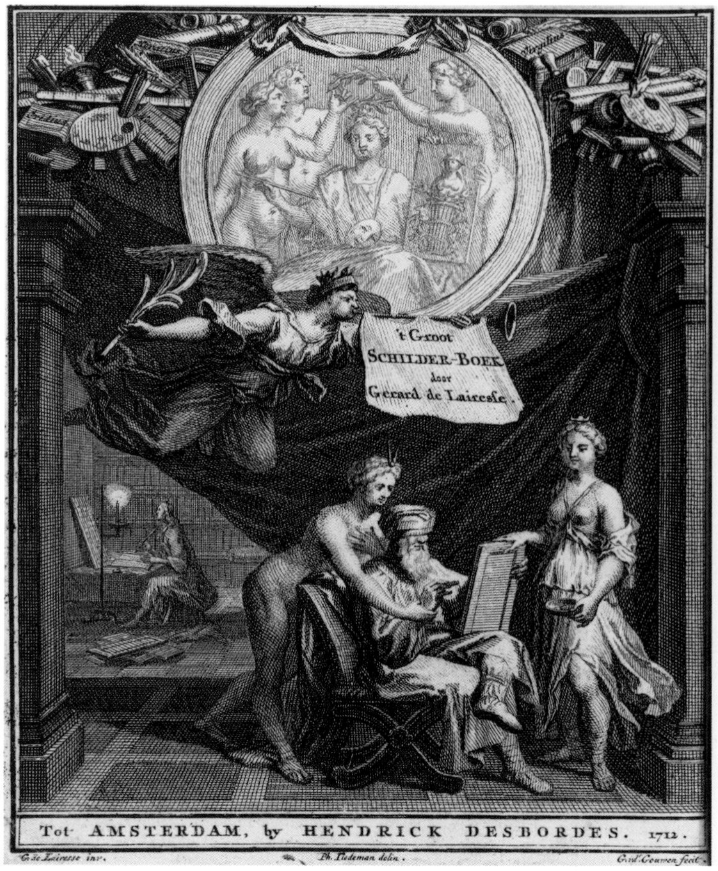

Fig. 61.2. Gilliam van der Gouwen after Philipp Tiedeman after Gerard de Lairesse. Frontispiece to Gerard de Lairesse, *Groot Schilderboek Waar in de Schilderkonst in al Haar Deelen Grondig werd onderweezen.* 1712. Etching, 182 x 140 mm (7⅛ x 5½ in.). Sarah Campbell Blaffer Foundation, Houston.

high moral purpose of depictions of ancient and biblical subjects to contemporary themes, and the amusing act of the little satyr in *Boys Peeping at Nature* anticipates the comedic content of the harlot series. In contrast, for the engravings after his more high-minded paintings, *Moses Brought to Pharaoh's Daughter* and *Paul before Felix,* Hogarth altered the subscription ticket substantially, eliminating the inquisitive satyr, and, as John Nichols avers, "with propriety, effaced all the wit in his original design."[5] The sculpture itself is rendered more classicizing with the change in headdress and the elimination of the necklace. Substituting for the satyr is a panel or canvas with a schematic, bust-length drawing of a woman. The drawing is an instructional type that had long been common—as in, for example, Odoardo Fialetti's *Il uero modo et ordine per dissegnar . . .* of 1608 (see cat. no. 24)—and was probably used in the Academy in Saint Martin's Lane, which Hogarth had attended under Thornhill, then run himself.[6] Its appearance here suggests Hogarth's adherence to the traditional idea that although art imitates nature, it must rely on conventions through which nature may be best apprehended and reproduced—conventions that can be taught.

JC

1. Paulson 1989, 75–76; see also Paulson 1995, 27–30.
2. Ireland 1791, 2:506–507.
3. Oppé 1948, 32; Paulson 1989, 75. For a sixteenth-century Italian depiction, see Goldstein 1996, fig. 6, p. 19. Daniel Chodowiecki (cat. nos. 46, 63) used Diana of Ephesus for his personal bookplate in 1777 (Engelmann 192).
4. Paulson 1989, 75.
5. Nichols 1785, 320. Paulson 1989, 155, suggests that Hogarth thus "proclaims that he was no longer concerned with gross contemporary reality." Ireland 1791, 2:506, delicately misconstrues the original action: "the boy . . . was . . . represented as curiously stooping down to examine the fringe [of Nature's garment]. Some of the artist's friends, suggesting that this was too ludicrous an idea for the public, the copper was thrown aside." But he implies otherwise in describing the transformation of the image for a new subscription: "to have given him [Paul] the *Peeping Boys,* in their original state, would have been a species of sacrilege; they were *chastened,* grouped as they now are, and transferred from the *Harlot* to the *Apostle*" (Ireland 1791, 2:507).
6. Oppé 1948, 32, sees it as Hogarth's "paying homage to Thornhill by scheming out, on Thornhill's lines, a portrait head."

Giovanni David (1743–1790)

62. *Painting, Sculpture*

c. 1775–76

Etchings on a single sheet, 124 x 85 mm (4⅞ x 3⅜ in.) and 126 x 91 mm (5 x 3⅝ in.), respectively

Reference: Grasso 43 i/ii; 44 i/ii

Inscriptions: lower left on each: *David Gen Inv fecit*

Purchased from C. G. Boerner

1998.18.1-2

Giovanni David's *Painting* is represented by a female figure with long, loosely bound hair, who works on a painting of a human figure. A mask rests on the side of her head. Her right hand raises a brush to the painting on an easel; her left holds a palette and other brushes. She is seated on an architectural fragment which includes a sculptured relief with two figures visible. In the background, smoke rises from an altar-like structure with a bucranium on its corner, reminiscent of the smoking urn in Salvator Rosa's *Genius* (cat. no. 58). In the lower right corner, a monkey sits, looking at itself in a mirror.

Although a mask was associated with various allegorical figures, from several of the Muses to Fraud and Deceit, Cesare Ripa included one in his description of Painting, as a pendant on a golden chain, and it often appears in allegorical representations of the art. For Ripa, it refers to the "imitation of real things," in that it is a "portrait of the human face."[1] A mask was also an attribute of Imitation, as was an ape, both demonstrating "the imitation of human actions."[2] The ape had been a metaphor for painters and other artists (including writers) since the late Middle Ages, first negatively, as deceivers and forgers of reality, then positively, for their imitative skill.[3] The idea retained its positive meaning through the sixteenth century, but it had to be interpreted more broadly: art is not just a slavish and thoughtless imitation of nature but an imitation of the ideals of nature, of nature's own creative powers, learned by the artist through observation of created nature. In the seventeenth century the metaphor took a negative turn once again, so that artists who only imitated what they saw before their eyes, who could not improve nature according to an ideal in their mind, were simply craftsmen and not true artists, and were despised as mere apes of nature (see cat. no. 56). Thus the vignette by Charles Errard at the beginning of the Life of Anthony van Dyck in Giovan Pietro Bellori's *Vite de pittori, scultori et architetti moderni* of 1672

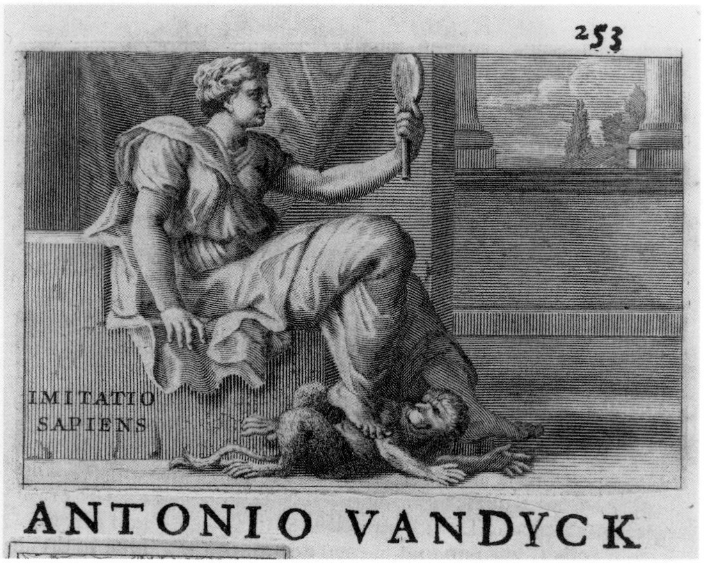

Fig. 62.1. Charles Errard. *Imitatio Sapiens* from Giovan Pietro Bellori, *Vite de pittori, scultori et architetti moderni*. 1672. Engraving, 85 x 120 mm (3⅜ x 4¾ in.). Research Library, The Getty Research Institute, Los Angeles.

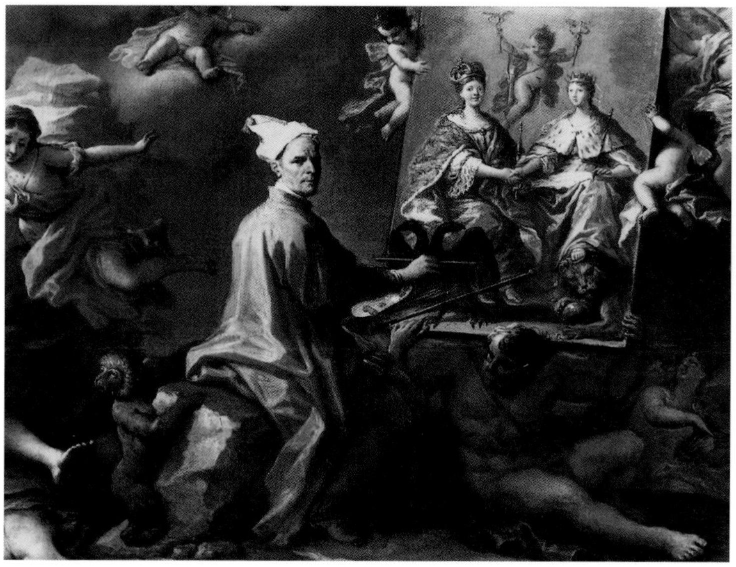

Fig. 62.2. Paolo de Matteis. *Allegory of the Peace of Utrecht* (detail). After 1714. Oil on canvas, 76.2 x 101.6 cm (30 x 40 in.). Sarah Campbell Blaffer Foundation, Houston.

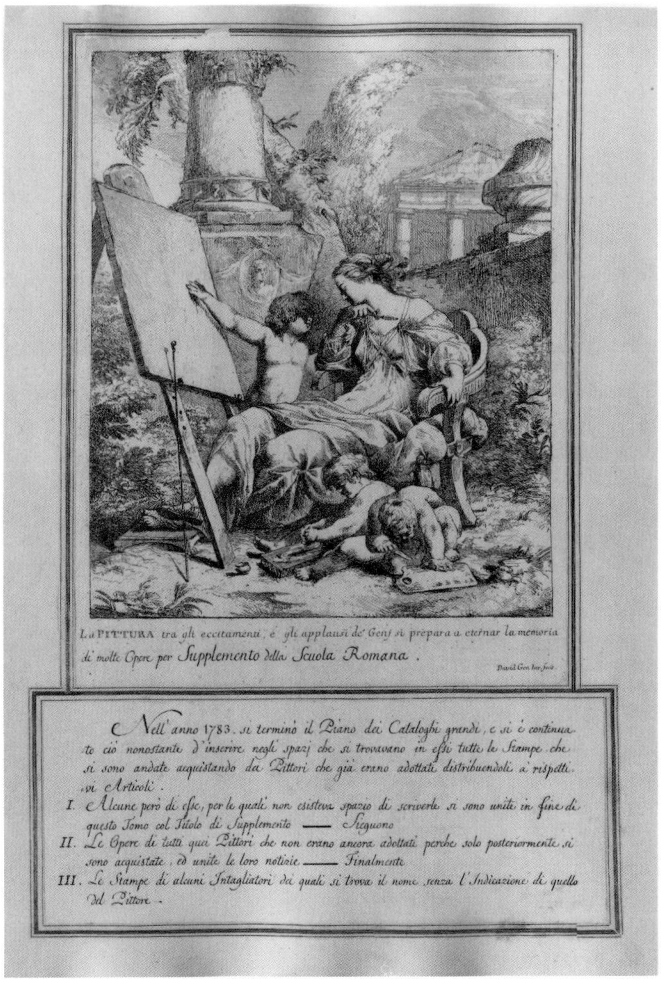

Fig. 62.3. Giovanni David. *Allegory of Painting.* Etching, 308 x 231 mm (12⅛ x 9⅛ in.). C. G. Boerner, Inc., New York.

portrays the allegorical figure of Wise Imitation (*imitatio sapiens*), who holds a mirror while trampling on an ape—that is, unwise imitation (fig. 62.1).[4] The unusual motif of an ape holding a mirror in David's *Painting* thereby doubles the allusion to imitation. Embracing the imitative meaning of the ape rather than disparaging it was possible, however, even in a self-portrait of an ambitious history painter such as Paolo de Matteis from around 1714 (fig. 62.2); David's etching seems to present imitation in positive, or at least neutral, terms.

David's *Sculpture* is also characterized by a female figure with loosely bound hair, this time standing. She rests her hands on a mallet as she gazes at a sculptured bust, which may represent Homer, as he was known from a famous Hellenistic sculpture that was widely copied.[5] In addition to the mallet, other tools of the art are present: compass and chisels on the pedestal, and a straight edge and drill leaning against it. In the background at right is a substantial structure crowned by the classical sculptural group known as the *Wrestlers* (in reverse), which had been discovered in Rome in 1583 and was installed in the Tribuna of the Uffizi in Florence by 1688. It was much copied and recommended for academic study, in particular because of the intertwining of the two bodies.[6]

The purpose of David's etchings of *Painting and Sculpture* is not known. In the brief period in which he made most of his etchings, 1775 to 1776, his most important patron, Count Giacomo Durazzo, had recently begun a massive project to collect both original and reproductive prints as a way of documenting the development of European art. Durazzo was a career diplomat, first in the service of his native Genoa as ambassador to Vienna, then, from 1774, as the emperor's ambassador to Venice, where he began the print collection, on behalf of Duke Albert of Saxe-Teschen until 1776, then for himself. Durazzo ultimately acquired more than thirty thousand prints—arranging them according to national and regional schools—which subsequently formed the core of the Graphische Sammlung Albertina in Vienna. In 1775, David had moved to Venice to be close to Durazzo, and he was certainly aware of Durazzo's print project, if not directly involved in it. David produced another etching on a related theme, a more elaborate *Allegory of Painting,* in which a female figure sits at a canvas, chalk holder in hand, accompanied by nude children (fig. 62.3). One child grinds pigments, another prepares the palette, and a third pulls on the woman's arm and gestures toward the canvas. The woman seems to be immobile in a melancholic desuetude, looking down rather than at the blank canvas facing her, in spite of the inscription below the image that reads: "Painting, among the excitements and applause of the geniuses, prepares to immortalize the memory of many works . . . ." Further inscription in manuscript follows, indicating the use of the print as a frontispiece for a print-collecting project like Durazzo's.[7]

JC

1. Ripa 1603, 405. On the mask as an attribute of Painting, see Georgel and Lecoq 1987, 52–53.
2. Ripa 1603, 223.
3. See Janson 1952, 287–325; Georgel and Lecoq 1987, 56–59; Vidal 1992, 152–55; Asemissen and Schweikhart 1994, 178–83; and cat. no. 72.
4. In holding a mirror, Imitation conforms to the traditional characterization of Vision; see Sluijter 2000, 90–99, and cat. no. 36.
5. See Held 1991a, 32.
6. Haskell and Penny 1981, 337–39.
7. In this instance, for a supplement to the works of modern Roman painters; an impression used for Dutch and Flemish works is also known (Schmid and Haunton 2000, 10, 39; Newcome Schleier and Grasso 2003, 184–86).

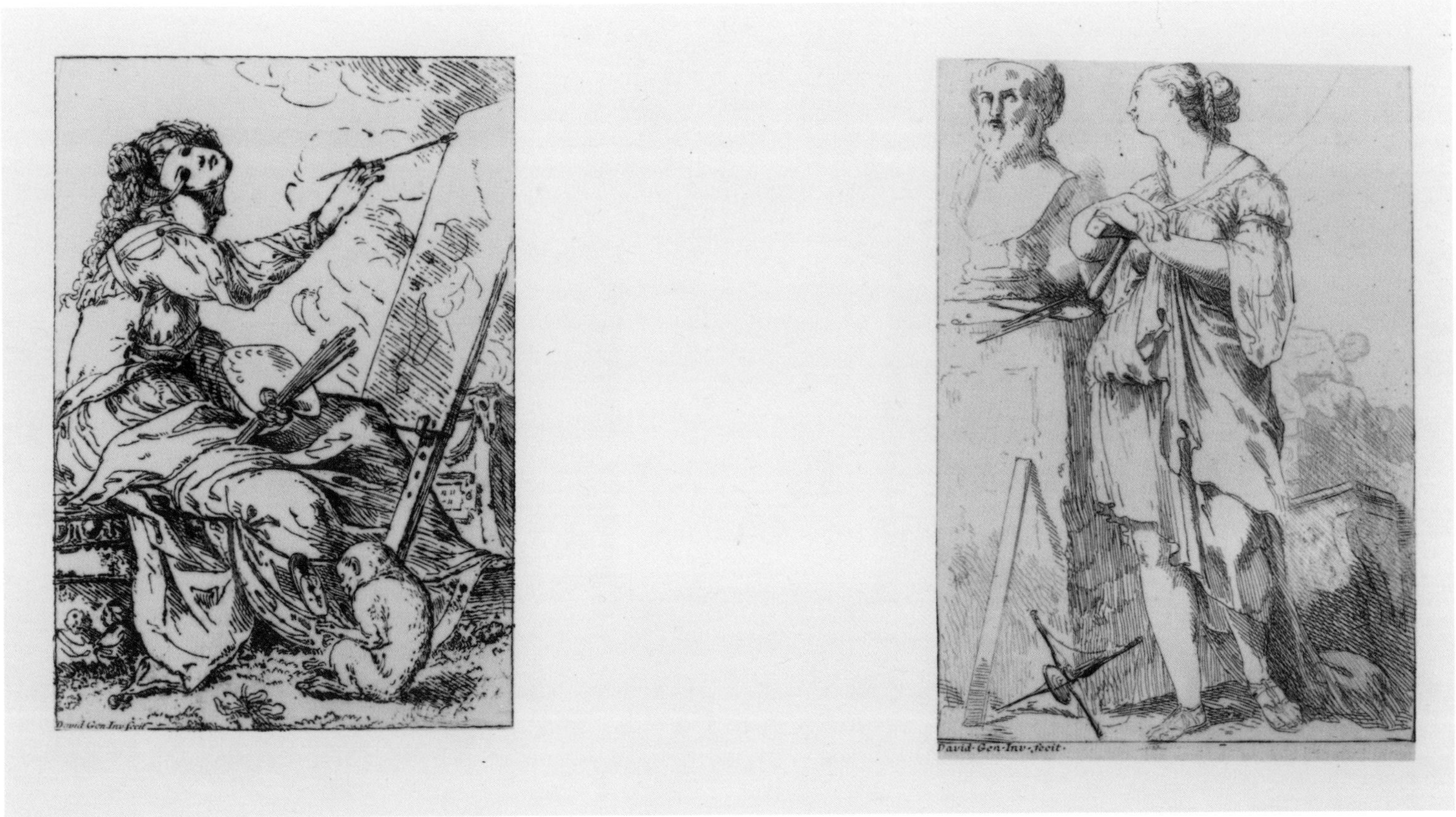

Cat. no. 62

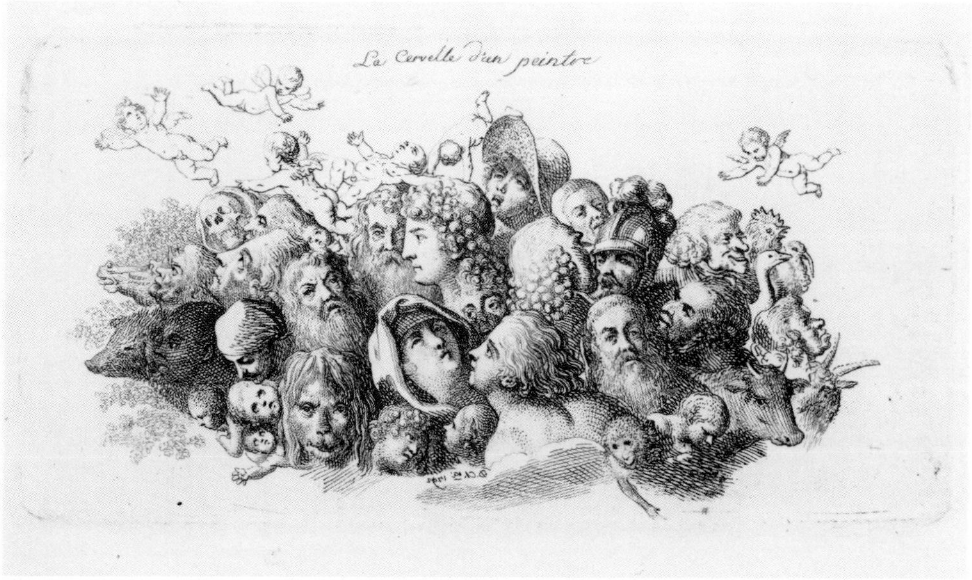

Cat. no. 63

Daniel Nikolaus Chodowiecki (1726–1801)

63. *The Brain of a Painter*

1792

Etching, 45 x 85 mm (1¾ x 3⅜ in.)

References: Engelmann 696 ib/ii; Bauer 1629

Inscriptions: above image: *La Cervelle d'un peintre*; lower center (in reverse): *D. Ch*^{ki} *1792*

Purchased from C. G. Boerner, New York

2000.19

Daniel Chodowiecki assembled more than thirty human and animal heads in apparent disorder but conforming to the oblong shape, and even suggesting the surface irregularities, of a brain, around which putti fly and frolic. A few faces are recognizable: Frederick the Great, King of Prussia (at left, below the skull); Voltaire (at right, caricatured); and, perhaps, Moses Mendelssohn (below Voltaire),[1] all three of whom were contemporaries of Chodowiecki but had died years before the production of the print. It may be Chodowiecki himself peering at the viewer from behind the helmeted head to the right of center, but the image as a whole can be construed as an allegorical self-portrait. The variety of figures recalls Chodowiecki's prolific and highly varied work as an illustrator.[2] The sculptural male head dominating the center of the composition is a nod to the classical tradition in art, and the skull and knight suggest allegory and history, but most of the figures derive from the artist's observation of nature, a practice Chodowiecki continually emphasized and which is amply evident in his hundreds of depictions of contemporary life,[3] including the self-portrait with his family called the *Cabinet d'un peintre* (cat. no. 46). If the *Cabinet d'un peintre (Chamber of a Painter)* exemplifies the artist's observation, then the *Cervelle d'un peintre (Brain of a Painter)* can exemplify his power of invention, an indispensable partner to observation, which turns Nature into art, suggested by the coherent image rising out of the chaos of heads. The depiction of the artist's inner world functions as a counterpart to the depiction of his outer world.[4]

Chodowiecki sent an impression of his *Brain of a Painter* to Countess Christiane von Solms-Laubach (1754–1815), with whom he corresponded from 1780 until at least 1795.[5] Solms-Laubach, an amateur pastelist, oil painter, and miniaturist, initiated the correspondence by sending the famous artist an example of her work. In response, Chodowiecki sent a drawn self-portrait and the *Cabinet d'un peintre,* and the two exchanged many friendly letters and small works over the years, although they never met.[6] With a letter of October 24, 1795, Chodowiecki enclosed the *Brain of a Painter* and remarked that "*The Brain of a Woman* [*La Cervelle d'une femme*] would be indeed a rich theme for a pendant, and I would be much obliged to Your Highness if you would send me a design for it. I would certainly with much pleasure etch it [*zu Kupfer bringen*] and would provide a good pendant for the other one. I beseech you for it!"[7] It is not known if the Countess responded to Chodowiecki's request. The known correspondence ceases at this point, and Chodowiecki does not seem to have produced such an etching. JC

1. Börsch-Supan 1986, 113; Akademie der Künste, Hochschule der Künste 1996, 190. For Frederick's profile, cf. Chodowiecki's proposal for an equestrian monument (Netzer 1989, 126–27); for Voltaire's head, cf. his (non-caricatured) drawing of 1780–81 for a title page (Netzer 1989, 106–107); for Mendelssohn, cf. his design of c. 1774 for a medallion (Müller 2000, 104, 174).
2. Börsch-Supan 1986, 113, who sees the etching as "eine humoristisch vorgetragene Klage über seine Arbeitsüberlastung."
3. See ibid., 111–12.
4. Cf. ibid., 112–13.
5. See Steinbrucker 1927.
6. Ibid., 6 (letter of October 24, 1780).
7. Ibid., 184. *The Brain of a Painter* had been exhibited at the Royal Academy of Arts in Berlin in 1793 (Börsch-Supan 1971, 1:n.p.).

E. Le Sueur (active c. 1775–1800)

64. *The Painter Creator (Le Peintre Créateur)*

c. 1790–1800

Etching, 326 x 377 mm (12⅞ x 14⅞ in.) (trimmed)

Inscriptions: on the bust at right: ΑΠΟΛΛΟΝ; on plinth below bust: *Celui qui méprise / Les Arts / et n'en Sent pas / Lutilité / est*; below image at left: *E. Le Sueur P.^{tre} Sculp.*; below image at center: *Le Peintre Créateur, que le génie inspire, / Par de Savants Tableaux peut Charmer et instruire; / De L'immortalité, il S'ouvre le Chemin, / En dépit des Efforts d'un Jaloux Ecrivain. / a Paris Rue des marais N.º16. D^{on} Bondy.*

Purchased from Hill-Stone, New York

2000.13

In a low-ceilinged room, a painter faces a canvas on an easel. He leans back sharply, his wide-eyed, open-mouthed expression suggesting astonishment or even fear. One arm is held across his chest, the other embraces a large bust of Apollo, almost as if seeking protection.[1] In his left hand he holds a branch of laurel, sacred to Apollo, that is tipped as a drawing instrument.[2] On the canvas is a nude male figure, apparently an ancient Greek hero, his sword, shield, and helmet by his side. The same helmet, a studio prop, sits on the floor behind the easel. On one side of the artist is a work box with palette and brushes; on the other, is a still-life consisting of a large jug, a partial loaf of bread, a large sheet of paper, the cast of a leg, and a thick branch. Against the back wall of the studio are arranged further studio appurtenances, including sculptures and an *écorché* arm. The print is undated, and little is known of the artist, E. Le Sueur, including his first name. The strong planarity of the central figure, and even his pose, which may echo Jean-Germain Drouais's figure of Marius in a famous painting of 1786 (Paris, Louvre), as well as the style of his hair and clothing, suggest a date late in the eighteenth century.

The context of the print is not known, except that it was published in Paris, but the inscriptions suggest that it is polemical. The poem below the image reads, in translation, "The Painter Creator, whom genius inspires, can charm and instruct through wise paintings. He opens to himself the road to immortality, despite the efforts of a jealous writer." This "jealous writer" may be an art critic—a type that flourished, gaining considerable public importance, during the eighteenth century and into the nineteenth—who was critical of Le Sueur, his colleagues, or his profession. This writer is implied in the inscription on the plinth at right: "He who despises [or scorns] the arts and does not understand the usefulness of them is . . . ." The sentence may be completed by the still-life in some way, perhaps a partial rebus. The

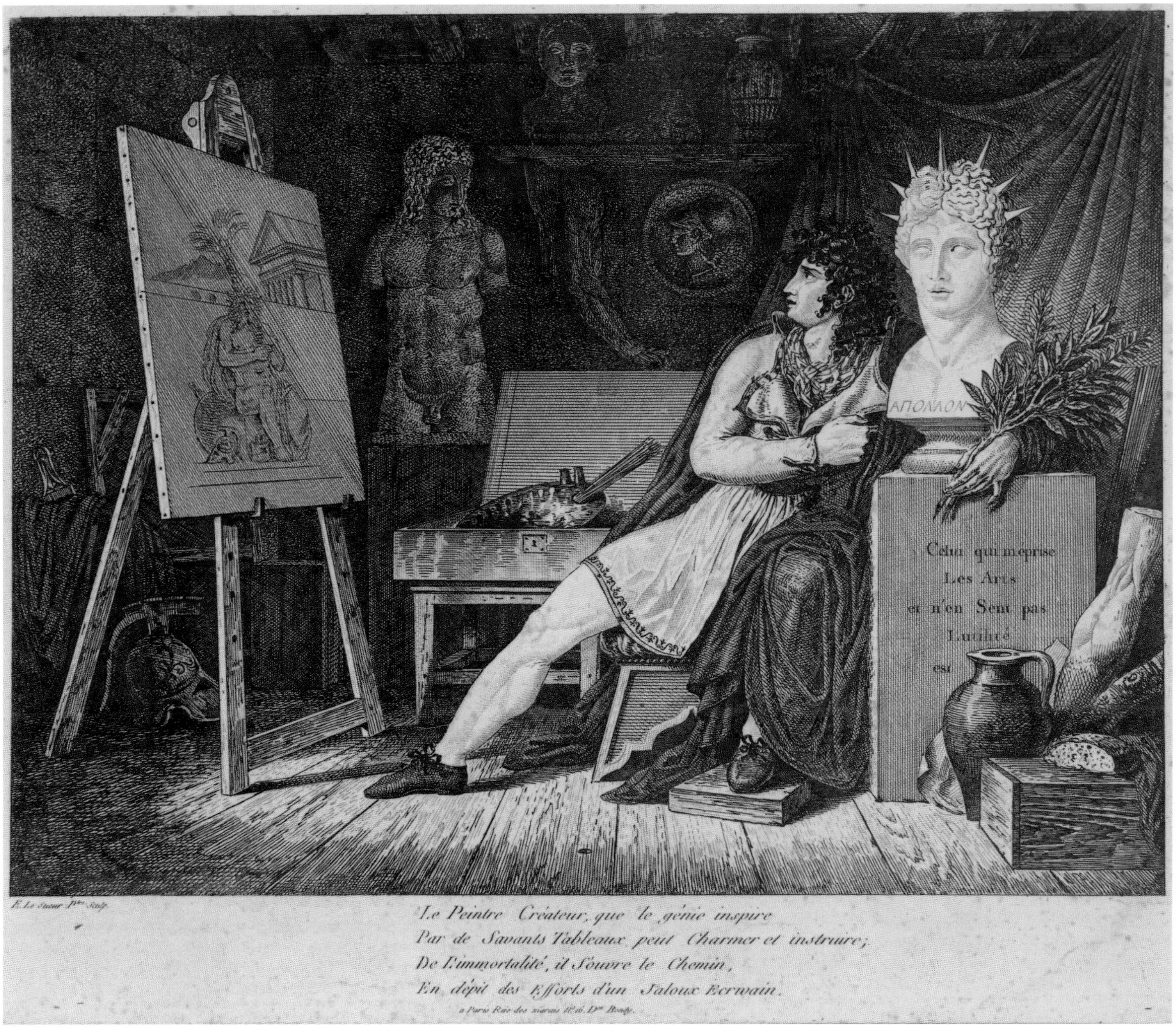

Cat. no. 64

poem invokes truisms that were used in the Renaissance and after in defense of painting; namely, that the purpose of art is to instruct and delight (ultimately from Horace),[3] and that the artist's renown will live on into eternity (overly optimistic in this case, since virtually nothing is known of E. Le Sueur). The term "painter creator" is a product of the eighteenth century: until then, creative acts (as distinct from acts of making) were almost universally reserved for God alone, notwithstanding the occasional sobriquets of divinity attached to some writers or artists such as Dante and Michelangelo.[4] The use of "genius" as inspiring the artist occupies an ambiguous middle ground between an earlier idea of an animating spirit and the Romantic and modern idea of preternatural abilities, but, given its conjunction with "creator," may be inclined to the latter.

Each line of Le Sueur's poem, as an alexandrine, includes a caesura after the sixth syllable, matching the compositional caesura in the middle of the image above. *The Painter Creator* contains several such carefully conceived compositional elements, like the elided inscription and still life at the lower right and the repetition of a classical profile in the figure and the relief sculpture behind him. Some are witty: the *écorché* arm is positioned as if it has opened the paint box; a palm tree seems to grow out of the head of the figure on the canvas. These, along with eerie lighting of the back wall, the overly dramatic figure of the painter,[5] and perhaps even the grandiose characterization of the "painter creator," might indicate that the print is ironic, demonstrating bemusement at the pretensions of painters. JC

1. Minerva and Mercury are the gods usually associated with artists, but Apollo may have been chosen here for his association with reason, Parnassus, music, and the Muses.
2. Two tips project below his hand, presumably an uncorrected pentimento.
3. See Lee 1967, 32–34.
4. Kristeller 1983. De Dominici 1742–45, 3:526, 529, 540, clearly thought it an example of Paolo de Matteis's arrogance that he would call himself "creator."
5. A tension of creative uncertainty is sometimes seen in images of an artist facing a canvas, especially a blank one as in Rembrandt's early painting in Boston, but here the artist faces a rather tame composition, whose figure possibly derives from an ancient Jupiter (cf. Goldstein 1996, 139, for a drawing of it by Charles Le Brun) and anticipates the more monumental enthroned figures (Napoleon, Jupiter, Homer) by Ingres.

Johann Friedrich Bolt (1769–1836)

65. *The Daughter of Butades Drawing the Silhouette of Her Lover*

1804

Lithograph, 253 x 176 mm (10 x 6⅞ in.) (image)

Reference: Dussler 1

Inscriptions: at lower left (reversed): *Fried. Bolt i et de. [?] 1804*; in lower margin: *Polÿautographische Zeichnung von Fr. Bolt.*

Purchased from Kunsthandlung Helmut H. Rumbler, Frankfurt

1999.5

In 1804, when the painter Wilhelm Reuter (1768–1834) began publishing a series of lithographs in Berlin, the process was still in its infancy. Reuter, who ultimately produced over a hundred lithographs of his own, persuaded several artists to participate in the project, which consisted of twenty-three lithographs and extended through 1808.[1] He titled the series *Polyautographische Zeichnungen vorzüglicher Berliner Künstler (Polyautographic Drawings of Leading Berlin Artists),* using the term prevalent during the earliest history of the process. The experimental nature of Reuter's project is evident in the present sheet, which consists of *The Daughter of Butades Drawing the Silhouette of Her Lover* by Johann Friedrich Bolt on one side and a group of unrelated images by Carl Franz Jacob Heinrich Schumann (1767–1827) on the other: on the left, the busts of two ancient figures and, rotated ninety degrees, a male head; on the right, Aeneas and the Cumaean Sibyl (fig. 65.1), a composition derived from an etching by Gerard de Lairesse.[2] Working with pen and ink, Bolt used a variety of relatively coarse marks for his composition, from cross-hatching to stipple, not yet exploiting the extensive possibilities of the medium available through the use of crayon, which was just at that time being introduced. In printing, the ink was squeezed out of dark areas, leaving tonal gaps or irregularities, as in the hair of the male figure. Given the nascent status of the technique, the experimental nature of the work, and its designation as a drawing (*Zeichnung*), Bolt's subject was well chosen: the origin of the art of drawing and painting.

In the *Natural History,* Pliny considered the origins of painting: "As to the Greeks, some of them say it was discovered at Sicyon, others in Corinth, but all agree that it began with tracing an outline round a man's shadow and consequently that pictures were originally done in this way. . . ."[3] Later in the same text, he recounted a related tale:

> It was through the service of that same earth that modelling portraits from clay was first invented by Butades, a potter of Sicyon, at Corinth. He did this owing to his daughter, who was in love with a young man; and she, when he was going abroad, drew in outline on the wall the shadow of his face thrown by a lamp. Her father pressed clay on this and made a relief, which he hardened by exposure to fire with the rest of his pottery; and it is said that this likeness was preserved in the Shrine of the Nymphs until the destruction of Corinth by Mummius.[4]

Although Pliny does not assert that the daughter of Butades was the first to trace such a silhouette, the two passages were conflated in the seventeenth century, and his anecdote was taken up as one

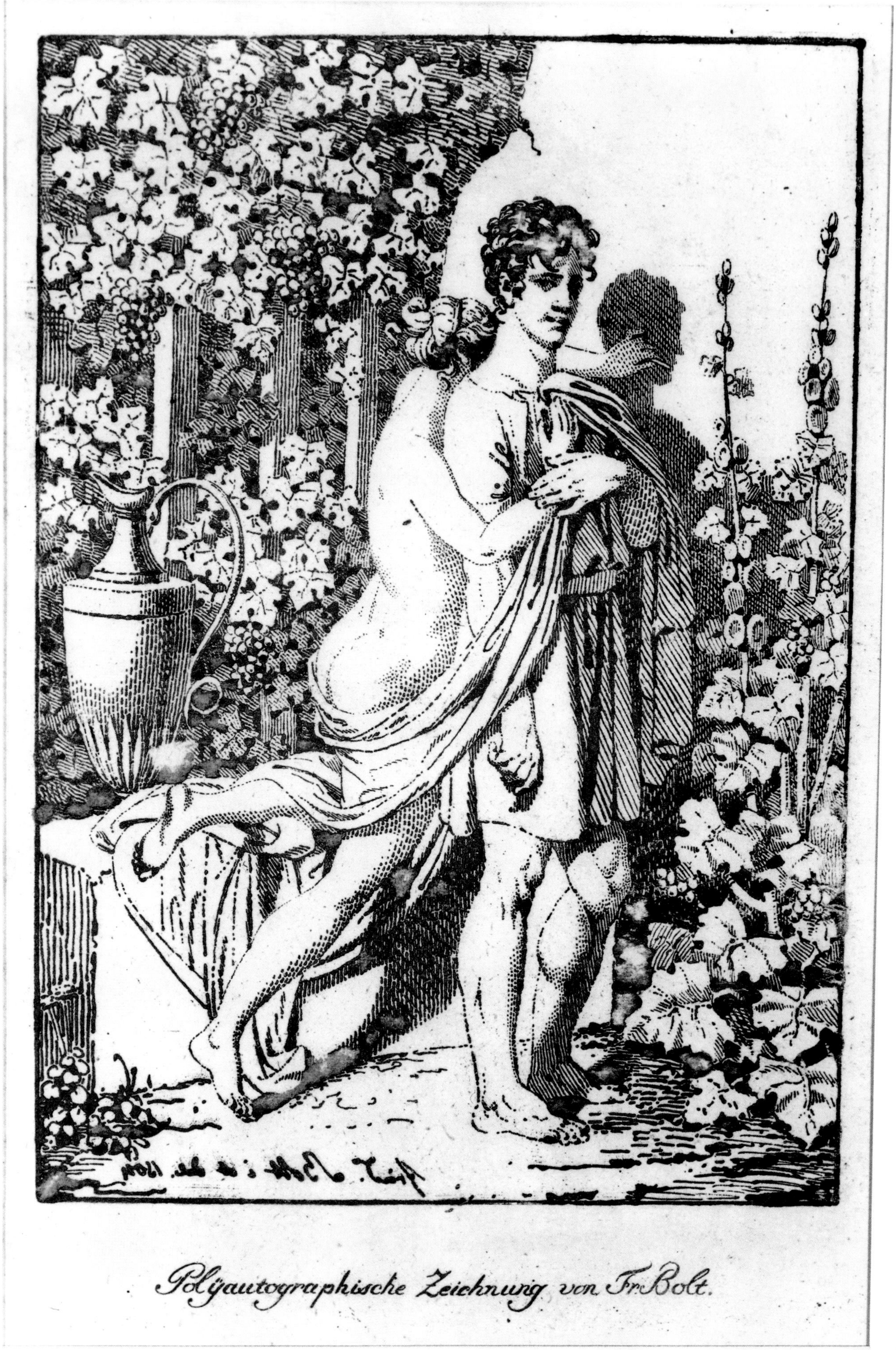

Cat. no. 65

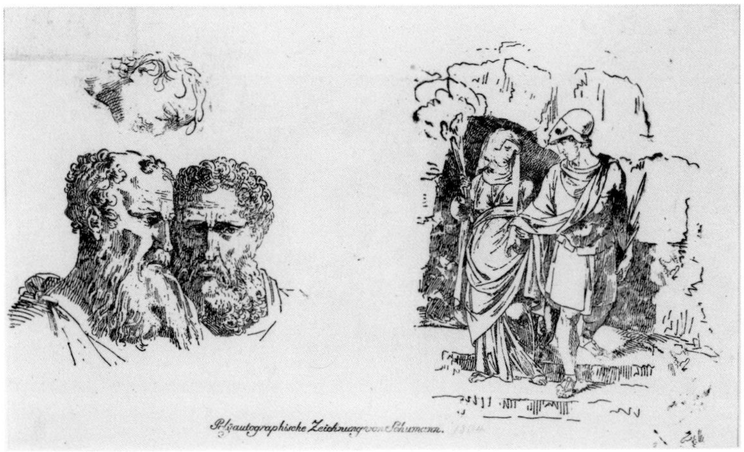

Fig. 65.1. Carl Franz Jacob Heinrich Schumann. *Various Figures*. Lithograph, 305 x 439 mm (12 x 17¼ in.) (sheet). Sarah Campbell Blaffer Foundation, Houston.

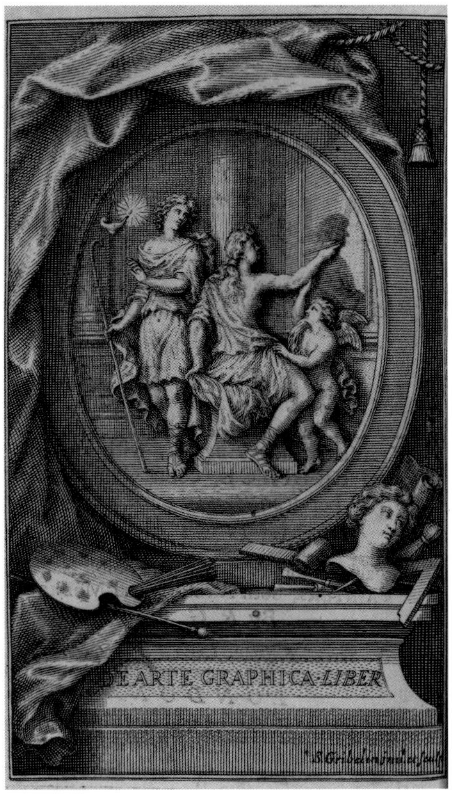

Fig. 65.2. Simon Gribelin. *De Arte Graphica Liber*, frontispiece to Charles-Alphonse Du Fresnoy, *The Art of Painting*, trans., John Dryden (1685, 2nd edition, 1716). Engraving, 148 x 90 mm (5⅞ x 3½ in.). Sarah Campbell Blaffer Foundation, Houston.

of several accounts of the origins of drawing or painting.[5] The focus, as a consequence, was on the young woman's tracing of the silhouette of her lover rather than on her father's putative invention of sculptural relief. By the second half of the eighteenth century, Diderot could assert that everyone was familiar with the story of the Corinthian maiden, but it was only infrequently depicted until the 1770s and again fell into disfavor in the 1820s,[6] its heyday corresponding with the fashion for drawn or cut-out silhouettes.

The story of the daughter of Butades was one of three possible tales regarding the origins of the art of painting that involved the tracing of shadows that were recounted in the early modern period. In one of the others, of uncertain source but recounted by Giorgio Vasari and depicted in his houses in Arezzo (1548) and Florence (c. 1570–73), a Lydian named Gyges, by a fire, notices his shadow on the wall and traces it with a piece of charcoal. In the third, a shepherd traces with his staff a sheep's shadow (or, later, his own) on the ground. All three were illustrated in Joachim von Sandrart's important *Teutsche Akademie* (1675).[7] Sandrart's depiction of the daughter of Butades may have been the earliest representation of the subject. In attributing the origins of painting to the colorless tracing of a shadow, all three stories emphasize the fundamental importance of drawing, what Vasari called the father of the arts.

But the appeal of the story of the daughter of Butades for a broader audience probably lay elsewhere. In the fifteenth century, Leon Battista Alberti had remarked on painting's ability to make the absent present, which became a truism in the literature of art and was often suggested in artworks—especially portraits—themselves. The story of the daughter of Butades sharpens the point of the concept, granting love an essential role in the making of art. The two lovers are often shown embracing as she traces the outline, as in Friedrich Bolt's lithograph. In Simon Gribelin's engraved frontispiece for John Dryden's translation of Charles-Alphonse Du Fresnoy's *The Art of Painting* (1685; 2nd edition, 1716), the maiden's efforts are literally supported and guided by Cupid (fig. 65.2), a motif that became quite common.[8] That Bolt's artist is nearly completely nude—her minimal drapery slipping considerably—adds to the sensual potential of the story.[9]

JC

1. See Keil 1963, esp. 66, 71.
2. Mezzotints after Lairesse's etching of c. 1670 (Hollstein 54) were made by Adriaan Schoonebeek (Hollstein 78) and an unknown artist with the initials G. L. Schumann's lithograph, because it, like the mezzotints, reverses Lairesse's composition, probably derives directly from that etching rather than through the intermediary of one of the mezzotints. I am grateful to James Ganz for pointing out the source of Bolt's composition.
3. Pliny 1984, 271 (35.15).
4. Ibid., 371–73 (35.151).
5. Franciscus Junius, in his *De pictura veterum libri tres* (Amsterdam 1637), seems to be the first to have credited the Corinthian maiden with the invention of art (Muecke 1999, 299). On the story of the daughter of Butades and its illustration, see Rosenblum 1957; Levitine 1958; Wille 1960; Wille 1972; Pigler 1974, 2:348–49; Asemissen and Schweikhart 1994, 11–12; Georgel and Lecoq 1997, 100–103; Bätschmann 1990, 45; Bermingham 1992; Akademie der Künste, Hochschule der Künste 1996, 233–34; Muecke 1999.
6. Diderot's comment appears in the *Encyclopédie,* quoted by Rosenblum 1957, 281 n. 20.

7. The *Teutsche Akademie* was reissued in Latin in 1683, with a new illustration of the daughter of Butades, which was also used in the 1768–75 German edition (see Rosenblum 1957, 280–81 n. 14). On Sandrart's importance for the subsequent depiction of the story, especially in Germany, see Wille 1960, 280. In Wille's review of the German examples, Bolt's lithograph seems to have escaped notice (indeed, the notice of the other writers on the subject as well), so that he could claim in regard to Franz Ignatz Oefele's etching of 1769, that "Darstellungen dieser Art, bei denen das Liebespaar steht, finden in späterer Zeit keine Nachfolge" (p. 287).

8. See also the epigram of Karl Wilhelm Ramler, a writer of great importance to late eighteenth- and early nineteenth-century Berlin artists, which reads in part: "Wer schuf das erste Bild aus Schatten an der Wand? / Die Liebe" (quoted by Wille 1960, 298). Daniel Chodowiecki focused, unusually, on a different moment in the story, in a drawing of the parting of the lovers after the silhouette had been traced (known from correspondence, May 11, 1787 [Steinbrucker 1927, 125]).

9. Joseph Wright of Derby altered his depiction of the story, adding more clothing, when some female visitors to his studio objected to the "divisions of the [maid's] posteriors appearing too plain through the drapery and its sticking so close" (quoted by Bermingham 1992, 140).

Pierre-Narcisse Guérin (1774–1833)

66. *The Vigilant One (Le Vigilant)*

c. 1820

Crayon lithograph, 270 x 198 mm (10⅝ x 7¾ in.) (image)

References: Beraldi 7:6; *Inventaire du fonds français* 9:465

Inscriptions: on table at left: *RE. / PG.*; below image: *Le Vigilant.*

Purchased from Carolyn Bullard, Dallas

1998.12

The figure in Pierre-Narcisse Guérin's *The Vigilant One* turns from drawing at a board on his lap and raises his arm to attempt to ward off winged Sleep. The sand in the hourglass at his side has run low, and a cock crowing in the window announces the dawn. Scrolls of paper, like the one on his drawing board, lie on the table and floor, discarded examples of his perhaps unsuccessful work. At the artist's feet, Cupid sleeps, his arrows—on which the single-minded artist treads—spilled uselessly on the ground. The three protagonists in the lithograph recall the figures in two paintings by Guérin: the *Aurora and Cephalus* of 1810 (Paris, Louvre) and the *Iris and Morpheus* of the following year. The latter was commissioned by the diplomat and avid collector Prince Nicolai Yousoupoff along with, and as a pendant to, an autograph copy of the *Aurora and Cephalus* (both St. Petersburg, Hermitage).[1] In the print, however, where the cloud-borne visitor tries to induce sleep, the situation and action are reversed from the paintings. There, the sensual, curly-haired male nudes are asleep, and the goddesses will rouse them: Cupid tugs on the finger of the mortal Cephalus, whom he induces to return the love of Aurora, the goddess of dawn; and Iris, the goddess of the rainbow, descends, in the company of Cupid, to bring a message from Juno to Morpheus, the god of dreams.

Industry, study, and labor were seen as fundamental to the early modern artist's highest professional achievement.[2] Giorgio Vasari included a yoked figure of Labor (*Fatica*) in the fresco decoration of his own house in Arezzo in 1548. Over two centuries later, "Labor et Ingenium" was inscribed on the diplomas of the members of the Royal Academy of Arts in London (see cat. no. 75). For Vasari, Michelangelo was the paragon of the artist devoted to his work, with scarcely any other consideration, who as a young man slept in his work clothes when too tired to continue (quite the opposite from Guérin's nude figure of the Vigilant One), and as an old man wore dogskin buskins for months at a time, so that when he removed them the skin would come off as well.[3] According to Vasari, Perino del Vaga worked on Sundays, feast days, and through most of the night, "thus stealing time from time itself."[4] In the illustration to the first of Vicente Carducho's *Diálogos de la pintura* (1633), the inscription avers that it is "by reason and labor, not pleasure and leisure" that the pictured artist progresses, and a cock—seemingly anticipating Guérin's—appears as "the symbol of that diligent wakefulness necessary for *studio*."[5]

Misguided labor, however, could be unproductive. Many artists were criticized for overworking compositions or attending too closely to peripheral issues. According to a Vasari anecdote, Paolo Uccello, stung by criticism, shut himself up in his house to study perspective; his wife said that he "would stay in his study all night, seeking to solve the problems of perspective, and that when she called him to come to bed, he would say: 'Oh, what a sweet thing is this perspective!'"[6] Guérin's young artist is likewise not necessarily

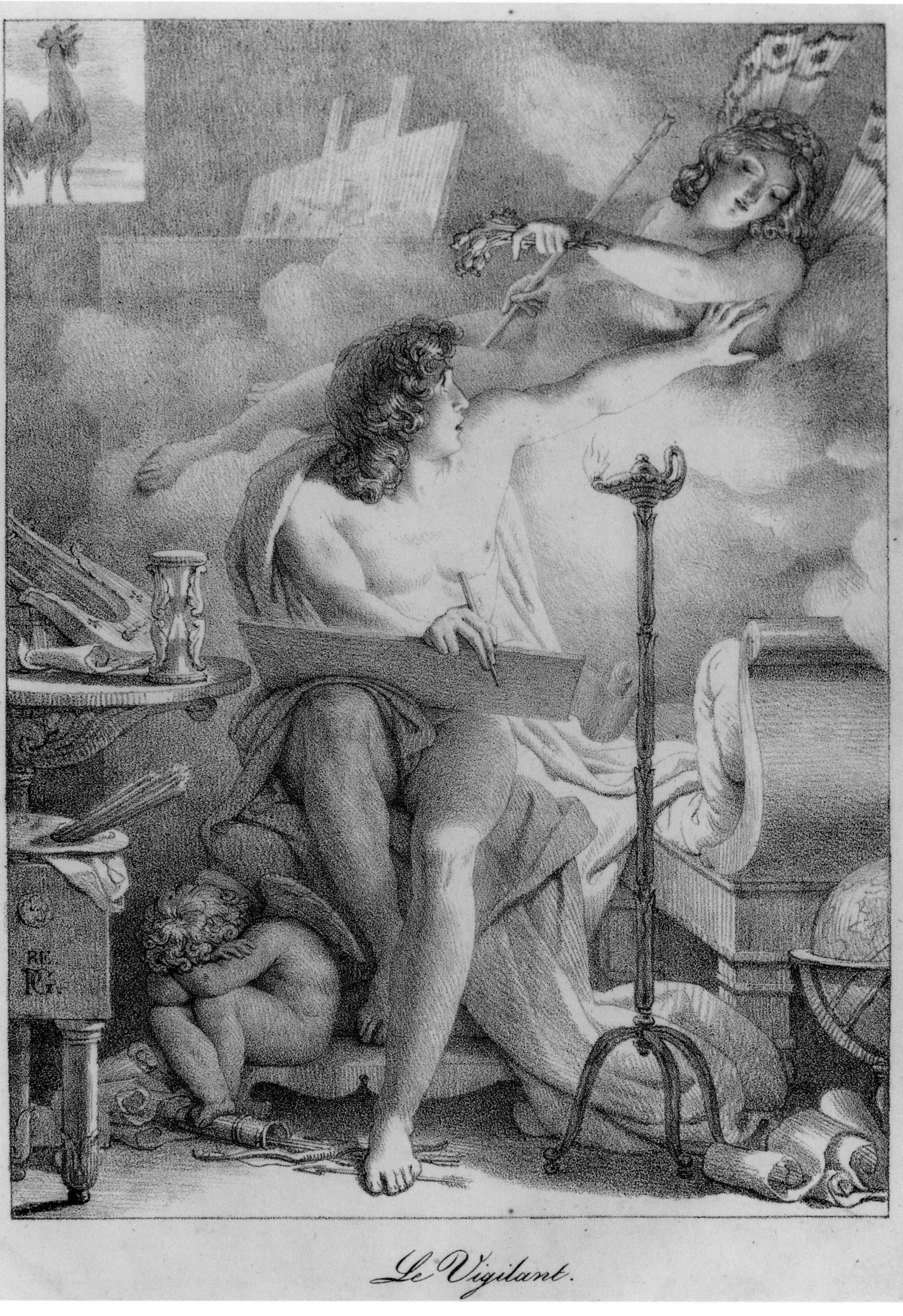

Cat. no. 66

Pierre Woeiriot (1532–1599)

67. *Phalaris Condemning Perillus to the Bronze Bull*

c. 1556

Engraving, 223 x 172 mm (8¾ x 6¾ in.)

References: Robert-Dumesnil 205, i/ii; *Inventaire du fonds français* 21, i/ii

Purchased from Kunsthandlung Helmut H. Rumbler, Frankfurt

1997.29

Several ancient authors recount the story of the sixth-century-B.C. Sicilian tyrant, Phalaris of Agrigentum, who punished his enemies, real or merely suspected, with ingenious tortures. The sculptor Perillus made for him a brazen bull, whose hollow interior could hold a victim to be slowly roasted alive. For the bull's inauguration, Phalaris had Perillus himself placed inside and killed, establishing early in the history of art a low point in patron-artist relations. Yet in recounting the story, Pliny calls Perillus more cruel than the tyrant: "such were the depths to which the sculptor had diverted this most humane of arts from images of gods and men!"[1] Phalaris's subjects eventually tired of his cruelty, revolted, and used the bull for their liberating tyrannicide. Dante used the story to describe the cry of Guido da Montefeltro in hell: "As the Sicilian bull which bellowed for the first time . . . with the cry of him who had shaped it with his file used to bellow with the voice of the victim, so that, though it was of brass, it yet seemed pierced with pain."[2] Much later, Johann Georg Hertel found the story exemplary for illustrating "Cruelty" in his 1758-60 edition of Cesare Ripa's *Iconologia,* noting that the sculptor's tongue was first cut out.[3] In Pierre Woeiriot's engraving, Phalaris is enthroned on a raised platform, watching as Perillus is shoved headlong into the belly of the bull, a fire already blazing under it. The bull's neck is stretched upward, its eyes wide and its mouth open, so that the victim's screams seem to bring the sculpture, bellowing, to life.

Woeiriot's engraving was part of a suite of three horrific subjects whose only mutual element is the burning of human bodies. In one, the wife of Hasdrubal, the Carthagian general who surrendered to the Romans to end the Third Punic War (146 B.C.), throws herself and her two children into the flames of the burning temple of Aesculapius, preferring death to capture. In the other, the deposed Byzantine emperor Phocas (reigned 602-610) is brought before his usurper, Heraclius, who beheaded him, severed his right arm, disemboweled him, and burned his corpse.

JC

1. Pliny 1984, 9:193 (34.89).
2. *Inferno,* canto XXVII, vv. 7-12 (Dante 1939, 335).
3. Maser 1971, pl. 77.

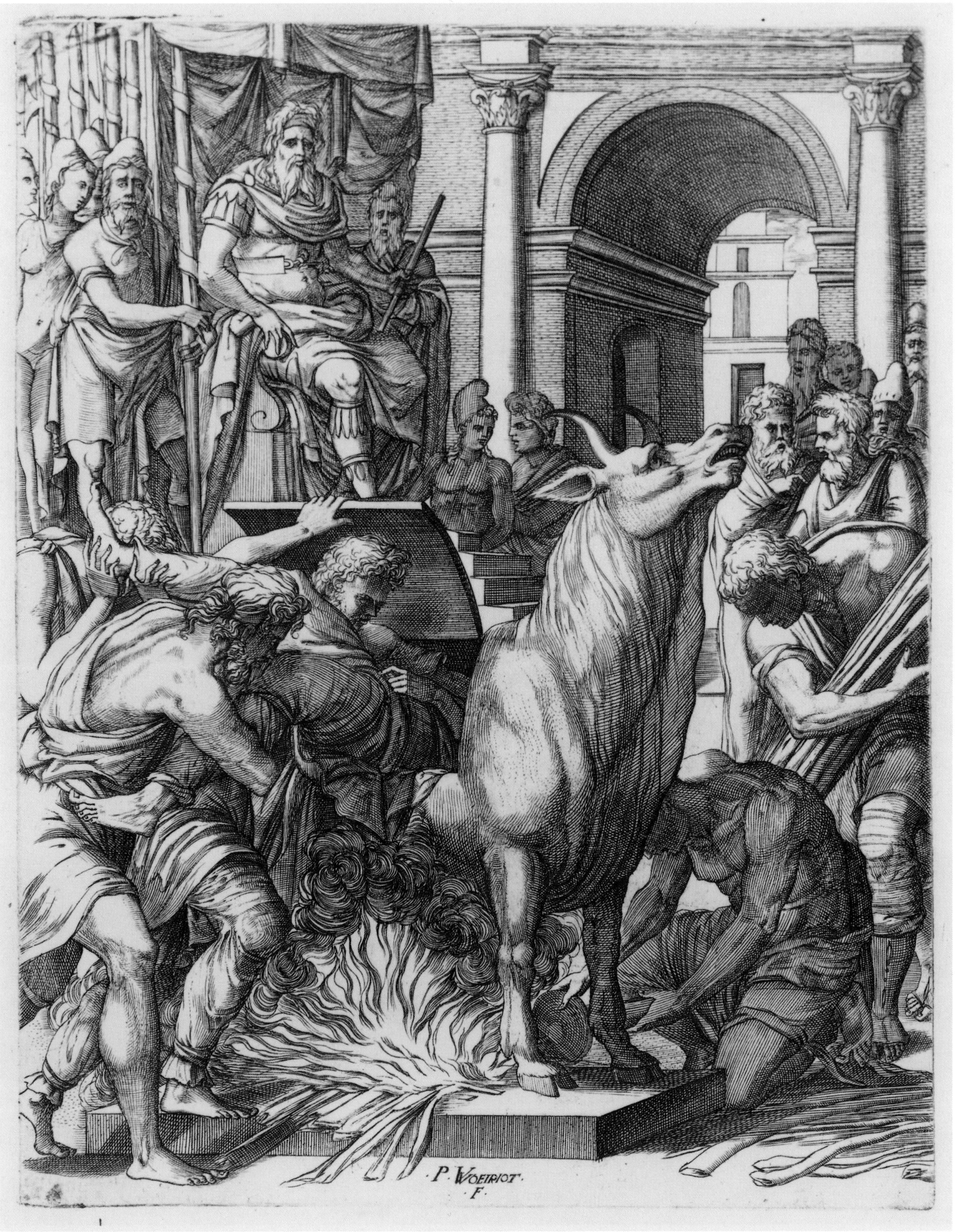

Cat. no. 67

Abraham Bosse (1602–1676)

68. *A Sculptor in His Studio*

1642

Etching, 257 x 326 mm (10⅛ x 12⅞ in.)

References: Duplessis 1386; Blum 204

Inscription: *Voicy la representation d'un Sculpteur dans son Attelier / Les Choses dont il forme ses ouurages sont diuerses, de diferente nature, et il y procede en diferentes facons, les dures Com[m]e la pierre et le bois il les faconne / en ostant de la matiere auec le cizeau le maillet et au[tr]es outilz, et les molles Comme la Cire et largile, il les faconne en mettant de la matiere auec le / poulce et le bauchoir, souuent il se fait un modelle de sa pensee com[m]e il en tient a la main et quapres il Coppie en une au[tr]e grandeur / fait a leau forte par ABoße, a Paris en Lisle du palais, lan 1642, auec Priuilege*

Purchased from R.E. Lewis, Larkspur, California

1996.16

Bosse was one of the busiest artists in seventeenth-century France; in addition to etching about one thousand five hundred plates, he was a tireless theorist, lecturer, and writer of the best-known and most-translated treatise on printmaking ever written, the *Traité des manières de graver en taille-douce* (1645), based on the etching technique he learned from Jacques Callot. Bosse was admitted as an honorary member of the Académie Royale de Peinture et de Sculpture in 1651, and was ultimately expelled from it in 1662 after unwisely accusing its leader Charles Le Brun of improperly applying the rules of perspective. An etcher of varied subject matter, Bosse is best known for secular scenes (or biblical scenes set in contemporary surroundings). These were sometimes issued singly, and sometimes arranged in series like the five senses, the four seasons, or as here, as part of a series of four prints treating the subjects of painting, sculpture, and printmaking. These scenes are most often set in wealthy interiors and populated with well-dressed people, and most offer a moralizing or instructive message.

Whether Bosse was aware of the idea of the *paragone,* or theoretical competition, between painting and sculpture, popular in the sixteenth century and mentioned in Castiglione's *Book of the Courtier,*[1] it seems at first glance quite clear in his series of prints that painting takes the prize. *The Noble Painter* (cat. no. 69), so identified by an inscription, is celebrated by a florid poem praising his abilities, whereas the print of the sculptor presents the rather

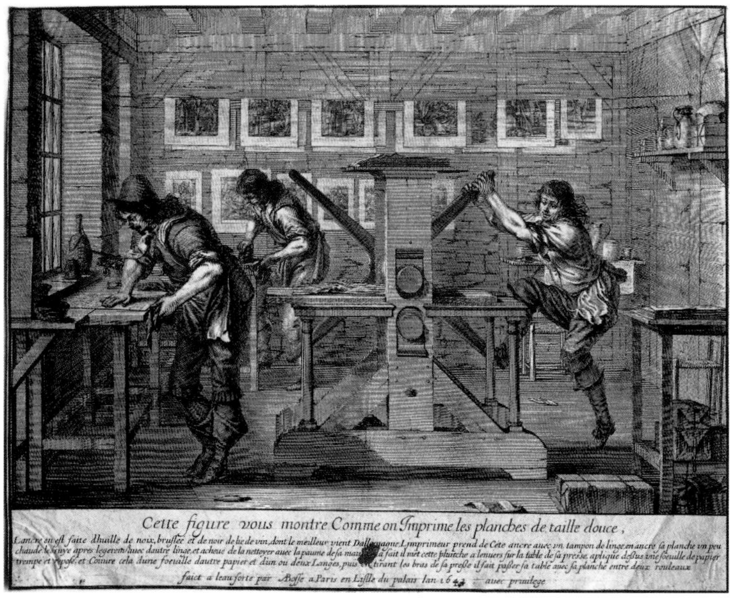

Fig. 68.1. Abraham Bosse. *The Engravers Workshop.* 1642. Etching-engraving, 260 x 327 mm (10¼ x 12⅞ in.). Fine Arts Museums of San Francisco; California State Library long loan, A032079.

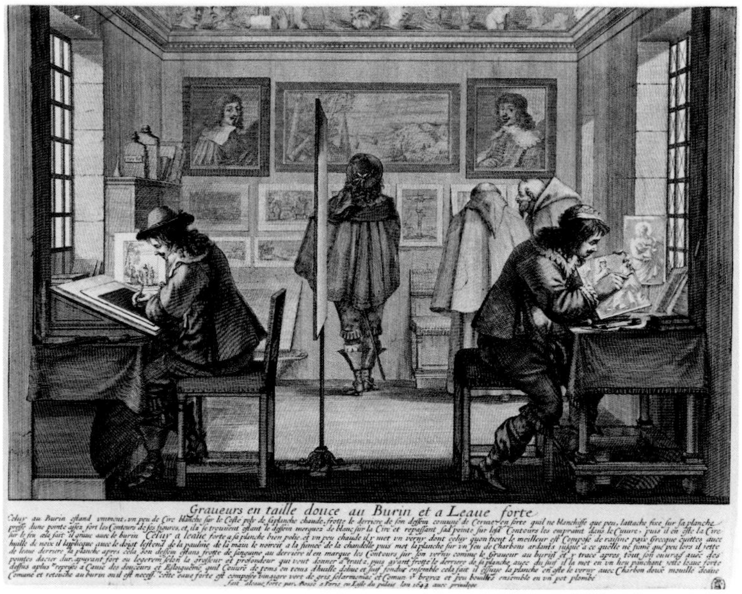

Fig. 68.2. Abraham Bosse. *Les Graveurs.* 1643. Etching-engraving, 257 x 313 mm (10⅛ x 12⅜ in.). Fine Arts Museums of San Francisco; gift of Dr. Ludwig A. Emge, 1971.17.725.

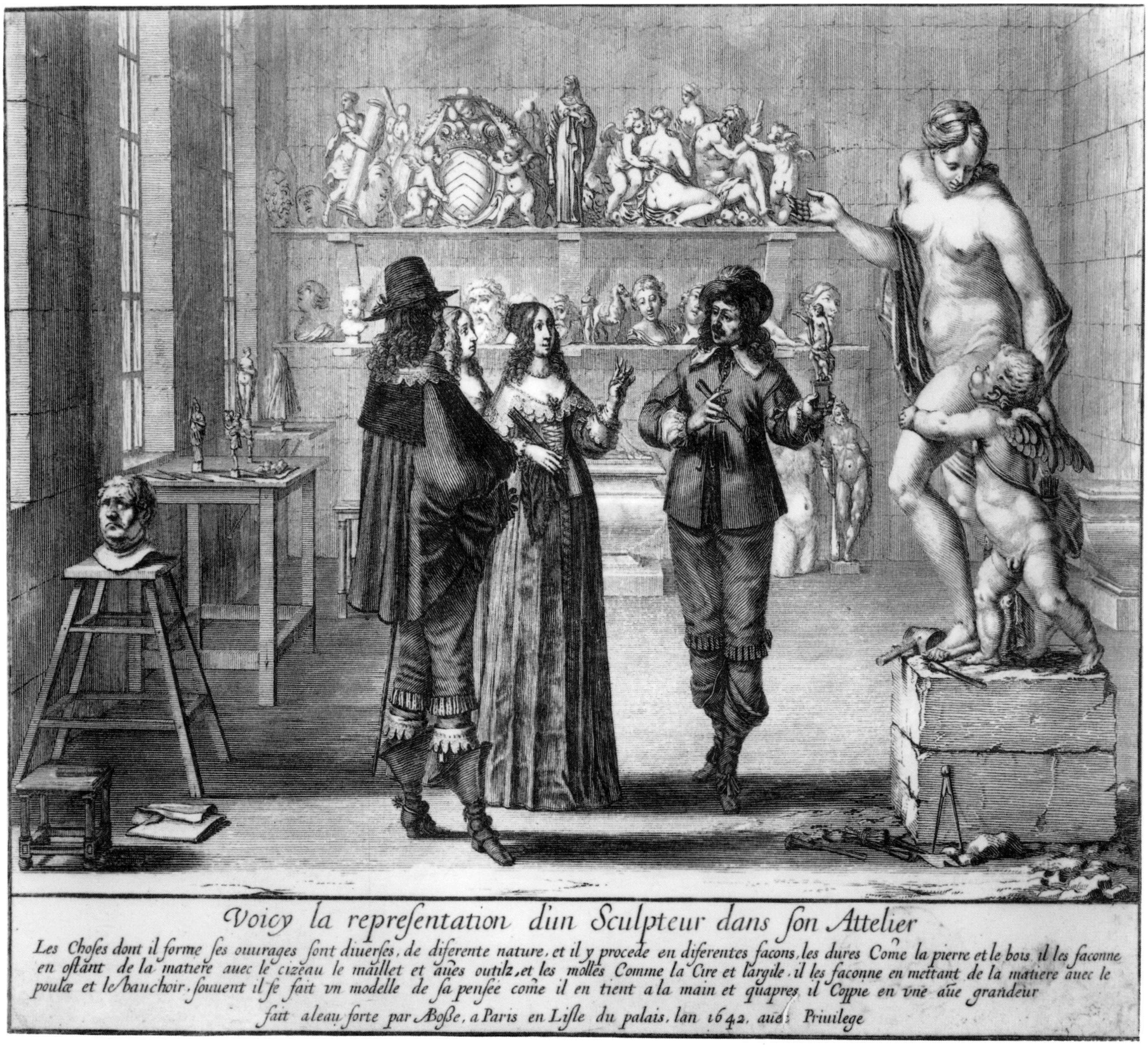
Voicy la representation d'un Sculpteur dans son Attelier
Les Choses dont il forme ses ouurages sont diuerses, de diferente nature, et il y procede en diferentes facons, les dures Come la pierre et le bois il les faconne en ostant de la matiere auec le cizeau le maillet et aues outilz, et les molles Comme la Cire et largile, il les faconne en mettant de la matiere auec le poulce et le bauchoir, souuent il se fait vn modelle de sa pensée come il en tient a la main et quapres il Coppie en vne aue grandeur
fait a leau forte par A Bosse, a Paris en Lisle du palais, lan 1642, auec Priuilege

Cat. no. 68

bland title "Here is the representation of a sculptor in his studio," followed by a dry description of the sculptor's materials and process[2] and no laudatory statements of any kind. The print dedicated to the sculptor and the two prints dedicated to printmaking (figs. 68.1, 68.2) have plain black line borders instead of the illusionistic gilt frame studded with fleurs-de-lis surrounding the scene of the painter's studio. Although Leonardo's *Trattato della Pittura* was not published in Paris until 1651, this scene perfectly epitomizes Leonardo's rationale for preferring painting to sculpture: "the well-dressed painter sits at great ease in front of his work, and moves a very light brush, which bears attractive colors, and he is adorned with such garments as he pleases. His dwelling is full of fine paintings and is clean and often filled with music, or the sound of different beautiful works being read, which are often heard with great pleasure, unmixed with the pounding of hammers or other noises."[3]

In fact, this etching of the sculptor seems in many ways poised between the lavish life of the painter and the assiduous, artisanal toil of the etcher, engraver, and printers, who are all shown concentrating on their work. The sculptor is not seated at ease, his walls and floor are bare, and his windows are devoid of draperies. However, as Sue Welsh Reed has noted, he, like the painter, is not shown actually working, but instead engaging in a discussion with his three guests that centers around the inventive nature of his calling.[4] He holds a chisel, but its position in his hand mimics that of the lady's folded fan to his right, and so it appears more as courtly prop than tool of his trade. In his left hand, he holds the small model for the over-life-sized statue, apparently of Venus and Cupid. As the text below explains, this is the initial model of his *pensée,* or conception, for the work, which he then has scaled up to its full, impressive size, partly by means of the dividers leaning against the statue's base. The lady at center raises her hand in admiration, looking at the sculpture as if astonished by this miraculous magnification. Bosse seems to have understood that the correct enlargement of the model to the finished statue is the part of the process most demanding of the sculptor's imagination and mathematical acumen, a point emphatically stated in the *Treatise on Sculpture* of Benvenuto Cellini, who deemed it the greatest success when there was no visible discrepancy between the small model and the full-sized work.[5]

In addition, Bosse communicates the sculptor's connection to his great predecessors in antiquity. We see many of the products of his studio—for example, on the top shelf a figure of Fortitude holding a column, a carved crest for an entryway bearing the arms of Cardinal Richelieu, and a female saint in monastic habit—interspersed with casts from antique sculpture, such as a bearded face, a head, and a leg clustered at the far left end of the top shelf. Whether many of these figures on the shelves are ancient or modern is left intentionally ambiguous.

Perhaps most interesting is Bosse's evocation of the sculptor's working and learning process and its important ties to ancient sculpture. At far left, a frowning male head (the so-called Vitellius, on which see cat. no. 40) stands on a support near the window. The placement there is purposeful, because the raking light from the window creates deep shadows at the left corner of the mouth, the left eye, and the left cheek, making these modeled forms more instructive to draw. That this is a scene set for sketching is further confirmed by the leather case of drawing instruments perched on the stool and the sketchbooks lying on the floor. This stool is sized for a child, indicating that our sculptor drew from casts of antique sculpture as a boy, but the drawing case and sketchbooks are now closed to show that his training is accomplished. This memory of the sculptor's proper education from the correct sources is balanced on the right side of the composition by the small model in his hand and the full-sized sculpture, a statement about what he can now achieve thanks to his lessons from the ancients. The tools on the floor at the right (especially the prominent dividers, which are also a geometer's and an architect's tool and therefore demonstrate intellect and not just manual skill) complete the parallel with his first tools on the left. The sculptor's lot seems to be long study and considerable physical labor in less than ideal conditions, but he does have the advantage of a fount of ancient inspiration to draw on at any moment.

AW

1. Castiglione's *Libro del cortegiano* was available in French beginning with the translation by Denys de Harsy, printed in Lyon in 1537.
2. The full inscription is translated as follows: "This is the representation of a sculptor in his studio / The things he uses to shape his works are many and of different natures, and he proceeds in various manners with them. The hard ones, like stone and wood, he shapes by removing material with the chisel, the mallet, and with other tools, and the soft ones, like wax and clay, he shapes by adding material with his thumb and a shaping tool. Often he makes a model of his conception, like the one he holds here in his hand, that afterwards he copies in a larger size." Present author's translation.
3. Leonardo 1956, 1:37.
4. Reed 1998, 54.
5. Cellini 1967, 141. These treatises were originally published in Florence in 1568, and were undoubtedly known in French academic circles.

Abraham Bosse (1602–1676)

69. *The Noble Painter (Le Noble Peintre)*

c. 1642

Etching, 257 x 327 mm (10⅛ x 12⅞ in.)

References: Duplessis 1385; Blum 1076, i/ii

Inscriptions: below image: *le Noble Peintre / A Bosse in et fe / le Blond excud auec Priuilege du Roy.*; in cartouche: *Que le Graueur jngenieux / Faict bien icy voir à nos yeux / Lexcellence de la peinture! / Et que c'et [sic] Art me semble beau, / Quand il jmite la nature. / Par les merueilles du pinceau! / Celuy dont la noble maniere / Joint les ombres à la lumiere / En mille tableaux differans; / N'est pas de ces Peintres vulgaires, / Qui passent pour des ignorans / Dans leurs Ouurages ordinaires / Il execute, & au jour / Tout ce que la Guerre et l'Amour / Ont de memorable et d'estrange; / Et semble à qui voit ses dessains, / Que c'est Apelle ou Michel l'Ange / Qui guide son Art et ses mains. / Soit qu'il represente Bellonne, / Ou Pallas aue [sic] sa Gorgonne, / Ou Cupidon armé de traits; / Il se met si fort en estime / Par ses admirables portraits, / Que châcun dict qu'il les anime. / Mais quand il nous peint les lauriers / De Lovys, honneur des Guerriers, / Et vray portrait de la Victoire / Il fait vn chef-doeuure sans prix / Pour ce grand Roy, qui dans l'histoire / Est l'objet des meilleurs Esprits*

Purchased from Paul Prouté, Paris

1999.31

The "noble painter" in Abraham Bosse's print is dressed as finely as the nobleman who is visiting his neat, spacious, and airy studio. Among the paintings lining the wall is a shelf of books, suggesting the artist's learning, which is unusual but recalls the books in Enea Vico's depiction of Baccio Bandinelli's academy (cat. no. 21), and Bosse's painter embodies the image and social status to which many early modern artists, like Bandinelli, aspired. Missing are the appurtenances and activities often found in depictions of artists' studios, such as the nearly ubiquitous color grinder, which tend to emphasize the painter's status as a master craftsman (and successful businessman) rather than, as here, a gentlemanly intellectual. He sits comfortably on a cushion, one slippered foot propped on his easel, in front of a portrait of King Louis XIII that he has been finishing.[1] Among the paintings against the wall are a couple of portraits on the floor, recognizable as likenesses of Anne of Austria and Cardinal Richelieu.[2] The painter pauses to look at a print held up to him by a boy. It is after a painting by Andries Both that depicts a poor painter at an easel with his wife and children; both the bedraggled figures and the wretched environment are the polar opposite of Bosse's painter and studio. The composition was very popular, reproduced in print at least six times; Bosse probably made use of Nicolas Viennot's engraving.[3] The poem inscribed on Viennot's print is a dialogue among the family in which the painter blames his failures on fate, his wife chastises him for his affection for "the pipe and the bottle," and the children bemoan the fact that they were not born to "those brave workers like a Zeuxis, Apelles, a Parrhasius, a Timanthes and a hundred other painters who with a learned hand . . . have changed their brushes into laurels."

The lengthy poem inscribed on Bosse's print, by contrast, lauds the painter and his profession. It appears as if on a strip of paper pinned to the surface of a painting, which is set in a frame decorated with fleurs-de-lis. The print is thus quite different from Bosse's other representations of artists and craftsmen in their studios and workshops, which are enclosed by a simple border (cat. no. 68). This simple trompe-l'oeil echoes the inscription's exclamation that the art is lovely "when it imitates nature by the marvels of the brush." The laudatory poem continues: in "a thousand different paintings," the art can depict "all that war and love have that is memorable and strange." It is as if Apelles or Michelangelo guides the artist's hands. (It may be a depiction of Apelles painting Alexander the Great's lover Campaspe in the center of the wall [for the subject, see cat. no. 70], and the painting next to it may be the Bellona or Minerva with her gorgon shield also named in the inscription.) The painter is particularly admired for his portraits, and when he paints "the laurels of Louis, honor of warriors, and true portrait of victory, he makes a priceless masterpiece."

The elegant visitor at left, who looks at the viewer and gestures toward the painter, may be "speaking" the inscription, extolling the virtues of painting.[4] Since at least the early sixteenth century, an understanding of the arts was considered to be essential for the constitution of a proper gentleman, and an even narrower segment

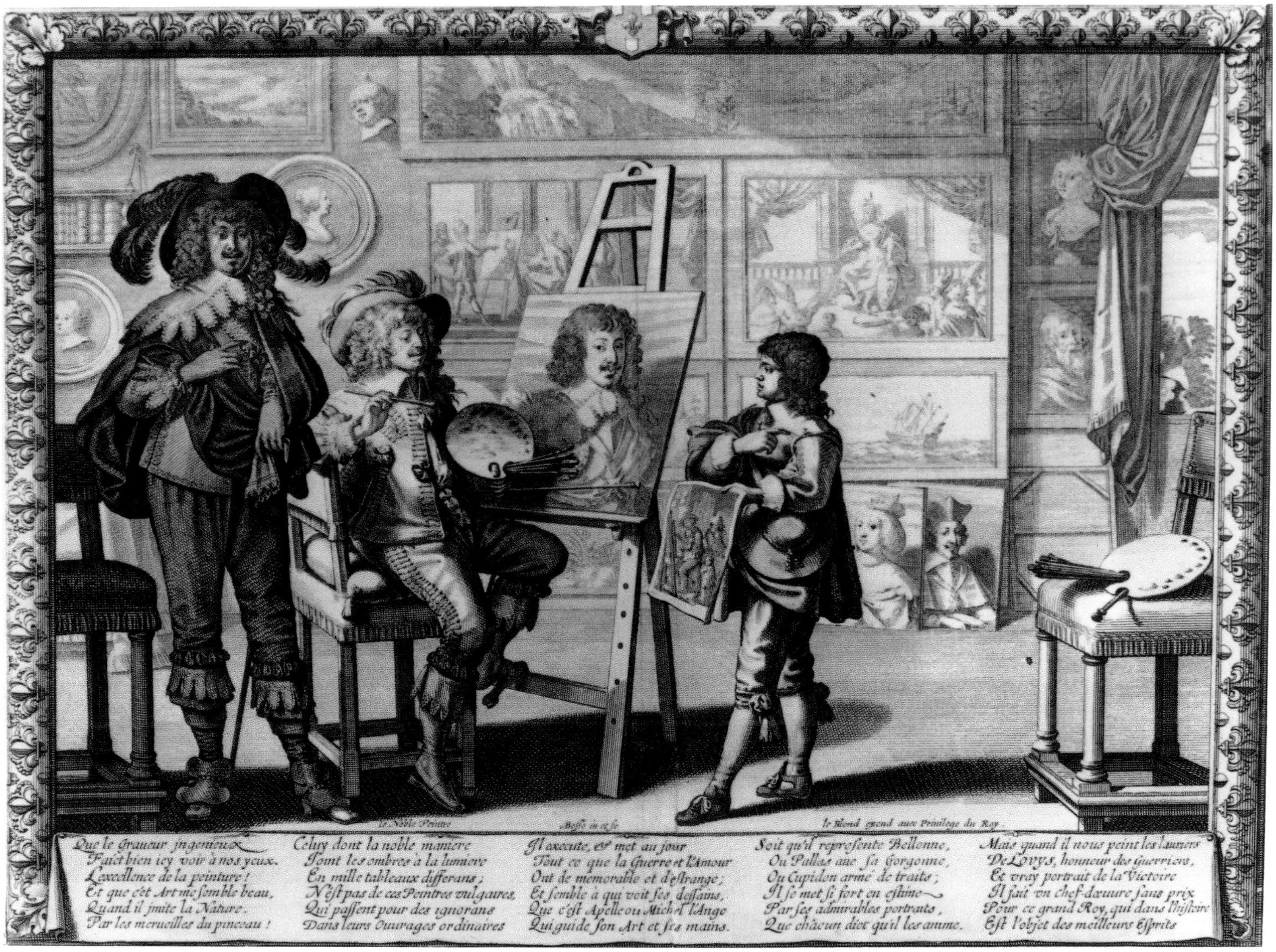

Cat. no. 69

of society, which became increasingly coherent in the seventeenth century, could be considered "art lovers."[5] Visits to artists' studios became common and were often represented, as both historical and genre subjects.[6] A French writer in 1635 told the art lover that "to know how to discourse on this noble profession [painting], you must have visited the studio and disputed with the masters, have seen the magic effects of the pencil, and the unerring judgement with which the details are worked out."[7]

JC

1. The portrait is also sometimes taken to be that of the gentleman at left, said by Költzsch 2000, 235, who could be, for example, visiting to check on the progress of the painting. Vidal 1992, 165, characterizes the artist as "the worldly gentleman leisurely producing an image with the time and intelligence to converse about art with other *gens de qualité*."
2. Goldfarb 2002, 371.
3. See De Jongh and Luijten 1997, 247–52; Költzsch 2000, 236–37.
4. Suggested by Stoichita 1997, 233–34.
5. See Van de Wetering 1999, 22–25.
6. See Raupp 1984, 329–31; Asemissen and Schweikhart 1994, 204–209.
7. Quoted from the so-called *Brussels Manuscript* by Van de Wetering 1999, 24. Van de Wetering's observation that "the knowledge gained from studio visits mainly concerned the miracle of the illusion of reality on a flat surface" is supported in part by the inscription on Bosse's *Noble Painter*.

Salvator Rosa (1615–1673)

70. *Alexander the Great in the Studio of Apelles*

c. 1662

Etching and drypoint, 459 x 277 mm (18⅛ x 10⅞ in.) (trimmed)

References: Bartsch 4; Wallace 114, ii/ii

Inscription: *Alexandro M. multa imperite in officina disserenti / silentium comiter suadebat Apelles, rideri eum dicens / a pueris, qui colores tererent. / Saluator Rosa inu. scul.*

Purchased from C. G. Boerner, New York

1997.8

The story illustrated by Salvator Rosa is taken from Pliny's *Natural History,* which is quoted almost exactly in Rosa's inscription: "In fact, he also possessed great courtesy of manners, which made him more agreeable to Alexander the Great, who frequently visited his studio—for, as we have said, Alexander had published an edict forbidding any other artist to paint his portrait; but in the studio Alexander used to talk a great deal about painting without any real knowledge of it, and Apelles would politely advise him to drop the subject, saying that the boys engaged in grinding the colours were laughing at him: so much power did his authority exercise over a King who was otherwise of an irascible temper."[1] Alexander, seated at right and accompanied by soldiers, points to Apelles's work. The painter cautions him to silence with a finger to his lips and a gesture toward his apprentices beside and behind the painting, who smile and laugh. The boys are not grinding pigments, as Pliny and Rosa's inscription say, but one of them holds a drawing board. On the large canvas (an anachronism) resting on the floor in front of Apelles appears, lightly etched, a painting identifiable as a *Diana in the Midst of a Band of Maidens Offering a Sacrifice,* which Pliny describes as one of Apelles's most famous works, in which he may be thought to have surpassed Homer's verse on the same subject.[2]

Apelles, whose skill was legendary, was probably the ancient artist most frequently referred to and depicted in early modern Europe. Beginning in the fifteenth century, many artists were called a "new Apelles," although artists, exercising some (possibly false) modesty, did not refer explicitly to themselves as such, and even the audacious Rosa admitted in his poem *Invidia,* "I am not an Apelles."[3] Nonetheless, the *Alexander the Great in the Studio of Apelles* is one of several self-referential works by Rosa, including his contemporaneous *Genius* (cat. no. 58).

The conventional naming of a painter as a "new Apelles" not only flattered the artist but was also a reminder of the high esteem in which a great king held an artist. This esteem is best exemplified by Pliny's story of Alexander's request of Apelles that he paint a portrait of the king's mistress, Campaspe. Apelles fell in love with Campaspe, and Alexander, with royal generosity, gave Campaspe to the painter. The subject of Alexander in the studio while Apelles painted the portrait of Campaspe was often depicted in the early modern

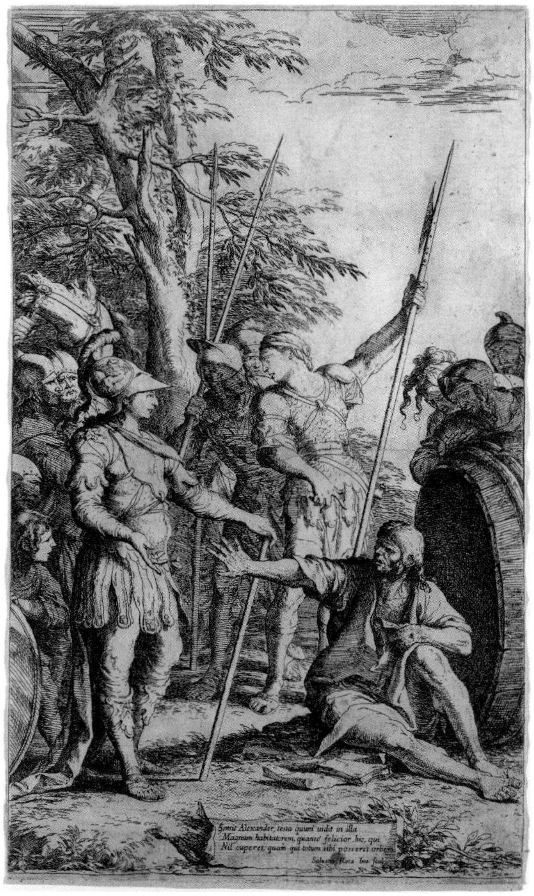

Fig. 70.1. Salvator Rosa, Italian, 1615–1673. *Diogenes and Alexander.* 1662. Etching and drypoint. Catalogue raisonné: B 6 I; W 108 I. 458 x 276 mm (18 1/16 x 10⅞ in.) (platemark). Museum of Fine Arts, Boston. Katherine E. Bullard Fund in memory of Francis Bullard. 1970.651. Photograph copyright 2004 Museum of Fine Arts, Boston.

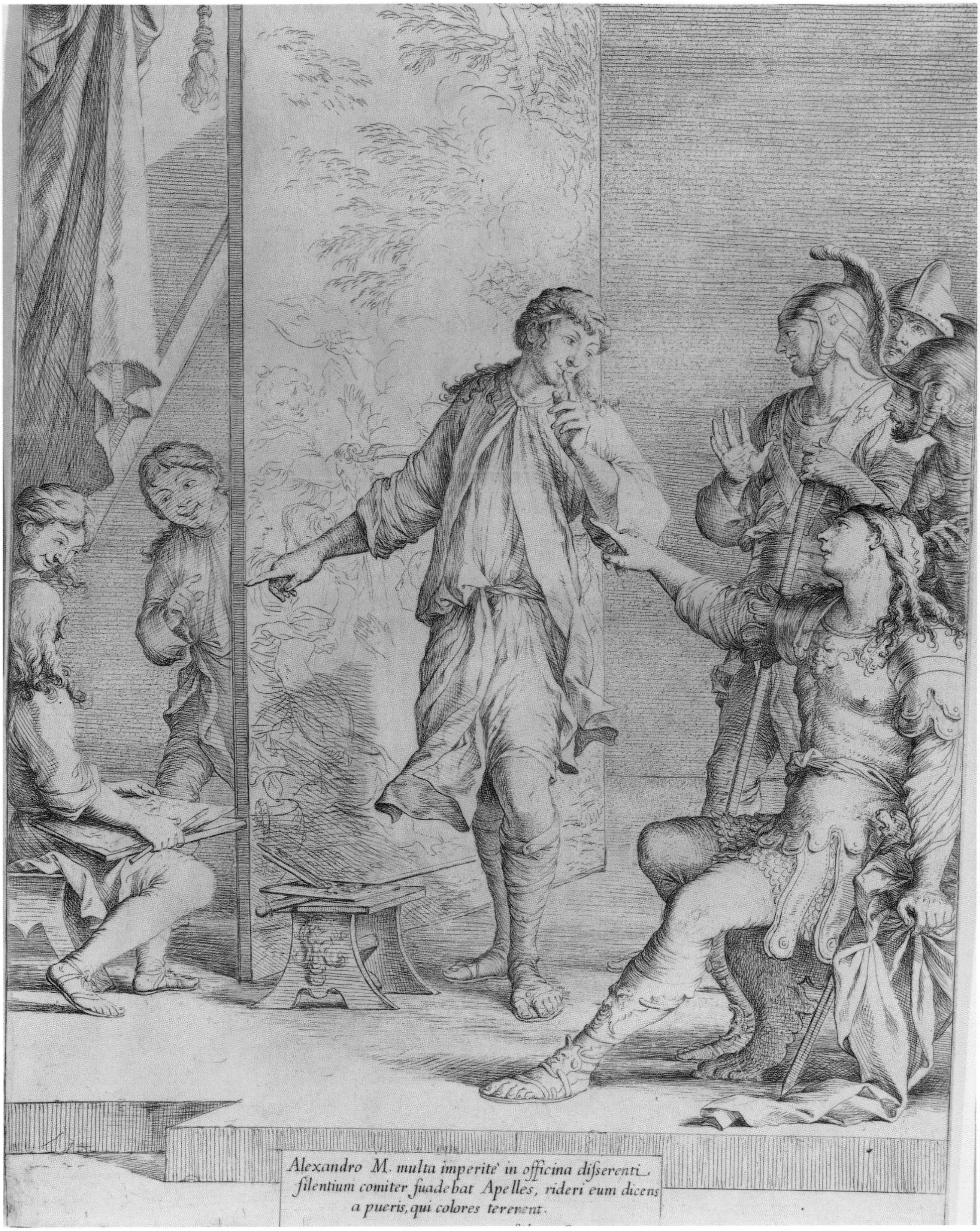
Alexandro M. multa imperite in officina disserenti
silentium comiter suadebat Apelles, rideri eum dicens
a pueris, qui colores tererent.

Cat. no. 70

era[4] and spawned numerous stories of royal visits to painters' studios, which were used to argue for the nobility of painting. The subject of Rosa's etching, however, was almost never depicted, presumably because of the poor light in which it casts patrons.[5] In the story, Apelles reminds the viewer of his aesthetic ignorance, albeit more gently with the august Alexander than with the humble cobbler who appears in a similar anecdote of Apelles, also told by Pliny (see cat. no. 71). Rosa had, notoriously, little patience with pretentious and ignorant patrons, regardless of their social status. Filippo Baldinucci, Rosa's contemporary and one of his earliest biographers, recounts the story of Rosa's encounter with a doctor who was tending to a prince and patron of Rosa's. The doctor remarked that he would like a work by Rosa but asked him not to start it "until I will have provided [*somministrato,* the same term used for administering medicine] the idea and concept of the painting that I want from you." Rosa did not answer until the doctor began to write a prescription for the prince, at which point he told the doctor not to write further until he could suggest to him how to proceed. The doctor, not understanding the joke, said that it was something that he, not Rosa, knew how to do. The painter replied, "better and much better do I know how to suggest prescriptions to you than you know how to provide thoughts for my paintings to me." The prince laughed and applauded, the doctor was mortified, "and the negotiation for the painting died on its own bed."[6]

Rosa depicted another humbling moment for Alexander, this time by the cynic philosopher Diogenes, another alter ego for the artist, in an etching that may have been intended as a pendant to the *Alexander the Great in the Studio of Apelles* (fig. 70.1).[7] Alexander sought out Diogenes, who rejected virtually all material possessions and lived in a barrel. When the emperor asked if he could do anything for him, Diogenes responded: "Yes, stand a little out of my sun." Rather than being angry at the impudence, Alexander was impressed by the philosopher's disdain for his grandeur, an analogue for Rosa's independence from his critics and patrons.

JC

1. Pliny 1984, 9:325 (35, 85–86).
2. Pliny 1984, 9:333 (35, 96); see Wallace 1979, 92.
3. For comparisons to Apelles, see Kennedy 1964; Warnke 1993, 40–41, and passim; see also cat. nos. 39, 69. In the satire *Invidia,* Rosa considers executing a painting akin to Apelles's famous depiction of Calumny, but admits, "Un Apelle io non son" (Cesareo 1892, 1:303).
4. See Georgel and Lecoq 1987, 65–69; Asemissen and Schweikhart 1994, 19–25; Költzsch 2000, 87–102, 109–17.
5. In fact, Cast 1981, 187, identifies only two known representations of the subject, Rosa's and one by the eighteenth-century Venetian painter Antonio Novelli. See also Georgel and Lecoq 1987, 64–65. For a seventeenth-century reference to the story in France with the purpose of encouraging patrons to educate themselves in the arts, see Posner 1993, 594.
6. Baldinucci 1974, 5:488–89; cf. pp. 485, 486. See also cat. no. 58.
7. See Roworth 1977, 303–37.

Christian Bernhard Rode (1725–1797)

71. *Apelles and the Cobbler*

1773

Etching, 174 x 223 mm (6⅞ x 8¾ in.)

References: Nagler 105, i/ii; Le Blanc 132, i/ii; Jacobs 98

Purchased from C. G. Boerner, New York

2001.5

The story of Apelles, the fourth-century B.C. Greek painter, and a cobbler was told by the ancient Roman writer, Pliny the Elder:

> [A] habit of his was when he had finished his works to place them in a gallery in the view of passers by [*in pergula transeuntibus*], and he himself stood out of sight behind the picture and listened to hear what faults were noticed, rating the public as a more observant critic than himself. And it is said that he was found fault with by a shoemaker because in drawing a subject's sandals he had represented the loops in them as one too few, and the next day the same critic was so proud of the artist's correcting the fault indicated by his previous objection that he found fault with the leg, but Apelles indignantly looked out from behind the picture and rebuked him, saying that a shoemaker in his criticism must not go beyond the sandal [*ne sutor ultra crepidam*]—a remark that has also passed into a proverb.[1]

represent the flourishing of the arts, or, as Rubens himself put it, "the flourishing of the Kingdom of France, with the resuscitation of the sciences and arts thanks to the liberality and splendor of Her Majesty."[6] In *The Queen Triumphant,* Marie wears a fleur-de-lis mantle and a plumed helmet, stands on discarded arms and armor, and holds a statuette of Victory.[7] She appears with attributes of Minerva, one of her mythological tutelaries, who presided over the arts of both war and peace; in fact, it was quite common in seventeenth-century France to portray women in the guise of Minerva.[8] More generally, the flourishing of the arts under wise governance and in times of peace (and, conversely, their languishing and destruction in times of war) was a common theme of early modern allegorical imagery.

The print is dedicated to Jean-Paul Bignon (1662–1743), Abbot of Saint-Quantin (or Quentin), Councillor of State and Master of Louis XIV's library, and President of the Royal Academy of Sciences and of the Royal Academy of Inscriptions and Medals, whose regulations he helped to set in 1701.[9] Bignon was the grandson of the renowned scholar and lawyer Jerôme Bignon and the son of Jerôme Bignon II. Like Jean-Paul after them, Jerôme I and Jerôme II were each Councillor of State and Master of the royal library.[10]

JC

1. See Aulanier 1958, 47–48, and figs. 15–16; Montagu 1963, 401, 407; Wildenstein 1965, 3–31; Beauvais 2000, 1:45, 531.
2. The *France Triumphant* is self-published ("Chez lauteur"). Heinecken 1778–90, 1:237, though noting that Simon died in 1677, ascribed the engravings of the Galerie d'Apollon to him, making no mention of their date of 1695, or of Augustin Jacques.
3. Described by Guillet de Saint-Georges (Aulanier 1958, 47), whose authority is, however, suspect; see below.
4. Cited by Aulanier 1958, 47, and quoted by Beauvais 2000, 531.
5. See Dowley 1955, 278, for the definition of *Minerve gauloise* as "La France and Minerva in one." For the snake as an ancient attribute of Minerva, see Haskell and Penny 1981, 269.
6. Quoted by Millen and Wolf 1989, 165.
7. On the painting, see Millen and Wolf 1989, 224–27.
8. See Dowley 1955, who interprets Rubens's *The Queen Triumphant* as "a *Minerve gauloise,* who is just shedding her role as goddess of war to resume her patronage of the arts of peace" (p. 264). In 1663 Simon Renard de Saint-André presented to the Royal Academy of Painting and Sculpture as his reception piece just such a painting: a double portrait of Anne of Austria as Minerva and Marie Thérèse as Abundance or Concord (Dowley 1955, 265). A later inventory attributes another double portrait, now lost, to Saint-André, this of Marie de Medici as Minerva, with Louis XIII (Dowley 1955, 275).
9. The inscription on a medallion from 1704 featuring Bignon's portrait is similar to that on the print: *IEAN PAVL BIGNON ABBÉ DE St QUENTIN CONSEILLER D'ÉTAT ORDINAIRE PRÉSIDENT DE L'ACADÉMIE ROYALLE DES INSCRIPTIONS ET DE CELLE DES SCIENCES* (Administration des monnaies et médailles 1892, 203). In 1716, the academy was renamed as the "Académie des inscriptions et belles-lettres."
10. See Perrault 1696–1700, 1:43–44, who mentions Jerôme I's appointment in 1642 as *Grand Maistre* of the king's library and indicates that one of Jerôme I's sons was currently (1696) Councillor of State and the other *Premier President du Grand Conseil,* without naming either one; Carey 1972, 219, 232, 247 n. 130, who notes that Jean-Paul Bignon's nephew and great-nephew were also royal librarians. P. Van Schuppen's engraved portrait of Jerôme Bignon I (Perrault 1696–1700, 1: opposite p. 43) carries the same family coat-of-arms found on Saint-André's print.

Giandomenico Tiepolo (1727–1804)

74. *The Arts Paying Homage to Pius VI*

1775

Etching, 431 x 318 mm (17 x 12½ in.)

References: Rizzi 158; De Vesme 98

Inscription: on open book at lower left: *DOMENICO / TIEPOLO / INVENT / E INCISE / ANNO / 1775*

Purchased from Hill-Stone, New York

1999.18

This dynamic allegory prominently displays the coat of arms of Pope Pius VI (Giovanni Angelo Braschi, 1717–1799), surmounted by the papal tiara and the keys of Saint Peter and borne aloft by a congregation of putti, while below a personification of the Church elevates a chalice with the Eucharist. At the bottom right, personifications of Painting—identifiable by her conventional attributes, paintbrushes and a palette, Music, and Architecture pay homage to the papal authority of Pius VI, and various symbols of

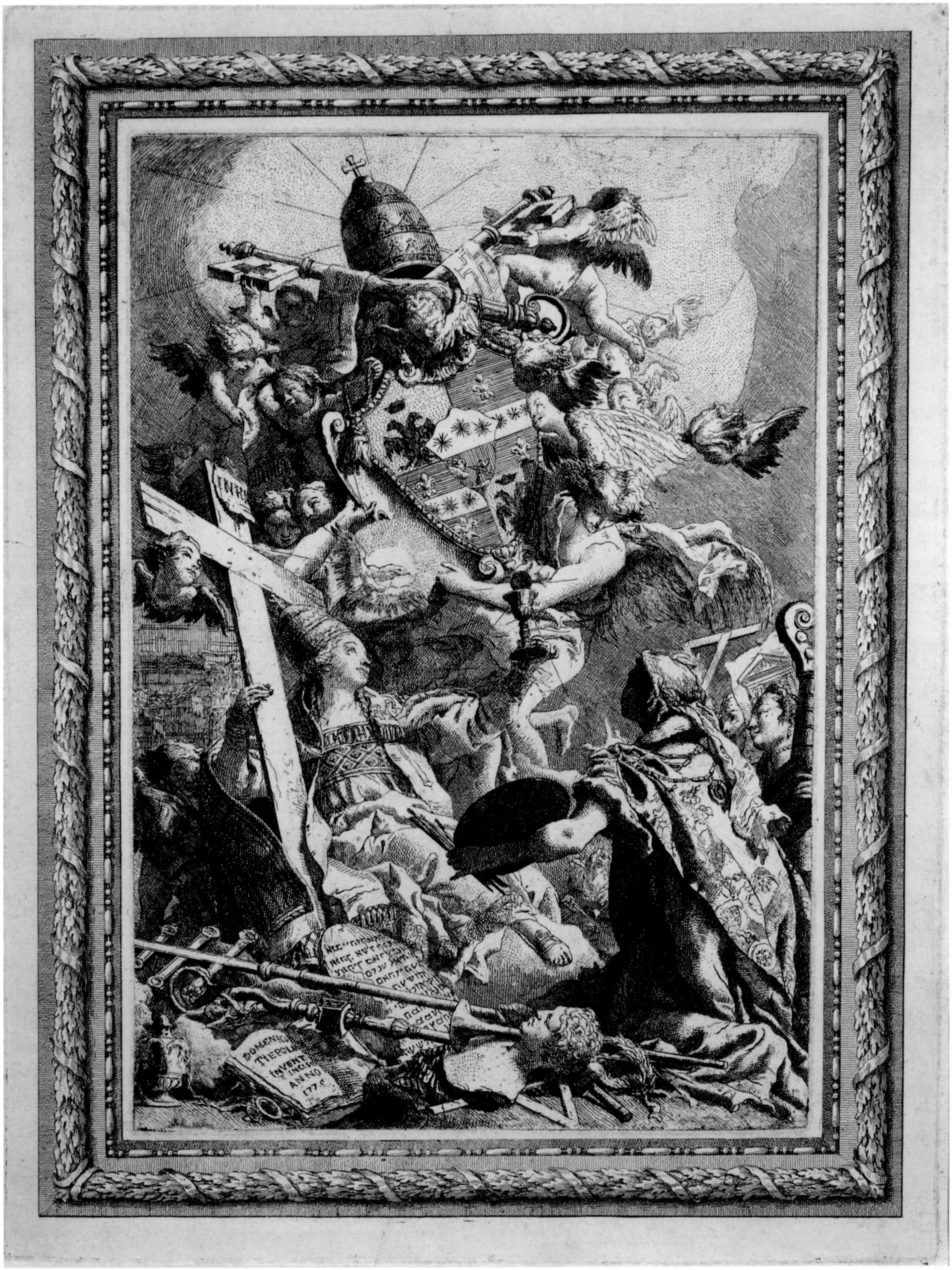

Cat. no. 74

77. *Time Smoking a Picture*

1761

Etching and mezzotint, 246 x 183 mm (9⅝ x 7¼ in.)

REFERENCE: Paulson 208, iii/iii

INSCRIPTIONS: on picture frame: *Crates____ : Χρονος γαρ 'ον τεχτωγ σοφος, / 'Απαντα δ'εργαζομενο–ςαθενεξερα / See Spectator / Vol: II: Page 83.*; on urn: *VARNISH.*; at lower right: ______ *As Statues moulder into Worth. P:W:*; below image: *To Nature and your Self appeal, / Nor learn of others, what to feel. Anon:.*

Purchased from Andrew Edmunds, London

1983.5.92

Time Smoking a Picture was originally intended to function as a subscription ticket for an engraving after Hogarth's painting *Sigismunda,* now in the Tate Gallery, London (on Hogarth's subscription tickets, see cat. no. 61); when the project foundered, the subscription information was removed from the plate, which Hogarth then printed as a fully independent image. The immediate occasion for the print explains its caustic tone: Hogarth had been irritated by the high price raised at auction in London in 1758 by a painting of Sigismunda (or Ghismonda), a tragic lover from Boccaccio's *Decameron,* that he considered inferior (the painting at the time was attributed to Correggio but in the twentieth century was reattributed to Francesco Furini and is now lost). He executed a picture of the same subject as a means of proving the abilities of modern English artists in competition with continental artists of the past, painting it for his patron, Richard Grosvenor, who, however, refused the work. The print after *Sigismunda* was begun by James Basire under Hogarth's direction but not completed by the time of Hogarth's death in 1764.[1]

In *Time Smoking a Picture,* Hogarth turns on its head the notion that the passage of time, with its attendant yellowing and muting of varnish, enhanced the appearance of paintings, an idea expressed succinctly by Joseph Addison in 1711 in the *Spectator,* to which Hogarth refers in the inscription on the frame in the etching. Addison describes a vision in which an old man (Time) "wore off incensibly every little disagreeable Gloss that hung upon a Figure: He also added such a beautiful brown to the Colours, that he made every Picture appear more perfect than when it came fresh from the Master's Pencil." In the chapter "Of Colouring" in *The Analysis of Beauty* (1753), Hogarth had alluded to Addison's text in arguing the contrary: "time disunites, untunes, blackens, and by degrees destroys even the best preserved pictures."[2] The point is further made by the Greek text on the picture frame, which derives from the ancient Greek poet Crates (with some modification): "For time is not a great artist, but weakens all he touches."[3]

Hogarth's figure of Time sits before a painting of a sparse landscape on an easel, assuming the standard pose of an artist, as in Hogarth's own self-portrait painting a figure of Comedy (cat. no. 12). But Time's actions are destructive rather than creative: his scythe punctures the canvas, and smoke pours onto the picture from his mouth and the bowl of the pipe. His effect on the picture is likened to the excessive darkening caused by the aging of varnish present in the large jar at lower left. Time is equally unkind to sculpture: he sits on sculptural fragments, parts of classical nudes. A noseless face stares disconsolately at the viewer. Hogarth draws on a visual tradition of the ill effects of time on art, evident, for example, in the title page to François Perrier's well-known compendium of images of ancient sculptures, first published in 1638 and subsequently in several editions (fig. 77.1), in which Time gnaws on the Torso Belvedere. But his application of the theme to painting rather than sculpture (or architecture) is unusual or even unprecedented.[4]

The single line below Time—"As Statues moulder into Worth"—is attributed to "P.W.," presumably Hogarth's friend, Paul Whitehead.[5] It condenses the irony of an epistolary poem on the *Sigismunda* affair from Hogarth to Whitehead, a poem in which Hogarth further attacks the obsession with aged paintings:

> Let the picture rust,
> Perhaps Time's price-enhancing dust,—
> As statues moulder into earth,
> When I'm no more may mark its worth,
> And future connoisseurs may rise,
> Honest as ours, and full as wise,
> To puff the piece and painter too,
> And make me *then,* what Guido's now.[6]

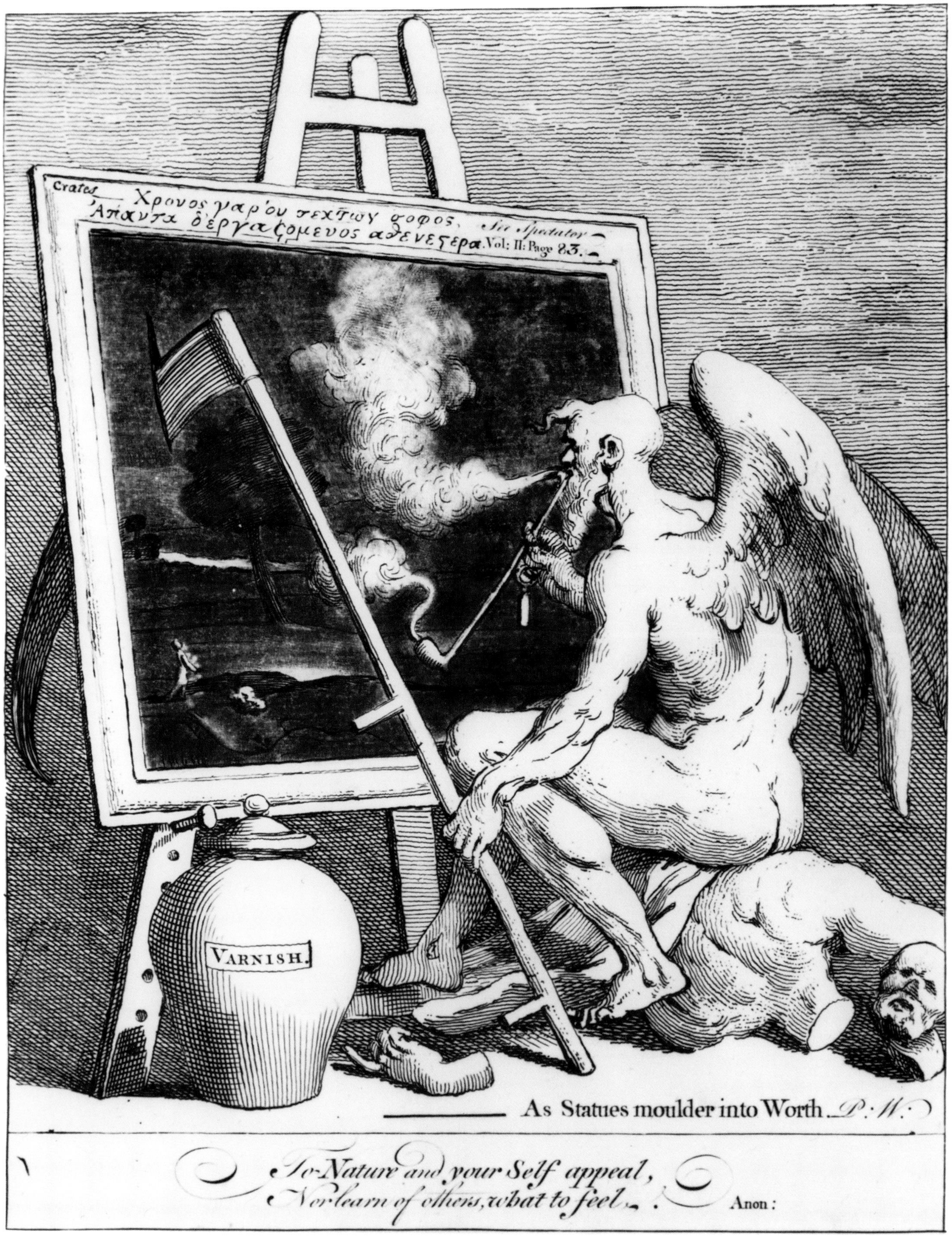

Crates
Χρονος γαρ'ου τεκτων σοφος,
Ἀπαντα δ'εργαζομενος ασθενεστερα
See Spectator Vol: II: Page 83.
VARNISH.
As Statues moulder into Worth P: W:
To Nature and your Self appeal,
Nor learn of others, what to feel.
Anon:

Cat. no. 77

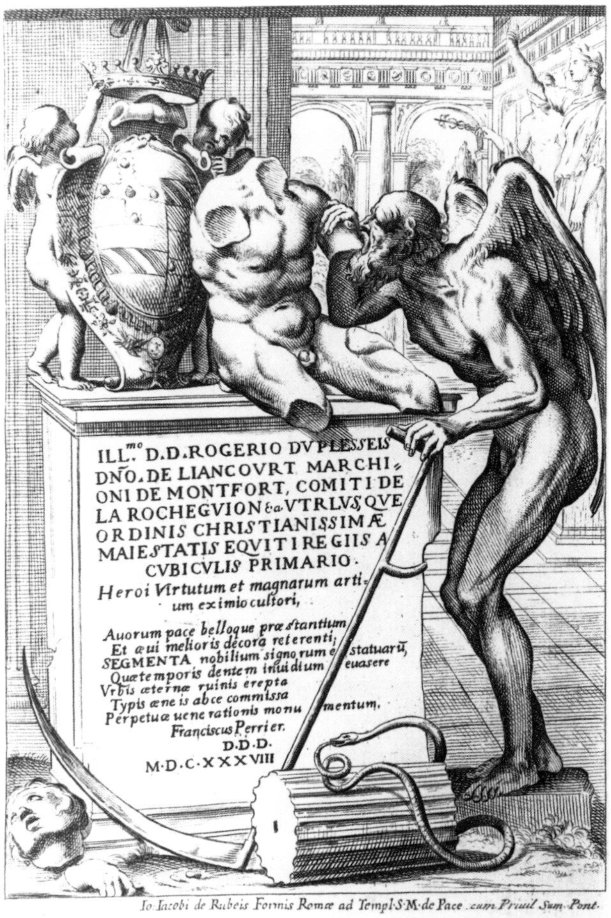

Fig. 77.1. François Perrier. Title page of François Perrier, *Segmenta nobilium signorum et statuarum quae Temporis dentem inuidium euasere, Urbis Aeternae erepta.* 1638. Etching. Private collection.

Without irony, the couplet below the image summarizes Hogarth's disdain for excessive reverence (and value) given to Old Master paintings and ancient sculpture, advocating instead attention to nature and personal experience. In this, Hogarth counters the centuries-long tradition of looking to the past for artistic instruction and inspiration. The line, "Nor learn of others, what to feel," may serve as a warning not just to artists, but to patrons and collectors as well, lest they be misled by the "dealers in dark pictures" against whom Hogarth persistently railed and who were known literally to age pictures artificially with smoke for marketing purposes.[7] His criticism was emphasized by John Ireland in 1791: "Mr. Hogarth frequently asserted, that no man was so ill qualified to form a true judgment of pictures as the professed Connoisseur; whose taste being originally formed upon IMITATIONS, and confined to the MANNERS of Masters, had seldom any reference to Nature."[8]

JC

1. Ireland 1791, 1:lxxxvi-lxxxvii, reports that Grosvenor "unluckily gave him an order for the same subject" as the "Correggio," but the commission was conditional, and the painting was returned because the subject "must excite melancholy ideas." But according to Hogarth's autobiographical notes (Hogarth 1955, 220), Grosvenor had left the subject and the price up to Hogarth, probably expecting an entertaining piece like *The Lady's Last Stake,* which Hogarth had painted for Lord Charlemont under the same terms. Grosvenor then balked at both the subject and the price, which was set at what the earlier painting had achieved at auction. See further Paulson 1989, 194-95, including for Basire's print.
2. Hogarth 1997, 91n. On *Time Smoking a Picture* as a response to Addison, including the quotation from the *Spectator,* see Klotz 1959.
3. Trans. Paulson 1989, 173, who identifies Hogarth's probable source and notes Hogarth's alteration of it.
4. See especially Arndt 1972, 334-40.
5. On Whitehead and the line, see Paulson 1989, 174.
6. Quoted by Ireland 1791, lxxxvii. The reference in the last line is to the Italian painter Guido Reni (1575-1642), whose works were particularly prized in eighteenth-century England.
7. Paulson 1989, 174. Ireland 1791, 1:xlv, quotes a passage from an anonymous manuscript which describes the production of paintings in Britain to be sold as Old Masters ("modern antiques"): "Every picture is at present most sacredly preserved from the public eye, but in the course of a few months will be smoked into antiquity. . . ." On the contemporaneous *Enthusiasm Delineated* as a satire on connoisseurs and dealers, see Krysmanski 1996, and, more concisely, Krysmanski 1998.
8. Ireland 1791, 1:n.p. ("Introduction").

William Hogarth (1697-1764)

78. *Tail Piece: The Bathos*

1764

Etching and engraving, 317 x 335 mm (12½ x 13¼ in.)

Reference: Paulson 216

Inscriptions: above image: *TAIL PIECE.*; on gallows arm: *The Worlds End.*; in smoke: *FINIS.*; above seal at lower left: *H. Nature / Bankrupt.*; in book at lower left: *Exeunt Omnes.*; on scroll at lower center: *all and every / Atom there- / of to [. . . obscured] / Chaos whom / I appoint my / sole / Excecutor. / Witness Clothq. / Lacbesis. / Atropos.*; on print at lower right: *THE TIMES*; below image, lower left: *Design'd and Engrav'd by Wm Hogarth. / The Conic Form in wch the Goddess of / Beauty was worship'^d by the Ancients / at Paphos in ye Island of Cyprus. / See the Medals struck when / a Roman Emperor visited / the Temple.*; below image, center: *THE BATHOS, / or Manner of Sinking, in Sublime Paintings, / inscribed to the Dealers in Dark Pictures. / "Simulacrum Deae non effigie humanâ: / continuus orbislatiore initie tenuem in / ambitum, metae modo, exsurgens et ratio / in obscuro." Tacit: Hist: Lib: 2. / "Venus a Paphiis colitur, cujus simula- / crum nulli rei magis affimile, quam / albae Pyramidi. / Maximus Tyrius: Anna 157. / See the manner of disgracing ye most Se- / rious Subjects, in many celebrated Old / Pictures; by introducing Low, absurd, ob- / scene & often prophane Circumstances into them.*; below image, at right: *Published according to Act of Parliam.^t March 3.^d 1764. / A Copy of the precise line of Beauty, as it is represented on the 1st explanatory / *Plate of the Analysis of Beauty, / Note, the similarity of these two / Conic Figures, did not occur to / the Author, till two or three Years / after his publication of the Analy- / sis, in 1754. / *fig:26*

Purchased from Andrew Edmunds, London

1983.05.77

The last print Hogarth executed, *Tail Piece: The Bathos* is one of his most complex. It served as a tailpiece to the folio of his engravings, for which first *Gulielmus Hogarth* (cat. no. 12) and then *Hogarth Painting the Comic Muse* (cat. no. 41) served as frontispiece. John Ireland summarized its purpose: "The aim of this OMEGA *to his own alphabet,* was two-fold; to bring together every object which denoted *the end of time,* and throw a ridicule upon the *bathos and profundity* of the ancients."[1] A moribund figure of Time slumps among a jumble of fractured and fragmented objects. Hogarth had featured this figure three years earlier in his *Time Smoking a Picture* (cat. no. 77), but now Time exhales a final cloud of smoke from a broken pipe; a shattered hourglass sits at his side, and his scythe, which had sliced a canvas in the earlier print, is now itself broken. His hand rests on his will, witnessed by the three Fates, which names Chaos as his beneficiary. Hogarth gathers multiple references to the ends of things: in addition to broken objects, there is a teetering sign of a ruined pub called "The World's End" with a logo of an Earth in flames; a grave stone; a sinking ship; Apollo and his horses no longer able to drive the chariot of the Sun across the sky; the end of a play marked "Exeunt Omnes"; a candle igniting his controversial print *The Times*; and so on.[2] The artist's palette, which had featured prominently in *Gulielmus Hogarth,* lies abandoned, its "line of beauty" replaced by a crack. Hogarth puns on the term "last" with the cobbler's wooden last below the hourglass, which might also be a reference to Pliny's story of the painter Apelles and an irritating viewer (see cat. no. 71) and thus to Hogarth's critics.[3] The still-life elements in the foreground form a wrecked version of Hogarth's etching, *Crowns, Mitres, Maces, etc.* of 1754 (fig. 78.1), which celebrated governmental "Encouragement of the Arts of Designing Engraving &c" through the passage in 1735 of the Engravers' Act protecting copyright, commonly known as Hogarth's Act because of the artist's advocacy of it.[4]

Hogarth's career-long confrontation with a restrictive tradition in the visual arts, which valued continental art over English and history painting over genre, and the purveyors of works in that tradition culminates in this print. The print is "inscribed to the Dealers in Dark Pictures," those who promoted a taste which was, in Hogarth's view, ill-founded, and against which he struggled, as he made manifest in his *Battle of the Pictures* and *Time Smoking a Picture* (cat. nos. 76, 77). Ireland noted that "a more heterogeneous compound of ludicrous and serious objects was never displayed in one print,"[5] and the ironic footnote—"See the manner of disgracing ye most Serious Subjects, in many celebrated Old Pictures; by introducing Low, absurd, obscene & often prophane Circumstances

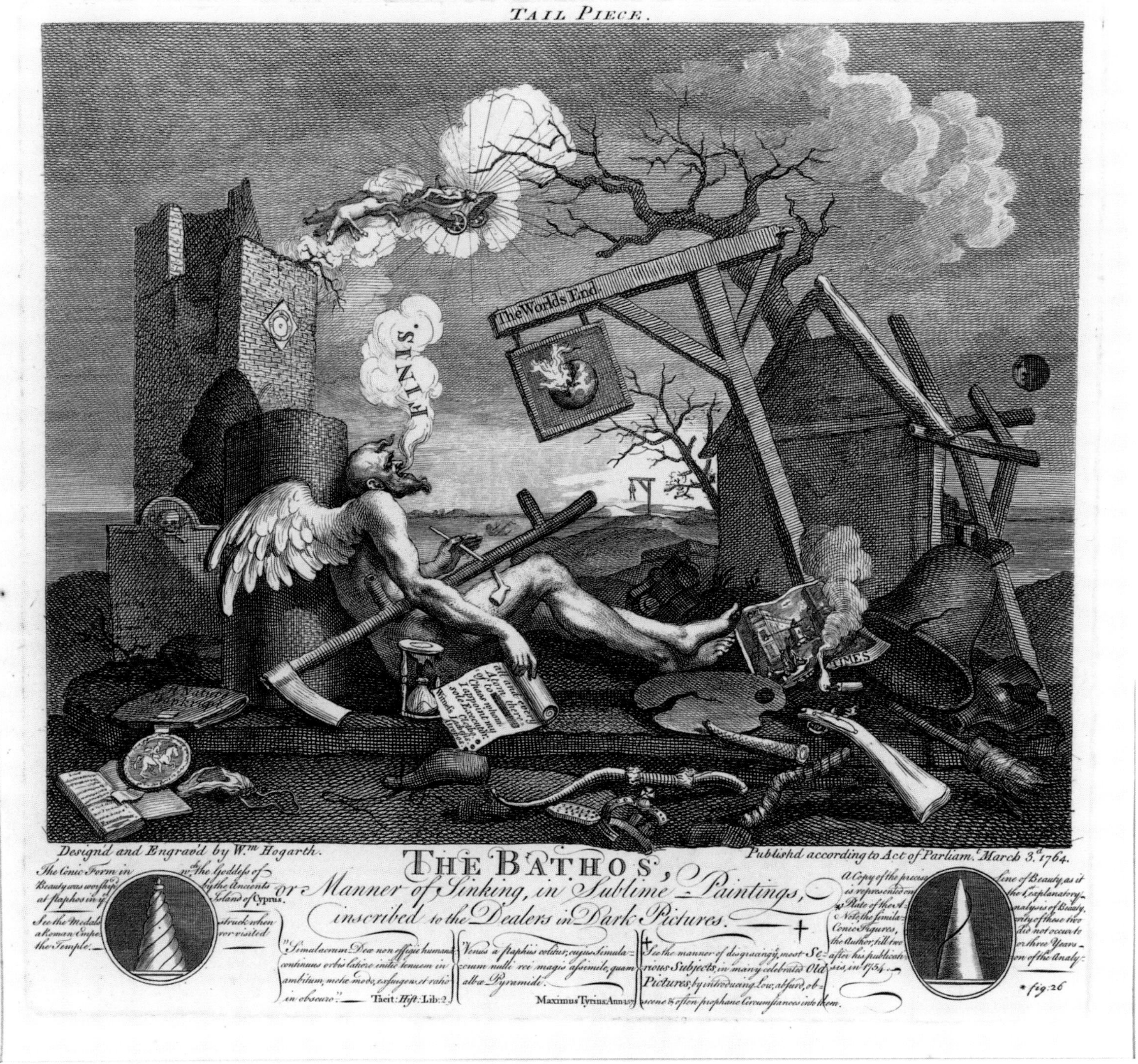
TAIL PIECE.
The Worlds End
FINIS.
Design'd and Engrav'd by Wm Hogarth.
Publish'd according to Act of Parliam.t March 3.d 1764.
THE BATHOS,
or Manner of Sinking, in Sublime Paintings,
inscribed to the Dealers in Dark Pictures.
"Simulacrum Deæ non effigie humanâ continuus orbis latiore initio tenuem in ambitum, metæ modo, exsurgens et ratio in obscuro." Tacit: Hist: Lib:2.
Venus a Paphiis colitur, cujus Simulacrum nulli rei magis assimile, quam albæ Pyramidi.
Maximus Tyrius Ann.
See the manner of disgracing ye most Serious Subjects, in many celebrated Old Pictures; by introducing Low, absurd, obscene & often prophane Circumstances into them.
* fig:26

Cat. no. 78

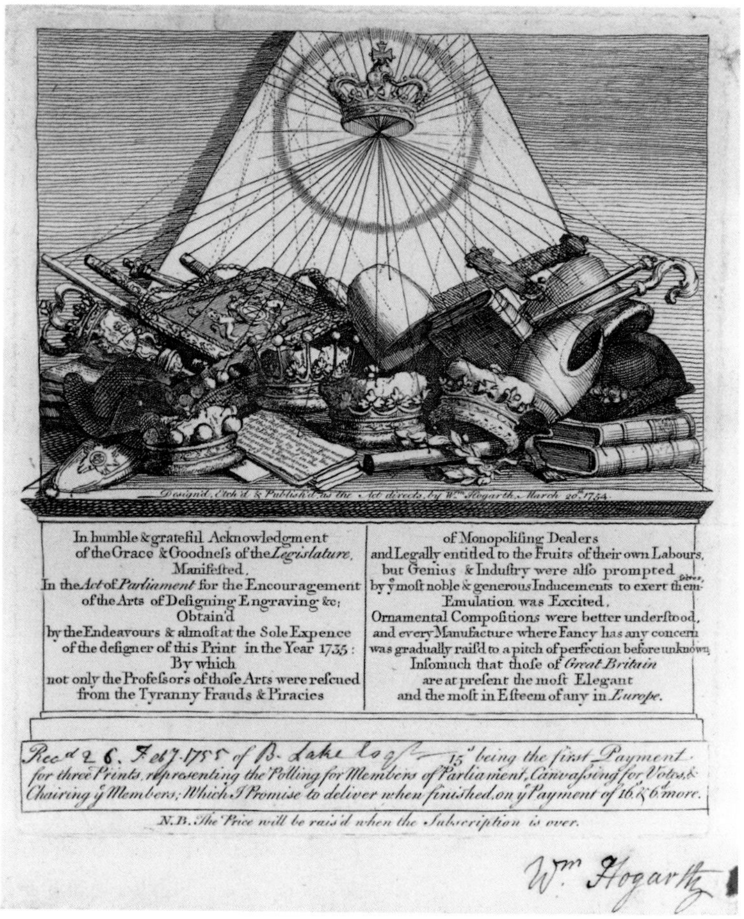

Fig. 78.1. William Hogarth. *Crowns, Mitres, Maces, etc.* 1754. Etching, fourth state, 229 x 191 mm (9 x 7½ in.). Sarah Campbell Blaffer Foundation, Houston.

into them"—parrots the criticism of Hogarth that was still reiterated after his death. Joshua Reynolds, in his Discourse of 1770 to the Royal Academy, averred: "The painters who have applied themselves more particularly to low and vulgar characters, and who express with precision the various shades of passion, as they are exhibited by vulgar minds, (such as we see in the works of Hogarth,) deserve great praise; but as their genius has been employed on low and confined subjects, the praise which we give must be as limited as its object."[6] Hogarth's reference to "Sublime Paintings" brings to mind Edmund Burke's *A Philosophical Enquiry into the Origin of Our Ideas of the Sublime and Beautiful,* first published in 1757. For Burke, the sublime, born of terror and a sense of danger, is "the strongest emotion which the mind is capable of feeling" and is not the result of terrible subjects treated with clarity; rather, "in painting a judicious obscurity in some things contributes to the effect of the picture; because the images in painting are exactly similar to those in nature; and in nature dark, confused, uncertain images have a greater power on the fancy to form the grander passions than those have which are more clear and determinate."[7] Alexander Pope had already parodied the taste for the sublime in his *Peri Bathous* of 1728, to which Hogarth's title refers. Hogarth employs the language of history painting and the sublime to ridicule the taste to which such work appealed.

JC

1. Ireland 1791, 2:596. On an anecdote recounting the origin of the print, see the Introduction.
2. For a detailed description of the motifs in the composition, see Paulson 1989, 185–86.
3. Wind 1984. Ireland 1791, 2:595, refers to the *Tail Piece: The Bathos* as Hogarth's "concluding aenigmatical and pun-ical print."
4. On *Crowns, Mitres, Maces, etc.,* see Paulson 1989, 161–62; on Hogarth's Act, see Paulson 1991–93, 2:36ff.
5. Ireland 1791, 2:604.
6. Reynolds 1975, 51.
7. Burke 1958, 39, 62.

Pierre Aveline (1702–1760)

after Antoine Watteau (1684–1721)

79. *L'Enseigne de Gersaint (Signboard of Gersaint)*

c. 1732

Engraving and etching, 579 x 857 mm (22¾ x 33¾ in.)

References: Goncourt 95; Dacier and Vuaflart 115, iii/iii

Inscriptions: below image: *A. Watteau pinxit. P. Aveline sculp. / L'ENSEIGNE / Gravée d'apres le Tableau en Platfond peint par Watteau pour Mr Gersain son amy Marchand / sur le Pont Nôtre Dame, haut de 5. pieds sur 9. pieds 6. pouces de large, qui est a present / dans le Cabinet de Mr De Jullienne. / a Paris Avec Privilege du Roy. / Watteau, dans cette enseigne, à la fleur de ses ans, / Des Maestres de son Art Imite la maniere; / Leurs caracteres differens, / Leurs touches et leur goût Composent la matiere / De ces Esquisses Elegans. / Que n'attendions-nous point de tant d'heureux Talens! / Si le Ciel eut voulû prolonger sa carriere / Il auroit surpassé ses Modeles charmants.*

Purchased from Kunsthandlung Helmut H. Rumbler, Frankfurt

1997.14

The collector and amateur engraver, Jean de Jullienne, published two collections of reproductive prints by major engravers after the work of his friend Antoine Watteau: the drawings (*Figures de différens caractères de paysages et d'études, dessinés d'après nature par Antoine Watteau,* 1726) and the paintings (*Oeuvre gravé de Watteau,* 1736).[1] The latter is composed of nearly three hundred plates by around two dozen engravers, the largest print of which is Pierre Aveline's engraving (reversed) of Watteau's *L'Enseigne de Gersaint (Signboard of Gersaint)* of 1721, which had been displayed for two weeks outside the shop of his friend, the art dealer Edme Gersaint.[2] The title page of the *Oeuvre gravé* claims that one hundred exemplars were produced, but *L'Enseigne* was already offered for sale in November 1732, according to the *Mercure de France.*[3] The production of the print had been announced in the *Mercure* in March and July of the same year, which referred to the painting each time as "famous," in one instance as "the masterpiece of this excellent painter."[4] Most of the engravings in the project were made directly from Watteau's paintings, but, owing to the great size of *L'Enseigne* (even cut down, it is still 306 centimeters [120½ inches] across), an intermediary painted copy was made by Watteau's former pupil Jean-Baptiste Pater to the size of the projected engraving, augmenting the upper area somewhat in the process.[5]

Jullienne may have been unusual in the degree of his dedication to the work of a single artist, both in collecting it—he owned over five hundred drawings and forty paintings by Watteau, including *L'Enseigne*—and in disseminating it. But the reproduction of paintings as prints was a practice that was initiated in the sixteenth century and became quite common by the eighteenth and early nineteenth centuries. At first, individual pictures were copied, sometimes under the aegis of, or even by, the painters themselves, but in the seventeenth century and following, reproductive prints took on broader connotations for art historical understanding and for collecting, as they appeared in groups, whether of the works of a single artist, such as Hogarth (cat. nos. 76–78; see also cat. no. 74), of a single collection (an early example of which is David Teniers's *Theatrum pictorium,* 1660, of the collection of Archduke Leopold Wilhelm in Brussels; see also cat. nos. 31, 59),[6] or of dispersed works, organized according to regional schools (see cat. no. 62). Even though Jullienne's *Oeuvre gravé de Watteau* was not a financial success,[7] the increased frequency of such projects in the eighteenth century paralleled the expansion of a class of people, including at its core *amateurs,* for whom a knowledge, and even collection, of art was socially desirable, precisely the kind of people depicted in Watteau's *L'Enseigne de Gersaint.*

Watteau presented an art gallery as open fronted, virtually a stage set, with walls covered by paintings of various subjects that evoke, without reproducing, works by sixteenth-century Venetians and seventeenth-century Flemings—that is, artists admired by Watteau. It recalls numerous seventeenth-century Flemish paintings of galleries, themselves a testament to the rise of interest in collecting (fig. 79.1).[8] A gentleman offers to help a woman step into the shop, but she turns her head to look at a portrait of Louis XIV (after a Hyacinthe Rigaud painting, and a reference to the name of Gersaint's shop, Au Grand Monarque) being packed or perhaps unpacked, while another worker hefts a mirror and a porter watches. On the other side of the shop, a salesman shows a couple—the woman dressed as a widow—an oval painting of nudes in a landscape (she peers at the trees, he at the bodies). Next

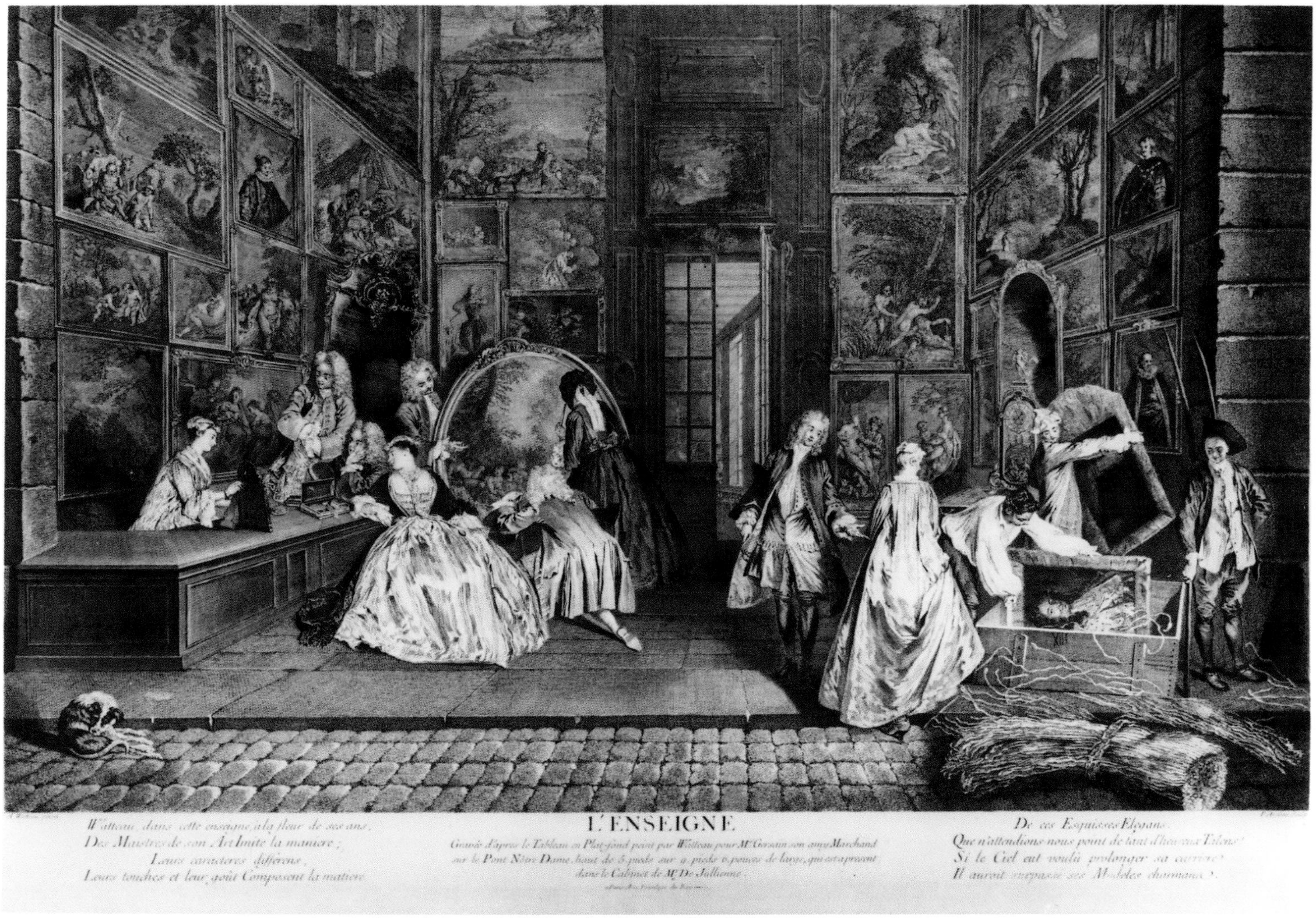

Cat. no. 79

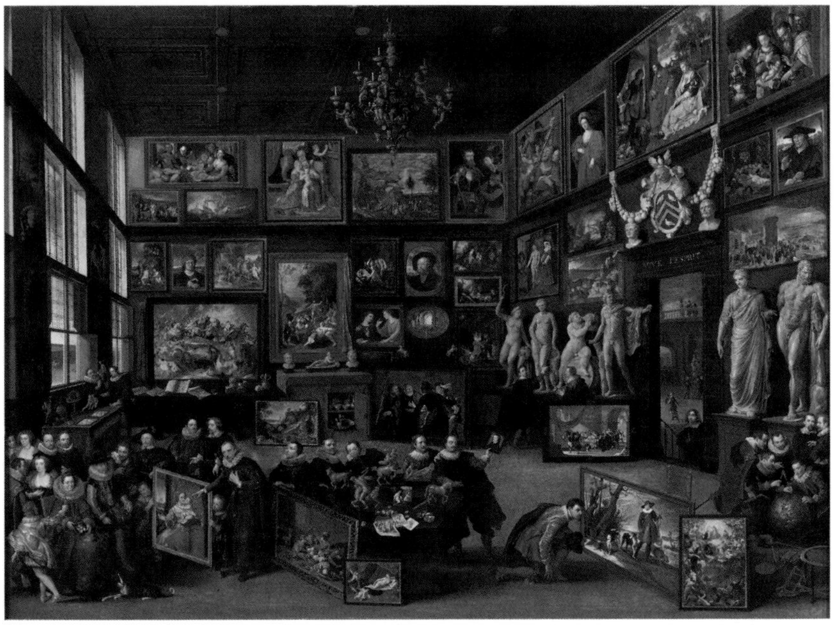

Fig. 79.1. Willem van Haecht. *De Kunstkamer van Cornelis van der Geest (The Cabinet of Cornelis van der Geest).* 1628. Oil on panel, 104 x 139 cm (41 x 54¾ in.). Rubenshuis, Antwerp.

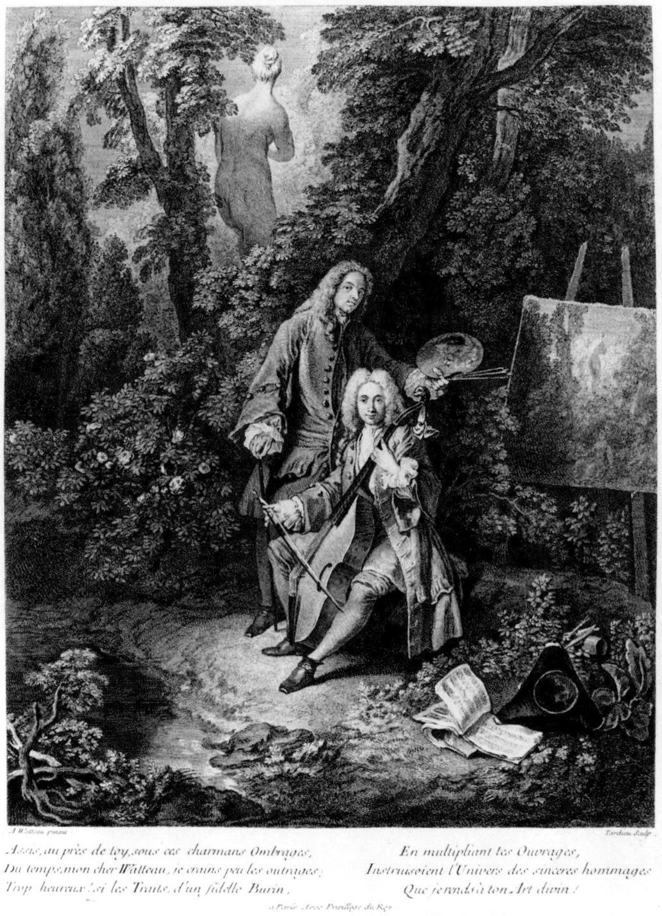

Fig. 79.2. N. H. Tardieu after Antoine Watteau (?). *Assis, au près de toy (Portrait of Watteau and Jullienne).* Etching, 428 x 311 mm (16⅞ x 12¼ in.). École nationale supérieure des Beaux-Arts, Paris.

to them, two gentlemen and a woman look at a mirror held by a saleswoman, who has also shown them the grooming items on the counter. Their attention to their own appearance matches that of the couple inspecting the painting, raising the fashionable person to the level of artwork.[9] As far as one can tell, all the visitors to the shop, as well as the sales personnel, are young and attractive. A dog, lifted from Rubens's *Coronation of Marie de Medici,* is curled on the cobblestones outside the shop. As the woman at center steps into the shop, into the art world, the viewer is invited to accompany her. As Gersaint wrote in 1744, even the bourgeois of modest income could aspire to an elite status through art:

> What advantages can a *Curieux* customarily derive from his curiosity? . . . His title of *Curieux* gives him access to the most famous collections and he can go to divert himself there; in the capacity of *Curieux* he becomes equal to those same people given over to this noble passion whose rank or condition is beyond his: as such he is invited to and received with pleasure at their gatherings established for the purpose of communicating to one another their discoveries or their acquisitions; he benefits from and rejoices with them over these novelties and he acquires daily some information and knowledge thus enlightening himself in the course of entertaining himself.[10]

Jean de Jullienne was just such a *curieux,* a textile manufacturer who pursued an early interest in art, but never professionally. His double portrait with Watteau, etched by Nicolas-Henry Tardieu, ostensibly after a painting by Watteau himself, shows the friends not as professionals, but as members of the leisure class, in the unlikely activities of painting and playing the cello outdoors (fig. 79.2).[11] Jullienne was ennobled in 1736, the year he issued the *Oeuvre gravé de Watteau.*

JC

1. For the *Oeuvre gravé,* see Dacier and Vuaflart 1921–29.
2. On Aveline's *L'Enseigne* in particular, see Dacier and Vuaflart 1921–1929, 3:56–57; Baltimore Museum of Art and Minneapolis Institute of Arts 1984, 82. Aveline's was also one of the five most costly prints in the *Oeuvre* when impressions were sold individually in 1770, selling for 6 *livres* (the next most expensive group sold for 3 *livres*) (Dacier and Vuaflart 1921–29, 2:129–32). Aveline was one of the principal collaborators in the project, producing twelve engravings.
3. "[L]a Vve de F. Chereau & Surugue annoncent la mise en vente de deux estampes: L'une a pour titre, & c. . . . L'autre est l'*Engseigne. . . .*" (Quoted by Dacier and Vuaflart 1921–29, 3:56.)
4. Dacier and Vuaflart 1921–1929, 3:56.
5. Ibid., 2:76. It has also been suggested that Pater was responsible for transforming Watteau's painting itself from an arched-top to a rectangular form, adding passages as needed. On the painting, see Grasselli and Rosenberg 1984, 446–58; Vidal 1992, 173–96; Plax 2000, 154–83.
6. Another prominent example is the illustrated folio catalogue, in 57 volumes, of the collection of the Ducs d'Orléans (*Galerie du Palais Royal gravée d'après les Tableaux des differentes Ecoles qui la composent,* Paris, 1786–1808).
7. Dacier and Vuaflart 1921–29, 1:233.
8. Filipczak 1987; Vidal 1992, 183–84.
9. See Vidal 1992, 188–92.
10. Trans. Plax 2000, 172.
11. See Vidal 1992, 158–67.

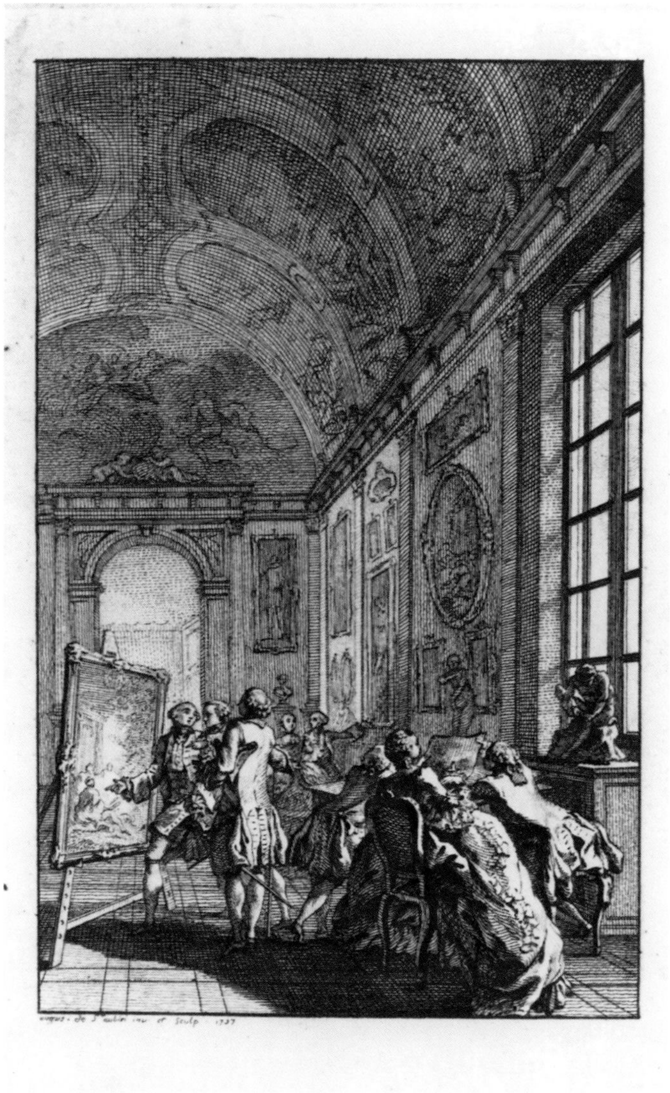

Cat. no. 80

AUGUSTIN DE SAINT-AUBIN (1736–1807)

80. *La Galerie de Heinecken*

1757

Etching, 144 x 87 mm (5⅝ x 3⅜ in.)

REFERENCES: Portalis and Béraldi 231; Bocher 546, i/ii

INSCRIPTION: below image: *augus. de S^t aubin inv et sculp 1757*

Purchased from C. G. Boerner, New York

1998.16

In a large, barrel-vaulted gallery, eight elegantly dressed men and women look at art. At right, two men hold up a large print, while a woman, her voluminous skirt projecting well over the sides of the chair in which she sits, looks on. At left, three men discuss a painting set on an easel, and in the background a man turns to his female companion as he gestures toward a painting on the wall. Three sculptures are visible: a bust against the back wall, and two full figures at the right, recognizable as copies of popular ancient sculptures: a Venus Pudica and the Spinario (the latter reversed).[1] Saint-Aubin's composition recalls, on a more intimate scale, an

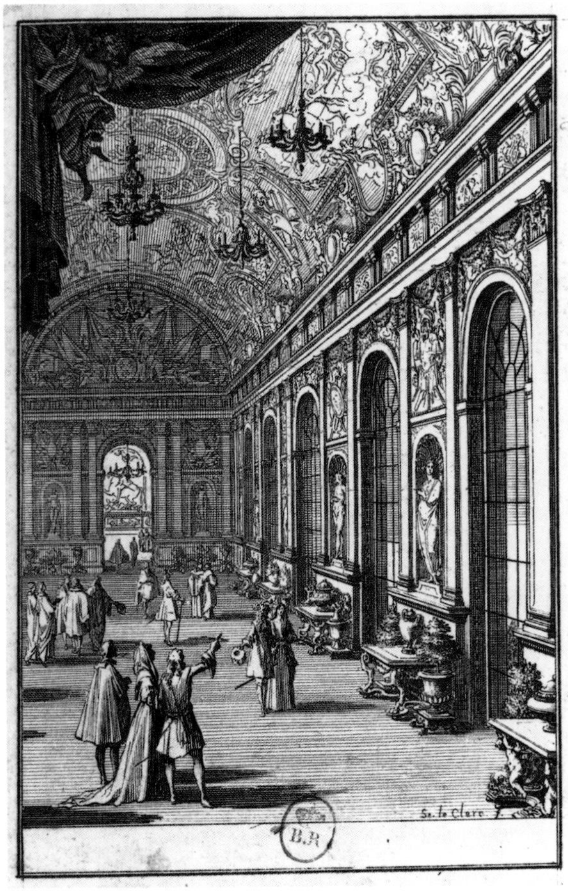

Fig. 80.1. Sébastien Leclerc. *La Galerie des Glaces (The Hall of Mirrors), Versailles*. 1684. Engraving, 143 x 90 mm (5⅝ x 3½ in.). Bibliothèque nationale de France, Paris.

engraving by Sébastien Leclerc of the Galerie des Glaces of the château of Versailles, which had been used as the frontispiece to Pierre Rainssant's *Explication des tableaux de la galerie de Versailles* of 1687 (fig. 80.1).[2] Here, as elsewhere (see cat. nos. 68, 79, 81–83), art viewing is presented as an activity of the wealthy and fashionable, members of a class with the leisure to learn about and discuss art.[3] Saint-Aubin did not depict a particular place but confirmed more generally these associations for an art-buying public.

Saint-Aubin's etching was created to serve as the frontispiece of a sale catalogue of paintings, drawings, and prints belonging to Carl Heinrich von Heinecken (1706–1791), auctioned in Paris under the direction of Pierre Remy on December 12, 1757, and February 13–18, 1758.[4] The present impression was used as a frontispiece to the sale catalogue of the De Selle collection, also by Remy, in Paris, February 19–28, 1761.[5] Heinecken was one of the most important print collectors and connoisseurs of the eighteenth century, appointed by the Saxon Elector Friedrich Augustus II in 1746 as the director of the Kupferstichkabinett in Dresden, whose collection he augmented by some fifty thousand prints. He was a prolific writer on prints and printmakers, publishing several monumental works later in life aimed at *amateurs*: three volumes of *Nachrichten von Künstlern und Kunst-Sachen* and *Neue Nachrichten . . .* (1768–69, 1786); the *Idée générale d'une collection complette d'estampes* (1771); and the *Dictionnaire des artistes,* in thirty volumes (1778–90).[6] Heinecken was personally acquainted with Saint-Aubin. As part of his investigation into early printed book illustration, he examined several copies of the *Speculum humanae salvationis* in Paris and had Saint-Aubin copy the first and last images in the work, presumably as drawings, which he then sent to scholars in Holland to compare against editions there.[7] Saint-Aubin produced a portrait of Heinecken in 1769.[8] Heinecken included the sale catalogue frontispiece in the list of works by Saint-Aubin in his *Dictionnaire* but was laconic: "*Titre* ou Frontispice pour un Catalogue de tableaux, inventé & gravé en 1757. in-12."[9]

JC

1. See Haskell and Penny 1981, 308–10, 318–20, 325–28.
2. *Inventaire du fonds français* 3061; the print was originally used as the frontispiece of Madeleine de Scudéry's *Conversations nouvelle sur divers sujets* (Paris, 1684).
3. See Vidal 1992.
4. *Catalogue raisonné, de tableaux, desseins & estampes, des meilleurs maîtres d'Italie, des Païs-Bas, d'Allemagne, d'Angleterre et de France*; Lugt 1938–87, 1:n.p. (nos. 979, 986). For an even more intimate gathering of potential collectors, see the frontispiece by C.-N. Cochin II to the catalogue of the Quentin de Lorangere sale of 1744 (reproduced in Dacier and Vuaflart 1921–29, 1:139).
5. Lugt 1938–87, 1:n.p. (no. 1137). The verso of the impression carries a manuscript inscription: *De Selle 1761.*
6. See Griffiths and Carey 1994, 17, who call Heinecken "the doyen of German print scholars . . . whose *Idée générale d'une collection d'estampes* of 1771 was perhaps the most important single text of the period in defining what the purpose and scope of print collecting should be."
7. Heinecken 1771, 443.
8. Heinecken 1778–90, 1:496, where Heinecken refers to himself as an *Amateur.*
9. Ibid., 1:497. Heinecken also mentions a frontispiece produced by Saint-Aubin for the catalogue of a natural history collection auctioned by Remy on November 21, 1757, and following (Heinecken 1778–90, 1:497; Portalis and Béraldi 230; Lugt 1938–87, 1:n.p. [no. 974]).

Pietro Antonio Martini (1738–1797)

81. *Coup-d'oeil exact de l'arrangement des Peintures au Salon du Louvre, en 1785*

1785

Etching, 296 x 489 mm (11⅝ x 19¼ in.) (trimmed)

Reference: Portalis and Béraldi 12

Inscription: below image: *Coup d'oeil exact de l'arrangement des Peintures au Salon du Louvre, en 1785.*

Purchased from Kunsthandlung Helmut H. Rumbler, Frankfurt

1999.3

Pietro Antonio Martini (1738–1797)

82. *Exposition au Salon du Louvre en 1787*

1787

Etching, 380 x 510 mm (15 x 20⅛ in.) (trimmed)

Reference: Portalis and Béraldi 12

Inscription: below image: *P.A. Martini Parm^s Faciebat / LAUDA-CONATUM / EXPOSITION AU SALON DU LOUVRE EN 1787. / à Paris, chez Bornet, Peintre, Rue Guénégaud N° 24, et à Londres N° 7. St George's Row, Hyde Park*

Purchased from Kunsthandlung Helmut H. Rumbler, Frankfurt

1999.4

Exhibitions of the Royal Academy of Painting and Sculpture in Paris were sporadic events in the late seventeenth and early eighteenth century, but in 1737 they became regular events, at first annually, then soon biannually, mounted in late August and September.[1] They took place in the Galerie d'Apollon and the Salon Carrée (from which they took their popular name) of the Louvre. The Salons were packed with both paintings and people. The paintings (as well as drawings, prints, and sculptures), widely ranging in both subject and scale, were stacked up to six high, from below eye level to the springing of the vault, and crammed into the staircase leading up to the Salon.[2] The exhibitions were open to the public, free of charge, and attracted viewers (of both paintings and people) from all classes. An observer, Pidansat de Mairobert, in 1777 described the scene:

> You emerge through a stairwell like a trapdoor, which is always choked despite its considerable width. Having escaped that painful gauntlet, you cannot catch your breath before being plunged into an abyss of heat and a whirlpool of dust. Air so pestilential and impregnated with the exhalations of so many unhealthy persons should in the end produce either lightning or plague. Finally you are deafened by a continuous noise like that of the crashing waves in an angry sea. But here nevertheless is a thing to delight the eye of an Englishman: the mixing, men and women together, of all the orders and all the ranks of the state. . . . This enchanting spectacle pleases me even more than the works displayed in this temple of the arts. Here the Savoyard odd-job man rubs shoulders with the great noble in his *cordon bleu*; the fishwife trades her perfumes with those of a lady of quality, making the latter resort to holding her nose to combat the strong odor of cheap brandy drifting her way; the rough artisan, guided only by natural feeling, comes out with a just observation, at which an inept wit nearby bursts out laughing only because of the comical accent in which it was expressed; while an artist hiding in the crowd unravels the meaning of it all and turns it to his profit.[3]

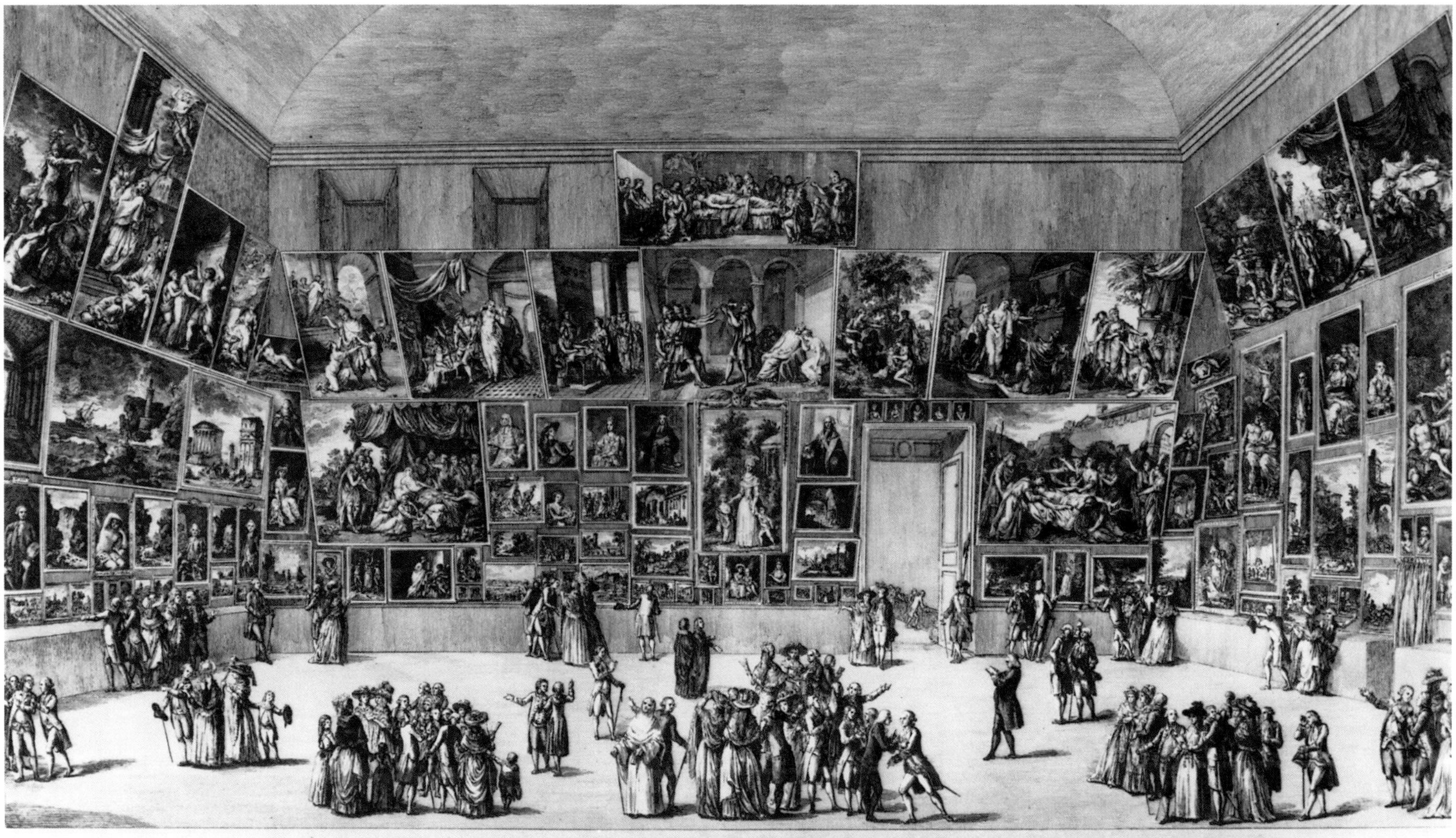

Coup-d'œil exact de l'arrangement des Peintures au Salon du Louvre, en 1785.

Cat. no. 81

Aside from the mixing of male and female, it is difficult to reconcile Mairobert's description with Pietro Antonio Martini's depiction of the Salons of slightly later: virtually all the figures are elegant and well-behaved, although the 1787 print includes some mildly rambunctious children, three dogs, and possibly a bird. Although numerous, the visitors scarcely crowd the great hall, especially in the 1785 print with its slightly smaller figure scale and more open floor space. In the right rear of both prints, a few figures look over the balustrade into the stairwell. Many of the figures look at the paintings—one, in the left rear of the 1787 print, even with the aid of a magnifying glass—and discuss them; some figures carry open volumes, presumably the official Salon *livret* (guidebook and catalogue). But the scenes ultimately resemble promenades, although without the satire injected into them by Martini's contemporaries, Philibert-Louis Debucourt and Louis Le Coeur.[4]

The prints may have been useful for those interested in the Salons, whether they had attended or not, as either souvenirs or possibly complements to the *livrets,* which sold in the thousands, as well as the many reviews and reports of the exhibitions (although the etchings naturally do not show all four walls of the Salon). Although the inscription on the 1785 print (trimmed in this impression but known from others) admits that the work was engraved from memory, it is also careful to note that it was finished during the time of the exhibition, presumably so that the final image could be checked against the actual appearance, and claims to reproduce the precise installation of the paintings ("coup-d'oeil exact").[5] Careful depictions of the Salons, or of other large exhibitions for that matter, are rare, and it is probable that the market did not justify the great labor necessary to produce such images, in spite of the evident popularity of the Salons for both visitors (21,940 copies of the *livret* were sold in 1787)[6] and readers throughout Europe. Martini's efforts must have been painstaking, since the miniature reproductions of the individual pictures are reasonably accurate and detailed, although there are a few infelicities; for example, Martini apparently did not allow enough room for Jacques-Louis David's *Oath of the Horatii* in the center of the 1785 etching,

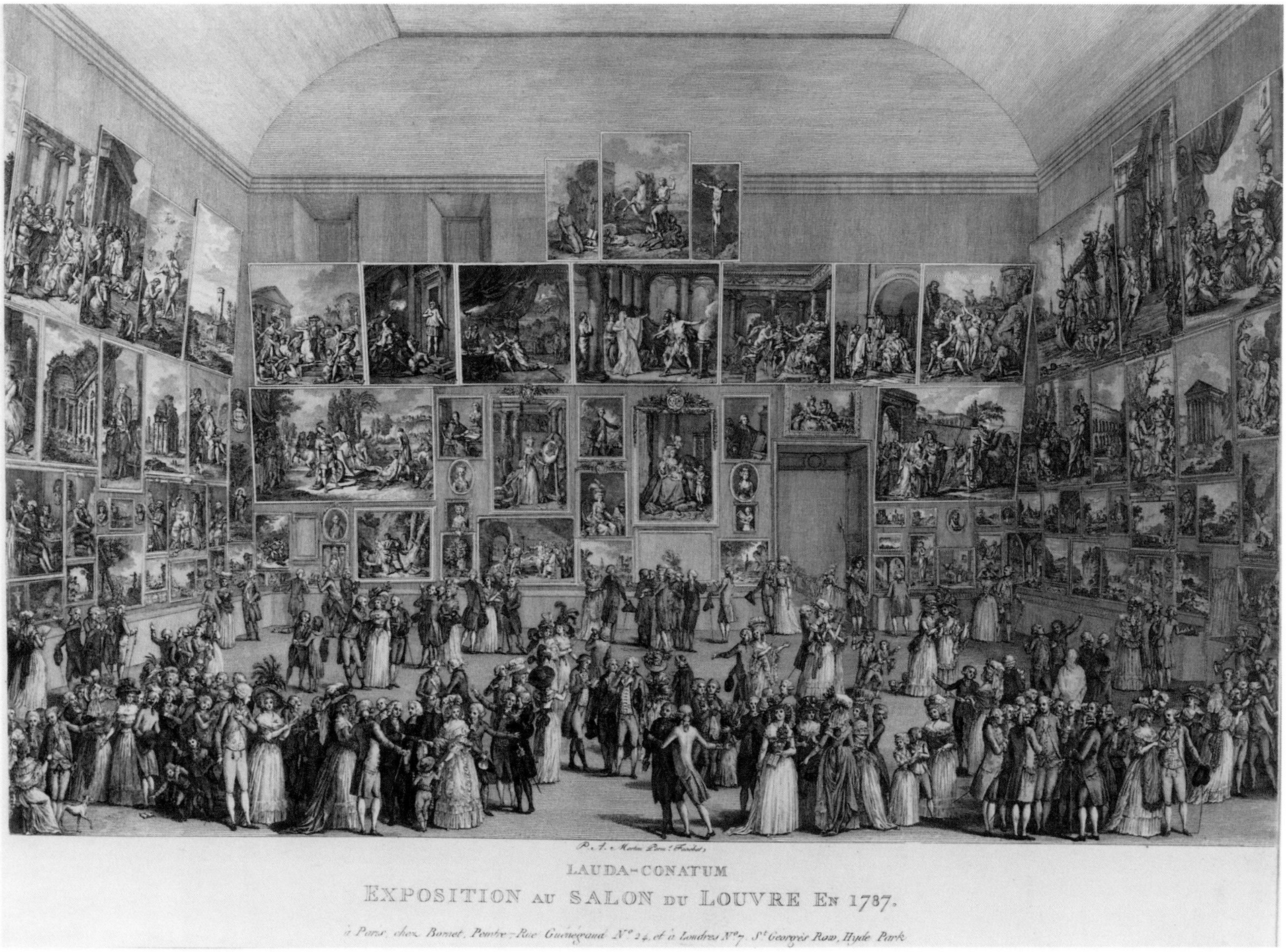

Cat. no. 82

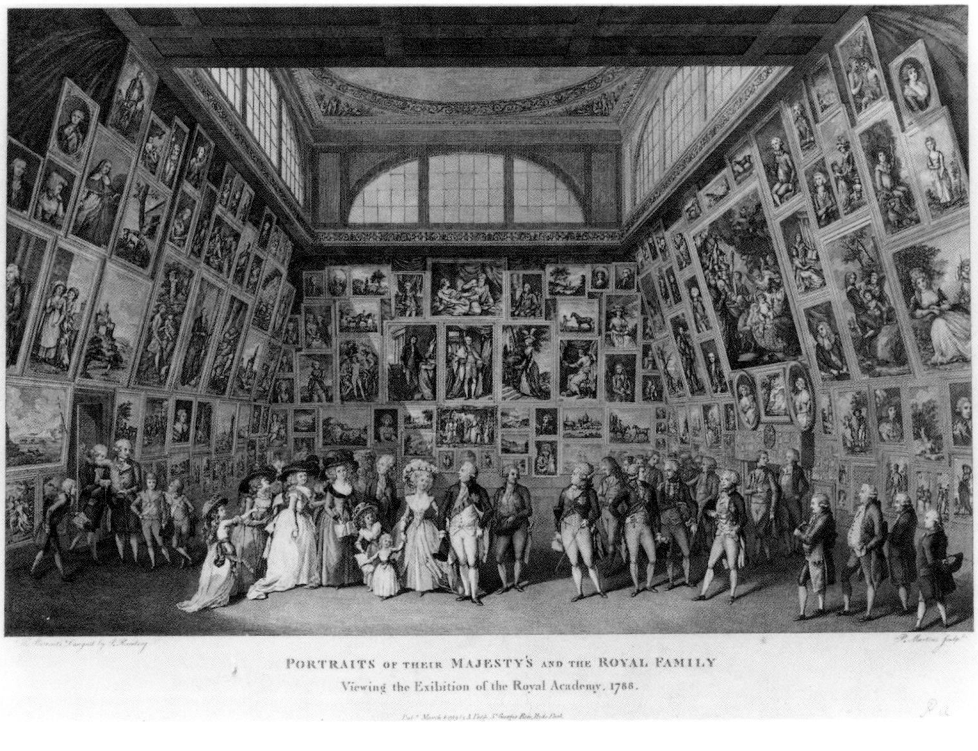

Fig. 81.1. Pietro Antonio Martini after J. H. Ramberg. *Portraits of their Majesty's and the Royal Family Viewing the Exhibition of the Royal Academy, 1788* [sic]. Published 1789. Engraving, 323 x 490 mm (12¾ x 19¼ in.). Royal Academy of Arts, London.

or made the figures too large, so that Horatius is no longer able to extend his arms fully toward his sons.

Martini also engraved views of two of the annual summer exhibitions of the Royal Academy of Arts in London, in 1787 and 1788, with drawings of the figures supplied by Johann Heinrich Ramberg (fig. 81.1).[7] In these instances, particular moments and persons are depicted: Joshua Reynolds escorting the Prince of Wales (subsequently King George IV) through the exhibition, and the visit of the royal family to the exhibition, respectively. JC

1. On the Salon in the eighteenth century, see Crow 1985, passim; Berger 1999, 157-91.
2. See Gabriel-Jacques de Saint-Aubin's etching of the *Staircase of the Salon,* 1753, which he reworked to depict the 1767 Salon (Baltimore Museum of Art and Minneapolis Institute of Arts 1984, 120-21; Crow 1985, 3).
3. Trans. Crow 1985, 4. The stairwell was enlarged in 1780 (Berger 1999, 168).
4. See Baltimore Museum of Art and Minneapolis Institute of Arts 1984, 279-82, 290-91.
5. The remainder of the inscription reads: *Gravée de mémoire, et terminé durant le temps de l'exposition. / A Paris, chez Bornet, peintre en miniature, Rue Guénégaud N° 24.* (see Berger 1999, 169).
6. Berger 1999, 168.
7. Hutchison 1968, 66-67, who mentions Ramberg's drawings in the British Museum.

James Gillray (1757-1815)

83. *A Peep at Christies; _or_ Tally-ho, & His Nimeney-Pimmeney Taking the Morning Lounge*

1796

Etching and aquatint, hand colored, 354 x 253 mm (13⅞ x 10 in.) (trimmed)

Reference: Wright and Evans 429

Inscriptions: on picture frame at left: *Susan[nah and the] Elders*; on picture frame at upper right: *Zenocrates & Phryne*; on picture frame at lower right: *The Death*; on the open volume: *Catalogue*; in margin below image: *J.s G.y ad vivam fecit / Pub. Sept. 24th 1796. by H. Humphrey, New Bond Street / A Peep at Christies; _or_Tally-ho, & his Nimeney-pimmeny taking / the Morning Lounge.*

Purchased from Kunsthandlung Helmut H. Rumbler, Frankfurt

1997.31

Among James Gillray's extensive satirical oeuvre are several images lampooning the public viewing and buying art, a group taken to task by William Hogarth and others (see cat. nos. 76, 77). The great feathered hat of the woman in the background of *A Peep at Christies* who studies a painting of *Susannah and the Elders* suggests the ridiculousness of the viewers at James Christie's auction house at 84 Pall Mall, where the fashionable were wont to take a "morning lounge," in the words of the print's inscription.[1] In the foreground, a tall, thin woman with pearls in her hair and around her neck raises a quizzing-glass to view a painting a few feet away. Her very round companion, about two-thirds her height, looks at a painting lower on the wall, at his eye level. In this instance, Gillray is using an art exhibition to provide metaphorical ammunition for an attack on two of his repeated targets, the Whig politician Edward Smith-Stanley, 12th Earl of Derby (1752-1834), and the actress Elizabeth Farren (1762-1829). In 1786, Farren had been acclaimed in the role of Lady Emily in John Burgoyne's *The Heiress,* which was dedicated to Derby. In the passage that gave rise to the reference in Gillray's inscription, she explained to the young Miss Alscrip how she was "preparing the cast of the lips for the ensuing winter," averring that "it is done by one cabalistical word, like a metamorphosis in the fairy tales. You have only, when before your glass, to keep pronouncing to yourself nimini-primini—the lips cannot fail of taking their plie."[2] Farren and Derby had developed a relationship as early as 1781 that was ostensibly platonic but that Gillray characterizes as more intimate. The painting she inspects depicts the ancient Greek philosopher Xenocrates (396-314 B.C.), a disciple of Plato, and Phryne, a famous courtesan who was said to have been the model for famous works by Apelles and Praxiteles and to have tested Xenocrates's continence. Diogenes Laertius recounts how Xenocrates shared his small bed with her, believing her to be seeking refuge from some people chasing her, but when he refused her advances, she went away, later saying that she had been with a statue and not a man.[3] Here she appears

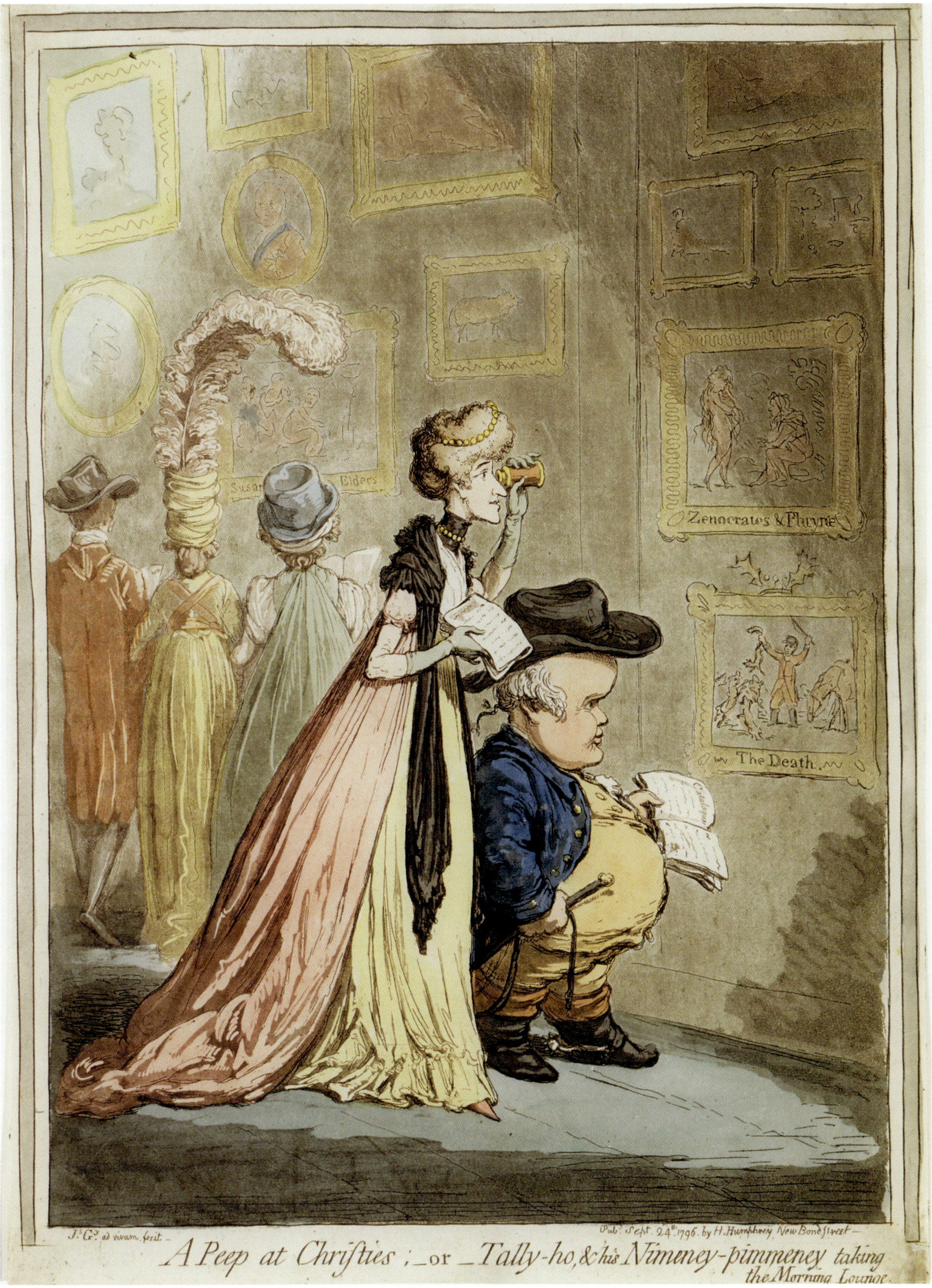
Zenocrates & Phryne
The Death.
Js. Gy. ad vivam. fecit –
Pubd. Sept. 24th. 1796. by H. Humphrey, New Bond Street –
A Peep at Christies ; – or – Tally-ho, & his Nimeney-pimmeney taking the Morning Lounge.

Cat. no. 83

nude before the bearded philosopher. In drawing the connection between the actress and putative mistress Farren and the courtesan Phryne—one suggested perhaps by the consonance of their names—Gillray may have recalled John Donne's epigram: "Thy flattering picture, Phryne, is like thee, / Only in this, that you both painted be." The object of Derby's attention is a painting called *The Death,* in which a fox is held aloft in front of baying hounds. It may be, as has been suggested, "a cruel reference to the illness and impending death of his wife," after which the earl married Farren,[4] but it more directly indicates his interest in blood sports, to which his whip and spurs, as well as the inscribed "Tally-ho" also refer.[5] The title of the painting is hyperbolically dramatic for a hunting scene but matches the excess of the coronet and antlers crowning the frame.

Gillray's inscription asserts that he made the image "from life" (*ad vivam fecit*). The claim had long been used to help persuade the viewer that he or she was presented with an accurately reproduced, experienced reality.[6] In this instance, Gillray employs the art-theoretical convention—undermined by the obvious distortions and manipulations of the caricature—to sharpen his satire.

JC

1. Gillray revisited the location over a decade later in *Maecenas in Pursuit of the Fine Arts* of May 9, 1808, depicting the Duke of Sutherland (Wright-Evans 560). For the fashionable and art, see cat. nos.79–82.
2. Miss Alscrip, after practicing the phrase, pronounces: "Oh, its [sic] delightfully enfantine! and so innocent, to be kissing one's own lips" (Burgoyne 1808, 2:77–78, Act III, scene ii).
3. Diogenes Laertius 1925, 1:380–83.
4. Godfrey 2001, 189; see also Hill 1966, 167; Hasse and Unverfehrt 1986, 217. The marriage was the subject of another Gillray print, dated May 3, 1797 (two days after the wedding), called *The Marriage of Cupid and Psyche* and based on an antique gem of the subject known as the Marlborough Gem (Wright and Evans 432). In commenting on a later print by Gillray (*Dilettanti-Theatricals* of 1803), a writer in the German journal *London und Paris* recognized "the fat-cheeked little Lord Derby, who seduced the famous comic actress, . . . Miss Farren, from the theatre into the marriage bed. . . . [A]lthough the character of the present Lady Derby has always been pure and unsullied, both when she was an actress before her marriage and afterwards under the earl's coronet, the hidebound English nobility can never forget this mistake, and is always whispering things it would never dare say aloud. The dissipation of his first wife, Miss Farren's predecessor, plays a large part in this gossip, and is said to have contributed to the lengthening of the troublesome outgrowth on the brow of her husband." (Trans. Banerji and Donald 1999, 147.)
5. *The Death* might also allude to the political demise of Charles James Fox, of whom Derby was a partisan and with whom he appeared in several Gillray satires.
6. See Clifton 1995, 114–15.

Nicolas-Toussaint Charlet (1792–1845)

84. *Soldier at a Print-seller's Stand (Seriez-vous sensible?)*

1823

Lithograph, image: 174 x 188 mm (6⅞ x 7⅜ in.)

Reference: La Combe 532

Inscriptions: above image at right: *15.*; at lower left on bottom step: *Charlet*; in margin below image: *chez Gihaut b[ard] des Italiens n[o] 5; I. lith. de Villain*; below: *seriez vous sensible*

Purchased from Jan Johnson, Montreal

1999.9

The invention of lithography in Germany in the last years of the eighteenth century revolutionized the world of printmaking, allowing for a more direct translation of the artist's ideas into print. Large editions could be pulled from a single lithographic stone, making the medium less time intensive and more affordable than intaglio or relief prints. Within five years of lithography's viability in France (1815–20), the medium was adopted by loyal Bonapartists in opposition to the Restoration. The flood of Napoleonic images, depicting everything from uniforms and quotidian activities in camp to battle scenes, catered to the working-class market composed largely of retired and discharged soldiers of the Grande Armée.[1] Lithography's role in the cultivation and propagation of Napoleonic legend cannot be underestimated, and one of the leading military artists of the day was Nicolas-Toussaint Charlet, a staunch Bonapartist who fought as a national guardsman in the defense of the Clichy Barricade in 1814 and was the son of

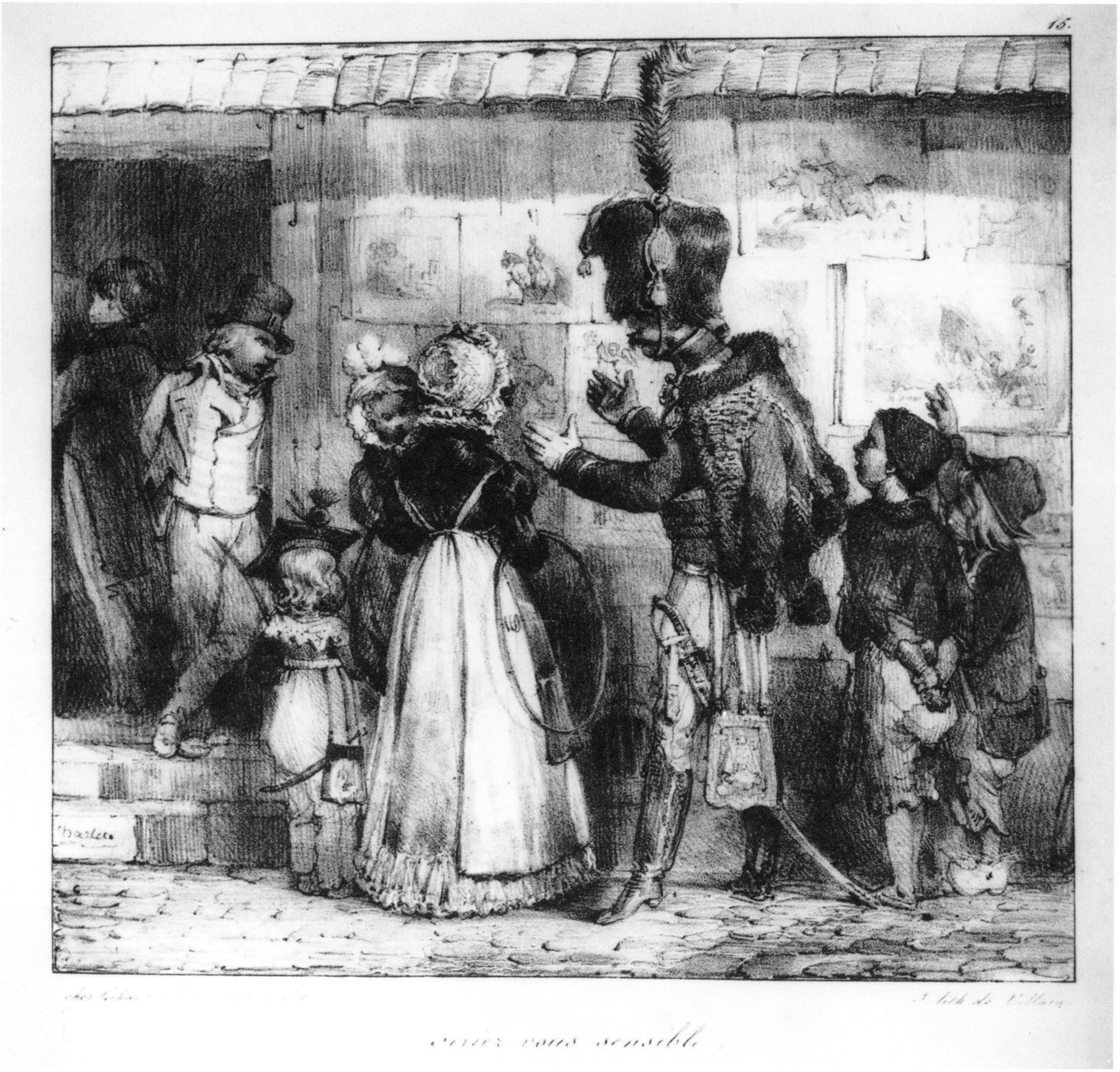

Cat. no. 84

a Republican soldier.[2] Charlet was particularly sensitive to the plight of the unemployed and often impoverished Napoleonic veteran under the Restoration, a theme that occurs repeatedly in the artist's extensive oeuvre.[3]

In *Seriez-vous sensible?* a soldier wearing the uniform of a *chasseur au cheval de la garde,* a member of the imperial light cavalry, is engaged in an animated discussion with a young maid in front of a print-seller's stand as the vendor looks on from the steps of his shop. The finely dressed children in the care of the maid contrast with the two indigent young street urchins at right, who are enamored by the display. The young boy at the maid's side is dressed up in military accoutrements, including a miniature sword and sabretache, symbolizing the respect soldiers were generally accorded by the French public.

The motif of a retired soldier telling stories in front of a print stand is not uncommon in Charlet's work. In both *Le Marchand de dessins lithographiques* from 1818–19 (La Combe 85) and *Tu vois Austerlitz au moment du tremblement* from 1827 (La Combe 673), a Napoleonic veteran expounds on his former exploits to a young soldier in front of a backdrop of military prints, which serve to complement the narrative. In *Seriez-vous sensible?,* however, an anonymous maid stands in place of the young soldier. While it is difficult to identify the particular prints displayed in the stall in *Seriez-vous sensible?,* one can make out the signature "H. Vernet" on the apparent battle scene pointed out by the child at right and "Géricault" on the equestrian print to the left of the soldier's fur cap. The prominently placed print of Cupid who is pointing his bow and arrow directly at the maid may elucidate the title of the work, which can be understood as a question of not only whether the woman would be sensitive or compassionate to the veteran's situation, but whether she would be receptive to his advances as well. The juxtaposition of the soldier's phallic sword with the maid's hoop, presumably a child's toy, further underscores the sexual innuendo. This reading of Charlet's lithograph is not meant to compete with, but rather to complement the artist's more common theme of the predicament of the neglected veteran.

Seriez-vous sensible?, inscribed under the text on the print, is plate fifteen (noted in the upper-right corner) of a lithographic album by Charlet consisting of a frontispiece and sixteen plates of varying subject matter, published by the Gihaut brothers in 1823.[4] The frontispiece, *Quand il n'y auras plus, il y en aura encore* (La Combe 515), depicts a young print seller leaning on a shovel before a veritable deluge of albums that are being delivered incessantly in large baskets. Frontispieces often commented in a reflexive and sometimes humorous manner on various aspects of the lithographic album, such as its development, public reception, and the role of the print-seller in its popularity.[5]

Charlet's lithographs were very popular in his own day, and he earned the respect and friendship of the leading artists of the time.[6] His depictions of soldiers were both objects of admiration and sources of inspiration. Emile de la Bédollière's account of 1840–42 of the military under the July Monarchy describes some old army officers who know no life other than the military, stating that they "aspirent à se donner le *chique* des soldats de Charlet, étudient les caricatures, en copient les poses, et en intercalent les légendes dans leur discours, comme des épices dans un ragoût."[7]

Charlet was not without his detractors, though. Charles Baudelaire, while acknowledging Charlet's popularity, criticized him sharply for being an inadequate draftsman and for catering to the taste of the masses. Baudelaire states that "a drawing by Charlet is seldom a truth; . . . There is no beauty, goodness, nobility, kindness or wit but in the soldier."[8] He asks the reader, ". . . What was this man but a manufacturer of nationalist nursery-rhymes, a licensed purveyor of political catchwords. . . ?"[9] Though Baudelaire's opinion of Charlet may have been tainted by his own political inclinations, he was not far off course when he stated that Charlet's reputation would soon ". . . slumber in the waste-paper basket of indifference, like this sheet of paper which I have needlessly soiled and which is now only fit for pulping."[10] Although Charlet was a prominent artist in the first half of the nineteenth century, his reputation has long since fallen into decline. His artistic corpus, however, has left us with an invaluable glimpse into social issues and conditions, particularly those concerning veterans, during the Restoration and the July Monarchy.

LS

1. Farwell 1989, 18.
2. Unless otherwise noted, all biographical details are taken from La Combe 1856. Charlet's portrait was included in the painting *La Barrière de Clichy,* 1820, by Horace Vernet, who also participated as a national guardsman in this event. On the painting, see Académie de France à Rome and Ecole nationale supérieure des Beaux-Arts 1980, no. 34.
3. When the Grande Armée was disbanded shortly after Waterloo, most officers were forced into retirement or put on inactive duty at half-pay. These *demi-soldes,* as they were called, were not permitted to work and were forced to survive on their reduced salary. Many turned to farming, which was not considered regular work, and the neglected *soldat laboureur* became an immensely popular theme in the art and literature of the Restoration. See Athanassoglou-Kallmyer 1986; and Woloch, 1979, esp. 295–303.
4. On the Gihaut brothers, see Bouquin 1989. For a list and brief description of the prints in the album, see La Combe 1856, nos. 515–533.
5. Bouquin 1989, 8.
6. La Combe 1856, 17, relates that Géricault sought out and introduced himself to Charlet in 1818, after which time they remained friends for life. Baudelaire 1956, 332, tells us that Delacroix came to Charlet's defense after Baudelaire published his blistering commentary on Charlet.
7. Quoted from Farwell 1983, 88.
8. Baudelaire 1956, 157.
9. Ibid., 159.
10. Ibid., 160.

Artists' Biographies

Pierre Aveline (Paris 1702–1760 Paris)
The son of a Parisian engraver of topographical views, Aveline studied with Jean-Baptiste de Poilly. He was approved by the Académie Royale on two separate occasions but was never accepted as a full academician. Aveline's best-known prints reproduce the works of Antoine Watteau, but he also made engravings after paintings by Boucher, Natoire, Oudry, and others.

Ludolf Bakhuizen (Emden 1630–1708 Amsterdam)
Calligrapher, painter, draftsman, and printmaker, Bakhuizen was a multifaceted artist. He had established himself as a painter of seascapes by 1658, and was the leading marine painter in the Netherlands after the departure of the van de Veldes for England in 1672. Many of his works glorify Amsterdam and the mercantile source of her prosperity, such as his first set of etchings, *D'Y Stroom en Zeegezichten (The River Ij and Seascapes),* produced when the artist was seventy-one. His noteworthy patrons included Frederick I of Prussia, Cosimo III de' Medici, and Peter the Great, who visited Bakhuizen's studio and is said to have received drawing instruction from him.

Baccio Bandinelli (Gaiole 1488–1560 Florence)
Born to a prominent Florentine goldsmith who was loyal to the Medici, Bandinelli remained a favorite of the family and received major commissions from the Medici popes, Leo X and Clement VII. Bandinelli studied sculpture in the studio of Giovanni Francesco Rustici, where he came in contact with the work of Leonardo da Vinci. He was knighted in the Order of Santiago by Charles V, becoming the first artist to receive this honor. Bandinelli's political views and megalomania led to harsh criticism and feuds with prominent artists such as Benvenuto Cellini and Michelangelo.

Pierre-Charles Baquoy (Paris 1759–1829 Paris)
Baquoy learned printmaking from his father, Jean-Charles (1721-1777), and is best known for his vignettes. In the later part of his career, he also produced some independent reproductive prints while still maintaining his work as a book illustrator. His two daughters, Angélique and Henriette, continued in their father's career path.

Nicolas Beatrizet (Thionville 1507 or Lunéville 1515–c. 1565 Rome)
A French engraver who was active in Italy, Beatrizet worked for several prominent Roman publishers, specializing in views of the ancient city and reproductive engravings after Italian masters, such as Michelangelo, Raphael, and Baccio Bandinelli. Drawing inspiration from Agostino Musi, Enea Vico, and the Ghisi brothers, Beatrizet's own skillful prints earned him the praise of Vasari.

Isaac Beckett (possibly Kent c. 1653–possibly 1715 or 1719 London)
Beckett was the first English-born professional mezzotint practitioner and was the most accomplished of the early mezzotint artists in England. He eventually set up shop as a publisher and print-seller as well. Beckett is best known for his sophisticated portraits but also produced religious and mythological scenes.

Stefano della Bella (Florence 1610–1664 Florence)
Della Bella, the youngest of five children, was born into a family of artists. His father was a sculptor in the studio of Giambologna, and each of his three older brothers became artists as well. Della Bella's formal training was brief. He was apprenticed to Orazio Vanni and other Florentine goldsmiths and also studied painting before deciding to become a printmaker. Della Bella learned etching from Callot's teacher, Remigio Cantagallina. He found patrons in the Medici, who funded his extended sojourn in Rome. His Roman period, from 1633 to 1639, was fundamental to the development of his individual style. In 1639, della Bella moved to Paris, where he produced the majority of his prints. He returned to Florence in 1650 and served as drawing teacher to Cosimo III. In 1656 he was elected to the literary society, Accademia degli Apatisti.

Abraham Blooteling (Amsterdam 1640–1690 Amsterdam)
A pupil of Cornelis van Dalen, Blooteling produced his earliest dated prints in 1665. He worked in a wide variety of genres but is perhaps best known for his portraits. Blooteling moved to London in 1672, where he increasingly embraced and even advanced the mezzotint technique. He mastered the dramatic tonal capabilities of the medium and greatly influenced later generations of English mezzotint practitioners. Blooteling moved back to Amsterdam by autumn 1678 and in his later years focused more on business activities, especially publishing and selling maps and prints.

Louis-Léopold Boilly (La Bassée 1761–1845 Paris)
Boilly received his earliest artistic instruction from his father, a wood carver, before studying trompe l'œil painting in Arras. In 1785/56 he moved to Paris, where he exhibited works at the Salon from 1791 to 1824, earning a gold medal in 1804. Boilly was successful as a painter of moralizing and amorous subjects influenced by Greuze and Fragonard, and of genre scenes whose detail and realism reflect his knowledge of seventeenth-century Dutch genre painting. Boilly is also known as a pioneer of lithography in France and is credited with producing the country's first dated lithograph in 1802.

Jean-Jacques de Boissieu (Lyon 1736–1810 Lyon)
A largely self-taught artist, Boissieu was a talented printmaker and draftsman who produced both reproductive prints and those of his own invention. He also dabbled in painting, though his works in this medium exhibit less skill and are often copies after his prints. Boissieu was influenced by Rembrandt, and vestiges of the Dutch school are to be found in his rustic landscapes. His works influenced such prominent artists as Félix Bracquemond and Adolph Menzel, and the dissemination of his prints in the nineteenth century helped create a vogue for works inspired by seventeenth-century Dutch art.

Johann Friedrich Bolt (Berlin 1769–1836)
Bolt was a draftsman and printmaker influenced largely by Daniel Chodowiecki (1726-1801). His book illustrations and numerous other designs include many contemporary portraits, which have some significance as historical documents.

Abraham Bosse (Tours 1602–1676 Paris)
Bosse most likely trained with the Flemish printmaker Melchior Tavernier (possibly 1564-1641) in Paris, where he settled permanently in 1632. Regardless of the subject matter, Bosse's works almost always depict figures in contemporary garb, and his large corpus of more than one thousand five hundred prints is an important source of documentation of seventeenth-century French society and social history. His theories on etching were set forth in his treatise of 1645, *Traité des manières de graver en taille-douce.* In 1648, Bosse began lecturing on perspective at the Académie Royale, and he was given an honorary membership in 1651. However, after having published several works promoting views directly opposed to the teachings of the Académie and becoming increasingly unorthodox and quarrelsome, Bosse was expelled from the institution in 1661.

François Boucher (Paris 1703–1770 Paris)
Perhaps more than any other artist, Boucher embodied the refined superficiality of court culture in mid-eighteenth-century France. He was a prolific painter, draftsman, designer, and printmaker, and is credited with reviving the pastoral landscape. His picturesque detail, painterly style, and saturated colors made him a favorite of Louis XV's powerful mistress, Madame de Pompadour. Boucher was

a versatile artist, designing stage sets, tapestries, and porcelain figurines. In 1755 he was named director of the Gobelins factory, and he became director of the Académie Royale and *premier peintre du roi* in 1765. His most notable student was Jean-Honoré Fragonard (1732–1806).

Dirck de Braij (Haarlem c. 1635–1694 Brabant)
Born into a family of artists in Haarlem, Dirck de Braij was trained as a printmaker and bookbinder. While he did produce a small corpus of oil paintings—mostly still lifes—he is most known for his woodcuts of various subjects, which he created both from his own designs and those of his brothers and father. Dirck de Braij served as secretary of the Guild of Saint Luke in Haarlem in 1671.

Jan de Braij (Haarlem c. 1627–1697 Haarlem)
Jan de Braij spent the majority of his life in Haarlem, where he learned to paint from his father, Salomon (1597–1664). He is best known as a portraitist and history painter, sometimes blurring the line between the two genres to create historiated portraits. From 1667 to 1684 de Braij served on the board of the Guild of Saint Luke. He was married three times and was declared bankrupt in 1689.

Pierre Brebiette (Mantes-la-Jolie c. 1598–c. 1650 Paris)
Brebiette was living in Rome by 1617 and remained in Italy until 1625, when he returned to Paris and was married the following year. His printed oeuvre is comprised of both reproductive engravings—after such Italian masters as Michelangelo, Raphael, and Veronese—and those of his own design. He particularly excelled in his inventive prints of bacchanals and allegorical and mythological scenes.

Nicolò della Casa (active 1543–48)
Little is known about the life of this French engraver from Lorraine. While working in Rome from 1543 to 1548, he italianized his surname. He is known to have produced only five engravings: a Last Judgment after Michelangelo, and portraits of Henry II, Charles V, Cosimo de' Medici, and Baccio Bandinelli.

Giovanni Benedetto Castiglione (Genoa 1609–1664 Mantua)
An eclectic and versatile artist, Castiglione is noted for the rich tones and vibrant brushstrokes of his paintings, while his etchings often exhibit dramatic chiaroscuro effects inspired by Rembrandt. His works display a wide range of themes, including journeys of biblical patriarchs and philosophical subjects, and he is credited with the development of the monotype. Castiglione was patronized by the Gonzaga court in Mantua, where his duties were not limited to producing paintings, but also included traveling to purchase artwork on behalf of the duke.

Nicolas-Toussaint Charlet (Paris 1792–1845 Paris)
Charlet was the son of a Republican soldier and received his early education in Napoleonic public schools. He was a loyal Bonapartist and fought in the defense of Clichy in 1814 during the fall of the First Empire. Charlet's first formal artistic instruction came from Charles Jacques Lebel, a student of Jacques-Louis David. In 1817, he entered the studio of Antoine-Jean Gros, a favorite painter of Napoleon, where he remained until 1820. Although Charlet was a competent painter and draftsman, he is best known for his military lithographs, particularly those representing Napoleonic veterans. In 1836, Charlet was admitted to the Académie des Beaux-Arts, and he was named professor at the Ecole Polytechnique in Paris in 1839.

Daniel Nikolaus Chodowiecki (Danzig 1726–1801 Berlin)
In 1743 Chodowiecki moved to Berlin, where he came into contact with local artists while training to become a salesman. There he learned the art of enamel painting from Johann Lorenz Haid and participated in life drawing sessions hosted by Christian Bernhard Rode. He joined the Berlin Kunstakademie in 1764 and was elevated to the position of director in 1797. Chodowiecki was an accomplished and prolific illustrator, working on both literary and pedagogical texts.

Giovanni Battista Cipriani (Florence 1727–1785 London)
Cipriani moved to England in 1755, where he was active as a designer and decorative painter in the Neoclassical style. He was a founding member of London's Royal Academy, where he taught and exhibited works between 1769 and 1779. Cipriani designed stage sets as well as ceiling paintings and other decorative elements for public and private buildings. He was also employed in the restoration of Rubens's ceiling at the Whitehall banqueting house in 1778. Cipriani was a prolific draftsman whose drawings were often engraved by his friend Francesco Bartolozzi (1727–1815).

Claude Gellée, called Claude Lorrain (Chamagne 1604–1682 Rome)
Claude Lorrain was the leading proponent of the ideal landscape, whose practitioners sought to surpass the beauty and order of nature itself. He spent most of his life and career in Rome and often made drawings outdoors in the Roman countryside. Although influenced by northern landscape painters in Rome, like Bartholomeus Breenbergh (1589–1657) and Paul Bril (c. 1554–1626), Claude created a landscape type all his own. His works are infused with dramatic light and ephemeral atmospheric effects and exude a sense of peaceful calm. Claude produced forty-four etchings, most of them based on his own paintings. His poetic landscapes were highly sought after, and his reputation earned him such distinguished patrons as Pope Urban VIII and King Philip IV of Spain.

Alexandre Clément (active late 18th–early 19th centuries)
Almost nothing is known of this stipple engraver, who was active in Paris. He printed several portraits and provided illustrations for the Parisian publisher, Defer de Maisonneuve, which appeared in books such as a 1792 edition of Milton's *Paradise Lost*.

Hans Collaert II (Antwerp 1566–1628 Antwerp)
Hans Collaert II was born into a family of Flemish artists. In 1585 he entered the Guild of Saint Luke in Antwerp and served as its dean from 1610 to 1613. Collaert worked primarily as a reproductive printmaker—engraving the works of Hans Bol, Hendrick Goltzius, Marten de Vos, and others—but was also a renowned designer of ornamental prints.

Jean Daullé (Abbeville 1703–1763 Paris)
A specialist in engraved portraits, Daullé became the preferred engraver of Hyacinthe Rigaud (1659–1743) and produced his finest prints after Rigaud's portraits. He was among the best reproductive engravers of his day, and his skill was such that he was both admitted and received by the Académie Royale in one day, June 2, 1742. From 1748 to 1755, Daullé concentrated more on genre scenes and mythological subjects, reproducing works by David Teniers the Younger, Joseph Vernet, François Boucher, and others. Daullé began to publish prints around 1754, and from that point on he engraved less frequently.

Giovanni David (Cabella Ligure 1743–1790 Genoa)
David moved to Rome around 1770, where he studied with Domenico Corvi (1721–1803), a prominent Neoclassical painter. In 1775, David's painting, *Moses Giving the Law,* earned him first prize at Rome's Accademia di San Luca. That same year, David moved to Venice, where he concentrated on printmaking and also served as a scene designer for La Fenice, the famed Venetian theater. David settled in Genoa in 1780, where he produced many paintings for churches and palazzi. He spent the rest of his life there, apart from excursions to England, France, and Holland.

Gilles Demarteau (Liège 1722–1776 Paris)
An early exponent of crayon manner prints, Demarteau first used improvised goldsmith's tools to create areas of shading on the plate that, when printed, closely imitated chalk drawing. In fact, the renowned French art critic Denis Diderot praised his prints for their marked resemblance to drawing. Demarteau's oeuvre consists of nearly six hundred plates, around half of which were printed after designs by François Boucher (1703–1770). He was admitted to the Académie Royale in 1769 and was appointed *graveur des dessins du cabinet du roi* in 1770.

Simon Du Bois (Antwerp 1632–1708 London)
In 1652–53, Du Bois trained with Philips Wouwerman (1619–1668) before moving to Italy with his brother. He is documented in Haarlem by 1661, and he finally settled in London around 1680. Du Bois painted portraits as well as battle scenes and landscapes. He also functioned as a dealer and made reproductions of old master paintings, which were sold as originals.

Anthony van Dyck (Antwerp 1599–1641 London)
Van Dyck began an apprenticeship with Hendrick van Balen in Antwerp before entering the workshop of Peter Paul Rubens (1577–1640), where he remained for two years. Rubens had a profound impact on van Dyck's style, which was also influenced by the works of Titian. He traveled extensively in Italy, where he developed a more refined manner characteristic of his mature works. While he produced a small number of etchings himself, van Dyck commanded an array of reproductive printmakers to work after his paintings and designs. In 1632, van Dyck moved to England and served as court painter to King Charles I, who knighted him in the same year. He remained in England the rest of his life, producing mainly portraits. He had a profound influence on Thomas Gainsborough and generations of British portrait painters who looked to his works as a standard of courtly portraiture.

Richard Earlom (London 1743–1822 London)
A pupil of Giovanni Battista Cipriani (1727–1785), Earlom worked mainly in mezzotint and etching. His reproductive prints include works after Jan van Huysum, Joseph Wright of Derby, Johann Zoffany, and George Stubbs. His most important prints, published in 1777, were produced after a volume of Claude Lorrain's drawings of his own paintings, the so-called *Liber Veritatis*.

Gérard Edelinck (Antwerp 1640–1707 Paris)
Edelinck studied engraving with Gaspar Huybrechts and Cornelis Galle II before moving to Paris in 1666. A specialist in portraiture, which accounts for about two-thirds of his oeuvre, Edelinck reproduced works for such prominent portrait painters as Nicolas de Largillierre and Hyacinthe Rigaud. He was appointed *premier dessinateur du cabinet du roi* and is counted among the best engravers of his day.

Odoardo Fialetti (Bologna 1573–1638 Venice)
Fialetti trained in Tintoretto's workshop in Venice and developed a style that incorporated elements of Flemish art and the realism characteristic of the Carracci. He fulfilled several commissions to paint works for Italian churches and engraved around two hundred fifty plates. Some of his prints reproduce paintings by Italian Renaissance and Baroque masters, whereas others were produced after his own designs.

James Gillray (London 1757–1815 London)
Gillray engraved more than one thousand five hundred compositions in the course of his career and established political caricature as an artistic genre in Great Britain. By 1775 Gillray was engraving satires for the publisher William Humphrey in London. In 1778 he enrolled at the Royal Academy Schools, where he was exposed to the Italian engraver Francesco Bartolozzi (1727–1815). While a student, Gillray supported himself with income from his engravings, and his first political satire appeared in 1778. Over the next several years he developed a style that changed the face of British caricature. Whereas previous artists had largely depicted types instead of individuals, Gillray was among the first to exaggerate the recognizable physical features of his subjects and to combine these distinctive likenesses with complex political and social satires. Despite his often scathing caricatures, Gillray was able to avoid censure for the most part, giving expression to a generation of public opinion.

Jacob Gole (Amsterdam 1660–c. 1737 Amsterdam)
Very little is known about the life of Gole, a printmaker and publisher from Amsterdam. He probably spent some time in Haarlem, becoming closely associated with Cornelis Dusart (1660–1704), for whom he sometimes provided preparatory drawings and acted as publisher. In 1688 Gole accompanied the Prince of Orange to England, where the latter ascended the throne as King William III. Gole is known for his portraits and genre scenes, and many of his prints reflect the compositions of artists like Jan Steen, Adriaen van Ostade, Adriaen Brouwer, and Anthony van Dyck.

Hendrick Goltzius (Mülbracht 1558–1617 Haarlem)
Perhaps the finest and best-known engraver of his day, Goltzius received his training first from his father, a glass painter, and then from Dirck Coornhert, a prominent Dutch politician, humanist, and printmaker. Early in his career, Goltzius was the leading proponent of Mannerism in the northern Netherlands, but after a trip to Italy in 1590/91, his style began to incorporate more classical influences. Goltzius was known for his virtuosic ability to adapt to various artistic styles, despite the fact that his right hand was disabled from a childhood accident. From about 1600, Goltzius virtually abandoned engraving in favor of painting, although his printmaking style continued to flourish under his adept pupils Jan Muller, Jacques de Gheyn II, Jacob Matham, and Jan Saenredam.

Francisco Goya (Fuendetodos 1746–1828 Bordeaux)
Goya served three kings of Spain during his long and productive career, and his artistic style spanned from Rococo to Romanticism and to the brink of Impressionism. In addition to his talent as a painter, Goya was also a gifted graphic artist, producing some nine hundred drawings and nearly three hundred prints. In 1792, a serious illness left him deaf and seems to mark a crossroads in his career. From that point on, Goya's compositions became increasingly morbid and brutal. Although he was revered for his portraits in his own time, he is best known today for his vivid social satire and nightmarish visions of the cruelty of war.

Pierre-Narcisse Guérin (Paris 1774–1833 Rome)
Though not a prolific painter, Guérin was one of the most successful artists of his day. He made his Salon debut in 1795 and was awarded the Rome Prize in 1797. In 1822, Guérin assumed the directorship of the French Academy in Rome. During the 1820s, he dabbled in lithography but only executed four prints. While he was rooted in the Neoclassical tradition—admiring Poussin and David and drawing inspiration from the tales of Greek mythology—Guérin also trained the next generation of painters, including Delacroix and Géricault, who would become pivotal figures in the Romantic movement.

Johann Jakob Haid (Kleineislingen 1704–1767 Augsburg)
Born to a family of artists, Haid began working with the German animal painter Johann Elias Ridinger early in his career. He later established a publishing house and was known mainly for a series of mezzotint portraits produced after his drawings and those of other artists. His son and pupil, Johann Elias Haid, continued his father's publishing house and eclipsed him in artistic importance.

Francesco Hayez (Venice 1791–1882 Milan)
Hayez made his first trip to Rome in 1809, where he studied ancient sculpture as well as Raphael's frescoes in the Vatican. There he came into contact with Antonio Canova (1757–1822), who had a profound influence on him, as well as with foreign artists like Ingres (1780–1867). Hayez spent most of his career in Milan, where was active as both a painter and printmaker specializing in portraits and history scenes. He was an important figure in the transition from Neoclassicism to Romanticism, eventually becoming Italy's leading exponent of the latter movement. During the period of Italy's unification, Hayez was considered by many a great patriot, and his historical paintings were often laden with contemporary political significance.

Johann Georg Hertel the Elder (1700–1775, active in Augsburg)
The patriarch of a family of engravers, Hertel was a maker of plaster casts in his youth. Later on, he owned a share of a publishing house before finally founding his own publishing establishment. Around 1760, he published a German translation of the immensely popular *Iconologia* by Cesare Ripa.

William Hogarth (London 1697–1764 London)
William Hogarth earned a living as a commercial engraver in London by 1720. Later that year, he enrolled in the Saint Martin's Lane Academy. In 1724, Hogarth began studying painting with James Thornhill, whose daughter he would later marry. Well known for his moral progresses and social satires, Hogarth lent an original and distinctive character to British art, helping to forge a uniquely English school. Many of Hogarth's paintings were created with the intention of being reproduced. He successfully published and sold his own engravings from 1724, demonstrating that artists could free themselves from dependence on patrons by publishing reproductive prints of their own paintings. His treatise *The Analysis of Beauty* (1753) rails against academicism and claims that the views and theories of the professional artist should outweigh those of the dilettante or connoisseur.

Johann Jacobe (Vienna 1733–1797 Vienna)
After his early training in the mezzotint technique in Vienna, Jacobe was sent on a state-sponsored trip to London in 1778 to perfect his skills in the medium. While there, he made reproductive prints after Joshua Reynolds (1723–1792) and George Romney (1734–1802). In 1782, Jacobe was named professor of mezzotint at the Viennese Academy, where he taught for the remainder of his life and had a considerable influence in the dissemination of the mezzotint.

Louis-Félix de La Rue (Paris 1730–1777 Paris)
Primarily known for his sculptural work, de La Rue won the Rome Prize in 1750. He was employed for a time at the porcelain factory at Vincennes, modeling figures after drawings by Boucher. De La Rue entered Paris's Academy of Saint Luke in 1760 and exhibited works at its salons in 1762 and 1764.

Charles Le Brun (Paris 1619–1690 Paris)
Charles Le Brun was the dominant painter working in France during the reign of Louis XIV. In 1642 he traveled with Poussin to Rome and absorbed his artistic theories, which he later attempted to codify. Le Brun was one of the twelve founding members of the Académie Royale, where he presented influential lectures that helped shape the principles of academicism. He was in charge of the decoration of Versailles, which, along with the Galerie d'Apollon in the Louvre, is among his most notable accomplishments.

Sébastien Leclerc I (Metz 1637–1714 Paris)
Leclerc was trained as a draftsman, painter, and military engineer. He moved to Paris around 1664–65, where he found a mentor in Charles Le Brun and entered into the king's service. His popularity and numerous commissions eventually led him to leave the royal service to work independently. Leclerc was a prolific artist who produced prints of the highest quality, mostly after his own designs. He worked mainly in small formats and was highly sought after for his book illustrations, which account for over half of his oeuvre.

E. Le Sueur (active in France c. 1775–1800)
Almost nothing is known about Le Sueur, who was a designer of prints active in France. His work includes scenes of Venus chastising Cupid, Pygmalion admiring his sculpture of Galatea, and the Imprudence of Candaule.

Pietro Antonio Martini (Trecasali 1738–1797 Parma)
Martini moved to Paris at a young age, where he entered the workshop of Jacques-Philippe Lebas and executed engravings after Flemish masters. He also worked for a time in England before eventually returning to Parma. Martini worked in various genres, engraving history pieces, views, and scenes of everyday life.

Jacob Matham (Haarlem 1571–1631 Haarlem)
Matham was apprenticed to Hendrick Goltzius after his mother married the master printmaker in 1579. He worked very closely with Goltzius but did not clearly develop his own artistic identity. Matham traveled to Italy between 1593 and 1597 and executed many prints after the Italian masters upon his return. He was elected dean of Haarlem's Guild of Saint Luke in 1605.

Theodor Matham (Haarlem 1605/6–1676 Amsterdam)
Theodor Matham, along with his two brothers, was trained by his father, Jacob Matham, according to methods the latter learned in the workshop of Goltzius. Theodor engraved many portraits and figural settings. He also participated in campaigns to reproduce in prints the Reynst art collection in Amsterdam and the Giustiniani sculpture collection in Rome.

Henri Mauperché (possibly Paris c. 1602–1686 Paris)
Mauperché traveled to Rome in 1634 and returned to Paris by 1639, when he worked on a commission to paint landscapes and views for Cardinal Richelieu at the Palais-Royal. He was accepted to the Académie Royale in 1648 and became a professor there in 1655. In the 1660s, Mauperché executed eight landscape paintings for the apartments of Maria Teresa, wife of Louis XIV, in the Louvre. He is best known, however, for his intricate and lively engravings.

Anton Raphael Mengs (Aussig 1728–1779 Rome)
Mengs is widely recognized as a leader of the Neoclassical movement. He served as court painter in Dresden and later in Madrid but spent most of his career in Rome, where he formed a reputation as a distinguished portraitist and history painter. In Rome he came into contact with the antiquarian Johann Winckelmann (1717–1768), who became his mentor and fostered his interest in the antique. Mengs recorded his thoughts and theories on art, which were published shortly after his death, translated into various languages, and widely disseminated.

Frans van Mieris the Elder (Leiden 1635–1681 Leiden)
One of the undisputed masters of seventeenth-century Dutch genre painting, Frans van Mieris was born to a family of silver- and goldsmiths and served an early apprenticeship in this field. He was already painting by 1651, however, and in 1658 he joined Leiden's Guild of Saint Luke. Van Mieris was the most distinguished pupil of the Leiden "fine painter" Gerrit Dou (1613–1675), from whom he learned his painstakingly meticulous technique. Van Mieris's style and subject matter influenced other great genre painters of his own day, and the esteem in which he was held is reflected both in the reviews of contemporary critics and in the exceedingly high prices paid for his works. His polished manner of painting was carried on by his children, Jan and Willem, and his grandson, Frans II.

Pierre Mignard (Troyes 1612–1695 Paris)
After arriving in Paris, Mignard joined the workshop of Simon Vouet in 1633, becoming one of his most successful students. Mignard lived in Italy from 1635 to 1657, where he absorbed the influence of the Carracci and Francesco Albani, among others. After his return to Paris, Mignard became highly sought after for his vivid and elegant portraits. Following the death of his rival Charles Le Brun in 1690, Mignard succeeded him as *premier peintre du roi* and director of the Académie Royale.

Jean-Michel Moreau, called Le Jeune (Paris 1741–1814 Paris)
In 1758 Moreau traveled to St. Petersburg, where he served as drawing professor at the Academy of Fine Arts. He returned to Paris in 1759 and entered the studio of the printmaker Jacques-Philippe Lebas, providing drawings to be engraved after both contemporary artists and the old masters. In 1770 Moreau was appointed *dessinateur des menus plaisirs du roi* and in 1781 was named *dessinateur et graveur du cabinet du roi*. He was a successful book illustrator, and his drawings of court activities provide a record of French fashion and etiquette in the twilight of the *ancien régime*. In 1789 he was received in the Académie Royale and remained active during the French Revolution. Among his notable students was his grandson Horace Vernet (1789–1863).

Jacob Neeffs (Antwerp 1610–after 1660 Antwerp)
Neeffs was one of the last followers of Rubens to work directly for the master. An etcher and engraver, he made many book illustrations and reproductive prints after Annibale Carracci, Jacob Jordaens, and others. Neeffs also contributed to Anthony van Dyck's compendium of illustrious men, the *Iconography*.

Adriaen van Ostade (Haarlem 1610–1685 Haarlem)
As a pupil of Frans Hals in Haarlem, van Ostade was primarily influenced by the subject matter of his fellow student Adriaen Brouwer. Van Ostade was active in Haarlem's Guild of Saint Luke and in 1662 was appointed dean of that organization. He became a leading specialist in Dutch genre and peasant scenes, taking a more sympathetic attitude toward his subjects than did many of his contemporaries. His prominence as an etcher in Holland was eclipsed only by Rembrandt. A highly productive and prosperous artist, more than eight hundred paintings and four hundred drawings by van Ostade are extant today. He also added figures to works by artists such as Jacob van Ruisdael and Pieter Saenredam. Although he did not maintain a large workshop, van Ostade did train some notable pupils, including his brother Isaak van Ostade, Cornelis Bega, Cornelis Dusart, and Jan Steen.

Philippe-Louis Parizeau (Paris 1740–1801)
Parizeau studied printmaking in the studio of Jean-Georges Wille (1715–1808), which was one of the most respected engraving centers in Paris. Parizeau's etchings and aquatints generally depict mythological and historical subjects, as well as genre scenes, replicating the paintings of Salvator Rosa, François Boucher, and others.

Jean Pesne (Rouen 1623–1700 Paris)
Known more for his engravings and etchings than for his paintings, Jean Pesne made prints after many of Poussin's works. He also reproduced paintings by such masters as Raphael, van Dyck, and the Carracci.

William Pether (Carlisle c. 1738–1821 Bristol)
Known for the rich tonal quality of his mezzotints, William Pether engraved more than fifty plates, reproducing the paintings of old masters and contemporaries alike. He was particularly drawn to the works of Rembrandt and Joseph Wright of Derby. In a lesser known aspect of his career, Pether also produced chalk portraits, which he exhibited at the Society of Artists and the Free Society.

Jean-Baptiste-Marie Pierre (Paris 1714–1789 Paris)
Pierre primarily painted large-scale religious works and subjects from history but also depicted a number of genre scenes. He adapted his style according to his subject matter: his early history and religious paintings often drew upon the intensity of the Italian Baroque, while his mythological paintings tended toward the light and graceful forms of the Rococo. Pierre trained with Charles-Joseph Natoire (1700–1777) and earned the Rome Prize in 1734. In 1740 he was back in Paris and was appointed professor at the Académie Royale in 1744. In 1770 Pierre was named *premier peintre du roi* and director of the Académie Royale.

Giovanni Andrea Podestà (Genoa 1608–c. 1674 Genoa)
After his early training in Genoa, Podestà moved to Rome, where he was influenced by the paintings of Titian and became a follower of Gaspard Dughet. Podestà's preferred subjects for both paintings and etchings included bacchanals and frolicking children or putti in landscapes. His works have often been confused with those of Gaspard Dughet and Pietro Testa, both of whom were also active in Rome at the same time.

Nicolas Poussin (Les Andelys 1594–1665 Rome)
Poussin spent most of his career in Rome, where he became the leading exponent of the classical mode of Baroque painting. Though not a student of Domenichino, Poussin drew in his studio and by 1632 was a member of the Academy of Saint Luke. He painted scenes from history and mythology, and later took a serious interest in landscapes. His works are known for their rational order as well as their emphasis on gesture and clearly articulated emotion. Poussin believed that painting should appeal more to the mind than the eye, and his principles were to become the central tenets of classicism, which would later be codified by Le Brun and taught in academies.

Martin Ferdinand Quadal (Niemtschitz, Moravia 1736–1808 St. Petersburg)
An itinerant painter who traveled widely, Quadal trained in Vienna's Akademie der Bildenden Künste and studied in Paris in 1767. He worked in a variety of genres and exhibited hunting pictures and portraits at the Royal Academy in London during the 1770s. Many of his paintings were reproduced in engravings and mezzotints.

Rembrandt van Rijn (Leiden 1606–1669 Amsterdam)
Rembrandt attended Latin school in Leiden and enrolled in the university there before entering the workshop of Jacob van Swanenburgh, where he remained for about three years. He then studied with Pieter Lastman in Amsterdam for six months. Unlike many of his contemporaries, he never traveled to Italy. In 1631 Rembrandt settled in Amsterdam, where he quickly became the city's foremost portrait painter. He is highly regarded for his facility in various genres, and his mature paintings are characterized by expressive, broad handling and emotional depth. In addition to his eminence as a painter, Rembrandt has been considered by many the finest etcher in history, and his prints display an unparalleled range of dramatic tonal effects. Despite his success, in 1656 Rembrandt declared bankruptcy. He was forced to sell his collection and move out of his house. Rembrandt made around four hundred paintings, nearly three hundred prints, and over one thousand drawings. His notable pupils included Dou, Bol, Flinck, and de Gelder.

Christian Bernhard Rode (Berlin 1725–1797 Berlin)
After early training in Germany, Rode moved to Paris where he studied with Jean Restout and Carle Vanloo between 1750 and 1752. He was in Italy between 1754 and 1756, where he painted oil sketches after Italian masters like Tintoretto, Titian, and Giordano. After returning to Germany, Rode received commissions to paint works for various German churches and aristocratic residences. He served as director of Berlin's Akademie der Künste in 1783. Rode was comfortable working in different artistic genres, producing history paintings, portraits, genre scenes, and landscapes. His graphic oeuvre includes more than three hundred etchings.

Salvator Rosa (Naples 1615–1673 Rome)
After receiving his early training in Naples, which may have included an apprenticeship with Jusepe de Ribera (1591-1652), Rosa departed for Rome in 1635. Although he strove to be a successful history painter, his most popular works—and those with which he made his most significant contribution to art history—were his rugged landscapes. These expressive and dramatic works contrast sharply with the more serene, classically inspired landscapes of Claude Lorrain and Nicolas Poussin. Rosa developed a scorn for society in general and refused to succumb to the demands of patrons, preferring to create works without a commission which would then be sold through dealers or displayed at public exhibitions. Rosa may have begun to etch in the 1630s, but his most successful and ambitious prints date from the 1660s, when he used them to publicize his paintings.

William Wynne Ryland (London 1732–1783 London)
The first significant stipple artist in England, Ryland was named engraver to King George III in 1762. He was a popular printmaker, producing around fifty stipples, most of them after Angelica Kauffman. He also worked as a print publisher and seller at different points in his career. Despite his success, Ryland accrued great debts and was eventually executed for forging bills of exchange.

Aegidius Sadeler II (Antwerp c. 1570–1629 Prague)
Aegidius Sadeler II was born into a family of Flemish engravers, print dealers, and publishers. Aegidius studied with his uncle, Jan Sadeler I, and around 1587 accompanied him to Munich, where he came into contact with many influential artists, including Joris Hoefnagel, Hans von Aachen, and Hendrick Goltzius. While living in Munich, Aegidius visited Italy twice and sold many of his copper plates to support his travels. In 1597 Aegidius moved to Prague and entered the circle of prominent Mannerist artists gathered at the court of the Holy Roman Emperor Rudolf II. He served as imperial engraver to Rudolf II and his successors, Matthias and Ferdinand II. His official portraits, often laced with allegorical allusions, are characterized by their delicate rendering and psychological penetration. His pupil and biographer, Joachim von Sandrart, described his friend as a "phoenix among engravers."

Jan Saenredam (Zaandam c. 1565–1607 Assendelft)
Saenredam worked in the circles of two celebrated Dutch graphic artists, Jacques de Gheyn II and Hendrick Goltzius. Though Saenredam was apprenticed to de Gheyn rather late in life—the master and student were the same age—he was his most gifted pupil. His earliest prints were executed after drawings made by Goltzius in Rome and bear the date 1593. In fact, he worked primarily from Goltzius's drawings, and Saenredam's early engravings reflect his influence. Saenredam's most original works date from 1600 on, when he began to engrave many compositions of his own design. The attention to individual detail and spatial relationships in his prints of this period exhibit a marked difference from Goltzius's more abbreviated style. His son Pieter was a highly successful painter who specialized in the depiction of church interiors.

Augustin Jacques Renard de Saint-André (active c. 1695–1705)
Almost nothing is known of this printmaker, whose work is often confused with that of Simon Renard de Saint-André. He engraved a collection of forty-four prints after Charles Le Brun's paintings in the Galerie d'Apollon in the Louvre, which was published in 1695.

Augustin de Saint-Aubin (Paris 1736–1807 Paris)
Although Saint-Aubin never became a full member of the Académie Royale due to his failure to submit a reception piece, he did exhibit prints and drawings at the annual Salon between 1771 and 1793. He designed some of his own prints, made drawings to be printed by other artists, and engraved plates after the designs of others, particularly Charles-Nicolas Cochin and François Boucher. In 1776 he was appointed draftsman and engraver of the Bibliothèque Royale, and then served in the same capacity for the Duc d'Orléans, where he was responsible for printing reproductions of the Orléans collection of gems.

Georg Frederic Schmidt (Berlin 1712–1775 Berlin)
After training with Georg Paul Busch (d. 1756) and a six-year military stint, Schmidt left Berlin for Paris in 1736. There he worked as a portrait engraver, eventually securing commissions from the foremost French portrait painter, Hyacinth Rigaud (1659-1743). In 1746 Schmidt was back in Berlin, where he stayed until accepting an invitation from Empress Elizabeth of Russia to engrave her portrait and found a school for engraving at the Imperial Academy in St. Petersburg. Later in his career, Schmidt began to focus more on etching, producing a number of book illustrations and many prints in the style of Rembrandt.

Heinrich Sintzenich (Mannheim 1752–1812 Munich)
Sintzenich first studied at Mannheim's drawing academy before traveling to London to learn the art of stipple engraving from Francesco Bartolozzi. After his return to Germany, he helped popularize the new technique and was named court engraver by the Elector of Mannheim.

Bartholomaeus Spranger (Antwerp 1546–1611 Prague)
Spranger received his early training in Antwerp before setting out for Paris in 1565 and then moving on to Italy. In Rome Spranger received commissions from Cardinal Alessandro Farnese and Pope Pius V, who named him a papal painter. He also worked for Emperor Maximilian II in Vienna before becoming one of the central artists at the court of his successor, Rudolf II, in Prague. Spranger's paintings, known widely through reproductive engravings, combined Netherlandish realism with Italian Mannerism to form a highly sophisticated and intellectual style.

Joannes Stradanus (Bruges 1523–1605 Florence)
After receiving his early training in Flanders, Stradanus set out for Italy and was employed designing cartoons for the Medici tapestry factory in Florence from 1546 to 1550. After a three-year stint in Rome he returned to Florence and from 1557 worked under the supervision of Giorgio Vasari (1511-1574) on decorations for the Palazzo Vecchio. While still occupied with work for the Palazzo Vecchio, Stradanus produced cartoons for a set of tapestries depicting hunting scenes, which was so popular that he designed two more hunting series to be engraved.

Willem van Swanenburg (Leiden 1580–1612 Leiden)
Van Swanenburg was trained in painting by his father and may have learned engraving from Jacques de Gheyn. Although he died young, van Swanenburg was one of the most promising Dutch engravers of his day, executing prints after Peter Paul Rubens, Joachim Wtewael, and Abraham Bloemaert.

Pietro Testa (Lucca 1612–1650 Rome)
Testa spent most of his career in Rome, where he trained in Domenichino's workshop before entering the studio of Pietro da Cortona (1596-1669). While in Rome, he provided drawings for the project to engrave the antiquities collection of Vincenzo Giustiniani and for Cassiano dal Pozzo's Paper Museum. Among the many artists with whom Testa came in contact in Rome was Nicolas Poussin, who was a significant influence throughout his career. While Testa strove to become a respected history painter, he was more gifted as a draftsman and printmaker and etched some forty plates. Testa began writing a treatise outlining his artistic theory and principles, but the work was never finished and is only known through his notes. Testa drowned in the Tiber River at the age of thirty-seven in an apparent suicide.

Giandomenico Tiepolo (Venice 1727–1804 Venice)
Tiepolo trained in the workshop of his father, Giambattista, and later served as both his assistant and collaborator. He produced a small number of original etchings, but most of his prints are reproductions of his own paintings as well as those of his father. He traveled to Spain with his father in 1762 and served as president of the Academy in Venice from 1780 to 1783.

Wallerant Vaillant (Lille 1623–1677 Amsterdam)
Vaillant learned the art of mezzotint engraving from the purported inventor of the technique, Prince Rupert of the Rhine (1619–1682), in Frankfurt. Vaillant achieved great success and is considered the first professional mezzotint practitioner. He produced more than two hundred plates after works from the Italian and Dutch schools as well as his own paintings. His most notable student was Abraham Blooteling.

Carle Vanloo (Nice 1705–1765 Paris)
In 1714 Vanloo moved with his brother from Turin to Rome, where he studied with Benedetto Lutti and Pierre Legros (the younger). The two brothers went to Paris in 1719, but Vanloo was back in Rome in 1728 after winning the Rome Prize in 1724. Vanloo returned to France in 1734 along with his new wife, and he was admitted to the Académie Royale in 1735. He worked for both the French court and the aristocracy and tailored his style to the particular subject or commission, sometimes working in the monumental Grand Manner, while at others opting for the sensuous Rococo. Vanloo was very successful in his day and accumulated many distinctions, including being named *premier peintre du roi* in 1762 and director of the Académie Royale in 1763. Perhaps the most notable of his students was Jean-Honoré Fragonard (1732–1806).

Dirk Vellert (possibly Amsterdam c. 1480/85–after 1547 Antwerp)
Vellert is best known as a designer and painter of stained glass and as a printmaker. He served as dean of Antwerp's Guild of Saint Luke in 1518 and 1526 and supervised six pupils between 1512 and 1530. Vellert produced both monumental stained-glass windows for churches as well as smaller roundels popular in the decoration of private residences. His prints often combine the techniques of engraving and etching and exhibit the influence of Albrecht Dürer, Lucas van Leyden, Jan Gossaert, and Marcantonio Raimondi. Dürer cites him three times in his journal of his visit to the Netherlands (1520–21), mentioning an exchange of pigments and a dinner hosted by Vellert.

Enea Vico (Parma 1523–1567 Ferrara)
After receiving his early training in Parma, Vico settled in Rome by 1541, where he studied under the tutelage of the printmaker and publisher Tommaso Barlacchi, with whom he produced his first set of engravings. In Rome he was influenced by the prints of Marcantonio Raimondi (c. 1470–c. 1527), whose fame was derived from his creative reproductions after Raphael and the antique. Vico was also an important scholar of antiquities, a penchant he combined with his talent as a printmaker. He was particularly interested in ancient medals and produced several volumes of engravings after the antique. Vasari notes that Vico's diligent records of ancient statues, portrait medals, vases, cameos, and gems earned him great praise in his own day. He enjoyed the patronage of Grand Duke Cosimo I de' Medici in Florence and spent his last years in the service of Duke Alfonso II d'Este in Ferrara.

Reinier Vinkeles (Amsterdam 1741–1816 Amsterdam)
Vinkeles studied with the Amsterdam painter and printmaker Jan Punt (1711–1779) for ten years. He became well known both in Holland and throughout Europe, earning entrance into four foreign academies as well as the Amsterdam Stadstekenacademie. Vinkeles went to Paris in 1770, but returned to Amsterdam a year later. In 1771, he declined an offer from Catherine the Great to head the St. Petersburg Academy of Arts. Vinkeles was extremely prolific, producing over three thousand prints encompassing a range of diverse subjects.

Antoine Watteau (Valenciennes 1684–1721 Nogent-sur-Marne)
In 1702 Watteau settled in Paris and shortly thereafter began working for Claude Gillot, from whom he developed an interest in theatrical subjects, including characters and scenes from the *commedia dell'arte.* After parting with Gillot, Watteau joined the ornamental painter Claude Audran III, who also served as the curator of Luxenbourg Palace. This association allowed Watteau access to Rubens's famous Marie de' Medici cycle in the palace, which had a profound influence on him. Watteau was a prolific draftsman who bound his sketches and used them as source material for his paintings. He is credited with the invention of a new type of painting, the *fête galante,* in which elegant people socialize in a pastoral setting, creating an atmosphere of detached frivolity.

Pierre Woeiriot (Neufchâteau, Vosges, 1532–1599 Damblain, Haute-Marne)
Woeiriot initially worked as a goldsmith, following the family trade. From about 1555, though, he functioned primarily as a printmaker, producing well over four hundred engravings as well as a smaller corpus of woodcuts. Woeiriot's subject matter included religious scenes, ornamental designs, and portraits. He was influenced by Giorgio Ghisi, Bernard Salomon, and Maarten van Heemskerck.

Joseph Wright of Derby (Derby 1734–1797 Derby)
Wright studied painting in the London workshop of Thomas Hudson on two separate occasions. He made a living as a portraitist, though in the 1760s he began to paint dramatic candlelit scenes, often scientific in subject, whose rich chiaroscuro is derived from Dutch masters and Caravaggio. He also developed a penchant for nocturnal scenes and landscapes. Wright arrived in Rome in 1774, where he sketched antiquities, the Sistine Chapel, and an eruption of Mount Vesuvius at Naples, which inspired some thirty paintings. Later in his career, Wright increasingly depicted literary subjects and in the 1780s contributed three works to the Shakespeare Gallery in London.

Johann Zoffany (near Frankfurt am Main 1733–1810 Strand-on-the-Green)
After working in Rome for about ten years, Zoffany moved to England in 1760 to pursue a career in decorative painting. He became known for his conversation pieces as well as his paintings of theatrical scenes, often depicting his patron, the actor David Garrick, in one of his roles. Zoffany traveled to Italy in 1772, and found upon his return that the demand for his conversation pieces had waned. He went to India in 1783 in the hopes of securing fresh commissions and was immensely successful, returning to England in 1789 a wealthy man.

Leslie Scattone

References

Bartsch
Bartsch, Adam von. *Le peintre graveur.* 21 vols. Vienna: Degen, 1803–21.

Bauer
Bauer, Jens-Heiner. *Daniel Nikolaus Chodowiecki: Das druckgraphische Werk.* Hannover: Verlag Galerie J. H. Bauer, 1982.

Bellini
Bellini, Paolo. *L'opera incisa di Giovanni Benedetto Castiglione.* Exh. cat. Milan: Castello Sforzesca, 1982.
and
Bellini, Paolo. *L'opera incisa di Pietro Testa.* Vicenza: N. Pozza, 1976.

Béraldi
Béraldi, Henri. *Les graveurs du XIX siècle: Guide de l'amateur d'estampes modernes.* 12 vols. Paris: L. Conquet, 1885–92.

Bleackley
Bleackley, Ruth. "A List of William Wynne Ryland's Engravings." *Connoisseur* 12 (1905): 110–11.

Blum
Blum, André. *L'oeuvre gravé d'Abraham Bosse.* Paris: A. Morancé, 1924.

Bocher
Bocher, Emmanuel. *Les gravures françaises de XVIIIe siècle.* . . . 6 fasc. in 3. Paris: Librairie des bibliophiles, 1875–82.

Chaloner Smith
Chaloner Smith, John. *British Mezzotint Portraits.* . . . 4 vols. London: Henry Sotheran, 1878–84.

Clayton
Clayton, Tim. "A Catalogue of the Engraved Works of Joseph Wright of Derby." In *Wright of Derby,* edited by Judy Egerton, 231–58. Exh. cat. New York: Metropolitan Museum of Art, 1990.

Dacier and Vuaflart
Dacier, Émile, and Albert Vuaflart. *Jean de Jullienne et les graveurs de Watteau au XVIIIe siècle.* 4 vols. Paris: Societé pour l'étude de la gravure française, 1921–29.

Delteil
Delteil, Loys. *Le peintre-graveur illustré (XIXe et XXe siècles).* 32 vols. Paris: Chez l'auteur, 1906–1930.

De Vesme
De Vesme, Alexandre. *Le peintre-graveur italien.* 1906. Reprint, Mansfield Centre, Conn.: Martino, 2001.

De Vesme and Massar
De Vesme, Alexandre, and P. D. Massar. *Stefano della Bella: Catalogue raisonné.* 2 vols. New York: Collectors Editions, 1971.

Duplessis
Duplessis, Georges. *Catalogue de l'oeuvre de Abraham Bosse.* Paris: A. Labroue, 1859.

Dussler
Dussler, Luitpold. *Die Incunabeln der deutschen Lithographie (1796–1821).* Berlin: H. Tiedemann, 1925.

Engelmann
Engelmann, Wilhelm. *Daniel Chodowiecki's sämmtliche Kupferstiche.* Leipzig: Verlag von Wilh. Engelmann, 1857.

Firmin-Didot
Firmin-Didot, Ambroise. *Les graveurs de portraits en France* . . . . 2 vols. Paris: Firmin-Didot, 1875–77.

Goncourt
Goncourt, Edmond de. *Catalogue raisonné de l'oeuvre peint, dessiné et gravé d'Antoine Watteau.* Paris: Rapilly, 1875.

Grasso
Grasso, Giovanni. "Incisioni." In *Giovanni David: Pittore e incisore della famiglia Durazzo,* by Mary Newcome Schleier and Giovanni Grasso, 105–91. Turin: Artema, 2003.

Harris
Harris, Tomás. *Goya Engravings and Lithographs.* Oxford: Bruno Cassirer, 1964 (republished in reduced format, San Francisco: Alan Wofsy Fine Arts, 1983).

Heller and Andresen
Heller, Joseph, and Andreas Andresen. *Handbuch für Kupferstichsammler* . . . . 2 vols. Leipzig: T. O. Weigel, 1870–73.

Hirschmann
Hirschmann, Otto. *Verzeichnis des graphischen Werks von Hendrick Goltzius, 1558–1617.* Leipzig: Klinkhardt & Biermann, 1921.

Hollstein
Hollstein, F. W. H. *Dutch and Flemish Etchings, Engravings, and Woodcuts, ca. 1450–1700.* Amsterdam: M. Hertzberger, 1949–.
and
Hollstein, F. W. H. *German Engravings, Etchings and Woodcuts, ca. 1400–1700.* Amsterdam: M. Hertzberger, 1954–.

Inventaire du fonds français
Bibliothèque nationale, Département des estampes. *Inventaire du fonds français: Graveurs du XVIe siècle.* Paris: Bibliothèque nationale, 1932–.
and
Bibliothèque nationale, Département des estampes. *Inventaire du fonds français: Graveurs du XVIIe siècle.* Paris: Bibliothèque nationale, 1939–.
and
Bibliothèque nationale, Département des estampes. *Inventaire du fonds français: Graveurs du XVIIIe siècle.* Paris: Bibliothèque nationale, 1930–.

Jacobs
Jacobs, Renate. *Das graphische Werk Berhard Rodes (1725–1797).* Münster: Lit, 1990.

La Combe
La Combe, Joseph Félix Leblanc de. *Charlet, sa vie, ses lettres suivie d'une description raisonnée de son oeuvre lithographique.* Paris: Paulin et Le Chevalier, 1856.

Le Blanc
Le Blanc, Charles. *Manuel de l'amateur des estampes.* . . . 4 vols. Paris: E. Bouillon, 1854–90.

Leymarie
Leymarie, Léo de. *L'oeuvre de Gille Demarteau.* . . . Paris: Rapilly, 1896.

Mannocci
Mannocci, Lino. *The Etchings of Claude Lorrain.* New Haven: Yale University Press, 1988.

Mauquoy-Hendrickx
Mauquoy-Hendrickx, Marie. *L'Iconographie d'Antoine van Dyck: Catalogue Raisonné.* 2 vols. 2nd ed. Brussels: Bibliothèque royale Albert 1, 1991.

Nagler
Nagler, G. K. *Neues allgemeines Künstler-Lexicon.* . . . 22 vols. Munich: E. A. Fleischmann, 1835–52.

Paulson
Paulson, Ronald. *Hogarth's Graphic Works.* 3rd ed. London: The Print Room, 1989.

Perez
Perez, Marie-Félice. *L'oeuvre gravé de Jean-Jacques de Boissieu 1736–1810.* Geneva: Cabinet des estampes, Editions du Tricorne, 1994.

Portalis and Béraldi
Portalis, Roger, and Henri Béraldi. *Les graveur du dix-huitième siècle.* 3 vols. Paris: D. Morgan and C. Fatout, 1880–82.

Rizzi
Rizzi, Aldo. *The Etchings of the Tiepolos: Complete Edition.* London: Phaidon, 1971.

Robert-Dumesnil
Robert-Dumesnil, A. P. F. *Le peintre-graveur français.* . . . 8 vols. Paris: G. Warée et al., 1835–50.

Baroni Vannucci 1997
Baroni Vannucci, Alessandra. *Jan Van Der Straet detto Giovanni Stradano: Flandrus pictor et inventor.* Milan: Jandi Sapi, 1997.

Barryte 1989
Barryte, Bernard. "History and Legend in T. J. Barker's *The Studio of Salvator Rosa in the Mountains of the Abruzzi,* 1865." *Art Bulletin* 71 (1989): 660–73.

Barthes 1977
Barthes, Roland. "The Death of the Author." In his *Image, Music, Text,* edited and translated by Stephen Heath, 142–48. New York: Hill and Wang, 1977.

Barzman 1991
Barzman, Karen-edis. "Perception, Knowledge, and the Theory of Disegno in Sixteenth-Century Florence." In *From Studio to Studiolo: Florentine Draftsmanship under the First Medici Grand Dukes,* edited by Larry J. Feinberg, 37–48. Exh. cat. Oberlin, Ohio: Allen Memorial Art Museum, Oberlin College, 1991.

Barzman 2000
Barzman, Karen-edis. *The Florentine Academy and the Early Modern State: The Discipline of Disegno.* Cambridge: Cambridge University Press, 2000.

Basan c. 1789–97
Basan, Pierre-François. *Recueil de quatre-vingt-cinq estampes originales . . . dessinées et gravées par Rembrandt.* Paris: Basan, n.d., c. 1789–97.

Bätschmann 1990
Bätschmann, Oskar. *Nicolas Poussin: Dialectics of Painting.* London: Reaktion Books, 1990.

Bätschmann 1992
Bätschmann, Oskar. "Pygmalion als Betrachter: Die Rezeption von Plastik und Malerei in der zweiten Hälfte des 18. Jahrhunderts." In *Der Betrachter ist im Bild: Kunstwissenschaft und Rezeptionsästhetik,* edited by Wolfgang Kemp, 237–78. 2nd ed. Berlin: Dietrich Reimer Verlag, 1992.

Baudelaire 1956
Baudelaire, Charles. *The Mirror of Art.* Edited and translated by Jonathan Mayne. Garden City, New York: Doubleday, 1956.

Baxandall 1988
Baxandall, Michael. *Painting and Experience in Fifteenth-Century Italy: A Primer in the Social History of Pictorial Style.* 2nd ed. Oxford and New York: Oxford University Press.

Beauvais 2000
Beauvais, Lydia. *Charles Le Brun, 1619–1690.* Inventaire général des dessins, école française, Musée du Louvre, Département des arts graphiques. 2 vols. Paris: Réunion des Musées Nationaux, 2000.

Bedaux and van Gool 1974
Bedaux, J. B., and A. van Gool. "Bruegel's Birthyear, Motive of an Ars/ Natura Transmutation." *Simiolus* 7 (1974): 133–56.

Bell Gallery 1984
Bell Gallery. *Children of Mercury: The Education of Artists in the Sixteenth and Seventeenth Centuries.* Exh. cat. Providence, Rhode Island: Bell Gallery, List Art Center, 1984.

Bellini 1976
Bellini, Paolo. *L'opera incisa di Pietro Testa.* Vicenza: N. Pozza, 1976.

Bellini 1982
Bellini, Paolo. *L'opera incisa di Giovanni Benedetto Castiglione.* Exh. cat. Milan: Castello Sforzesca, 1982.

Bellini 1985
Bellini, Paolo. *Italian Masters of the Seventeenth Century.* Vol. 46 of *The Illustrated Bartsch.* New York: Abaris Books, 1985.

Bellori 1976
Bellori, Giovan Pietro. *Le vite de' pittori, scultori e architetti moderni.* Edited by Evelina Borea. Turin: Giulio Einaudi editore, 1976.

Berger 1999
Berger, Robert W. *Public Access to Art in Paris: A Documentary History from the Middle Ages to 1800.* University Park, Pa.: Pennsylvania State University Press, 1999.

Bermingham 1992
Bermingham, Ann. "The Origin of Painting and the Ends of Art: Wright of Derby's Corinthian Maid." In *Painting and the Politics of Culture: New Essays on British Art 1700–1850,* edited by John Barrell, 135–65. Oxford and New York: Oxford University Press, 1992.

Bernsmeier 1986
Bernsmeier, Uta. "Die Nova Reperta des Jan van der Straet: Ein Beitrag zur Problemgeschichte der Entdeckungen und Erfindungen im 16. Jahrhundert." PhD diss., Universität Hamburg, 1986.

Biard 1997
Biard, Bernard. "Henri Mauperché: Paysagiste au long cours." *L'Estampille,* no. 316 (1997): 32–41.

Bignamini 1986–87
Bignamini, I. "The 'Academy of Art' in Britain before the Foundation of the Royal Academy in 1768." In "Academies of Art between Renaissance and Romanticism." Special issue, *Leids Kunsthistorisch Jaarboek* 5–6 (1986–87): 434–50.

Bignamini and Postle 1991
Bignamini, Ilaria, and Martin Postle. *The Artist's Model: Its Role in British Art from Lely to Etty.* Exh. cat. Nottingham: University Art Gallery, and Kenwood: The Iveagh Bequest, 1991.

Bloom 2001
Bloom, James J. "Mastering the Medium: Reference and Audience in Goltzius's Print of the *Circumcision.*" In "Prentwerk, 1500–1700," edited by Jan de Jong, Mark Meadow, Bart Ramakers, and Frits Scholten. Special issue, *Nederlands Kunsthistorisch Jaarboek* 52 (2001): 79–103.

Blunt 1940
Blunt, Anthony. *Artistic Theory in Italy 1450–1600.* Oxford: Clarendon Press, 1940.

Blunt 1954
Blunt, Anthony. *The Drawings of G. B. Castiglione and Stefano della Bella in the Collection of Her Majesty the Queen at Windsor Castle.* London: Phaidon Press, 1954.

Blunt 1958
Blunt, Anthony. "Poussin dans les Musées de Province." *La Revue des Arts* 8 (1958): 5–16.

Blunt 1960
Blunt, Anthony. "Poussin Studies X: Karel Philips Spierincks, the First Imitator of Poussin's Bacchanals." *Burlington Magazine* 102 (1960): 308–11.

Blunt 1966
Blunt, Anthony. *The Paintings of Nicolas Poussin: A Critical Catalogue.* London: Phaidon, 1966.

Blunt 1967
Blunt, Anthony. *Nicolas Poussin.* 2 vols. Bollingen Series 35. New York: Pantheon Books, 1967.

Boehm 1985
Boehm, Gottfried. *Bildnis und Individuum: Über den Ursprung der Porträtmalerei in der italienischen Renaissance.* Munich: Prestel-Verlag, 1985.

Börsch-Supan 1971
Börsch-Supan, Helmut. *Die Kataloge der Berliner Akademie-Ausstellungen 1786–1850.* 3 vols. Quellen und Schriften zur bildenden Kunst 4. Berlin: B. Hessling, 1971.

Börsch-Supan 1986
Börsch-Supan, Helmut. "Die Originalität Chodowieckis." In *Chodowiecki und die Kunst der Aufklärung in Polen und Preußen: Vorträge der 4. Internationalen Konferenz des "Komitees" vom 30.11. bis zum 3.XII.1983 in Wolfenbüttel,* edited by Hans Rothe and Andrzej Ryszkiewicz, 99–114. Cologne: Böhlau, 1986.

Bouquin 1989
Bouquin, Corinne. "Les frères Gihaut: éditeurs, marchands d'estampes et imprimeurs lithographes (1815–1871)." *Nouvelles de l'estampe* 108 (December 1989): 4–13.

Boyer 1929
Boyer, F. "Un inventaire inédit des antiques de la Villa Médicis (1598)." *Revue Archéologique* 30 (1929): 256–70.

Brann 2002
Brann, Noel L. *The Debate over the Origin of Genius during the Italian Renaissance: The Theories of Supernatural Frenzy and Natural Melancholy in Accord and in Conflict on the Threshold of the Scientific Revolution.* Leiden: Brill, 2002.

Bromley 1793
Bromley, Henry. *A Catalogue of Engraved British Portraits, from Egbert the Great to the Present Time.* London: T. Payne, J. Edwards, W. Otridge and Son, and R. Faulder, 1793.

Broos, Vorstman, and van de Watering 1985
Broos, Ben, Robert Vorstman, and Willem L. van de Watering. *Ludolf Bakhuizen 1631–1708, schryfmeester–teyckenaer–schilder.* Exh. cat. Amsterdam: Rijksmuseum Nederlands Scheepvaart Museum, 1985.

Brown 1978
Brown, Jonathan. *Images and Ideas in Seventeenth-Century Spanish Painting.* Princeton: Princeton University Press, 1978.

Bruand and Hébert 1970
Bruand, Yves, and Michèle Hébert. *Inventaire du fonds français: Graveurs du XVIIIe siècle.* Vol. 11, *Greuze—Jahandier.* Paris: Bibliothèque nationale, 1970.

Brunner 1994
Brunner, Michael. "Alcune note sulla commissione dei disegni danteschi di Giovanni Stradano." In *Giovanni Stradano e Dante,* edited by Corrado Gizzi, 123–32. Milan: Electa, 1994.

Brusati 1990–91
Brusati, Celeste. "Stilled Lives: Self-Portraiture and Self-Reflection in Seventeenth-Century Netherlandish Still-Life Painting." *Simiolus* 20 (1990–91): 168–82.

Burckhardt 1958
Burckhardt, Jacob. *The Civilization of the Renaissance in Italy.* Translated by S. G. C. Middlemore, and introduced by Benjamin Nelson and Charles Trinkaus. 2 vols. New York: Harper & Row, 1958.

Burckhardt 1959
Burckhardt, Jacob. "Die Anfänge der neuern Porträtmalerei. 10 März 1885." In his *Kulturgeschichtliche Vorträge,* edited by Rudolf Marx, 209–27. Stuttgart: Alfred Kröner Verlag, 1959.

Burgoyne 1808
Burgoyne, John. *The Dramatic and Poetical Works.* 2 vols. London: G. Whittingham for Scratcherd and Letterman, 1808.

Burke 1958
Burke, Edmund. *A Philosophical Enquiry into the Origin of Our Ideas of the Sublime and Beautiful.* Edited by J. T. Boulton. London: Routledge and Kegan Paul, 1958.

Burke 1987
Burke, Peter. *The Italian Renaissance: Culture and Society in Italy.* Rev. ed. Princeton: Princeton University Press, 1987.

Burke 1988
Burke, Peter. Review of *Bildnis und Individuum: Über den Ursprung der Porträtmalerei in der italienischen Renaissance,* by Gottfried Boehm. *Kunstchronik* 41 (1988): 24–26.

Burke 1995
Burke, Peter. "The Renaissance, Individualism and the Portrait." *History of European Ideas* 21 (1995): 393–400.

Burke 1997
Burke, Peter. "Representations of the Self from Petrarch to Descartes." In *Rewriting the Self: Histories from the Renaissance to the Present,* edited by Roy Porter, 17–28. London and New York: Routledge, 1997.

Burke 1998
Burke, Seán. *The Death and Return of the Author: Criticism and Subjectivity in Barthes, Foucault and Derrida.* 2nd ed. Edinburgh: Edinburgh University Press, 1998.

Campbell 1981
Campbell, Lorne. "The Early Netherlandish Painters and Their Workshops." In *Dessin sous-jacent dans la peintur: Colloque III, Le problème Maître de Flémalle-van der Weyden,* edited by Dominique Hollanders-Favart and R. van Schoute, 43–61. Louvain: Collège Érasme, 1981.

Campbell 1984–85
Campbell, Richard. "The Portrait Print: Traditions and Transformations." In Carlson and Ittman 1984–85, 28–35.

Capecchi 1993
Capecchi, Gabriele. *Il Giardino di Boboli: Un anfiteatro per la gioia dei Granduchi.* Florence: Edizioni Medicea, 1993.

Carey 1972
Carey, Richard J., trans. and ed. "'Bibliotheques': An Extract from Essais sur l'histoire des sciences des belles lettres et des arts of Felixe de Juvenel de Carlencas (1679–1760)." *The Journal of Library History* 7 (1972): 208–50.

Carlson and Ittmann 1984–85
Carlson, Victor I., and John W. Ittmann. *Regency to Empire: French Printmaking 1715–1814.* Exh. cat. Baltimore: The Baltimore Museum of Art; Minneapolis: The Minneapolis Institute of Arts, 1984–85.

Carrier 1991
Carrier, David. "Poussin's Self-Portraits." *Word and Image* 7 (1991): 127–48.

Cast 1981
Cast, David. *The Calumny of Apelles: A Study in the Humanist Tradition.* New Haven and London: Yale University Press, 1981.

Castelnuovo 1990
Castelnuovo, Enrico. "The Artist." In *Medieval Callings,* edited by Jacques Le Goff and translated by Lydia G. Cochrane, 210–41. Chicago and London: University of Chicago Press, 1990.

Castiglione 1959
Castiglione, Baldassare. *The Book of the Courtier.* Translated by Charles S. Singleton. New York: Anchor Books, 1959.

Cazort, Kornell, and Roberts 1996
Cazort, Mimi, Monique Kornell, and K. B. Roberts. *The Ingenious Machine of Nature: Four Centuries of Art and Anatomy.* Exh. cat. Ottawa: National Gallery of Canada, 1996.

Cellini 1956
Cellini, Benvenuto. *The Autobiography of Benvenuto Cellini.* Translated by George Bull. Harmondsworth, UK: Penguin Books, 1956.

Cellini 1967
Cellini, Benvenuto. *Treatises of Benvenuto Cellini on Goldsmithing and Sculpture.* Translated by C. R. Ashbee. New York: Dover, 1967.

Cesareo 1892
Cesareo, G. A., ed. *Poesie e lettere edite e inedite di Salvator Rosa.* 2 vols. Naples: Tipografia della Regia Università, 1892.

Chantelou 1985
Fréart de Chantelou, Paul. *Diary of the Cavaliere Bernini's Visit to France.* Edited by Anthony Blunt, annotated by George C. Bauer, and translated by Margery Corbett. Princeton: Princeton University Press, 1985.

Chapman 1990
Chapman, H. Perry. *Rembrandt's Self-Portraits: A Study in Seventeenth-Century Identity.* Princeton: Princeton University Press, 1990.

Chapman 1996
Chapman, H. Perry. "Jan Steen, Player in His Own Paintings." In *Jan Steen: Painter and Storyteller,* edited by H. Perry Chapman, Wouter Th. Kloek, and Arthur K. Wheelock, Jr., 11–23. Exh. cat. Washington, D.C.: National Gallery of Art, 1996.

Chong and Klock 1999
Chong, Alan, and Wouter Klock. *Still-Life Paintings from the Netherlands: 1550–1720.* Exh. cat. Amsterdam: Rijksmuseum, 1999.

Choux 1975
Choux, Jacques. "Nicolas de La Case graveur lorrain du XVIe siècle." *Le Pays Lorrain* 56 (1975): 175–80.

Ciofalo 2001
Ciofalo, John. *The Self-Portraits of Francisco Goya.* Cambridge and New York: Cambridge University Press, 2001.

Clark 1966
Clark, Kenneth. *Rembrandt and the Italian Renaissance.* New York: New York University Press, 1966.

Clifton 1995
Clifton, James. "'Ad vivum mire depinxit': Toward a Reconstruction of Ribera's Art Theory." *Storia dell'arte* 83 (1995): 111–32.

Clifton 1996
Clifton, James. "Vasari on Competition." *Sixteenth Century Journal* 27 (1996): 23–41.

Colantuono 1989
Colantuono, Anthony. "Titian's Tender Infants: On the Imitation of Venetian Painting in Baroque Rome." *I Tatti Studies* 3 (1989): 207–34.

Collins 2004
Collins, Jeffrey. *Papacy and Politics in Eighteenth-Century Rome: Pius VI and the Arts.* Cambridge and New York: Cambridge University Press, 2004.

Colombier 1929
Du Colombier, Pierre, ed. *Lettres de Poussin.* Paris: Cité des Livres, 1929.

Coquery 2000
Coquery, Emmanuel. "I pittori francesi a Roma nella prima metà dell '600 e l'antico." In *Intorno a Poussin: Ideale classico e epopea tra Parigi e Roma,* edited by Olivier Bonfait and Jean-Claude Boyer, 41–53. Exh. cat. Rome: Accademia di Francia, 2000.

Cropper 1984
Cropper, Elizabeth. *The Ideal of Painting: Pietro Testa's Düsseldorf Notebook.* Princeton: Princeton University Press, 1984.

Cropper 1988
Cropper, Elizabeth. *Pietro Testa 1612–1650: Prints and Drawings.* Exh. cat. Philadelphia: Philadelphia Museum of Art, 1988.

Cropper 1992
Cropper, Elizabeth. "Painting and Possession: Poussin's Portrait for Chantelou and the *Essais* of Montaigne." In *Der Künstler über sich in seinem Werk: Internationales Symposium der Bibliotheca Hertziana, Rom 1989,* edited by Mattias Winner, 485–509. Weinhaim: VCH, Acta Humaniora, 1992.

Cropper and Dempsey 1996
Cropper, Elizabeth, and Charles Dempsey. *Nicolas Poussin: Friendship and the Love of Painting.* Princeton: Princeton University Press, 1996.

Crow 1985
Crow, Thomas E. *Painters and Public Life in Eighteenth-Century Paris.* New Haven: Yale University Press, 1985.

Crow 1995
Crow, Thomas. *Emulation: Making Artists for Revolutionary France.* New Haven and London: Yale University Press, 1995.

Dacier and Vuaflart 1921–29
Dacier, Émile, and Albert Vuaflart. *Jean de Jullienne et les graveurs de Watteau au XVIIIe siècle.* 4 vols. Paris: Societé pour l'étude de la gravure française, 1921–29.

Dalen 1900
Dalen, J. L. "Matthys van de Merwede, Heer van Clootwijck." *Oud Holland* 18 (1900), 95–111.

Dandré-Bardon 1973
Dandré-Bardon, M. F. *Vie de Carle Vanloo.* 1765. Reprint, Geneva: Minkoff Reprint, 1973.

Dante 1939
Dante Alighieri. *The Divine Comedy.* Translated by John D. Sinclair. Vol. 1, *Inferno.* New York: Oxford University Press, 1939.

Davis 1988
Davis, Bruce. *Mannerist Prints: International Style in the Sixteenth Century.* Exh. cat. Los Angeles: Los Angeles County Museum of Art, 1988.

De Dominici 1742–45
De Dominici, Bernardo. *Vite de' pittori, scultori, ed architetti napoletani.* 3 vols. Naples: Nella stamperia del Ricciardi, 1742–45.

De Jongh 1982
De Jongh, E. *Still-Life in the Age of Rembrandt.* Exh. cat. Auckland, New Zealand: Auckland City Art Gallery, 1982.

De Jongh and Luijten 1997
De Jongh, Eddy, and Ger Luijten. *Mirror of Everyday Life: Genre Prints in the Netherlands 1550–1700.* Exh. cat. Amsterdam: Rijksmuseum, 1997.

De Klerk 1986–87
De Klerk, E. A. "'Academy-beelden' and 'Teekenschoolen' in Dutch Seventeenth-Century Treatises on Art." In "Academies of Art between Renaissance and Romanticism." Special issue, *Leids kunsthistorisch Jaarboek* 5–6 (1986–87): 283–88.

Delignières 1873
Delignières, Em. *Catalogue raisonné de l'oeuvre gravé de Jean Daullé d'Abbeville précédé d'une notice sur sa vie et ses ouvrages.* Paris: Rapilly, Libraire et marchand d'estampes, 1873.

Dempsey 1968
Dempsey, Charles. "'Et nos cedamus amori': Observations on the Farnese Gallery." *Art Bulletin* 50 (1968): 363–74.

Den Blaauwen 1979
Den Blaauwen, A. L., ed. *Dutch Silver, 1580–1830.* Amsterdam: Rijksmuseum, 1979.

Depauw and Luijten 1999
Depauw, Carl, and Ger Luijten. *Anthony van Dyck as a Printmaker.* Exh. cat. Antwerp: Antwerpen Open; Amsterdam: Rijksmuseum, 1999.

De Rinaldis 1939
De Rinaldis, Aldo, ed. *Lettere inedite di Salvator Rosa a G. B. Ricciardi.* Rome: Fratelli Polombi Editori, 1939.

De Smet 1988
De Smet, R. *Hadrianus Beverlandus (1650–1716): Non unus e multis peccator: Studie over het leven en werk van Hadriaan Beverland.* Brussels: WLSK, 1988.

De Vesme 1906
De Vesme, Alexandre. *Le peintre-graveur italien.* 1906. Reprint, Mansfield Centre, Conn.: Martino, 2001.

De Vesme and Massar 1971
De Vesme, Alexandre, and P. D. Massar. *Stefano della Bella: Catalogue Raisonné.* 2 vols. New York: Collectors Editions, 1971.

Dingwall 1962
Dingwall, Eric John. *Very Peculiar People: Portrait Studies in the Queer, the Abnormal and the Uncanny.* New Hyde Park, New York: University Books, 1962.

Diogenes Laertius 1925
Diogenes Laertius. *Lives of Eminent Philosophers.* Translated by R. D. Hicks. The Loeb Classical Library. 2 vols. Cambridge, Mass.: Harvard University Press, 1925.

Dowley 1955
Dowley, Francis H. "French Portraits of Ladies as Minerva." *Gazette des Beaux-Arts,* 6th ser., 45 (1955): 261–86.

Duffy 1995
Duffy, Michael H. "Michelangelo and the Sublime in Romantic Art Criticism." *Journal of the History of Ideas* 56 (1995): 217–38.

Edwards 1808
Edwards, Edward. *Anecdotes of Painters Who Have Resided or Been Born in England.* London: Leigh and Sotheby, W. J. and J. Richardson, R. Faulder, T. Payne, and J. White, 1808.

Egerton 1990
Egerton, Judy. *Wright of Derby.* Exh. cat. New York: Metropolitan Museum of Art, 1990.

Einberg and Egerton 1988
Einberg, Elizabeth, and Judy Egerton. *The Age of Hogarth: British Painters Born 1675–1709.* Tate Gallery Collections 2. London: The Tate Gallery, 1988.

Elmer 2000
Elmer, Peter. "Inventing the Renaissance: Burckhardt as Historian." In *The Impact of Humanism,* edited by Lucille Kekewich, 1–22. New Haven and London: Yale University Press, 2000.

Emmens 1968
Emmens, J. A. *Rembrandt en de Regels van de Kunst (Rembrandt and the Rules of Art).* Utrecht: Haentjens Dekker & Gumbert, 1968.

Engelmann 1857
Engelmann, Wilhelm. *Daniel Chodowiecki's sämmtliche Kupferstiche.* Leipzig: Verlag von Wilh. Engelmann, 1857.

Enggass and Brown 1970
Enggass, Robert, and Jonathan Brown, eds. *Italy and Spain 1600–1750: Sources and Documents.* Englewood Cliffs, N.J.: Prentice-Hall, 1970.

Eschenburg 2001
Eschenburg, Barbara. *Pygmalions Werkstatt: Die Erschaffung des Menschen im Atelier von der Renaissance bis zum Surrealismus.* Exh. cat. Munich: Lehnbachhaus, 2001.

Evelyn 1955
Evelyn, John. *The Diary of John Evelyn.* Edited by E. S. de Beer. 6 vols. Oxford: Clarendon Press, 1955.

Fader 1977
Fader, Martha Alice Agnew. "Sculpture in the Piazza della Signoria as Emblem of the Florentine Republic." PhD diss., University of Michigan, 1977.

Fagiolo dell'Arco 1996
Fagiolo dell'Arco, Maurizio. *Jean Lemaire: Pittore "antiquario."* Rome: U. Bozzi, 1996.

Farago 1992
Farago, Claire J. *Leonardo da Vinci's Paragone: A Critical Interpretation with a New Edition of the Text in the Codex Urbinas.* Leiden: Brill, 1992.

Farwell 1983
Farwell, Beatrice. *French Popular Lithographic Imagery, 1815–1870.* Vol. 3, *Genre: Urban and Military.* Chicago: University of Chicago Press, 1983.

Farwell 1989
Farwell, Beatrice. *The Charged Image. French Lithographic Caricature 1816–1848.* Exh. cat. Santa Barbara, Cal.: Santa Barbara Museum of Art, 1989.

Filedt Kok 1996
Filedt Kok, Jan Piet. "Artists Portrayed by Their Friends: Goltzius and His Circle." *Simiolus* 24 (1996): 161–81.

Filipczak 1987
Filipczak, Zirka Zaremba. *Picturing Art in Antwerp, 1550–1700.* Princeton: Princeton University Press, 1987.

Fiorentini 1999
Fiorentini, Erna. *Ikonographie eines Wandels: Form und Intention von Selbstbildnis und Porträt des Bildhauers im Italien des 16. Jahrhunderts.* Berlin: Tenea, 1999.

Fiorentini and Rosenberg 2002
Fiorentini, Erna, and Raphael Rosenberg. "Baccio Bandinelli's Self-Portrait." *Print Quarterly* 19 (2002): 34–44.

Firenze e la Toscana dei Medici 1980
Firenze e la Toscana dei Medici nell'Europa del Cinquecento. *Il primato del disegno.* Milan: Electa, and Florence: Centro Di, Edizioni Alinari, Scala, 1980.

Forlani Tempesti 1989
Forlani Tempesti, Anna. "Il David di Michelangelo nella tradizione grafica bandinelliana." *Antichità viva* 28 (1989): 19–25.

Foucault 1984
Foucault, Michel. "What Is an Author?" In *The Foucault Reader,* edited by Paul Rabinow, 101–20. New York: Pantheon Books, 1984.

Freedberg 1998
Freedberg, David. "Rubens and Titian: Art and Politics." In *Titian and Rubens: Power, Politics, and Style,* edited by Hilliard T. Goldfarb, David Freedberg, and Manuela B. Mena Marqués, 29–66. Boston: Isabella Stewart Gardner Museum, 1998.

Friesen 1980
Friesen, James. "Kupferstecher der Wiener Akademie im späteren achtzehnten Jahrhundert." *Mitteilungen der Gesellschaft für vergleichende Kunstforschung in Wien* 32 (1980): 1–7.

Gahtan and Jacks 1994
Gahtan, Maia W., and Philip J. Jacks. *Vasari's Florence: Artists and Literati at the Medicean Court.* Exh. cat. New Haven: Yale University Art Gallery, 1994.

Galicka and Sygietyńska 1992
Galicka, Izabella, and Hanna Sygietyńska. "A Newly Discovered Self-Portrait by Baccio Bandinelli." *Burlington Magazine* 134 (1992): 805–807.

Gaspari 1991
Gaspari, Carlo. "La collection d'antiques du cardinal Ferdinand." In *La Villa Médicis,* 2:443–85. Rome: Académie de France à Rome, Ecole française de Rome, 1991.

Geismeier 1993
Geismeier, Willi. *Daniel Chodowiecki.* Leipzig: E. A. Seemann, 1993.

References

Bartsch
Bartsch, Adam von. *Le peintre graveur.* 21 vols. Vienna: Degen, 1803–21.

Bauer
Bauer, Jens-Heiner. *Daniel Nikolaus Chodowiecki: Das druckgraphische Werk.* Hannover: Verlag Galerie J. H. Bauer, 1982.

Bellini
Bellini, Paolo. *L'opera incisa di Giovanni Benedetto Castiglione.* Exh. cat. Milan: Castello Sforzesca, 1982.
and
Bellini, Paolo. *L'opera incisa di Pietro Testa.* Vicenza: N. Pozza, 1976.

Béraldi
Béraldi, Henri. *Les graveurs du XIX siècle: Guide de l'amateur d'estampes modernes.* 12 vols. Paris: L. Conquet, 1885–92.

Bleackley
Bleackley, Ruth. "A List of William Wynne Ryland's Engravings." *Connoisseur* 12 (1905): 110–11.

Blum
Blum, André. *L'oeuvre gravé d'Abraham Bosse.* Paris: A. Morancé, 1924.

Bocher
Bocher, Emmanuel. *Les gravures françaises de XVIIIe siècle.* . . . 6 fasc. in 3. Paris: Librairie des bibliophiles, 1875–82.

Chaloner Smith
Chaloner Smith, John. *British Mezzotint Portraits.* . . . 4 vols. London: Henry Sotheran, 1878–84.

Clayton
Clayton, Tim. "A Catalogue of the Engraved Works of Joseph Wright of Derby." In *Wright of Derby,* edited by Judy Egerton, 231–58. Exh. cat. New York: Metropolitan Museum of Art, 1990.

Dacier and Vuaflart
Dacier, Émile, and Albert Vuaflart. *Jean de Jullienne et les graveurs de Watteau au XVIIIe siècle.* 4 vols. Paris: Societé pour l'étude de la gravure française, 1921–29.

Delteil
Delteil, Loys. *Le peintre-graveur illustré (XIXe et XXe siècles).* 32 vols. Paris: Chez l'auteur, 1906–1930.

De Vesme
De Vesme, Alexandre. *Le peintre-graveur italien.* 1906. Reprint, Mansfield Centre, Conn.: Martino, 2001.

De Vesme and Massar
De Vesme, Alexandre, and P. D. Massar. *Stefano della Bella: Catalogue raisonné.* 2 vols. New York: Collectors Editions, 1971.

Duplessis
Duplessis, Georges. *Catalogue de l'oeuvre de Abraham Bosse.* Paris: A. Labroue, 1859.

Dussler
Dussler, Luitpold. *Die Incunabeln der deutschen Lithographie (1796–1821).* Berlin: H. Tiedemann, 1925.

Engelmann
Engelmann, Wilhelm. *Daniel Chodowiecki's sämmtliche Kupferstiche.* Leipzig: Verlag von Wilh. Engelmann, 1857.

Firmin-Didot
Firmin-Didot, Ambroise. *Les graveurs de portraits en France* . . . . 2 vols. Paris: Firmin-Didot, 1875–77.

Goncourt
Goncourt, Edmond de. *Catalogue raisonné de l'oeuvre peint, dessiné et gravé d'Antoine Watteau.* Paris: Rapilly, 1875.

Grasso
Grasso, Giovanni. "Incisioni." In *Giovanni David: Pittore e incisore della famiglia Durazzo,* by Mary Newcome Schleier and Giovanni Grasso, 105–91. Turin: Artema, 2003.

Harris
Harris, Tomás. *Goya Engravings and Lithographs.* Oxford: Bruno Cassirer, 1964 (republished in reduced format, San Francisco: Alan Wofsy Fine Arts, 1983).

Heller and Andresen
Heller, Joseph, and Andreas Andresen. *Handbuch für Kupferstichsammler* . . . . 2 vols. Leipzig: T. O. Weigel, 1870–73.

Hirschmann
Hirschmann, Otto. *Verzeichnis des graphischen Werks von Hendrick Goltzius, 1558–1617.* Leipzig: Klinkhardt & Biermann, 1921.

Hollstein
Hollstein, F. W. H. *Dutch and Flemish Etchings, Engravings, and Woodcuts, ca. 1450–1700.* Amsterdam: M. Hertzberger, 1949–.
and
Hollstein, F. W. H. *German Engravings, Etchings and Woodcuts, ca. 1400–1700.* Amsterdam: M. Hertzberger, 1954–.

Inventaire du fonds français
Bibliothèque nationale, Département des estampes. *Inventaire du fonds français: Graveurs du XVIe siècle.* Paris: Bibliothèque nationale, 1932–.
and
Bibliothèque nationale, Département des estampes. *Inventaire du fonds français: Graveurs du XVIIe siècle.* Paris: Bibliothèque nationale, 1939–.
and
Bibliothèque nationale, Département des estampes. *Inventaire du fonds français: Graveurs du XVIIIe siècle.* Paris: Bibliothèque nationale, 1930–.

Jacobs
Jacobs, Renate. *Das graphische Werk Berhard Rodes (1725–1797).* Münster: Lit, 1990.

La Combe
La Combe, Joseph Félix Leblanc de. *Charlet, sa vie, ses lettres suivie d'une description raisonnée de son oeuvre lithographique.* Paris: Paulin et Le Chevalier, 1856.

Le Blanc
Le Blanc, Charles. *Manuel de l'amateur des estampes.* . . . 4 vols. Paris: E. Bouillon, 1854–90.

Leymarie
Leymarie, Léo de. *L'oeuvre de Gille Demarteau.* . . . Paris: Rapilly, 1896.

Mannocci
Mannocci, Lino. *The Etchings of Claude Lorrain.* New Haven: Yale University Press, 1988.

Mauquoy-Hendrickx
Mauquoy-Hendrickx, Marie. *L'Iconographie d'Antoine van Dyck: Catalogue Raisonné.* 2 vols. 2nd ed. Brussels: Bibliothèque royale Albert 1, 1991.

Nagler
Nagler, G. K. *Neues allgemeines Künstler-Lexicon.* . . . 22 vols. Munich: E. A. Fleischmann, 1835–52.

Paulson
Paulson, Ronald. *Hogarth's Graphic Works.* 3rd ed. London: The Print Room, 1989.

Perez
Perez, Marie-Félice. *L'oeuvre gravé de Jean-Jacques de Boissieu 1736–1810.* Geneva: Cabinet des estampes, Editions du Tricorne, 1994.

Portalis and Béraldi
Portalis, Roger, and Henri Béraldi. *Les graveur du dix-huitième siècle.* 3 vols. Paris: D. Morgan and C. Fatout, 1880–82.

Rizzi
Rizzi, Aldo. *The Etchings of the Tiepolos: Complete Edition.* London: Phaidon, 1971.

Robert-Dumesnil
Robert-Dumesnil, A. P. F. *Le peintre-graveur français.* . . . 8 vols. Paris: G. Warée et al., 1835–50.

Baroni Vannucci 1997
Baroni Vannucci, Alessandra. *Jan Van Der Straet detto Giovanni Stradano: Flandrus pictor et inventor.* Milan: Jandi Sapi, 1997.

Barryte 1989
Barryte, Bernard. "History and Legend in T. J. Barker's *The Studio of Salvator Rosa in the Mountains of the Abruzzi,* 1865." *Art Bulletin* 71 (1989): 660–73.

Barthes 1977
Barthes, Roland. "The Death of the Author." In his *Image, Music, Text,* edited and translated by Stephen Heath, 142–48. New York: Hill and Wang, 1977.

Barzman 1991
Barzman, Karen-edis. "Perception, Knowledge, and the Theory of Disegno in Sixteenth-Century Florence." In *From Studio to Studiolo: Florentine Draftsmanship under the First Medici Grand Dukes,* edited by Larry J. Feinberg, 37–48. Exh. cat. Oberlin, Ohio: Allen Memorial Art Museum, Oberlin College, 1991.

Barzman 2000
Barzman, Karen-edis. *The Florentine Academy and the Early Modern State: The Discipline of Disegno.* Cambridge: Cambridge University Press, 2000.

Basan c. 1789–97
Basan, Pierre-François. *Recueil de quatre-vingt-cinq estampes originales . . . dessinées et gravées par Rembrandt.* Paris: Basan, n.d., c. 1789–97.

Bätschmann 1990
Bätschmann, Oskar. *Nicolas Poussin: Dialectics of Painting.* London: Reaktion Books, 1990.

Bätschmann 1992
Bätschmann, Oskar. "Pygmalion als Betrachter: Die Rezeption von Plastik und Malerei in der zweiten Hälfte des 18. Jahrhunderts." In *Der Betrachter ist im Bild: Kunstwissenschaft und Rezeptionsästhetik,* edited by Wolfgang Kemp, 237–78. 2nd ed. Berlin: Dietrich Reimer Verlag, 1992.

Baudelaire 1956
Baudelaire, Charles. *The Mirror of Art.* Edited and translated by Jonathan Mayne. Garden City, New York: Doubleday, 1956.

Baxandall 1988
Baxandall, Michael. *Painting and Experience in Fifteenth-Century Italy: A Primer in the Social History of Pictorial Style.* 2nd ed. Oxford and New York: Oxford University Press.

Beauvais 2000
Beauvais, Lydia. *Charles Le Brun, 1619–1690.* Inventaire général des dessins, école française, Musée du Louvre, Département des arts graphiques. 2 vols. Paris: Réunion des Musées Nationaux, 2000.

Bedaux and van Gool 1974
Bedaux, J. B., and A. van Gool. "Bruegel's Birthyear, Motive of an Ars/ Natura Transmutation." *Simiolus* 7 (1974): 133–56.

Bell Gallery 1984
Bell Gallery. *Children of Mercury: The Education of Artists in the Sixteenth and Seventeenth Centuries.* Exh. cat. Providence, Rhode Island: Bell Gallery, List Art Center, 1984.

Bellini 1976
Bellini, Paolo. *L'opera incisa di Pietro Testa.* Vicenza: N. Pozza, 1976.

Bellini 1982
Bellini, Paolo. *L'opera incisa di Giovanni Benedetto Castiglione.* Exh. cat. Milan: Castello Sforzesca, 1982.

Bellini 1985
Bellini, Paolo. *Italian Masters of the Seventeenth Century.* Vol. 46 of *The Illustrated Bartsch.* New York: Abaris Books, 1985.

Bellori 1976
Bellori, Giovan Pietro. *Le vite de' pittori, scultori e architetti moderni.* Edited by Evelina Borea. Turin: Giulio Einaudi editore, 1976.

Berger 1999
Berger, Robert W. *Public Access to Art in Paris: A Documentary History from the Middle Ages to 1800.* University Park, Pa.: Pennsylvania State University Press, 1999.

Bermingham 1992
Bermingham, Ann. "The Origin of Painting and the Ends of Art: Wright of Derby's Corinthian Maid." In *Painting and the Politics of Culture: New Essays on British Art 1700–1850,* edited by John Barrell, 135–65. Oxford and New York: Oxford University Press, 1992.

Bernsmeier 1986
Bernsmeier, Uta. "Die Nova Reperta des Jan van der Straet: Ein Beitrag zur Problemgeschichte der Entdeckungen und Erfindungen im 16. Jahrhundert." PhD diss., Universität Hamburg, 1986.

Biard 1997
Biard, Bernard. "Henri Mauperché: Paysagiste au long cours." *L'Estampille,* no. 316 (1997): 32–41.

Bignamini 1986–87
Bignamini, I. "The 'Academy of Art' in Britain before the Foundation of the Royal Academy in 1768." In "Academies of Art between Renaissance and Romanticism." Special issue, *Leids Kunsthistorisch Jaarboek* 5–6 (1986–87): 434–50.

Bignamini and Postle 1991
Bignamini, Ilaria, and Martin Postle. *The Artist's Model: Its Role in British Art from Lely to Etty.* Exh. cat. Nottingham: University Art Gallery, and Kenwood: The Iveagh Bequest, 1991.

Bloom 2001
Bloom, James J. "Mastering the Medium: Reference and Audience in Goltzius's Print of the *Circumcision.*" In "Prentwerk, 1500–1700," edited by Jan de Jong, Mark Meadow, Bart Ramakers, and Frits Scholten. Special issue, *Nederlands Kunsthistorisch Jaarboek* 52 (2001): 79–103.

Blunt 1940
Blunt, Anthony. *Artistic Theory in Italy 1450–1600.* Oxford: Clarendon Press, 1940.

Blunt 1954
Blunt, Anthony. *The Drawings of G. B. Castiglione and Stefano della Bella in the Collection of Her Majesty the Queen at Windsor Castle.* London: Phaidon Press, 1954.

Blunt 1958
Blunt, Anthony. "Poussin dans les Musées de Province." *La Revue des Arts* 8 (1958): 5–16.

Blunt 1960
Blunt, Anthony. "Poussin Studies X: Karel Philips Spierincks, the First Imitator of Poussin's Bacchanals." *Burlington Magazine* 102 (1960): 308–11.

Blunt 1966
Blunt, Anthony. *The Paintings of Nicolas Poussin: A Critical Catalogue.* London: Phaidon, 1966.

Blunt 1967
Blunt, Anthony. *Nicolas Poussin.* 2 vols. Bollingen Series 35. New York: Pantheon Books, 1967.

Boehm 1985
Boehm, Gottfried. *Bildnis und Individuum: Über den Ursprung der Porträtmalerei in der italienischen Renaissance.* Munich: Prestel-Verlag, 1985.

Börsch-Supan 1971
Börsch-Supan, Helmut. *Die Kataloge der Berliner Akademie-Ausstellungen 1786–1850.* 3 vols. Quellen und Schriften zur bildenden Kunst 4. Berlin: B. Hessling, 1971.

Börsch-Supan 1986
Börsch-Supan, Helmut. "Die Originalität Chodowieckis." In *Chodowiecki und die Kunst der Aufklärung in Polen und Preußen: Vorträge der 4. Internationalen Konferenz des "Komitees" vom 30.11. bis zum 3.XII.1983 in Wolfenbüttel,* edited by Hans Rothe and Andrzej Ryszkiewicz, 99–114. Cologne: Böhlau, 1986.

Bouquin 1989
Bouquin, Corinne. "Les frères Gihaut: éditeurs, marchands d'estampes et imprimeurs lithographes (1815–1871)." *Nouvelles de l'estampe* 108 (December 1989): 4–13.

Boyer 1929
Boyer, F. "Un inventaire inédit des antiques de la Villa Médicis (1598)." *Revue Archéologique* 30 (1929): 256–70.

Brann 2002
Brann, Noel L. *The Debate over the Origin of Genius during the Italian Renaissance: The Theories of Supernatural Frenzy and Natural Melancholy in Accord and in Conflict on the Threshold of the Scientific Revolution.* Leiden: Brill, 2002.

Bromley 1793
Bromley, Henry. *A Catalogue of Engraved British Portraits, from Egbert the Great to the Present Time.* London: T. Payne, J. Edwards, W. Otridge and Son, and R. Faulder, 1793.

Broos, Vorstman, and van de Watering 1985
Broos, Ben, Robert Vorstman, and Willem L. van de Watering. *Ludolf Bakhuizen 1631–1708, schryfmeester–teyckenaer–schilder.* Exh. cat. Amsterdam: Rijksmuseum Nederlands Scheepvaart Museum, 1985.

Brown 1978
Brown, Jonathan. *Images and Ideas in Seventeenth-Century Spanish Painting.* Princeton: Princeton University Press, 1978.

Bruand and Hébert 1970
Bruand, Yves, and Michèle Hébert. *Inventaire du fonds français: Graveurs du XVIIIe siècle.* Vol. 11, *Greuze—Jahandier.* Paris: Bibliothèque nationale, 1970.

Brunner 1994
Brunner, Michael. "Alcune note sulla commissione dei disegni danteschi di Giovanni Stradano." In *Giovanni Stradano e Dante,* edited by Corrado Gizzi, 123–32. Milan: Electa, 1994.

Brusati 1990–91
Brusati, Celeste. "Stilled Lives: Self-Portraiture and Self-Reflection in Seventeenth-Century Netherlandish Still-Life Painting." *Simiolus* 20 (1990–91): 168–82.

Geissler 1979
Geissler, Heinrich. *Zeichnung in Deutschland 1540–1640.* Exh. cat. 2 vols. Stuttgart: Staatsgalerie Stuttgart, 1979.

Georgel and Lecoq 1987
Georgel, Pierre, and Anne-Marie Lecoq. *La peinture dans la peinture.* Paris: Editions Adam Biro, 1987.

Gilpin 1768
Gilpin, William. *An Essay upon Prints. . . .* London: J. Robson, 1768.

Giltaij and Lammertse 2001
Giltaij, Jeroen, and Friso Lammertse. "Maintaining a Studio Archive: Drawn Copies by the De Braij Family." *Master Drawings* 39 (2001): 367–94.

Goddard and Ganz 2001
Goddard, Stephen H., and James A. Ganz. *Goltzius and the Third Dimension.* Exh. cat. Williamstown, Mass.: Sterling and Francine Clark Art Institute, 2001.

Godefroy 1990
Godefroy, Louis. *The Complete Etchings of Adriaen van Ostade.* San Francisco: Alan Wofsy Fine Arts, 1990.

Godfrey 2001
Godfrey, Richard. *James Gillray: The Art of Caricature.* Exh. cat. London: Tate Britain, 2001.

Goldfarb 2002
Goldfarb, Hilliard Todd, ed. *Richelieu: Art and Power.* Exh. cat. Montreal: The Montreal Museum of Fine Arts; Cologne: The Wallraf-Richartz-Museum-Foundation Corboud of the City of Cologne, 2002.

Goldstein 1996
Goldstein, Carl. *Teaching Art: Academies and Schools from Vasari to Albers.* Cambridge and New York: Cambridge University Press, 1996.

Gombrich 1961
Gombrich, E. H. *Art and Illusion: A Study in the Psychology of Pictorial Representation.* 2nd ed. Princeton: Princeton University Press, 1961.

Gozzoli and Mazzocca 1983
Gozzoli, Maria Cristina, and Fernando Mazzocca, eds. *Hayez.* Exh. cat. Milan: Palazzo Reale and Accademia Pinacoteca Biblioteca di Brera, 1983.

Gramaccini and Meier 2003
Gramaccini, Norberto, and Hans Jakob Meier. *Die Kunst der Interpretation: Französische Reproduktionsgraphik 1648–1792.* Munich: Deutscher Kunstverlag, 2003.

Grand Palais, Detroit Institute of Arts, and Metropolitan Museum of Art 1975
Grand Palais, Detroit Institute of Arts, and Metropolitan Museum of Art. *French Painting 1774–1830: The Age of Revolution.* Exh. cat. Paris: Grand Palais; Detroit: Detroit Institute of Arts; New York: Metropolitan Museum of Art, 1975.

Grasselli and Rosenberg 1984
Grasselli, Margaret Morgan, and Pierre Rosenberg. *Watteau 1684–1721.* Exh. cat. Washington, D.C.: National Gallery of Art, 1984.

Greenblatt 1980
Greenblatt, Stephen. *Renaissance Self-Fashioning: From More to Shakespeare.* Chicago and London: University of Chicago Press, 1980.

Griffiths 1996
Griffiths, Antony, ed. *Landmarks in Print Collecting: Connoisseurs and Donors at the British Museum since 1753.* Exh. cat. Houston: The Museum of Fine Arts, Houston, 1996.

Griffiths and Carey 1994
Griffiths, Antony, and Frances Carey. *German Printmaking in the Age of Goethe.* Exh. cat. London: The British Museum, 1994.

Grohn 1980
Grohn, Hans Werner. "Ein neuerworbenes Bildnis der nidersächsischen Landesgalerie Hannover und die Selbstporträts des Wallerant Vaillant." *Niederdeutsche Beiträge zur Kunstgeschichte* 19 (1980): 137–54.

Harris and Lord 1970
Harris, Ann Sutherland, and Carla Lord. "Pietro Testa and Parnassus." *Burlington Magazine* 112 (1970): 15–21.

Haskell 1980
Haskell, Francis. *Patrons and Painters: A Study in the Relations between Italian Art and Society in the Age of the Baroque.* Rev. ed. New Haven and London: Yale University Press, 1980.

Haskell 1987
Haskell, Francis. "The Old Masters in 19th Century Painting." In his *Past and Present in Art and Taste: Selected Essays,* 90–115. New Haven: Yale University Press, 1987.

Haskell and Penny 1981
Haskell, Francis, and Nicholas Penny. *Taste and the Antique: The Lure of Classical Sculpture 1500–1900.* New Haven and London: Yale University Press, 1981.

Hasse and Unverfehrt 1986
Hasse, Max, and Gerd Unverfehrt. *James Gillray 1757–1815: Meisterwerke der Karikatur.* Exh. cat. Hannover: Wilhelm-Busch-Museum Hannover, Staatsgalerie Stuttgart; Hamburg: Museum für Kunst und Gewerbe, 1986.

Hayes 1972
Hayes, John. *Rowlandson Watercolours and Drawings.* London: Phaidon, 1972.

Heikamp 1972
Heikamp, Detlef. "Appunti sull'Accademia del Disegno." *Arte Illustrata* 5 (1972), 298–304.

Heinecken 1771
[Heinecken, Carl Heinrich von.] *Idée générale d'une collection complette d'estampes. Avec une Dissertation sur l'origine de la Gravure & sur les premiers Livres d'Images.* Leipzig and Vienna: Jean Paul Kraus, 1771.

Heinecken 1778–90
[Heinecken, Carl Heinrich von.] *Dictionnaire des artistes, dont nous avons des estampes, avec une notice detaillée de leurs ouvrages gravés.* 30 vols. Leipzig: Jean-Gottlob-Immanuel Breitkopf, 1778–90.

Heinecken 1786
Heinecken, Carl Heinrich von. *Neue Nachrichten von Künstlern und Kunstsachen.* Dresden and Leipzig: Johann Gottlob Immanuel Breitkopf, 1786.

Held 1991a
Held, Julius S. "Aristotle." In his *Rembrandt Studies,* 17–58. Rev. ed. Princeton: Princeton University Press, 1991.

Held 1991b
Held, Julius S. "Rembrandt's Interest in Beggars." In his *Rembrandt Studies,* 153–63. Rev. ed. Princeton: Princeton University Press, 1991.

Herzog Anton Ulrich-Museum 1980
Herzog Anton Ulrich-Museum. *Selbstbildnisse und Künstlerporträts von Lucas van Leyden bis Anton Raphael Mengs.* Exh. cat. Braunschweig: Herzog Anton Ulrich-Museum, 1980.

Herzog Anton Ulrich-Museum 1993
Herzog Anton Ulrich-Museum. *Bilder vom alten Menschen in der niederländischen und deutschen Kunst 1550–1750.* Exh. cat. Braunschweig: Herzog Anton Ulrich-Museum, 1993.

Hill 1966
Hill, Draper. *Fashionable Contrasts: Caricatures by James Gillray.* London: Phaidon, 1966.

Hinterding, Luijten, and Royalton-Kisch 2000
Hinterding, Erik, Ger Luijten, and Martin Royalton-Kisch. *Rembrandt the Printmaker.* Exh. cat. London: The British Museum, 2000.

Hofstede de Groot 1976
Hofstede de Groot, C. *A Catalogue Raisonné of the Works of the Most Eminent Dutch Painters of the Seventeenth Century.* 10 vols. in 3. Teaneck, N.J., and Cambridge: Somerset House, 1976.

Hogarth 1955
Hogarth, William. "The Autobiographical Notes." In *The Analysis of Beauty with the Rejected Passages from the Manuscript Drafts and Autobiographical Notes,* edited by Joseph Burke, 201–31. Oxford: Clarendon Press, 1955.

Hogarth 1997
Hogarth, William. *The Analysis of Beauty.* Edited by Ronald Paulson. New Haven and London: Yale University Press, 1997.

Holsten 1978
Holsten, Siegmar. *Das Bild des Künstlers: Selbstdarstellungen.* Hamburg: Hans Christians Verlag, 1978.

Houbraken 1753
Houbraken, Arnold. *De Groote Schouburgh der Nederlantsche Konstschilders en Schilderessen.* 3 vols. 2nd ed. The Hague: J. Swart, C. Boucquet, and M. Gaillard, 1753.

Howard 1973
Howard, Seymour. "An Antiquarian Handlist and Beginnings of the Pio-Clementino." *Eighteenth-Century Studies* 7 (1973): 40–61.

Huber 1797–1808
Huber, M. *Manuel des curieux et des amateurs de l'art, contenant une notice abrégée des principaux graveurs. . . .* 9 vols. Zurich: Orell, Gessner, Fuesslin, 1797–1808.

Hughes 1990
Hughes, Anthony. "The Cave and the Stithy: Artists' Studios and Intellectual Property in Early Modern Europe." *Oxford Art Journal* 13 (1990), 34–48.

Hülsen and Egger 1913–16
Hülsen, Christian, and Hermann Egger. *Die römischen Skizzenbücher von Marten van Heemskerck im Königlichen Kupferstichkabinett zu Berlin.* 2 vols. Berlin: Bard, 1913–16.

Hutchison 1968
Hutchison, Sidney C. *The History of the Royal Academy 1768–1968.* New York: Chapman & Hall, 1968.

Hutchison 1986–87
Hutchison, S.C. "The Royal Academy of Arts in London: Its History and Activities." In "Academies of Art between Renaissance and Romanticism." Special issue, *Leids Kunsthistorisch Jaarboek* 5–6 (1986–87): 451–63.

Ireland 1791
Ireland, John. *Hogarth Illustrated.* 2 vols. London: J. & J. Boydell, 1791.

Ivins 1953
Ivins, William M., Jr. *Prints and Visual Communication.* Cambridge, Mass.: Harvard University Press, 1953.

Jacobowitz and Stepanek 1983
Jacobowitz, Ellen S., and Stephanie Loeb Stepanek. *The Prints of Lucas van Leyden and His Contemporaries.* Exh. cat. Washington, D.C.: National Gallery of Art, 1983.

Janda 1958
Janda, Karl-Heinz. "Daniel Chodowiecki als Sammler." In *Festschrift Johannes Jahn zum XXII. November MCMLVII,* 293–98. Leipzig: E. A. Seemann, 1958.

Janson 1937
Janson, Horst W. "The Putto with the Death's Head." *Art Bulletin* 19 (1937): 423–49.

Janson 1952
Janson, H. W. *Apes and Ape Lore in the Middle Ages and the Renaissance.* London: Warburg Institute, University of London, 1952.

Jitta 1972
Jitta, A. N. Zadoks-Josephus. "A Creative Misunderstanding." *Nederlands Kunsthistorisch Jaarboek* 23 (1972): 3–12.

Johnson 1982
Johnson, W. McAllister. *French Royal Academy of Painting and Sculpture: Engraved Reception Pieces 1672–1789.* Exh. cat. Kingston, Ontario: Agnes Etherington Art Centre, 1982.

Johnson 2000
Johnson, Geraldine A. "The Lion on the Piazza: Patrician Politics and Public Statuary in Central Florence." In *Secular Sculpture, 1300–1550,* edited by Phillip Lindley and Thomas Frangenberg, 54–71. Stamford, Conn.: Shaun Tyas, 2000.

Joslyn 1996
Joslyn, Catherine R. "Tapestry, II, 2: 1500–1620." In *The Dictionary of Art,* edited by Jane Turner, 30:314–20. New York: Grove, 1996.

Kahr 1975
Kahr, Madlyn Millner. "Velazquez and Las Meninas." *Art Bulletin* 57 (1975): 236–39.

Kauffmann 1960
Kauffmann, Georg. *Poussin-Studien.* Berlin: De Gruyter, 1960.

Kaufmann 1982
Kaufmann, Thomas DaCosta. "The Eloquent Artist: Towards an Understanding of the Stylistics of Painting at the Court of Rudolf II." *Leids Kunsthistorisch Jaarboek* 1 (1982): 119–48.

Keil 1963
Keil, N. "Wilhelm Reuter und die Anfänge der Lithographie." *Albertina-Studien* 2 (1963): 63–74.

Kemp 1977
Kemp, Martin. "From 'Mimesis' to 'Fantasia': The Quattrocento Vocabulary of Creation, Inspiration and Genius in the Visual Arts." *Viator* 8 (1977), 347–98.

Kemp 1987
Kemp, Martin. "'Equal excellences': Lomazzo and the Explanation of Individual Style in the Visual Arts." *Renaissance Studies* 1 (1987): 1–26.

Kemp 1989
Kemp, Martin. "The 'Super-artist' as Genius: The Sixteenth-Century View." In *Genius: The History of an Idea,* edited by Penelope Murray, 32–53. Oxford: Basil Blackwell, 1989.

Kennedy 1964
Kennedy, Rose Wedgwood. "Apelles Redivivus." In *Essays in Memory of Karl Lehmann,* 160–70. New York: Institute of Fine Arts, New York University, 1964.

Kerslake 1977
Kerslake, John. *Early Georgian Portraits: National Portrait Gallery.* 2 vols. London: H. M. Stationery Off., 1977.

Klinger Aleci 1998
Klinger Aleci, Linda. "Images of Identity: Italian Portrait Collections of the Fifteenth and Sixteenth Centuries." In *The Image of the Individual: Portraits in the Renaissance,* edited by Nicholas Mann and Luke Syson, 67–79, 204–13. London: British Museum Press, 1998.

Klotz 1959
Klotz, Günther. "Hogarth und Addison: 'Time Smoking a Picture' und 'The Spectator.'" *Zeitschrift für Kunstgeschichte* 22 (1959): 102–107.

Knolle 1979
Knolle, Paul. "De Amsterdamse stadstekenacademie, een 18de-eeuwse 'oefenschool' voor modeltekenaars. Met een lijst van redevoeringen." "Kunstoderwijs in Nederland." Special issue, *Nederlands Kunsthistorisch Jaarboek* 30 (1979): 1–41.

Knolle 1986–87
Knolle, Paul. "Dilettanten en hun rol in 18de-eeuwse noordnederlandse tekenacademies." In "Academies of Art between Renaissance and Romanticism." Special issue, *Leids kunsthistorisch Jaarboek* 5–6 (1986–87): 289–301.

Knox 1976
Knox, George. *Etchings by the Tiepolos: Domenico Tiepolo's Family Etchings. . . .* Exh. cat. Ottawa: The National Gallery of Canada, 1976.

Koerner 1993
Koerner, Joseph Leo. *The Moment of Self-Portraiture in German Renaissance Art.* Chicago and London: University of Chicago Press, 1993.

Költzsch 2000
Költzsch, Georg-W. *Maler Modell: Der Maler und sein Modell. Geschichte und Deutung eines Bildthemas.* Cologne: Dumont, 2000.

Köstler 1998
Köstler, Andreas. "Das Portrait: Individuum und Image." In *Bildnis und Image: Das Portrait zwischen Intention und Rezeption,* edited by Andreas Köstler and Ernst Seidl, 9–14. Cologne: Böhlau Verlag, 1998.

Kraut 1986
Kraut, Gisela. *Lukas malt die Madonna: Zeugnisse zum künstlerischen Selbstverständnis in der Malerei.* Worms: Wernersche Verlagsgesellschaft, 1986.

Kris and Kurz 1979
Kris, Ernst, and Otto Kurz. *Legend, Myth, and Magic in the Image of the Artist: A Historical Experiment.* New Haven and London: Yale University Press, 1979.

Kristeller 1951–52
Kristeller, Paul Oskar. "The Modern System of the Arts: A Study in the History of Aesthetics." *Journal of the History of Ideas* 12 (1951): 496–527, 13 (1952): 17–46.

Kristeller 1983
Kristeller, Paul Oskar. "'Creativity' and 'Tradition.'" *Journal of the History of Ideas* 44 (1983): 105–13.

Krysmanski 1996
Krysmanski, Bernd. *Hogarth's Enthusiasm Delineated: Nachahmung als Kritik am Kennertum: Eine Werkanalyse, Zugleich ein Einblick in das sarkastisch-aufgeklärte Denken eines 'Künstlerrebellen' im englischen 18. Jahrhundert.* 2 vols. Hildesheim: Georg Olms Verlag, 1996.

Krysmanski 1998
Krysmanski, Bernd. "We See a Ghost: Hogarth's Satire on Methodists and Connoisseurs," *Art Bulletin* 80 (1998): 292–310.

Kubler 1965
Kubler, George. "Vicente Carducho's Allegories of Painting." *Art Bulletin* 47 (1965): 439–45.

Kuijpers 1986–87
Kuijpers, J. T. C. "Hofpreise der K. K. Adademie der bildenden Künste in Wien, 1772–1794." In "Academies of Art between Renaissance and Romanticism." Special issue, *Leids kunsthistorisch Jaarboek* 5–6 (1986–87): 378–405.

La Combe 1856
La Combe, Joseph Félix Leblanc de. *Charlet, sa vie, ses lettres suivie d'une description raisonnée de son oeuvre lithographique.* Paris: Paulin et Le Chevalier, 1856.

Lamb 1935
Lamb, W. R. M. *The Royal Academy: A Short History of Its Foundation and Development to the Present Day.* London: Alexander Maclehose, 1935.

Lampsonius 1956
Lampsonius, Domenicus. *Les effigies des peintres célèbres des Pays-Bas.* Edited by Jean Puraye. Paris: Desclée De Brouwer, 1956.

Langedijk 1992
Langedijk, Karla. *Die Selbstbildnisse der holländischen und flämischen Künstler in der Galleria degli Autoritratti der Uffizien in Florenz.* Florence: Edizioni Medicea, 1992.

Langemeyer and Schleier 1976
Langemeyer, Gerhard, and Reinhart Schleier. *Bilder nach Bildern: Druckgrafik und die Vermittlung von Kunst.* Exh. cat. Münster: Westfälisches Landesmuseum für Kunst und Kulturgeschichte, 1976.

Laurentius 1998
Laurentius, Theo. "Adriaen van Ostade: The Watermarks." In *Everyday Life in Holland's Golden Age. The Complete Etchings of Adriaen van Ostade,* edited by Peter van der Coelen, 61–68. Exh. cat. Amsterdam: Museum het Rembrandthuis, 1998.

Laveissière 1988
Laveissière, Sylvain. "L'Atelier d'Isabey: Un panthéon de l'amitié." In *Boilly 1761/1845: Un Grand Peintre Français de la Révolution à la Restauration,* 52–85. Exh. cat. Lille: Musée des Beaux-Arts de Lille, 1988.

Lee 1967
Lee, Rensselaer W. *Ut pictura poesis: The Humanistic Theory of Painting*. New York: W. W. Norton, 1967.

Leeflang and Luijten 2003
Leeflang, Huigen, and Ger Luijten. *Hendrick Goltzius (1558–1617): Drawings, Prints and Paintings*. Exh. cat. Amsterdam: Rijksmuseum; New York: The Metropolitan Museum of Art; Toledo, Ohio: The Toledo Museum of Art, 2003.

Leonardo 1956
Leonardo da Vinci. *Treatise on Painting*. Translated and edited by A. Philip McMahon. 2 vols. Princeton: Princeton University Press, 1956.

Levey 1981
Levey, Michael. *The Painter Depicted: Painters as a Subject in Painting*. London: Thames and Hudson, 1981.

Levine and Mai 1991
Levine, David A., and Ekkehard Mai, eds. *I Bamboccianti: Niederländische Malerrebellen im Rom des Barock*. Exh. cat. Cologne: Wallraf-Richartz-Museum; Utrecht: Centraal Museum, 1991.

Levitine 1958
Levitine, George. "Addenda to Robert Rosenblum's 'The Origin of Painting.'" *Art Bulletin* 40 (1958), 329–31.

Levitine 1984–85
Levitine, George. "French Eighteenth-Century Printmaking in Search of Cultural Assertion." In Carlson and Ittman 1984–85, 10–21.

Levy 1984
Levy, Evonne. "Ideal and Reality of the Learned Artist: The Schooling of Italian and Netherlandish Artists." In *Children of Mercury: The Education of Artists in the Sixteenth and Seventeenth Centuries,* 109–18. Exh. cat. Providence, Rhode Island: Bell Gallery, List Art Center, 1984.

Levy-Van Halm 1991–92
Levy-Van Halm, Koos, with Lucy L. E. Schlüter. "Schildertechniek: middel en doel? De 'Mercurius' en 'Minerva' van Hendrick Goltzius." In "Goltzius-Studies: Hendrick Goltzius (1558–1617)," edited by Reindert Falkenburg, Jan Piet Filedt Kok, and Huigen Leeflang. Special issue, *Nederlands Kunsthistorisch Jaarboek* 42–43 (1991–92): 499–508.

Limouze 1988
Limouze, Dorothy. "Aegidius Sadeler (1570–1629): Drawings, Prints, and the Development of an Art Theoretical Attitude." In *Prague um 1600: Beiträge zur Kunst und Kultur am Hofe Rudolfs II,* 183–92. Freren: Luca Verlag, 1988.

Limouze 1989
Limouze, Dorothy. "Aegidius Sadeler, Imperial Printmaker." *Bulletin, Philadelphia Museum of Art* 85 (1989), 1–24.

Limouze 1991–92
Limouze, Dorothy. "Engraving as Imitation: Goltzius and His Contemporaries." In "Goltzius-Studies: Hendrick Goltzius (1558–1617)," edited by Reindert Falkenburg, Jan Piet Filedt Kok, and Huigen Leeflang. Special issue, *Nederlands Kunsthistorisch Jaarboek* 42–43 (1991–92): 439–53.

Liverani 2000
Liverani, Paolo. "The Museo Pio-Clementino at the Time of the Grand Tour." *Journal of the History of Collections* 12 (2000), 151–59.

Logan 1979
Logan, Anne-Marie S. *The "Cabinet" of the Brothers Gerard and Jan Reynst*. Amsterdam and New York: North-Holland Publishing, 1979.

Lugt 1938–87
Lugt, Frits. *Répertoire des catalogue de ventes publiques, intéressant l'art ou la curiosité. . . .* 4 vols. The Hague: M. Nijhoff, 1938–87.

Lukes 1973
Lukes, Steven. *Individualism*. New York: Harper & Row, 1973.

Lyons 1989
Lyons, John D. *Exemplum: The Rhetoric of Example in Early Modern France and Italy*. Princeton: Princeton Univeristy Press, 1989.

Macfarlane 1978
Macfarlane, Alan. *The Origins of English Individualism: The Family, Property, and Social Transition*. Oxford: Blackwell, 1978.

MacLaren 1991
MacLaren, Neil. *The Dutch School 1600–1900*. 2 vols. London: National Gallery Publications, 1991.

Magurn 1955
Magurn, Ruth Saunders, trans. and ed. *The Letters of Peter Paul Rubens*. Cambridge, Mass.: Harvard University Press, 1955.

Mahon 1949–50
Mahon, Denis. "Notes on the 'Dutch Gift' to Charles II." *Burlington Magazine* 91 (1949): 303–305, 349–50, 92 (1950): 12–18.

Manners and Williamson 1920
Manners, Victoria, and G. C. Williamson. *John Zoffany, R.A.: His Life and Works, 1735–1810*. London and New York: John Lane, 1920.

Mannings 2000
Mannings, David. *Sir Joshua Reynolds: A Complete Catalogue of His Paintings*. 2 vols. New Haven and London: Yale University Press, 2000.

Mannocci 1988
Mannocci, Lino. *The Etchings of Claude Lorrain*. New Haven: Yale University Press, 1988.

Mansuelli 1958
Mansuelli, Guido A. *Galleria degli Uffizi: Le Sculture, Parte I*. Rome: Istituto poligrafico dello Stato, Libreria dello Stato, 1958.

Manuth 1999
Manuth, Volker. "Rembrandt and the Artist's Self-Portrait: Tradition and Reception." In *Rembrandt by Himself,* edited by Christopher White and Quentin Buvelot, 38–57. Exh. cat. London: The National Gallery, 1999.

Margolin 2001
Margolin, Jean-Claude. "À propos des Nova Reperta de Stradan." In *Esthétiques de la nouveauté à la Renaissance,* edited by François Laroque and Franck Lessay, 1–28. Paris: Presses de la Sorbonne nouvelle, 2001.

Marin 1999
Marin, Louis. "Variations on an Absent Portrait: Poussin's Self-Portraits, 1649–1650." In his *Sublime Poussin,* translated by Catherine Porter, 183–208, 258. Stanford, Cal.: Stanford University Press, 1999.

Martin 1965
Martin, John Rupert. *The Farnese Gallery*. Princeton: Princeton University Press, 1965.

Martindale 1988
Martindale, Andrew. *Heroes, Ancestors, Relatives and the Birth of the Portrait*. Maarssen: G. Schwartz; The Hague: SDU Publishers, 1988.

Maser 1971
Maser, Edward A., ed. *Cesare Ripa: Baroque and Rococo Pictorial Imagery: The 1758–60 Hertel Edition of Ripa's "Iconologia" with 200 Engraved Illustrations*. New York: Dover, 1971.

Maugeri 1982
Maugeri, Vincenza. "I manuali propedeutici al disegno, a Bologna e Venezia, agli inizi del Seicento." *Musei Ferraresi. Bollettino Annuale* 12 (1982): 147–56.

Mauquoy-Hendrickx 1991
Mauquoy-Hendrickx, Marie. *L'Iconographie d'Antoine van Dyck: Catalogue Raisonné*. 2 vols. 2nd ed. Brussels: Bibliothèque royale Albert 1, 1991.

Mazière de Monville 1730
Mazière de Monville, Simon Philippe. *La vie de Pierre Mignard, premier peintre du Roy*. Paris: Jean Boudout & Jacques Guerin, 1730.

Mazza 1998
Mazza, Angelo. "Negli anni di Cesare d'Este (1598–1628). Tendenze della pittura del ducato." In *Sovrane Passioni: Le raccolte d'arte della Ducale Galleria Estense,* edited by Jadranka Bentini, 44–56. Exh. cat. Modena: Galleria Estense, Palazzo dei Musei, 1998.

Mazzocca 1994
Mazzocca, Fernando. *Francesco Hayez: Catalogo ragionato*. Milan: F. Motta, 1994.

Melion 1991
Melion, Walter S. *Shaping the Netherlandish Canon: Karel van Mander's Schilder-Boeck*. Chicago and London: University of Chicago Press, 1991.

Melion 1992
Melion, Walter S. "Piety and Pictorial Manner in Hendrick Goltzius's Early Life of the Virgin." In *Hendrick Goltzius and the Classical Tradition,* edited by Glenn Harcourt, 44–51. Exh. cat. Los Angeles: Fisher Gallery, University of Southern California, 1992.

Melion 2001a
Melion, Walter S. "*Cordis circumcisio in spiritu*: Imitation and the Wounded Christ in Hendrick Goltzius's *Circumcision* of 1594." In "Prentwerk, 1500–1700," edited by Jan de Jong, Mark Meadow, Bart Ramakers, and Frits Scholten. Special issue, *Nederlands Kunsthistorisch Jaarboek* 52 (2001): 31–77.

Melion 2001b
Melion, Walter S. "*Vivae dixisses virginis ora*: The Discourse of Color in Hendrick Goltzius's *Pygmalion and the Ivory Statue*." *Word and Image* 17 (2001): 153–76.

Mengs 1787
Mengs, Anton Raphael. *Opere*. Edited by Giuseppe Niccola d'Azara, corrected and augmented by Carlo Fea. Rome: Stamperia Pagliarini, 1787.

Merrifield 1967
Merrifield, M. P., ed. *Original Treatises on the Arts of Painting.* 2 vols. New York: Dover, 1967.

Metropolitan Museum of Art 1986
Metropolitan Museum of Art. *François Boucher, 1703–1770.* Exh. cat. New York: Metropolitan Museum of Art, 1986.

Metropolitan Museum of Art 1992
Metropolitan Museum of Art. *Masterworks from the Musée des Beaux-Arts, Lille.* Exh. cat. New York: Metropolitan Museum of Art, 1992.

Meyer 1992
Meyer, Veronique. "Jean Daullé et l'édition." *Gazette des Beaux-Arts,* 6th ser., 99 (1992): 99–122.

Miedema 1973
Miedema, Hessel. "Karel van Mander's Grondt der Edel Vry Schilder-Const ('Foundations of the Noble and Free Art of Painting')." *Journal of the History of Ideas* 34 (1973): 653–68.

Mielke 1979
Mielke, Hans. *Manierismus in Holland um 1600: Kupferstiche, Holzschnitte und Zeichnungen aus dem Berliner Kupferstichkabinett.* Exh. cat. Berlin: Kupferstichkabinett, 1979.

Millen and Wolf 1989
Millen, Ronald Forsyth, and Robert Erich Wolf. *Heroic Deeds and Mystic Figures: A New Reading of Rubens' Life of Maria de' Medici.* Princeton: Princeton University Press, 1989.

Montagu 1963
Montagu, Jennifer. "The Early Ceiling Decorations of Charles Le Brun." *Burlington Magazine* 105 (1963): 395–408.

Montreal Museum of Fine Arts 2001
Montreal Museum of Fine Arts. *Francisco Goya: Los Caprichos, Los Desastres de la Guerra, Los Disparates.* Exh. cat. Montreal: Montreal Museum of Fine Arts, 2001.

Montrose 1992
Montrose, Louis. "New Historicisms." In *Redrawing the Boundaries: The Transformation of English and American Literary Studies,* edited by Stephen Greenblatt and Giles Gunn, 392–418. New York: The Modern Language Association of America, 1992.

Morgan 1824
Morgan, Lady (Sydney). *The Life and Times of Salvator Rosa.* 2 vols. London: H. Colburn, 1824.

Moxey 1994
Moxey, Keith. *The Practice of Theory: Poststructuralism, Cultural Politics, and Art History.* Ithaca, N.Y., and London: Cornell University Press, 1994.

Moxey 2001
Moxey, Keith. *The Practice of Persuasion: Paradox and Power in Art History.* Ithaca, N.Y.: Cornell University Press, 2001.

Muecke 1999
Muecke, Frances. "'Taught by Love': The Origin of Painting Again." *Art Bulletin* 81 (1999): 297–302.

Mukařovský 1976
Mukařovský, Jan. "The Essence of the Visual Arts." In *Semiotics of Art: Prague School Contributions,* edited by Ladislav Matejka and Irwin R. Titunik, 229–44. Cambridge, Mass., and London: MIT Press, 1976.

Müller 2000
Müller, Rebecca. *"Die Natur ist meine einzige Lehrerin, meine Wohltäterin": Zeichnungen von Daniel Nikolaus Chodowiecki (1726–1801) im Berliner Kupferstichkabinett.* Exh. cat. Berlin: Berliner Kupferstichkabinett, 2000.

Müller Hofstede 1984
Müller Hofstede, J. "'Non saturatur oculus visu'—Zur 'Allegorie des Gesichts' von Peter Paul Rubens und Jan Brueghel d. Ä." In *Wort und Bild in der niederländischen Kunst und Literatur des 16. und 17. Jahrhunderts,* edited by Herman Vekeman and Justus Müller Hofstede, 243–89. Erftstadt: Lukassen Verlag, 1984.

Müller Hofstede 1985
Müller Hofstede, Justus. "Rubens und die Porträtbüste des 'Vitellius' aus der Sammlung des Kardinals Grimani." In *Rubens and His World,* 109–22. Antwerp: Het Gulden Cabinet, 1985.

Musée de l'Ain 1967
Musée de l'Ain. *Jean-Jacques de Boissieu 1736–1810.* Exh. cat. Brou: Musée de l'Ain, 1967.

Museo del Prado 1949
Museo del Prado. *Museo del Prado: Catalogo de los Cuadros.* Madrid: Museo del Prado, 1949.

Museo del Prado 1980
Museo del Prado. *Anton Rafael Mengs, 1728–1779.* Exh. cat. Madrid: Museo del Prado, 1980.

Naumann 1978
Naumann, Otto. "Frans van Mieris as a Draughtsman." *Master Drawings* 16 (1978): 3–34.

Naumann 1981
Naumann, Otto. *Frans van Mieris (1635–1681) the Elder.* 2 vols. Doornspijk, Netherlands: Davaco, 1981.

Nesbitt 1992
Nesbitt, Elizabeth. "An Artist Picturing Art: Goltzius's *Portrait of the Painter Hans Bol* and *Pygmalion and Galatea.*" In *Hendrick Goltzius and the Classical Tradition,* 52–55. Exh. cat. Los Angeles: Fisher Gallery, University of Southern California, 1992.

Netzer 1989
Netzer, Susanne. *Daniel N. Chodowiecki 1726–1801: Drawings from the Collection of the Veste Coburg / Zeichnungen aus dem Besitz der Kunstsammlungen der Veste Coburg.* Exh. cat. London: Goethe-Institut, and Kunstsammlungen der Veste Coburg, 1989.

Newcome Schleier and Grasso 2003
Newcome Schleier, Mary, and Giovanni Grasso. *Giovanni David: Pittore e incisore della famiglia Durazzo.* Turin: Artema, 2003.

Nichols 1785
Nichols, John. *Biographical Anecdotes of William Hogarth; with a Catalogue of His Works Chronologically Arranged; and Occasional Remarks.* 3rd ed. London: John Nichols, 1785.

Nichols 1987
Nichols, Lawrence W. "Jan Govertsz. van der Aar: On the Identification of Goltzius's Patron." *Nederlands Kunsthistorisch Jaarboek* 38 (1987): 241–55.

Nicodemi 1962
Nicodemi, Giorgio. *Francesco Hayez.* 2 vols. Milan: Ceschina, 1962.

Nicolson 1954
Nicolson, Benedict. "Joseph Wright's Early Subject Pictures." *Burlington Magazine* 96 (1954): 72–80.

Nicolson 1968
Nicolson, Benedict. *Joseph Wright of Derby: Painter of Light.* 2 vols. London: Routledge and Kegan Paul, and New York: Pantheon Books, 1968.

Niemeijer 1962
Niemeijer, J. W. "De Portretten van Ploos van Amstel." *Nederlands Kunsthistorisch Jaarboek* 13 (1962): 181–215.

Nikolenko 1983
Nikolenko, Lada. *Pierre Mignard: The Portrait Painter of the Grand Siècle.* Munich: Nitz Verlag, 1983.

Nilsson 1978
Nilsson, Sten Åke. "The Ass Sequence in Los Caprichos." *Konsthistorisk Tidskrift* 47 (1978): 27–38.

Nochlin 1971
Nochlin, Linda. "Why Have There Been No Great Women Artists?" *Art News* 69 (1971): 22–39, 67–71.

O'Donoghue 1908–25
O'Donoghue, Freeman. *Catalogue of Engraved British Portraits Preserved in the Department of Prints and Drawings in the British Museum.* London: The British Museum, 1908–25.

Offerhaus 1979
Offerhaus, Johannes. "Van Isaac en Apollo: De prijswinnende tekeningen van de Amsterdamse stadstekenacademie." In "Kunstoderwijs in Nederland." Special issue, *Nederlands Kunsthistorisch Jaarboek* 30 (1979): 43–78.

Okayama 1992
Okayama, Yassu. *The Ripa Index: Personifications and their Attributes in Five Editions of the Iconologia.* Doornspijk, Netherlands: Davaco, 1992.

Olszewski 1981
Olszewski, Edward J. *The Draftsman's Eye: Late Italian Renaissance Schools and Styles.* Exh. cat. Cleveland: The Cleveland Museum of Art, 1981.

Oppé 1948
Oppé, A. P. *The Drawings of William Hogarth.* London: Phaidon, 1948.

Paas and Mertens 2003
Paas, Sigrun, and Sabine Mertens, eds. *Beutekunst under Napoleon: Die "französiche Schenkung" an Mainz 1803.* Exh. cat. Mainz: Landesmuseum, 2003.

Panofsky 1955
Panofsky, Erwin. *The Life and Art of Albrecht Dürer.* 4th ed. Princeton: Princeton University Press, 1955.

Pascoli 1730–36
Pascoli, Lione. *Vite de' pittori, scultori, ed architetti moderni.* 2 vols. Rome: Antonio de' Rossi, 1730–36.

Passeri 1772
Passeri, Giambattista. *Vite de' pittori, scultori, ed architetti che anno lavorato in Roma morti dal 1641. fino al 1673.* Rome: G. Settari, 1772.

Pastor 1923–69
Pastor, Ludwig Freiherr von. *The History of the Popes: From the Close of the Middle Ages.* 40 vols. St. Louis: Herder, 1923–69.

Paulson 1989
Paulson, Ronald. *Hogarth's Graphic Works.* 3rd ed. London: The Print Room, 1989.

Paulson 1991–93
Paulson, Ronald. *Hogarth.* 3 vols. New Brunswick, N.J.: Rutgers University Press, 1991–93.

Paulson 1995
Paulson, Ronald. "Hogarth and the Distribution of Visual Images." In *Towards a Modern Art World,* edited by Brian Allen, 27–46. New Haven and London: Yale University Press, 1995.

Pavoni 1985
Pavoni, Rosanna. "Paolo Giovio, et son musée de portraits: à propos d'une exposition." *Gazette des Beaux-Arts,* 6th ser., 105 (1985): 109–16.

Pelletier, Slatkes, and Stone-Ferrier 1994
Pelletier, S. William, Leonard J. Slatkes, and Linda Stone-Ferrier. *Adriaen van Ostade: Etchings of Peasant Life in Holland's Golden Age,* edited by Patricia Phagan. Exh. cat. Athens, Georgia: Georgia Museum of Art, University of Georgia, 1994.

Percy 1971
Percy, Ann. *Giovanni Benedetto Castiglione: Master Draughtsman of the Italian Baroque.* Exh. cat. Philadelphia: Philadelphia Museum of Art, 1971.

Perez 1994
Perez, Marie-Félice. *L'oeuvre gravé de Jean-Jacques de Boissieu 1736–1810.* Geneva: Cabinet des estampes, Editions du Tricorne, 1994.

Pérez Sanchez and Sayre 1989
Pérez Sanchez, Alfonso E., and Eleanor E. Sayre. *Goya and the Spirit of Enlightenment.* Exh. cat. Boston: Museum of Fine Arts, 1989.

Perrault 1696–1700
Perrault, [Charles]. *Les Hommes illustres qui ont paru en France pendant ce siècle.* 2 vols. Paris: Antoine Dezallier, 1696–1700.

Perrault 2003
Perrault, Charles. *Les Hommes illustres avec leurs portraits au naturel.* Edited by D. J. Culpin. Tübingen: Gunter Narr, 2003.

Perry 1978
Perry, Marilyn. "Cardinal Domenico Grimani's Legacy of Ancient Art to Venice." *Journal of the Warburg and Courtauld Institutes* 41 (1978): 215–44.

Persels 1997
Persels, Jeffery C. "Bragueta Humanística, or Humanism's Codpiece." *Sixteenth Century Journal* 28 (1997): 79–99.

Perry 1999
Perry, Gill. "'Mere face painters'? Hogarth, Reynolds and Ideas of Academic Art in Eighteenth-Century Britain." In *Academies, Museums and Canons of Art,* edited by Gill Perry and Colin Cunningham, 124–68. New Haven and London: Yale University Press, 1999.

Pevsner 1940
Pevsner, Nikolaus. *Academies of Art Past and Present.* Cambridge: The University Press, 1940.

Philadelphia Museum of Art 1994
Philadelphia Museum of Art. *Paintings from Europe and the Americas in the Philadelphia Museum of Art.* Philadelphia: Philadelphia Museum of Art, 1994.

Pigler 1974
Pigler, A. *Barockthemen: Eine Auswahl von verzeichnissen zur Ikonographie des 17. und 18. Jahrhunderts.* 2nd ed. 3 vols. Budapest: Akadémiai Kiadó, 1974.

Pilliod 1998
Pilliod, Elizabeth. "Representation, Misrepresentation, and Non-Representation: Vasari and His Competitors." In *Vasari's Florence: Artists and Literati at the Medicean Court,* 30–52, 254–63. Cambridge: Cambridge University Press, 1998.

Plax 2000
Plax, Julie Anne. *Watteau and the Cultural Politics of Eighteenth-Century France.* Cambridge: Cambridge University Press, 2000.

Pliny 1984
Pliny. *Natural History.* Translated by H. Rackham. The Loeb Classical Library. 10 vols. Cambridge, Mass.: Harvard University Press, 1984.

Pollock 1980
Pollock, Griselda. "Artists Mythologies and Media Genius, Madness and Art History." *Screen* 21 (1980): 57–96.

Posner 1993
Posner, Donald. "Concerning the 'Mechanical' Parts of Painting and the Artistic Culture of Seventeenth-Century France." *Art Bulletin* 75 (1993): 583–98.

Préaud 1983
Préaud, Maxime. "'L'Académie des sciences et des beaux-arts': le testament graphique de Sébastien Leclerc." *RACAR* 10 (1983): 73–81.

Prinz 1966
Prinz, Wolfram. *Vasaris Sammlung von Künstlerbildnissen: Mit einem kritischen Verzeichnis der 144 Vitenbildnisse in der zweiten Ausgabe der Lebensbeschreibungen von 1568.* Florence: Kunsthistorisches Institut, 1966.

Prinz 1971
Prinz, Wolfram. *Die Sammlung der Selbstbildnisse in den Uffizien: Geschichte der Sammlung.* Berlin: Mann, 1971.

Rambuss 1998
Rambuss, Richard. *Closet Devotions.* Durham, N.C.: Duke University Press, 1998.

Rassieur 1998
Rassieur, Tom. "Adriaen van Ostade, the Methodical Artist: Preparatory Drawings, a Chronology, and Rembrandt." In *Everyday Life in Holland's Golden Age: The Complete Etchings of Adriaen van Ostade,* edited by Peter van der Coelen, 31–53. Exh cat. Amsterdam: Museum het Rembrandthuis, 1998.

Raupp 1980
Raupp, Hans-Joachim. "Selbstbildnisse und Künstlerporträts—ihre Funktion und Bedeutung." In Herzog Anton Ulrich-Museum 1980, 7–35.

Raupp 1984
Raupp, Hans-Joachim. *Untersuchungen zu Künstlerbildnis und Künstlerdarstellung in den Niederlanden im 17. Jahrhundert.* Hildesheim: Georg Olms, 1984.

Reed 1998
Reed, Sue Welsh. *French Prints from the Age of the Musketeers.* Exh. cat. Boston: Museum of Fine Arts, 1998.

Reed and Wallace 1989
Reed, Sue Welsh, and Richard Wallace. *Italian Etchers of the Renaissance and Baroque.* Exh. cat. Boston: Museum of Fine Arts, 1989.

Reynolds 1975
Reynolds, Joshua. *Discourses on Art.* Ed. Robert R. Wark. New Haven and London: Yale University Press, 1975.

Reznicek 1960
Reznicek, Emil. "Het begin van Goltzius' loopbaan als schilder." *Oud Holland* 75 (1960): 30–49.

Reznicek 1984
Reznicek, E. K. J. "De overlevering van een verloren gegaan schilderij van Jan van Eyck." In *De arte et libris: Festschrift Erasmus 1934–1984,* 387–93. Amsterdam: Erasmus Antiquariaat en Boekhandel, 1984.

Riggs and Silver 1993
Riggs, Timothy, and Larry Silver. *Graven Images: The Rise of Professional Printmakers in Antwerp and Haarlem, 1540–1640.* Exh. cat. Evanston, Illinois: The Mary and Leigh Block Gallery, Northwestern University, 1993.

Rijksmuseum 1976
Rijskmuseum. *All the Paintings of the Rijksmuseum in Amsterdam: A Completely Illustrated Catalogue.* Amsterdam and Maarssen: Rijksmuseum, 1976.

Ripa 1603
Ripa, Cesare. *Iconologia overo descrittione di diverse imagini cauate dall'antichità, & di propria inuentione.* Rome: Lepido Facij, 1603.

Rizzi 1971
Rizzi, Aldo. *The Etchings of the Tiepolos. Complete Edition.* London: Phaidon, 1971.

Robinson 1980
Robinson, Franklin W. "Puns and Plays in Rembrandt's Etchings." *Print Collector's Newsletter* 11 (1980): 165–68.

Roethlisberger 1968
Roethlisberger, Marcel. *Claude Lorrain: The Drawings.* 2 vols. Berkeley: University of California Press, 1968.

Roettgen 1999–2003
Roettgen, Steffi. *Anton Raphael Mengs 1728–1779.* 2 vols. Munich: Hirmer, 1999–2003.

Rogers 2003
Rogers, Ben. *Beef and Liberty.* London: Chatto & Windus, 2003.

Roland Michel 1990
Roland Michel, Marianne. "Landscape Painting in the Eighteenth Century: Theory, Training, and Its Place in Academic Doctrine." In *Claude to Corot: The Development of Landscape Painting in France,* edited by Alan Wintermute, 99–109. Exh. cat. New York: Colnaghi, 1990.

Rosand 1970
Rosand, David. "The Crisis of the Venetian Renaissance Tradition." *L'Arte* 11–12 (1970): 5–53.

Rose-de Viejo 2000
Rose-de Viejo, Isadora. "Goya, the 'Aragonese Rembrandt." In *Etched on the Memory: The Presence of Rembrandt in the Prints of Goya and Picasso,* 14–27. Exh. cat. Amsterdam: The Rembrandt House Museum, 2000.

Westermann 1996
Westermann, Mariët. *A Worldly Art: The Dutch Republic, 1585–1718.* New York: Harry Abrams, 1996.

Wheelock 2000
Wheelock, Arthur K., Jr. "Rembrandt Inventing Himself." In *Rembrandt Creates Rembrandt: Art and Ambition in Leiden, 1629–1631,* 13–23. Exh. cat. Boston: Isabella Stewart Gardner Museum, 2000.

White 1969
White, Christopher. *Rembrandt as an Etcher.* University Park, Pa.: Pennsylvania State University Press, 1969.

White and Buvelot 1999
White, Christopher, and Quentin Buvelot, eds. *Rembrandt by Himself.* Exh. cat. London: The National Gallery, 1999.

Widerkehr 1991–92
Widerkehr, Léna. "JACOB MATHAM GOLTZIJ PRIVIGNUS: Jacob Matham graveur et ses rapports avec Hendrick Goltzius." In "Goltzius-Studies: Hendrick Goltzius (1558–1617)," edited by Reindert Falkenburg, Jan Piet Filedt Kok, and Huigen Leeflang. Special issue, *Nederlands Kunsthistorisch Jaarboek* 42–43 (1991–92): 219–260.

Wildenstein 1957
Wildenstein, Georges. *Les graveurs de Poussin au XVIIe siècle.* Paris: Les Beaux Arts, Presses universitaires de France, 1957.

Wildenstein 1965
Wildenstein, Daniel, ed. "Les Oeuvres de Charles Le Brun d'après les gravures de son temps." *Gazette des Beaux-Arts,* 6th ser., 66 (1965): 1–58.

Wille 1960
Wille, Hans. "Die Erfindung der Zeichenkunst." In *Beiträge zur Kunstgeschichte: Eine Festgabe für Heinz Rudolf Rosemann zum 9. Oktober 1960,* edited by Ernst Guldan, 279–300. Munich: Deutscher Kunstverlag, 1960.

Wille 1972
Wille, Hans. "Die Dibutades-Erzählung in der Kunst der Goethezeit." *Jahrbuch der Sammlung Kippenberg* 2 (1972): 328–51.

Wimsatt and Beardsley 1954
Wimsatt, W. K., and Monroe C. Beardsley. "The Intentional Fallacy." In *The Verbal Icon: Studies in the Meaning of Poetry,* 3–18. Lexington, Ky.: University of Kentucky Press, 1954.

Wind 1984
Wind, Barry. "The Last of the Tail Piece: Hogarth and Apelles." *Source* 3 (1984): 12–15.

Winner 1987
Winner, Matthias. "Poussins Selbstbildnis von 1649." In *"Il se rendit en Italie": Etudes offertes à André Chastel,* 371–94. Rome: Edizioni dell'Elefante, 1987.

Winters 2002
Winters, Laurie. *Leonardo da Vinci and the Splendor of Poland: A History of Collecting and Patronage.* Exh. cat. Milwaukee: Milwaukee Art Museum, 2002.

Wittkower 1961
Wittkower, Rudolf. "Individualism in Art and Artists: A Renaissance Problem." *Journal of the History of Ideas* 22 (1961): 291–302.

Wittkower 1963
Wittkower, Rudolf, and Margot Wittkower. *Born under Saturn: The Character and Conduct of Artists, A Documented History from Antiquity to the French Revolution.* New York and London: W. W. Norton, 1963.

Wolf 1991
Wolf, Reva. *Goya and the Satirical Print in England and on the Continent, 1730–1850.* Exh. cat. Chestnut Hill, Mass.: Boston College Museum of Art, 1991.

Woloch 1979
Woloch, Isser. *The French Veteran from the Revolution to the Restoration.* Chapel Hill: North Carolina University Press, 1979.

Wood 1990
Wood, Jeremy. "Van Dyck's 'Cabinet de Titien': The Contents and Dispersal of His Collection." *Burlington Magazine* 132 (1990): 680–95.

Woods-Marsden 1998
Woods-Marsden, Joanna. *Renaissance Self-Portraiture: The Visual Construction of Identity and the Social Status of the Artist.* New Haven and London: Yale University Press, 1998.

Wright 1994
Wright, Alison. "The Myth of Hercules." In *Lorenzo il Magnifico e il suo mondo: Convegno internazionale di studi (Firenze, 9–13 1992),* edited by Gian Carlo Garfagnini, 323–39. Florence: L. S. Olschki, 1994.

Würtenberger 1961
Würtenberger, Franzsepp. "Das Maleratelier als Kultraum im 19. Jahrhundert." In *Miscellanea Bibliotecae Herzianae zu Ehren von Leo Bruhns, Fransgraf Wolff Metternich, Ludwig Schudt,* 502–13. Munich: A. Schroll, 1961.

Zafran 2002
Zafran, Eric M. "Michael Sweerts in America: Collecting, Commerce and Scholarship." In *Michael Sweerts (1618–1664),* edited by Guido Jansen and Peter C. Sutton, 56–66. Exh. cat. Amsterdam: Rijksmuseum; San Francisco: Fine Arts Museums of San Francisco; Hartford, Conn.: Wadsworth Atheneum Museum of Art, 2002.

Index

Page numbers in **boldface** refer to illustrations.

Photographic Credits

Photographs of works of art in the collection of the Sarah Campbell Blaffer Foundation are by Thomas R. DuBrock.

Fig. 1: Erich Lessing/Art Resource, NY.

Fig. 3: Scala/Art Resource, NY.

Fig. 6: Photo: A. Idini.

Figs. 7, 8: Alinari/Art Resource, NY.

Fig. 10: Réunion des Musées Nationaux/Art Resource, NY. Photo: J.G. Berizzi.

Figs. 12, 15, 3.1, 6.1, 6.2, 7.3, 9.1, 15.1, 21.1, 21.2, 40.2, 47.2, 61.1, 66.2: © Copyright The British Museum.

Figs. 14, 66.1: Image © Board of Trustees, National Gallery of Art, Washington.

Fig. 18: Finsiel/Archivi Alinari, Firenze.

Fig. 20: © Christie's Images Limited 2004.

Fig. 26: © Sterling and Francine Clark Art Institute, Williamstown, Massachusetts.

Fig. 27: © Copyright Leiden Universiteits-bibliotheek.

Fig. 28: Réunion des Musées Nationaux/Art Resource, NY. Photo: Bulloz.

Fig. 30: Bildarchiv Preussischer Kulturbesitz/Art Resource, NY. Photo: Joerg P. Anders.

Figs. 31, 18.2, 26.1: Photograph, all rights reserved, The Metropolitan Museum of Art.

Fig. 10.1: Réunion des Musées Nationaux/Art Resource, NY. Photo: R.G. Ojeda.

Figs. 19.1, 43.1, 60.1: Réunion des Musées Nationaux/Art Resource, NY.

Figs. 23.1, 28.1: The Royal Collection © 2004, Her Majesty Queen Elizabeth II.

Figs. 28.3, 75.1, 81.1: © Royal Academy of Arts, London.

Fig. 30.1: Copyright The Frick Collection, New York.

Figs. 31.1, 31.2: Photo: Fine Arts Library, University of Texas Libraries, The University of Texas at Austin.

Fig. 49.1: Photograph © Copyright Fitzwilliam Museum, University of Cambridge.

Fig. 55.1: Archivio Fotografico Soprintendenza Speciale per il Polo Museale Romano.

Fig. 79.1: © Collectiebeleid Musea stad Antwerpen.